T0180733

Lecture Notes in Computer Science　13951

Founding Editors

Gerhard Goos
Juris Hartmanis

The series Lecture Notes in Computer Science (LNCS), including its subseries Lecture Notes in Artificial Intelligence (LNAI) and Lecture Notes in Bioinformatics (LNBI), has established itself as a medium for the publication of new developments in computer science and information technology research, teaching, and education.

LNCS enjoys close cooperation with the computer science R & D community, the series counts many renowned academics among its volume editors and paper authors, and collaborates with prestigious societies. Its mission is to serve this international community by providing an invaluable service, mainly focused on the publication of conference and workshop proceedings and postproceedings. LNCS commenced publication in 1973.

Foteini Baldimtsi · Christian Cachin
Editors

Financial Cryptography and Data Security

27th International Conference, FC 2023
Bol, Brač, Croatia, May 1–5, 2023
Revised Selected Papers, Part II

 Springer

Editors
Foteini Baldimtsi 🆔
George Mason University
Fairfax, VA, USA

Christian Cachin 🆔
University of Bern
Bern, Switzerland

ISSN 0302-9743   ISSN 1611-3349 (electronic)
Lecture Notes in Computer Science
ISBN 978-3-031-47750-8   ISBN 978-3-031-47751-5 (eBook)
https://doi.org/10.1007/978-3-031-47751-5

This Springer imprint is published by the registered company Springer Nature Switzerland AG
The registered company address is: Gewerbestrasse 11, 6330 Cham, Switzerland

Paper in this product is recyclable.

Preface

The 27th International Conference on Financial Cryptography and Data Security, FC 2023, was held from May 1 to May 5, 2023, at the Bluesun Hotel Elaphusa in Bol, on the island of Brač, Croatia. The conference is organized annually by the International Financial Cryptography Association (IFCA).

We received 182 papers (165 regular ones and 17 short papers) by the submission deadline for the conference, which was October 19th, 2022. Of these, 41 were accepted (39 regular papers and two short papers), resulting in an acceptance rate of 22.5%. The present proceedings volume contains revised versions of all the papers presented at the conference.

The review process lasted approximately two months and was double-blind. Each paper received a minimum of three reviews. The Program Committee used the HotCRP system to organize the reviewing process. The merits of each paper were discussed thoroughly and intensely on the online platform as we converged to the final decisions. In the end, a number of worthy papers still had to be rejected owing to the limited number of slots in the conference program.

The Program Committee (PC) consisted of 64 members with expertise in various aspects of financial cryptography, including representatives from both industry and academia. The PC additionally solicited reviews from 58 external reviewers. We are deeply grateful to all the members of the PC and the external reviewers for their dedication and thorough work. Their valuable insights and constructive feedback considerably strengthened the overall quality of the final program.

The main conference program lasted for four days. A half-day tutorial on the topic of "Constant Function Market Makers" took place a day before the main conference and a series of one-day workshops were held the day after the main conference. The main conference started with an invited keynote talk by George Danezis, University College London and Mysten Labs, titled "Combining broadcast and consensus in a production blockchain system." The accepted papers were presented in 10 sessions and there was also a Rump Session and a General Meeting. Finally, two posters were presented during the poster session.

We are grateful to the general chairs, Ray Hirschfeld and Carla Mascia, for an excellent organization. Additionally, we appreciate the dedication of the IFCA directors and Steering Committee for their service. We would also like to express our thankfulness to the conference sponsors whose generous support made this event possible. Our Platinum Sponsors: a16z Crypto Research, Casper Association, Chainlink Labs and Mysten Labs. Our Silver Sponsors: Evertas and Zcash Foundation. Finally, we would like to thank our sponsors in kind: the Croatian National Tourist Board, the Split-Dalmatia Tourist Board, the Bol Tourist Board, and Worldpay.

Lastly, our sincere gratitude goes to all the authors who submitted their papers to this conference, as well as to all the attendees who contributed to making this event a truly intellectually stimulating experience through their active participation. Their support is the most important factor for the success of the conference.

August 2023   Foteini Baldimtsi
                                                                 Christian Cachin

Organization

General Chairs

Rafael Hirschfeld   Unipay Technologies, The Netherlands
Carla Mascia   University of Trento, Italy

Steering Committee

Joseph Bonneau   New York University and a16z Crypto Research, USA
Sven Dietrich   City University of New York, USA
Rafael Hirschfeld   Unipay Technologies, The Netherlands
Andrew Miller   University of Illinois at Urbana-Champaign, USA
Monica Quaintance   Zenia Systems, USA
Burton Rosenberg   University of Miami, USA
Kazue Sako   Waseda University, Japan

Program Committee Chairs

Foteini Baldimtsi   George Mason University, USA
Christian Cachin   University of Bern, Switzerland

Program Committee

Ghada Almashaqbeh   University of Connecticut, USA
Zeta Avarikioti   Technical University of Vienna, Austria
Christian Badertscher   Input Output, Switzerland
Massimo Bartoletti   University of Cagliari, Italy
Rainer Böhme   University of Innsbruck, Austria
Joseph Bonneau   New York University and a16z Crypto Research, USA
Benedikt Bünz   Stanford University and Espresso Systems, USA
L. Jean Camp   Indiana University, USA
Srdjan Čapkun   ETH Zurich, Switzerland
Kostas Chalkias   Mysten Labs, USA
T.-H. Hubert Chan   University of Hong Kong, China
Panagiotis Chatzigiannis   Visa Research, USA

Jeremy Clark   Concordia University, Canada
Vanesa Daza   Universitat Pompeu Fabra, Spain
Rafael Dowsley   Monash University, Australia
Stefan Dziembowski   University of Warsaw, Poland
Karim Eldefrawy   SRI International, USA
Kaoutar Elkhiyaoui   IBM Research, Switzerland
Zeki Erkin   TU Delft, The Netherlands
Chaya Ganesh   Indian Institute of Science, Bangalore, India
Christina Garman   Purdue University, USA
Peter Gaži   Input Output, Slovakia
Rosario Gennaro   Protocol Labs, USA
Arthur Gervais   University College London, UK
Ethan Heilman   BastionZero, USA
Ari Juels   Cornell Tech, USA
Aniket Kate   Purdue University and Supra Research, USA
Lefteris Kokoris-Kogias   IST Austria, Austria
Evgenios M. Kornaropoulos   George Mason University, USA
Duc V. Le   University of Bern, Switzerland
Andrew Lewis-Pye   London School of Economics, UK
Ben Livshits   Imperial College and Brave Software, UK
Giorgia Azzurra Marson   NEC Labs Europe, Germany
Shin'ichiro Matsuo   Georgetown University, USA
Patrick McCorry   Infura, UK
Ian Miers   University of Maryland, USA
Andrew Miller   University of Illinois at Urbana-Champaign, USA
Pedro Moreno-Sanchez   IMDEA Software Institute, Spain
Kartik Nayak   Duke University, USA
Valeria Nikolaenko   a16z Crypto Research, USA
Anca Nitulescu   Protocol Labs, France
Giorgos Panagiotakos   Input Output, UK
Dimitris Papadopoulos   Hong Kong University of Science and
                                        Technology, China

Charalampos Papamanthou   Yale University, USA
Alexandros Psomas   Purdue University, USA
Elizabeth A. Quaglia   Royal Holloway, University of London, UK
Ling Ren   University of Illinois at Urbana-Champaign, USA
Ori Rottenstreich   Technion, Israel
Abhi Shelat   Northeastern University, USA
Alberto Sonnino   Mysten Labs, UK
Alessandro Sorniotti   IBM Research, Switzerland
Alexander Spiegelman   Aptos Labs, USA
Chrysoula Stathakopoulou   Chainlink Labs, Switzerland

Vanessa Teague   Thinking Cybersecurity and Australian National
                                University, Australia
Marie Vasek   University College London, UK
Roger Wattenhofer   ETH Zurich, Switzerland
Edgar Weippl   University of Vienna and SBA Research, Austria
Fan Zhang   Yale University, USA
Haibin Zhang   Beijing Institute of Technology, China
Ren Zhang   Cryptape Co. Ltd. and Nervos, China
Yupeng Zhang   Texas A&M University, USA
Hong-Sheng Zhou   Virginia Commonwealth University, USA
Dionysis Zindros   Stanford University, USA
Aviv Zohar   Hebrew University, Israel

Additional Reviewers

Hamza Abusalah   Joël Mathys
Amit Agarwal   Subhra Mazumdar
Jannik Albrecht   Liam Medley
Balaji Arun   Jovana Micic
Judith Beestermöller   Atsuki Momose
Adithya Bhat   Muhammad Haris Mudgees
Matteo Campanelli   Kamilla Nazirkhanova
Kevin Choi   Ben Riva
Sandro Coretti-Drayton   Schwinn Saereesitthipitak
Xiaohai Dai   Philipp Schindler
Sourav Das   Peiyao Sheng
Yepeng Michael Ding   Srivatsan Sridhar
Fatima Elsheimy   Shravan Srinivasan
Zhiyong Fang   Christo Stefo
Rati Gelashvili   Nicholas Stifter
Tiantian Gong   Ertem Nusret Tas
Florian Grötschla   Benjamin Terner
Lioba Heimbach   Athina Terzoglou
Javier Herranz   Phuc Thai
Yanxue Jia   Giorgos Tsimos
Aljosha Judmayer   Sarisht Wadhwa
Dimitris Karakostas   Chenghong Wang
David Lehnherr   Weijie Wang
Rujia Li   Zhuolun Xiang
Yunqi Li   Yuting Xiao
Yujie Lu   Tom Yurek
Zhichun Lu   Yuncong Zhang
Nikos Makriyannis   Ren Zhijie
Easwar Vivek Mangipudi   Zhelei Zhou
Deepak Maram

Contents – Part II

Empirical Studies and more Decentralized Finance

Game Theory and Protocols

Contents – Part I

Proof of X

SNACKs for Proof-of-Space Blockchains

Hamza Abusalah$^{(\boxtimes)}$ (iD)

IMDEA Software Institute, Madrid, Spain
hamza.abusalah@imdea.org

Abstract. SNACKs are succinct non-interactive arguments of chain knowledge. They allow for efficient and generic solutions to blockchain light-client bootstrapping. Abusalah et al. construct SNACKs in the random oracle model for any *single-chain* blockchain from any graph-labeling proof of sequential work (PoSW) scheme. Their SNACK construction is a PoSW-like protocol over the augmented blockchain.

Unlike single-chain blockchains, such as proof-of-work and proof-of-stake blockchains, proof-of-space (PoSpace) blockchains are composed of two chains: a *canonical* proof chain and a data chain. These two chains are related using a signature scheme.

In this work, we construct PoSW-enabled SNACKs for any PoSpace blockchain. Combined with the results of Abusalah et al., this gives the first solution to light-client bootstrapping in PoSpace blockchains. The space cost of our construction is *two* hash values in each augmented PoSpace block. Generating SNACK proofs for a PoSpace blockchain is identical to generating SNACK proofs for single-chain blockchains and amounts to looking up a succinct number of augmented blocks.

1 Introduction

Consider a blockchain protocol Π, say Bitcoin or the Chia Network, and a light client V, which is assumed to hold only minimal information about Π, say its genesis block ψ. A *bootstrapping* protocol [3,6] for a blockchain allows such V to hold a commitment to its stable prefix.

A succinct non-interactive argument of chain knowledge (SNACK) system is a computationally-sound proof system (P, V) that allows a prover P to give a succinct non-interactive proof that convinces a verifier V that P *knows* a *chain* of certain weight. Crucially, the SNACK proof is succinct, i.e., poly-logarithmic in the length of the blockchain.

In [3], secure bootstrapping is formalized and instantiated for any blockchain protocol Π for which (1) we have a secure SNACK system and (2) a natural and previously used assumption [6] on the adversarial mining power holds. This is captured in the (c, ℓ, ϵ)-fork assumption, which informally says that, except with probability ϵ, no adversary can produce a fork containing ℓ consecutive

© International Financial Cryptography Association 2024
F. Baldimtsi and C. Cachin (Eds.): FC 2023, LNCS 13951, pp. 3–17, 2024.
https://doi.org/10.1007/978-3-031-47751-5_1

blocks with more than a c-fraction of them being valid.[1] Furthermore, Abusalah et al. [3] construct SNACKs for single-chain blockchains, like Bitcoin, generically from any graph-labeling proof of sequential work (PoSW) scheme assuming the (c, ℓ, ϵ)-fork assumption holds for such chains.

SNACKs for PoSpace Blockchains. In this paper, we study SNACKs for PoSpace blockchains [8,12]. These blockchains are composed of two chains in tandem: a proof chain and a data chain – see Fig. 1. Both chains are bound by a signature scheme. The proof chain contains only *canonical* data, such as (unique) proofs of space [1,10] and verifiable-delay function [5] computations. The data chain contains transactions and any arbitrary data the blockchain protocol allows. The dual nature of these chains and the requirement that the proof chain must remain canonical make designing SNACKs for such chains more involved than their single-chain blockchain counterparts, say Bitcoin.

Contributions. In this work, we extend the framework of [3] and construct SNACKs for *any* PoSpace blockchain from any graph-labeling PoSW scheme. The cost of our construction is *two* hash values in each augmented block, one in the augmented proof block, and one in the augmented data block. Generating a SNACK proof is as efficient as generating a PoSW proof, which amounts to looking up a succinct[2] number of blocks.

(We mention that simply defining the PoSpace SNACK to be two SNACK systems, one for the proof chain, and one for the data chain, doesn't result in a secure SNACK, and extra care needs to be exercised in order to prove security of the SNACK and maintain the security of the underlying PoSpace blockchain.)

Therefore, by the results of [3], by plugging in our PoSpace SNACK construction into their generic bootstrapping protocol, we get, to the best of our knowledge, the first solution to bootstrapping in PoSpace blockchains that avoids setup assumptions. Our protocol, as outlined above, is also practically efficient.[3]

2   Preliminaries

In this section, we review the SNACK-related definitions from [3].

Notation. For a directed acyclic graph (DAG) $G = (V, E)$ on $n + 1$ vertices, we always number its vertices $V = [n]_0$ in topological order and often write G_n to make this explicit. For $v \in [n]_0$, we denote the parent vertices of v in G by $\mathsf{parents}_G(v)$, and their number (i.e., the indegree of v) by $\deg_G(v)$; thus, $\mathsf{parents}_G(v) = (v_1, \ldots, v_{\deg_G(v)})$. We also let $\deg(G) := \max_{v \in V}\{\deg_G(v)\}$. We drop the subscript G when it's clear from context.

---

[1] This assumption was first introduced in [6] in the PoW-blockchain setting and adopted in [3] generically, i.e., without reference to the Sybil-mechanism of the underlying blockchain protocol. Studying the (c, ℓ, ϵ)-fork assumption in various blockchain protocols, and possibly deriving it from their underlying security assumptions, is an interesting open problem that we don't address in this work.

[2] Depending on the PoSW scheme used, this number maybe $O(t \log n)$ where n is the length of the blockchain and t a security parameter.

[3] SNACKs are on par with Flyclient in terms of practical efficiency [3].

Graph Labeling. A *chain graph* is a DAG on $[n]_0$ vertices such that its edge set E contains a path $P := (0, \ldots, n)$ which goes through all $[n]_0$.

Definition 1 (Chain graphs). *A DAG $G_n = ([n]_0, E_n)$ is a chain graph if $E_n \supseteq \{(i - 1, i) : i \in [n]\}$.*

A DAG is weighted if its vertices have arbitrary weights that sum to 1. In SNACK constructions, the verifier's challenges are sampled according to the distribution induced by the weights of the underlying DAG.

Definition 2 (Weighted DAGs). *We call $\Gamma_n = (G_n, \Omega_n)$ a weighted DAG if $G_n = ([n]_0, E_n)$ is a DAG and $\Omega_n \colon [n]_0 \to [0, 1]$ is a function s.t. $\Omega_n([n]_0) = 1$, where for $S \subseteq [n]_0$, $\Omega_n(S) := \sum_{s \in S} \Omega_n(s)$.*

SNACK constructions are over labeled chain graphs. An augmented data corresponding to arbitrary blockchain data is infused into the random-oracle-based labeling of chain graphs that underlie SNACKs.

Definition 3 (Oracle-based graph labeling). *Let $G_n = ([n]_0, E_n)$ be a DAG and $\tau = (\tau_i)_{i \in [n]_0}$ be a tuple of oracles, with each $\tau_i \colon \{0, 1\}^* \to \{0, 1\}^\lambda$. For any $X = (x_0, \ldots, x_n) \in (\{0, 1\}^*)^{n+1}$ the X-augmented τ-labeling $L^\tau \colon [n]_0 \to \{0, 1\}^*$ of G_n is recursively defined as*

$$L^\tau(i) := \begin{cases} \tau_i(\varepsilon) \| x_i & \text{if } \mathsf{parents}(i) = \emptyset, \\ \tau_i\big(L^\tau(\mathsf{parents}(i))\big) \| x_i & \text{otherwise,} \end{cases} \tag{1}$$

where $L^\tau(\mathsf{parents}(i)) := L^\tau(i_1) \| \cdots \| L^\tau(i_k)$ for $(i_1, \ldots, i_k) := \mathsf{parents}(i)$. If $X = (\varepsilon, \ldots, \varepsilon)$, we call L^τ the τ-labeling of G_n.

SNACKs. A *valid path* is a labeled path whose labels are locally valid according to some poly-time relation R and globally consistent as in (2).

Definition 4 (Valid paths). *Let $G_n = ([n]_0, E_n)$ be a DAG, and $R \subseteq \mathbb{N}_0 \times (\{0, 1\}^*)^2$ a relation. Furthermore, let P be a path in G_n, L_P a labeling of P, and $(p_v)_{v \in P} \in (\{0, 1\}^*)^{|P|}$ a $|P|$-tuple of bitstrings with $p_v = (p_v[1], \ldots, p_v[\deg(v)])$. We say that $(P, L_P, (p_v)_{v \in P})$ is an R-valid path in G_n if $\forall v \in P$ with $(v_1, \ldots, v_{\deg(v)}) := \mathsf{parents}(v)$, we have*

$$R\big(v, L_P(v), p_v\big) = 1 \text{ and } \forall i \in [\deg(v)] \text{ if } v_i \in P \text{ then } p_v[i] = L_P(v_i). \tag{2}$$

For a weighted DAG $\Gamma_n = (G_n = ([n]_0, E_n), \Omega_n)$, we say $(P, L_P, (p_v)_{v \in P})$ is (α, R)-valid in Γ_n if in addition $\Omega_n(P) \geq \alpha$.

The language over which SNACKs are defined $\mathcal{L}_{\Gamma, R, \mathsf{Com}}$ is defined via a parameter-dependent ternary polynomial-time (PT) relation $\mathcal{R}_{\Gamma, R, \mathsf{Com}}$ over tuples (prm, η, w), where prm is generated by a parameter generation G algorithm. A statement $\eta = (\phi, n)$ in $\mathcal{L}_{\Gamma, R, \mathsf{Com}}$ consists of a position-binding Com commitment ϕ to an R-valid labeling of the graph $\Gamma_n \in \Gamma$. The labeling together with an opening of ϕ constitutes a witness w for η.

Definition 5 (Chain commitment language). *Let* $\Gamma = (\Gamma_n)_{n \geq 0}$ *be a family of weighted DAGs and* Com *a vector commitment scheme, define*

$$
\mathcal{R}^{(\alpha)}_{\Gamma, R, \mathsf{Com}} := \left\{ \begin{array}{l} (\mathsf{prm}, \eta = (\phi, n), \\ w = (P, L_P, (p_i)_{i \in P}, \rho)) \end{array} : \begin{array}{l} (P, L_P, (p_i)_{i \in P}) \text{ is } (\alpha, R) - valid\ in \\ \Gamma_n \wedge \mathsf{Com.ver}(\mathsf{pp}, \phi, L_P, P, \rho) = 1 \end{array} \right\}
$$
(3)

where $R \subseteq \mathbb{N}_0 \times (\{0,1\}^*)^2$ *is a PT relation that depends on* prm. *We let* $\mathcal{R}_{\Gamma, R, \mathsf{Com}} := \mathcal{R}^{(1)}_{\Gamma, R, \mathsf{Com}}$ *and* $\mathcal{L}_{\Gamma, R, \mathsf{Com}}$ *denote the language defined by* $\mathcal{R}_{\Gamma, R, \mathsf{Com}}$.

A SNACK system (P, V) for $\mathcal{L}_{\Gamma, R, \mathsf{Com}}$ in a non-interactive argument system satisfying completeness, (α, ϵ)-knowledge soundness, and succinctness. Completeness guarantees that an honest P holding a witness for a statement $(\phi, n) \in \mathcal{L}_{\Gamma, R, \mathsf{Com}}$ makes V accept. For an $\alpha \in (0, 1]$, (α, ϵ)-knowledge-soundness guarantees that from any convincing prover for a statement (ϕ, n) one can extract, except with probability ϵ, an R-valid labeling of a path P in Γ_n of weight at least α. In our SNACK constructions, due to the use of random-oracle graph-labeling, the labels of R will be guaranteed to be computed *sequentially*. Succinctness requires that the proof size as well as its verification time are polylogarithmic in n and polynomial in the security parameter.

Definition 6 (SNACK). *A tuple of PPT algorithms* (P, V) *is a succinct non-interactive argument of chain knowledge (SNACK) for* $\mathcal{L}_{\Gamma, R, \mathsf{Com}}$ *with parameter generator* G *from Definition 5 if the following properties hold:*

Completeness: $\forall \lambda \in \mathbb{N}$, $\mathsf{prm} \leftarrow \mathsf{G}(1^\lambda)$, $\eta, w \in \{0,1\}^*$ *with* $(\mathsf{prm}, \eta, w) \in \mathcal{R}_{\Gamma, R, \mathsf{Com}}$, *we have* $\Pr\left[\pi \leftarrow \mathsf{P}(\mathsf{prm}, \eta, w) : \mathsf{V}(\mathsf{prm}, \eta, \pi) = 1 \right] = 1$.
(α, ϵ)-**Knowledge soundness:** *For every PPT prover* $\tilde{\mathsf{P}}$ *there exists a PPT extractor* E *such that*

$$
\Pr \left[\begin{array}{l} \mathsf{prm} \leftarrow \mathsf{G}(1^\lambda); r \xleftarrow{\$} \{0,1\}^{\mathsf{poly}(\lambda)} \\ (\eta, \pi) := \tilde{\mathsf{P}}(\mathsf{prm}; r); \\ w' \leftarrow \mathsf{E}(\mathsf{prm}, r) \end{array} : \begin{array}{l} \mathsf{V}(\mathsf{prm}, \eta, \pi) = 1\ \wedge \\ \mathcal{R}^{(\alpha)}_{\Gamma, R, \mathsf{Com}}(\mathsf{prm}, \eta, w') = 0 \end{array} \right] \leq \epsilon(\lambda) ,
$$
(4)

with $\mathcal{R}^{(\alpha)}_{\Gamma, R, \mathsf{Com}}$ *from* (3).
Succinctness: *For all* $\mathsf{prm} \leftarrow \mathsf{G}(1^\lambda)$, $(\mathsf{prm}, \eta, w) \in \mathcal{R}_{\Gamma, R, \mathsf{Com}}$ *and* $\pi \leftarrow \mathsf{P}(n, t, \eta, w)$, *we have* $|\pi| \leq \mathsf{poly}(\lambda, \log n)$, P *runs in time* $\mathsf{poly}(\lambda, n)$, *and* V *runs in time* $\mathsf{poly}(\lambda, \log n)$.

Our SNACK construction relies on graph-labeling PoSW [3]. For lack of space, we give a high-level overview here and refer the reader to either [3] or the full version. A graph-labeling PoSW scheme $\mathsf{PoSW} = (\mathsf{PoSW.P} := (\mathsf{PoSW.label}, \mathsf{PoSW.open}), \mathsf{PoSW.V})$ is an (interactive) proof system in which $\mathsf{PoSW.P}$ on common input a weighted DAG (G_n, Ω_n) and a statement χ sampled by the verifier, computes a proof that convinces the verifier that a certain number of *sequential* computational steps with weight 1 according to Ω_n have been performed since χ was received. In particular, $\mathsf{PoSW.label}$ computes a τ labeling L of G_n and sends a vector commitment of L to $\mathsf{PoSW.V}$, which sends challenges to $\mathsf{PoSW.P}$, where PoSW.open replies by giving, among other things, commitment openings to these challenges. Finally PoSW.V accepts or rejects. (α, ϵ)-knowledge soundness of PoSW guarantees that from any convincing prover, a sequentially-labeled path of total weight $\geq \alpha$, can be extracted except with probability ϵ.

3 SNACKs for Proof-of-Space Blockchains

We extend the PoSW-enabled SNACK construction of [3] to the context of PoSpace blockchains. Our construction in a nutshell follows the simple outline of (1) defining an appropriate DAG (2) labeling it and (3) running a PoSW-like protocol over it.

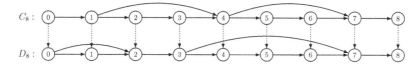

Fig. 1. Example DAGs $C_8 = ([8]_0, E_C)$ and $D_8 = ([8]_0, E_D)$.

3.1 Proof-of-Space Blockchains

We are aware of two PoSpace blockchains: SpaceMint [12] and Chia [8] and our treatment covers them both.

Unlike blockchains based on either proofs of work (PoW) or proofs of stake (PoS), proofs of space (PoSpace) based blockchains are composed of two chains: a *canonical* proof chain and a data chain. The proof chain contains unique proofs and hence is canonical. The data chain contains transactions and any arbitrary data that the blockchain permits. The data chain is bound to the proof chain by means of digital signatures.

Without loss of generality we can view a *PoSpace blockchain* as a tuple of labeled chains whose underlying DAG is $B_n = (C_n, D_n)$ where $C_n = ([n]_0, E_C)$ and $D_n = ([n]_0, E_D)$ are the chain graphs underlying the canonical proof and data chains, respectively. Both C_n and D_n are chain graphs in the sense of Definition 1, and we stress that E_C and E_D need not be equal. Furthermore, C_n is bound to D_n by a digital signature scheme SIG = (Gen, Sign, Vrfy) in a simple manner that we explain shortly below. Example chain graphs for C_n, D_n are shown in Fig. 1.

We view *blockchain mining* as the process of labeling the vertices of these chains. We let $(b_i := (c_i, d_i))_{i \in [n]_0}$ denote the labels of these chains, where c_i and d_i denote the ith labels of the canonical and data blocks, respectively. Although our treatment allows for arbitrary labeling, c_i and d_i, for simplicity of exposition, can be assumed to have the following format (which is faithful to existing PoSpace blockchains):

- $c_i = (i, \pi_i)$ where π_i is a canonical computation that depends on the labels of parent proof blocks $(c_{i_1}, \ldots, c_{i_q})$ where $(i_1, \ldots, i_q) = \mathsf{parents}_C(i)$. For simplicity, we assume that $\pi = (\delta_i, (\mathsf{VDF}_v^i, \mathsf{VDF}_p^i))$ where δ_i is a proof of space $[1, 10]$ and $(\mathsf{VDF}_v^i, \mathsf{VDF}_p^i)$ is a verifiable delay function [5] computation/proof pair.
- $d_i = (s_i, \mathsf{data}_i)$ where $s_i \leftarrow \mathsf{Sign}_{\mathsf{sk}}(d_{i_1} \| \ldots \| d_{i_p} \| \mathsf{data}_i \| c_i)$ is a signature on the parents data blocks $d_{i_1} \| \ldots \| d_{i_p}$ where $(i_1, \ldots, i_p) = \mathsf{parents}_D(i)$, the current data data_i, and the current proof block c_i.

These simplifying assumptions are without loss of generality. For example, in both Chia and SpaceMint, π_i contains a *unique* PoSpace δ_i. The PoSpace challenge chal_i for δ_i is uniquely determined by the labels of its parents $\mathsf{parents}_C(i)$. The value of δ_i is defined by chal_i and the public key pk associated with the signing key sk of SIG. In Chia, π_i additionally contains $(\mathsf{VDF}_v^i, \mathsf{VDF}_p^i)$ where VDF_v^i is a verifiable delay function evaluation on input x_i for a time parameter t_i and VDF_p^i is a unique proof of correctness of VDF_v^i; both x_i and t_i are uniquely defined by $\mathsf{parents}_C(i)$.[4]

3.2 SNACKs for PoSpace Blockchains: An Overview

Constructing SNACKs for PoSpace blockchains is more subtle than for PoW blockchains, mainly due to the requirement that proof chain blocks must remain canonical. That the proof chain must be canonical (non-grindable) is crucial for the security of PoSpace blockchains [8, 12].[5] (If such a requirement is relaxed, then simpler solutions are possible – see the full version.)

In the full version, we give a detailed account of the generic PoSW-enabled SNACK for single-chain blockchains of [3]. We give here a high-level overview. Let $H_n = ([n]_0, E_H)$ be the underlying chain graph of the blockchain in question and $G_n = ([n]_0, E_G)$ the chain graph of any (graph-labeling) PoSW scheme. Then, the SNACK construction works by first defining an augmented chain graph $K_n = ([n]_0, E_K = E_H \cup E_G)$ whose ith augmented label is $k_i = (g_i, h_i)$ where g_i is defined by the underlying PoSW scheme and h_i contains the actual content of the block including the publicly verifiable (say PoW) proof π_i. The SNACK then would essentially be a non-interactive augmented PoSW on this labeled K_n. The (α, ϵ)-knowledge soundness guarantees imply that from any successful prover, we can extract, except with probability ϵ, an (α, R)-valid path $(P, L_P, (p_v)_{v \in P})$ as defined in Definition 4, such that the labels of L_P are sequentially computed and have total weight α.

For notational simplicity, we refer to (α, R)-valid paths $(P, L_P, (p_v)_{v \in P})$ by (P, L_P), and when R is either clear from the context or irrelevant for the discussion, we call an (α, R)-valid path, α-valid.

---

[4] In fact, in Chia, the pair $(\mathsf{VDF}_v^i, \mathsf{VDF}_p^i)$ is a pair of tuples, i.e., $\mathsf{VDF}_v^i = (y_{i_1}, \ldots, y_{i_k})$ and $\mathsf{VDF}_p^i = (\rho_{i_1}, \ldots, \rho_{i_k})$ where (y_{i_j}, ρ_{i_j}) is a VDF evaluation/proof pair on a challenge and time parameter pair (x_{i_j}, t_{i_j}), which is uniquely defined by the proof chain so far $(c_0, \ldots, c_{i-1})$.

[5] In the full version, we highlight the need for canonical proofs in PoSpace blockchains.

(In the full version, we explore a few (insecure) natural approaches that resemble the PoSW-enabled SNACK construction for single-chain blockchains.)

Our SNACK. We construct a SNACK for $B_n = (C_n, D_n)$, by constructing two SNACKs *simultaneously*, one for C_n, call it CS, and one for the data chain D_n, call it DS. Both CS and DS are generic PoSW-enabled constructions following the blueprint of [3]. They also satisfy:

1. CS and DS both use PoSW, i.e., the same underlying PoSW scheme
2. PoSW uses a *deterministic* Com, and
3. CS is embedded into DS.

The final PoSpace SNACK is simply DS. The soundness guarantees of DS is that from any convincing prover, we can extract an α-valid path (P, L_P) where $L_P = ((c_{i_1}, d_{i_1}), \ldots, (c_{i_k}, d_{i_m}))$ is such that (c_{i_j}, d_{i_j}) is a valid blockchain block and that $(c_{i_1}, \ldots, c_{i_m})$ and $(d_{i_1}, \ldots, d_{i_m})$ are both sequentially computed. These are the guarantees that a SNACK should provide for a blockchain: sequentiality of its blocks.

Let's justify the design choice made above. Note that assuming the same PoSW chain graph in CS and DS simplifies the final construction, and requiring Com to be deterministic is necessary to preserve the canonical nature of the augmented proof chain.[6] To see the necessity of embedding CS into DS, let's see what guarantees one would get from these SNACKs individually, and why these guarantees falls short of our goal of ensuring the sequentiality of the combined PoSpace blockchain blocks.

From α-valid paths (P_c, L_{P_c}) and (P_d, L_{P_d}) extracted from CS and DS respectively, we would like to construct an α-valid path (P, L_P) as above. However, as it may be the case that $P_c \neq P_d$, i.e., P_c, P_d may not coincide, constructing (P, L_P) with weight α out of (P_c, L_{P_c}) and (P_d, L_{P_d}) may not be possible.

A natural first idea towards ensuring $P_c = P_d$ would be to fix the same PoSW scheme in both CS and DS. That is, we augment both C_n and D_n with the same PoSW chain graph G_n to arrive at augmented chain graphs K_n^c and K_n^d, respectively. However, this doesn't mean that $K_n^c = K_n^d$ as C_n need not be equal to D_n, and hence, the extracted paths may be such that $P_c \neq P_d$. But as we will show in Lemma 1 below, in any PoSW-enabled SNACK, over an augmented chain graph, say $K_n^c = ([n]_0, E_K = E_C \cup E_G)$, any *extractable* α-valid path (P_c, L_{P_c}) is such that P_c lies in G_n. Still, that P_c and P_d lie in G_n doesn't mean they coincide, but now we are a step closer towards ensuring they do.

---

[6] We remark that all PoSW schemes in the ROM [2–4,7,9,11] use deterministic Com anyway.

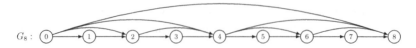

Fig. 2. An illustrative example DAG of a skiplist-based PoSW [3,4].

To be able to compose an α-valid path (P, L_P) from α-valid paths (P_c, L_{P_c}) and (P_d, L_{P_d}), not only we want to ensure that $P_c = P_d$, but also that their labels are valid and bound, i.e., let $L_{P_c} = (c_{i_1}, \ldots, c_{i_m})$ and $L_{P_d} = (d_{i_1}, \ldots, d_{i_m})$, then it must hold that (c_{i_j}, d_{i_j}) is a valid blockchain block including that d_{i_j} contains a signature on c_{i_j}. Recall that SIG binds C_n to D_n. Now because c_{i_j} is needed to validate d_{i_j}, DS can't simply be independent of CS.

To resolve all issues at once, that is, to make sure $P_c = P_d$ and that $L_P := ((c_{i_1}, d_{i_1}), \ldots, (c_{i_m}, d_{i_m}))$ is valid, where $P := P_c = P_d$, we require that CS and DS use the *same* underlying PoSW scheme, and furthermore, *embed* CS into DS. By embedding the augmented labeled proof chain K_n^c into the augmented labeled data chain K_n^d, and relying on Lemma 1 below, we ensure that the same labeled path in K_n^d contains a valid labeling in K_n^c at the same time.

3.3   SNACK for PoSpace Blockchains: The Main Construction

For simplicity, fix an integer n and let PoSW be any (graph-labeling) PoSW scheme and $\Gamma_n = (G_n = ([n]_0, E_G), \Omega_n)$ its underlying weighted chain graph, where G_n is a chain graph and $\Omega_n : [n]_0 \to [0, 1]$ s.t. $\Omega_n([n]_0) = 1$ is a weight function. We will use the PoSW from [3,4] in our *illustrative examples*. Its underlying DAG is depicted in Fig. 2. (We emphasize the our SNACK construction works for *any* graph-labeling PoSW scheme whose underlying graph is a chain graph.)

Furthermore, let $B_n = (C_n, D_n)$ be a PoSpace blockchain with ψ being its genesis block, and R_ψ^c and R_ψ^d be the polynomial-time validity relations for the (labeled) proof and data chains, respectively. That is, let $(i_1, \ldots, i_p) := \mathsf{parents}_C(i)$, then

$$R_\psi^c(i, c_i, (c_{i_1}, \ldots, c_{i_p})) = 1 \tag{5}$$

iff c_i is a valid proof chain block, and for $(i_1, \ldots, i_q) := \mathsf{parents}_D(i)$:

$$R_\psi^d(i, (c_i, d_i := (s_i, \mathsf{data}_i)), (d_{i_1}, \ldots, d_{i_q})) = 1 \tag{6}$$

iff d_i is a valid data chain block. In particular, (6) implies that

$$\mathsf{Vrfy}_{\mathsf{pk}}(d_{i_1} \| \ldots \| d_{i_q} \| \mathsf{data}_i \| c_i, s_i) = 1 \ . \tag{7}$$

The validity relation for B_n is simply the relation that checks that both (5) and (6) hold simultaneously. These validity relations are blockchain specific and they can be augmented or redefined to suite the specific instantiation of the PoSpace blockchain in question.

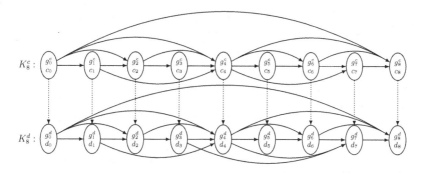

Fig. 3. Example K_8^c and K_8^d defined in (8) and (9) where C_n and D_n are from Fig. 1 and G_8 is from Fig. 2. CS and DS are w.r.t. K_8^c and K_8^d, respectively. The dashed arrows indicate the labels of the source are embedded into the labels of the target. The labels of these graphs are computed by SInit and SMine of Fig. 4.

Augmented Blockchains. We define *augmented chain graphs* K_n^c and K_n^d that respectively underlie CS and DS as follows:

$$K_n^c = ([n]_0, E_{K^c}) \quad \text{with} \quad E_{K^c} = E_G \cup E_C \tag{8}$$

$$K_n^d = ([n]_0, E_{K^d}) \quad \text{with} \quad E_{K^d} = E_G \cup E_D \cup E_C \tag{9}$$

Note that while K_n^c augments C_n with G_n, K_n^d augments the union of C_n and D_n with G_n. The reason for this is that we would like the DS extractor to succeed in extracting a labeled path in (the labeled) K_n^d such that it contains a labeled path in K_n^c, and for this to be possible, we make sure that (1) the (augmented) labels of K_n^c are embedded (as data) in the (augmented) labels of K_n^d and that (2) $E_{K^d} \supseteq E_{K^c}$. Examples of these graphs are depicted in Fig. 3.

Let τ be an oracle and χ a bitstring to be defined later, we define oracles $(\tau_i)_{i \in [n]_0}$ as $\tau_i(\cdot) := \tau(i, \chi, \cdot)$ and use these oracles to label our augmented blockchain.

The *augmented blockchain* is obtained by *labeling* the augmented chain graphs K_n^c and K_n^d at once, and furthermore, embedding K_n^c in K_n^d as data. This labeling is done using oracles $(\tau_i)_{i \in [n]_0}$, where $\tau_i(\cdot) := \tau(i, \chi, \cdot)$ for a random oracle τ and random bitstring χ.

This labeling is formalized by the augmented mining algorithms Init and SMine, in Fig. 4. In particular, from an initial genesis block ψ, we define in Init, an augmented genesis block $\sigma := L_K(0)$, which contains, in addition to ψ and pk_0, PoSW-related data such as χ and pp.

SMine, on input $(k_j^d := (g_j^d, d_j)_{j \in [i-1]_0}$, i.e., the augmented labels of the first i vertices of K_n^d, as well as the current data data_i including transactions and the signing/verification key pair $(\mathsf{sk}, \mathsf{pk})$ of an arbitrary space farmer, and some auxiliary information $\mathsf{aux}_{i-1}^c, \mathsf{aux}_{i-1}^d$ related to the commitment opening (which we explicitly state in Fig. 4, but ignore in this informal discussion for simplicity), computes the augmented labels of both the proof and data chain as follows.

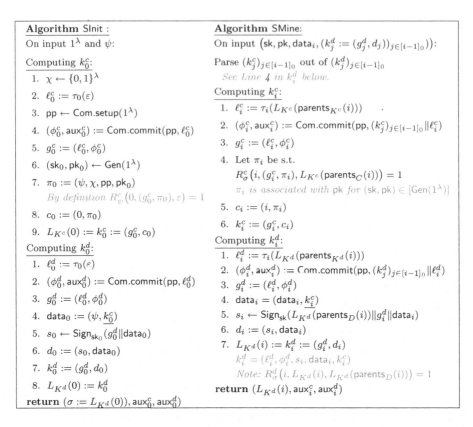

Algorithm SInit :

On input 1^λ and ψ:

Computing k_0^c:

1. $\chi \leftarrow \{0,1\}^\lambda$
2. $\ell_0^c := \tau_0(\varepsilon)$
3. $pp \leftarrow \mathsf{Com.setup}(1^\lambda)$
4. $(\phi_0^c, \mathsf{aux}_0^c) := \mathsf{Com.commit}(pp, \ell_0^c)$
5. $g_0^c := (\ell_0^c, \phi_0^c)$
6. $(\mathsf{sk}_0, \mathsf{pk}_0) \leftarrow \mathsf{Gen}(1^\lambda)$
7. $\pi_0 := (\psi, \chi, pp, \mathsf{pk}_0)$
   By definition $R_\psi^c\big(0, (g_0^c, \pi_0), \varepsilon\big) = 1$
8. $c_0 := (0, \pi_0)$
9. $L_{K^c}(0) := k_0^c := (g_0^c, c_0)$

Computing k_0^d:

1. $\ell_0^d := \tau_0(\varepsilon)$
2. $(\phi_0^d, \mathsf{aux}_0^d) := \mathsf{Com.commit}(pp, \ell_0^d)$
3. $g_0^d := (\ell_0^d, \phi_0^d)$
4. $\mathsf{data}_0 := (\psi, k_0^c)$
5. $s_0 \leftarrow \mathsf{Sign}_{\mathsf{sk}_0}(g_0^d \| \mathsf{data}_0)$
6. $d_0 := (s_0, \mathsf{data}_0)$
7. $k_0^d := (g_0^d, d_0)$
8. $L_{K^d}(0) := k_0^d$

return $(\sigma := L_{K^d}(0)), \mathsf{aux}_0^c, \mathsf{aux}_0^d)$

Algorithm SMine:

On input $\big(\mathsf{sk}, \mathsf{pk}, \mathsf{data}_i, (k_j^d := (g_j^d, d_j))_{j \in [i-1]_0}\big)$:

Parse $(k_j^c)_{j \in [i-1]_0}$ out of $(k_j^d)_{j \in [i-1]_0}$
See Line 4 in k_i^d below.

Computing k_i^c:

1. $\ell_i^c := \tau_i(L_{K^c}(\mathsf{parents}_{K^c}(i)))$
2. $(\phi_i^c, \mathsf{aux}_i^c) := \mathsf{Com.commit}(pp, (k_j^c)_{j \in [i-1]_0} \| \ell_i^c)$
3. $g_i^c := (\ell_i^c, \phi_i^c)$
4. Let π_i be s.t.
   $R_\sigma^c\big(i, (g_i^c, \pi_i), L_{K^c}(\mathsf{parents}_C(i))\big) = 1$
   π_i is associated with pk for $(\mathsf{sk}, \mathsf{pk}) \in [\mathsf{Gen}(1^\lambda)]$
5. $c_i := (i, \pi_i)$
6. $k_i^c := (g_i^c, c_i)$

Computing k_i^d:

1. $\ell_i^d := \tau_i(L_{K^d}(\mathsf{parents}_{K^d}(i)))$
2. $(\phi_i^d, \mathsf{aux}_i^d) := \mathsf{Com.commit}(pp, (k_j^d)_{j \in [i-1]_0} \| \ell_i^d)$
3. $g_i^d := (\ell_i^d, \phi_i^d)$
4. $\mathsf{data}_i = (\mathsf{data}_i, k_i^c)$
5. $s_i \leftarrow \mathsf{Sign}_{\mathsf{sk}}(L_{K^d}(\mathsf{parents}_D(i)) \| g_i^d \| \mathsf{data}_i)$
6. $d_i := (s_i, \mathsf{data}_i)$
7. $L_{K^d}(i) := k_i^d := (g_i^d, d_i)$
   $k_i^d := (\ell_i^d, \phi_i^d, s_i, \mathsf{data}_i, k_i^c)$
   Note: $R_\sigma^d\big(i, L_{K^d}(i), L_{K^d}(\mathsf{parents}_D(i))\big) = 1$

return $(L_{K^d}(i), \mathsf{aux}_i^c, \mathsf{aux}_i^d)$

Fig. 4. The mining algorithms Init and SMine for PoSpace-augmented blockchains.

As for the ith augmented proof chain label, SMine computes the PoSW label ℓ_i^c using the random oracle τ_i and the graph structure of K_n^c, computes a *deterministic* commitment ϕ_i^c of the labels $(k_j^c := (g_j^c, c_j))_{j \in [i-1]_0}$ and ℓ_i^c, and defines the label $g_i^c := (\ell_i^c, \phi_i^c)$. We stress that the commitment ϕ_i^c must be deterministic, for otherwise the proof chain becomes grindable. The label of the proof chain is defined as $c_i := (i, \pi_i)$ and the augmented label is defined as $L_{K^c}(i) := k_i^c := (g_i^c, c_i)$. For the sequentiality guarantees of the PoSW to carry on to the SNACKs, we must ensure that in the augmented blockchain, π_i is computed *after* ϕ_i^c – see [3] for a detailed discussion on this point. However, note that Line 4 in Fig. 4 doesn't make this explicit, as ensuring this condition is blockchain-specific.

As for the ith augmented data chain label, SMine computes the PoSW label ℓ_i^d using τ_i and the graph structure of K_n^d, computes a commitment ϕ_i^d of the labels $(k_j^d := (g_j^d, d_j))_{j \in [i-1]_0}$ and ℓ_i^d, and defines the label $g_i^d := (\ell_i^d, \phi_i^d)$. A space farmer/miner who generates a PoSpace proof δ_i using pk, computes a digital signature s_i, using the corresponding signing key sk, on $(L_{K^d}(\mathsf{parents}_D(i)) \| g_i^d \| \mathsf{data}_i)$, where $L_{K^d}(\mathsf{parents}_D(i))$ are the augmented labels of the parents of i in D, data_i is the current data including (the now embedded) k_i^c, transactions, and any arbitrary data that the original mining protocol allows. Finally set $d_i := (s_i, \mathsf{data}_i)$ and $L_{K^d} := k_i^d := (g_i^d, d_i)$.

Blockchain validity must be adapted to accommodate the augmentation. Therefore, we define the *augmented validity relations* R_σ^c and R_σ^d of the proof and data chains, by overriding R_ψ^c and R_ψ^d, respectively. Both R_σ^c and R_σ^d still consider the same graph structure as R_ψ^c and R_ψ^d but expect augmented labels. Concretely, we override R_ψ^c from (5) as

$$R_\sigma^c\big(i, L_{K^c}(i), L_{K^c}(\mathsf{parents}_C(i))\big) = 1 \ , \tag{10}$$

iff the augmented block is valid. Note that σ is defined by SInit and is the augmented genesis block. As before, this validity is blockchain specific. Similarly, we override R_ψ^d from (6) as

$$R_\sigma^d\big(i, L_{K^d}(i), L_{K^d}(\mathsf{parents}_D(i))\big) = 1 \tag{11}$$

iff the augmented data block is valid, which in particular, implies that

$$\mathsf{Vrfy}_{\mathsf{pk}}(L_{K^d}(\mathsf{parents}_D(i))\|g_i^d\|\mathsf{data}_i, s_i) = 1 \ . \tag{12}$$

Note that R_σ^d doesn't verify transaction consistency in data_i. The consistency of data_i is assumed, i.e., we assume honest miners would not finalize block i that contains data_i that is inconsistent with $\mathsf{data}_0, \ldots, \mathsf{data}_{i-1}$. The consistency of data in orthogonal to the SNACK construction.

As the ith augmented (proof/data) block contains, not only blockchain-specific, but also PoSW-specific data, we define augmented validity relations $\tilde{R}_\sigma^c$ and $\tilde{R}_\sigma^d$ that check the validity of (a) the blockchain-specific data using R_σ^c and R_σ^d, respectively, and check (b) the PoSW data. Concretely, define $\tilde{R}_\sigma^c, \tilde{R}_\sigma^d$ and R_σ:

$$\tilde{R}_\sigma^c\big(i, L_{K^c}(i), L_{K^c}(\mathsf{parents}_{K^c}(i))\big) = 1 \Leftrightarrow \exists\, x_i \text{ s.t.} \tag{13}$$
$$R_\sigma^c\big(i, L_{K^c}(i), L_{K^c}(\mathsf{parents}_C(i))\big) = 1 \wedge L_{K^c}(i) = \tau_i(L_{K^c}(\mathsf{parents}_{K^c}(i)))\|x_i.$$

$$\tilde{R}_\sigma^d\big(i, L_{K^d}(i), L_{K^d}(\mathsf{parents}_{K^d}(i))\big) = 1 \Leftrightarrow \exists\, x_i \text{ s.t.} \tag{14}$$
$$L_{K^d}(i) = \tau_i(L_{K^d}(\mathsf{parents}_{K^d}(i)))\|x_i \wedge R_\sigma^d\big(i, L_{K^d}(i), L_{K^d}(\mathsf{parents}_D(i))\big) = 1.$$

$$R_\sigma\big(i, L_{K^d}(i), L_{K^d}(\mathsf{parents}_{K^d}(i))\big) = 1 \Leftrightarrow$$
$$\tilde{R}_\sigma^c\big(i, L_{K^c}(i), L_{K^c}(\mathsf{parents}_{K^c}(i))\big) = 1 \ \wedge \ \tilde{R}_\sigma^d\big(i, L_{K^d}(i), L_{K^d}(\mathsf{parents}_{K^d}(i))\big) = 1 \ . \tag{15}$$

where by construction (see Fig. 4), $L_{K^c}(i)$ is contained in $L_{K^d}(i)$ as part of data_i and $\mathsf{parents}_{K^c}(i)$ is contained in $\mathsf{parents}_{K^d}(i)$ by definition of K_n^d (9).

Algorithm PoSW.ver$_{K^c}$:	Algorithm PoSW.open$_{K^c}$:
On input (χ, ι_i, o_i):	On input $(\chi, \mathsf{pp}, \phi_n, \mathsf{aux}_n, L, \iota_i)$:
1. Run $b_i := $ PoSW.ver(χ, ι_i, o_i) modified as follows: whenever it queries $\tau_j(L_{K^c}(\mathsf{parents}_G(j)))$ for some j, issue query $\tau_j(L_{K^c}(\mathsf{parents}_{K^c}(j)))$ instead. *(Missing labels are provided in $o_{i,2}$.)*	1. $o_{i,1} \leftarrow$ PoSW.open$(\chi, \mathsf{pp}, \phi_n, \mathsf{aux}_n, L, \iota_i)$ *(PoSW.open acts based on edges E_G.)*
	2. $\mathcal{J} := \{ j \in [n]_0 \colon L_{K^c}(\mathsf{parents}_G(j))$ which appear in $o_{i,1} \}$
2. **return** b_i	3. $o_{i,2} := \{ (j, L_{K^c}(\mathsf{parents}_C(j))) \}_{j \in \mathcal{J}}$
	4. **return** $o_i := (o_{i,1}, o_{i,2})$

Fig. 5. Algorithms PoSW.open$_{K^c}$ and PoSW.ver$_{K^c}$ defined based on PoSW.open and PoSW.ver, respectively. Algorithms PoSW.open$_{K^d}$ and PoSW.ver$_{K^d}$ are defined analogously by changing every occurrence of c to d and C to D.

Arguments for Augmented PoSpace Blockchains. We first define the witness relation $\mathcal{R}$ with respect to which we construct our SNACK.

Definition 7 (Augmented PoSpace chain language). *We define the augmented PoSpace chain relation $\mathcal{R}^{(1)}_{\Gamma^d_n, R_\sigma, \mathsf{Com}}$ for any $\alpha \in (0,1]$ as*

$$\mathcal{R}^{(\alpha)}_{\Gamma^d_n, R_\sigma, \mathsf{Com}} = \left\{ \begin{array}{l} ((\mathsf{prm} := (\sigma, \mathsf{pp}), \eta := ((\phi^c, \phi^d), n), \\ w := (P, L^d_P, (p^d_i)_{i \in P}, \rho^c, \rho^d)) \text{ s.t.} \\ (P, L^d_P, (p^d_i)_{i \in P}) \text{ is an } (\alpha, R_\sigma) - \text{valid path in } \Gamma^d_n \\ \wedge \mathsf{Com.ver}(\mathsf{pp}, \phi^c, L^c_P, P, \rho^c) = 1 \\ \wedge \mathsf{Com.ver}(\mathsf{pp}, \phi^d, L^d_P, P, \rho^d) = 1 \end{array} \right\} . \tag{16}$$

where R_σ is defined in (15) and $\Gamma^d_n := (K^d_n, \Omega_n)$ for K^d_n as in (9) and Ω_n from the underlying PoSW scheme PoSW. *We let $\mathcal{L}_{\Gamma^d, R_\sigma, \mathsf{Com}}$ (cf. Definition 5) be the language associated with $\mathcal{R}^{(1)}_{\Gamma^d_n, R_\sigma, \mathsf{Com}}$.*

Having formalized $\mathcal{L}_{\Gamma^d, R_\sigma, \mathsf{Com}}$, we now build for it a succinct Argument of Chain Knowledge[7] (ACK) system ACK := (ACK.P, ACK.V), which we later Fiat-Shamir to get our final DS. The ACK is given in Fig. 6. Note that the prover takes as input the labeling of K^d_n as its witness. Additionally, the SNACK parameter generator G outputs prm. Syntactically, ACK can be seen as two copies of the respective ACK construction of [3], one for the proof chain and one for the data chain. The difference is that we embed K^c_n into K^d_n, use the same underlying PoSW scheme as well as the same verifier challenges in these two copies.

Theorem 1. *Let* SNACK := (SNACK.P, SNACK.V) *be the non-interactive counterpart of* ACK *from Fig. 6, then in the ROM,* SNACK *is an (α, ϵ)-knowledge-sound SNACK for $\mathcal{L}_{\Gamma^d, R_\sigma, \mathsf{Com}}$ as in Definition 7 if* PoSW *is an (α, ϵ)-knowledge-sound τ-based GL-PoSW as in [3] with* Com *being its underlying deterministic commitment scheme, $(G_n = ([n]_0, E_G), \Omega_n)_{n \in \mathbb{N}}$ its weighted graph family, and τ modeled as a random oracle.*

---

[7] A SNACK is a succinct and non-interactive ACK.

Verifier ACK.V $= (V_1, V_2)$	Prover ACK.P:

Stage V_1: On input $(1^\lambda, \eta)$:

1. $\forall i \in [t]$ **do** $\iota_i \xleftarrow{\$} \Omega_n$
2. $\iota_0 := 0$
3. **send** $\iota := (\iota_i)_{i \in [t]_0}$ to P

Stage V_2: On input $\gamma := (\gamma_i)_{i \in [t]_0}$:

1. $\forall i \in [t]$ **do**:
   - (a) $b^c_{i,1} := \tilde{R}^c_\sigma(\iota_i, k^c_{\iota_i}, p^c_{\iota_i})$
   - (b) $b^c_{i,2} := \mathsf{PoSW.ver}_{K^c}(\chi, \iota_i, o^c_i)$
   - (c) $b^c_{i,3} := \mathsf{Com.ver}(\mathsf{pp}, \phi^c_n, k^c_{\iota_i}, \iota_i, \rho^c_i)$
   - (d) $b^d_{i,1} := \tilde{R}^d_\sigma(\iota_i, k^d_{\iota_i}, p^d_{\iota_i})$
   - (e) $b^d_{i,2} := \mathsf{PoSW.ver}_{K^d}(\chi, \iota_i, o^d_i)$
   - (f) $b^d_{i,3} := \mathsf{Com.ver}(\mathsf{pp}, \phi^d_n, k^d_{\iota_i}, \iota_i, \rho^d_i)$
2. **output** $\bigwedge_{i=0}^t b^c_{i,1} \wedge b^c_{i,2} \wedge b^c_{i,3} \wedge$
   $\qquad b^d_{i,1} \wedge b^d_{i,2} \wedge b^d_{i,3}$

Prover ACK.P:

On input $(1^\lambda, (\eta, (k^d_j)_{j \in [n]_0}, (\mathsf{aux}^c_n, \mathsf{aux}^d_n), \iota)$:

1. Parse η as $((\sigma, \mathsf{pp}), (\phi^c_n, \phi^d_n, n))$
2. Parse $(k^c_j)_{j \in [n]_0}$ out of $(k^d_j)_{j \in [n]_0}$
3. $\forall i \in [t]_0$ **do**:
   - (a) $o^c_i \leftarrow \mathsf{PoSW.open}_{K^c}$
     $\qquad (\chi, \mathsf{pp}, \phi^c_n, \mathsf{aux}^c_n, (k^c_j)_{j \in [n]_0}, \iota_i)$
   - (b) $o^d_i \leftarrow \mathsf{PoSW.open}_{K^d}$
     $\qquad (\chi, \mathsf{pp}, \phi^d_n, \mathsf{aux}^d_n, (k^d_j)_{j \in [n]_0}, \iota_i)$
     We assume o^d_i contains both $L_{K^d}(\iota_i)$
     and $p^d_i := L_{K^d}(\mathsf{parents}_{K^d}(\iota_i))$.
     Similarly for o^c_i.
   - (c) $\rho^c_i \leftarrow \mathsf{Com.open}(\mathsf{pp}, \phi^c_n, \mathsf{aux}^c_n, k^c_{\iota_i}, \iota_i)$
   - (d) $\rho^d_i \leftarrow \mathsf{Com.open}(\mathsf{pp}, \phi^d_n, \mathsf{aux}^d_n, k^d_{\iota_i}, \iota_i)$
   - (e) $\gamma_i := ((o^c_i, o^d_i), (\rho^c_i, \rho^d_i))$
4. **send** $\gamma := (\gamma_i)_{i \in [t]_0}$ to V_2

Fig. 6. The interactive proof system ACK which underlies our SNACK construction.

SNACK's Cost and Guarantees. We started with an underlying chain $B_n = (C_n, D_n)$ of a PoSpace blockchain, and augmented it to (K^c_n, K^d_n), on which we run ACK, whose non-interactive counterpart SNACK is the SNACK construction for the PoSpace blockchain. The space cost of SNACK is storing in each block in K^c_n a PoSW label and a commitment pair (ℓ^c_i, ϕ^c_i). The same holds for K^d_n. (Note that the embedding of $L_{K^c}(i)$ into $L_{K^d}(i)$ doesn't mean that we actually store $L_{K^c}(i)$ twice, in K^c_n and K^d_n; all what it means is that computing and verifying $L_{K^d}(i)$ requires having $L_{K^c}(i)$ explicitly given as input.) If we instantiate PoSW from either PoSW schemes in [3], then $\phi^c_i = \ell^c_i$ and $\phi^d_i = \ell^d_i$ and hence the space cost is ℓ^c_i and ℓ^d_i per (PoSpace) block. Setting $|\ell^c_i| = |\ell^d_i| = 256$ bits is a reasonable instantiation. Furthermore, modeling a hash function as a RO, ℓ^c_i and ℓ^d_i are efficient hash computations.

Generating SNACK proofs is identical to generating PoSW proofs in the underlying PoSW scheme when $E_C = E_D = \{(i - 1, i) : i \in [n]\}$. The more edges E_C and E_D contain, the bigger the proof size. Furthermore optimizations similar to those given in [3] are possible.

At this storage and computation costs, we get sequentiality guarantees on the blockchain: Fix prm and a statement $(\phi^c, \phi^d, n) \in \mathcal{L}_{\Gamma^d, R_\sigma, \mathsf{Com}}$, then from any convincing SNACK prover, a witness w can be extracted, and such a witness contains an (α, R_σ)-valid path in Γ^d_n, which is sequentially computed. That the extracted path lies in K^d_n is clear, but that it also lies in K^c_n is not. In the sequel, we show that extracted paths must be in K^c_n as well, and hence this shows that the extracted path contains valid blocks in the combined augmented blockchain.

This, in turn, allows us to talk of the PoSpace blockchain as a single sequentially mined chain.

Lemma 1 says that if P is a path extracted by the knowledge-soundness of SNACK from Theorem 1, then the edges of P lie in G_n.

Lemma 1. *Let* SNACK *be as in Theorem 1 and let*

$$\left(\sigma, \eta := (\phi^c, \phi^d, n), w := (P, L_P^d, (p_i^d)_{i \in P}, \rho^c, \rho^d)\right) \in \mathcal{R}_{\Gamma_n^d, R_\sigma, \mathsf{Com}}^{(\alpha)}$$

be such that w is output by the extractor guaranteed by the (α, ϵ)-knowledge soundness of SNACK, *then P is a path in G_n.*

The following lemma shows that SNACK contains an embedded SNACK system for $\mathcal{L}_{\Gamma_n^c, \tilde{R}_\sigma^c, \mathsf{Com}}$, where $\mathcal{L}_{\Gamma_n^c, \tilde{R}_\sigma^c, \mathsf{Com}}$ is as in Definition 5 and $\tilde{R}_\sigma^c$ as in (13).

Lemma 2. *Let* $\left(\mathsf{prm}, (\phi^c, \phi^d, n), (P, L_P^d, (p_i^d)_{i \in P}, \rho^c, \rho^d)\right) \in \mathcal{R}_{\Gamma_n^d, R_\sigma, \mathsf{Com}}^{(\alpha)}$ *and P be a path in G_n, then* $\left(\mathsf{prm}, (\phi^c, n), (P, L_P^c, (p_i^c)_{i \in P}, \rho^c)\right) \in \mathcal{R}_{\Gamma_n^c, \tilde{R}_\sigma^c, \mathsf{Com}}^{(\alpha)}$, *where* $\mathcal{R}_{\Gamma_n^c, \tilde{R}_\sigma^c, \mathsf{Com}}^{(\alpha)}$ *is defined as in Definition 5 and $L^c(i), p_i^c$ are embedded in and extracted from $L^d(i), p_i^d$.*

Theorem 1 and Lemma 2 imply Corollary 1, which shows that SNACK proves knowledge of sequentially computed and valid PoSpace blockchain.

Corollary 1. *Let* SNACK *be as in Theorem 1 and let*

$$\left(\sigma, \eta := (\phi^c, \phi^d, n), w := (P, L_P^d, (p_i^d)_{i \in P}, \rho^c, \rho^d)\right) \in \mathcal{R}_{\Gamma_n^d, R_\sigma, \mathsf{Com}}^{(\alpha)}$$

be s.t. w is output by the extractor guaranteed by the (α, ϵ)-knowledge soundness of SNACK, *then (P, L_P^d) is a sequentially-computed path containing valid PoSpace blocks, i.e., let $P = (i_0, \ldots, i_k)$, then $\forall j \in [k]_0$, $L_P^d(i_j)$ contains a valid augmented data chain block which contains a signature on a valid augmented proof chain block $L_P^c(i_j)$, and for every $j \in [k]$, $L_P^c(i_j)$ is computed after $L_P^c(i_{j-1})$ and $L_P^d(i_j)$ after $L_P^d(i_{j-1})$.*

Proofs of Theorem 1 and Lemmas 1 and 2 are, due to space constrains, given the full version.

Acknowledgements. I want to thank Karen Klein for a fruitful discussion at the beginning of the project and for her feedback on an early version of this paper. Parts of this work were done while the first author was at TUWien funded by the Vienna Science and Technology Fund (WWTF)[10.47379/VRG18002]. The project has also received funding in part from the European Research Council (ERC) under the European Union's Horizon 2020 research and innovation program under project PIC-OCRYPT (grant agreement No. 101001283), the Spanish Government under projects SCUM (ref. RTI2018-102043-B-I00), the Madrid Regional Government under project BLOQUES (ref. S2018/TCS-4339), and a research grant from Nomadic Labs and the Tezos Foundation.

References

1. Abusalah, H., Alwen, J., Cohen, B., Khilko, D., Pietrzak, K., Reyzin, L.: Beyond Hellman's time-memory trade-offs with applications to proofs of space. In: Takagi, T., Peyrin, T. (eds.) ASIACRYPT 2017, Part II. LNCS, vol. 10625, pp. 357–379. Springer, Cham (2017). https://doi.org/10.1007/978-3-319-70697-9_13
2. Abusalah, H., Cini, V.: An incremental POSW for general weight distributions. In: Hazay, C., Stam, M. (eds.) Advances in Cryptology - EUROCRYPT 2023, Part II. LNCS, vol. 14005, pp. 282–311. Springer, Cham (2023). https://doi.org/10.1007/978-3-031-30617-4_10
3. Abusalah, H., Fuchsbauer, G., Gaži, P., Klein, K.: Snacks: leveraging proofs of sequential work for blockchain light clients. Cryptology ePrint Archive, Paper 2022/240 (2022). https://eprint.iacr.org/2022/240
4. Abusalah, H., Kamath, C., Klein, K., Pietrzak, K., Walter, M.: Reversible proofs of sequential work. In: Ishai, Y., Rijmen, V. (eds.) EUROCRYPT 2019, Part II. LNCS, vol. 11477, pp. 277–291. Springer, Cham (2019). https://doi.org/10.1007/978-3-030-17656-3_10
5. Boneh, D., Bonneau, J., Bünz, B., Fisch, B.: Verifiable delay functions. In: Shacham, H., Boldyreva, A. (eds.) CRYPTO 2018. LNCS, vol. 10991, pp. 757–788. Springer, Cham (2018). https://doi.org/10.1007/978-3-319-96884-1_25
6. Bünz, B., Kiffer, L., Luu, L., Zamani, M.: Flyclient: super-light clients for cryptocurrencies. In: 2020 IEEE Symposium on Security and Privacy, SP 2020, San Francisco, CA, USA, May 18–21, 2020, pp. 928–946. IEEE (2020). https://doi.org/10.1109/SP40000.2020.00049
7. Cohen, B., Pietrzak, K.: Simple proofs of sequential work. In: Nielsen, J.B., Rijmen, V. (eds.) EUROCRYPT 2018, Part II. LNCS, vol. 10821, pp. 451–467. Springer, Cham (2018). https://doi.org/10.1007/978-3-319-78375-8_15
8. Cohen, B., Pietrzak, K.: The chia network blockchain (2019). https://www.chia.net/assets/ChiaGreenPaper.pdf
9. Döttling, N., Lai, R.W.F., Malavolta, G.: Incremental proofs of sequential work. In: Ishai, Y., Rijmen, V. (eds.) EUROCRYPT 2019, Part II. LNCS, vol. 11477, pp. 292–323. Springer, Cham (2019). https://doi.org/10.1007/978-3-030-17656-3_11
10. Dziembowski, S., Faust, S., Kolmogorov, V., Pietrzak, K.: Proofs of space. In: Gennaro, R., Robshaw, M. (eds.) CRYPTO 2015, Part II. LNCS, vol. 9216, pp. 585–605. Springer, Heidelberg (2015). https://doi.org/10.1007/978-3-662-48000-7_29
11. Mahmoody, M., Moran, T., Vadhan, S.P.: Publicly verifiable proofs of sequential work. In: Kleinberg, R.D. (ed.) ITCS 2013, pp. 373–388. ACM (2013). https://doi.org/10.1145/2422436.2422479
12. Park, S., Kwon, A., Fuchsbauer, G., Gaži, P., Alwen, J., Pietrzak, K.: SpaceMint: a cryptocurrency based on proofs of space. In: Meiklejohn, S., Sako, K. (eds.) FC 2018. LNCS, vol. 10957, pp. 480–499. Springer, Heidelberg (2018). https://doi.org/10.1007/978-3-662-58387-6_26

Proof of Necessary Work: Succinct State Verification with Fairness Guarantees

Assimakis Kattis[(✉)] and Joseph Bonneau

New York University, New York, NY 10012, USA
{kattis,jcb}@cs.nyu.edu

Abstract. Blockchain-based payment systems utilize an append-only log of transactions whose correctness can be verified by any observer. Classically, verification costs grow linearly in either the number of transactions or blocks in the blockchain (often both). Incrementally Verifiable Computation (IVC) can be used to enable constant-time verification, but generating the necessary proofs is expensive. We introduce the notion of Proof of Necessary Work (PoNW), in which proof generation is an integral part of the proof-of-work used in Nakamoto consensus, producing proofs using energy that would otherwise be wasted. We implement and benchmark a prototype of our system, enabling stateless clients to verify the entire blockchain history in about 40 milliseconds.

Keywords: proof-of-work · zero-knowledge proofs · consensus algorithms

1 Introduction

Balancing throughput with decentralization is a major challenge in modern cryptocurrencies. Current systems such as Bitcoin require participants to process the entire system history to verify that the current state (the most recent block in the chain) is correct. Despite strict limits on blockchain growth which cap total system throughput, verification costs are prohibitive for many clients. Joining the system requires downloading and verifying over 450 GB of blockchain history (as of 2022) which takes days on a typical laptop. In practice, most clients don't perform independent verification and rely on a trusted third party instead.

Succinct blockchains aim to support efficient verification of the system's entire history by any participant without trusting any third parties. Participants only need to obtain some fixed public parameters from a trusted source (e.g. the genesis block and the system's rules). Participants can then join the system at any time and receive a succinct validity proof for the most recent block in the system using minimal bandwidth and time. These proofs demonstrate both that there exists a sequence of valid transactions from the genesis state S_0 to the state committed in the current block, and that the block's *branch* (the sequence of predecessor blocks) is of quality q according to the consensus protocol. In this work we focus on aggregate proof-of-work (PoW) difficulty as the measure of

© The Author(s) 2024
F. Baldimtsi and C. Cachin (Eds.): FC 2023, LNCS 13951, pp. 18–35, 2024.
https://doi.org/10.1007/978-3-031-47751-5_2

branch quality, as used in Bitcoin consensus. Currently, systems such as Bitcoin require $O(t + h)$ work to completely verify a branch containing t transactions and h blocks. Succinct proofs enable optimal asymptotic performance of $O(1)$ verification costs for a client joining the system at any point in its history.

A key challenge for succinct blockchains is incentivizing the expensive costs of computing a validity proof for each block. Meanwhile, Bitcoin employs proof-of-work (PoW), which provides system security by verifying energy consumption. This energy, while necessary for the consensus protocol, is not used for anything else and hence is often described as 'wasted.' We propose a new approach to useful PoW in which the work aids in the verification of the system itself. We denote this as *proof of necessary work* (PoNW) and show how it can be used within a succinct blockchain architecture as a suitable PoW puzzle.

A synergistic benefit is directly incentivizing hardware acceleration of zero-knowledge proofs. This is relevant for many distributed payment systems in which proof generation time is a critical bottleneck limiting transaction throughput and/or latency [6,7,15,20]. Indeed, recent industry developments [2] based on our work have yielded interest in dedicating resources toward an industry-wide effort to maximize the performance of zero-knowledge proof systems. We believe this to be beneficial not only for distributed payments, but also for any application where high-throughput, low-latency and low-energy zero-knowledge proof generation is required.

Building a consensus algorithm which produces validity proofs for each block as a useful byproduct requires carefully designing the PoW process to replicate the security properties of Bitcoin's non-useful puzzle. Our main technical contribution is a method to deeply embed a nonce into the proof computation process, making it suitable as a *progress-free* PoW puzzle. We formalize this intuition by introducing the notion of ϵ-amortization resistance and propose a protocol which achieves this. Our results are based on the average-case hardness of multiexponentiation in the Generic Group Model (GGM) [32]. We build a prototype allowing a stateless client to rapidly verify a block (and thus its complete history) in milliseconds with 500 bytes of data downloaded. This also assists miners in quickly validating new blocks broadcast on the network, which may reduce the risk of block collisions and enable faster block frequency.

2   Proof of Necessary Work

To allow proof generation to serve as a PoW puzzle, we require (a) a proof π_i whose generation algorithm $\mathcal{P}$ is moderately difficult to compute and (b) a PoW puzzle $\mathsf{P}_V^{\mathcal{H},d}$ that requires the miner to fully recompute $\mathcal{P}$ to test a potential solution. The second property is necessary for the puzzle to be progress-free for fairness to miners of differing size. Indeed, if generating unique proofs π_i based on randomly sampled nonces n_i is sufficiently 'hard', then using $\mathsf{P}_V^{\mathcal{H},d}$ instead of a generic puzzle (such as computing the double SHA256 digest in Bitcoin) would allow us to not only perform PoW with the same theoretical guarantees, but also compute a valid proof π_i in the process.

We do not formally analyze any consensus properties, since our goal is not to design a new consensus protocol but to retain that used by Bitcoin (and similar systems) and inherit its properties. However, we would like the work done to be useful by producing proofs of each block's validity. We introduce the notion of performing PoW by proving the validity system state, denoted by *Proof of Necessary Work* (PoNW).

Definition 1. *(Proof of Necessary Work).* *Given a pseudorandom function* $\mathcal{H}$ *and a proof* $\pi_i \in \mathcal{Z}$ *in some RSM with transition tuple* (NewState, VerifyState), *we define the verification puzzle* $\mathsf{P}_V^{\mathcal{H},d} : \mathcal{S} \times \mathcal{S} \times \mathcal{Z} \to \{0,1\}$ *with difficulty* d *as the solution to the following function:*

$$\mathsf{P}_V^{\mathcal{H}}(\mathcal{S}_i, \mathcal{S}_{i+1}, \pi_{i+1}) = \mathbf{1} \left[\begin{array}{c} \mathsf{VerifyState}(\mathcal{S}_i, \mathcal{S}_{i+1}, \pi_{i+1}) = 1 \\ \mathcal{H}(\pi_{i+1}) < d \end{array} \right],$$

where $\mathbf{1}[\cdot]$ *is the indicator function.*

By having access to a proof generating algorithm $\mathcal{P}(\mathbf{t}, \mathcal{S}_i, \mathcal{S}_{i+1}, n_i) \to \pi_{i+1}$ that generates unique (yet valid) π_{i+1} for each n_i, we can generate π_{i+1} for $\mathcal{S}_{i+1} = \mathsf{NewState}(\mathbf{t}, \mathcal{S}_i, \pi_i)$ using a uniformly randomly sampled n_i until the puzzle condition is satisfied:

$$\mathsf{P}_V^{\mathcal{H}}(\mathcal{S}_i, \mathcal{S}_{i+1}, \mathcal{P}(\mathbf{t}, \mathcal{S}_i, \mathcal{S}_{i+1}, n_i)) = 1.$$

Then π_{i+1} suffices for public verification that PoW has been performed. This is because our prover will always fail with constant probability (when $\mathcal{H}(\pi_{i+1}) \geq d$), so iteratively sampling new proofs (by sampling new n_i) until a valid one is found can be shown, under the assumption that $\mathcal{P}$ is the most efficient way to find such an n_i, to be a memoryless exponential process and hence *fair*. Note that, by construction, we also guarantee that π_{i+1} is a valid witness for the RSM. The number of transactions verified is always *fixed* (with empty transactions still 'added') as otherwise miners would be incentivized to mine puzzles with the smallest blocks.

Like Nakamoto consensus, our puzzle needs the property that solutions are equally hard to test even after testing an arbitrary number of previous solutions. In other words, a miner should not be able to *amortize* costs while testing multiple potential solutions. This property is defined more formally below based on the μ-Incompressibility of [26], although we work in the bounded-size precomputation model. We model PoNW as a function $f^{\mathcal{O}}$ with limited access to some oracle $\mathcal{O}$ that performs a hard computation in an encoding of some group $\mathbb{G}$.

Definition 2. *(ϵ-Amortization Resistance).* *For inputs of length* λ *and ouputs* $q \in poly(\lambda)$, *function* $f^{\mathcal{O}} = \{f^{\mathcal{O}}(n)\}_{n \in \mathcal{N}}$ *is ϵ-amortization resistant on average with respect to a sampler* S *if for all adversaries* $\mathcal{A} = (\mathcal{A}_1^{\mathcal{O}}, \mathcal{A}_2^{\mathcal{O}})$ *with* $\mathcal{A}$ *performing less than* $(1-\epsilon)qN$ *queries to the oracle* $\mathcal{O}$ *on average, where* N *number of queries required for one evaluation of* $f^{\mathcal{O}}(n)$ *on average, the following is negligible in* λ:

$$\Pr\left[\forall i \in [q], \pi_i = f^{\mathcal{O}}(n_i) \,\middle|\, \begin{array}{l} \{n_i\}_{i=1}^q \leftarrow n, (n, \mathsf{aux}) \leftarrow \mathsf{S}(1^\lambda) \\ \mathsf{precomp} \leftarrow \mathcal{A}_1^{\mathcal{O}}(1^\lambda, \mathsf{aux}) \\ \{\pi_i\}_{i=1}^q \leftarrow \mathcal{A}_2^{\mathcal{O}}(1^\lambda, n, \mathsf{precomp}) \end{array}\right].$$

This definition captures the fact that computing multiple proofs does not come with marginal gains: indeed, provers cannot use larger computational resources to batch process proofs and achieve disproportionate performance improvements. By preventing large miners from achieving algorithmic returns-to-scale, this property is crucial in ensuring fairness. With the above objectives in mind, we now look at how to adapt our implementation to realize such a system.

Before we look at designing an amortization resistant PoNW system, we summarize the computationally expensive components of proof generation in the Quadratic Arithmetic Program (QAP) Non-Interactive Proof (NIPs) of [27] compiled with [21]. For an ℓ-size statement with m internal variables and n constraints, the prover $\mathcal{P}$ needs to (1) update inputs and witnesses, and (2) perform $9m + n$ exponentiations in $\mathbb{G}$ using elements from the proving key as bases. Since updating variable assignments is orders-of-magnitude faster, amortization resistance requires $\mathcal{P}$ to recompute (almost) all exponentiations for each new nonce.

Amortization of Multiexponentiation. Multiexponentiation is inherently amortizable [16,19] given enough memory, although space requirements scale exponentially with the number of computed elements. This is because we can precompute the exponents of specific basis elements and perform look-ups that can be used by multiple evaluations at once. We make precise the relationship between size and amortization gain to demonstrate that non-negligible amortization gains require an infeasibly large amount of space. Since we are interested in average-case guarantees, all input elements to the multiexponentiation algorithm (i.e. the enumerated exponents, or puzzle instances) are sampled uniformly randomly from some S.

We consider amortization in Shoup's Generic Group Model (GGM) [32],[1] in which the adversary can only compute products based on existing group elements (with non-negligible probability), or directly query the exponentiation of some index. The adversary has access to a multiplication oracle $\mathcal{O} : \mathbb{G} \times \mathbb{G} \to \mathbb{G}$, which returns the multiplication of the input elements over some random encoding $\sigma : \mathbb{Z}_p \to \mathbb{G}$. This oracle computes $\mathcal{O}(\sigma(i), \sigma(j)) = \sigma(i + j)$. The adversary may also use a polynomially-sized precomputation string. Since they don't have access to the exponents of the bases that are being multiplied together (so as to perform a direct look-up), computing some $\sigma(k)$ requires the generation of an addition chain ending with $\sigma(k)$.

However, this is the only assumption underlying the lower-bound results which prove the optimality of (the generalized) Pippenger's algorithm [19], as they obtain lower-bounds on the length of the minimal addition chain needed to

---

[1] Maurer proposed a slightly different GGM definition [25], for a comparison see [35].

compute some element. In short, our main formal contribution relies on adapting the packing lower-bound ideas of [14, 28] to formalize the relationship between amortization of multiexponentiation of random indices and the amount of space available to the adversary. We do this by making explicit the average-case lower bounds for multiexponentiation, which were only stated (but not proven) in [14, 28] to be a constant term away from the worst-case lower bounds.

Note that the notion of average-case hardness requires an underlying probability distribution over which the input indices are sampled. Obviously, the distribution of the sampled puzzle instances can affect the average-case bounds if, for example, the sampler provides structured output with high probability. Therefore, all results have to be taken with respect to the underlying distribution of the inputs, which is in turn specified by the choice of sampling algorithm S. Where this S is taken to be uniform (as in this work), the notion of average-case hardness defaults to the traditional average-case lower bound results.

In order to make formal statements about the amortization resistance of computing multiple NIPs, we need to show that there exists some sampling algorithm S_{NIP} outputting instance-witness pairs (ϕ, w) so that, on average over its public coins, these output puzzle instances require a minimum number of oracle calls each for computation of their corresponding proof π. Firstly, we construct the equivalent multiexponentiation problem that the above will reduce to. In the following, we restrict ourselves to the NIP of [27], in which the valid output proof consists of 9 group elements of the form $\sum_{k=1}^{\kappa} w_k G_k^i$ for $i \in [9], w_k \in [N]$ and an additional element $\sum_{m=1}^{\mu} g(w_1, ..., w_\kappa)_m H_m$, where g an m-dimensional n-variable polynomial encoding the instance's witness and $G_i, H_m \in \mathbb{G}$.

Since the hardness of the above computation depends on the structure of w and g, it becomes apparent that we need to restrict the types of *predicates* that we are looking at. In subsequent sections, we make precise the following construction: a circuit with an efficient sampler S such that (1) accepting witness elements $w_1, ..., w_\kappa \in [N]$ are randomly distributed, (2) for each valid instance ϕ there exists only one valid w, and (3) for each valid w, there exists a unique valid g. Note that (1) and (2) are properties of the predicate, while (3) requires a stronger result on the NIP's knowledge guarantees. We will show that predicates satisfying (1) and (2) are enough to reduce the computation of a NIP from [27] (which satisfies (3)) to a multiexponentiation problem (Definition 3) whose amortization we can bound.

Definition 3. *The (κ, μ)-length MultiExp function $f : [N]^\kappa \to \mathbb{G}^\nu$ of dimension ν for $\{G_i^{(1)}, ..., G_i^{(\nu-1)}\}_{i=1}^{\kappa}, \{G_i^{(\nu)}\}_{i=1}^{\mu}$, and function $g : [N]^\kappa \to K \subseteq [N]^\mu$ is*

$$f(x_1, ..., x_\kappa) := \left(\sum_{i=1}^{\kappa} x_i G_i^{(1)}, ..., \sum_{i=1}^{\kappa} x_i G_i^{(\nu-1)}, \sum_{i=1}^{\mu} g(x)_i G_i^{(\nu)} \right),$$

where the x_i are given by sampler S, based on its random coins.

In order to provide a reduction that exactly captures the average-case hardness of the above problem, the structure of g becomes important. This requires a more technical treatment, so here we work in the case where g is a weakly collision-resistant map from the witness elements $x = (x_1, ..., x_\kappa)$ to the values $(g(x)_1, ..., g(x)_\mu) \in K \subseteq [N]^\mu$. This defines a computationally unique correspondence between witness elements and representations of μ-degree polynomials with coefficients in $[N]$. We specifically require the mapping $g : [N]^\kappa \to K \subseteq [N]^\mu$ to be collision-resistant in each of its output coordinates, or that the following probability is negligible for all PPT adversaries $\mathcal{A}$:

$$\Pr\left[\exists i \text{ s.t. } g(\mathcal{A}(z))_i = z_i; z \leftarrow g(x), x \leftarrow_R [N]^\kappa\right] \approx 0,$$

where z_i denotes the i-th coordinate of z. This is enough to provide multiexponentiation amortization bounds, which are given below for the case when $\kappa = \mu$. Note that the general case for $\mu > \kappa$ can also be calculated in the exact same way, but has been omitted for simplicity.

Theorem 1. *The (κ, κ)-length MultiExp function (c.f. Definition 3) of dimension ν over index size $\lambda := \log(N)$, group $\mathbb{G}$ with $|\mathbb{G}| = 2^\lambda$, and storage size q is ϵ-amortization resistant with respect to the uniform sampler for all collision-resistant g, and for large enough κ, λ, ν, q satisfies:*

$$\epsilon \leq \frac{\log(q) + o(1)}{\log(q) + \log(\kappa) + \log(\nu) + \log(\lambda)}.$$

We prove Theorem 1 in Appendix A. This amortization gain is unavoidable for NIPs that reduce to multiexponentiation; such as by compilation with [21].

2.1   Amortization Resistance and Efficiency

We modify the DPS predicate Π to ensure that most of the proof variables change unpredictably with modifications of the nonce or state. This gives amortization resistance in exchange for increasing the number of variables and constraints in the predicate. The performance overhead originates from the need to commit to state and 'mask' the computation, which can be expensive for large predicates.

The naive approach would be to isolate each of the different circuits in the system and show that they can be modified to change unpredictably based on some seed. The design challenge here is how to make this happen while conserving the proof's correctness guarantees. For this, we ideally want to leverage a property specific to our predicate in order to 'mask' the computations and treat the proving system as a black box. We leverage the Pedersen hash function to transform our predicate Π to an amortization resistant version in Sect. 4.

Given some nonce n, the prover might only change a part of the input in order to (re)check difficulty. This is an issue if the same nonce can be used with many inputs (in our case, transactions), as an adversarial prover would compute a proof and then only switch out a single transaction (or bit!), rechecking difficulty with no expensive recomputation. Define $\rho := \mathsf{PRF}_n(\mathsf{state})$ that commits to state where PRF a pseudorandom function family. We need to commit to all block transactions, ensuring that changing one transaction changes ρ. This can be expensive if we exploit no information about the underlying predicate, since PRF would have to commit to every single original variable.

Fortunately, for our predicate the input to PRF is small: we use $\rho = \mathsf{PRF}_n(rt)$ where rt the root of the new state and n the given nonce. Since this input will anyways be computed as part of the protocol, we don't actually suffer any overhead apart from having to verify the above computation. Note that this is actually *constant* in predicate size. In the GGM, we can replace the PRF by a collision resistant hash function CRT instead, since the randomness of the group encoding is sufficient for the witness elements to look random to an adversary.

We can force unique changes to the Merkle path updating the account if we require n to be part of the leaf: since a change in the block (or nonce) would lead to a new n, all update paths need to be recomputed if any transaction is changed. However, we also need to enforce change to the *old* Merkle path checking account existence. This technique is thus not ideal, since these paths do not depend on the current nonce (or state) at all, meaning that around half our variables will remain the same, giving $\epsilon \approx 1/2$.

To get around this, we opt for a different approach. We 'mask' the input variables to $\mathcal{H}$ by interaction with ρ (which also commits to n) and transform the constraints of the hash function subcircuit $C_{\mathcal{H}}$ into a new circuit that retains the original Proof of Knowledge (PoK) guarantees by verifying the same underlying computation. By the unpredictability of ρ and randomness of n, we hope to achieve upper bounds for amortization resistance based on the security of the CRT. In this case, the sampler would need to provide valid witnesses for $C_{\mathcal{H}}$ of the form $w = (w_1, ..., w_m)$ whose encodings are indistinguishable from random, given n sampled uniformly randomly and access to a multiplication oracle $\mathcal{O}$ for a randomized encoding of some $\mathbb{G}$.

3   Implications for Nakamoto Consensus

PoNW introduces two novel effects on the consensus protocol due to the fact that checking a nonce (on the order of seconds to minutes) can now take a significant fraction of the average block frequency (ten minutes in the case of Bitcoin), whereas it was negligible for traditional PoW puzzles. We can evaluate these effects assuming a single puzzle solution takes time τ to check (with the mean block arrival time normalized to 1). When τ becomes a significant fraction of the average block generation time ($\tau \sim 1$), miners face a loss of efficiency as they will often be forced to discard a partially-checked puzzle solution when a block is broadcast while checking previous solutions. We prove the scale of this efficiency loss in a short theorem:

Theorem 2. *A miner in a PoW protocol with puzzle checking time τ will discard a fraction $1 - \frac{\tau}{e^{\tau}-1}$ of their work due to newly broadcast solutions.*

Note that as $\tau \to 0$ (fast puzzle checking time relative to block interval), the fraction of wasted work drops to 0. This is why this effect has never been considered in prior work. In the reverse direction, as $\tau \to \infty$ the fraction of wasted work approaches 1. For $\tau = 1$ (solutions take as long to check as the mean block interval), the fraction of wasted work is $\frac{e-2}{e-1} \approx 0.42$, suggesting that we should aim to keep the time (even for slow miners) to get a solution significantly shorter than the mean block time.

Slow puzzle checking time also introduces a concern that miners might refuse to stop working on a partially-checked solution (and hence discard partial work) even if a valid solution is found and broadcast. These *stubborn* miners might cause collisions in the blockchain (two blocks being found at the same height in the chain). We can analyse a worst-case scenario in which all miners are synchronized with identical proving time, in effect making all miners stubborn and maximizing the probability of simultaneous solutions. If miners aren't synchronized, they may opt to finish their current effort after a block is found, but even if all miners do so this reduces to the above case where all miners finish checking a solution simultaneously. We call each synchronized period in which all miners check a solution a *round*.

Theorem 3. *The expected number of solutions in a synchronized mining round is defined by a Poisson distribution with $\lambda = \tau$. The proportion of rounds with multiple solutions (of rounds with any solution) is upper bounded by $\tau/2$.*

By Theorem 3, our prototype unoptimized $100\,\mathrm{s}$ proving time (and $10\,\mathrm{min}$ block time) leads to less than $\frac{1}{12}$ worst case collisions.

4   Design and Instantiation

We prototype our system using libsnark [31], a C++ library implementing the IVC system in [4] using the construction from [27]. This is done using Succinct Non-Interactive Arguments of Knowledge (SNARKs) [3], non-interactive proofs of knowledge with the additional property of *succinctness*: producing constant-sized proofs that can be instantly verified. We can equivalently consider Π_S as an arithmetic circuit C_Π, evaluating to 1 on some input B_i if and only if B_i is a valid commitment to the output of UpdateState given some transaction set $\mathbf{t}$ and $\mathcal{S}_{i-1}$. In our implementation, C_Π is a QAP. Since this construction depends on SNARKs over pairs of elliptic curves that form *IVC-friendly cycles*, we use the same pair of non-supersingular curves of prime order as [4] with 80 bits of security and field size $\log p \approx 298$.

A tree depth of 32 for our implementation allows for 4.2 billion accounts. We compare this to 32 million unique used wallets on the Bitcoin blockchain after 10 years of operation. This requires $32 \cdot 4 = 128$ hash checks for each transaction. We use the circuits in libsnark to verify such proofs of inclusion and modification. We modify the Pedersen hash [13] to compute $\prod_{i=1}^{D} G_i^{1-2x_i}$ where $\{x_i\}_{i=1}^{D}$ is the bit representation of the input x and $\{G_i\}_{i=1}^{D}$ is a set of primitive roots for an elliptic curve group $E(\mathbb{F}_p)$. We use Schnorr signatures [30] over the same elliptic curve (EC), based on the hardness of DLP.

In addition to some input x of length n bits, our evaluation requires a pseudorandom seed $\rho \in \{0,1\}^n$. Consider the following modification, which can be thought of as masking the underlying evaluation by using two sets of input variables: $\mathcal{H}_G(\rho)^2 \cdot \mathcal{H}_H(\rho)$ and x_i for $i \in [n]$, where $\mathcal{H}_G(\cdot)$ the evaluation of the Pedersen function $\mathcal{H}_G(x) = \prod_{i=1}^{n} G_i^{1-2x_i}$.

The variable $h_0 = \mathcal{H}_G(\rho)^2 \cdot \mathcal{H}_H(\rho)$ forms the 'starting point' of the evaluation. In the beginning, the prover will have access to generator constants $\{H_i, H_i^{-1}, G_i^{-2}H_i^{-1}, G_i^2 H_i\}$ for the specific instance of the problem. It would then perform a 2-bit lookup based on x_i and ρ_i, multiplying the intermediate variable c_i by one of the above. By carefully choosing these q_i, we can design the circuit in such a way that unpredictability based on the seed is retained by all intermediate variables except the output y, which we ensure equals $\mathcal{H}_G(x)$.

Algorithm 1. MaskedPedersen

Require: $x, \rho \in \{0,1\}^n, G, H \in \mathbb{G}^n$
Ensure: $y \in \mathbb{G}$
 1: **procedure** CACHEGENERATORS(ρ, G, H)
 2:     Parse $\{\rho_i\}_{i=1}^{n} \leftarrow \rho$
 3:     Compute $h \leftarrow \mathcal{H}(\rho, G)$, $h_2 \leftarrow \mathcal{H}(\rho, H)$, $h_0 = h^2 \cdot h_2$
 4:     **return** h_0, h
 5: **end procedure**
 6: **procedure** MASKEDHASH(x, ρ, h_0, h)
 7:     Parse $\{x_i\}_{i=1}^{n} \leftarrow x$, $\{\rho_i\}_{i=1}^{n} \leftarrow \rho$
 8:     Define $q = \{q_i\}_{i=1}^{n}$, $c = \{c_i\}_{i=0}^{n}$ and set $c_0 = h_0$
 9:     **for** $i \leq n$ **do**
10:         **if** $\rho_i = 0, x_i = 0$ **then** $q_i = H_i^{-1}$
11:         **else if** $\rho_i = 0, x_i = 1$ **then** $q_i = G_i^{-2} \cdot H_i^{-1}$
12:         **else if** $\rho_i = 1, x_i = 0$ **then** $q_i = G_i^2 \cdot H_i$
13:         **else if** $\rho_i = 1, x_i = 1$ **then** $q_i = H_i$
14:         **end if**
15:         $c_i = c_{i-1} \cdot q_i$
16:     **end for**
17:     $y = c_n \cdot h^{-1}$
18:     **return** y
19: **end procedure**

Correctness follows from the following observation: at step 0, the variable $c_0 = \mathcal{H}_H(\rho) \cdot \mathcal{H}_G(\rho)^2 = \mathcal{H}_G(\rho) \cdot \prod_{i=1}^{n} G_i^{1-2\rho_i} \cdot H_i^{1-2\rho_i}$ is initialized as the hash of the seed. For all intermediate steps $j < n$, we have that $c_j = \mathcal{H}_G(\rho) \cdot \left(\prod_{i=1}^{j} G_i^{1-2x_i} \right) \cdot \left(\prod_{i=j+1}^{n} G_i^{1-2\rho_i} H_i^{1-2\rho_i} \right)$. Finally, after the n-th bit has been processed the final intermediate variable c_n is equal to the Pedersen hash of the original input x multiplied by (the unpredictable) $\mathcal{H}_G(\rho)$. By multiplying with $\mathcal{H}_G(\rho)^{-1}$, we get $\mathcal{H}_G(x)$. This follows easily from the fact that at every step we are performing the following operation: $c_i = c_{i-1} \cdot (H_i \cdot \mathbf{1}[\rho_i, x_i = 1] + H_i^{-1} \cdot \mathbf{1}[\rho_i, x_i = 0] + G_i^{-2}H_i^{-1} \cdot \mathbf{1}[\rho_i = 0, x_i = 1] + G_i^2 H_i \cdot \mathbf{1}[\rho_i = 1, x_i = 0])$.

It can be quickly checked that this computation ensures the previous recursive property when initialized with $c_0 = \mathcal{H}_H(\rho) \cdot \mathcal{H}_G(\rho)^2$. By induction, this implies that after the n-th bit, only $\mathcal{H}_G(\rho)$ and the exponentiations due to the bits of x remain in the output variable i.e. $c_n = \mathcal{H}_G(\rho) \cdot \prod_{i=1}^{n} G_i^{1-2x_i}$.

Where we know that the variable a_i has small support (when, for example, it is boolean $a_i \in \{0,1\}$), the prover can always precompute once and use the same answers without performing exponentiations. This is not a problem since all miners would know what the precomputed answers are from the very beginning and can incorporate them with a small memory cost. The problem with creating variables that become more and more 'deterministic' is that at some point their support becomes so small that an adversary will be able to precompute some oracle queries. However, since the end value of the sequence of variables $\{c_i\}_{i=1}^{n}$ is $h \cdot \mathcal{H}_G(x)$ which is also unpredictable due to h, it is not feasible to predict any index $i \in [n]$ without violating the security of the operation $\mathcal{H}_G(\rho) = h$ even if $\mathcal{H}_G(x)$ is previously known. Note that h can be 'offset' by a random element I as $h'_i = h + I_i$ for each path $i \in [N]$. This provides independence between authentication paths using the same nonce.

We must restrict the proof systems used because certain constructions are inherently insecure: Groth16 [17] can easily be re-randomized, for example, with only a few additional group multiplications. We thus need a notion akin to non-malleability, ensuring that we cannot construct proofs given access to previous valid proofs. To achieve this, we show that Pinocchio [27] satisfies *unique witness extractability*. This property requires the proof system to output proofs with unique encodings for each distinct statement-witness pair, and hence rules out malleability.

Definition 4. *Let* $\mathsf{NIP} := (\mathsf{Setup}, \mathsf{Prove}, \mathsf{Verify}, \mathsf{Simulate})$ *denote a NIP for relation* $\mathcal{R}$. *Define the PPT algorithm* $\mathcal{A}$ *with extractor* $\chi_{\mathcal{A}}$, $\mathbf{Adv}_{\mathcal{BG},R,\mathcal{A},\chi_{\mathcal{A}}}^{uwe}(\lambda) = \Pr[\mathcal{G}_{\mathcal{BG},R,\mathcal{A},\chi_{\mathcal{A}}}^{uwe}(\lambda)]$, *and* $\mathcal{G}_{\mathcal{BG},R,\mathcal{A},\chi_{\mathcal{A}}}^{uwe}(\lambda)$ *as:*

Main $\mathcal{G}_{\mathcal{BG},R,\mathcal{A},\chi_{\mathcal{A}}}^{uwe}(\lambda)$

$(p, \mathbb{G}_1, \mathbb{G}_2, \mathbb{G}_T, e, g) \leftarrow \mathcal{BG}(1^\lambda)$

$(\mathbf{crs}, \tau) \leftarrow \mathsf{Setup}(\mathcal{R})$

$(\phi, \pi_1, \pi_2) \leftarrow \mathcal{A}^{\mathcal{O}}(\mathbf{crs})$

$(w_1, w_2) \leftarrow \chi_{\mathcal{A}}(\mathsf{tr}_{\mathcal{A}})$

$b_1 \leftarrow (w_1 = w_2) \cup (\mathcal{R}(\phi, w_1) \neq 1) \cup (\mathcal{R}(\phi, w_2) \neq 1)$

$b_2 \leftarrow \mathsf{Verify}(\mathbf{crs}, \phi, \pi_1) \cap \mathsf{Verify}(\mathbf{crs}, \phi, \pi_2) \cap ((\phi, \pi_1) \notin Q) \cap ((\phi, \pi_1) \notin Q) \cap (\pi_1 \neq \pi_2)$

Return $b_1 \cap b_2$

$\mathcal{O}(\phi)$

$\pi \leftarrow \mathsf{Simulate}(\mathbf{crs}, \tau, \phi)$

$Q = (\phi, \pi) \cup Q$

Return π

NIP *is unique witness extractable if* $\forall \mathcal{A} \, \exists \chi_{\mathcal{A}} \, s.t. \, \mathbf{Adv}_{\mathcal{BG},R,\mathcal{A},\chi_{\mathcal{A}}}^{uwe}(\lambda) \in negl(\lambda)$.

Theorem 4. *Assume the q-PDH, 2q-SDH and d-PKE assumptions hold for* $q \geq \max(2d-1, d+2)$. *[27] satisfies unique witness extractability.*

The ability to resample witnesses for a statement-witness pair is advantageous to an adversary, since an 'easy' witness could be found by repeated sampling. We follow the definition of 2-hard instances in [12] and define *single witness hard* languages, for which it is hard to find a new witness given an existing one.

Definition 5. *Let R_L be a relation, and $\mathcal{L} = \{\phi | \exists w \text{ s.t. } R_L(\phi, w) = 1\}$ an NP language. $\mathcal{L}$ is a hard single-witness language if:*

1. **Efficient Sampling:** *There exists a PPT sampler $\mathsf{S}(1^\lambda)$ outputting a statement-witness pair $\langle \mathsf{S}^x, \mathsf{S}^w \rangle$ with $\mathsf{S}^x \in \{0,1\}^\lambda$ and $(\mathsf{S}^x, \mathsf{S}^w) \in R_L$.*
2. **Witness Intractability:** *For every PPT $\mathcal{A}$ there exists a negligible function $\mu(\cdot)$ such that:*

$$\Pr\left[\left(\mathsf{S}^x(1^\lambda), \mathcal{A}(\mathsf{S}(1^\lambda), 1^\lambda)\right) \in R_\mathcal{L}, \mathcal{A}(\mathsf{S}(1^\lambda), 1^\lambda) \neq \mathsf{S}^w(1^\lambda)\right] \leq \mu(\lambda).$$

A relation whose statements are outputs of a CRT hash function $\mathcal{H}$ defines a hard single-witness language. We show this for $\mathcal{L}(\mathcal{H}_P) = \{\phi : \exists w \text{ s.t. } \mathcal{H}^G_{P,|w|}(w) = \phi\}$ where $\mathcal{H}^G_{P,n}$ a weakly collision-resistant hash function.

We show that computing a [27] proof for the evaluation of MaskedHash (and our DPS predicate) will take on average a similar number of queries as a suitably parametrized MultiExp instance. We restrict to the case of outputs from a sampler S which samples a ρ randomly and generates valid witnesses. Since we are working in the GGM, the witness variables of the MaskedHash instance have an encoding that is indistinguishable from random. Therefore, the amortization bounds of Theorem 1 apply.

Theorem 5. *There exists a sampler S and QAP R evaluating N parallel instances of k-bit inputs of MaskedHash for which the [27] prover and the $(4N(k+1), 8N(k+1) + 2k)$-length MultiExp problem of dimension 10 are equivalent up to constant terms with respect to multiplicative hardness.*

The vast majority of the constraints and variables in the predicate of the designed system are hash evaluations, so Theorem 5 can be used to show that there exists a proof system verifying state transitions for the DPS with bounded amortization-resistance guarantees. This is because the DPS predicate spends the vast majority of its time computing a proof whose hardness can be bounded by Theorem 5, since it is a sequence of iterated Pedersen hashes over a unique simulation extractable NIP.

Corollary 1. *There exists a DPS with block size T, state tree depth d, and index size λ that admits a Proof of Necessary Work that is ϵ-amortization resistant w.r.t. a multiplication oracle and for which:*

$$\epsilon \lessapprox \frac{\log(q)}{\log(q) + \log(dT\lambda) + \log(\lambda)},$$

where q is memory size measured in proof elements.

Table 1. Prototype Times and Key Sizes for Predicates verifying different numbers of transactions: Average running times for setup $\mathcal{G}$, prover $\mathcal{P}$ and verifier $\mathcal{V}$ over 10 iterations are shown alongside proving/verification key and proof sizes.

Txs	Constraints	Generator	Prover	Verifier	Size		
#	#	Avg (s)	Avg (s)	Avg (ms)	pk (GB)	vk (kB)	π (B)
3	3658281	53.99	24.57	16.0	0.74	0.76	373
10	10071527	161.24	88.14		1.96		
20	19233307	268.93	185.10		3.74		
30	28395087	354.83	198.61		5.61		
40	37556867	485.52	286.50		7.15		
50	46718647	570.09	358.95		9.01		

We construct the DPS based on the above specifications and investigate its running time and memory consumption. Results are displayed in Table 1. Our benchmark machine was an Amazon Web Services (AWS) c5.24xlarge instance, with 96 vCPUs and 192GiB of RAM. The security properties of the DPS are based on the guarantee of Π-compliance provided by IVC. It is apparent that setup and proving times dominate both the running time and memory consumption in the protocol. Setup takes place once by a trusted third-party and hence is less critical for day-to-day system performance.

The prover is run by the miners, or full nodes. These generate PoW solutions repeatedly and would compute proof instances for many input nonces. Thus, larger storage requirements ($\sim$ 5.42GB key sizes) could be easily met by these nodes, as could the need for more parallelism and better computing power to bring down the proving rate. We normalize the block time to achieve $\tau = 1/3$ in the sense of Theorem 2 for a proof including 30 transactions. This gives us that a miner will discard in expectation 15.59% of their work for an efficiency of $\sim$ 84% if all miners operated based on the above benchmarks. Theorem 3 then gives an upper bound on the block orphan rate (or likelihood of block collisions) of 16.65%. Since we are keeping block times constant at 10 minutes, we note that any improvements in SNARK proof generation times will correspondingly decrease the amount of wasted work and orphan rate. Moreover, this does not depend on the way that the proofs are generated: distributed techniques among many participants (such as [34]) would also benefit efficiency through the corresponding decrease of average proof time.

5   Related Work

Several proposals have aimed to reduce verification costs for light clients; Chatzigiannis et al. provide a survey [9]. Most relevant to our work are Vault [24] and MimbleWimble [29] which speed up verifying transaction history and NIPoPoW [22] and FlyClient [8] which speed up verifying consensus. None of these proposals achieve constant-time verification, though they require significantly less work from provers. Succinct blockchains, which provide optimal $O(1)$ bandwidth and computation costs to verify both history and consensus, were proposed in 2020, simultaneously by this work and the Mina project [5] (formerly Coda). Mina takes a similar high-level approach, encoding state transitions in a recursive proof system for asymptotically optimal verification time. The two proposals vary in a number of technical details, but the main conceptual differences lie in our choice of consensus protocol. Mina implements proof-of-stake consensus, specifically a variant of Ouroboros [23] designed for succinct proofs, but does not incentivize efficient proof generation. By contrast, we implement a PoW variant specifically designed to incentivize proving efficiency.

Subsequent work has provided novel and efficient constructions for succinct blockchains, though not focused directly on prover incentivization. Chen et al. [10] propose a general framework for succinct blockchains over arbitrary transition functions, alongside benchmarks using the Marlin [11] proof system. Hegde et al. [18] tackle a related but critical problem: that of minimizing the total memory requirements of *full nodes*. Vesely et al. [33] propose Plumo, which leverages offline signature aggregation to design a cost and latency optimized light client for the Celo [33] blockchain. Abusalah et al. [1] propose SNACKS, a formal framework that adds knowledge extraction guarantees to Proofs of Sequential Work. We note that these contributions are orthogonal to our main focus of incentivizing efficient proving, and all could be incorporated in a practical PoNW implementation.

A   Security Proofs

Proof. (Proof of Theorem 2). Assume that a blocks are found in a Poisson process with a mean of $\lambda = 1$ and an individual miner can check one puzzle solution in time τ. Consider the expected number of blocks this individual miner is able to check before the network broadcasts a solution. A block will be found by the network in less than time τ with probability $\int_0^\tau e^{-x} dx = 1 - e^\tau$. In this case, the miner will not even finish checking a single block. If the network does not broadcast a block within time τ, the miner will check at least one block. The Poisson process then repeats, since it is memoryless. So the expected number of blocks checked is $\mathrm{E}_{blocks} = (1 - e^\tau) \cdot 0 + e^{-\tau} \cdot (1 + \mathrm{E}_{blocks})$ or:

$$e^\tau \cdot \mathrm{E}_{blocks} = 1 + \mathrm{E}_{blocks} \qquad \mathrm{E}_{blocks} = \frac{1}{e^\tau - 1}.$$

If no partially-checked solutions were wasted, the miner would always expect to check $\frac{1}{\tau}$ solutions. Thus, the fraction of wasted work is:

$$1 - \frac{\frac{1}{e^\tau - 1}}{\frac{1}{\tau}} = 1 - \frac{\tau}{e^\tau - 1}.$$

Proof. (Proof of Theorem 3). Since solutions are Poisson random variables:

$$\Pr[\mathsf{collision}] = [1 - \mathsf{Po}(1, \tau)/(1 - \mathsf{Po}(0, \tau))] \leq \tau/2.$$

We borrow notation from [28] and parametrize with q input indices, p outputs and maximum index size 2^λ. Where not specified, $H = pq\lambda$. Let $L(\mathbf{y})$ be the minimum number of multiplications to compute $\mathbf{y} = (y_1, ..., y_p)$ with $y_i \in [2^\lambda]^q$ and $[2^\lambda] = \{1, ..., 2^\lambda - 1\}$ from the inputs and unit vectors and $L(p, q, 2^\lambda)$ be the maximum over all of them.

Lemma 1. *For any value of $c \leq L(p, q, N)$, there are at most:*

$$\left(\frac{H^2}{c}\right)^c 2^{q+1} e^c (q+1) 2^{O(1)},$$

addition chains of length at most c.

Lemma 2. *Define $H := \kappa q \nu \lambda$, $\phi(q, \kappa, \nu, \lambda) :=$*

$$q\kappa\nu \log(q\kappa\nu) + \kappa \log(H) + q + \log(q+1) + 1,$$

and fix $\mu := \delta H$, corresponding to:

$$c_\delta := \frac{(1-\delta)H - \phi(q, \kappa, \nu, \lambda)}{\log(H) - \log(e) + \log(\mu) + \log(1/\delta)}.$$

For the (κ, κ)-length MultiExp function of dimension ν for CRT g:

$$\Pr_{\mathbf{x} \in_R [2^\lambda]^{\kappa \times q}, \mathbf{G} \in_R \mathbb{G}^{\kappa \times \nu}} [L(f(x_1), ..., f(x_q)) \leq c_\delta] \leq \left(\frac{1}{2}\right)^\mu.$$

Proof. Write $G_k^{(j)} = r_{jk}G$. As the $x_i \in [2^\lambda]^\kappa$ and $r_{jk} \in [2^\lambda]$ are sampled randomly, the values $x_{ik}G_k^{(j)} = x_{ik}r_{jk}G$ for $i \in [q], j \in [\nu-1], k \in [\kappa]$ will be distinct w.h.p. The $\kappa \cdot q$ values $g(x_i)_k \cdot r_{\nu k}G$ will also be distinct w.h.p. as g is collision resistant in each of its κ output coordinates.

Let M be the $q \times (\kappa\nu)$ sized matrix with these values as entries. As each entry is an element in $[2^\lambda]$, the number of matrices M with $q\kappa\nu$ distinct elements is:

$$\binom{2^\lambda}{q\kappa\nu} \geq \frac{2^{\lambda q\kappa\nu}}{(q\kappa\nu)^{q\kappa\nu}},$$

and to each M there corresponds a unique matrix $F = (f(x_1), ..., f(x_q))$ with dimension $q \times \nu$, where the κ products over random bases for each x_i have been computed. Note that $L(F) = L(M) + \kappa - 1$.

We can thus upper bound the minimal addition chain size $L(F)$ using $L(M)$ and the number of matrices M:

$$\Pr_{\mathbf{x} \in_R [2^\lambda]^{\kappa \times q}, \mathbf{G} \in_R \mathbb{G}^{\kappa \times \nu}} [L(F) \leq c] \leq \frac{|\{\mathbf{z} : L(\mathbf{z}) \leq c\}|}{2^{H - q\kappa\nu \log(q\kappa\nu)}}.$$

The numerator is upper bounded by Lemma 1 and the fact that a single chain corresponds to at most H^κ matrices, giving:

$$\Pr_{\mathbf{x} \in_R [2^\lambda]^{\kappa \times q}, \mathbf{G} \in_R \mathbb{G}^{\kappa \times \nu}} [L(F) \leq c] \leq \left(\frac{1}{2}\right)^{H - \psi(c)},$$

where $\psi(c) := c(2 \log H + \log e) + \phi(q, \kappa, \nu, \lambda) - c \log(c)$.

Suffices to show that for $c \leq c_\delta$, $\psi(c) \leq (1 - \delta)H$. Since $\psi(c)$ is increasing for $c \leq L(\kappa, \nu q, 2^\lambda)$, required to show that $\rho \geq c_\delta$ for $\psi(\rho) = (1 - \delta)H$:

$$\rho(2 \log H + \log e) + \phi(q, \kappa, \nu, \lambda) \geq (1 - \delta) \cdot H,$$

$$\log \rho \geq \log((1 - \delta) \cdot H - \phi(q, \kappa, \nu, \lambda)) - \log(2 \log H - \log(e)),$$

$$\therefore \rho \geq \frac{(1 - \delta)H - \phi(q, \kappa, \nu, \lambda)}{\log H - \log(e) + \log(\mu) + \log(1/\delta)},$$

since $\mu = \delta H$.

Corollary 2. *Fix $\delta > 0$ and let $\psi(\rho_\delta) - (1 - \delta) \cdot H = 0$.*

$$\mathbb{E}[L(f(x_1), ..., f(x_q))] \geq \rho_\delta \cdot (1 - 2^{-\delta H}).$$

Proof. By Markov's inequality:

$$\Pr[L(f(x_1), ..., f(x_q)) > \rho_\delta] \cdot \rho_\delta \leq \mathbb{E}[L(\mathbf{x})],$$

$$(1 - \Pr[L(f(x_1), ..., f(x_q)) < \rho_\delta]) \cdot \rho_\delta \leq \mathbb{E}[L(f(x_1), ..., f(x_q))].$$

Proof. (Proof of Theorem 1). Required to compute q iterations of the MultiExp function. Each iteration includes ν multiproducts over random bases, with the indices also sampled from $[2^\lambda]$.

Using c oracle queries to do this corresponds to knowledge of an addition chain of length c containing all of $F = (f(x_1), ..., f(x_q))$ with $x_i \in [2^\lambda]^\kappa$. Therefore, the probability that we compute F for $\mathbf{x} \in_R [2^\lambda]^{\kappa \times q}$ with less than c queries is upper bounded by the probability that $L(F) \leq c$.

Fix $\delta > 0$. Lemma 2 states that $\exists c_\delta$ s.t. this probability is negligible in $\mu := \delta \kappa \nu q \lambda$ for $c \leq c_\delta$. One function computation of dimension ν with κ inputs has an upper bound on the expected number of multiplications of:

$$\min(\kappa, \nu) \cdot \lambda + \frac{\kappa \nu \lambda}{\log(\kappa \nu \lambda)} \cdot (1 + o(1)).$$

Corollary 2 implies that:

$$\epsilon \leq 1 - q^{-1} \cdot \left(\min(\kappa, \nu) \cdot \lambda + \frac{\kappa \nu \lambda}{\log(\kappa \nu \lambda)} \cdot (1 + o(1)) \right)^{-1} \cdot (1 - 2^{-\delta \kappa \nu q \lambda}) \cdot c_\delta$$

$$\leq \frac{\log(q) + \delta \log(\kappa \nu \lambda) + o(1)}{\log(\kappa \nu q \lambda)} \leq \frac{\log(q) + o(1)}{\log(\kappa \nu q \lambda)},$$

where we have taken $\delta \leq 1/\log(\kappa \nu \lambda)$.

Proof. (Proof of Theorem 4). We know that the NIP has a PKE extractor from its security proof and so $\mathcal{A}$ can extract two witnesses almost surely using extractor $\chi_{\mathcal{A}}^{PKE}$. If the polynomials are distinct, so are their witnesses. This follows directly from the fact that, since $\pi_1 \neq \pi_2$, either (1) one of $u_i(X), v_i(X), w_i(X)$ differs in one of the proofs, or (2) the extracted witnesses differ. Since the predicate is the same, it follows that the witnesses must differ.

Lemma 3. *Let $\mathcal{H}_P = \{\mathcal{H}_{P,\lambda}^G\}_{\lambda \in \mathbb{N}_+}$ be a family of efficiently computable functions for which each $\mathcal{H}_{P,\lambda}^G : \{0,1\}^\lambda \to \mathbb{G}$ is weakly collision-resistant. $\mathcal{L}(\mathcal{H}_P)$ is hard single-witness.*

Proof. (*Proof of Lemma 3*). Define S in the natural way: fix $\lambda \in \mathbb{N}_+$ and define S to randomly sample an element $x \in \{0,1\}^\lambda$, outputting $(\mathcal{H}_{P,\lambda}(x), x)$. The sampler is efficient by the efficiency of $\mathcal{H}_{P,\lambda}(x)$, and $(\mathcal{H}_{P,\lambda}(x), x) \in R_{\mathcal{L}(\mathcal{H}_{P,\lambda})}\}$ by definition. Witness intractability (WI) follows from the collision resistance of $\mathcal{H}_{P,\lambda}$ on constant-size inputs. If some $\mathcal{A}$ exists that violates WI, then running S on 1^λ and then $\mathcal{A}$ on $S(1^\lambda)$ and 1^λ, we non-negligibly find a collision in $\mathcal{H}_{P,\lambda}^G$.

Proof. (*Proof of Theorem 5*). The MaskedHash QAP has $4N(k+1)$ intermediate witness variables (and $8N(k+1) + 2k$ constraints) which admits witnesses from a sampler S where the seed ρ is uniformly random and so all witness variables (with full support) also look random by the randomness of the group encoding. This is as the intermediate values are distinct powers of a group element that is random due to ρ and the independence of the I_j index elements. By unique witness extractability and single witness hardness of CRT functions, all valid witnesses have a unique encoding and hence a unique witness polynomial h.

We start with ℓ instances of N k-bit hash evaluations from S, and require ℓ valid proofs. We reduce to the $4N(k+1)$-length MultiExp problem for ℓ instances and g equal to the function evaluating the representation of h given the witness elements. We provide ℓ of the $4N(k+1)$ intermediate witness variables and the corresponding 9 sets of bases to the MultiExp function. The representation of h will be unique w.r.t. the witness (since the instance is single witness hard) and thus look random due to the inputs. Note that $\mu = 8N(k+1) + 2k$. We finally perform a linear in ℓ number of multiplications to add any witness variables that were not included (i.e. not randomly distributed). Since the MultiExp index distributions are also random, a proof verifies iff the MultiExp solution is valid.

Conversely, given ℓ $(4N(k+1), 8N(k+1) + 2k)$-length MultiExp instances of dimension 10 with inputs and bases sampled from the QAP's sampler and proving key respectively, we reduce to computing ℓ proofs for N k-bit hash evaluations. This is because the unassigned witness variables can be discerned from the auxiliary input to g, which comes from the QAP sampler. By the uniqueness of the proof's encoding, the set of ℓ valid proofs will have to equal the MultiExp instances after a linear in ℓ number of operations to 'undo' products by any of the additional variables.

References

1. Abusalah, H., Fuchsbauer, G., Gaži, P., Klein, K.: SNACKs: leveraging proofs of sequential work for blockchain light clients. Cryptology ePrint Archive, Paper 2022/240 (2022)
2. Announcing the ZPrize Competition. https://www.aleo.org/post/announcing-the-zprize-competition (2022). Accessed: 09 Aug 2022

3. Ben-Sasson, E., Chiesa, A., Tromer, E., Virza, M.: Succinct non-interactive zero knowledge for a von neumann architecture. In: USENIX Security (2014)
4. Ben-Sasson, E., Chiesa, A., Tromer, E., Virza, M.: Scalable zero knowledge via cycles of elliptic curves. Algorithmica **79**(4), 1102–1160 (2017)
5. Bonneau, J., Meckler, I., Rao, V., Shapiro, E.: Mina: decentralized cryptocurrency at scale. https://docs.minaprotocol.com/static/pdf/technicalWhitepaper.pdf (2020). Accessed: 09 Aug 2022
6. Bowe, S., Chiesa, A., Green, M., Miers, I., Mishra, P., Wu, H.: ZEXE: enabling decentralized private computation. Cryptology ePrint Archive, Report 2018/962 (2018)
7. Bünz, B., Agrawal, S., Zamani, M., Boneh, D.: Zether: towards privacy in a smart contract world. In: Bonneau, J., Heninger, N. (eds.) FC 2020. LNCS, vol. 12059, pp. 423–443. Springer, Cham (2020). https://doi.org/10.1007/978-3-030-51280-4_23
8. Bünz, B., Kiffer, L., Luu, L., Zamani, M.: Flyclient: super-light clients for cryptocurrencies. cryptology ePrint Archive, Report 2019/226 (2019)
9. Chatzigiannis, P., Baldimtsi, F., Chalkias, K.: SoK: Blockchain Light Clients. Cryptology ePrint Archive, Paper 2021/1657 (2021)
10. Chen, W., Chiesa, A., Dauterman, E., Ward, N.P.: Reducing participation costs via incremental verification for ledger systems. Cryptology ePrint Archive, Paper 2020/1522 (2020)
11. Chiesa, A., Hu, Y., Maller, M., Mishra, P., Vesely, P., Ward, N.: Marlin: preprocessing zksnarks with universal and updatable SRS. Cryptology ePrint Archive, Paper 2019/1047 (2019). https://eprint.iacr.org/2019/1047
12. Dahari, H., Lindell, Y.: Deterministic-prover zero-knowledge proofs. Cryptology ePrint Archive, Paper 2020/141 (2020)
13. Damgård, I.B., Pedersen, T.P., Pfitzmann, B.: On the existence of statistically hiding bit commitment schemes and fail-stop signatures. In: CRYPTO (1993)
14. Erdös, P.: Remarks on number theory III. On addition chains. Acta Arithmetica **6**, 77–81 (1960)
15. Fisch, B., Bonneau, J., Greco, N., Benet, J.: Scaling proof-of-replication for Filecoin mining. Stanford University, Technical Report (2018)
16. Gordon, D.M.: A survey of fast exponentiation methods. J. Algorithms **27**(1), 129–146 (1998)
17. Groth, J.: On the size of pairing-based non-interactive arguments. In: Eurocrypt (2016)
18. Hegde, P., Streit, R., Georghiades, Y., Ganesh, C., Vishwanath, S.: Achieving almost all blockchain functionalities with polylogarithmic storage. arXiv preprint arXiv:2207.05869 (2022)
19. Henry, R.: Pippenger's multiproduct and multiexponentiation algorithms. University of Waterloo, Technical Report (2010)
20. Kamvar, S., Olszewski, M., Reinsberg, R.: CELO: a multi-asset cryptographic protocol for decentralized social payments. https://celo.org/papers/whitepaper (2019)
21. Kate, A., Zaverucha, G.M., Goldberg, I.: Constant-size commitments to polynomials and their applications. In: Asiacrypt (2010)
22. Kiayias, A., Lamprou, N., Stouka, A.P.: Proofs of proofs of work with sublinear complexity. In: Financial Crypto (2016)
23. Kiayias, A., Russell, A., David, B., Oliynykov, R.: Ouroboros: a provably secure proof-of-stake blockchain protocol. In: CRYPTO (2017)
24. Leung, D., Suhl, A., Gilad, Y., Zeldovich, N.: Vault: fast bootstrapping for the algorand cryptocurrency. In: NDSS (2018)

25. Maurer, U.: Abstract models of computation in cryptography. In: IMA International Conference on Cryptography and Coding (2005)
26. Miller, A., Kosba, A., Katz, J., Shi, E.: Nonoutsourceable scratch-off puzzles to discourage bitcoin mining coalitions. In: ACM CCS (2015)
27. Parno, B., Gentry, C., Howell, J., Raykova, M.: Pinocchio: nearly practical verifiable computation. Cryptology ePrint Archive, Report 2013/279 (2013)
28. Pippenger, N.: On the evaluation of powers and monomials. SIAM J. Comput. **9**(2), 230–250 (1980)
29. Poelstra, A.: Mimblewimble. https://download.wpsoftware.net/bitcoin/wizardry/mimblewimble.pdf (2016). Accessed 09 Aug 2022
30. Schnorr, C.P.: Efficient identification and signatures for smart cards. In: Eurocrypt (1989)
31. SCIPRLab: libsnark: a c++ library for zksnark proofs. https://github.com/scipr-lab/libsnark (2017)
32. Shoup, V.: Lower bounds for discrete logarithms and related problems. In: Eurocrypt (1997)
33. Vesely, P., et al.: Plumo: an ultralight blockchain client. Cryptology ePrint Archive, Paper 2021/1361 (2021)
34. Wu, H., Zheng, W., Chiesa, A., Popa, R.A., Stoica, I.: DIZK: a distributed zero knowledge proof system. In: USENIX Security (2018)
35. Zhandry, M.: To label, or not to label (in generic groups). Cryptology ePrint Archive, Paper 2022/226 (2022)

Proof of Availability and Retrieval in a Modular Blockchain Architecture

Shir Cohen[1], Guy Goren[2], Lefteris Kokoris-Kogias[3,6], Alberto Sonnino[3,5(✉)], and Alexander Spiegelman[4]

[1] Technion IIT, San Francisco, USA
shirco@campus.technion.ac.il
[2] Protocol Labs, San Francisco, USA
guy.goren@protocol.ai
[3] Mysten Labs, Palo Alto, USA
lefteris@mystenlabs.com
[4] Aptos Labs, Palo Alto, USA
sasha@aptoslabs.com
[5] University College London (UCL), London, UK
alberto@mystenlabs.com
[6] IST, Sydney, Austria

Abstract. This paper explores a modular design architecture aimed at helping blockchains (and other SMR implementation) to scale to a very large number of processes. This comes in contrast to existing monolithic architectures that interleave transaction dissemination, ordering, and execution in a single functionality. To achieve this we first split the monolith to multiple layers which can use existing distributed computing primitives. The exact specifications of the data dissemination part are formally defined by the *Proof of Availability & Retrieval* (PoA&R) abstraction. Solutions to the PoA&R problem contain two related sub-protocols: one that "pushes" information into the network and another that "pulls" this information. Regarding the latter, there is a dearth of research literature which is rectified in this paper. We present a family of pulling sub-protocols and rigorously analyze them. Extensive simulations support the theoretical claims of efficiency and robustness in case of a very large number of players. Finally, actual implementation and deployment on a small number of machines (roughly the size of several industrial systems) demonstrates the viability of the architecture's paradigm.

1 Introduction

Blockchain systems are currently supporting a trillion-dollar economy. New use cases emerge every day and with the promise of "Web 3.0" powering the future digital societies, the number of users grows rapidly. Nevertheless, more than a decade after Bitcoin's invention, blockchains' scalability remains one of the prevalent problems. This problem exists in two dimensions. First, the number of

© International Financial Cryptography Association 2024
F. Baldimtsi and C. Cachin (Eds.): FC 2023, LNCS 13951, pp. 36–53, 2024.
https://doi.org/10.1007/978-3-031-47751-5_3

transactions per second a blockchain can process with low latency, enabling real-time payments as well as robustness under high load. Second, the level of decentralization of the system that manages to achieve that high performance. This is important even in permissioned settings since to increase trust blockchains should be as decentralized as possible.

Most of the implementations of blockchain protocols in a permissioned setting are currently using leader-based SMR protocols such as PBFT [12], Tendermint [7], Hotstuff [40], and Jolteon [23]. Although Tendermint and Hotstuff reduce the total load of the system when the leader is good to $O(n)$, they are still challenging to scale. This is because of the monolithic architecture proposed by current SMR designs, where the leader is expected to propose already executed valid operations and disperse them directly to all nodes on the critical path, quickly using up the computing, storage, and networking resources of the leader node.

One good approach to tackle the network bottleneck is to reduce the traffic on the critical path by running consensus on the metadata instead of on the full blocks. This is evident by its abundant use in literature and industry (e.g., [5,7,12,17]). In many works, achieving consensus on the metadata and disseminating the full blocks are deeply intertwined (which may help performance in a particular system but hinders attempts to reuse in other systems). Some works gain efficiency mostly thanks to not being deployed in real adversarial settings. If, for example, we use a gossip network to disseminate the block like Tendermint [7] or Filecoin [39] then the liveness of the consensus is dependant on the performance and robustness of the gossip network which in their majority are not Byzantine Fault tolerant

Nevertheless, the idea of splitting responsibilities is a natural one, for example, Narwhal [17,37] embed a mechanism to disseminate the data to ensure its future availability and then causally order the meta data to form a mempool for consensus. Narwhal reports a tremendous speedup over the standard approach, however, since the data dissemination mechanism is deeply embedded in the code it is not trivial to modify it and to explore possible trade offs with other implementations. In this paper, we explore a *modular SMR* architecture that composes existing sub-protocols towards building an SMR. This allows for better usage of resources and exposes a key unexplored bottleneck, that of post-ordering retrieval of data. Specifically, we split the responsibilities of data dissemination, data ordering, and data execution into different modules. Data dissemination is done through a disperse&retrieve module that can be implemented by any Asynchronous Verifiable Information Dispersal (AVID) protocol [10]. Data ordering is done through any kind of Byzantine Atomic Broadcast (AB) protocol [10,19,28,35] and execution is done through any deterministic execution engine [1,4,26,38].

Once we have this explicit layering it becomes apparent that there is a gap of research on the retrieval step. This step is supposed to take the totally ordered proofs of availability that the AB outputs and retrieve the actual data to be executed. Current AVID protocols focus on scaling the disperse phase, but the retrieval protocols either ask the initial source for the data or collect from a supermajority of parties error-corrected chunks. Both of these protocols impose an $O(n)$ cost per node for retrieval and do not try to load-balance. We address this gap in the literature with our scalable retrieval protocol; we investigate how to efficiently run the retrieve sub-protocol of AVID. Unlike existing designs that cost $O(n)$ messages per node, we show how, using a probabilistic retrieval algorithm, we achieve complete retrieval with an expected $O(\log n)$ messages per node.

The Proof of Availability and Retrieval Problem
In a nutshell, the PoA&R problem detaches the act of "sending" a block from the part in which nodes "receive" it. Thus, a significant amount of the costs is transferred from the critical path to a time of the recipient's choice. To do so, each block is translated into a (short) proof π and when a node aims to inform the network of a new block of information (or transactions in our blockchain example) it disseminates π instead of the actual block. This can be done, for example, by broadcasting π, which is cheaper than broadcasting the block itself when using an efficient proof generator. A node that receives π stores it and is essentially convinced that when the actual block is needed it will be retrievable.[1]

To obtain the block itself, processes can retrieve it at their own time. In this sub-protocol they reconstruct the initial block, using the stored proof π. Since we alleviate the costs of dispersing the block's evidence into the network, the act of retrieving the block must incur additional costs. However, this kind of paradigm equips systems designers with the flexibility to decide when to undertake such costs. Specifically in blockchains systems, in times of congestion processes can progress by making consensus decisions on proofs alone, whereas the block retrieval and execution can be updated when the load decreases. Retrieval can also catch up when leaders are slow or changing.

In our proposed solution, the creation of the proof π is done using an erasure code scheme and a vector commitment scheme. When a process aims to share a block, it uses erasure coding to create a vector of n code words. It then creates a commitment that binds each word to the entire vector and sends each word (together with the commitment) to a different process. Processes that receive a commitment return a signature to the sender. Once the sender collects "enough" signatures, it forms the proof π that the block can be reconstructed. This is the basic "push" part in several AVID protocols [10,19,35].

In existing AVID protocols, retrieving the block (corresponding to the proof π) from the network is done via collecting a large number of code words and reconstructing the block. This might be too costly in large-scale systems. Instead, for the retrieval part, we propose a randomized solution that is deterministically safe and provides liveness with probability 1. Our proposed protocol incorporates vector reconstruction with random sampling. That is, a process that attempts to retrieve a block, occasionally samples a random subset of processes

---

[1] Notice that, unlike for AVID, the node does not need to reliably broadcast π. The AB layer takes care of that.

and asks them for the block. Clearly, when processes first try to retrieve the block, the creator of the block is the only process that knows it, thus, more communication rounds are needed. However, the spread of information is typically very fast. This intuitive claim is formally proved in Sect. 5. Moreover, we analyze different sample sizes that allow for different trade-offs in the cost structure.

Main Contributions

- Considering a modular architecture for the design of blockchains, we recognize a gap in research regarding the retrieval sub-protocol and present a family of (possibly) probabilistic protocols that offer a variety of cost structures. In particular, by using a probabilistic approach, we can reduce the expected cost of messages per node from $\Theta(n)$ to $\Theta(\log n)$.
- We analyze the behavior of our protocols both theoretically and with extensive simulations for large-scale systems. For smaller-sized systems, we implement and deploy our architecture on a network of AWS machines and show its viability in practice.

2   Model

We consider a standard asynchronous message-passing model with Byzantine faults and a computationally bounded adversary [8,9,32]. There is a fixed set Π of $n = 3f + 1$ processes, at most f of them are faulty. These faulty processes are called *Byzantine* and are not bound to the protocol. The rest of the processes are *correct* and act according to the protocol. Until a process first deviates from the protocol, it is called *so-far correct*. Each pair of processes is connected via reliable albeit asynchronous links. That is, messages among correct processes eventually arrive but there is no bound on message delays. We consider an adversary that is exposed to all of the network communication, fully controls the Byzantine processes, and can adaptively choose which processes to corrupt. In particular, even after a so-far correct process has sent a message, if the message is yet to be delivered the adversary can view this message, choose to corrupt the sending process, and change/delete the message.

We model the computations made by all system components as probabilistic Turing machines and bound the number of computational basic steps allowed by the adversary by a polynomial in a security parameter λ. We further assume a trusted setup, namely, before the start of the protocol, each party is dealt its own secret key share and the public keys as internal states. This can be achieved by a trusted dealer or distributed key generation protocols [2,18,25,30].

Our protocols employ several standard cryptographic primitives with the following abstractions. (A reference to a full definition is given per primitive.)
Erasure Code. We use an erasure code scheme that consists of two algorithms, EC.*encode* and EC.*decode*. EC.*encode* takes a block b and returns a vector of n code words such that any $n - 2f$ out of the n code words suffice for EC.*decode* to fully reconstruct the original block b. (See [6].)

Threshold Signature. This scheme allows processes to combine different signatures on the same message, into a single compact signature. It consists of the *SignShare* and *Combine$_t$* algorithms. The first is used by each individual to produce its individual signature, while *Combine$_t$* is used to produce a single compact signature from t valid individual signatures. Individual/full signatures are $O(\lambda)$-bit long. (See [31].)

Vector Commitment. The vector commitment (VC) scheme is comprised of three algorithms: 1) VectorCommit(**c**) which takes an n-element vector **c** and returns a commitment to that vector vc_{sig}; 2) PositionalCommitProof(**c**, vc_{sig}, c_i, i) which takes the vector **c**, its commitment vc_{sig}, the element c_i and its position i in **c**, and returns a positional proof π_i; and 3) VerifyElement(vc_{sig}, c_i, π_i) that uses the proof π_i to check whether c_i is indeed the ith element in the vector whose commitment is vc_{sig}. Both vc_{sig} and π_i bit lengths are in $O(\lambda)$. (See [13].)

3   Modular SMR Architecture

We propose a layered architecture for SMR that enables plug-and-play use of PoA&R, Atomic Broadcast, and deterministic execution protocols (see Fig. 1). We first define the *proof of availability & retrieval* abstraction that is required for our architecture in a format that conforms with distributed-computing literature. A similar definition, in a more information-theoretic format, can be found in a concurrent work [35]. The rest of the paper focuses on the PoA&R protocol. For completeness, we also briefly describe below the rest of the layers in the architecture.

3.1   The Proof of Availability and Retrieval Problem Definition

In this section, we formally define the Proof of Availability & Retrieval (PoA&R) abstraction. This abstraction should capture the ability to disseminate a block in a fashion that enables reducing the cost on the critical path (the consensus module). Roughly speaking, we detach the act of "sending" a block from the part in which processes "receive" it. Thus, a significant amount of the costs can be transferred from the critical path to a time of the recipient's choice. The PoA&R abstraction exposes an interface with two operations and two callbacks:

PoA_push(b): an operation invoked by a process to push (disseminate) a proof for block b.

PoA_commit(π): a callback triggered to commit a proof π. (For the availability of a block b.)

PoA_pull(π): an operation invoked by a process to pull (retrieve) a block that corresponds to the proof π.

PoA_deliver(b): a callback triggered to handle the delivery of a block b.

We only define the single-sender problem (with a given known sender p_s), since this specification can easily be extended to the case with multiple senders that push/pull blocks. For the multiple-senders problem, many single-senders instances can be active in parallel (by using source tags, for example).

We assume the existence of two functions `CreateProof` and `Verify` that satisfy the following conditions. For any arbitrary blocks b, b_1 and b_2, it holds that $\mathtt{CreateProof}(b_1) = \mathtt{CreateProof}(b_2)$ iff $b_1 = b_2$, and $\mathtt{Verify}(b, \pi) = true$ if $\pi = \mathtt{CreateProof}(b)$ and $\mathtt{Verify}(b, \pi) = false$ otherwise. Given these standard cryptographic functions, the PoA&R problem is defined by the following properties that must be satisfied at all the possible executions.

Definition 1. Proof of Availability & Retrieval:

- **Push-Validity:** If p_s is correct and invokes `PoA_push`(b), then every correct process eventually performs `PoA_commit`(π) such that $\mathtt{Verify}(b, \pi) = true$.
- **Pull-Validity:** If a correct process p_i had performed `PoA_commit`(π) and invokes `PoA_pull`(π), then:
  (liveness) – p_i eventually performs `PoA_deliver`(b) with probability 1. Moreover,
  (safety) – b and π satisfy $\mathtt{Verify}(b, \pi) = true$.

Our definition separates the *Pull* property into a safety part and a liveness part. This facilitates the analysis of deterministically safe protocols that are probabilistically live. Most notably, since PoA&R is defined as part of a blockchain architecture, we are able to capture exactly what is necessary without redundant properties. For example, we do not need the agreement property of AVID, which in turn enables us to design more efficient protocols.

Complexity Measures. A PoA&R protocol satisfies the validity and termination properties even in cases of asynchrony and Byzantine faulty processes, which means it is robust by design. However, executions with failures and asynchrony are not the majority in the routine operation of systems. In fact, the "nice case" in which no failures occur and the network is almost synchronous can be quite common in practice. It is therefore desired to design systems that minimize costs in these common "nice" conditions while allowing for increased costs when having to deal with troubles. We assume that the common-case execution of the considered blockchain system has the following properties:

- **Good processes.** All process are correct.
- **Synchrony.** The roundtrip of messages in the network is within Δ.
- **Concurrency.** Processes start the pulling sub-protocol at the same time.

The last assumption is crucial for the stochastic analysis of the protocols. It is a justified approximation since in the normal modus operandi a process pulls immediately after the consensus decision, and synchrony causes these decisions to happen within a short time span at almost all processes.

We henceforth use the following (per process) complexity metrics:

Message Complexity. The expected number of messages a process sends during a common-case execution.

Bit Complexity. The expected number of bits a process sends during a common-case execution.

Round Complexity (Running Time). We define an asynchronous round in the standard way (see [11]). Essentially, this measurement counts the number of messaging "rounds", when the protocol is embedded into a lock-step timing model. The round complexity is then the expected number of asynchronous rounds it takes a process to complete the protocol (deliver a block) during a common-case execution.

3.2   Atomic Broadcast

The classic definition of Atomic Broadcast states that every execution of a protocol solving AB should satisfy:

- **Validity:** If a correct process *broadcasts* msg then all correct processes eventually deliver *msg*.
- **Agreement:** If a correct process *delivers* msg then all correct processes eventually deliver *msg*.
- **Integrity:** *msg* is delivered by a correct process at most once, and only if it was previously broadcast.
- **Total order:** If two correct processes deliver both *msg* and *msg'*, they deliver them in the same order.

However, it is well-known that AB is impossible to solve in an asynchronous model even with one possible crash failure [22]. Since we are dealing with an asynchronous setting with Byzantine failures, these properties must be relaxed. There are varied relaxations and protocols solving them in the literature, e.g., [3, 12,23,29,34,40]. We leave the choice of desired relaxation and implementing protocol for the system designer, but remark that this crucial choice determines the basic theoretical guarantees provided by the SMR system.

3.3   Execution

The execution layer simply takes as input the total ordered set of operations and updates the state. The only property required by this layer to implement SMR is that of determinism. Solutions such as [14,16,21,36,38] can be used to provide a scalable execution layer.

3.4   Bringing Them All Together

Our SMR works in layers. First, every process that has a batch of operations transmits it through PoA&R and collects a proof of availability π. These proofs are then submitted to the AB layer which totally orders the proofs without having to incur the cost of handling the data. The totally ordered proofs are then fed into the Retrieval sub-protocol that recovers any batches not locally available at each process. Once a batch is available and at the head of the ordering queue, the process locally executes it and updates the state. Figure 1 gives an overview of the architecture.

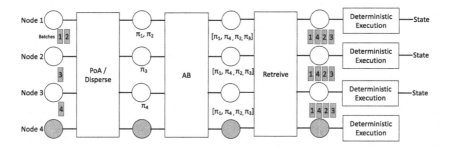

Fig. 1. Overview of the Layered SMR approach

4 Proof of Availability and Retrieval Protocols

Many protocols can implement the abstraction of Definition 1, for example, AVID protocols. As we have observed, the retrieval (pulling) part significantly affects the performance of the system. Thus, we propose a PoA&R module with a family of pulling sub-protocols that offer different trade-offs in terms of time vs. communication costs. Clearly, any pulling sub-protocol depends on the dispersal (push) sub-protocol, therefore, it is defined with relation to a given push-commit protocol.

In a trivial PoA&R scheme, when a process wishes to push a block b, it simply sends it to all processes. Upon receiving the block, a correct process commits b as the proof for itself (i.e., $\texttt{CreateProof}(b) = b$), and when it wants to pull it, it immediately delivers b. It is straightforward that this simple algorithm satisfies Definition 1 and is also optimal in the number of messages and the round complexity. However, it is far from being optimal in terms of bit complexity. More importantly, this solution does not allow the desired goal of removing the load from the consensus module. That is, processes take the block itself as an input for a single consensus decision. In typical systems, a single block contains a large number of transactions in order to increase throughput, which implies large block sizes. This renders the above sub-protocol impractical for large systems with a high level of decentralization (i.e. large n).

To bypass this problem several works suggested using erasure coding and vector commitments [32,35] in their protocols, that can be interpreted as push-commit sub-protocols. We use this single (standard) push sub-protocol and focus instead on the pulling sub-protocol. For completeness, we first detail the standard push-commit protocol and briefly explain the standard deterministic pull protocol. We then present a pulling protocol that improves the standard one by satisfying pull-termination with probability 1 instead of deterministically.

4.1 Erasure Coded PoA&R

A full pseudo-code can be found in the long version of the paper [15].

Push-Commit Protocol. In this algorithm, the sender erasure-codes the block b into n code words from which any $n - 2f$ words suffice for reconstructing b. These n code words are treated as a vector from hereon. The sender then uses a vector commitment mechanism to create a binding proof for each vector element. Each code word and proof are then sent to a process corresponding to the vector position. A process that receives a valid vector commitment proof, returns to the sender a signed share for a threshold signature on the vector signature (denoted as vc_{sig}). When the sender collects enough shares ($n - f$ this time), it combines them into a valid threshold signature on vc_{sig} and sends that signature to all as the proof. A process that receives a valid threshold signature commits it as a "proof for the availability of a block".

The bit and message complexities of the protocols are in $\Theta(|B|+n\lambda)$ and $\Theta(n)$ respectively. Since the sender must transmit $\Omega(|B|)$ bits and must send at least f messages to enable the correct reconstruction of b, the Push-Commit protocol is asymptotically optimal in the number of bits it communicates as well as in the number of messages.[2]

Deterministic Pull-Deliver Protocol. A natural pull-deliver protocol that complements the push algorithm is as follows. A process that initiates PoA_pull(π) sends to all other processes a request to reconstruct the block associated with π. Each of the processes answers with its share of the data and the vector commitment proof attached to it. When the puller collects $f + 1$ valid replays, it reconstructs b. It then verifies that b is valid by computing the vector commitment procedure on b and comparing the resulting vc_{sig} to the one in π. If the block is valid, it can be delivered. Otherwise, deliver $\perp$ which indicates that the sender of the block is faulty and no valid block exists.

This algorithm costs $\Theta(|B| + \lambda n)$ bits per puller and is very efficient in moderately large systems where $n < |B|$. For larger-scale systems, however, the linear number of messages per puller might hinder performance. A "strawman" solution to this issue is the following. A puller first asks the sender for the block. If the sender does not respond timely, then the puller initiates the deterministic pull-deliver protocol. Although this protocol seems to cost on average only a single message and $O(|B|)$ bits per puller, it fails in practice because many pullers ask the sender for the block concurrently, thus causing it to stall and become a fatal bottleneck. This is because there is a process (the sender) that experiences an $\Omega(n)$ message and $\Omega(n|B|)$ bits complexity. The acute imbalance of costs leads to a severe bottleneck in large systems. We deal with this imbalance problem by proposing a family of randomized pull-deliver protocols. These protocols combine rumor spreading in a "reverse gossiping" manner for common-case performance together with erasure-code reconstruction to ensure safety.

---

[2] We note that the cryptographic primitives for vector commitment might be heavy in local computations and could slow down a system. In comparison, simpler commitment primitives such as Merkle trees [33] can prove a better match as long as n is not "too large". However, they incur a $\Theta(\lambda \log n)$ bit complexity per commitment in comparison to the constant (λ) complexity of the vector commitment primitive.

Probabilistic Pull-Deliver Protocols. A process that initiates `PoA_pull`(π) and does not have the block locally does the following. It flips a (biased) coin with a probability of k/n of getting heads. If heads is flipped, then the puller sends a reconstruction request to all. Regardless of the coin's outcome, the puller randomly selects a set $\mathcal{S}$ of k processes and sends them a block request (for the transmission of the block associated with π). A process that receives a reconstruction request answers with its code word. A process that receives a "block-transmission" request answers with the block if it has it, otherwise, it informs the puller that it does not have the block (via a "NACK" message). If the puller receives a "NACK" from a process $p_j \in \mathcal{S}$, it removes p_j from $\mathcal{S}$ and randomly chooses a new process, sends this process a block-transmission request, and adds it to $\mathcal{S}$. If the puller does not receive any reply from $p_j \in \mathcal{S}$ within some predefined time (say Δ), it randomly chooses a process not in $\mathcal{S}$, sends this process a block-transmission request, and adds it to $\mathcal{S}$. After every new k block requests, the puller flips the coin again to decide whether to attempt a reconstruction from all or not.

These pull protocols offer a variety of cost structures for the system designer to choose from. The cost is comprised of the expected message, bit and round complexities in the common case. These complexities are determined by the choice of k, as we show in the theoretical analysis in Sect. 5. While using our probabilistic pulling protocols cannot significantly reduce the bit complexity in comparison to the deterministic counterpart, in terms of expected message complexity we can gain an exponential improvement. Specifically, we prove that for $k \in \Theta(1)$ we get a message complexity in $O(\log n)$, for $k \in \Theta(\log n)$ the message complexity is in $O\left(\frac{\log^2 n}{\log \log n}\right)$, and in for $k \in \Theta(\sqrt{n})$ we get a message complexity in $O(\sqrt{n})$. However, the reduced message complexity does not come for free. Either the round complexity increases (for $k \in \Theta(1)$), or the bit complexity increases (for $k \in \Theta(\sqrt{n})$). Therefore, different choices of k fit different systems according to where the system bottleneck is. (See Table 1.)

Table 1. Expected Costs per Process for different choices of k

k values	Messages	Bits	Rounds
$k \in \Theta(1)$	$O(\log n)$	$O(|B|\log n + \lambda \log n)^{\dagger}$	$O(\log n)$
$k \in \Theta(\log n)$	$O\left(\frac{\log^2 n}{\log \log n}\right)$	$O\left(|B|\log n + \frac{\lambda \log^2 n}{\log \log n}\right)$	$O\left(\frac{\log n}{\log \log n}\right)$
$k \in \Theta(\sqrt{n})$	$O(\sqrt{n})$	$O(|B|\sqrt{n})$	$O(1)$
$k = n^*$*	$O(n)$	$O(|B| + \lambda n)$	$O(1)$

†Only for the sender, others' expected bit-complexity is actually in $O(|B| + \lambda \log n)$.

** Deterministic Pull-deliver (without block requests).

5   Theoretical Analysis

We analyze the complexity of the common-case in which all processes attempt to synchronize at the same time, the sender is correct, and in addition, the network is in a stable "nice" period. Concretely, we analyze the complexity in cases where no faults occur and a message round-trip time takes exactly 1 time-unit throughout the network.

5.1   One Sample Per Round

With $k = 1$ (a single sample per round), our model resembles the random phone-call model of [20]. There is an elegant analysis for address-oblivious rumor spreading in this model that was made by Karp, Schindelhauer, Shenker, and Vocking in [27]. Our analysis is inspired by their techniques and therefore shares similar structure. Nevertheless, their analysis yields slightly different quantities than ours, since they consider a protocol in which processes both actively tell the rumor (send the block) as well as passively inform others who ask for the rumor. In contrast, we allow only to passively inform those who ask. Moreover, the analysis in [27] only holds for large enough n, a restriction we do not have since we bound the expected values rather than the probability of higher costs.

Theorem 1. *In a common-case execution of the pull protocol with $k = 1$, the pulling terminates within $O(\log n)$ expected rounds.*

Proof. A complete proof can be found in the long version of the paper [15]

From Theorem 1 we immediately get the following.

Corollary 1. *In the common-case,*

1. *the expected number of messages per process is in $O(\log n)$, and*
2. *the expected number of bits per process is in $O(|B| + \lambda \log n)$ with only the sender having a higher load of $\Theta(|B| \log n + \lambda \log n)$.*

We remark that since we use only passive spreading without actively gossiping, our expected bit complexity is better than that of [27] which is $\Theta(|B| \log \log n + \log n)$ per receiving process (and the same as ours for the sender). Moreover, we are able to bypass the lower bound for address-oblivious protocols which is also presented in [27]. We do so by analysing the expected cost rather than the cost w.h.p. Applying a Chernoff bound on our result will show that we are optimal for the cost w.h.p.

5.2   Sampling $\log n$ per Round

For a different trade-off, one may choose the pulling protocol with $k \in \Theta(\log n)$. We show here the resulting expected costs of such choice.

Theorem 2. *In a common-case execution of the pull protocol with $k = \log n$, the pulling terminates within $O\left(\frac{\log n}{\log \log n}\right)$ expected rounds.*

Proof. The spread of information can be modeled by a Markov process, with states $\{1, \ldots, n\}$ which represent how many process currently have the block. Denote the random variable $X_r \in \{1, \ldots, n\}$ to be the number of informed processes at the end of round r and $Y_r \triangleq n - X_r$ is the number of uninformed processes at the end of round r. Observe that $X_r \geq X_{r-1}$, $X_0 = 1$, and that if $Y_r = 1$ then $Y_{r+1} = 0$ deterministically. Given X_r we have that $\Delta_{r+1} \triangleq X_{r+1} - X_r$ follows a binomial distribution with $n - X_r$ experiments and some success probability P_r. I.e., $\Delta_{r+1} \mid X_r \sim B(n - X_r, P_r)$, and we wish to bound P_r from below.

For each of the $Y_r = n - X_r$ experiments we denote by $\mathcal{S}$ the sampled set of processes. $|\mathcal{S}| = \log n$ and the samples are without replacement which increases the hitting probability. Therefore, P_r is bounded from below by sampling with replacement.

$$
\begin{aligned}
P_r = P(&\text{at least one out of} \log n \text{samples without replacement} \\
&\qquad\qquad \text{hits one of} X_r \text{options)} \\
\geq P(&\text{at least one out of} \log n \text{samples with replacement} \\
&\qquad\qquad \text{hits one of} X_r \text{options)} \triangleq \tilde{P}_r.
\end{aligned}
\tag{1}
$$

By the inclusion–exclusion principle

$$
\begin{aligned}
\tilde{P}_r =P(&\bigcup_{i=1}^{\log n} \text{a sample from n-1 possibilities hits on of} X_r \text{options)} \\
&- P(\text{at least two samples from} n - 1 \text{possibilities hits} \\
&\quad \text{one of} X_r \text{options)} \\
&\geq \log n \cdot \frac{X_r}{n-1} - \binom{\log n}{2}\left(\frac{X_r}{n-1}\right)^2 \\
&= \frac{X_r}{n-1}\left(\log n - \frac{(\log n)(\log n - 1)}{2} \cdot \frac{X_r}{n-1}\right),
\end{aligned}
\tag{2}
$$

where the last inequality is due to the union bound which implies that the probability of at least two samples hitting is at most $P\left(\bigcup_{i=1}^{\binom{\log n}{2}}\left(\frac{X_r}{n-1}\right)^2\right)$. Now, for $X_r \leq \frac{n}{\log n}$ we have that

$$
\begin{aligned}
\tilde{P}_r &\geq \log n \cdot \frac{X_r}{n-1}\left(1 - \frac{\log n - 1}{2} \cdot \frac{X_r}{n-1}\right) \\
&\geq \log n \cdot \frac{X_r}{n-1}\left(1 - \frac{1}{2}\right) = \frac{\log n}{2} \cdot \frac{X_r}{n-1}.
\end{aligned}
\tag{3}
$$

And using the expectation of a binomial variable, we obtain

$$\mathbb{E}[X_{r+1} \mid X_r] = X_r + \mathbb{E}[\varDelta_{r+1} \mid x_r] = X_r + (n-X_r)P_r = (1-P_r)X_r + nP_r$$
$$\geq n \cdot P_r \geq n \cdot \tilde{P}_r \geq n \cdot \frac{\log n}{2} \cdot \frac{X_r}{n-1} \geq \frac{\log n}{2} \cdot X_r, \tag{4}$$

and by the law of total expectation

$$\mathbb{E}[X_{r+1}] \geq \frac{\log n}{2} \cdot \mathbb{E}[X_r]. \tag{5}$$

Let r_1 be the first round at the end of which $X_r \geq \frac{n}{\log n}$. By applying (5) recursively we have

$$n \geq \mathbb{E}[X_{r_1}] \geq \left(\frac{\log n}{2}\right)^{r_1} \cdot \mathbb{E}[X_0]. \tag{6}$$

Taking the log of both sides yields

$$\log n \geq r_1 \cdot \log\left(\frac{\log n}{2}\right) \iff r_1 \leq \frac{\log n}{\log\log n - 1}. \tag{7}$$

We thus have that $\mathbb{E}[r_1] \in O\left(\frac{\log n}{\log\log n}\right)$.

We now turn to analyze the behavior of $Y_r \triangleq n - X_r$. It follows a binomial distribution $Y_{r+1} \mid Y_r \sim B(Y_r, Q_r)$, where Q_r is the probability that all of the $\log n$ samples miss. Again we bound it using sampling with replacement and get

$$Q_r \leq \left(\frac{Y_r - 1}{n - 1}\right)^{\log n} \leq \left(\frac{Y_r}{n}\right)^{\log n}. \tag{8}$$

Recall that at the end of round r_1 it holds that $X_{r_1} \geq \frac{n}{\log n}$ and therefore,

$$Q_{r_1} \leq \left(\frac{Y_{r_1}}{n}\right)^{\log n} \leq \left(\frac{n - n/\log n}{n}\right)^{\log n} = \left(1 - \frac{1}{\log n}\right)^{\log n} \leq \frac{1}{e}. \tag{9}$$

This, in turn, implies

$$\mathbb{E}[Y_{r_1+1} \mid Y_{r_1}] = Y_{r_1} \cdot Q_{r_1} \leq \left(n - \frac{n}{\log n}\right) \cdot \frac{1}{e} \leq \frac{n}{2}. \tag{10}$$

We denote the first round at which $Y_r \leq \frac{n}{2}$ by r_2. According to the above, it is expected that $r_2 - r_1 \in O(1)$.

Moreover, denote the round when $Y_r \leq 1$ by r_3. We have that

$$\mathbb{E}[Y_{r_2+1} \mid Y_{r_2}] = Y_{r_2} \cdot Q_{r_2} \leq Y_{r_2}\left(\frac{Y_{r_2}}{n}\right)^{\log n} \leq \frac{n}{2} \cdot \left(\frac{1}{2}\right)^{\log n} = \frac{n}{2} \cdot \frac{1}{n} \leq 1. \tag{11}$$

Clearly, $\mathbb{E}[r_3 - r_2] \in O(1)$. Finally, denote by r_{end} the round at the end of which all processes have been informed. We recall that if $Y_r \leq 1$ then $Y_{r+1} = 0$ deterministically. As a result, the linearity of expectation yields

$$\mathbb{E}[r_{end}] \leq 1 + \mathbb{E}[r_3] = 1 + \mathbb{E}[r_3 - r_2] + \mathbb{E}[r_2 - r_1] + \mathbb{E}[r_1]$$
$$= 1 + O(1) + O(1) + O\left(\frac{\log n}{\log \log n}\right), \tag{12}$$

and $\mathbb{E}[r_{end}] \in O\left(\frac{\log n}{\log \log n}\right)$.

This result implies:

Corollary 2. *In the common-case,*

1. *the expected number of messages per process is in* $O\left(\frac{\log^2 n}{\log \log n}\right)$, *and*
2. *the expected number of bits per process is in* $O\left(|B| \log n + \frac{\lambda \log^2 n}{\log \log n}\right)$.

5.3 Sampling $\sqrt{n}$ per Round

For the fastest termination, that is within $O(1)$ expected asynchronous rounds, it is possible to use our retrieval protocol with $k \in \Theta(\sqrt{n})$ samples. To prove this we use a Markov process, similarly to the previous proofs, with a binomial state-transfer distribution. Specifically, $\Delta_{r+1} \mid X_r \sim B(n - X_r, P_r)$ where we bound P_r to be at least $1 - e^{-\frac{X_r}{\sqrt{n}}}$. Roughly speaking, since $\mathbb{E}[X_r] \in \Omega(\sqrt{n})$, we will get that, in expectation, all processes complete their pull in a constant number of rounds.

Theorem 3. *In a common-case execution of the pull protocol with $k = \sqrt{n}$, the pulling terminates within $O(1)$ expected rounds.*

Proof. The complete proof can be found in the long version of the paper [15]. $\square$

The consequent message and bit complexities for a process are as follows.

Corollary 3. *In the common-case,*

1. *the expected number of messages per process is in* $O(\sqrt{n})$, *and*
2. *the expected number of bits per process is in* $O(|B|\sqrt{n})$.

5.4 Simulations

We complement the rigorously proven complexities with extensive simulations for systems with a large number of participants. All of the simulations begin with only a randomly chosen sender that posses the block while all other processes have their corresponding code word. We measure the time at which the last process is informed (i.e., delivers the block). For each system, we run 5 simulations and average the end results. The outcome is on par with the theoretical

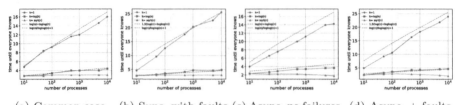

(a) Common-case   (b) Sync. with faults (c) Async. no failures   (d) Async. + faults

Fig. 2. Simulation results for the retrieval sub-protocol in different systems. The x-axis states the number of processes n, and the y-axis the time in units of Δ (the expected roundtrip delay). The graphs depict the time at which the **last** correct process delivers the block as a function of n. The network assumption are: (a) The assumed common case, i.e., synchrony and no failures; (b) Synchrony but $1/3$ non-responsive processes; (c) Asynchronous delay that follows a Poisson distribution with parameter Δ and no failures; and (d) Asynchronous delay that follows a Poisson distribution with parameter Δ with a $1/3$ of the processes that are non-responsive. The system sizes always vary between 10 to 10^4 processes.

expectations which are depicted by the dashed lines. Moreover, since our protocols are address oblivious and do not rely on synchrony for correctness, they are very robust by design. To demonstrate this, we have also simulated a degraded form of asynchrony by employing stochastic delays that follow a Poisson distribution and set Δ to be the expected delay. Besides the fact that it allows for unbounded delays, the choice of the distribution is arbitrary. (We make no claim as to what best models delays in practical networks.) The results in Figs. 2c and 2d suggest that, for Δ that equals the expected delay, the protocols are robust to asynchrony and achieve essentially the same complexities as in synchronous settings. There is even a slight improvement in comparison to synchronous networks, possibly because fast processes are able to answer slower processes in the same "asynchronous round" when they first obtain the block. Finally, we have also simulated the protocol's behavior under faults. Specifically, we run simulations in which a random $1/3$ of the processes have crashed. The results appear in Figs. 2, and 2d. Again, the simulations indicate the robustness of our protocols, with only a $\frac{3}{2}$x slowdown in performance which is expected since on average third of the samples are wasted on faulty processes. To conclude, our simulations suggest that the pulling sub-protocol is as efficient as expected and is robust under different network conditions.

There are several questions that have arisen during this work. One natural direction to consider is more complex choices for $\mathcal{S}$, such as giving higher probability to sampling a process that we have not previously sampled, or randomly choosing k instead of having it fixed a priori. However, it is not obvious how to analyze such stochastic mechanisms. More practical directions to explore are: what choice of PoA&R module best suits a system based on the system's size? Can we use cloud-based solutions for an optimistic and more scalable PoA&R? Finally, while our definition covers some settings, others are left to be defined, for example, what are the properties of PoA&R in a permissionless setting?

On a general note, formally defining modularity in blockchains is an important endeavour. It would facilitate combining contributions from different parts of the community to establish a truly distributed ecosystem.

Acknowledgements. This work is partially supported by Meta. Eleftherios Kokoris-Kogias is partially supported by Austrian Science Fund (FWF) grant No: F8512-N. Shir Cohen is supported by the Adams Fellowship Program of the Israel Academy of Sciences and Humanities.

References

1. Abadi, D.J., Faleiro, J.M.: An overview of deterministic database systems. Commun. ACM **61**(9), 78–88 (2018)
2. Abraham, I., Jovanovic, P., Maller, M., Meiklejohn, S., Stern, G., Tomescu, A.: Reaching consensus for asynchronous distributed key generation. In: Proceedings of the 2021 ACM Symposium on Principles of Distributed Computing, pp. 363–373 (2021)
3. Abraham, I., Malkhi, D., Spiegelman, A.: Asymptotically optimal validated asynchronous byzantine agreement. In: Proceedings of the 2019 ACM Symposium on Principles of Distributed Computing, pp. 337–346 (2019)
4. Antonopoulos, A.M., Wood, G.: Mastering Ethereum: Building Smart Contracts and Dapps. O'reilly Media, Sebastopol (2018)
5. Biely, M., Milosevic, Z., Santos, N., Schiper, A.: S-paxos: Offloading the leader for high throughput state machine replication. In: 2012 IEEE 31st Symposium on Reliable Distributed Systems, pp. 111–120. IEEE (2012)
6. Blahut, R.E.: Theory and Practice of Error Control Codes, vol. 126. Addison-Wesley Reading, Boston (1983)
7. Buchman, E.: Tendermint: byzantine fault tolerance in the age of blockchains. Ph.D. thesis, University of Guelph (2016)
8. Cachin, C., Kursawe, K., Petzold, F., Shoup, V.: Secure and efficient asynchronous broadcast protocols. In: Kilian, J. (ed.) CRYPTO 2001. LNCS, vol. 2139, pp. 524–541. Springer, Heidelberg (2001). https://doi.org/10.1007/3-540-44647-8_31
9. Cachin, C., Kursawe, K., Shoup, V.: Random oracles in constantinople: practical asynchronous byzantine agreement using cryptography. J. Cryptol. **18**(3), 219–246 (2005)
10. Cachin, C., Tessaro, S.: Asynchronous verifiable information dispersal. In: 24th IEEE Symposium on Reliable Distributed Systems (SRDS 2005), pp. 191–201. IEEE (2005)
11. Canetti, R., Rabin, T.: Fast asynchronous byzantine agreement with optimal resilience. In: Proceedings of the Twenty-Fifth Annual ACM Symposium on Theory of Computing, pp. 42–51 (1993)
12. Castro, M., Liskov, B., et al.: Practical byzantine fault tolerance. In: OSDI, vol. 99, pp. 173–186 (1999)
13. Catalano, D., Fiore, D.: Vector commitments and their applications. In: Kurosawa, K., Hanaoka, G. (eds.) PKC 2013. LNCS, vol. 7778, pp. 55–72. Springer, Heidelberg (2013). https://doi.org/10.1007/978-3-642-36362-7_5
14. Chen, Y., et al.: Forerunner: constraint-based speculative transaction execution for Ethereum. In: Proceedings of the ACM SIGOPS 28th Symposium on Operating Systems Principles, pp. 570–587 (2021)

15. Cohen, S., Goren, G., Kokoris-Kogias, L., Sonnino, A., Spiegelman, A.: Proof of availability & retrieval in a modular blockchain architecture. Cryptology ePrint Archive (2022)
16. Cowling, J., Liskov, B.: Granola: low-overhead distributed transaction coordination. In: USENIX Annual Technical Conference (2012)
17. Danezis, G., Kokoris-Kogias, L., Sonnino, A., Spiegelman, A.: Narwhal and tusk: a DAG-based mempool and efficient BFT consensus. In: Proceedings of the Seventeenth European Conference on Computer Systems, pp. 34–50 (2022)
18. Das, S., Xiang, Z., Ren, L.: Asynchronous data dissemination and its applications. In: Conference on Computer and Communications Security (2021)
19. Das, S., Xiang, Z., Ren, L.: Balanced quadratic reliable broadcast and improved asynchronous verifiable information dispersal. Cryptology ePrint Archive (2022)
20. Demers, A., et al.: Epidemic algorithms for replicated database maintenance. In: Symposium on Principles of Distributed Computing (1987)
21. Faleiro, J.M., Abadi, D.J., Hellerstein, J.M.: High performance transactions via early write visibility. Proc. VLDB Endowment 10(5) (2017)
22. Fischer, M.J., Lynch, N.A., Paterson, M.S.: Impossibility of distributed consensus with one faulty process. J. ACM (JACM) 32(2), 374–382 (1985)
23. Gelashvili, R., Kokoris-Kogias, L., Sonnino, A., Spiegelman, A., Xiang, Z.: Jolteon and ditto: network-adaptive efficient consensus with asynchronous fallback. In: Financial Cryptography and Data Security (2022)
24. Guerraoui, R., Kuznetsov, P., Monti, M., Pavlovic, M., Seredinschi, D.A.: Scalable byzantine reliable broadcast. In: Symposium on Distributed Computing (2019)
25. Günther, C.U., Das, S., Kokoris-Kogias, L.: Practical asynchronous proactive secret sharing and key refresh. Cryptology ePrint Archive (2022)
26. Haas, A., et al.: Bringing the web up to speed with webassembly. In: Proceedings of the 38th ACM SIGPLAN Conference on Programming Language Design and Implementation, pp. 185–200 (2017)
27. Karp, R., Schindelhauer, C., Shenker, S., Vocking, B.: Randomized rumor spreading. In: Proceedings 41st Annual Symposium on Foundations of Computer Science, pp. 565–574. IEEE (2000)
28. Keidar, I., Kokoris-Kogias, E., Naor, O., Spiegelman, A.: All you need is DAG. In: Symposium on Principles of Distributed Computing (2021)
29. Kokoris Kogias, E., Jovanovic, P., Gailly, N., Khoffi, I., Gasser, L., Ford, B.: Enhancing bitcoin security and performance with strong consistency via collective signing. In: USENIX Association (2016)
30. Kokoris Kogias, E., Malkhi, D., Spiegelman, A.: Asynchronous distributed key generation for computationally-secure randomness, consensus, and threshold signatures. In: Conference on Computer and Communications Security (2020)
31. Libert, B., Joye, M., Yung, M.: Born and raised distributively: fully distributed non-interactive adaptively-secure threshold signatures with short shares. In: Theoretical Computer Science (2016)
32. Lu, Y., Lu, Z., Tang, Q., Wang, G.: Dumbo-mvba: Optimal multi-valued validated asynchronous byzantine agreement, revisited. In: Symopsium on Principles of Distributed Computing (2020)
33. Merkle, R.C.: Secrecy, Authentication, and Public Key Systems. Stanford University, Stanford (1979)
34. Nakamoto, S.: Bitcoin: A peer-to-peer electronic cash system. Decentralized Business Review, p. 21260 (2008)
35. Nazirkhanova, K., Neu, J., Tse, D.: Information dispersal with provable retrievability for rollups. arXiv preprint arXiv:2111.12323 (2021)

36. Qin, D., Brown, A.D., Goel, A.: Caracal: contention management with deterministic concurrency control. In: Symposium on Operating Systems Principles (2021)
37. Spiegelman, A., Giridharan, N., Sonnino, A., Kokoris-Kogias, L.: Bullshark: Dag BFT protocols made practical. In: Computer and Communications Security (2022)
38. Stefo, C., Xiang, Z., Kokoris-Kogias, L.: Executing and proving over dirty ledgers. Cryptology ePrint Archive (2022)
39. Vyzovitis, D., Napora, Y., McCormick, D., Dias, D., Psaras, Y.: Gossipsub: attack-resilient message propagation in the filecoin and eth2.0 networks. ArXiv preprint (2020)
40. Yin, M., Malkhi, D., Reiter, M.K., Gueta, G.G., Abraham, I.: HotStuff: BFT consensus with linearity and responsiveness. In: Symposium on Principles of Distributed Computing (2019)

Limits on Revocable Proof Systems, With Implications for Stateless Blockchains

Miranda Christ[1,3](✉) ⓘ and Joseph Bonneau[2,3] ⓘ

[1] Columbia University, New York, USA
mchrist@cs.columbia.edu
[2] New York University, New York, USA
jcs@cs.nyu.edu
[3] a16z Crypto Research, San Francisco, USA

Abstract. Motivated by the goal of building a cryptocurrency with succinct global state, we introduce the abstract notion of a revocable proof system. We prove an information-theoretic result on the relation between global state size and the required number of local proof updates as statements are revoked (e.g., coins are spent). We apply our result to conclude that there is no useful trade-off point when building a stateless cryptocurrency: the system must either have a linear-sized global state (in the number of accounts in the system) or require a near-linear rate of local proof updates. The notion of a revocable proof system is quite general and also provides new lower bounds for set commitments, vector commitments and authenticated dictionaries.

Keywords: Stateless Blockchains · Authenticated Data Structures

1 Introduction

Modern cryptocurrencies prevent double-spending attacks using a public, append-only log called a blockchain. Classically, a blockchain records *all* transactions, and validating a new transaction requires checking that it doesn't conflict with any prior transaction. This approach was first successfully deployed by Bitcoin [22] though it was proposed earlier [14].

A challenge of the blockchain paradigm is that each validator traditionally must store the entire *state* of the system. In Bitcoin, this consists of a set of unspent transaction outputs (UTXOs), which has consistently grown and now contains 80 million elements, requiring several GB to store. Ethereum's state is even larger [31], requiring roughly 35 GB to represent 200 million accounts.

The requirement that validators store this large (and growing) state raises concerns about centralization if the state grows so large that only well-funded organizations can afford to store it. As a result, most blockchain systems impose strict limits on state growth, which in turn limit transaction throughput. Famously, Bitcoin originally imposed a maximum size of 1 MB per block, limiting throughput to about three transactions per second.

© International Financial Cryptography Association 2024
F. Baldimtsi and C. Cachin (Eds.): FC 2023, LNCS 13951, pp. 54–71, 2024.
https://doi.org/10.1007/978-3-031-47751-5_4

The tension between throughput and state growth leads to a natural question: can we achieve high throughput with a small (perhaps even constant-sized) global state? This led to the proposal of *stateless* blockchain designs [27], although this term is a misnomer: they typically assume validators store a store a small commitment to the global state of the system (e.g., a Merkle root committing to the set of unspent coins). Users wishing to make a transaction must publish a *witness* that their transaction is valid given the current state commitment (e.g., a Merkle proof that a coin is included in the valid set). Validators can then accept transactions without knowing the full state of the system. Since Todd's original proposal using Merkle trees, several other designs have been proposed using Merkle-tree-based accumulators [6,16], RSA accumulators [4], and vector commitments [12,18,26,28,30]. Stateless blockchains are distinct from *succinct blockchains* [1,11,20] such as the Mina protocol [5]. Succinct blockchains use verifiable computation to achieve $O(1)$ storage and verification costs for light clients, but still require validators to store the entire system state in order to process new transactions and build (and prove correct) new blocks.

Unfortunately, all known stateless blockchain designs introduce a new problem: users' witnesses can become invalid as other (unrelated) transactions update the global state, requiring users to monitor the network and periodically refresh their witnesses. This is a departure from the traditional blockchain model, in which users can stay offline for long periods of time and then successfully create and broadcast a transaction. This is not simply a matter of convenience; there are important security benefits of supporting offline participation, as private keys can be kept in air-gapped machines such as hardware wallets.

In this work we show that, regrettably, the trade-off between a large global state and requiring frequent witness changes is fundamental. More specifically, in Theorem 1 we show a lower bound on the global state size as a function of the number of revoked statements and the desired maximum number of witness changes. In Corollary 1, we show that there is no trade-off which does not require either an (asymptotically) linear-sized global state or an (asymptotically) near-linear number of witness updates as a constant fraction of coins are spent.

Model. To analyze the efficiency of stateless blockchains and similar authenticated data structures, we introduce a new cryptographic notion: a *revocable proof system* (RPS, Sect. 2). An RPS is a simple abstraction capturing a class of schemes that involve a *global state* V encapsulating a set S of *valid statements*. Correctness ensures that each valid statement $s_i \in S$ has a corresponding *proof* π_i which can be efficiently verified given s_i, the public parameters, and the global state. A subset $T \subseteq S$ of the initial set of valid statements may later be *revoked*, yielding an updated global state V'. Security requires that these revoked statements' proofs no longer verify. This functionality is quite natural and captures a wide range of useful cryptographic notions, including accumulators and vector commitments. We discuss these connections in Sect. 4.

Contributions. Using our revocable proof system definition we prove a trade-off between the size of the global state and the frequency with which proofs must be updated (Theorem 1). We do so using a compression argument: if the global state is small and with constant probability there are few ($\leq k$) proof updates, an adversary can use the global state and a small amount of additional information to encode the revoked set. We apply Shannon's Coding Theorem to show a lower bound on the size of the global state given the number of proof updates k.

As a corollary, we observe that there is no useful asymptotic trade-off between the size of the global state and the number of proof changes: either the state size is linear, or a (nearly) linear number of proofs must change (Sect. 3.1). As a second corollary, we show that a useful notion of *persistence* (proofs of certain statements never change) requires linear storage for these persistent statements. In Sect. 4, we show that accumulators, vector commitments, and authenticated dictionaries fit the framework of a revocable proof system and thus our lower bound applies to them, giving results of independent interest.

Implications. Finally, we discuss the implications of our results on stateless blockchain proposals (Sect. 5). We plot the minimum number of required witness changes per day for blockchains with practical transaction rates and global state sizes. For a blockchain with a transaction rate on the scale of Visa, the number of witness changes is infeasibly large for any meaningfully compressed global state. We discuss three ideas for mitigating the witness update issue and analyze them in light of our impossibility result. The first idea is a versioning system, which stores explicitly all transactions occurring during the current epoch and consequently requires no witness updates within this epoch. The second is a scheme where users lock up their coins for a period of time in exchange for a guarantee that their witnesses will remain unchanged during that time. The third and most promising is the introduction of new state-storing third parties, which are neither users nor validators, called proof-serving nodes.

2   Model

Notation. We use λ to denote the security parameter. We use lg to denote a logarithm with the base 2. Right $\rightarrow$ and left $\leftarrow$ arrows denote the output of a (possibly randomized) algorithm.

A *revocable proof system* (RPS) maintains a *global state* V, a *valid set* S, and a set of proofs π_i for each element $s_i \in S$ which we'll also call a *statement*. The global state commits to the valid set, such that proofs of elements s_i in S can be verified. More formally, a *revocable proof system* is a tuple of algorithms (Setup, ComputeState, Revoke, Verify) where:

Setup(1^λ) $\rightarrow$ pp is a randomized algorithm that takes as input 1^λ, where λ is the security parameter, and outputs public parameters pp.

ComputeState(pp, S) $\rightarrow V, (\pi_1, \pi_2, \ldots, \pi_n)$ is a deterministic algorithm that takes as input the public parameters pp and a valid set S of size n. It outputs the corresponding global state V and a list of proofs $(\pi_1, \pi_2, \ldots, \pi_n)$ where π_i is the proof for $s_i \in S$.

$\mathsf{Revoke}(\mathsf{pp}, S, T, V, (\pi_1, \pi_2, \ldots, \pi_n)) \rightarrow V', (\pi_1', \pi_2', \ldots, \pi_n')$

is a deterministic algorithm that takes as input the public parameters pp, the initial valid set S, a revoked set $T \subseteq S$, an initial global state V, and a list of proofs for elements in S. It outputs an updated global state V' and updated proofs.[1]

$\mathsf{Verify}(\mathsf{pp}, V, s_i, \pi_i) \rightarrow \{\mathsf{true}, \mathsf{false}\}$ is a deterministic algorithm that takes as input the public parameters pp, a global state V, a statement s_i, and a proof π_i. It outputs true or false.

A revocable proof system must be correct and secure. By correct, we mean that genuine proofs for valid elements should verify against the corresponding global state. By secure, we mean that it should be difficult to find a proof for a revoked element; that is, it should be computationally hard for an adversary to produce a revoked set such that a proof for a revoked element still verifies against the updated global state. More formally, correctness and security are defined as follows:

Definition 1 (Correctness[2]). A revocable proof system is *correct* if for every set S, every set $T \subseteq S$, and every $s_i \in S \setminus T$,

$$
\Pr \left[
\begin{array}{c}
\mathsf{pp} \leftarrow \mathsf{Setup}(1^\lambda) \\
V, (\pi_1, \pi_2, \ldots, \pi_n) \leftarrow \mathsf{ComputeState}(\mathsf{pp}, S) \\
V', (\pi_1', \pi_2', \ldots, \pi_n') \leftarrow \mathsf{Revoke}(\mathsf{pp}, S, T, V, (\pi_1, \pi_2, \ldots, \pi_n)) \\
\mathsf{Verify}(\mathsf{pp}, V, s_i, \pi_i) = \mathsf{true} \\
\mathsf{Verify}(\mathsf{pp}, V', s_i, \pi_i') = \mathsf{true}
\end{array}
\right] = 1
$$

Definition 2 (Security). A revocable proof system is *secure* if for every p.p.t. adversary A,

$$
\Pr \left[
\begin{array}{c}
\mathsf{pp} \leftarrow \mathsf{Setup}(1^\lambda) \\
S, T, s^*, \pi^* \leftarrow \mathsf{A}(1^\lambda, \mathsf{pp}) \\
V, (\pi_1, \pi_2, \ldots, \pi_n) \leftarrow \mathsf{ComputeState}(\mathsf{pp}, S) \\
V', (\pi_1', \pi_2', \ldots, \pi_n') \leftarrow \mathsf{Revoke}(\mathsf{pp}, S, T, V, (\pi_1, \pi_2, \ldots, \pi_n)) \\
s^* \in T \\
\mathsf{Verify}(\mathsf{pp}, V', s^*, \pi^*) = \mathsf{true}
\end{array}
\right] \leq \mathsf{negl}
$$

3   Main Result

Our main result is an inequality describing the relationship between the size of the global state and the number of proofs of valid statements which must be

---

[1] Although for ease of notation the output includes n proofs, security dictates that proofs for elements in T should not verify.

[2] While correctness with probability 1 is standard for the schemes we consider, our main result (Theorem 1) still holds for a relaxed notion of correctness which holds with overwhelming probability. In fact, it does not rely on correctness at all and rather on the prevalence of a notion of a k-good revoked set. A revocable proof system that is secure, correct with overwhelming probability, and has few witness changes should have many k-good revoked sets.

updated. We first introduce the notion of a k-good revoked set; that is, a set of statements such that when these statements are revoked, none of their proofs still verify, and at most k still-valid statements' proofs must be changed.

Definition 3 (k-good revoked set). We say a revoked set T is k-*good* given a revocable proof system RPS, an initial valid set S, size parameter $n = |S|$, and public parameters pp if, for $V, (\pi_1, \pi_2, \ldots, \pi_n) \leftarrow$ ComputeState(pp, S) and $V', (\pi_1', \pi_2', \ldots, \pi_n') \leftarrow$ Revoke(pp, V, T) if:

1. For every revoked statement $s_i \in T$, Verify(pp, V', s_i, π_i) = false
2. There are at most k non-revoked statements $s_j \in (S \setminus T)$ such that Verify(pp, V', s_j, π_j) = false

Condition (1), that the original proof of a revoked statement no longer verifies, is a consequence of the security requirement that should hold for most revoked sets. Condition (2) is that few ($\leq k$) proofs of non-revoked statements no longer verify (i.e., need to be updated). Suppose that we want to have a secure revocable proof system such that most of the time, at most k non-revoked statements change when a set of size m is revoked. This is equivalent to having many k-good revoked sets of size m. By security (regardless of $|V|$), an overwhelming fraction of sets of size m must satisfy condition (1); otherwise an adversary could choose a set of size m at random, revoke it, and succeed in finding a proof for a revoked element. Condition (2) is exactly the other property we want: that at most k non-revoked statements change when our set is revoked. Therefore, our desired revocable proof system must have many k-good revoked sets of size m.

We now show that if any public parameters yield many k-good revoked sets, the size of the global state must be large. In other words, if the size of the global state is small, many proofs of non-revoked statements must change when an average set is revoked.

Theorem 1. *Let* RPS $=$ (Setup, ComputeState, Revoke, Verify) *be a revocable proof system satisfying correctness, and let* pp *be any public parameters occurring with nonzero probability over* Setup(1^λ). *Let* S *be a set of size* n, *and let* $\mathcal{X}_k^*$ *denote the set of subsets* $T \subseteq S$ *that are* k-good *given* RPS, S, *and public parameters* pp. *Then* $|V|$, *the size of the global state in bits, satisfies*

$$|V| \geq \lg |\mathcal{X}_k^*| - \lceil k \lg n \rceil$$

Proof. We show that if $|V|$ is any smaller, there exists an efficient encoding of $\mathcal{X}_k^*$ using fewer than $\lg |\mathcal{X}_k^*|$ bits, contradicting Shannon's Coding Theorem [25]. Note that $\mathcal{X}_k^*$ can be computed by trying every revoked set $T \subseteq S$ and determining whether it fits the conditions of a k-good revoked set. While this algorithm is not efficient, it does not need to be as the contradiction we derive is compression beyond information theoretic limits, which poses no computational bounds on the communicating parties.

Consider two parties A and B interacting with a challenger in a game given as input S and pp. The goal is for A to succinctly encode a uniformly chosen revoked set $T \subseteq S$ for B to decode. The challenger computes the initial global state and proofs $V_0, (\pi_1, \pi_2, \ldots, \pi_n) \leftarrow \mathsf{ComputeState}(\mathsf{pp}, S)$. The challenger passes $V_0, (\pi_1, \pi_2, \ldots, \pi_n)$ to both A and B. A chooses T uniformly at random from $\mathcal{X}_k^*$ and computes the updated global state $V \leftarrow \mathsf{Revoke}(\mathsf{pp}, V_0, T)$. Then, for each $s_i \in (S \backslash T)$, A checks whether its proof verifies; i.e., whether $\mathsf{Verify}(\mathsf{pp}, V, s_i, \pi_i) = \mathsf{true}$. If *not*, A adds s_i to a list L of still-valid statements with changed proofs. A sends V and L to B.

We now show that given V and L, B can decode T exactly. Let B's decoding be the set T' consisting of all statements s_i such that $\mathsf{Verify}(\mathsf{pp}, V, s_i, \pi_i) = \mathsf{false}$ and $s_i \notin L$. First, any statement $s_i \in T$ must be in T', since by definition of a k-good revoked set[3], no proofs for revoked statements verify. Therefore, $T \subseteq T'$. Next, B's decoding algorithm ensures any statement $s_i \in T'$ is not in L, and $\mathsf{Verify}(\mathsf{pp}, V, s_i, \pi_i) = \mathsf{false}$. All elements s_j that were not revoked (i.e., not in T) and whose proofs no longer verify ($\mathsf{Verify}(\mathsf{pp}, V, s_i, \pi_i) = \mathsf{false}$) are included in L. Since s_i is not in L, it must in fact have been revoked, so $s_i \in T$. Therefore, $T' \subseteq T$, which implies that $T' = T$.

Finally, we observe that A can encode L by listing a $(\lg n)$-bit representation of each of its elements. Since $|L| \leq k$ by definition of $\mathcal{X}_k^*$, this encoding takes at most $\lceil k \lg n \rceil$ bits, and A sends $|V| + \lceil k \lg n \rceil$ bits in total after choosing T. Since T was chosen uniformly from $\mathcal{X}_k^*$, and the entropy of the uniform distribution over $\mathcal{X}_k^*$ is $\lg |\mathcal{X}_k^*|$, we have by Shannon's Coding Theorem that $|V| + \lceil k \lg n \rceil \geq \lg |\mathcal{X}_k^*|$. $\qquad\square$

3.1   No Useful Trade-Offs for Sublinear State Size

We show that under certain regimes (when $|\mathcal{X}_k^*|$ includes at least a constant fraction of subsets of size m for $\lg n \leq m \leq \frac{n}{2}$), there is no useful trade-off between the global state size and the frequency of proof changes when m elements are deleted. That is, the global state size is either linear in the size of the stored set, or $\Omega\left(\frac{m}{\lg n}\right)$ proofs must be updated.

Corollary 1 (No useful trade-offs). *Let n be the size of the initial valid set S and $m \leq \frac{n}{2}$ be the number of deleted elements.[4] If $|\mathcal{X}_k^*|$ includes at least a constant fraction of subsets $T \subseteq S$ of size m, and the global state size is $|V| = o(\lg \binom{n}{m})$, then $k = \Omega\left(\frac{m}{\lg n}\right)$.*

Proof. This holds by a straightforward application of Theorem 1. First, observe that the number of possible $T \subseteq S$ of size m is $\binom{n}{m} \geq \frac{n^m}{m^m} \geq 2^m$. $\mathcal{X}_k^*$ includes at least a constant fraction of these subsets T of size m, so $\lg |\mathcal{X}_k^*| = \Omega(\lg \binom{n}{m}) =$

---

[3] It is tempting to instead cite security of a revocable proof system here, but security guarantees only that for *most* revoked sets T, proofs of revoked statements do not verify. Our definition of k-good gives us exactly what we need.

[4] If more than $\frac{n}{2}$ elements are deleted in sequence, as in stateless blockchains, we can set $m = \frac{n}{2}$ since there must be an intermediate point where $\frac{n}{2}$ elements were deleted, and this bound still applies.

$\Omega(m)$. In order for the inequality from Theorem 1 to hold, we must have $k \lg n \geq \Omega(\lg \binom{n}{m}) - o(\lg \binom{n}{m})$, or $k = \frac{\Omega(\lg \binom{n}{m})}{\lg n} = \Omega\left(\frac{m}{\lg n}\right)$.

This bound on k holds for *any* global state size $|V|$ that is sublinear in $\lg \binom{n}{m}$. Once the global state size becomes $\Omega(\lg \binom{n}{m})$, we can (asymptotically) store the full list of deleted elements and require no witness updates. One especially interesting regime for this bound is when $m = \Theta(n)$ and $|V| = o(n)$. Then Corollary 1 implies that $k = \Omega\left(\frac{n}{\lg n}\right)$. In other words, if we want to avoid a near-constant fraction of proof updates, we need a linear global state size, at which point we can (asymptotically) store the full state naively and require no witness updates. This suggests that there is no asymptotically useful trade-off between global state size and number of proof changes in this regime; at least one of the two must be (nearly) linear.

3.2 Persistence Requires Linear Storage

We now show that another desirable property, which we call *persistence*, is also not possible without linear global state. Suppose that we want proofs of certain statements to always verify as long as those statements remain true. This guarantee would be very useful in cryptocurrencies, allowing a user to stay offline until she is ready to make a transaction, without fear of her proof becoming stale. We call this notion *persistence* and formalize it below.

Definition 4 (Persistence). A statement $s_i \in S$ is *persistent* given initial valid set S of size n and public parameters pp if for all $T \subseteq S$ such that $s_i \notin T$,

- $V, (\pi_1, \pi_2, \ldots, \pi_n) \leftarrow \mathsf{ComputeState}(\mathsf{pp}, S)$
- $V', (\pi_1', \pi_2', \ldots, \pi_n') \leftarrow \mathsf{Revoke}(\mathsf{pp}, S, T, V, (\pi_1, \pi_2, \ldots, \pi_n))$
- $\mathsf{Verify}(\mathsf{pp}, V', s_i, \pi_i) = \mathsf{true}$

A corollary of Theorem 1 shows that there can be very few persistent statements:

Corollary 2 (Persistence requires linear storage). *Let* RPS *be a secure and correct revocable proof system such that there exists an initial set S and a set $S^* \subseteq S$ such that*

$$\Pr_{\mathsf{pp} \leftarrow \mathsf{Setup}(1^\lambda)} [\text{every } s \in S^* \text{ is persistent}] > \frac{1}{2}$$

Then the the global state of RPS *has size at least $|S^*| - 1$.*

Proof. Let S be any initial set and S^* be any subset of S. We wish to show that with high probability, $\mathcal{X}_0^*$ is large, where $\mathcal{X}_0^*$ is the family of revoked sets that require no witness changes and for which proofs of revoked statements do not verify. We first argue that by security, few revoked sets $T \subseteq S^*$ yield proofs of revoked statements that still verify. Then it follows that $\mathcal{X}_0^*$ contains all other revoked subsets of S^*, since by definition of persistence they require no witness changes.

Suppose for the sake of contradiction that for *all* parameters $\mathsf{pp} \leftarrow \mathsf{Setup}(1^\lambda)$ that occur with nonzero probability and for which every $s \in S^*$ is persistent, more than half of the revoked sets $T \subseteq S^*$ yield a global state such that the proof of a revoked statement verifies. Then the following adversary A forges a proof with non-negligible probability, breaking security. Let A compute $\mathsf{pp} \leftarrow \mathsf{Setup}(1^\lambda)$ and $V, (\pi_1, \pi_2, \dots, \pi_n) \leftarrow \mathsf{ComputeState}(\mathsf{pp}, S)$. A then chooses $T \subseteq S^*$ uniformly at random, computes $V', (\pi'_1, \pi'_2, \dots, \pi'_n) \leftarrow \mathsf{Revoke}(\mathsf{pp}, V, T)$, and checks whether $\mathsf{Verify}(\mathsf{pp}, V', s_i, \pi_i)$ for each $s_i \in T$. If A finds such an s_i, it outputs S, T, s_i, π_i. Independently, A chooses pp such that all of S^* is persistent with probability at least $\frac{1}{2}$ and T such that the proof of a revoked statement verifies with probability at least $\frac{1}{2}$. Thus, A is efficient and succeeds with probability $\frac{1}{4}$, contradicting security. Therefore, there must be some parameters pp occurring with nonzero probability such that all of S^* is persistent and at least half of the revoked sets $T \subseteq S^*$ have no revoked statements whose original proofs verify. The family of these sets is exactly $\mathcal{X}_0^*$, whose size is at least $\frac{1}{2} \cdot 2^{|S^*|}$.

Thus, there exist public parameters pp occurring with nonzero probability such that $|\mathcal{X}_0^*| \geq \frac{1}{2} \cdot 2^{|S^*|}$. Applying Theorem 1 for $k = 0$, we have that the size of the global state is at least $\lg |\mathcal{X}_k^*| = |S^*| - 1$.

4   Implications for Authenticated Data Structures

We show that cryptographic accumulators, vector commitments, and authenticated dictionaries, are instances of revocable proof systems. Thus, our lower bound from Theorem 1 applies. This result is of interest since these data structures are frequently used in distributed settings, in which users maintain proofs of portions of the committed data that are verified against a global state. Our bound dictates that these users must update their proofs frequently as the global state changes.

4.1   Cryptographic Accumulators

A cryptographic *accumulator* [3,9], also called a *set commitment*, commits to an accumulated set X via a succinct digest A. Different accumulator schemes support efficiently proving various properties about the accumulated set X, such as membership or non-membership of elements. Some schemes may also allow X to be modified and the corresponding proofs updated. A typical accumulator supports additions, deletions, and membership proofs. That is, given a set X there is a function computing a digest A and a membership proof (also called a *witness*) w_i for each $x_i \in X$, corresponding to the $\mathsf{ComputeState}$ function of a revocable proof system. When a new element x is added to X, a new global state A' can be computed using x and A. Furthermore, each membership proof w_i can be updated given x and A. When an element $x_i \in X$ is deleted, a new global state A' can be computed using x_i, A, and the membership proof w_i for

x_i. The membership proofs of the other elements of X can be updated using the same information. Some accumulator schemes also allow batch updates, where multiple elements can be efficiently added and/or deleted at once [4].

Constructing a Revocable Proof System Using an Accumulator. We show how an RPS can be constructed using an accumulator scheme Acc supporting addition, deletion, and membership proofs. Addition is only necessary for the initial set S. The Setup function for our RPS calls the Setup function for Acc. The ComputeState function for our RPS, given public parameters pp and a valid set S, adds S to our accumulator given pp to obtain a digest A and a membership witness w_i for each $s_i \in S$. We let the proof π_i for s_i be this membership witness w_i. We implement Revoke for our RPS by, given a set $T \subseteq S$, removing T from the accumulated set and updating all witnesses according to the accumulator scheme. The resulting global state is the resulting accumulator value A', and the resulting proofs π_i' are the updated witnesses w_i'. We let the Verify function for our RPS be the same as the Verify function for the accumulator scheme.

Accumulator schemes have correctness and security definitions that are analogous to those of a revocable proof system; full definitions can be found in [8]. By correctness of the accumulator, membership witnesses for elements of the accumulated set (equivalently, valid statements) verify. By security of the accumulator, it is hard for an adversary to find verifying membership witnesses for elements not in the accumulated set (equivalently, revoked or invalid statements). Thus, this construction is indeed a revocable proof system, and our lower bound from Theorem 1 applies.

We note that we can also construct a revocable proof system using an accumulator that supports only addition and non-membership witnesses (but not deletion). Given a finite data universe U and a set $X \subseteq U$, a delete/membership accumulator storing X can be implemented using an add/non-membership accumulator storing $U \setminus X$.

Camacho-Hevia Result. Our accumulator lower bound is reminiscent of a lower bound proved by Camacho and Hevia [8]. They consider a dynamic accumulator supporting addition, deletion, and membership proofs. Their model allows batch updates: if $w_1, \ldots, w_n$ are witnesses for an initial accumulated set X, after deletion of a set T the state-update function outputs a string $Upd_{X,X \setminus T}$ that can be used to update all witnesses to $w_1', \ldots, w_n'$ to reflect the updated state. They show that if there are $|T| = m$ deletions, $Upd_{X,X \setminus T}$ must have length $\Omega(m)$. Baldimtsi et al. show an analogous result for a universal accumulator supporting addition, deletion, and *non-membership* proofs, using the same proof style [2]. While these results are similar in spirit to ours, they do not address how this string $Upd_{X,X \setminus T}$ is incorporated into the new witnesses or how many witnesses must change. It is possible in this model that some elements require very long witness changes, while nearly all other witnesses can remain the same. Our result addresses the separate question of how many witness changes are required.

We note a small gap in the Camacho-Hevia proof (and similarly in the Baldimtsi et al. proof) in the appendix of the full version of this paper. In our proof, we address this issue by defining the notion of a k-good revoked set.

4.2   Vector Commitments

A *vector commitment (VC)* [10] stores a vector $\mathbf{v} = [v_1, \ldots, v_k]$ in the form of a succinct digest C. For each index i and corresponding component v_i, the scheme produces a proof π_i that can be used alongside C to verify that $\mathbf{v}_i = v_i$. When a component is changed, the digest and proofs of some or all components may change. Correctness dictates that properly generated proofs of true components verify with their corresponding digests. Security dictates that it is hard to find a proof for an incorrect component. Recently several vector commitment schemes have been constructed with cryptocurrency applications in mind; see [12,18,26, 28,30].

Constructing a Revocable Proof System Using a Vector Commitment Scheme. Our construction commits to a vector storing valid statements. In describing our construction, we use the syntax for a VC scheme from [26]. Let q be an upper bound on the total number of valid statements. Let $\perp$ be some special value used to denote that there is no statement stored at that vector position. The Setup function for our RPS calls the KeyGen function of the VC scheme with security parameter λ and vector length n (the size of our initial valid set) to obtain public parameters pp. The ComputeState function, given pp and an initial valid set S of size n, first calls the commitment function of the VC scheme on the vector $[s_1, s_2, \ldots, s_n, \perp, \ldots, \perp]$ (using some arbitrary ordering of S). This outputs a commitment C that is the global state, along with auxiliary information aux. To generate the proof w_i for each s_i, ComputeState then calls the Open function of the VC given i, s_i, and aux. It outputs the commitment C and a proof w_i for each s_i. The Revoke function of our RPS, given $T \subseteq S$, revokes each statement $s_i \in T$ by setting the corresponding position of the committed vector to $\perp$. We describe how to do so assuming no batch updates, updating the state and all proofs for each revocation before moving onto the next. More precisely, for each $s_i \in T$, it calls VC.Update$(C, s_i, \perp, i)$ to obtain an updated state C' and update information U. It then updates the proof w_j for each other component s_j using VC.ProofUpdate given C, w_j, s_i, i, U. After all updates have been made, it outputs all proofs and the resulting commitment. Finally, the Verify function of our RPS, given C, s_i, w_i, calls VC.Ver(C, s_i, j, w_i) for each vector component j. Verify outputs true if and only if there exists a j such that VC.Ver outputs true.

We give an overview of how correctness and security for a VC scheme relate to the corresponding definitions for a revocable proof system; full definitions of correctness and security for a VC scheme are given in [10]. VC schemes offer correctness with overwhelming probability, ensuring that properly generated proofs for committed components verify. See footnote 2 for a discussion of how this compares to correctness with probability 1 for a revocable proof system. The security definition for a VC guarantees that it's hard for an adversary to find two valid proofs for different values s_i and s_i' of the ith component. This implies security of our constructed revocable proof system: if an adversary finds a proof w^* of a statement s^* that is *not* in the valid set, it has succeeded in finding a proof that the value of the vector at some index i is s^*. Since s^* is not in the valid set, the actual value at i must be $\bot$ or some other s'. The proof w of this other value yields a pair of proofs that verify for different values at index i. Thus, our constructed scheme is an RPS.

4.3   Authenticated Dictionary

A related notion is an *authenticated dictionary* [17,23], which produces a commitment to a set of key-value pairs, such that proofs of these stored pairs can be generated and verified against the commitment. Throughout time, more key-value pairs can be added, and existing pairs can be modified. When the dictionary is updated, a new shared commitment is generated, potentially invalidating old proofs. The existence of these proofs both for the original data and the updated data corresponds to correctness for a revocable proof system. Security of an authenticated dictionary guarantees that it is difficult to generate proofs of a key-value pair that is not in the stored set. The argument that we can construct a revocable proof system from an authenticated dictionary is along the same lines as the arguments from vector commitments and accumulators. One way to see this is to observe that we can construct a vector commitment scheme using an authenticated dictionary, by storing the vector index-value pairs as key-value pairs in the dictionary. Authenticated dictionaries therefore fit the framework of a revocable proof system, and thus our lower bound holds, implying that proofs must be updated often.

Aardvark [21], a recently proposed distributed authenticated dictionary with applications to stateless blockchains, proposes an interesting versioning scheme to overcome the need to change witnesses enough to accommodate many users making transactions concurrently. We discuss this idea further in Sect. 5.2.

5   Implications for Blockchains

Blockchains typically operate in one of two models: the *unspent transaction output (UTXO)* model or the *account-based* model. A stateless blockchain functions slightly differently in each of these models. We describe the models below and argue that each requires the functionality of a revocable proof system, meaning that our lower bound from Theorem 1 holds.

UTXO Model. In the UTXO model, the global state stores the set of unspent coins. When a user wants to make a transaction, they must specify the coin(s) (UTXOs) they wish to spend and submit a proof that these coins are unspent. A stateless blockchain needs to satisfy correctness: a proof for an unspent coin should verify against the corresponding global state. If the transaction is successful, the global state is updated, and the spent coins' proofs should no longer verify. In order to prevent users from double spending, it should be computationally hard to produce a proof for a spent coin—this is equivalent to the definition of security for a revocable proof system. A stateless blockchain in the UTXO model is commonly constructed using a dynamic accumulator, where the accumulated set is the set of valid UTXOs. Such accumulators include RSA accumulators [4], Merkle-tree-based accumulators [7,16], and Verkle trees [6].

Account-Based Model. In the account-based model, the global state stores a list of account-balance pairs. Each account owner, or user, maintains a proof of their account balance. When a user u wants to make a transaction, they submit a proof π that their account-balance pair is included in the global state. The validator verifies the user's account balance using this proof, and they check that the balance is high enough to make the desired transaction. The amount spent is then deducted from the user's balance, and the global state is updated accordingly.

In the context of a revocable proof system, the valid set is the set of account-balance pairs. An account-balance pair is revoked when the corresponding user makes a transaction, changing their account balance. Security ensures that it is hard to generate a proof for an incorrect account-balance pair. Correctness ensures that every user can prove that their true account balance is valid. An account-based blockchain is often constructed using a vector commitment or authenticated dictionary, where each index of the vector represents an account and the value is that account's balance (e.g., [26]).

5.1 Interpreting Our Bound in Practice

An interesting question is exactly what implications Theorem 1 has for practical stateless blockchains. Toward answering this, we graph the number of witness (or proof) changes for various parameter values.

We first apply Theorem 1 to obtain a lower bound on the number of witness changes required after some number m deletions, given an initial valid set of size n. The number of possible deleted sets of size m is $\binom{n}{m} \geq \frac{n^m}{m^m}$ (by, e.g., [13]). Ideally, we would like at least half of these sets to (1) require few ($\leq k$ for some k) witness changes, and (2) allow no deleted elements to be double spent. These are exactly the conditions for a k-good revoked set; thus, in our application of Theorem 1 we can set $|\mathcal{X}_k^*| = \frac{1}{2}\binom{n}{m} \geq \frac{n^m}{2m^m}$. Our next step is to obtain a lower bound for k, showing that many witnesses must change.

Rearranging, we have $\lceil k \lg n \rceil \geq \lg \frac{n^m}{2m^m} - |V|$. Simplifying further,

$$k \lg n \geq m \lg n - m \lg m - |V| - 2$$

$$k \geq m - \frac{|V| + m \lg m}{\lg n} - \frac{2}{\lg n} \tag{1}$$

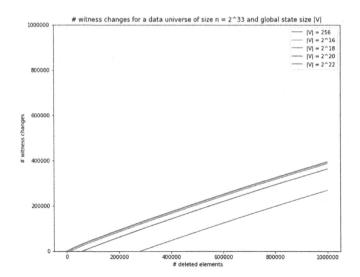

Fig. 1. Number of witness changes $f(m,n,|V|)$ given $0 \leq m \leq 10^6$ deleted elements, a data universe of size $n = 2^{33}$, and varying global state size $|V|$.

Let $f(m,n,|V|)$ denote the right hand side of Eq. 1. We graph f, showing that if at least half of the sets of size m are k-good revoked sets, k must be at least $f(m,n,|V|)$. In our graphs, we use two natural values of n. The first is 2^{33}, approximately the world's current human population. The second is 2^{26}, approximately the current number of UTXOs in Bitcoin [15]; these graphs are included in the appendix of the full version of this paper.

In Fig. 1, we can see that the relationship between f and m is approximately linear, with the $\frac{m \lg m}{\lg n}$ term having little impact since m is small relative to n in our ranges. Furthermore, increasing the size of the global state V results in a horizontal shift of the curve and has little benefit until it becomes very large.

Like Fig. 1 and Fig. 2 shows that there is not a useful trade-off between the global state size and the number of witness changes per day. The global state size must become very large, at least 2^{22} for most throughput values, before there is much impact on the number of witness changes. This concrete effect mirrors the asymptotic relation of by Corollary 1.

While the number of witness changes may seem small in comparison to the number of UTXOs or accounts in the system, without some additional recovery mechanism, the consequences of a user missing their witness update are severe as they will no longer be able to make transactions. Furthermore, if the system has enough throughput to adequately serve the data universe, there will be many more witness changes: for 24,000 transactions per second (the maximum throughput supported by Visa [29]) the number of witness changes per day for $n = 2^{33}$ becomes roughly 1.25×10^8. Our graphs show that if most users are not willing to refresh their witnesses continually, hundreds of thousands of these users will lose their coins per day. As a result, most stateless blockchain proposals

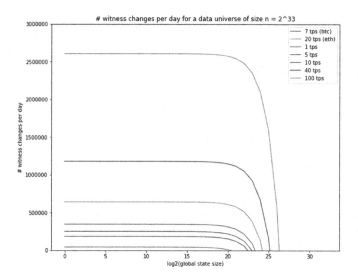

Fig. 2. Number of witness changes per day for a data universe of size $n = 2^{33}$ and varying global state size, for blockchains with various throughput. In particular, Bitcoin and Ethereum support roughly 7 and 20 transactions per second respectively.

have included a way for lazy users to obtain updated proofs, at the cost of more storage for certain parties; the most prominent such solution uses proof-serving nodes (PSNs). Below, we discuss two more limited solutions (a versioning model and a partially persistent model), then conclude with a discussion of PSNs and potential future work relating to them.

5.2   Versioning Model

An issue arises when at some time t, many users simultaneously provide a proof of their account balance (an element in the authenticated dictionary) and a transaction that they wish to make (an update of their element in the dictionary). If the transactions are executed in sequence, each user's transaction requires updating the dictionary, invalidating the other users' proofs. One solution is to store this set of transactions temporarily, so we can verify each user's proof against the global state at time t and then check manually that none of the subsequent transactions changed that user's account balance. We call this a versioning system.

Aardvark [21], an authenticated dictionary designed with cryptocurrency applications in mind, does essentially this: it stores all transactions that happen in the next τ time, for some tunable time parameter τ. The current state commitment at time t is also stored. At a future time up to $t + \tau$, any proof at least as recent as time t can still be verified by checking it against the state commitment at time t, then naively checking that it does not conflict with the cached transactions. This approach essentially ensures that proofs do not need to change for k transactions by storing k additional state, where k is the number of transactions happening in time τ. This matches our lower bound from Corollary 2 (up to constants), which when translated to this setting says that if we want no proof changes when deleting k elements, we must store at least k state. Thus, this versioning scheme is essentially the best one can hope to achieve without introducing parties such as PSNs storing more state (see, e.g., [24,26,28]).

5.3   Partially Persistent Model

A desirable feature of a stateless blockchain is that users know in advance when their proofs will need to change, so they can go online only at that time. Perhaps users could pay a fee for the guarantee that their proofs will remain valid for some number of transactions in the future. A natural question is how much additional state is necessary to accommodate these special requests.

This property is exactly our notion of *persistence*: the persistent set S^* corresponds to the set of proofs that are guaranteed to remain valid. Unfortunately, Corollary 2 says that any secure and correct revocable proof system with a persistent set S^* must have global state size at least $|S^*| - 1$. If any significant portion of the user base wants persistent proofs, the stateless blockchain model does essentially no better than storing the full state.

We can achieve persistence if users are willing to lock up their coins for a set period of time. That is, a user wanting their proof to remain valid for at least a day would sacrifice their ability to spend their coin during that day. We could then separate the blockchain into two state commitments: one state S_1 storing the set of locked coins and another state S_2 storing all other (liquid) coins. Since locked coins can only be spent at the end of the day, S_1 remains the same and no proofs of locked coins change throughout the day. At the end of the day, users may unlock their coins and move them from S_1 to S_2. We could extend this scheme to support other time ranges, incurring the cost of extra storage as more time ranges are supported.

While potentially helpful in limited settings, this model has serious drawbacks for general use. The most obvious is the fact that users cannot spend their locked coins. Furthermore, the benefits are all-or-nothing in the following way: If a user wants to maintain *any* liquid coins, they must continually update these liquid coins' witnesses, at which point updating their locked coins' witnesses would require minimal additional effort.

5.4   Proof-Serving Node Model

Prior work proposes offloading witness updates to a *proof-serving node (PSN)* [24,26,28]. Instead of maintaining its proof itself, a user can delegate this task to a PSN and come online only when it wishes to make a transaction. In any revocable proof system, the PSN can update a user's proof simply by using the Revoke algorithm. The storage required for this simple approach scales with the number of users: the PSN can serve k users by storing only these users' proofs and constantly checking for updates. This property that PSNs can use storage proportional to the number of proofs they maintain somewhat mitigates the centralization issues posed by requiring storing a large state, allowing anyone to operate a small PSN. PSNs also interact nicely with *hybrid nodes*, a newly introduced [19] type of node that stores much less state than full nodes yet can perform nearly all full node functionalities. The PSN model is especially promising in light of our result that there is no holy grail revocable proof system achieving few witness updates on its own.

However, centralization is still a major concern with PSNs, and the PSN model raises interesting questions regarding incentives. PSNs must be incentivized in some way to do this work. Hyperproofs [26] suggests a PSN model where users pay PSNs to maintain their proofs for them. This payment model seems to have an interesting relationship with batch updates, which hyperproofs also allow. That is, while it takes a user time t to update a single proof, a PSN can update the proofs of all n users in the system in time $t \cdot f(n)$ (for some sublinear function f). PSNs that serve enough users to take advantage of batch updates can offer much cheaper prices than small PSNs. There can only be a few PSNs that serve this many users. The resulting system will have a few PSNs storing the full state, and the users they serve will store nothing. This is a significant risk: an adversary that attacks these PSNs can compromise the entire blockchain, preventing many users from spending their coins.

Acknowledgments. This research was conducted primarily at a16z crypto research. Miranda Christ was also supported in part by NSF Award CCF-2107187, by JPMorgan Chase & Co, by LexisNexis Risk Solutions, and by the Algorand Centres of Excellence programme managed by Algorand Foundation. Joseph Bonneau was also supported by NSF Award CNS-1940679 and DARPA Award HR00112020022, and served as a technical advisor to Mina. Any opinions, findings, and conclusions or recommendations expressed in this material are solely those of the authors.

References

1. Abusalah, H., Fuchsbauer, G., Gaži, P., Klein, K.: SNACKs: leveraging proofs of sequential work for blockchain light clients. Cryptology ePrint Archive, Paper 2022/240 (2022)
2. Baldimtsi, F., et al.: Accumulators with applications to anonymity-preserving revocation. In: IEEE Euro S&P (2017)
3. Benaloh, J., de Mare, M.: One-way accumulators: a decentralized alternative to digital signatures. In: Helleseth, T. (ed.) EUROCRYPT 1993. LNCS, vol. 765, pp. 274–285. Springer, Heidelberg (1994). https://doi.org/10.1007/3-540-48285-7_24
4. Boneh, D., Bünz, B., Fisch, B.: Batching techniques for accumulators with applications to IOPs and stateless blockchains. In: Boldyreva, A., Micciancio, D. (eds.) CRYPTO 2019. LNCS, vol. 11692, pp. 561–586. Springer, Cham (2019). https://doi.org/10.1007/978-3-030-26948-7_20
5. Bonneau, J., Meckler, I., Rao, V., Shapiro, E.: Mina: decentralized cryptocurrency at scale (2020). https://docs.minaprotocol.com/static/pdf/technicalWhitepaper.pdf. Accessed 9 Aug 2022
6. Buterin, V.: A state expiry and statelessness roadmap. https://notes.ethereum.org/@vbuterin/verkle_and_state_expiry_proposal

7. Buterin, V.: The stateless client concept (2017). https://ethresear.ch/t/the-stateless-client-concept/172
8. Camacho, P., Hevia, A.: On the impossibility of batch update for cryptographic accumulators. In: Abdalla, M., Barreto, P.S.L.M. (eds.) LATINCRYPT 2010. LNCS, vol. 6212, pp. 178–188. Springer, Heidelberg (2010). https://doi.org/10.1007/978-3-642-14712-8_11
9. Camenisch, J., Lysyanskaya, A.: Dynamic accumulators and application to efficient revocation of anonymous credentials. In: Yung, M. (ed.) CRYPTO 2002. LNCS, vol. 2442, pp. 61–76. Springer, Heidelberg (2002). https://doi.org/10.1007/3-540-45708-9_5
10. Catalano, D., Fiore, D.: Vector commitments and their applications. In: Kurosawa, K., Hanaoka, G. (eds.) PKC 2013. LNCS, vol. 7778, pp. 55–72. Springer, Heidelberg (2013). https://doi.org/10.1007/978-3-642-36362-7_5
11. Chen, W., Chiesa, A., Dauterman, E., Ward, N.P.: Reducing participation costs via incremental verification for ledger systems. Cryptology ePrint Archive, Paper 2020/1522 (2020). https://eprint.iacr.org/2020/1522
12. Chepurnoy, A., Papamanthou, C., Srinivasan, S., Zhang, Y.: EDRAX: a cryptocurrency with stateless transaction validation. Cryptology ePrint Archive, Paper 2018/968 (2018)
13. Cormen, T.H., Leiserson, C.E., Rivest, R.L., Stein, C.: Introduction to Algorithms. MIT Press, Cambridge (2022)
14. Dai, W.: b-money (1998). https://www.weidai.com/bmoney.txt
15. Delgado-Segura, S., Pérez-Solà, C., Navarro-Arribas, G., Herrera-Joancomartí, J.: Analysis of the Bitcoin UTXO set. In: Zohar, A., et al. (eds.) FC 2018. LNCS, vol. 10958, pp. 78–91. Springer, Heidelberg (2019). https://doi.org/10.1007/978-3-662-58820-8_6
16. Dryja, T.: Utreexo: a dynamic hash-based accumulator optimized for the Bitcoin UTXO set. Cryptology ePrint Archive, Paper 2019/611 (2019)
17. Goodrich, M.T., Shin, M., Tamassia, R., Winsborough, W.H.: Authenticated dictionaries for fresh attribute credentials. In: Nixon, P., Terzis, S. (eds.) iTrust 2003. LNCS, vol. 2692, pp. 332–347. Springer, Heidelberg (2003). https://doi.org/10.1007/3-540-44875-6_24
18. Gorbunov, S., Reyzin, L., Wee, H., Zhang, Z.: Pointproofs: aggregating proofs for multiple vector commitments. In: ACCM CCS (2020)
19. Hegde, P., Streit, R., Georghiades, Y., Ganesh, C., Vishwanath, S.: Achieving almost all blockchain functionalities with polylogarithmic storage. In: Eyal, I., Garay, J. (eds.) Financial Cryptography and Data Security: 26th International Conference, FC 2022, Grenada, 2–6 May 2022, Revised Selected Papers, pp. 642–660. Springer, Cham (2022). https://doi.org/10.1007/978-3-031-18283-9_32
20. Kattis, A., Bonneau, J.: Proof of necessary work: succinct state verification with fairness guarantees. In: Financial Crypto (2023). https://eprint.iacr.org/2020/190.pdf
21. Leung, D., Gilad, Y., Gorbunov, S., Reyzin, L., Zeldovich, N.: Aardvark: an asynchronous authenticated dictionary with applications to account-based cryptocurrencies. In: USENIX Security (2022)
22. Nakamoto, S.: Bitcoin: a peer-to-peer electronic cash system (2008)
23. Papamanthou, C., Tamassia, R.: Time and space efficient algorithms for two-party authenticated data structures. In: Qing, S., Imai, H., Wang, G. (eds.) ICICS 2007. LNCS, vol. 4861, pp. 1–15. Springer, Heidelberg (2007). https://doi.org/10.1007/978-3-540-77048-0_1

24. Reyzin, L., Meshkov, D., Chepurnoy, A., Ivanov, S.: Improving authenticated dynamic dictionaries, with applications to cryptocurrencies. Cryptology ePrint Archive, Paper 2016/994 (2016)
25. Shannon, C.E.: A mathematical theory of communication. Bell Syst. Tech. J. **27**(3), 379–423 (1948)
26. Srinivasan, S., Chepurnoy, A., Papamanthou, C., Tomescu, A., Zhang, Y.: Hyperproofs: aggregating and maintaining proofs in vector commitments. IACR Cryptol. ePrint Arch. **2021**, 599 (2021)
27. Todd, P.: Making UTXO Set Growth Irrelevant with Low-Latency Delayed TXO Commitments (2016). https://petertodd.org/2016/delayed-txo-commitments
28. Tomescu, A., Abraham, I., Buterin, V., Drake, J., Feist, D., Khovratovich, D.: Aggregatable subvector commitments for stateless cryptocurrencies. Cryptology ePrint Archive, Paper 2020/527 (2020)
29. Visa: Visa acceptance for retailers. https://usa.visa.com/run-your-business/small-business-tools/retail.html
30. Wang, W., Ulichney, A., Papamanthou, C.: BalanceProofs: maintainable vector commitments with fast aggregation. Cryptology ePrint Archive, Paper 2022/864 (2022)
31. Wood, G., et al.: Ethereum: a secure decentralised generalised transaction ledger (2014)

Layer 2

State Machines Across Isomorphic Layer 2 Ledgers

Maxim Jourenko[1,2]([⊠]) and Mario Larangeira[1,2]

[1] Department of Mathematical and Computing Sciences School of Computing,
Tokyo Institute of Technology, Tokyo, Japan
mario@c.titech.ac.jp
[2] Input Output Global, Singapore, Singapore
jourenko.m.ab@m.titech.ac.jp
http://iohk.io

Abstract. With the ever greater adaptation of blockchain systems, smart contract based ecosystems have formed to provide financial services and other utility. This results in an ever increasing demand for transactions on blockchains, however, the amount of transactions per second on a given ledger is limited. Layer-2 systems attempt to improve scalability by taking transactions off-chain, with building blocks that are two party channels which are concatenated to form networks. Interaction between two parties requires (1) routing such a network, (2) interaction with and collateral from all intermediaries on the routed path and (3) interactions are often more limited compared to what can be done on the ledger. In contrast to that design, recent constructions such as Hydra Heads (FC'21) are both multi-party and isomorphic, allowing interactions to have the same expressiveness as on the ledger making it akin to a ledger located on Layer-2. The follow up Interhead Construction (MARBLE'22) further extends the protocol to connect Hydra Heads into networks by means of a "virtual" Hydra Head construction. This work puts forth an even greater generalization of the Interhead Protocol, allowing for interaction across different Layer-2 ledgers with a multitude of improvements. As concrete example, our design is modular and lightweight, which makes it viable for both full virtual ledger constructions as well as straightforward one-time interactions and payments systems.

Keywords: Blockchain · State Channel · Channel Network

1 Introduction

Blockchain technology as introduced by Nakamoto [19] was a breakthrough in scaling byzantine consensus to a point where operation of decentralized ledgers among a large number of mutually distrustful parties became viable. While Bitcoin, Nakamoto's implementation of a decentralized ledger, remains one of the

This work was supported by JST CREST Grant Number JPMJCR2113, Japan.

F. Baldimtsi and C. Cachin (Eds.): FC 2023, LNCS 13951, pp. 75–91, 2024.
https://doi.org/10.1007/978-3-031-47751-5_5

largest blockchain implementations by market capitalization[1] to date further blockchains such as Ethereum and Cardano expanded on the technology by enabling arbitrary smart contracts and state machines. This improved the utility of their ledgers which facilitated the creation of financial ecosystems. However, albeit blockchain's ability to scale to a seemingly arbitrary amount of users, the amount of transactions that can be performed on their ledgers is limited [5]. If there are more transactions being committed to a blockchain than its consensus mechanism can handle, transaction issuer can include a fee to their transactions to increase their priority. At times of high demand this can result in unfeasible high fees for an average transaction. One approach to mitigate this are Layer-2 protocols [4,6,20,21] such as Bitcoin's payment channel network Lightning [21]. Parties can move their coins into a Layer-2 structure which locks these coins on the ledger. Then, they can interact and perform payments with other parties that participate in the Layer-2 structure offchain, i.e. without requiring any transactions on the ledger itself. Only at the end, when a party wishes to move their coins back and unlock on the ledger another transaction is committed to the ledger that summarizes the transactions that occurred offchain. However, a common drawback of Layer-2 protocols is a lack of expressiveness of the interactions that can occur on Layer-2. For instance, payment channel networks are restricted to simple payments. State Channels [7,8] improve on that by allowing execution of smart contracts. Moreover, earlier versions of Layer-2 protocols operate on channels between two parties which can be concatenated by means of Hash Timelocked Contracts (HTLCs) [21] to perform payments or two parties in the network can connect by means of virtual channels [7,8,12,13], i.e. a channel that is created on Layer 2 instead of the ledger. This can be impractical since if two parties want to interact with another, it requires the intermediaries, i.e. the parties on the path between them, to lock away a large amount of collateral which ensures security of these protocols, however, such a path might not exist. Other approaches attempt to connect multiple parties, for instance Rollups – albeit not entirely Layer-2 as they require a small amount of data to be committed to the ledger per transaction – can directly connect an arbitrary amount of parties, however, making the expressiveness of interactions on Rollups on par to the ledger is ongoing research. Hydra [4] is a Layer-2 protocol that forms an isomorphic state channel called Hydra *Head* for an arbitrary amount of parties which allows interaction to have the same expressiveness as on the ledger itself. This makes Hydra Heads akin to a ledger located in Layer-2. However, while interaction between different Hydra heads by utilizing intermediaries is possible it is either limited to payments (HTLCs) or requires iterative construction of virtual Hydra heads [14], which construction is heavy as it requires partial execution of the Hydra Head state machine. Moreover, the construction is complex making it difficult to verify its security and also making it prone to implementation errors. It is inflexible because all UTxO that are available on the Interhead have to be moved into it at the very beginning of the protocol. Since it is tightly related to the Hydra State Machine construction, adaptation

---

[1] https://coinmarketcap.com.

of any changes to the Hydra State Machine would require additional work and careful consideration to ensure security of the Interhead construction.

Our Contributions. The aim of this work is to create a lightweight *ad-hoc ledger* to enable arbitrary interactions between parties on separate Layer-2 ledgers, i.e. Layer-2 structures containing an arbitrary amount of parties and which have the same expressiveness as a smart-contract capable ledger. Our work is based on the Interhead [14] construction and in fact is a generalized version of it. Similarly we assume two Layer-2 ledger based on the Unspent Transaction Output (UTxO) paradigm and utilize a set of intermediaries, i.e. parties that participate in both Layer-2 ledgers, to facilitate payments as well as execution of arbitrary state machines. However, in addition to the previous work our construction provides a multitude of improvements: (1) There is no time limit to the ad-hoc ledger, (2) setup is done only once and can be reused for future interactions, (3) UTxO can be moved between Layer-2 ledgers and the ad-hoc ledger at any time compared to only at the beginning and the end of the Interhead construction making the ad-hoc ledger more flexible, (4) disputes are local only affecting individual UTxO instead of the whole structure, (5) a modular and therefore significantly simpler construction. (6) While we present the core of our construction in this work, we also present multiple potential extensions to further improve on the scalability of the construction. Additionally, as with the Interhead construction, collateral does not need to be paid by single individual intermediaries but instead any collateral can be paid by multiple intermediaries. Although a tradeoff of our construction is that we require interaction with all intermediaries for each transaction on the ad-hoc ledger, we are able to execute the Hydra Head state machine within it creating a virtual Hydra Head where interaction with the intermediaries is no longer necessary. This gives us the same function and benefits as the Interhead allowing our construction to be both a generalization of the Interhead construction as well as the Hydra Head construction. While our work assumes a UTxO based ledger we argue that any Layer-2 ledger that can implement an adaptation of the state machine presented in this work can execute our construction thus it is not limited to be used with Hydra Heads alone, but aims to enhance interoperability between any Layer-2 ledgers.

Related Work. Layer 2 or *offchain* structures are scalability solutions for ledgers. Early approaches are payment channels [6,20] where two parties, first, lock coins on the ledger via a transaction and then perform an offchain protocol to perform payments between another without requiring to commit any further transactions. Only at the very end, one last transaction is committed to the ledger that summarizes all payments and unlocks the two parties' coins. Protocols such as Hash Timelocked Contracts (HTLCs) [21] enable payments across multiple adjacent channels allowing for the formation of payment channel networks. An efficiency requirement for Layer 2 structures and protocols is that when performing $\mathcal{O}(n), n \in \mathbb{N}$ transactions then only $\mathcal{O}(1)$ transactions are committed to the ledger. More recent approaches such as Hydra [4] allow for an arbitrary amount of parties to interact offchain with the same expressiveness as on the ledger itself instead of being limited to simple payments, effectively forming a sub-ledger on Layer 2. Another notable approach are Rollups[2] where an arbitrary amount of parties can interact offchain with a few caveats: To our knowledge, rollups based on Zero-Knowledge proofs do not yet support full expressiveness of the ledger although there is active research to achieve this. Moreover, for reasons of data availability, each transaction within a rollup produces some data that has to be committed to the ledger therefore it is akin to a Hybrid protocol rather than a full Layer 2 protocol. The Interhead [14] allows parties across two Hydra Heads to interact with another with the aid of intermediaries, i.e. parties participating on both Hydra Heads, by creation of a virtual Hydra head. Our work aims to provide a lightweight, flexible and modular generalization to the Interhead construction not only allowing for the creation of a virtual Hydra Head, but also providing a low-overhead framework for brief interactions.

2   Background

Notation. In this work we consider structured data. If we assume a value $\beta \in \mathcal{B}$ of form $(\beta_0, \ldots, \beta_n)$, $n \in \mathbb{N}$, then $\beta.\beta_i$ is the value of β with label β_i, $i \in \mathbb{N}$, $0 \leq i \leq n$. Moreover, parties within a protocol are denoted using $\mathcal{P}$. Lastly $\mathcal{H}$ denotes a cryptographic hash function.

Signatures. We assume a cryptographic signature scheme [1,9,10] with existential unforgeability under a chosen message attack (EU-CMA) consisting of algorithms (key_gen, verify, sign). Then key_gen(1^λ) = (vk, sk) generates a verification key vk and a private key sk using security parameter 1^λ, sign(sk, m) = σ takes sk and a message $m \in \{0,1\}*$ as input and creates a signature $\sigma \in \{0,1\}*$ and verify(vk, m', σ') takes vk, a message m and a signature σ' as input and outputs 1 on successful verification and 0 otherwise. We assume a secure multisignature scheme [11,18] with algorithms (ms_setup, ms_key_gen, ms_agg_vk, ms_sign, ms_agg_sign, ms_verify). Algorithm ms_setup($1^{\lambda'}$) = Π creates public parameters Π, algorithm ms_key_gen(Π) = (vk, sk) creates a new set of verification key vk' and private key sk, algorithm ms_agg_vk(Π, V) = vk_{agg} takes Π and a set of verification keys V as input and outputs an aggregate verification key vk_{agg}, algorithm ms_sign(Π, sk, m) = σ creates a signature σ on message m, algorithm ms_agg_sign(Π, V, S, m) = σ_{agg} aggregates a set of signatures S on message m to an aggregate signature σ_{agg} and lastly ms_verify($\Pi, m', vk_{agg}, \sigma_{agg}$) verifies an aggregate signature on a message to a aggregate verification key where it outputs 1 upon success and 0 otherwise.

The UTxO Ledger and Extensions. In UTxO based ledgers such as Bitcoin [19] coins that are in circulation are represented using a tuple (b, ν) where $b \in \mathbb{N}$ is an amount of coins and ν is a verification script that evaluates to a value in $\{0, 1\}$ such that the coins within a UTxO can be spent if presented a witness w where $\nu(w) = 1$. The ledger's state is represented as a set U of all currently circulating

---

[2] https://ethereum.org/en/developers/docs/scaling/zk-rollups/.

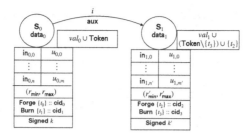

Fig. 1. A general state machine transition moving it from state S_0 to S_1 on input symbol i and auxiliary input data aux. Each state is represented by a UTxO on the ledger, in the case of S_0 with data field data$_0$, coins val_0 and (non-) fungible token Token. The box below a state represents constraints to transactions creating that UTxO. The left-hand side contains UTxO inputs that are spent and the right-hand side UTxO outputs that are created. The transaction is valid only in time (r_{min}, r_{max}), burns token t_1 while minting token t_0 and is signed corresponding to public verification key k.

UTxO. Transactions can be used to spend UTxO and thereby perform a state transition on the ledger. A transaction is of form $(\mathsf{In}, \mathsf{Out}, t)$ where In is a set of tuples of form (ref, w) where ref is a pointer to an UTxO that exists on the ledger and w is a witness as above, Out is a list of new UTxO and timelock $t \in \mathbb{N}$ is a point in time such that a transaction can be applied on the ledger only after time t. A transaction is included in the ledger after being submitted after at most time $\Delta \in \mathbb{N}$. Note that even though UTxO might be similar, the ledger ensures that all UTxO are unique by assigning them unique addresses. The Extended UTxO model [2] adds an arbitrary data field $\delta \in \{0,1\}^*$ to UTxOs. Moreover, the verification script ν is extended to additionally receive δ as well as a context $\mathsf{ctx} \in \{0,1\}^*$ consisting of the transaction that creates the UTxO as well as the UTxO that are referenced within the transaction's inputs. Doing so ν can enforce constraints on transactions. Lastly, timelocks are extended to form time ranges $[r_0, r_1]$, $r_0, r_1 \in \mathbb{N}$ where a transaction can be committed onto the ledger within this time range. It has been shown [2] that there exists a weak bi-simulation between Constraint Emitting Machines (CEM), which are state machines derived from Mealy automata, such that it is possible to execute state machines defined as CEMs as in Fig. 1 on EUTxO based ledgers. Further work [3] adds multi-asset support such that they not only contain coins, but also fungible and non-fungible token. In this work we consider EUTxO with multi-asset support, but for simplicity refer to them as UTxO.

3   Overview

We assume two layer 2 ledgers $\mathcal{L}_0^2$ and $\mathcal{L}_1^2$ created on a common ledger $\mathcal{L}$. Let parties $P_b = \{\mathcal{P}_{b,0}, \ldots, \mathcal{P}_{b,i}\} \ldots, \mathcal{P}_{b,n_b}$ for $b \in \{0,1\}$ be an arbitrary, non-empty subset of the parties who participate in ledgers $\mathcal{L}_0^2$ and $\mathcal{L}_1^2$ respectively and $P = P_0 \cup P_1$, where $|P| = n$, $|\mathcal{P}_0| = n_0$ and $|\mathcal{P}_1| = n_1$ $i, n, n_0, n_1 \in \mathbb{N}$. Let $P_{\mathsf{int}} = P_0 \cap P_1 \neq \varnothing$ with $|P_{\mathsf{int}}| = n_{\mathsf{int}}$, $n_{\mathsf{int}} \in \mathbb{N}$ be the set of intermediaries.

Communication Model and Time. We assume synchronized communication between parties which happens in rounds such that, if a message is send within one round it is available to the recipient at the beginning of the next round. We assume a relation between communication rounds and time [15–17].

Adversarial Model. We assume an malicious adversary $\mathcal{A}$ who can statically corrupt $n-1$ out of n parties where $n \in \mathbb{N}$. Corrupted parties leak their internal state including their secret keys to the adversary and communication from and $\mathcal{A}$ receives all communication from and to that party. $\mathcal{A}$ can dictate the corrupted party's behaviour and make them deviate from the protocol arbitrarily.

Layer 2 Ledgers. We assume the existence of a Layer 2 ledger construction for a UTxO based ledger. Moreover, we assume that the Layer 2 ledger can implement CEMs or allows for execution of state machines with sufficient expressiveness. As is the case with regular ledgers, we assume that all UTxO on the Layer 2 ledger are unique. Moreover, if a Layer 2 ledger $\mathcal{L}^2$ is instantiated on a UTxO based ledger $\mathcal{L}$, then there exists $\Delta_{\mathcal{L}^2} \in \mathbb{N}$ such that any UTxO can be moved from $\mathcal{L}^2$ to $\mathcal{L}$ within time $t \in \mathbb{N}$ with $t \leq \Delta_{\mathcal{L}^2}$. We note that a construction that fulfills these requirements is Hydra [4].

Semantic UTxO Equality. Any well defined ledger makes sure that each UTxO is unique by assigning unique addresses to each newly created UTxO. In our construction we are considering multiple instances of the same UTxO where two UTxO are *semantically equal* if they are equal except for their address. For instance, we consider two UTxO that each award 5 coins to a party $\mathcal{P}$ to be semantically equal even though their addresses are distinct.

3.1   The Goal

The aim of this work is to allow interaction between an arbitrary set of parties P with the same expressiveness as on any Layer 2 ledger. In the following we denote interaction between parties in P as interaction on an *ad-hoc* ledger $\mathcal{L}_P$. We define the properties we desire in our construction consistent with related work as follows.

Definition 1. (Offchain Efficiency). No transactions are committed to $\mathcal{L}$ except in the case of dispute where $\mathcal{O}(1)$ transactions are committed to $\mathcal{L}$.

Definition 2. (Liveness). There exists $t \in \mathbb{N}$ such that upon a party's request any UTxO in $\mathcal{L}_P$ can be made available on $\mathcal{L}$ or $\mathcal{L}_0^2$ and $\mathcal{L}_1^2$ after at most time t. If there exists an honest intermediary the same holds true for collateral.

Definition 3. (Balance Security). Any honest party loses access to their collateral and UTxO without their consent at most with negligible probability.

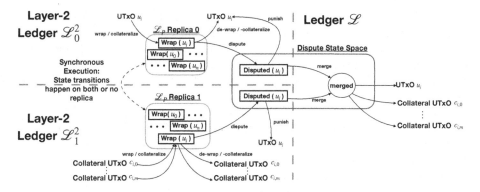

Fig. 2. Overview of our Setting with two Layer-2 ledger $\mathcal{L}_0^2$, $\mathcal{L}_0^2$ and the ledger $\mathcal{L}$ they are created on all separated using dashed lines. We display the lifecycle of a UTxO u_i which is moved into replicas of the ad-hoc ledger $\mathcal{L}_P$ and which can either be moved out of it regularly or through dispute.

Consensus. If a UTxO can be spent by two different transactions, then these transactions are in conflict as any UTxO can only be spent once. In the remainder we assume a mechanism that decides which transactions to perform, e.g. a leader-based approach as in approach in Hydra [4]. If we relax security by allowing the adversary to corrupt only less than a third of participants, then another approach are byzantine consensus protocols as HotStuff [22]. However, this is an orthogonal problem to our work and we do not further address it in this work.

3.2 Approach

The construction consists of three components. (1) UTxOs are moved into and out of $\mathcal{L}_P$. (2) Perform arbitrary transactions that consume and create UTxOs in $\mathcal{L}_P$. (3) Any UTxO in $\mathcal{L}_P$ can be disputed and made available on the underlying ledger $\mathcal{L}$ or in $\mathcal{L}_0^2$ and $\mathcal{L}_1^2$. Recall that in the EUTxO model, coins, (non-) fungible token as well as CEMs, i.e. state machines, are represented as UTxO such that showing the above steps for any UTxO is sufficient to show that it is not only possible to perform payments but also to execute CEMs on $\mathcal{L}_P$.

Wrapped UTxO. Figure 2 illustrates the lifecycle of any UTxO in $\mathcal{L}_P$. Each ledger $\mathcal{L}_b$ maintains a *replica* $\mathcal{R}_b$ – a copy – of $\mathcal{L}_P$. In the following we look at the example of moving a UTxO from $\mathcal{L}_0^2$ to $\mathcal{L}_P$. We consider a UTxO to be in $\mathcal{L}_P$ by *wrapping* it inside a CEM that (1) makes sure that if a UTxO is moved into $\mathcal{L}_P$ on legder $\mathcal{L}_i^2$, $i \in \{0,1\}$, then it is moved into $\mathcal{L}_P$ on $\mathcal{L}_{1-i}^2$ by collecting collateral from a subset of the intermediaries $P_i \subseteq P_{\text{int}}$ on $\mathcal{L}_{1-i}^2$. (2) Likewise it can be *de-wrapped* and moved into $\mathcal{L}_j^2$, $j \in \{0,1\}$ by returning the collateral to the intermediaries on $\mathcal{L}_{1-j}^2$.

Dispute Mechanism. Correctness is facilitated through collaboration with the intermediaries in P_{int}. If any intermediary in P_{int} misbehaves or fails to collaborate, a UTxO can be *disputed* by any participating party. A dispute has two outcomes: (1) If there is at least one honest intermediary they move both instance of the wrapped UTxO from $\mathcal{L}_0^2$ and $\mathcal{L}_1^2$ respectively and onto the underlying ledger $\mathcal{L}$. Afterwards, they can use both UTxO as input into a *merge* transaction which has the original UTxO in its outputs as well as all collateral that was committed with it. (2) If no intermediary is honest such that none perform the steps in (1), then after a timeout enforced through a timelock, two semantically equal instances of the UTxO are moved into both $\mathcal{L}_0^2$ and $\mathcal{L}_1^2$ using the collateral of the intermediaries to finance it and in the process punish the intermediaries. This ensures that the UTxO is always available to their owners independent on which Layer 2 ledger they participate in.

Atomic Transactions. Intermediaries collaborate to perform transactions on $\mathcal{L}_P$ atomically, meaning it is performed on both or on no replica. Otherwise, if a UTxO is spent on $\mathcal{R}_0$ but not on $\mathcal{R}_1$, it can be spent by a different transaction on $\mathcal{R}_1$ effectively double spending the UTxO in which process the collateral of the intermediaries is implicitly consumed and lost. Atomic transactions have to be performed for spending already wrapped UTxO, as well as for wrapping and de-wrapping of UTxO. Transactions are performed atomically by splitting them into two steps, where each step is performed by a dedicated transaction. (1) First, we verify that the transactions can be performed through the *verify-transaction*. The verify-transaction collects all the (wrapped) UTxOs on both replica as well as any witnesses, and forges token if necessary. Moreover it evaluates the UTxOs verification scripts. Note that this step is reversible, i.e. we can create another transaction that re-creates all input UTxOs by creating semantically equal ones within its outputs and burns all forged tokens. This transaction requires an aggregate signature signed by all intermediaries. We proceed only if this transaction has been performed on both replica. (2) Only afterwards we can be sure that the transaction can be done on both replica ensuring it is atomic. This is done through a perform transaction that creates all UTxO within its outputs and burns any token if required. To ensure that any honest intermediary can prevent wrongful execution of the perform transaction, i.e. before the replica are synchronized, we require an aggregate signature signed by all intermediaries to create the perform transaction. This aggregate signature is the only witness required to perform the transactions. This step is irreversible, we might not be able to create a transaction that can reforge burned token, or claim all UTxO we created as input as they might be spent by different transactions by then.

We can resolve disputes through a merge-transaction, (1) either if the UTxO in both replica are in the same state, (2) one replica has performed only the verify-transaction while the other hasn't since we can revert this step by outputting the UTxO in the merge transaction's outputs and (3) if the perform transaction was performed on one replica while only the verify-transaction was performed on the other replica since we have the required witness, i.e. the aggregate signature, to do the perform transaction bringing the UTxO of both replica into the same state. Acting as mentioned above any honest intermediary can ensure that a merge-transaction can be performed on disputed UTxO.

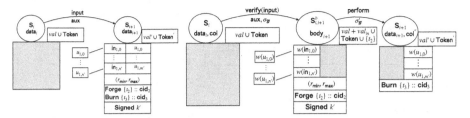

(a) The original transaction.   (b) Atomic transaction on each replica.

Fig. 3. Derivation of a atomic two-step transaction in Fig. 3b from an arbitrary transaction in Fig. 3a.

Limitations. We require UTxO that are moved to $\mathcal{L}_P$ to be collateralized, i.e. the intermediaries have to commit collateral equal to the number of coins and token present. This limits us to UTxO that contain coins or fungible token, however, we cannot move non-fungible token into $\mathcal{L}_P$ without any additional workaround.

4 The Ad-Hoc Ledger State Machine

In the following we give a description of the state machine that governs the lifecycle of each UTxO within an ad-hoc ledger $\mathcal{L}_P$ between parties P. Note that while we do not specify the exact storage of data, however, to reduce the size of UTxO a potential data structure are Patricia Merkle trees[3].

4.1 Setup

Recall that we aim to setup an ad-hoc ledger between parties P with the help of intermediaries P_{int}. For setup, each party $\mathcal{P}$ creates an individual key pair $(vk_{\mathcal{P}}, sk_{\mathcal{P}})$. Moreover, the parties collaborate to setup public parameter Π_P and use them to create aggregate verification key V_P where $(\text{sk}_{P,\mathcal{P}}, \text{vk}_{P,\mathcal{P}})$ are the individual keys of $\mathcal{P}$. Analogously the intermediaries collaborate to setup public parameter Π_{int} to create aggregate verification key V_{int} where $(\text{sk}_{\text{int},\mathcal{P}'}, \text{vk}_{\text{int},\mathcal{P}'})$ are the individual keys of $\mathcal{P}' \in P_{\text{int}}$. Then, the parties sample a random nonce $r \in \mathbb{N}$ and negotiate a dispute time $t_d \geq \Delta_{\mathcal{L}^2} + \Delta$. This data is stored within the data field of each wrapped UTxO. A cryptographic hash h_{MP} of the execution parameters, public keys and nonce r serves to bind them to the ad-hoc ledger and in addition they are used as a unique identifier for the ad-hoc ledger itself.

4.2 Atomic Transactions

Transactions are executed on all replica atomically, i.e. they are executed either on all or none, by splitting them up into two transactions, (1) the verify-transaction verifying that the transaction can be executed on each replica and

---

[3] https://ethereum.org/en/developers/docs/data-structures-and-encoding/patricia-merkle-trie/.

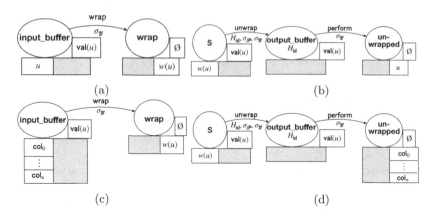

Fig. 4. Illustration of wrapping a UTxO in Figs. 4a and 4c and unwrapping in Figs. 4b and 4d.

(2) the perform-transaction which executes the transaction. This is illustrated in Fig. 3b where the original-transaction depicted in Fig. 3a is executed atomically. These transactions are executed on all replica to keep their states equal. Both transactions require an aggregate signature corresponding to verification key V_{int}. (1) The first transaction is labeled verify(input) where input is the label of the original-transaction that should be performed. The transaction collects all UTxO that are required for the transaction in its inputs while verifying their validator scripts and forges all token that are required. It verifies the validator script of the input transition using auxilliary information aux. However, note that since the verify-transaction does not contain the outputs of the original-transaction, we cannot directly verify the transaction constraints that are required by the validator. Instead, we store the body of the original-transaction that we perform in the $body_{i+1}$ verify that it confirms the constraints and that the inputs of the verify-transaction confirm with the original-transaction. (2) After the verify-transaction is performed on each replica we proceed with the perform-transaction. This transaction burns all required token and creates the UTxO outputs of the original-transaction. We use $body_{i+1}$ that is available through $S^b_{i,i+1}$'s data field to verify that the perform-transaction is consistent with the original-transaction. The field col stores how the coins and tokens associated with that UTxO $val \cup$ Token are collateralized by the intermediaries as discussed in Sect. 4.4.

4.3 Wrapping UTxO

All UTxO that are used within $\mathcal{L}_P$ are wrapped using a state machine that has two purposes. (1) It manages the lifecycle of the UTxO as shown in Fig. 2 and ensures it is only spent through verify-/ and perform-transactions and (2) it ensures sufficient collateral was committed as well as it tracks how much collateral was committed by the individual parties. Figures 4a and 4c depicts how UTxO are wrapped and made available on $\mathcal{L}_P$ wheres Figs. 4b and 4d depict how they are unwrapped and moved out of $\mathcal{L}_P$ back into either $\mathcal{L}_0^2$ or $\mathcal{L}_1^2$. All operations have to be done atomically and thus are executed using the framework described in Sect. 4.2. When wrapping a UTxO u, it is committed into the input-buffer transaction on the ledger it originates from, whereas for the other replica the intermediaries $\mathcal{P}_{\text{int},0}, \ldots, \mathcal{P}_{\text{int},n_{\text{int}}}$ commit collateral $\text{col}_0, \ldots, \text{col}_{n_{\text{int}}}$ respectively such that $\text{val}(u) \leq \sum_{i=0}^{n_{\text{int}}} \text{col}_i$ where $\text{val}(u)$ is the amount of coins and token in u. Only after the input_buffer transaction has been committed to both replica, the intermediaries collaborate to create the wrap-transactions which are analogous to the perform-transaction in Sect. 3b and make the wrapped UTxO available in $\mathcal{L}_P$. Lastly, each wrapped UTxO contains a nonce u_{id} that is unique to $\mathcal{L}_P$ to make it uniquely identifiable, however, which is equal for the same wrapped UTxO on each replica. Unwrapping of a UTxO is analogous with a few differences. For one, we require that the unwrap-transaction in addition contains information H_{id} which designates that the UTxO will be moved to $\mathcal{L}_{H_{\text{id}}}^2$ as depicted in Fig. 4b and the collateral associated with it is released on the other layer 2 ledger as depicted in Fig. 4d. Moreover, to trigger unwrapping of a UTxO we additionally require a group signature corresponding to the aggregate verification key of all participants V_P of the message (unwrap, u_{id}, H_{id}).

4.4 Collateral

The wrapping itself is a unique UTxO living in $\mathcal{L}_0^2$ and $\mathcal{L}_1^2$. It's datafield contains the amount of collateral committed by each intermediary. Let $\text{col}(\mathcal{P}, w(u))$ be the collateral intermediary $\mathcal{P}$ has contributed to wrapped UTxO $w(u)$. If a transaction consumes wrapped UTxOs $w_{\text{in}}(u_0), \ldots, w_{\text{in}}(u_n)$, and creates wrapped UTxOs $w_{\text{out}}(u_0), \ldots, w_{\text{out}}(u_m)$ $n, m \in \mathbb{N}$, then for each intermediary $\mathcal{P}_i$, $0 \leq i \leq n_{\text{int}}$ holds that the sum of their committed collateral does not change, i.e. $\sum_{j=0}^{n} \text{col}(w_{\text{in}}(u_j)) = \sum_{l=0}^{m} \text{col}(w_{\text{in}}(u_l))$. It has to hold that each wrapped UTxO remains sufficiently collateralized, i.e. the inequation $\text{val}(u) = \sum_{i=0}^{n_{\text{int}}} \text{col}_i$ holds. How collateral is distributed within the new UTxOs is to be negotiated between the intermediaries. In Layer-2 protocols intermediaries receive a fee for locking their collateral. While not addressing it in detail we argue that we can adapt the handling of fees from the Interhead [14] where intermediaries receive fee proportional to the collateral locked whereas parties pay out a fee to the intermediaries proportional to the value of UTxO they request moving to $\mathcal{L}_P$.

4.5 Dispute

Dispute resolution is similar to Interhead Hydra [14]. At any point, any party can create a transaction that consumes a wrapped UTxO and outputs a semantically equal UTxO to which a dispute flag is added. A dispute might be required if the intermediaries fail to perform a transaction atomically on all replica, or if the intermediaries stop collaborating to perform any further transaction which is required to ensure liveness.. A UTxO with such a flag can be spent in two ways. (1) As depicted in Fig. 5a a merge-transaction consumes one instance of the

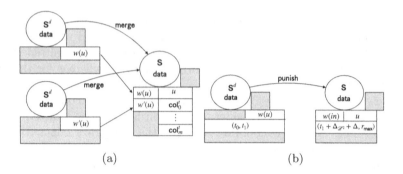

$$(a) \qquad\qquad (b)$$

Fig. 5. Figure 5a shows dispute resolution through merge of its two wrapped UTxO instances. Figure 5b shows timeout and punishment of the intermediaries.

wrapped UTxO from each replica and outputs the UTxO as well as all collateral associated with it. This requires moving the flagged UTxO out of $\mathcal{L}_0^2$ and $\mathcal{L}_1^2$ and to the underlying ledger which can be done by any party which takes at most time $\Delta_{\mathcal{L}^2}$. Recall that committing any transaction on the ledger takes time Δ. Therefore any intermediary can perform this within time $\Delta_{\mathcal{L}^2} + \Delta$. However, the above dispute resolution requires that both wrapped UTxO are available. If dispute is triggered while a UTxO is involved in a atomic transaction it might be only available on one replica. Recall the atomic transaction in Fig. 3b where a UTxO is first in state S_i, then a verify-transaction moves it to a buffer state $S_{i,i+1}^b$ and lastly the UTxO is moved with a perform-transaction to state S_{i+1}. Since the intermediaries synchronize after each transaction as mentioned in Sect. 4.2 and described in Sect. 5 the states can only diverge by one state transition and we can proceed as follows. If both states are at least in state $S_{i,i+1}^b$ we already verified on all replica that the original-transaction can be performed thus the merge-transaction outputs a UTxO in state S_i and burning token as well as outputting wrapped UTxO on the ledger consistent to $body_{i+1}$. Otherwise one UTxO is in state S_i while the other is in state $S_{i,i+1}^b$. Then the merge transaction outputs a UTxO in state S_i while reversing the verify-transaction, i.e. it for each UTxO in the verify-transaction's inputs it outputs semantically equal wrapped UTxO on the ledger, as well as it burns all token that were forged in that transaction. (2) As shown in Fig. 5b a timelock expires after time $\Delta_{\mathcal{L}^2} + \Delta$ which allows the flagged UTxO to be spent by a transaction that consumes it and outputs the UTxO directly and without outputting any collateral. Note that if a UTxO is in state $S_{i,i+1}^b$ the UTxO that will be output is in state S_{i+1}.

4.6 Extensions

Batch Transaction. To improve efficiency of the construction multiple wrap and de-wrap transactions could be batched into one transaction. Moreover, instead of requiring wrapped UTxO as input, a sync-transaction can take UTxO and collateral as input and implicitly wrapping the UTxO in the same step.

Multiple Replica. Our construction can be extended to $n \geq 2$, $n \in \mathbb{N}$ replica. As in the case of $n = 2$ all replica require to synchronize at *sync-transactions* and merge-transactions have to be adapted to merge not two but n disputed UTxOs. However, this naive extension to multiple replica requires that the collateral committed by each intermediary for each UTxO in each replica is equal. The option of having variable collateral is left as an open question.

Recovery from Disputes. If UTxOs are disputed within each replica, but are either in the same state or can be brought into the same state through reversing a sync-transaction or doing a perform transaction they could be moved back into their respective replicas and thus into L$_P$ thus resolving the disupte. However, to ensure correctness and liveness, we require an aggregate signature of the intermediaries as well an aggregate signature of all remaining parties, i.e. all parties must verify and consent to recover from a dispute as otherwise corrupted parties might prevent a correct dispute resolution.

Virtual Ledgers. Since our construction requires interaction with all intermediaries in P for each transaction it cannot be considered a virtual ledger. However, layer 2 ledger constructions such as Hydra [4] can be performed within our framework effectively creating virtual ledgers.

5   The Protocols

We require that all transactions performed on $\mathcal{L}_P$ are either performed on all replica or on none which is ensured through ATOMIC_TRANSACTION protocol shown in Algorithm 1 which is executed by the intermediaries. This protocol is executed for general transactions and (un-) wrapping of UTxOs. If this fails, there would be UTxO that are on only one replica, i.e. UTxO are not spent on the replica that did not perform the transaction, whereas new UTxO are created only on the replica that did perform the transaction. Any UTxO that exists on only one replica can be claimed by their owner by setting a dispute flag on the UTxO which allows it to be claimed directly after time $\Delta_{\mathcal{L}^2} + \Delta$. A dispute might also be triggered to ensure liveness, if the intermediaries stop collaboration to perform further transactions. However, if a disputed UTxO exists on all replica, the intermediaries can perform the DISPUTE_UTXO protocol shown in Algorithm 2 to move the UTxO out of $\mathcal{L}_P$ and into the common ledger $\mathcal{L}$.

Atomic Transactions. Algorithm 1 describes how all Intermediaries collaborate to perform a transaction atomically on all replica. Whenever a participant of $\mathcal{L}_P$ requests a transaction to be performed they submit the original transaction tr$_o$. First, we verify whether tr$_o$ is a valid transaction in lines 2 and 3 tr$_o$ and terminate if this is not the case. In line 4 we derive the verify − transactions tr$_{v,0}$ and tr$_{v,1}$ for the replicas in $\mathcal{L}_0^2$ and $\mathcal{L}_1^2$ respectively and in line 5 we derive the perform − transactions tr$_{v,0}$ and tr$_{v,1}$. In lines 6 - 8 the intermediaries collaborate to create group signatures for the verify − transactions, commit them

Algorithm 1 Transaction Protocol	**Algorithm 2** Dispute Protocol
1: **function**	1: **function** DISPUTE_UTXO(u)
ATOMIC_TRANSACTION(tr_o)	2: **if** ¬DISPUTED(u) **then return**
2: **if** ¬VERIFY(tr_o) **then return**	3: **end if**
3: **end if**	4: DECOMMIT($\mathcal{L}_0^2, u$)
4: $(\text{tr}_{v,0}, \text{tr}_{v,1}) \leftarrow$ VRFY_TR(tr_o)	5: DECOMMIT($\mathcal{L}_1^2, u$)
5: $(\text{tr}_{p,0}, \text{tr}_{p,1}) \leftarrow$ PRFRM_TR(tr_o)	6: WAIT_DECOMMITTED(u)
6: AGGREGATE_SIG($V_{\text{int}}, \text{tr}_{v,0}, \text{tr}_{v,1}$)	7: $\text{tr}_m \leftarrow$ MERGE_TX(u)
7: COMMIT($(\mathcal{L}_0^2, \text{tr}_{v,0}), (\mathcal{L}_1^2, \text{tr}_{v,1})$)	8: COMMIT($\mathcal{L}, \text{tr}_m$)
8: WAIT_COMITTED($\text{tr}_{v,0}, \text{tr}_{v,1}$)	9: **end function**
9: AGGREGATE_SIG($V_{\text{int}}, \text{tr}_{p,0}, \text{tr}_{p,1}$)	
10: COMMIT($(\mathcal{L}_0^2, \text{tr}_{p,0}), (\mathcal{L}_1^2, \text{tr}_{p,1})$)	
11: WAIT_COMITTED($\text{tr}_{p,0}, \text{tr}_{p,1}$)	
12: **end function**	

Fig. 6. Algorithm 1 is executed by intermediaries to perform transactions whereas Algorithm 2 is done by any one intermediary to resolve a dispute.

and wait until they are confirmed by the respective layer 2 ledgers. In line 6, AGGREGATE_SIG takes an aggregate verification key and two transactions as input and outputs aggregate signatures for both transactions corresponding to that verification key. Then, COMMIT takes tuples of form $(\mathcal{L}, \text{tr})$ as input and commits transaction tr onto (layer 2) ledger $\mathcal{L}$. In line 8 WAIT_COMMITTED takes a list of transactions as input and makes the protocol participants wait until these transactions are processed on their respective ledgers. After this is done the same is repeated for the perform − transactions in lines 9–11 (Fig. 6).

Dispute. Algorithm 2 describes how a dispute can be resolved by any one intermediary without them losing their collateral. This algorithm can only be executed if a disputed UTxO is present on all replica. The algorithm takes a wrapped UTxO as input. First, the intermediary checks whether the UTxO's dispute flag is set in lines 2 - 4 and terminates the algorithm otherwise. If the UTxO is disputed the wrapped UTxOs are decommitted from $\mathcal{L}_0^2$ and $\mathcal{L}_1^2$ respectively and moved to the common ledger $\mathcal{L}$ within time $\Delta_{\mathcal{L}^2}$. Then, in line 6 the intermediary observes $\mathcal{L}$ and waits until both replica of the UTxO are present on $\mathcal{L}$ after which in line 7 a merge − transaction for the disputed UTxO is created that takes the decommitted wrapped UTxOs and outputs the UTxO as well as all collateral that is associated with it as depicted in Fig. 5a. Lastly in line 8 the merge − transaction is committed to $\mathcal{L}$ and is processed within time Δ.

6   Analysis

Theorem 1. (*Offchain Efficiency*). *If $\mathcal{L}^2$ can de-commit a UTxO to the ledger in $\mathcal{O}(1)$ transactions, $\mathcal{L}_P$ has offchain efficiency.*

Proof. The only occasion in which UTxO are committed to $\mathcal{L}$ is when an intermediary executes DISPUTE_UTXO in Algorithm 2. In that case the disputed UTxO is de-commited from both, $\mathcal{L}_0^2$ and $\mathcal{L}_1^2$ which happens in $\mathcal{O}(1)$ transactions. Afterwards one merge-transaction is committed to the ledger.

Theorem 2. (*Liveness*). *$\mathcal{L}_P$ has the liveness property.*

Proof. At any point within a UTxOs lifecycle within $\mathcal{L}_P$ including during wrapping and unwrapping it can be disputed by any party including any intermediary. If there is a honest intermediary, they will proceed to make the UTxO and the associated collateral available on the ledger by executing Algorithm 2. This happens within time $\Delta_{\mathcal{L}^2} + \Delta$. Otherwise, at time $\Delta_{\mathcal{L}^2} + \Delta$ a semantically equal UTxO is available in Layer 2 ledgers $\mathcal{L}_0$ and $\mathcal{L}_1$ respectively.

Theorem 3. (*Balance Security*). *$\mathcal{L}_P$ has the balance security property.*

Proof. In the following we assume that all UTxO are well formatted, i.e. a owner of a UTxO has given consent to spent the UTxO to any computationally polynomially bound party that can compute a valid witness for the UTxO. Moreover, in the following we consider a honest party $\mathcal{P}$ and a UTxO u that is present in $\mathcal{L}_P$ and either $\mathcal{P}$ can spend u by computing a witness within polynomial time, or u contains $\mathcal{P}$'s collateral. A honest party can lose access to their coins either (1) by having a UTxO and its associated collateral be locked within $\mathcal{L}_P$ indefinitely such that the party cannot move it to $\mathcal{L}_0$, $\mathcal{L}_1$ or $\mathcal{L}$, or (2) if a party without consent to spend can use the UTxO as input in a transactions spending it in the process. Note that since by construction, if a UTxO is spent in any way on $\mathcal{L}_P$ its collateral is moved to another UTxO. Thus, to show balance security for collateral we need to show that case (1) cannot occur. To show balance security for the coins in u itself we have to show that (1) cannot occur and that (2) can only occur with negligible probability. Since $\mathcal{L}_P$ has the liveness property, case (1) cannot occur. In the following, we assume that there exists a computationally polynomially bound party that attempts to spend u without receiving consent. This requires creation of a witness for u. As they have no consent to spend the UTxO they cannot compute a witness within polynomial time, thus the probability they can spend it is negligible.

7   Conclusion

In this work we presented a means for parties on two Layer-2 ledgers to interact with another ad-hoc and with little in advance setup. We showed properties *balance security*, *liveness* and *offchain efficiency* hold in the presence of a malicious adversary corrupting all but one parties. While we presented only the core of the construction, we proposed multiple potential extensions as improving efficiency through batching of transactions, recovery from disputes, creation of virtual ledgers and connecting more than two Layer-2 ledgers. We argue that the construction can be used as a framework for secure interaction and individual uses cases can be optimized to facilitate low-overhead interactions.

References

1. Canetti, R.: Universally composable signature, certification, and authentication. In: Proceedings of 17th IEEE Computer Security Foundations Workshop, 2004, pp. 219–233. IEEE (2004)
2. Chakravarty, M.M., Chapman, J., MacKenzie, K., Melkonian, O., Jones, M.P., Wadler, P.: The extended UTXO model. In: 4th Workshop on Trusted Smart Contracts (2020)
3. Chakravarty, M.M.T., et al.: Native custom tokens in the extended UTXO model. In: Margaria, T., Steffen, B. (eds.) ISoLA 2020. LNCS, vol. 12478, pp. 89–111. Springer, Cham (2020). https://doi.org/10.1007/978-3-030-61467-6_7
4. Chakravarty, M.M., et al.: Hydra: fast isomorphic state channels. In: International Conference on Financial Cryptography and Data Security. Springer (2021)
5. Croman, K., et al.: On scaling decentralized blockchains. In: Clark, J., Meiklejohn, S., Ryan, P.Y.A., Wallach, D., Brenner, M., Rohloff, K. (eds.) FC 2016. LNCS, vol. 9604, pp. 106–125. Springer, Heidelberg (2016). https://doi.org/10.1007/978-3-662-53357-4_8
6. Decker, C., Wattenhofer, R.: A fast and scalable payment network with bitcoin duplex micropayment channels. In: Pelc, A., Schwarzmann, A.A. (eds.) SSS 2015. LNCS, vol. 9212, pp. 3–18. Springer, Cham (2015). https://doi.org/10.1007/978-3-319-21741-3_1
7. Dziembowski, S., Eckey, L., Faust, S., Malinowski, D.: Perun: virtual payment hubs over cryptocurrencies. In: Perun: Virtual Payment Hubs over Cryptocurrencies. IEEE (2017)
8. Dziembowski, S., Faust, S., Hostáková, K.: General state channel networks. In: Proceedings of the 2018 ACM SIGSAC Conference on Computer and Communications Security, pp. 949–966. ACM (2018)
9. Goldwasser, S., Micali, S., Rivest, R.L.: A paradoxical solution to the signature problem. In: Proceedings of the 25th Annual Symposium OnFoundations of Computer Science, pp. 441–448 (1984). SFCS '84, IEEE Computer Society, USA (1984). https://doi.org/10.1109/SFCS.1984.715946
10. Goldwasser, S., Micali, S., Rivest, R.L.: A digital signature scheme secure against adaptive chosen-message attacks. SIAM J. Comput. **17**(2), 281–308 (1988). https://doi.org/10.1137/0217017
11. Itakura, K.: A public-key cryptosystem suitable for digital multisignatures. NEC J. Res. Dev. 71 (1983)
12. Jourenko, M., Larangeira, M., Tanaka, K.: Lightweight virtual payment channels. Cryptology ePrint Archive, Report 2020/998 (2020). https://eprint.iacr.org/2020/998
13. Jourenko, M., Larangeira, M., Tanaka, K.: Payment trees: low collateral payments for payment channel networks. In: Borisov, N., Diaz, C. (eds.) FC 2021. LNCS, vol. 12675, pp. 189–208. Springer, Heidelberg (2021). https://doi.org/10.1007/978-3-662-64331-0_10

14. Jourenko, M., Larangeira, M., Tanaka, K.: Interhead hydra: Two heads are better than one. In: The 3rd International Conference on Mathematical Research for Blockchain Economy (2022)
15. Katz, J., Maurer, U., Tackmann, B., Zikas, V.: Universally composable synchronous computation. In: Sahai, A. (ed.) TCC 2013. LNCS, vol. 7785, pp. 477–498. Springer, Heidelberg (2013). https://doi.org/10.1007/978-3-642-36594-2_27
16. Kiayias, A., Litos, O.S.T.: A composable security treatment of the lightning network. IACR Cryptology ePrint Archive **2019**, 778 (2019)
17. Kiayias, A., Zhou, H.S., Zikas, V.: Fair and robust multi-party computation using a global transaction ledger. In: Fischlin, M., Coron, J.S. (eds.) Advances in Cryptology - EUROCRYPT 2016, pp. 705–734. Springer, Berlin Heidelberg (2016). https://doi.org/10.1007/978-3-662-49896-5_25
18. Micali, S., Ohta, K., Reyzin, L.: Accountable-subgroup multisignatures. In: Proceedings of the 8th ACM Conference on Computer and Communications Security, pp. 245–254 (2001)
19. Nakamoto, S.: Bitcoin: a peer-to-peer electronic cash system (2008)
20. PDecker, C., Russel, R., Osuntokun, O.: eltoo: a simple layer2 protocol for bitcoin. https://blockstream.com/eltoo.pdf (2017)
21. Poon, J., Dryja, T.: The bitcoin lightning network: scalable off-chain instant payments. https://lightning.network/lightning-network-paper.pdf (2016)
22. Yin, M., Malkhi, D., Reiter, M.K., Gueta, G.G., Abraham, I.: Hotstuff: BFT consensus with linearity and responsiveness. In: Proceedings of the 2019 ACM Symposium on Principles of Distributed Computing, pp. 347–356 (2019)

Get Me Out of This Payment! `Bailout`: An HTLC Re-routing Protocol

Oğuzhan Ersoy[1,3]([✉]), Pedro Moreno-Sanchez[2], and Stefanie Roos[3]

[1] Radboud University, Nijmegen, The Netherlands
`oguzhan.ersoy@ru.nl`
[2] IMDEA Software Institute, Madrid, Spain
`pedro.moreno@imdea.org`
[3] Delft University of Technology, Delft, The Netherlands
`s.roos@tudelft.nl`

Abstract. The Lightning Network provides almost-instant payments to its parties. In addition to direct payments requiring a shared payment channel, parties can pay each other in the form of multi-hop payments via existing channels. Such multi-hop payments rely on a 2-phase commit protocol to achieve balance security; that is, no honest intermediary party loses her coins. Unfortunately, failures or attacks in this 2-phase commit protocol can lead to coins being committed (locked) in a payment for extended periods of time (in the order of days in the worst case). During these periods, parties cannot go offline without losing funds due to their existing commitments, even if they use watchtowers. Furthermore, they cannot use the locked funds for initiating or forwarding new payments, reducing their opportunities to use their coins and earn fees.

We introduce `Bailout`, the first protocol that allows intermediary parties in a multi-hop payment to unlock their coins before the payment completes by re-routing the payment over an alternative path. We achieve this by creating a circular payment route starting from the intermediary party in the opposite direction of the original payment. Once the circular payment is locked, both payments are canceled for the intermediary party, which frees the coins of the corresponding channels. This way, we create an alternative route for the ongoing multi-hop payment without involving the sender or receiver. The parties on the alternative path are incentivized to participate through fees. We evaluate the utility of our protocol using a real-world Lightning Network snapshot. Bailouts may fail due to insufficient balance in alternative paths used for re-routing. We find that attempts of a node to bailout typically succeed with a probability of more than 94% if at least one alternative path exists.

1 Introduction

Payment channels have emerged as one of the most promising mitigations to the blockchain scalability problem [22]. A payment channel enables two users to perform many payments between them while requiring only two transactions to be published on the blockchain. In a bit more detail, Alice and Bob open a channel between each other by submitting a transaction to the blockchain that locks

© International Financial Cryptography Association 2024
F. Baldimtsi and C. Cachin (Eds.): FC 2023, LNCS 13951, pp. 92–109, 2024.
https://doi.org/10.1007/978-3-031-47751-5_6

coins in a shared deposit. A (off-chain) payment only requires that Alice and Bob exchange an authenticated agreement of a new deposit's balance, i.e., the split of the funds in the deposit between the two. This off-chain payment operation can be repeated arbitrarily often until the channel is closed by publishing a transaction on the blockchain that releases the deposited coins according to the last authorized balance. However, opening a channel only pays off if parties transact with each other repeatedly.

To enable parties to conduct a transaction without establishing a new channel, payment channel networks (PCNs) [3–5,15,16,31,38] allow routing payments from a sender to a receiver via multiple channels. In such a *multi-hop* payment, each channel in the route is updated with the payment amount (and a fee) from the sender to the receiver. The most important requirement for a multi-hop payment protocol is balance security [5,18,31], i.e., no honest party other than the sender should lose coins and the sender should only lose the payment amount and the fees. While there exist several proposals to achieve balance security [5,18,32,38], *hash-time lock contracts* (HTLC) are currently implemented in the Lightning Network (LN).

An HTLC-based multi-hop payment works as follows: When agreeing to conduct a payment, the receiver chooses a random value and then gives the hash of that value to the sender. The sender decides on one payment path. The first node on each channel making up the path commits to paying the second node if the second node provides the preimage of the hash within a certain time. The time, which depends on the node's individual preference and its position in the path, is called the timelock of the conditional payment. More details on the HTLC construction and timelocks are given in Sect. 2. Once all the commitments are made, the receiver provides the preimage and the preimage is forwarded along the path back to the sender, concluding the promised payments.

While the protocol provides balance security, it causes issues with regard to the availability of coins. After a node has committed to a payment, neither the node nor their successor on the path can use the payment amount for concurrent payments, as it is not yet known whether the coins will be successfully transferred. The typical amount of time funds can be *locked* in this manner is in the order of seconds, assuming that all parties are responsive. However, there can sometimes be delays in the order of days [36].

The delays can be caused by nodes being offline or payment failure. Thus, the locked coins can severely limit a node's liquidity and prevent them both from initiating payments of their own and from forwarding other payments due to the lack of available funds, which can drastically reduce the ability of the network to conduct payments [36,40]. Also, if there are several locked HTLCs, the parties may not able to accept new HTLCs (even if they have enough funds) because of the upper limit in the number of concurrent HTLC [11]. Moreover, it is important to note that intermediary parties cannot go offline until all the locked payments are released. This holds even with watchtowers, as there is no watchtower protocol that updates the channel state without the presence of the channel owner [7,8,14,24,26,34].

These negative effects of unexpectedly long-locked coins give rise to the question: *Is it possible to unlock coins of an intermediary party if the multi-hop payment is not completed and the timelock has not expired?*

Our Contributions. In this work, we positively answer this question by providing Bailout, which allows an intermediary party, who has locked her coins for an unfinished multi-hop payment, to unlock her coins before the expiration of the corresponding timelock. In a nutshell, Bailout allows the intermediary party to re-route the on-going multi-hop payment, so that other nodes with a better availability situation take over the payment, freeing up coins for the intermediary party to use in other payments. We incentivize the other parties to take over the payment through offering them extra fees, typically higher than the standard fee for routing a payment. In this manner, we offload payments from overloaded nodes to nodes with a low load and available funds. Our contributions are:

- We introduce Bailout, the first protocol that allows intermediary parties to unlock their coins from an ongoing HTLC payment and provably achieves balance security. Bailout re-routes the payment over an alternative path that connects the neighboring parties of the intermediary. It is compatible with HTLC-based multi-hop payments in Lightning: (i) it can be implemented with the scripting language of Bitcoin, (ii) it does not require any additional information than the existing knowledge in Lightning, e.g., the intermediary party knows only her neighbors on the payment path.
- We evaluate our protocol in the face of parties that want to go offline and bailout of their ongoing payments. The level of concurrency and the frequency of long delays determine the amount of locked collateral in the network and hence affect the ability of a party to find an alternative path with sufficient funds. Still, even for high concurrency and frequent delays, less than 6% of bailouts fail.

2 Building Blocks

Transactions and Ledger. In this work, we utilize a simplified version of Bitcoin to model transactions and the ledger as in [3]. The transactions are based on the *unspent transaction output* (UTXO) model, where the coins are represented by outputs. An output $\vec{\theta}$ is defined as a tuple (cash, θ) where cash denotes the number of coins in the output and θ is the corresponding spending condition. For readability, we extract away the details of the ledger functionality. We require that the ledger handles the notion of time in rounds, and the round number corresponds to the number of blocks on the ledger. Also, we assume that a valid transaction is included in a block on the ledger after at most Δ rounds. Details of transactions and ledger functionality are given in [21].

Payment Channels. A payment channel is defined as a tuple of $\gamma := (id, \mathsf{users}, \mathsf{cash}, \mathsf{st})$ where $\gamma.id$ is the id of the channel between parties $P \in$

γ.users, γ.cash denotes the capacity of the channel and γ.st:=$(\vec{\theta}_1, \ldots, \vec{\theta}_n)$ is the state of the channel. We denote channel between A and B as $\gamma_{A,B}$. A channel has three phases: (i) *create* where the channel is opened by publishing the funding transaction on the ledger, (ii) *update* where parties update the state of the channel, and (iii) *close* where parties close the channel by publishing the latest channel state on-chain. The payment channel functionality is given in [21].

Payment Channel Networks. A payment channel network is a network where parties are nodes and channels are edges. One can route payments from a payer to a payee along multiple channels without requiring a direct channel between them. A Multi-hop payment (MHP) is constructed over a path of channels path:=(path[0], \ldots, path[$n-1$]) and conditional payments (MHP[0], \ldots, MHP[$n-1$]) (one for each channel) where n is the payment route length. path[i] is the ith channel in the payment route and path[i].payer (and also MHP[i].payer) denotes the ith party in the path who pays to the $(i+1)$th party, path[i].payee.

We present the ideal functionality of MHP $\mathcal{F}_{MHP}$ in [21], which has two phases: Setup and Lock, and Pay or Revoke phases. In the Setup and Lock phase, the payment path is created and the channels on the path lock the corresponding amounts. More concretely, at each channel path[i], amt[i] coins of path[i].payer are locked. Here, the order of the locking corresponds to the order of channels on the path, starting with the channel adjacent to the sender. If the locking fails in a channel on the path, then the locking stops. When all channels in the path are locked, this phase is finished. In the Pay (or Revoke) phase, for each channel of path[i], the locked coins are paid to path[i].payee. Unlike in the previous phase, the channel updates are executed in the order from the receiver to the sender. If the payment is not completed before TL[i], then the locked coins can be revoked and given back to the path[i].payer.

Lightning Network achieves multi-hop payments via the HTLC (hash time locked contract) protocol. An HTLC is a *conditional payment* where the receiving party can claim the payment amount by providing the preimage of the given hash value. If the preimage is not provided within a certain time, the payment amount returns to the sending party. We write an HTLC tuple with the following attributes HTLC:=(mid, cpid, γ, payer $\rightarrow$ payee, cond, TL, amt) where HTLC.cpid is the id of the HTLC in channel HTLC.γ between the payer HTLC.payer and the payee HTLC.payee. If the HTLC is part of a multi-hop payment, then HTLC.mid stores the corresponding id, otherwise it is $\perp$. The payment amount of the HTLC is HTLC.amt that is locked for the condition HTLC.cond. If the HTLC is part of a MHP, the amount is deducted from the available coins of HTLC.payer. If a witness witness is provided s.t. $\mathcal{H}$(witness) = cond until time HTLC.TL, then the payment amount is given to HTLC.payee. Otherwise, at time HTLC.TL, the amount is returned to HTLC.payer. Note that a channel γ can have several ongoing HTLCs at the same time. For readability, unless it is necessary, we skip the first three attributes of the HTLC tuple, also we omit the payer and payee in figures where they are visually ascertainable. The scripts of an HTLC are given in [21].

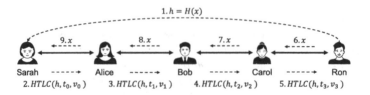

Fig. 1. A multi-hop payment with HTLCs. h denotes $MHP[i].cond$ where x is the corresponding preimage, and t_i and v_i represents $MHP[i].TL$ and $MHP[i].amt$.

As explained previously, a MHP in Lightning is done by locking HTLCs in the payment path from sender to receiver wrt. the condition cond chosen by the receiver. Note that each intermediary party P_i plays the role of payee in the channel (of $MHP[i]$) closer to sender, and the role of payer in the subsequent channel (of $MHP[i+1]$), which is closer to the receiver. Party $MHP[i+1].payer$ accepts locking the conditional payment $MHP[i+1]$ if the following conditions are satisfied: (i) the previous channel should be updated first with the same hash condition, $MHP[i+1].cond = MHP[i].cond$, (ii) the locked amount should be equal to the one in previous channel minus the fee, i.e., $MHP[i].amt - MHP[i+1].amt$ is equal to the fee amount chosen by the channel, and the locked amount can be at most the channel balance, and (iii) the timelock of the HTLC is less than or equal to the timelock of the previous channel plus the timelock of the channel chosen by the intermediary, $MHP[i+1].TL = MHP[i].TL - T_i$ where T_i is the timelock of the channel. In Lightning Network, the timelock and fee values of a channel is publicly known. An illustrative example of a MHP is given in Fig. 1.

After the last channel before the receiver has been updated with an HTLC condition, the receiver reveals the preimage and obtains the payment. Subsequently, all intermediaries forward the preimage to their predecessor. If the receiver does not share the preimage, each channel returns to its initial state after the timelock. In this case, the coins in each channel will be locked and cannot be used until the timelock is over.

3   The Bailout Protocol

Assume there is an ongoing multi-hop payment (MHP_0) including the channels from A to B and B to C (seen at the Initial State of Fig. 2). Let $HTLC_A$ and $HTLC_C$ be the existing HTLCs with condition h and amounts amt_A and amt_C in channels $\gamma_{A,B}$ and $\gamma_{B,C}$, defined as: $HTLC_A := (A \rightarrow B, h, TL_A, amt_A)$ and $HTLC_C := (B \rightarrow C, h, TL_C, amt_C)$, where $TL_C < TL_A$ and $amt_C < amt_A$. In both channels, coins have been locked for longer than expected by B. If the payment is not completed, B has to wait until the timelock of $HTLC_C$ expires, which can be days.

Motivation. Here, we list some of the potential reasons that B may request to be removed from the long-lasting payment. First, B may want to go offline with minimal monitoring of the blockchain. If there are no ongoing payments locked, B only needs to monitor the blockchain (wrt. the channel timelock, once per day) for potential fraud of the other party of the channel, and this can even be delegated to a watchtower [26]. However, if there are ongoing HTLCs, the channel needs to be updated wrt. the outcome of them, and this cannot be delegated. Note that even if every party in the MHP is honest and online but B is offline, then the MHP cannot be completed until B is online again or the timelocks of B are expired. Thus, other parties also benefit from removing B from the ongoing payment as B's absence may delay the payment further.

Secondly, B may want to close his channels and spend the coins immediately. Even though, B can close the channel with ongoing payments, he needs to wait for them to be finalized. Thirdly, B may want to make an off-chain payment but due to the ongoing payment and the locked coins, there are not enough funds available. In the last scenario, B could also want to unlock his funds to participate in off-chain payments as an intermediary and make profits in the form of fees from other payments using the currently locked coins.

Security and Compatibility Requirements. Here, we aim to design a protocol that unlocks the coins of B, which is compatible with Bitcoin's scripting language and the Lightning Network. The protocol requires the participation of B's neighbors A and C as they need to be involved in unlocking previously made commitments. Without the cooperation of these neighbors, B cannot update the channels. The Lightning Network uses onion routing such that the intermediary only learns the identity of the previous and next node on the path. Thus, our protocol should also not require the identities of other parties on the path, in particular the sender and receiver. Finally, but most importantly, the protocol should provide balance security to every honest intermediary, meaning that no honest party should lose coins regardless of the acts of other parties.

3.1   Overview of `Bailout`

In this work, we design `Bailout` and show that it satisfies all the requirements given above. `Bailout` *re-routes* the ongoing locked HTLCs via an alternative path such that coins of B are released. In a nutshell, the idea is creating new HTLCs in the opposite direction with the same payment amounts and then cancelling them out. For that reason, we create a circular MHP (MHP_1) of length four starting from B that goes through A, D (party in the new route, called a *bailout party*), C and ends at B again (see Step 2 in Fig. 2).[1] Once the new MHP is locked, both payments are canceled for B, which frees the coins of the corresponding channels, which is illustrated in the Step 3 of Fig. 2. The

---

[1] Here, we require that there is an alternative path between Alice and Carol via only one intermediary, Dave. Later on, we generalize it to multiple intermediaries.

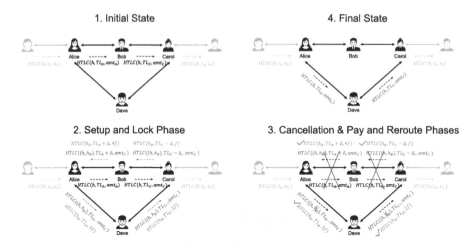

Fig. 2. Simplified protocol phases for the full cancellation/re-routing. In Setup and Lock Phase, the new multi-hop payments (MHP$_1$ and MHP$_2$) are locked. In Cancellation Phase, the HTLCs of B are cancelled in the channels with A and C. In Pay and Reroute Phase, MHP$_2$ is payed by sharing the preimage of h_B and the condition of MHP$_1$ is reduced to h. For simplification of the figure, we use a constant fee f, which can actually differ among parties. HTLCs of MHP$_0$, MHP$_1$ and MHP$_2$ are colored with black, blue and green respectively. (Color figure online)

re-routing of the original payment can be seen in the path difference between the Initial and Final State given in Fig. 2.

Naive Approach. A naive solution is creating a circular MHP$_1$ with the same condition as MHP$_0$, then HTLC$_A$ and MHP$_1$[0] have the same amount and the same hash condition but in opposite directions. Then, for the parties A and B, it would be the same if they cancel both of them, rather than waiting for the payments to be completed. It is similar for the channel between B and C. However, there is a security problem: if the preimage of h is known to A during the locking phase of MHP$_1$, then B loses his coins. More specifically, just after locking MHP$_1$[0], and before locking the other hops in MHP$_1$, if A knows the preimage[2], A can claim the payment in MHP$_1$[0] from B. Yet, if the last hop MHP$_1$[3] is not locked, then B is not be compensated in MHP$_1$.

To overcome the aforementioned problem, the conditional payments in MHP$_1$ should include an additional condition chosen by B, say h_B. In this way, if MHP$_0$ is completed during the process, then the new MHP (MHP$_1$) cannot be spent, and B does not lose his coins. In this case, MHP$_1$ is cancelled since there is no need to execute the protocol. With the additional condition, after re-routing, we need to ensure that parties A and C do not lose their coins because of the

---

[2] A can learn the preimage from B (or the other parties on the path if she is colluding with them).

differences in conditions of MHP_0 and MHP_1. From A's perspective, since A is the payer for conditions (h, h_B) in $MHP_1[1]$, and payee for h in MHP_0 (if she is not the sender), she is guaranteed that after paying in $MHP_1[1]$, she can get paid in MHP_0. However, for C, it is the opposite. For that reason, we have an interim step for the update between B and C where B needs to reveal the preimage of h_B, which we explain in more detail while presenting the protocol phases.

Incentives. Note that the reason of re-routing HTLCs of B in MHP_0 is that it was not completed in the expected time. The delay can be due to i) a node not forwarding the payment or preimage, ii) a node not peacefully settling the payment that she knows will fail and instead waiting for the timelock to expire, and iii) a receiver (intentionally) not providing the preimage, e.g., in a griefing attack. In case ii) and iii), the payment fails and the cancellation happens at the last possible moment, leading to very long delays. If the payment fails, intermediaries do not receive fees. As a consequence, the bailout party D is unlikely to agree to take over the payment if a fee is only paid when the original payment is successful. For this reason, there should be an additional incentive for D to be involved in the re-routing.

We introduce a secondary MHP, MHP_2 with the sole purpose of paying fees to the bailout party D, as well as A and C, for their involvement in the protocol. The condition of MHP_2 is h_B, which is revealed by B to C after the cancellation of HTLCs in their channel. Thus, the intermediary parties will get paid just after the HTLCs of B are cancelled, which is independent of the completion of MHP_0. D can negotiate its fee with B.

A simplified overview of Bailout steps is given in Fig. 2. The locking of the new MHPs, MHP_1 and MHP_2, is done in the Setup and Lock phase. After that, the Cancellation phase starts. In this phase, the previous HTLCs, $HTLC_A$ and $HTLC_C$, together with the new ones in MHP_1 belonging to channels $\gamma_{A,B}$ and $\gamma_{B,C}$ are cancelled, i.e., they are simultaneously revoked. Thus, the coins of B are released. Then, in the last phase, B reveals the secret x_B, so that each party can claim the payment in MHP_2 and also reduce the conditions of HTLCs in MHP_1 to only h.

Extension I - Multiple Bailout Parties and Timelocks. So far we explained the protocol for only one bailout party D that connects A and C. However, such a party may not exist because of the network topology or insufficient balance. Thus, we extend the protocol to multiple bailout parties, D_i's. For the multiple case, the protocol steps do not change. The only concern of having multiple D_i's is that the timelocks of the re-routing payments (MHP_1) have to be divided by the number of new parties. In practice, a default timelock of a channel is either 40 or 144 blocks, with one block being published roughly every 10 min [36]. The average transaction confirmation time is not higher than one hour in the last three months (as of Oct. 17, 2022), yet, in the past, it had spikes higher than five days [10]. Thus, we assume the bailout parties can assess a safe timelock value regarding the transaction confirmation time at the moment, and whether they are willing to participate in the protocol with a lower timeout.

Extension II - Partial Re-routing (or Cancellation). Until now, Bailout is defined over the scenario where HTLC_A and HTLC_C of MHP_0 are completely cancelled and MHP_0 is re-routed over the bailout parties. Yet, it is also possible that the payment is partially re-routed and the HTLCs in $\gamma_{A,B}$ and $\gamma_{B,C}$ are updated accordingly. Let amt_{cxl} be the amount that party B aims to re-route via the new path. We can achieve partial re-routing by replacing the amount locked in MHP_1 with amt_{cxl} (instead of the amount in MHP_1). Then, during the cancellation phase, instead of completely cancelling the corresponding HTLCs in $\gamma_{A,B}$ and $\gamma_{B,C}$, we replace HTLC_A and HTLC_C with HTLC_A^{new} and HTLC_C^{new} with the only difference of amount reduction by amt_{cxl}. Hereby, we re-route the amount amt_{cxl} over the channels of bailout parties and keep the remaining in channels $\gamma_{A,B}$ and $\gamma_{B,C}$.

3.2   The Phases of Bailout

In [21], we give the protocol, Π_{BO} in the UC framework. Here, we explain the phases of Bailout: *Setup and Lock, Cancellation* and *Pay and Reroute.*

First, we should discuss the path of new multi-hop payments. The protocol requires existence of bailout parties, D_i's, that connect A and C. Here, finding an alternative path is not sufficient, it is also necessary that all channels on the new path have sufficient funds and the new bailout parties charge a fee that is acceptable. Also, as mentioned in the previous section, the more parties are involved, the lower the timelock values are. Thus, having only one bailout party is preferable to not shortening the timelock values. For completeness, we write the protocol for multiple ones.

Setup and Lock Phase. In this phase, the new MHPs are created and locked wrt. to the initial HTLCs, HTLC_A and HTLC_C. B constructs the new MHPs of length n with $\mathsf{mhpInfo}_1 := (\mathsf{amt}_1, \mathsf{TL}, \mathsf{path})$ and $\mathsf{mhpInfo}_2 := (\mathsf{amt}_2, \mathsf{TL}, \mathsf{path})$ such that:

- $\mathsf{path}[0].\mathsf{payer} = \mathsf{path}[n-1].\mathsf{payee} = B$, $\mathsf{path}[0].\mathsf{payee} = \mathsf{path}[1].\mathsf{payer} = A$, $\mathsf{path}[n-2].\mathsf{payee} = \mathsf{path}[n-1].\mathsf{payer} = C$ and $\mathsf{path}[i].\mathsf{payee} = \mathsf{path}[i+1].\mathsf{payer} = D_i$ for $i \in [1, n-3]$.
- For $i \in [0, n-1]$, $\mathsf{amt}_1[i] := amt_{cxl} \leq amt_C$, and $\mathsf{amt}_2[i] = \sum_{j=i}^{n-1} f_j$ where f_j is the fee of channel $\mathsf{path}[j]$.
- $\mathsf{TL}[0] = TL_A + \Delta$, $\mathsf{TL}[n-1] = TL_C - \Delta$, and for $i \in [1, n-2]$, $\mathsf{TL}[i] = \frac{(n-2-i)}{n-3} \times (TL_A - TL_C) + TL_C$.

B chooses a random value x_B and computes $h_B = \mathcal{H}(x_B)$. Then, B computes the HTLCs of MHP_1 and MHP_2 (for $i \in [0, n-1]$):

$$\mathsf{MHP}_1[i] = (\mathsf{payer}_i \rightarrow \mathsf{payee}_i, \{h, h_B\}, \mathsf{TL}[i], \mathsf{amt}_1[i]),$$
$$\mathsf{MHP}_2[i] = (\mathsf{payer}_i \rightarrow \mathsf{payee}_i, \{h_B\}, \mathsf{TL}[i], \mathsf{amt}_2[i]),$$

where $\mathsf{payer}_i = \mathsf{path}[i].\mathsf{payer}$ and $\mathsf{payee}_i = \mathsf{path}[i].\mathsf{payee}$.

Once the HTLCs are created, starting from $i = 0$ to $n - 1$, each channel of $\mathsf{path}[i]$ is locked with both $\mathsf{MHP}_1[i]$ and $\mathsf{MHP}_2[i]$. In the locking phase, parties follow the standard Lightning MHP locking procedure with the only difference being the two parallel HTLCs. If there is failure in any of them, the parties do not continue. Once both MHPs are successfully locked, the phase is completed.

Cancellation Phase. In this phase, B updates his channels with both parties $P \in \{A, C\}$ by (partially or fully) canceling the existing HTLCs and unlocking the coins in his channels. B updates his channels $\gamma_{A,B}$ and $\gamma_{B,C}$. To ensure balance security of B, both channels are updated atomically. Also, the new states of both channels should not be publishable on the blockchain until the old ones are revoked. Otherwise, an old state of one channel (e.g., $\gamma_{A,B}$) and a new state of the other channel ($\gamma_{B,C}$) can be published. To achieve this, we use the idea presented in [4] where the updated states have an additional timelock condition. This additional timelock gives enough time for B to make sure that the previous state of both channels are revoked. If not, then he can publish the old states of both channels before the timelocks of the new states.

Another atomicity is required in the channel update of $\gamma_{B,C}$. The update of the channel $\gamma_{B,C}$ and revealing of x_B should be atomic. On the one hand, B should not share x_B with C before updating their channel. Otherwise, a malicious C can stop the update, and if x is revealed between $\mathsf{MHP}_1[n-1].TL$ and $\mathsf{MHP}_1[2].TL$, C can get paid by B from HTLC_C of MHP_0 without paying $\mathsf{MHP}_1[n-1]$. On the other hand, C should not update the channel without learning x_B. Otherwise, if a malicious B does not share x_B, then C might pay for MHP_0 when receiving x (assuming C is not the receiver of MHP_0), but cannot claim the payment from D_{n-3} in $\mathsf{MHP}_1[n-2]$. For that reason, we have an additional condition payment HTLC'_C that updates the channel where B needs to reveal x_B to claim his coins with the timelock of $\mathsf{MHP}_1[n-1].TL$:

$$\mathsf{HTLC}'_C \leftarrow (C \to B, h_B, TL_C - \Delta, amt_C) \tag{1}$$

where Δ is the time required to publish a transaction on the ledger. It is important to note that, unlike other HTLCs, the amount amt_C in HTLC'_C is not deducted from C, but B, which is the released amount in HTLC_C. It is better to interpret HTLC'_C as a conditional payment that uses collateral of B, and B can re-claim it by revealing x_B, otherwise, it goes to C after the timelock period.

For the channel $\gamma_{B,C}$, there are three existing HTLCs: HTLC_C has condition h for the amount of amt_C from B to C, $\mathsf{MHP}_1[n-1]$ has conditions $\{h, h_B\}$ for the amount of amt_{cxl} from C to B and $\mathsf{MHP}_2[n-1]$ has condition $\{h_B\}$ for the amount of f_{n-1} from C to B. For full cancellation where the amounts are the same, i.e., $amt_C = amt_{cxl}$, B and C update $\gamma_{B,C}$ by canceling HTLC_C and $\mathsf{MHP}_1[n-1]$, and locking HTLC'_C. Otherwise, for partial cancellation where $amt_C > amt_{cxl}$, parties additionally lock HTLC^{new}_C where $\mathsf{HTLC}^{new}_C := (B \to C, h, TL_C, amt_C - amt_{cxl})$.

For the channel $\gamma_{A,B}$, there are also three ongoing HTLCs: HTLC$_A$ has condition h for the amount of amt_A from A to B, MHP$_1[0]$ has conditions $\{h, h_B\}$ for the amount of amt_C from B to A and MHP$_2[0]$ has condition $\{h_B\}$ for the amount of $\sum_{j=0}^{n-1} f_j$ from B to A. For full cancellation, since atomic reveal of x_B is not necessary for A, A and B will update $\gamma_{A,B}$ by canceling HTLC$_A$ and MHP$_1[0]$. Here, the difference of cancelling HTLC$_A$ and MHP$_1[0]$, $amt_A - amt_C$, can be seen as an additional fee gain for A. For partial cancellation, parties lock HTLC$_A^{new}$ where HTLC$_A^{new}:=(A \rightarrow B, h, TL_A, amt_A - amt_{cxl})$.

In the honest case where both channels of B are updated, B can reveal x_B to C and update their transitory state by unlocking HTLC$_C'$ and receiving payment MHP$_2[n-1]$. Here, B can also share x_B with A and execute MHP$_2[0]$.

If a malicious A or C does not complete the channel update, then B publishes the previous state of both channels, which includes the pending HTLCs of MHP$_0$, MHP$_1$ and MHP$_2$. Then, B does not reveal x_B and waits until the end of all timelocks that require x_B. For the initial HTLCs, HTLC$_A$ and HTLC$_C$, he follows the standard HTLC protocol. Hence, even if A and/or C are malicious, B doesn't lose any funds.

Pay and Reroute. In this phase, the bailout parties get paid by MHP$_2$ once B reveals x_B. Here, parties follow the standard MHP payment procedure. Also, the intermediaries update the locking condition of MHP$_1$ by eliminating h_B there. For each $i \in [1, n-2]$, MHP$_1[i]$ is updated with

$$\text{MHP}_1^{new}[i] = (\text{payer}_i \rightarrow \text{payee}_i, h, \text{TL}[i], \text{amt}_1[i]). \tag{2}$$

This implies that MHP$_0$ is re-routed. In the full cancellation case, HTLC$_A$ and HTLC$_C$ are replaced by MHP$_1^{new}[1], \ldots,$ MHP$_1^{new}[n-2]$. In other words, the new payment path goes via $D_1, \ldots, D_{n-3}$, and B is no longer involved in the payment. In partial cancellation case, the locked amounts in channels $\gamma_{A,B}$ and $\gamma_{B,C}$ are reduced by amt_{cxl}, which is now locked in the alternative path.

3.3   Security Discussion

Here, we briefly argue the balance security of the parties. For parties A and C, they are replacing their existing HTLCs of MHP$_0$ with the ones in MHP$_1$ where the timelocks are hash conditions are the same. Thus for them, only the path is changing. For the bailout intermediaries, the balance security mainly relies on the security of MHPs since they are regular intermediaries. For B, the balance security comes from the fact that the new MHPs depend on the secret x_B chosen by him. Thus, if the HTLC updates and the cancellation phase are incomplete, then B can always ignore the new HTLCs since only he has the witness x_B of them. Because of the page limitations, we present the detailed security discussion of the HTLC updates with timelines in [21]. Also, in [21], we provide the ideal functionality $\mathcal{F}_{BO}$ and we show that our protocol Bailout (Π_{BO}) emulates the ideal functionality $\mathcal{F}_{BO}$.

4   Evaluation

We consider the scenario that a party (Bob) wants to go offline and *bailout of all of his payments*. In [21], we also treat the case of a party wanting to bailout to re-gain liquidity. While in the first scenario, the party wants to get out of all ongoing payments, for the second case he only wants to bailout of a subset of payments that allows him to freely use a certain amount of locked funds.

Metrics. Our evaluation is focused on the rate of successful bailouts. For this, we classify the result of a bailout in three categories:

1. *No Loop*: the network does not contain an alternative path that can be used for bailout for at least one of the payments the party aims to bailout from.
2. *Failed*: the party finds an alternative path for all payments but the bailout fails nevertheless, e.g., due to insufficient balance on the alternative paths.
3. *Successful*: the party managed to bailout of all payments.

During a simulation, we count the number of occurrences of each of the above, and the sum of all these three numbers (called *number of bailout events*).

The first possible cause of failure, 'No Loop', results from the topology of the network. Our algorithm does not directly impact the topology, since no new channel is created or deleted during the protocol execution. However, it stands to reason that if parties have the option to use `Bailout`, they ensure that bailout parties are present by establishing channels such that alternative paths exist. Consequently, we expect a lower amount of 'No Loop' cases when our protocol is deployed than for the current Lightning topology, which we use as a model in our evaluation. In order to focus on protocol-related rather than topology-related aspects, we compute the *failure ratio* as $(Failed)/(Successful + Failed)$.

Simulation Model. We implemented the protocol by extending a known simulator, and the code is open-source[3]. We simulate the Lightning Network by using real-world topology snapshots. As 92% of parties use the LND client [36], our simulation implements the routing behavior of LND. Other clients differ slightly in the path selection but otherwise execute the same behavior.

Payments are executed concurrently. For simplicity, we disregard the time required for local operations and only add network latency for the communication. As Lightning only requires relatively fast operations such as encryption and decryption of messages of 1300 bytes as well as hashing [12], the network latency should dominate the local computation time.

Generally, the latency of payments that are properly executed are chosen such that parties do not bailout during this time but only if additional delays happen. In order for parties to use `Bailout`, we consider the following behaviors that cause additional delays:

---

[3] https://github.com/stef-roos/PaymentRouting/tree/bailout.

- *Delaying*: with a certain probability p, an intermediary or receiver delays the payment (e.g., by being offline) until the maximal timeout.
- *Not settling*: a fraction p of intermediaries does not cancel failed payments but rather waits until the timeout expires.

Parameters. We run our simulation on a real-world Lightning snapshot [39]. We restricted our evaluation to the largest connected component with nearly 7,000 nodes and about 65,000 channels to ensure that every node had a path to every other node. For each channel and direction, we choose the balance exponentially with an average of 4 million satoshi, similar to the statistics of Lightning from early 2022 [1]. For the normal Lightning fees, we roughly approximated the statistics as follows: More than 75% of the parties choose a base fee of 0 or 1, so we chose each with a probability of 50%. For the fee rate, the probability to have a rate of 0.000001 was 25%, otherwise the fee rate followed an exponential distribution with parameter $\lambda = 1/0.000004$. We chose the local timelock of each party to be the widely used value of 144 blocks. We generated 100,000 transactions with random source-destination pairs, an exponentially distributed payment value of 10% of the average channel balance, and an average of 10 transactions per party and hour. There is no real-world data on transactions in Lightning as they are considered private. Thus, we took the same parameters as previous work [18]. For the additional delays, i.e., Delaying and Not Settling, p was varied between 0.1 and 0.5 in steps of 0.1. All results were averaged over 10 runs. When the last transaction is initiated, a party B decides that he wants to go offline. He waits 60 s such that any ongoing payments without additional delays can terminate. 60 s was chosen as Lightning payments should terminate within a minute [2]. During the 60 s, he no longer forwards new payments. After the 60 s, he attempts to bailout of all remaining payments. For simplicity, we assume that bailout parties are not paid fees here, but we consider them in [21].

The party aiming to use `Bailout` considers each ongoing payment and first determines a list of alternative paths for the payment. The discovery of alternative paths works as follows: We initialize a queue containing paths, with the first path in the queue being a path containing only the party A, i.e., the party preceding the party B that aims to go offline. We want to find loop-free path from A to B's successor C, which does not contain B. In each step of the path discovery algorithm, we remove the first path from the queue. We iterate over all neighbors I of the last node in the path. If $I = C$, we extend the path by I and add it to the list of alternative paths. Otherwise, if I is not B and appending it to the path does not create a loop, we add the path with I appended to the queue. For efficiency reasons, we limit the alternative path length to at most 4 and the maximal queue size to 1000. If no alternative paths are found, we record 'No Loop' to note that the bailout failed due to the absence of alternative paths.

After determining a list of alternative paths, the party checks whether he can bailout of the payment using one or several of the alternative paths. Concretely, we consider the first path and determine the amount of funds that can be sent via it in accordance with the balance constraints. If the balance is sufficient to take over the complete payment value, we bailout out of the payment by moving the value to this alternative paths. Note that the balance of the path is accordingly reduced. Otherwise, we split the payment value and execute `Bailout` for the amount that can be moved to the alternative path. For the remaining funds, we consider the second path found, for which we repeat the same process. We continue the algorithm until we have either moved all funds to another path or there are no alternative paths left. In the later case, the bailout fails.

The party executes the above process for all ongoing payments he is an intermediary for. Note that the party can only go offline if he can bailout of all these payments. Thus, we mark the bailout as 'Successful' if all separate bailouts are successful. If we experience 'No Loop' for any of them, we terminate and record 'No Loop' as the result of the overall bailout attempt. Otherwise, the bailout is 'Failed'. We count the number of 'No Loop', 'Failed', and 'Successful' by executing the above bailout protocol for every party that has at least one ongoing payment. Based on these value, we compute the success ratio of bailouts. Note that parties cannot bailout of payments that they are the source off. However, as they do not need to relay a preimage to their predecessor when they are the source, these payments do not prevent them from going offline, so that we do not consider them in the set of ongoing payments.

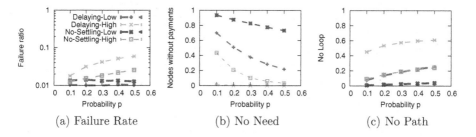

Fig. 3. a) Failure ratio for bailing out of all ongoing payments; b)+c) Fraction of parties that do not attempt to bailout because they b) do not have ongoing payments or c) do not have an alternative path.

As concurrency has a major impact on the number of ongoing payments, we consider a low-concurrency and a high-concurrency scenario. In the former, a party on average sends 0.04 transactions per hour, or roughly 1 transaction per day. In the latter, parties send an average of 10 transactions per hour.

Results. Figure 3a shows the failure ratio. Note that since few payments fail, the figure uses a log scale. High concurrency indicates that at any time, there is more collateral locked and hence the probability that an alternative path has sufficient collateral is lower. Furthermore, *Delaying* can be executed during any payment and by any party whereas *Not Settling* only happens when payments fail, which is less frequent. As a consequence, there are less ongoing payments to bail out for *Not Settling*, resulting in a lower failure ratio.

The main difference between the various parameter selections lies in the number of parties that attempt to bailout. Parties may not attempt a bailout because they do not need to as they have no ongoing payments or because they cannot find an alternative path. Thus, we divide the parties in the snapshot in four classes: 'No Loop', 'Successful', and 'Failed', as defined in Sect. 4, as well as 'No Need', the parties without ongoing payments. Figures 3b and 3c show the fraction of parties that all fall into the 'No Need' and 'No Loop' category, respectively. As there are more concurrent payments and a higher probability of delay, more parties have ongoing payments and consequently, the fraction of parties not discovering an alternative path increases. In particular, when few parties have ongoing parties, ongoing payments mainly affect central parties with a large number of links. These parties can easily find alternative paths. As more parties are affected, parties with few connections that are not part of any loops have ongoing payments as well. Establishing channels such that alternative paths are possible is hence an important aspect when aiming to use `Bailout`. We can see that as long as alternative paths exist, `Bailout` is nearly always successful.

5   Related Work

There have been several works on the different channel constructions: Lightning channels [38], generalized channels [3,17], and virtual channels [4,6,15,16,23,25]. A network of channels can be used for atomic multi-channel updates and multi-hop payments over parties who do not have a direct channel [5,18,19,32,35,38].

An important aspect regarding multi-hop payments concerns the channel balances. The balance in each side of a channel determines the usability of that channel in a multi-hop payment in that direction. Thus, if a channel is depleted in one direction, then that direction cannot be used for multi-hop payments. There have been studies on reducing depletion by (i) *active re-balancing* with circular payments [9,28,37,42], and (ii) *passive re-balancing* with fees and incentive mechanisms [13,20,41]. It is also possible to change the capacity, and thereby the balance, of a channel by Loop-in and Loop-out protocols [27], which require on-chain transactions. Recently, Spider [40] has been proposed to improve channel balances and network throughput. It utilizes a packet-switched architecture that allows splitting transactions into smaller units for better load balancing. These re-balancing protocols re-locate the available (unlocked) coins in the channels, yet they do not solve the unavailability of locked coins.

The existing multi-hop payment protocols require locking coins in each channel in the path for a period of time, which can be days. The coins can be unlocked if the payment is completed (with success or honest immediate cancellation). However, the locking period can be abused by griefing and congestion attacks [29,36,43], which lock the available balances in the channels, and limit their usability for the period of time. The attacks can be against the whole network or some specific parties/channels. The effect of the griefing attack can be reduced by changing the path selection algorithm [43], limiting the number of hops [36], or decreasing the locked time [5,35]. Also, recently, an alternative HTLC protocol with a griefing-penalty mechanism is proposed [33], which requires the receiving parties (payees) to lock coins as well, which are paid in the case of griefing. With this mechanism, the budget of executing the griefing attack is increased by a factor of 4 for a path length of 4. Note that all these (partial) countermeasures are *preventive*, i.e., they aim to reduce the effect of the attack before the payment is locked. To the best of our knowledge, there was no *reactive* countermeasure that frees (unlocks) the locked coins of a party from an ongoing multi-hop payment.

Watchtowers [7,8,14,24,26,34] address the issue of offline parties for single payment channels. In a single channel, one party may publish an invalid balance on the blockchain with the goal of earning more coins than their actual balance. Then, the other party has to publish a dispute including the correct balance within a certain time. In a watchtower protocol, the responsibility of raising a dispute is delegated to third party. However, watchtowers are not designed for relaying multi-hop payments as they are observing the blockchain rather than local payments. Indeed, multi-hop payments aim for *value privacy* [30,31], meaning that no party not involved in the payment should learn the payment value, which seems to contradict the involvement of an outside party.

Acknowledgements. This work has been partially supported by Madrid regional government as part of the program S2018/TCS-4339 (BLOQUES-CM) co-funded by EIE Funds of the European Union; by grant IJC2020-043391-I/MCIN/AEI/10.13039/501100011033; by PRODIGY Project (TED2021-132464 B-I00) funded by MCIN/AEI/10.13039/501100011033/ and the European Union NextGenerationEU/PRTR; and by Ripple's University Blockchain Research Initiative. The Distributed ASCI supercomputer (https://www.cs.vu.nl/das5/) was used to run the experiments.

References

1. Lightning network statistics. https://1ml.com/statistics
2. Antonopoulos, A.M.: Mastering Bitcoin: Programming the Open Blockchain. O'Reilly Media, Inc., Boston (2017)
3. Aumayr, L.: Generalized channels from limited blockchain scripts and adaptor signatures. In: Tibouchi, M., Wang, H. (eds.) ASIACRYPT 2021. LNCS, vol. 13091, pp. 635–664. Springer, Cham (2021). https://doi.org/10.1007/978-3-030-92075-3_22
4. Aumayr, L., et al.: Bitcoin-compatible virtual channels. In: IEEE SP (2021)
5. Aumayr, L., Moreno-Sanchez, P., Kate, A., Maffei, M.: Blitz: secure multi-hop payments without two-phase commits. In: USENIX Security Symposium (2021)
6. Aumayr, L., Moreno-Sanchez, P., Kate, A., Maffei, M.: Donner: utxo-based virtual channels across multiple hops. IACR Cryptol. ePrint Arch., p. 855 (2021)
7. Avarikioti, G., Laufenberg, F., Sliwinski, J., Wang, Y., Wattenhofer, R.: Towards secure and efficient payment channels. In: FC (2018)
8. Avarikioti, Z., Litos, O.S.T., Wattenhofer, R.: Cerberus channels: incentivizing watchtowers for bitcoin. In: FC (2020)
9. Awathare, N., Suraj, Akash, Ribeiro, V.J., Bellur, U.: REBAL: channel balancing for payment channel networks. In: MASCOTS, pp. 1–8. IEEE (2021)

10. Blockchain.com: average confirmation time (2022). https://www.blockchain.com/charts/avg-confirmation-time
11. Community, L.N.: Lighning network specification. https://github.com/lightning/bolts/blob/master/02-peer-protocol.md#rationale-7
12. Community, L.N.: Lightning network specification. https://lightning-bolts.readthedocs.io/en/latest/
13. Conoscenti, M., Vetrò, A., Martin, J.C.D.: Hubs, rebalancing and service providers in the lightning network. IEEE Access **7**, 132828–132840 (2019)
14. Dryja, T., Milano, S.B.: Unlinkable outsourced channel monitoring. Scaling Bitcoin Milan (2016)
15. Dziembowski, S., Eckey, L., Faust, S., Hesse, J., Hostáková, K.: Multi-party virtual state channels. In: Ishai, Y., Rijmen, V. (eds.) EUROCRYPT 2019. LNCS, vol. 11476, pp. 625–656. Springer, Cham (2019). https://doi.org/10.1007/978-3-030-17653-2_21
16. Dziembowski, S., Eckey, L., Faust, S., Malinowski, D.: Perun: virtual payment hubs over cryptocurrencies. In: IEEE SP (2019)
17. Dziembowski, S., Faust, S., Hostáková, K.: General state channel networks. In: CCS, pp. 949–966. ACM (2018)
18. Eckey, L., Faust, S., Hostáková, K., Roos, S.: Splitting payments locally while routing interdimensionally. IACR Cryptol. ePrint Arch. **2020**, 555 (2020)
19. Egger, C., Moreno-Sanchez, P., Maffei, M.: Atomic multi-channel updates with constant collateral in bitcoin-compatible payment-channel networks. In: CCS (2019)
20. van Engelshoven, Y., Roos, S.: The merchant: avoiding payment channel depletion through incentives. In: DAPPS, pp. 59–68. IEEE (2021)
21. Ersoy, O., Moreno-Sanchez, P., Roos, S.: Get me out of this payment! bailout: an htlc re-routing protocol (full version). Cryptology ePrint Archive, Paper 2022/958 (2022). https://eprint.iacr.org/2022/958
22. Gudgeon, L., Moreno-Sanchez, P., Roos, S., McCorry, P., Gervais, A.: SoK: layer-two blockchain protocols. In: Bonneau, J., Heninger, N. (eds.) FC 2020. LNCS, vol. 12059, pp. 201–226. Springer, Cham (2020). https://doi.org/10.1007/978-3-030-51280-4_12
23. Jourenko, M., Larangeira, M., Tanaka, K.: Lightweight virtual payment channels. In: CANS (2020)
24. Khabbazian, M., Nadahalli, T., Wattenhofer, R.: Outpost: a responsive lightweight watchtower. In: ACM AFT (2019)
25. Kiayias, A., Litos, O.S.T.: Elmo: recursive virtual payment channels for bitcoin. IACR Cryptol. ePrint Arch., p. 747 (2021)
26. Lab, T.M.D.C.I..M.: Watchtower - watch channels for fraudulent transactions (2018). https://github.com/mit-dci
27. Labs, L.: Loop. https://lightning.engineering/loop/
28. Li, P., Miyazaki, T., Zhou, W.: Secure balance planning of off-blockchain payment channel networks. In: INFOCOM, pp. 1728–1737. IEEE (2020)
29. Lu, Z., Han, R., Yu, J.: General congestion attack on HTLC-based payment channel networks. IACR Cryptol. ePrint Arch., p. 456 (2020)
30. Malavolta, G., Moreno-Sanchez, P., Kate, A., Maffei, M.: Silentwhispers: enforcing security and privacy in credit networks. In: NDSS (2017)
31. Malavolta, G., Moreno-Sanchez, P., Kate, A., Maffei, M., Ravi, S.: Concurrency and privacy with payment-channel networks. In: ACM CCS (2017)
32. Malavolta, G., Moreno-Sanchez, P., Schneidewind, C., Kate, A., Maffei, M.: Anonymous multi-hop locks for blockchain scalability and interoperability. In: NDSS (2019)

33. Mazumdar, S., Banerjee, P., Ruj, S.: Griefing-penalty: countermeasure for griefing attack in lightning network. arXiv preprint arXiv:2005.09327 (2020)

34. McCorry, P., Bakshi, S., Bentov, I., Meiklejohn, S., Miller, A.: Pisa: arbitration outsourcing for state channels. In: ACM AFT (2019)

35. Miller, A., Bentov, I., Bakshi, S., Kumaresan, R., McCorry, P.: Sprites and state channels: payment networks that go faster than lightning. In: FC (2019)

36. Mizrahi, A., Zohar, A.: Congestion attacks in payment channel networks. In: Borisov, N., Diaz, C. (eds.) FC 2021. LNCS, vol. 12675, pp. 170–188. Springer, Heidelberg (2021). https://doi.org/10.1007/978-3-662-64331-0_9

37. Pickhardt, R., Nowostawski, M.: Imbalance measure and proactive channel rebalancing algorithm for the lightning network. In: IEEE ICBC, pp. 1–5. IEEE (2020)

38. Poon, J., Dryja, T.: The bitcoin lightning network: scalable off-chain instant payments (2016). https://lightning.network/lightning-network-paper.pdf

39. roher: discharged-pc-data (github project). https://git.tu-berlin.de/rohrer/discharged-pc-data/

40. Sivaraman, V., et al.: High throughput cryptocurrency routing in payment channel networks. In: NSDI, pp. 777–796. USENIX Association (2020)

41. Stasi, G.D., Avallone, S., Canonico, R., Ventre, G.: Routing payments on the lightning network. In: iThings/GreenCom/CPSCom/SmartData. IEEE (2018)

42. Subramanian, L.M., Eswaraiah, G., Vishwanathan, R.: Rebalancing in acyclic payment networks. In: PST, pp. 1–5. IEEE (2019)

43. Tochner, S., Zohar, A., Schmid, S.: Route hijacking and dos in off-chain networks. In: AFT, pp. 228–240. ACM (2020)

Extras and Premiums: Local PCN Routing with Redundancy and Fees

Yu Shen[1(✉)], Oğuzhan Ersoy[1,2], and Stefanie Roos[1]

[1] Delft University of Technology, Delft, The Netherlands
{y.shen-5,s.roos}@tudelft.nl
[2] Radboud University, Nijmegen, The Netherlands
oguzhan.ersoy@ru.nl

Abstract. Payment channel networks (PCNs) are a promising solution to the blockchain scalability problem. In PCNs, a sender can route a multi-hop payment to a receiver via intermediaries. Yet, Lightning, the only prominent payment channel network, has two major issues when it comes to multi-hop payments. First, the sender decides on the path without being able to take local capacity restrictions into account. Second, due to the atomicity of payments, any failure in the path causes a failure of the complete payment. In this work, we propose **F**orward-**U**pdate-**Fi**nalize (FUFi): The sender adds redundancy to a locally routed payment by initially committing to sending a higher amount than the actual payment value. Intermediaries decide on how to forward a received payment, potentially splitting it between multiple paths. If they cannot forward the total payment value, they may reduce the amount they forward. If paths for sufficient funds are found, the receiver and sender jointly select the paths and amounts that will actually be paid. Payment commitments are updated accordingly and fulfilled. In order to guarantee atomicity and correctness of the payment value, we use a modified Hashed Time Lock Contract (HTLC) for paying that requires both the sender and the receiver to provide a secret preimage. FUFi furthermore is the first local routing protocol to include fees and specify a fee policy to intermediaries on how to determine their fair share of fees. We prove that the proposed protocol achieves all key security properties of multi-hop payments. Furthermore, our evaluation on both synthetic and real-world Lightning topologies shows FUFi outperforms existing algorithms in terms of fraction of successful payments by about 10%.

1 Introduction

Payment channel networks (PCNs) enable blockchain scalability by increasing the throughput of transactions and reducing latency, and fees [14]. They move payments off-chain, i.e., not all payments have to be included in the blockchain. Thus, they do not require that every payment is broadcast to all participants and verified by them.

© International Financial Cryptography Association 2024
F. Baldimtsi and C. Cachin (Eds.): FC 2023, LNCS 13951, pp. 110–127, 2024.
https://doi.org/10.1007/978-3-031-47751-5_7

Two parties fund a payment channel by depositing coins into a joined account using a blockchain transaction, and then they can make direct transactions in the channel [4]. Opening such a channel only pays off for frequent transaction partners due to the need for the initial blockchain transaction. If a sender S wants to send funds to a receiver R without having a direct channel, they can route the funds via multiple existing channels. For instance if both S and R have a channel with P, P can act as intermediary. It is important that both the channel between S and P and the one between P and R have sufficient funds [17].

Designing routing algorithms to find sufficiently funded paths between senders and receivers successfully and swiftly is thus the key for a usable PCN. In the literature, there are two types of routing algorithms: source routing, in which the sender decides on the path, and local routing, where intermediaries decide on which neighbor they forward the payment to. Lightning, Bitcoin's PCN, uses source routing: The sender determines one path to the receiver based on a publicly available snapshot of the network topology [14]. However, the snapshot does not include the exact amount of funds available in each channel. So payments may fail due to channels in the path having insufficient funds.

There are approaches for the sender to split payments into multiple subpayments, each routed via a different path [13,20]. Smaller payments are less likely to exceed the amount of available funds in a channel and congestion information can be utilized to determine the most suitable paths [20]. Yet, if only one channel in one path has insufficient funds, the payment fails. You can retry the payment using different paths and splits of the total payment amount but it might take a large number of tries until you find a distribution of funds on paths that works. Boomerang [3] adds redundancy to the payment, i.e., the sender initially sends more funds than the actual payment value. In this manner, some failures along individual paths do not result in the overall payment failing. If more than the payment value arrive at the receiver, they are returned to the sender.

Boomerang mitigates the lack of knowledge about local distributions of funds but does not fundamentally address it. In contrast, local routing protocols leave the decision of how to find a path to the intermediaries of a payment, who are clearly aware of the amount of funds in their channels [6,17]. However, failures are still possible if the routing ends up at a node that does not have any outgoing channels with sufficient funds. So, redundancy should be included here as well. Applying Boomerang is possible, however, it requires that the sender splits the payment whereas local routing protocols leave the splitting to intermediaries [6]. In addition, intermediaries typically receive a fee to incentivize participation. In source routing, the sender can compute the required fee as they know the path or paths but in local routing, the sender cannot know the fee in advance and it is challenging to find a suitable algorithm for fee computation. So, local routing due to its awareness of local constraints is more suitable for PCNs than source routing but the existing local routing algorithms are not useful in practice due to their lack of redundancy and incentives.

We here address both issues by presenting **Forward-Update-Finalize(FUFi)**. We integrate fees into local routing by having the sender add a separate amount dedicated to fees to each payment, which they compute based on the expected number of intermediaries. Intermediaries know how much of the payment they receive is dedicated to fees and can then subtract an amount as their own fees. We suggest but do not enforce a policy on how to choose the amount, which provides more fees to the parties early on in the path who take a higher risk as they need to lock up funds for longer than parties close to the receiver. While we do not enforce the policy as such, taking more funds than suggested results in insufficient fees for successors on the path who then do not forward the payment. If a payment fails, no fees are paid, so nodes are disincentivized from deviating from the fee policy.

For redundancy in FUFi, the sender increases the payment amount by a factor r. Intermediaries may then reduce the amount they forward. Concretely, when an intermediary receives amount a to **forward**[1], they determine a set of neighbors that can provide them with a path to the receiver. If the amount a can be split between these neighbors, the intermediary splits the amount a; otherwise, a smaller amount is split. In the first phase of routing, only commitments are made to pay the respective amounts but payments and amounts are not yet finalized. Once sufficient funds reach the receiver, commitments are **updated** such that incoming funds (minus fees) at an intermediaries match the outgoing funds and any redundant funds are returned to the sender. In order to ensure updated commitments, parties are incentivized to revoke the old commitment as the alternative is a failed payment, which implies no fees. After the amounts are updated, the payments can be **finalized**. In Lightning, finalization means that the receiver reveals a hash preimage that allows them and all intermediaries to claim their funds. However, with redundancy present, a rational receiver should reveal the secret before updating to gain additional funds. To prevent this loss of funds, the sender needs to also provide a second hash preimage, which they only provide once all commitments are updated.

We prove that intermediaries do not lose any funds by participating in FUFi, the sender only loses the original payment value plus fees, and the payment terminates. Furthermore, the sender loses funds only if they obtain a signed receipt of the receiver. In turn, if the receiver provides a receipt, they are indeed paid. To show that FUFi indeed achieves better performance than state-of-the-art routing algorithms, we extend an existing payment channel network simulator. Our results on both real-world Lightning snapshots and synthetic topologies indicates that a redundancy factor $r = 1.8$ achieves the best results. Furthermore, for such redundancy values, FUFi improves upon Boomerang and the local routing protocol Interdimensional SpeedyMurmurs [6] by about 10% in terms of fraction of successful payments.

---

[1] so a is the amount after they subtracted their fees.

2   Background and Related Work

In this section, we first provide the necessary background on PCNs and the routing of the payments. Then, we discuss closely related works on routing protocols.

2.1   Payment Channel Networks

A payment channel allows two parties to exchange transactions without publishing them on the blockchain [9]. First, two parties open a channel by publishing a funding transaction on the blockchain. Then, they can send and receive coins by exchanging authenticated messages to update the channel state. Assume in a channel between v_1 and v_2, v_1 contributes c_1 and v_2 contributes c_2 coins. Then v_1 can send up to c_1 coins to P_2 locally. After sending a coins, v_1 can now still send $c_1 - a$ coins but there are more coins available for v_2, mainly $c_2 + a$. We call $c = c_1 + c_2$ the capacity of the channel. The balance in the direction of v_1 to v_2 is the maximum amount that can be sent by v_1 and changes with every local payment. Later on, parties can close the channel by publishing the latest state of the channel on the blockchain. Disputes about the balance are also handled on the blockchain.

A payment channel network (PCN) allows parties (nodes) who do not have a direct channel (edge) to make payments by using the channels in the network. In such a *multi-hop payment* (MHP), the payment between the sender and the receiver is forwarded via a path of connected channels [2,8,12,14,23,24]. The Lightning Network [14], a PCN on top of Bitcoin, realizes MHPs via Hash-Time-Locked-Contracts (HTLCs). A HTLC between a payer and a payee is defined wrt. a payment amount a, a hash value h and a timelock t, and implements the following two logical conditions:

1. If a value x is given such that $H(x) = h$ (where H is a hash function), then the payee can claim the a coins.
2. If t has expired, then the payer can claim the a coins.

An HTLC-based MHP works as follows: First, the receiver chooses a random value x shares $h = H(x)$ with the sender. Then, each channel on the path (from the sender to the receiver) locks coins wrt. hash condition h, corresponding payment value (plus fee), and a timelock. The first of two subsequent nodes on the path acts a the payer and the second as the payee for the HTLC. Once the last channel has locked coins, the receiver reveals the value x to the last intermediary in the path and claims the payment amount. The last intermediary shares the same x with the previous party and obtains the corresponding amount of coins in their channel. This continues until the sender has paid the first intermediary.

Routing protocols find a path between a sender and a receiver. In Lightning, the sender decides on the path based on snapshot of the network topology [21]. Apart from the nodes and edges/channels, the snapshot includes the following information per channel: the fee policy, i.e., how to determine the fee claimed by the nodes for a given payment value, the timelock t that the nodes in the channel want to use for a HTLC, and the capacity c. Based on the provided information, the sender determines a least costly path. The cost function used to evaluate the cost of a path differs between Lightning clients [22].

We abstract payment channel functionalities through APIs. Possible realizations of these APIs are discussed in [6], including realizations that can be instantiated over Bitcoin. Different parties can call those APIs to communicate and make payments. We use four APIs for different events:

- *cPay* is called when a party wants to establish an HTLC with a neighbor. Unlike the HTLC of Lightning Network, two hashes are passed to cPay as our payments require both the agreement of the sender and the receiver to be finalized, as detailed below.
- *updateHTLC* is called when a party wants to modify the amount locked in a HTLC.[2] Modifying the payment amount can be necessary to remove redundancy after paths have been found.
- *cPay-unlock* is called when a party provides the two preimages of an HTLC and wants to unlock the funds in this HTLC.
- *refund* is used if the time-lock expires and a party wants to have their locked coins returned.

For simplicity, we denote the calling to an API as $API \longrightarrow F$ where F is a Turning machine that implements those APIs. Yu Shen's master thesis [19] gives the formal descriptions of the APIs.

2.2   State-of-the-Art PCN Routing Protocols

To improve the success ratio of multi-hop payments, there have been several works that can be divided into two categories: splitting the payment amount [13, 20] with redundancy [3,15] and local routing [5,6,17]. Here, we briefly explain the most important state-of-the-art protocols.

AMP [13]: The Atomic Multi-Path payment (AMP) protocol allows a sender to forward a payment through multiple paths to improve the success ratio of Lightning's single-path HTLCs. Since the payment is divided into smaller amounts, the probability of having sufficient funds is higher for one channel. However, if any channel involved in the payment does not have a positive balance, the payment still fails.

Boomerang [3]: Boomerang extends the AMP protocol by adding redundancy to payments. Concretely, Boomerang makes k sub-payments of an equal amount b such that $k \cdot b > a$ for payment amount a. Thus, even if some of the sub-payments fail, the amount reaching the receiver may still be sufficient. Boomerang ensures that receivers cannot claim more than amount a, i.e., any funds reaching the receiver that exceed a are returned to the sender. However, for

---

[2] We introduce *updateHTLC* API since FUFi allows parties to modify the locked amount in the update phase. The realization of *updateHTLC* can be done by simply revoking the existing HTLC while creating the new one in the same channel update.

the protocol to work, all sub-payments have to be of the same size and splitting can only be done by the sender, not by intermediaries.

Spear [15]: Spear, like Boomerang, integrates redundancy into source routing. It is more flexible than Boomerang as it can have sub-payments of varying amounts. Spear uses a modified HTLC to realize the redundancy of payments. Each HTLC has two hash conditions: one chosen by the sender and one chosen by the receiver. Spear still requires that the amount of each sub-payment and the path taken by the payment are fixed by the sender before starting the routing. We use the idea of the two hash conditions in FUFi but only require one hash from the sender for all sub-payments. By using local routing, we enable flexibility and allow parties to adapt the sub-payment amount.

Spider [20]: Spider splits a payment into small sub-payments at the source and forwards them separately. Rather than forwarding these sub-payments at once, a sender can forward them over a longer period of time. During this time, they react to feedback about congestion along the paths used to forward and adjust the rate using a waterfilling algorithm to balance between paths. Communication load and latency are drastically increased and the authors do not provide a concrete method on how to achieve atomicity, i.e., ensure that either all sub-payments are claimed by the receiver or all funds are returned to the sender.

Ethna [5]: Ethna is a local routing protocol that supports payment splitting without atomicity. Intermediaries can split a payment into sub-payments and forward them to different neighbors, and they can decrease the payment amount. In this case, the payment can still be partly completed with a smaller payment size. It is unclear which applications can profit from such partial payments as usually the full payment value is expected for a purchase. Furthermore, Ethna requires smart contract functionality that PCNs over Bitcoin, like the Lightning Network, do not provide.

SpeedyMurmurs [17]: SpeedyMurmurs is a local routing algorithm: It establishes spanning trees in a distributed manner. Intermediaries then locally determine which of their neighbors provide short paths to the receiver based on the spanning tree positions of the neighbors and the receiver. They forward to one neighbor that provides a path to the receiver and has a channel with sufficient balance. If no such channels exist, the routing fails. Splitting at the source is possible but not at intermediaries. The paper only focuses on the routing and does not specify the cryptography used to achieve atomicity.

Splitting Payments Locally [6]: Eckey et al. designed a protocol to enable intermediate nodes to split a payment and still achieve atomicity. They show how the protocol can be integrated into a number of routing protocols, including SpeedyMurmurs. For deciding how much funds to give to each neighbor they present two variants: SplitIfNecessary only locally splits payments if there is no single channel that can handle the payment. SplitClosest minimizes the path length and forwards as much as possible to the neighbor that is closest to the receiver, in terms of the path length in the spanning trees. In contrast to original

SpeedyMurmurs, the paper provides a cryptographic protocol to guarantee that payments are atomic and intermediaries do not lose funds. However, if only one of the split subpayments fails, the complete payment still fails.

3 Our Protocol

After specifying our system and threat model, we first present the protocol without fees. Afterwards, we show how to integrate fees into the protocol.

3.1 System and Threat Model

Let V be the set of nodes in a PCN and $E \subset V \times V$ be the set of channels. We model a PCN as a directed graph $G = (V, E)$ with a capacity function $C \colon V \times E \to \mathbb{R}$. The function C returns the balance in a channel, i.e., $C(v_i, (v_i, v_j))$ gives the available coins of v_i in the channel (v_i, v_j). We assume that there is synchronous communication and the protocol advances in rounds, which correspond to the maximal delay of communication. It takes at Δ rounds to publish information (e.g., disputes) on the chain.

We assume a local internal active adversary, i.e., the adversary can compromise nodes in the network and adapt their behaviour arbitrarily. The attacker cannot observe and control the behaviour of uncompromised parties. They further do not control the network, e.g., they cannot delay messages of uncompromised parties to cause time-locks to expire. The set of corrupted parties is static during the execution of the protocol. The adversary is computationally bounded and hence cannot break cryptographic primitives.

We focus on a rational adversary that aims to gain funds through an attack. Thus, denial-of-service attacks where the adversary refuses to forward payments to undermine the routing without causing other parties to lose funds are not treated here. Such denial-of-service attacks have been evaluated in the context of local routing [25]. We furthermore assume that all parties communicate via secure authenticated channels.

3.2 Security Goals

We now define our security goals. Concretely, we modify the security goals — balance security, bounded loss for the sender, atomicity, and finality — from [6] to include fees. Informally, balance security implies that no honest node, excluding the sender, loses funds during a payment. Bounded loss for the sender means that the sender loses at most the payment value plus any fees paid. Atomicity means that i) the sender only loses funds if they obtain a valid receipt in return and ii) the receiver only provides the sender with a valid receipt if they are paid. Last, finality states that the payment terminates.

The formal definitions of the above properties require us to first define the concept of a receipt formally. Note that in contrast to [6], in line with our "c-Pay" operation, two preimages are used for a receipt. Payments are routed from sender

S to receiver R. We assume a EUF-CMA-secure signature algorithm, which is given by a triple of algorithms $(KGen, Sign, Verify)$ for key generation, signing, and verification, and a preimage-resistant hash function H.

Definition 1. *A receipt is defined as*

$$receipt(S, R, a, h_s, h_r) = Sign_{sk_R}(S, R, a, h_s, h_r) \tag{1}$$

where sk_R is the secret key of the receiver R with pk_R being the corresponding public key, a indicates the payment amount and h_s and h_r are two hash values. We define a validation function validate such that

$$validate(receipt(S, R, a, h_s, h_r)) = true \; iff$$

1. $Verify(pk_R, receipt(S, R, a, h_s, h_r)) = true$
2. *S provides $receipt(S, R, a, h_s, h_r)$, x_s, x_r, where $H(x_s) = h_s$, $H(x_r) = h_r$.*

In our security definitions, we look at the capacity function C before a payment is executed and the function C' after the execution of the payment. For clarity, we here assume that there are no concurrent payments that affect the function C. Our evaluation considers concurrency. Let furthermore B be the set of honest or benign nodes.

Definition 2 (Balance security for intermediaries).
$\forall \; v_i \in B \setminus \{S\}, \quad \sum_{(v_i, v_j) \in E} C'(v_i, (v_i, v_j)) - \sum_{(v_i, v_j) \in E} C(v_i, (v_i, v_j)) \geq 0$

Definition 3 (Bounded lose for sender). *For a payment of amount a with fee f: if $S \in B$, then $\sum_{(S, v_j) \in E} C(S, (S, v_j)) - \sum_{(S, v_j) \in E} C'(S, (S, v_j)) \leq a + f$*

Definition 4 (Atomicity). *For a payment of amount a:*

1. *if $\sum_{(S, v_j) \in E} C'(S, (S, v_j)) - \sum_{(S, v_j) \in E} C(S, (S, v_j)) < 0 \; \wedge S \in B$*
   then $validate(receipt(S, R, size, h_s, h_r)) = true$
2. *if $validate(receipt(S, R, size, h_s, h_r)) = true \; \wedge R \in B$*
   then $\sum_{(R, v_j) \in E} C'(R, (R, v_j)) - \sum_{(R, v_j) \in E} C(R, (R, v_j)) \geq a$

Definition 5 (Finality). *The protocol terminates for all honest parties, i.e., on all locked channels, either "refund" or "cPay-unlock" is eventually executed.*

3.3 Protocol Description

The key idea of FUFi is to forward payments with redundancy and revoke those redundant payments later. For this purpose, we divide the protocol into three phases: Forward, Update, and Finalize. In the forward phase, sender and intermediaries split a payment into several sub-payments and forward them to neighbors until the receiver is reached. In the update phase, intermediaries and the receiver may modify the payment size. Only if the correct payment amount arrives at the receiver, the payment can go through. The update phase is the key difference of FUFi to previous routing algorithms, as it enables the use of redundancy. The last phase, the finalize phase, completes the payment or revokes it. Figure 1 displays an example of the forward and update phase of FUFi, the finalize phase merely executes the red payments that are agreed upon during the update phase. We now go over each of the phases. Detailed pseudocode is given in Yu Shen's thesis [19]. In the following, we refer to HTLCs for which a node is a payee as incoming HTLCs while outgoing HTLCs are those for which they are a payer.

Initialization. Before starting the actual routing, the sender S first uses a random value x_S and sends the hash $h_S = H(x_S)$ to the receiver R. In response, the receiver chooses their own random value x_R and sends the corresponding hash h_R to S. Both preimages are necessary to obtain the funds promised in the HTLCs applied during the finalize phase. Afterwards, S decides on the amount they want to send, which is the payment amount a times a redundancy factor r. Once the amount is fixed, the actual routing of the payment starts.

Forward. During the routing, both sender and intermediaries have to decide which of their neighbours they forward sub-payments to. In [6], multiple methods are proposed for splitting the payment such that the combined amount of all sub-payments equals the total payment value. Since we include redundancy in our payment, FUFi can also proceed if the amounts of the sub-payments sum up to less than the total amount, as the total amount includes redundancy.

We abstract the splitting procedure as follows: A party P — sender or intermediary — calls a function $Route_G(a_P, P, R, aux)$ where a_P is the total amount P wants to forward and aux is any auxiliary information the routing algorithm may require. For instance, Interdimensional SpeedyMurmurs requires the set of nodes that have previously been on the path to prevent routing loops. $Route_G(a_P, P, R, aux)$ returns i) a set of tuples (e_j, a_j), such that e_j indicates a payment channel adjacent to P and a_j the amount to be forwarded via this channel, and ii) an amount a_{Rest} that is not forwarded. We have $a_{Rest} + \sum_j a_j = a_P$, so the payment value is split over adjacent channels with a possible leftover. There are many possible instantiations for $Route_G(a_P, P, R, aux)$, some of which are introduced in Sect. 4 for our evaluation. The function is mostly identical to [6] but in [6], $a_{Rest} = 0$ or the payment fails.

For each (e_j, a_j), P establishes a HTLC for the channel e_j by calling "cPay" stating that P will pay a_j if they receive preimages for h_S and h_R within a certain time. We will discuss how to choose the time-lock at the end of this section. R keeps track of all sub-payments that arrive. If less than the payment amount a arrives, the payment fails. After a HTLC timeouts, all involved parties call "refund" to have their invested funds returned. Otherwise, if enough funds reach R, the payment proceeds to the update phase.

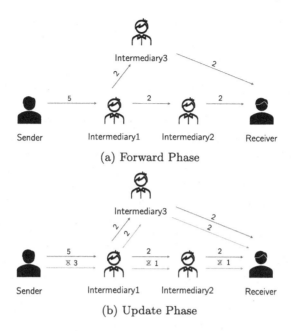

(a) Forward Phase

(b) Update Phase

Fig. 1. Forward and update phase of FUFi. Sender wants to make a payment of value 3 but initially sends 5 (blue). The first intermediary only forwards 4, split into two payments of 2. After 4 coins arrive at the receiver, one payment path has to be updated to only have 1 coin. Red indicates final payment after update. (Color figure online)

Update. The update phase, which is a new phase that none of the previous protocols have, has to deal with the fact that S in the end only agrees to paying a while initially sending $r \cdot a$. S thus only provides the preimage for h_S, which is necessary to complete the payment, if the HTLCs are updated such that S loses at most a coins.

At the end of the forward phase, let $a + \delta$ coins being locked in R's channels. R has to update the HTLCs such that only a coins are locked. They hence select HTLCs whose values are to be reduced. The HTLCs can also be completely cancelled. Any method of choosing which HTLCs to reduce or cancel can be applied as long as the final results restricts the incoming funds from the payment at R to a. For the HTLCs that should be changed, R calls "updateHTLC" to change the locked amount. One straight-forward method that we use in the evaluation is to simply keep the HTLCs that are established first.

Now, for the sender's outgoing HTLCs to have a combined value of a as well, intermediaries have to update their HTLCs. During the update phase, intermediaries check whether the funds they promise in their outgoing HTLCs, i.e., the funds they pay if the payment succeeds, is lower than the amount they are promised to receive from incoming HTLCs. The two may differ for two reasons: i) a successor updated one of the outgoing HTLCs and ii) they were unable to split the total incoming amount among their neighbors in the forward phase.

Independently of the reason, the intermediary updates their incoming HTLCs such that incoming and outgoing funds match. Like for the receiver, the exact protocol used to decide on which HTLCs to update does not matter for the protocol to work. Once the incoming and outgoing funds of all intermediaries match, the HTLCs of S should amount to exactly a because no funds are 'lost' to intermediaries.

The above protocol relies on the fact that intermediaries may not be willing to update the HTLC, an operation that requires the agreement of both payer and payee. In such a case, the funds are not reduced and the payment fails as the sender does not provide their preimage x_S. Intermediaries hence do not gain fees if they refuse to update. Note that they even receive fees if the HTLC is cancelled (e.g., modified to have an amount of 0), as we detail in Sect. 3.4.

Finalize. Once all the HTLCs are updated, the finalize phase completes the payment: S provides the preimage x_S to R. R then provides both x_S and x_R to resolve the HTLCs with their neighbors, which then forward the preimages to their predecessors on the path until all payments have been executed.

Time-Locks. Now, we can discuss the choice of time-locks. For HTLCs, we need to ensure there is enough time for honest parties to update payments and publish their HTLCs on chain in a dispute. It takes $(\Delta + 1)$ rounds for an intermediary to know that its payment is published on chain by neighbours in the worst case. To get money back, this node needs another $(\Delta+1)$ rounds to publish the HTLC with its predecessors on chain. So, if we want to make sure honest nodes have enough time to publish their HTLCs, the difference of time-locks for subsequent nodes on a path should be at least $2 \cdot (\Delta+1)$. Besides the time to publish HTLCs, there is also one round of communication for both establishing the original HTLC and possibly for updating it. Thus, the time-lock set by the sender should be $t_0 + n \cdot (2 + 2 \cdot (\Delta + 1))$ where n is an upper bound on the expected number of nodes on a path, with n depending on the routing algorithm, and t_0 is the current time.

3.4   Fees

In PCNs, nodes are incentivized by fees to participate. Yet, previous local routing protocols disregard fees and how to assign them [6,17]. In the Lightning network, fees are computed in advance and added to the payment amount. However, the computation is only possible as the source decides on the path and knows the fee policies of all nodes. As the paths in local routing are determined by intermediaries, the exact fee cannot be computed in advance. In addition to this known challenge in local routing, FUFi suffers from a second challenge: nodes need to be incentivized to revoke their HTLCs. Such revocation fees need to be paid even if the receiver decides not to use a channel for routing as the nodes would otherwise refuse to revoke and let the payment fail.

We use a relatively simple idea for fees: The sender S decides on an amount f they are willing to pay as fees and then route the amount $a + r + f$ consisting of the actual payment amount, the redundancy, and the maximal fee. Intermediaries learn the amount f and can then decide how much they take as a fee. They forward the remaining fees to the subsequent nodes. If they take a large amount, subsequent nodes may refuse to route the payment due to insufficient compensation, meaning that greedy intermediaries may not receive funds due to the payment failing. Moreover, the more fee they take, the less likely the receiver will choose theirs in the case of receiving more than a amount.

Ersoy et al. [7] analyzed how to determine propagation fees for forwarding transactions in the Bitcoin network. Two requirements defined in their fee policy: i) nodes should not gain more fees by acting maliciously like introducing Sybil nodes, ii) rational nodes should benefit from forwarding. They showed that honest intermediary nodes are incentivized to claim a fraction C of the remaining fee that they receive, and the receiver obtains the remaining part. Here, C is a globally agreed-upon constant. Any remaining fees are taken by the receiver. We apply this fee policy in our evaluation.

Note that the previously discussed fees are only paid upon success. We now discuss the revocation fees. Revocation fees should not exceed the fees for a successful payment to prevent intermediaries from intentionally failing payments. We use a separate transaction with a new HTLC for the same two hash conditions to forward revoke fees. So, two transactions with different temporary secret keys are required for one sub-payment: one for the normal payment and the other one for revoking fees. With this construction, the transaction for revocation fees still exists after the revocation of a normal payment and the node can claim their fee once the preimages are revealed. If a party refuses to revoke, the payment amount exceeds v and the sender S does not provide their preimage, meaning that the party does not gain any fees, not even revocation fees.

We have now specified the phases of our protocol and how it handles fees. Yu Shen's thesis shows that FUFi indeed achieves the claimed security goals [19]. In the security proofs, we prove termination separately for sender, intermediaries, and receiver. For balance security, we note that parties never promise to pay more than they are promised to receive and if they pay, they are also paid. Similarly, for bounded loss for the sender, we argue that the sender does not reveal their preimage unless the bounded loss is guaranteed. Atomicity is argued similarly to [6].

4   Evaluation

We simulate FUFi's performance in a simulator by extending a known PCN simulator[3]. Our simulator[4] executes payments concurrently. We adapt routing algorithms from previous work to include an update phase and compute their success ratio.

---

[3] https://github.com/stef-roos/PaymentRouting.

[4] https://github.com/tokisamu/PaymentRouting.

4.1   Routing Algorithms

The performance of three different routing protocols is compared in our simulations. *SplitClosest* is a local routing protocol with splitting, introduced as a variant of SpeedyMurmurs [6]. It consumes channels' capacities in the order of closeness to the receiver and has been shown to have the best success ratio of all the algorithms evaluated in [6].

A new routing algorithm has been designed for FUFi. Like SplitClosest, it is a variant of SpeedyMurmurs with splitting. It differs from SplitClosest in two aspects: i) it utilizes redundancy and fees as introduced in Sect. 3 and ii) it uses a waterfilling algorithm for splitting the forwarded amount between neighbors that offer a shorter path to the receiver. Concretely, a node splits the payment value to forward such that the available funds in the channels are as close to equal as possible. As stated in Sect. 3, parties may have to update incoming HTLCs. They choose the HTLC in order of arrival, i.e., they prioritise older HTLCs and revoke the ones most recently established. To determine the impact of each of the two changes i) and ii), we also consider SplitClosest with redundancy, i.e., only change i), and FUFi without redundancy, i.e., only change ii). As a third algorithm, we use Boomerang. It is a source routing algorithm with redundancy. In our simulations, we use the parameters that achieved the best performance in the original paper (100 sub-payments redundancy 1.33 [3]).

4.2   Setup

We evaluate the different routing algorithms on a snapshot of the Lightning network and a randomly generated scale-free graph. The Lightning Network snapshot is from December 30, 2021. We delete disconnected nodes and channels without capacity. Then, we obtain a graph with 18081 nodes and 76427 channels. To simulate the size of the Lightning Network in the future, we use the Barabasi-Albert (BA) model [1] to generate the topology of network. BA graph is a scale-free model that means only a few nodes have a high degree, similar to Lightning [16]. We use the BA graph to approximate Lightning in the future, with a larger network size, and generate a graph with 25000 nodes where each new node is connected to 6 existing nodes. Most of channels in the Lightning Network snapshot have a low capacity. To simulate the capacity distribution of the Lightning Network, we use an exponential distribution with an average value of 200 to generate channels' balances in the random graph.

In our simulations, the delay of payment forwarding is set to 10 s and C is set to 0.4. In [7], C is chosen in relation to the average degree of the nodes, which is 9 for the snapshot. $C = 0.4$ has been identified as a good choice for incentivizing intermediaries to forward if the average degree is 9 or higher. For redundancy in FUFi, we consider 1.1, 1.4, and 1.8. In our first experiment, we change the payment amount and simulate 100000 payments in 1000 s. We start from a relatively small payment amount that is smaller than a single channel's capacity on average. To study the impact of payment splitting and redundancy, the payment amount is increased to a larger number that makes payment splitting necessary. For the random graph, the payment size varies from 50 to 400

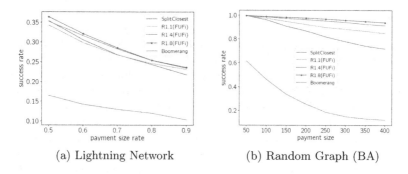

(a) Lightning Network   (b) Random Graph (BA)

Fig. 2. Success rate with different payment sizes

because the expected capacity of a channel is 200. In the Lightning network, the capacity of channels varies a lot. Thus, using a constant payment amount frequently results in the payment amount exceeding the total capacities of outgoing channels of the sender, meaning that the payment fails in the first step regardless of the protocol. To exclude such unavoidable failures, we instead set a payment amount rate $p \in (0, 1)$. When a sender starts a payment, the payment amount is p times the combined balance.

In the second experiment, we simulate 300000 payments in 3000 s and monitor how the success rate changes over time. The payment amount rate of the Lightning Network is 0.8 while the payment amount is set to 400 in the random graph.

Finally, we have an experiment to measure the influence of redundancy and the waterfilling algorithm separately. In this experiment, the redundancy is set to 1.4, payment amount rate of the Lightning Network is 0.8, payment amount of the random graph is 400, and 100000 payments are simulated in 1000 s.

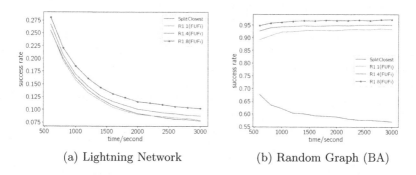

(a) Lightning Network   (b) Random Graph (BA)

Fig. 3. The change of success rate over time

4.3 Simulation Results

Figure 2a and Fig. 2b show the success ratio of different payment amounts. In the Lightning Network, FUFi with 1.8 redundancy improves the success ratio of SplitClosest by about 10%. Boomerang is outperformed by other protocols because it uses a source routing algorithm that can not adapt to the changes of channels' capacities. This result shows the effectiveness of combining local splitting and redundancy. The result of the random graph is similar to the Lightning Network. However, the differences in performance between the protocols are more pronounced, which can be explained by the better connectivity of the random graph. Nodes have more choices to forward and hence the payment is less likely to fail.

Figure 3a shows the success rate over time, which decreases over time in the Lightning Network. However, FUFi's success rate is retained at a higher level than SplitClosest because of the use of waterfilling. SplitClosest tends to use up all the funds in channels to have short paths whereas waterfilling tries to balance the funds. For the random graph, there is no negative impact over time for waterfilling. The higher number of paths enables nodes to better balance their channels and hence avoid depletion, i.e., channels with no or hardly any funds on one direction. For SplitClosest, there still is a negative impact as it does actively deplete channels.

Figure 4 compares the impact of our two changes, with the result that redundancy has more impact than waterfilling, which has no significant impact on Lightning and a smaller impact on the random graph.

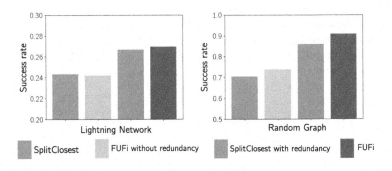

Fig. 4. Impact of redundancy in comparison to varying splitting protocol.

5 Conclusion

We have introduced FUFi, which increases the performance of local routing by about 10% and is the first local routing protocol for PCNs that integrates fees.

Yet, we mainly disregarded the aspect of privacy: Hiding the identity of sender and receiver as well as channel capacities are important privacy properties for PCNs [11]. While Lightning was initially thought to be private, it has been shown that it is vulnerable to multiple attacks [10,18]. The exact attacks are not possible for local routing; yet, it is likely that FUFi is vulnerable to similar attacks. In future work, we thus aim to investigate which privacy attacks are possible, how they affect FUFi, and how to defend against the attacks.

Acknowledgments. This research was partially funded by Ripple's University Blockchain Research Initiative. Experiments were run on the Distributed ASCI super-computer (https://www.cs.vu.nl/das5/).

References

1. Albert, R., Barabási, A.L.: Statistical mechanics of complex networks. Rev. Mod. Phys. **74**, 47–97 (2002). https://doi.org/10.1103/RevModPhys.74.47
2. Aumayr, L., Moreno-Sanchez, P., Kate, A., Maffei, M.: Blitz: secure multi-hop payments without two-phase commits. In: Bailey, M., Greenstadt, R. (eds.) 30th USENIX Security Symposium, USENIX Security 2021, 11–13 August 2021, pp. 4043–4060. USENIX Association (2021). https://www.usenix.org/conference/usenixsecurity21/presentation/aumayr
3. Bagaria, V., Neu, J., Tse, D.: Boomerang: redundancy improves latency and throughput in payment-channel networks. In: Bonneau, J., Heninger, N. (eds.) FC 2020. LNCS, vol. 12059, pp. 304–324. Springer, Cham (2020). https://doi.org/10.1007/978-3-030-51280-4_17
4. Decker, C., Wattenhofer, R.: A fast and scalable payment network with bitcoin duplex micropayment channels. In: Pelc, A., Schwarzmann, A.A. (eds.) SSS 2015. LNCS, vol. 9212, pp. 3–18. Springer, Cham (2015). https://doi.org/10.1007/978-3-319-21741-3_1
5. Dziembowski, S., Kedzior, P.: Ethna: Channel network with dynamic internal payment splitting. IACR Cryptol. ePrint Arch., 166 (2020). https://eprint.iacr.org/2020/166
6. Eckey, L., Faust, S., Hostáková, K., Roos, S.: Splitting payments locally while routing interdimensionally. IACR Cryptol. ePrint Arch., 555 (2020). https://eprint.iacr.org/2020/555
7. Ersoy, O., Ren, Z., Erkin, Z., Lagendijk, R.L.: Transaction propagation on permissionless blockchains: incentive and routing mechanisms. In: Crypto Valley Conference on Blockchain Technology, CVCBT 2018, Zug, Switzerland, 20–22 June 2018, pp. 20–30. IEEE (2018). https://doi.org/10.1109/CVCBT.2018.00008
8. Green, M., Miers, I.: Bolt: anonymous payment channels for decentralized currencies. In: Thuraisingham, B., Evans, D., Malkin, T., Xu, D. (eds.) Proceedings of the 2017 ACM SIGSAC Conference on Computer and Communications Security, CCS 2017, Dallas, TX, USA, October 30 - November 03 2017, pp. 473–489. ACM (2017). https://doi.org/10.1145/3133956.3134093
9. Gudgeon, L., Moreno-Sanchez, P., Roos, S., McCorry, P., Gervais, A.: SoK: layer-two blockchain protocols. In: Bonneau, J., Heninger, N. (eds.) FC 2020. LNCS, vol. 12059, pp. 201–226. Springer, Cham (2020). https://doi.org/10.1007/978-3-030-51280-4_12

10. Herrera-Joancomartí, J., Navarro-Arribas, G., Ranchal-Pedrosa, A., Pérez-Solà, C., Garcia-Alfaro, J.: On the difficulty of hiding the balance of lightning network channels. In: Proceedings of the 2019 ACM Asia Conference on Computer and Communications Security, pp. 602–612 (2019)
11. Malavolta, G., Moreno-Sanchez, P., Kate, A., Maffei, M., Ravi, S.: Concurrency and privacy with payment-channel networks. In: Proceedings of the 2017 ACM SIGSAC Conference on Computer and Communications Security, pp. 455–471 (2017)
12. Malavolta, G., Moreno-Sanchez, P., Schneidewind, C., Kate, A., Maffei, M.: Anonymous multi-hop locks for blockchain scalability and interoperability. In: 26th Annual Network and Distributed System Security Symposium, NDSS 2019, San Diego, California, USA, 24–27 February 2019. The Internet Society (2019). https://www.ndss-symposium.org/ndss-paper/anonymous-multi-hop-locks-for-blockchain-scalability-and-interoperability/
13. Osuntokun, O.: AMP: atomic multi-path payments over lightning. Accessed 06 Feb 2018
14. Poon, J., Dryja, T.: The bitcoin lightning network: scalable off-chain instant payments (2016). https://www.bitcoinlightning.com/wp-content/uploads/2018/03/lightning-network-paper.pdf
15. Rahimpour, S., Khabbazian, M.: Spear: fast multi-path payment with redundancy. In: Baldimtsi, F., Roughgarden, T. (eds.) AFT '21: 3rd ACM Conference on Advances in Financial Technologies, Arlington, Virginia, USA, 26–28 September 2021, pp. 183–191. ACM (2021). https://doi.org/10.1145/3479722.3480997
16. Rohrer, E., Malliaris, J., Tschorsch, F.: Discharged payment channels: quantifying the lightning network's resilience to topology-based attacks. In: 2019 IEEE European Symposium on Security and Privacy Workshops (EuroS&PW), pp. 347–356. IEEE (2019)
17. Roos, S., Moreno-Sanchez, P., Kate, A., Goldberg, I.: Settling payments fast and private: efficient decentralized routing for path-based transactions. In: 25th Annual Network and Distributed System Security Symposium, NDSS 2018, San Diego, California, USA, 18–21 February 2018. The Internet Society (2018). https://wp.internetsociety.org/ndss/wp-content/uploads/sites/25/2018/02/ndss2018_09-3_Roos_paper.pdf
18. Sharma, P.K., Gosain, D., Diaz, C.: On the anonymity of peer-to-peer network anonymity schemes used by cryptocurrencies. arXiv preprint: arXiv:2201.11860 (2022)
19. Shen, Y.: Revoke and update: a more flexible payment protocol for payment channel networks (2022). https://repository.tudelft.nl/islandora/object/uuid:5f9ee6f5-7f8b-4889-80b5-b641f15de9b5
20. Sivaraman, V., Venkatakrishnan, S.B., Alizadeh, M., Fanti, G., Viswanath, P.: Routing cryptocurrency with the spider network. In: Proceedings of the 17th ACM Workshop on Hot Topics in Networks, HotNets 2018, Redmond, WA, USA, 15–16 November 2018, pp. 29–35. ACM (2018). https://doi.org/10.1145/3286062.3286067
21. Sunshine, C.A.: Source routing in computer networks. Comput. Commun. Rev. 7(1), 29–33 (1977). https://doi.org/10.1145/1024853.1024855
22. Tochner, S., Zohar, A., Schmid, S.: Route hijacking and dos in off-chain networks. In: Proceedings of the 2nd ACM Conference on Advances in Financial Technologies, pp. 228–240 (2020)
23. Tripathy, S., Mohanty, S.K.: MAPPCN: multi-hop anonymous and privacy-preserving payment channel network. In: Bernhard, M., et al. (eds.) FC 2020. LNCS, vol. 12063, pp. 481–495. Springer, Cham (2020). https://doi.org/10.1007/978-3-030-54455-3_34

24. Tsabary, I., Yechieli, M., Manuskin, A., Eyal, I.: MAD-HTLC: because HTLC is crazy-cheap to attack. In: 42nd IEEE Symposium on Security and Privacy, SP 2021, San Francisco, CA, USA, 24–27 May 2021, pp. 1230–1248. IEEE (2021). https://doi.org/10.1109/SP40001.2021.00080
25. Weintraub, B., Nita-Rotaru, C., Roos, S.: Structural attacks on local routing in payment channel networks. In: 2021 IEEE European Symposium on Security and Privacy Workshops (EuroS&PW), pp. 367–379. IEEE (2021)

An Efficient Algorithm for Optimal Routing Through Constant Function Market Makers

Theo Diamandis[1](✉)(ID), Max Resnick[2](ID), Tarun Chitra[3](ID),
and Guillermo Angeris[4](ID)

[1] Massachusetts Institute of Technology, Cambridge, USA
tdiamand@mit.edu
[2] Risk Harbor, San Jose, USA
max@riskharbor.com
[3] Gauntlet Networks, New York, USA
tarun@gauntlet.network
[4] Bain Capital Crypto, Boston, USA
gangeris@baincapital.com

Abstract. Constant function market makers (CFMMs) such as Uniswap have facilitated trillions of dollars of digital asset trades and have billions of dollars of liquidity. One natural question is how to optimally route trades across a network of CFMMs in order to ensure the largest possible utility (as specified by a user). We present an efficient algorithm, based on a decomposition method, to solve the problem of optimally executing an order across a network of decentralized exchanges. The decomposition method, as a side effect, makes it simple to incorporate more complicated CFMMs, or even include 'aggregate CFMMs' (such as Uniswap v3), into the routing problem. Numerical results show significant performance improvements of this method, tested on realistic networks of CFMMs, when compared against an off-the-shelf commercial solver.

1 Introduction

Decentralized Finance, or DeFi, has been one of the largest growth areas within both financial technologies and cryptocurrencies since 2019. DeFi is made up of a network of decentralized protocols that match buyers and sellers of digital goods in a trustless manner. Within DeFi, some of the most popular applications are decentralized exchanges (DEXs, for short) which allow users to permissionlessly trade assets. While there are many types of DEXs, the most popular form of exchange (by nearly any metric) is a mechanism known as the constant function market maker, or CFMM. A CFMM is a particular type of DEX which allows anyone to propose a trade (*e.g.*, trading some amount of one asset for another). The trade is accepted if a simple rule, which we describe later in §2.1, is met.

The prevalence of CFMMs on blockchains naturally leads to questions about routing trades across networks or aggregations of CFMMs. For instance, suppose that one wants to trade some amount of asset A for the greatest possible amount of asset B. There could be many 'routes' that provide this trade. For example,

© International Financial Cryptography Association 2024
F. Baldimtsi and C. Cachin (Eds.): FC 2023, LNCS 13951, pp. 128–145, 2024.
https://doi.org/10.1007/978-3-031-47751-5_8

we may trade asset A for asset C, and only then trade asset C for asset B. This routing problem can be formulated as an optimization problem over the set of CFMMs available to the user for trading. Angeris et al. [5] showed that the general problem of routing is a convex program for concave utilities, ignoring blockchain transactions costs, though special cases of the routing problem have been studied previously [13, 22].

This Paper. In this paper, we apply a decomposition method to the optimal routing problem, which results in an algorithm that easily parallelizes across all DEXs. To solve the subproblems of the algorithm, we formalize the notions of swap markets, bounded liquidity, and aggregate CFMMs (such as Uniswap v3) and discuss their properties. Finally, we demonstrate that our algorithm for optimal routing is efficient, practical, and can handle the large variety of CFMMs that exist on chain today.

2   Optimal Routing

In this section, we define the general problem of optimal routing and give concrete examples along with some basic properties.

Assets. In the optimal routing problem, we have a global labeling of n assets which we are allowed to trade, indexed by $j = 1, \ldots, n$ throughout this paper. We will sometimes refer to this 'global collection' as the *universe* of assets that we can trade.

Trading Sets. Additionally, in this problem, we have a number of markets $i = 1, \ldots, m$ (usually constant function market makers, or collections thereof, which we discuss in §2.1) which trade a subset of the universe of tokens of size n_i. We define market i's behavior, at the time of the trade, via its *trading set* $T_i \subseteq \mathbb{R}^{n_i}$. This trading set behaves in the following way: any trader is able to propose a *trade* consisting of a basket of assets $\Delta_i \in \mathbb{R}^{n_i}$, where positive entries of Δ_i denote that the trader receives those tokens from the market, while negative values denote that the trader tenders those tokens to the market. (Note that the baskets here are of a subset of the universe of tokens which the market trades.) The market then *accepts* this trade (*i.e.*, takes the negative elements in Δ_i from the trader and gives the positive elements in Δ_i to the trader) whenever

$$\Delta_i \in T_i.$$

We make two assumptions about the sets T_i. One, that the set T_i is a closed convex set, and, two, that the zero trade is always an acceptable trade, *i.e.*, $0 \in T_i$. All existing DEXs that are known to the authors have a trading set that satisfies these conditions.

Local and Global Indexing. Each market i trades only a subset of n_i tokens from the universe of tokens, so we introduce the matrices $A_i \in \mathbb{R}^{n \times n_i}$ to connect the local indices to the global indices. These matrices are defined such that $A_i \Delta_i$ yields the total amount of assets the trader tendered or received from market i, in the global indices. For example, if our universe has 3 tokens and market i trades the tokens 2 and 3, then

$$A_i = \begin{bmatrix} 0 & 0 \\ 1 & 0 \\ 0 & 1 \end{bmatrix}.$$

Written another way, $(A_i)_{jk} = 1$ if token k in the market's local index corresponds to global token index j, and $(A_i)_{jk} = 0$ otherwise. We note that the ordering of tokens in the local index does not need to be the same as the global ordering.

Network Trade Vector. By summing the net trade in each market, after mapping the local indices to the global indices, we obtain the *network trade vector*

$$\Psi = \sum_{i=1}^{m} A_i \Delta_i.$$

We can interpret Ψ as the net trade across the network of all markets. If $\Psi_i > 0$, we receive some amount of asset i after executing all trades $\{\Delta_i\}_{i=1}^{m}$. On the other hand, if $\Psi_i < 0$, we tender some of asset i to the network. Note that having $\Psi_i = 0$ does not imply we do not trade asset i; it only means that, after executing all trades, we received as much as we tendered.

Network Trade Utility. Now that we have defined the network trade vector, we introduce a utility function $U : \mathbb{R}^n \to \mathbb{R} \cup \{-\infty\}$ that gives the trader's utility of a net trade Ψ. We assume that U is concave and increasing (*i.e.*, we assume all assets have value with potentially diminishing returns). Furthermore, we will use infinite values of U to encode constraints; a trade Ψ such that $U(\Psi) = -\infty$ is unacceptable to the trader. We can choose U to encode several important actions in markets, including liquidating or purchasing a basket of assets and finding arbitrage. See [2, §5.2] for several examples.

Optimal Routing Problem. The *optimal routing problem* is then the problem of finding a set of valid trades that maximizes the trader's utility:

$$\begin{array}{ll} \text{maximize} & U(\Psi) \\ \text{subject to} & \Psi = \sum_{i=1}^{m} A_i \Delta_i \\ & \Delta_i \in T_i, \qquad i = 1, \dots, m. \end{array} \qquad (1)$$

The problem variables are the network trade vector $\Psi \in \mathbb{R}^n$ and trades with each market $\Delta_i \in \mathbb{R}^{n_i}$, while problem data are the utility function $U : \mathbb{R}^n \to \mathbb{R} \cup \{\infty\}$, the matrices $A_i \in \mathbb{R}^{n \times n_i}$, and the trading sets $T_i \subseteq \mathbb{R}^{n_i}$, where $i = 1, \ldots, m$. Since the trading sets are convex and the utility function is concave, this problem is a convex optimization problem. In the subsequent sections, we will use basic results of convex optimization to construct an efficient algorithm to solve problem (1).

2.1 Constant Function Market Makers

Most decentralized exchanges, such as Uniswap v2, Balancer, Curve, among others, are currently organized as *constant function market makers* (CFMMs, for short) or collections of CFMMs (such as Uniswap v3) [2,3]. A constant function market maker is a type of permissionless market that allows anyone to trade baskets of, say, r, assets for other baskets of these same s assets, subject to a simple set of rules which we describe below.

Reserves and Trading Functions. A constant function market maker, which allows r tokens to be traded, is defined by two properties: its *reserves* $R \in \mathbb{R}_{+}^r$, where R_j denotes the amount of asset j available to the CFMM, and a *trading function* which is a concave function $\varphi : \mathbb{R}_{+}^r \rightarrow \mathbb{R}$, which specifies the CFMM's behavior and its *trading fee* $0 < \gamma \leq 1$.

Acceptance Condition. Any user is allowed to submit a trade to a CFMM, which is, from before, a vector $\Delta \in \mathbb{R}^r$. The submitted trade is then accepted if the following condition holds:

$$\varphi(R - \gamma \Delta_- - \Delta_+) \geq \varphi(R), \tag{2}$$

and $R - \gamma \Delta_- - \Delta_+ \geq 0$. Here, we denote Δ_+ to be the 'elementwise positive part' of Δ, i.e., $(\Delta_+)_j = \max\{\Delta_j, 0\}$ and Δ_- to be the 'elementwise negative part' of Δ, i.e., $(\Delta_-)_j = \min\{\Delta_j, 0\}$ for every asset $j = 1, \ldots, r$. The basket of assets Δ_+ may sometimes be called the 'received basket' and Δ_- may sometimes be called the 'tendered basket' (see, *e.g.*, [2]). Note that the trading set T, for a CFMM, is exactly the set of Δ such that (2) holds,

$$T = \{\Delta \in \mathbb{R}^r \mid \varphi(R - \gamma \Delta_- - \Delta_+) \geq \varphi(R)\}. \tag{3}$$

It is clear that $0 \in T$, and it is not difficult to show that T is convex whenever φ is concave, which is true for all trading functions used in practice. If the trade is accepted then the CFMM pays out Δ_+ from its reserves and receives $-\Delta_-$ from the trader, which means the reserves are updated as $R \leftarrow R - \Delta_- - \Delta_+$. The acceptance condition (2) can then be interpreted as: the CFMM accepts a trade only when its trading function, evaluated on the 'post-trade' reserves with the tendered basket discounted by γ, is at least as large as its value when evaluated on the current reserves.

It can be additionally shown that the trade acceptance conditions in terms of the trading function φ and in terms of the trading set T are equivalent in the sense that every trading set has a function φ which generates it [3], under some basic conditions.

Examples. Almost all examples of decentralized exchanges currently in production are constant function market makers. For example, the most popular trading function (as measured by most metrics) is the product trading function:

$$\varphi(R) = \sqrt{R_1 R_2},$$

originally proposed for Uniswap [23] and a 'bounded liquidity' variation of this function:

$$\varphi(R) = \sqrt{(R_1 + \alpha)(R_2 + \beta)}, \tag{4}$$

used in Uniswap v3 [1], with $\alpha, \beta \geq 0$. Other examples include the weighted geometric mean (as used by Balancer [18])

$$\varphi(R) = \prod_{i=1}^{r} R_i^{w_i}, \tag{5}$$

where r is the number of assets the exchange trades, and $w \in \mathbb{R}_+^r$ with $\mathbf{1}^T w = 1$ are known as the weights, along with the Curve trading function

$$\varphi(R) = \alpha \mathbf{1}^T R - \left(\prod_{i=1}^{r} R_i^{-1}\right),$$

where $\alpha > 0$ is a parameter set by the CFMM [16]. Note that the 'product' trading function is the special case of the weighted geometric mean function when $r = 2$ and $w_1 = w_2 = 1/2$.

Aggregate CFMMs. In some special cases, such as in Uniswap v3, it is reasonable to consider an *aggregate CFMM*, which we define as a collection of CFMMs, which all trade the same assets, as part of a single 'big' trading set. A specific instance of an aggregate CFMM currently used in practice is in Uniswap v3 [1]. Any 'pool' in this exchange is actually a collection of CFMMs with the 'bounded liquidity' variation of the product trading function, shown in (4). We will see that we can treat these 'aggregate CFMMs' in a special way in order to significantly improve performance.

3   An Efficient Algorithm

A common way of solving problems such as problem (1), where we have a set of variables coupled by only a single constraint, is to use a decomposition method [8, 14]. The general idea of these methods is to solve the original problem by splitting it into a sequence of easy subproblems that can be solved independently. In this section, we will see that applying a decomposition method to the optimal routing problem gives a solution method which parallelizes over all markets. Furthermore, it gives a clean programmatic interface; we only need to be able to find arbitrage for a market, given a set of reference prices. This interface allows us to more easily include a number of important decentralized exchanges, such as Uniswap v3.

3.1 Dual Decomposition

To apply the dual decomposition method, we first take the coupling constraint of problem (1),

$$\Psi = \sum_{i=1}^{m} A_i \Delta_i,$$

and relax it to a linear penalty in the objective, parametrized by some vector $\nu \in \mathbb{R}^n$. (We will show in §3.2 that the only reasonable choice of ν is a market clearing price, sometimes called a no-arbitrage price, and that this choice actually results in a relaxation that is tight; $i.e.$, a solution for this relaxation also satisfies the original coupling constraint.) This relaxation results in the following problem:

$$\begin{array}{ll} \text{maximize} & U(\Psi) - \nu^T(\Psi - \sum_{i=1}^{m} A_i \Delta_i) \\ \text{subject to} & \Delta_i \in T_i, \quad i = 1, \ldots, m, \end{array}$$

where the variables are the network trade vector $\Psi \in \mathbb{R}^n$ and the trades are $\Delta_i \in \mathbb{R}^{n_i}$ for each market $i = 1, \ldots, m$. Note that this formulation can be viewed as a family of problems parametrized by the vector ν.

A simple observation is that this new problem is actually separable over all of its variables. We can see this by rearranging the objective:

$$\begin{array}{ll} \text{maximize} & U(\Psi) - \nu^T\Psi + \sum_{i=1}^{m}(A_i^T\nu)^T\Delta_i \\ \text{subject to} & \Delta_i \in T_i, \quad i = 1, \ldots, m. \end{array} \tag{6}$$

Since there are no additional coupling constraints, we can solve for Ψ and each of the Δ_i with $i = 1, \ldots, m$ separately.

Subproblems. This method gives two types of subproblems, each depending on ν. The first, over Ψ, is relatively simple:

$$\text{maximize} \quad U(\Psi) - \nu^T\Psi, \tag{7}$$

and can be recognized as a slightly transformed version of the Fenchel conjugate [10, §3.3]. We will write its optimal value (which depends on ν) as

$$\bar{U}(\nu) = \sup_{\Psi} \left(U(\Psi) - \nu^T\Psi \right).$$

The function $\bar{U}$ can be easily derived in closed form for a number of functions U. Additionally, since $\bar{U}$ is a supremum over an affine family of functions parametrized by ν, it is a convex function of ν [10, §3.2.3]. (We will use this fact soon.) Another important thing to note is that unless $\nu \geq 0$, the function $\bar{U}(\nu)$ will evaluate to $+\infty$. This can be interpreted as an implicit constraint on ν.

The second type of problem is over each trade Δ_i for $i = 1, \ldots, m$, and can be written, for each market i, as

$$\begin{array}{ll} \text{maximize} & (A_i^T\nu)^T\Delta_i \\ \text{subject to} & \Delta_i \in T_i. \end{array} \tag{8}$$

We will write its optimal value, which depends on $A_i^T \nu$, as $\mathbf{arb}_i(A_i^T \nu)$. Problem (8) can be recognized as the *optimal arbitrage problem* (see, *e.g.*, [2]) for market i, when the external market price, or reference market price, is equal to $A_i^T \nu$. Since $\mathbf{arb}_i(A_i^T \nu)$ is also defined as a supremum over a family of affine functions of ν, it too is a convex function of ν. Solutions to the optimal arbitrage problem are known, in closed form, for a number of trading functions. (See Appendix A for some examples.)

Dual Variables as Prices. The optimal solution to problem (8), given by $\Delta_i^\star$, is a point $\Delta_i^\star$ in T_i such that there exists a supporting hyperplane to the set T_i at $\Delta_i^\star$ with slope $A_i^T \nu$ [10, §5.6]. We can interpret these slopes as the 'marginal prices' of the n_i assets, since, letting $\delta \in \mathbb{R}^{n_i}$ be a small deviation from the trade $\Delta_i^\star$, we have, writing $\tilde{\nu} = A_i^T \nu$ as the weights of ν in the local indexing:

$$\tilde{\nu}^T(\Delta_i^\star + \delta) \leq \tilde{\nu}^T \Delta_i^\star,$$

for every δ with $\Delta_i^\star + \delta \in T_i$. (By definition of optimality.) Canceling terms gives

$$\tilde{\nu}^T \delta \leq 0.$$

If, for example, δ_i and δ_j are the only two nonzero entries of δ, we would have

$$\delta_i \leq -\frac{\tilde{\nu}_j}{\tilde{\nu}_i}\delta_j,$$

so the exchange rate between i and j is at most $\tilde{\nu}_i/\tilde{\nu}_j$. This observation lets us interpret the dual variables $\tilde{\nu}$ (and therefore the dual variables ν) as 'marginal prices', up to a constant multiple.

3.2   The Dual Problem

The objective value of problem (6), which is a function of ν, can then be written as

$$g(\nu) = \bar{U}(\nu) + \sum_{i=1}^{m} \mathbf{arb}_i(A_i^T \nu). \tag{9}$$

This function $g : \mathbb{R}^n \to \mathbb{R}$ is called the *dual function*. Since g is the sum of convex functions, it too is convex. The *dual problem* is the problem of minimizing the dual function,

$$\text{minimize} \quad g(\nu), \tag{10}$$

over the dual variable $\nu \in \mathbb{R}^n$, which is a convex optimization problem since g is a convex function.

Dual Optimality. While we have defined the dual problem, we have not discussed how it relates to the original routing problem we are attempting to solve, problem (1). Let $\nu^\star$ be a solution to the dual problem (10). Assuming that the dual function is differentiable at $\nu^\star$, the first order, unconstrained optimality conditions for problem (10) are that

$$\nabla g(\nu^\star) = 0.$$

(The function g need not be differentiable, in which case a similar, but more careful, argument holds using subgradient calculus.) It is not hard to show that if $\bar{U}$ is differentiable at $\nu^\star$, then its gradient must be $\nabla \bar{U}(\nu^\star) = -\Psi^\star$, where $\Psi^\star$ is the solution to the first subproblem (7), with $\nu^\star$. (This follows from the fact that the gradient of a maximum, when differentiable, is the gradient of the argmax.) Similarly, the gradient of $\mathbf{arb}_i$ when evaluated at $A_i^T \nu^\star$ is $\Delta_i^\star$, where $\Delta_i^\star$ is a solution to problem (8) with marginal prices $A_i^T \nu^\star$, for each market $i = 1, \ldots, m$. Using the chain rule, we then have:

$$0 = \nabla g(\nu^\star) = -\Psi^\star + \sum_{i=1}^{m} A_i \Delta_i^\star. \tag{11}$$

Note that this is exactly the coupling constraint of problem (1). In other words, when the linear penalties $\nu^\star$ are chosen optimally (i.e., chosen such that they minimize the dual problem (10)) then the optimal solutions for subproblems (7) and (8) automatically satisfy the coupling constraint. Because problem (6) is a relaxation of the original problem (1) for any choice of ν, any solution to problem (6) that satisfies the coupling constraint of problem (1) must also be a solution to this original problem. All that remains is the question of finding a solution $\nu^\star$ to the dual problem (10).

3.3 Solving the Dual Problem

The dual problem (10) is a convex optimization problem that is easily solvable in practice, even for very large n and m. In many cases, we can use a number of off-the-shelf solvers such as SCS [20], Hypatia [12], and Mosek [7]. For example, a relatively effective way of minimizing functions when the gradient is easily evaluated is the L-BFGS-B algorithm [11,19,24]: given a way of evaluating the dual function $g(\nu)$ and its gradient $\nabla g(\nu)$ at some point ν, the algorithm will find an optimal $\nu^\star$ fairly quickly in practice. (See §6 for timings.) By definition, the function g is easy to evaluate if the subproblems (7) and (8) are easy to evaluate. Additionally the right hand side of equation (11) gives us a way of evaluating the gradient ∇g, essentially for free, since we typically receive the optimal $\Psi^\star$ and $\Delta_i^\star$ as a consequence of computing $\bar{U}$ and $\mathbf{arb}_i$.

Interface. In order for a user to specify and solve the dual problem (10) (and therefore the original problem) it suffices for the user to specify (a) some way of evaluating $\bar{U}$ and its optimal Ψ for problem (7) and (b) some way of evaluating the arbitrage problem (8) and its optimal trade $\Delta_i^\star$ for each market i that the user wishes to include. New markets can be easily added by simply specifying how to arbitrage them, which, as we will see next, turns out to be straightforward for most practical decentralized exchanges. The Julia interface required for the software package described in §5 is a concretization of the interface described here.

4   Swap Markets

In practice, most markets trade only two assets; we will refer to these kinds of markets as *swap markets*. Because these markets are so common, the performance of our algorithm is primarily governed by its ability to solve (8) quickly on these two asset markets. We show practical examples of these computations in Appendix A. In this section, we will suppress the index i with the understanding that we are referring to a specific market i.

4.1   General Swap Markets

Swap markets are simple to deal with because their trading behavior is completely specified by the *forward exchange function* [2] for each of the two assets. In what follows, the forward trading function f_1 will denote the maximum amount of asset 2 that can be received by trading some fixed amount δ_1 of asset 1, *i.e.*, if $T \subseteq \mathbb{R}^2$ is the trading set for a specific swap market, then

$$f_1(\delta_1) = \sup\{\lambda_2 \mid (-\delta_1, \lambda_2) \in T\}, \quad f_2(\delta_2) = \sup\{\lambda_1 \mid (\lambda_1, -\delta_2) \in T\}.$$

In other words, $f_1(\delta_1)$ is defined as the largest amount λ_2 of token 2 that one can receive for tendering a basket of $(\delta_1, 0)$ to the market. The forward trading function f_2 has a similar interpretation. If $f_1(\delta_1)$ is finite, then this supremum is achieved since the set T is closed.

Trading Function. If the set T has a simple trading function representation, as in (3), it is not hard to show that the function f_1 is the unique (pointwise largest) function that satisfies

$$\varphi(R_1 + \gamma\delta_1, R_2 - f_1(\delta_1)) = \varphi(R_1, R_2). \tag{12}$$

whenever φ is nondecreasing, which may be assumed for all CFMMs [3], and similarly for f_2. (Note the equality, compared to the inequality in the original (2).)

Properties. The functions f_1 and f_2 are concave, since the trading set T is convex, and nonnegative, since $0 \in T$ by assumption. Additionally, we can interpret the directional derivative of f_j as the current marginal price of the received asset, denominated in the tendered asset. Specifically, we define

$$f_j'(\delta_j) = \lim_{h \to 0^+} \frac{f_j(\delta_j + h) - f_j(\delta_j)}{h}. \tag{13}$$

This derivative is sometimes referred to as the price impact function [4]. Intuitively, $f_1'(0)$ is the current price of asset 1 quoted by the swap market before any trade is made, and $f_1'(\delta)$ is the price quoted by the market to add an additional ε units of asset 1 to a trade of size δ, for very small ε. We note that in the presence of fees, the marginal price to add to a trade of size δ, *i.e.*, $f_1'(\delta)$, will be lower than the price to do so after the trade has been made [3].

Swap Market Arbitrage Problem. Equipped with the forward exchange function, we can specialize (8). Overloading notation slightly by writing $(\nu_1, \nu_2) \geq 0$ for $A_i^T \nu$ we define the swap market arbitrage problem for a market with forward exchange function f_1:

$$
\begin{array}{ll}
\text{maximize} & -\nu_1 \delta_1 + \nu_2 f_1(\delta_1) \\
\text{subject to} & \delta_1 \geq 0,
\end{array} \tag{14}
$$

with variable $\delta_1 \in \mathbb{R}$ We can also define a similar arbitrage problem for f_2:

$$
\begin{array}{ll}
\text{maximize} & \nu_1 f_2(\delta_2) - \nu_2 \delta_2 \\
\text{subject to} & \delta_2 \geq 0,
\end{array}
$$

with variable $\delta_2 \in \mathbb{R}$. Since f_1 and f_2 are concave, both problems are evidently convex optimization problems of one variable. Because they are scalar problems, these problems can be easily solved by bisection or ternary search. The final solution is to take whichever of these two problems has the largest objective value and return the pair in the correct order. For example, if the first problem (14) has the highest objective value with a solution $\delta_1^\star$, then $\Delta^\star := (-\delta_1^\star, f(\delta_1^\star))$ is a solution to the original arbitrage problem (8). (For many practical trading sets T, it can be shown that at most one problem will have strictly positive objective value, so it is possible to 'short-circuit' solving both problems if the first evaluation has positive optimal value.)

Problem Properties. One way to view each of these problems is that they 'separate' the solution space of the original arbitrage problem (8) into two cases: one where an optimal solution $\Delta^\star$ for (8) has $\Delta_1^\star \leq 0$ and one where an optimal solution has $\Delta_2^\star \leq 0$. (Any optimal point $\Delta^\star$ for the original arbitrage problem (8) will never have both $\Delta_1^\star < 0$ and $\Delta_2^\star < 0$ as that would be strictly worse than the 0 trade for $\nu > 0$, and no reasonable market will have $\Delta_1^\star > 0$ and $\Delta_2^\star > 0$ since the market would be otherwise 'tendering free money' to the trader.) This means that, in order to find an optimal solution to the original optimal arbitrage problem (8), it suffices to solve two scalar convex optimization problems.

Optimality Conditions. The optimality conditions for problem (14) are that, if

$$
\nu_2 f_1'(0) \leq \nu_1, \tag{15}
$$

then $\delta_1^\star = 0$ is a solution. Otherwise, we have $\delta_1^\star = \sup\{\delta \geq 0 \mid \nu_2 f_1'(\delta) \geq \nu_1\}$. Similar conditions hold for the problem over δ_2. If the function f_1' is continuous, not just semicontinuous, then the expression above simplifies to finding a root of a monotone function:

$$
\nu_2 f_1'(\delta_1^\star) = \nu_1. \tag{16}
$$

If there is no root and condition (15) does not hold, then $\delta_1^\star = \infty$. However, the solution will be finite for any trading set that does not contain a line, *i.e.*, the market does not have 'infinite liquidity' at a specific price.

No-Trade Condition. Note that using the inequality (15) gives us a simple way of verifying whether we will make any trade with market T, given some prices ν_1 and ν_2. In particular, the zero trade is optimal whenever

$$f_1'(0) \leq \frac{\nu_1}{\nu_2} \leq \frac{1}{f_2'(0)}.$$

We can view the interval $[f_1'(0), 1/f_2'(0)]$ as a type of 'bid-ask spread' for the market with trading set T. (In constant function market makers, this spread corresponds to the fee γ taken from the trader.) This 'no-trade condition' lets us save potentially wasted effort of computing an optimal arbitrage trade as, in practice, most trades in the original problem will be 0.

Bounded Liquidity. In some cases, we can easily check not only when a trade will not be made (say, using condition (15)), but also when the 'largest possible trade' will be made. (We will define what this means next.) Markets for which there is a 'largest possible trade' are called bounded liquidity markets. We say a market has *bounded liquidity in asset 2* if there is a finite δ_1 such that $f_1(\delta_1) = \sup f_1$, and similarly for f_2. In other words, there is a finite input δ_1 which will give the maximum possible amount of asset 2 out. A market has *bounded liquidity* if it has bounded liquidity on both of its assets. A bounded liquidity market then has a notion of a 'minimum price'. First, define

$$\delta_1^- = \inf\{\delta_1 \geq 0 \mid f_1(\delta_1) = \sup f_1\},$$

i.e., δ_1^- is the smallest amount of asset 1 that can be tendered to receive the maximum amount the market is able to supply. We can then define the *minimum supported price* as the left derivative of f_1 at δ_1^-:

$$f_1^-(\delta_1^-) = \lim_{h \to 0^+} \frac{f(\delta_1^-) - f(\delta_1^- - h)}{h}.$$

The first-order optimality conditions imply that δ_1^- is a solution to the scalar optimal arbitrage problem (14) whenever

$$f_1^-(\delta_1^-) \geq \frac{\nu_1}{\nu_2}.$$

In English, this can be stated as: if the minimum supported marginal price we receive for δ_1^- is still larger than the price being arbitraged against, ν_1/ν_2, it is optimal to take all available liquidity from the market. Using the same definitions for f_2, we find that the only time the full problem (14) needs to be solved is when the price being arbitraged against ν_1/ν_2 lies in the interval

$$f_1^-(\delta_1^-) < \frac{\nu_1}{\nu_2} < \frac{1}{f_2^-(\delta_2^-)}. \tag{17}$$

(It may be the case that $f_2^-(\delta_2^-) = 0$ in which case we define the right hand side to be ∞.) We will call this interval of prices the *active interval*.

Example. In the case of Uniswap v3 [1], we have a collection of, say, $i = 1, \ldots, s$ bounded liquidity product functions (4), where the parameters $\alpha_k, \beta_k > 0$ are chosen such that all of the active price intervals, as defined in (17), are disjoint. (An explicit form for this trading function is given in the appendix, equation (18).) Solving the arbitrage problem (14) over this collection of CFMMs is relatively simple. Since all of the intervals are disjoint, any price ν_1/ν_2 can lie in at most one of the active intervals. We therefore do not need to compute the optimal trade for any interval, except the single interval where ν_1/ν_2 lies, which can be done in closed form. We also note that this 'trick' applies to any collection of bounded liquidity markets with disjoint active price intervals.

5   Implementation

We implemented this algorithm in `CFMMRouter.jl`, a Julia [9] package for solving the optimal routing problem. Our implementation is available at

$$\text{https://github.com/bcc-research/CFMMRouter.jl}$$

and includes implementations for both weighted geometric mean CFMMs and Uniswap v3. In this section, we provide a concrete Julia interface for our solver.

5.1   Markets

Market Interface. As discussed in §3.3, the only function that the user needs to implement to solve the routing problem for a given market is

$$\text{find\_arb!}(\Delta, \Lambda, \text{mkt}, \text{v}).$$

This function solves the optimal arbitrage problem (8) for a market `mkt` (which holds the relevant data about the trading set T) with dual variables `v` (corresponding to $A_i^T \nu$ in the original problem (8)). It then fills the vectors Δ and Λ with the negative part of the solution, $-\Delta_-^\star$, and positive part, $\Delta_+^\star$, respectively.

For certain common markets (*e.g.*, geometric mean and Uniswap v3), we provide specialized, efficient implementations of `find_arb!`. For general CFMMs where the trading function, its gradient, and the Hessian are easy to evaluate, one can use a general-purpose primal-dual interior point solver. For other more complicated markets, a custom implementation may be required.

Swap Markets. The discussion in §4 and the expression in (16) suggests a natural, minimal interface for swap markets. Specifically, we can define a swap market by implementing the function `get_price`(Δ). This function takes in a vector of inputs $\Delta \in \mathbb{R}_+^2$, where we assume that only one of the two assets is being tendered, *i.e.*, $\Delta_1 \Delta_2 == 0$, and returns $f_1'(\Delta_1)$, if $\Delta_1 > 0$ or $f_2'(\Delta_2)$ if $\Delta_2 > 0$. With this *price impact* function implemented, one can use bisection to compute the solution to (16). When price impact function has a closed form and is readily differentiable by hand, it is possible to use a much faster Newton method to solve this problem. In the case where the function does not have a simple closed form, we can use automatic differentiation (*e.g.*, using `ForwardDiff.jl` [21]) to generate the gradients for this function.

Aggregate CFMMs. In the special case of aggregate, bounded liquidity CFMMs, the price impact function often does not have a closed form. On the other hand, whenever the active price intervals are disjoint, we can use the trick presented in §4.1 to quickly arbitrage an aggregate CFMM. For example, a number of Uniswap v3 markets are actually composed of many thousands of bounded liquidity CFMMs. Treating each of these as their own market, without any additional considerations, significantly increases the size and solution complexity of the problem.

In this special case, each aggregate market 'contains' s trading sets, each of which has disjoint active price intervals with all others. We will write these intervals as (p_i^-, p_i^+) for each trading set $i = 1, \ldots, s$, and assume that these are in sorted order $p_{i-1}^+ \le p_i^- < p_i^+ \le p_{i+1}^+$. Given some dual variables ν_1 and ν_2 for which to solve the arbitrage problem (8), we can then run binary search over the sorted intervals (taking $O(\log(s))$ time) to find which of the intervals the price ν_1/ν_2 lies in. We can compute the optimal arbitrage for this 'active' trading set, and note that the remaining trading sets all have a known optimal trade (from the discussion in §4.1) and require only constant time. For Uniswap v3 and other aggregate CFMMs, this algorithm is much more efficient from both a computational and memory perspective when compared with a direct approach that considers all s trading sets separately.

Other Functions. If one is solving the arbitrage problem multiple times in a row, it may be helpful to implement the following additional functions:

1. `swap!(cfmm, `Δ`)`: updates `cfmm`'s state following a trade Δ.
2. `update_liquidity!(cfmm, [range,] L)`: adds some amount of liquidity `L` $\in \mathbb{R}_+^2$, optionally includes some interval `range = (p1, p2)`.

5.2   Utility Functions

Recall that the dual problem relies on a slightly transformed version of the Fenchel conjugate, which is the optimal value of problem (7). To use L-BFGS-B (and most other optimization methods), we need to evaluate this function $\bar{U}(\nu)$ and its gradient $\nabla \bar{U}(\nu)$, which is the solution $\Psi^\star$ to (7) with parameter ν. This means that, to implement a utility function `objective`, we only need to define

- `f(objective, v)` evaluates $\bar{U}$ at `v`.
- `grad!(g, objective, v)` evaluates $\nabla \bar{U}$ at `v` and stores it in `g`.
- `lower_limit(objective)` returns the lower bound of the objective.
- `upper_limit(objective)` returns the upper bound of the objective.

The lower and upper bounds can be found by deriving the conjugate function. For example, for the 'total arbitrage' objective $U(\Psi) = c^T \Psi - I(\Psi \ge 0)$, where a trader wants to tender no tokens to the network, but receive any positive amounts out with value proportional to some nonnegative vector $c \in \mathbb{R}_+^n$, has $\bar{U}(\nu) = 0$ if $\nu \ge c$ and ∞ otherwise. Thus, we have the bounds $c \le \nu < \infty$, and gradient $\nabla \bar{U}(\nu) = 0$. We provide implementations for arbitrage and for basket liquidations in our Julia package. (See [5, §3] for definitions.)

6   Numerical Results

We compare the performance of our solver against the commercial, off-the-shelf convex optimization solver Mosek, accessed through JuMP [15,17]. We use real, on-chain data to illustrate the benefit of routing an order through multiple markets rather than trading with a single market. Our code is available at

https://github.com/bcc-research/router-experiments.

Performance. We first compare the performance of our solver against Mosek [7], a widely-used, performant commercial convex optimization solver. We generate m swap markets over a global universe of $2\sqrt{m}$ assets. Each market is randomly generated with reserves uniformly sampled from the interval between 1000 and 2000, denoted $R_i \sim \mathcal{U}(1000, 2000)$, and is a constant product market with probability 0.5 and a weighted geometric mean market with weights $(0.8, 0.2)$ otherwise. (These types of swap markets are common in protocols such as Balancer [18].) We run arbitrage over the set of markets, with 'true prices' for each asset randomly generated as $p_i \sim \mathcal{U}(0, 1)$. For each m, we use the same parameters (markets and price) for both our solver and Mosek. Mosek is configured with default parameters. All experiments are run on a MacBook Pro with a 2.3GHz 8-Core Intel i9 processor. In Fig. 1, we see that as the number of pools (and tokens) grow, our method begins to dramatically outperform Mosek and scales quite a bit better. We note that the weighted geometric mean markets are especially hard for Mosek, as they must be solved as power cone constraints. Constant product markets may be represented as second order cone constraints, which are quite a bit more efficient for many solvers. Furthermore, our method gives a higher objective value, often by over 50%. We believe this increase stems from Mosek's use of an interior point method and numerical tolerances. The solution returned by Mosek for each market will be strictly inside the associated trading set, but we know that any rational trader will choose a trade on the boundary.

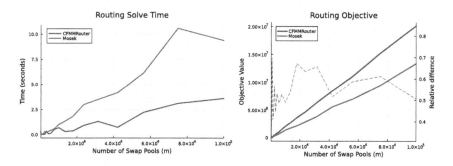

Fig. 1. Solve time of Mosek vs. `CFMMRouter.jl` (left) and the resulting objective values for the arbitrage problem, with the dashed line indicating the relative increase in objective provided by our method (right).

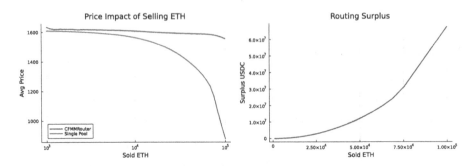

Fig. 2. Average price of market sold ETH in routed vs. single-pool (left) and routed vs. single-pool surplus liquidation value (right).

Real Data: Trading on Chain. We show the efficacy of routing by considering a swap from WETH to USDC (*i.e.*, using the basket liquidation objective to sell WETH for USDC). Using on-chain data from the end of a recent block, we show in Fig. 2 that as the trade size increases, routing through multiple pools gives an increasingly better average price than using the Uniswap v3 USDC-WETH .3% fee tier pool alone. Specifically, we route orders through the USDC-WETH .3%, WETH-USDT .3%, and USDC-USDT .01% pools. This is the simplest example in which we can hope to achieve improvements from routing, since two possible routes are available to the seller: a direct route through the USDC-WETH pool; and an indirect route that uses both the WETH-USDT pool and the USDC-USDT pool.

7   Conclusion

We constructed an efficient algorithm to solve the optimal routing problem. Our algorithm parallelizes across markets and involves solving a series of optimal arbitrage problems at each iteration. To facilitate efficient subproblem solutions, we introduced an interface for swap markets, which includes aggregate CFMMs.

We note that we implicitly assume that the trading sets are known exactly when the routing problem is solved. This assumption, however, ignores the realities of trading on chain: unless our trades execute first in the next block, we are not guaranteed that the trading sets for each market are the same as those in the last block. Transactions before ours in the new block may have changed prices (and reserves) of some of the markets we are routing through. This observation naturally suggests *robust routing* as a natural direction for future research. Furthermore, efficient algorithms for routing with fixed transaction costs (*e.g.*, gas costs) are another interesting direction for future work (see [5, §5] for the problem formulation).

Acknowledgements. We thank Francesco Iannelli and Jiahao Song for contributing to the package's documentation and the Financial Cryptography 2023 reviewers for helpful comments on this paper.

A   Closed Form Solutions

Here, we cover some of the special cases where it is possible to analytically write down the solutions to the arbitrage problems presented previously.

Geometric Mean Trading Function. Some of the most popular swap markets, for example, Uniswap v2 and most Balancer pools, which total over \$2B in reserves, are geometric mean markets (5) with $n = 2$. This trading function can be written as

$$\varphi(R) = R_1^w R_2^{1-w},$$

where $0 < w < 1$ is a fixed parameter. This very common trading function admits a closed-form solution to the arbitrage problem (8). Using (12), we can write

$$f_1(\delta_1) = R_2 \left(1 - \left(\frac{1}{1 + \gamma\delta_1/R_1} \right)^\eta \right)$$

where $\eta = w/(1 - w)$. (A similar equation holds for f_2.) Using (15) and (16), and defining

$$\delta_1 = \frac{R_1}{\gamma} \left(\left(\eta\gamma\frac{\nu_2}{\nu_1}\frac{R_2}{R_1} \right)^{1/(\eta+1)} - 1 \right),$$

we have that $\delta_1^\star = \max\{\delta_1, 0\}$ is an optimal point for (14). Note that when we take $w = 1/2$ then $\eta = 1$ and we recover the optimal arbitrage for Uniswap given in [6, App. A].

Bounded Liquidity Variation. The bounded liquidity variation (4) of the product trading function satisfies the definition of bounded liquidity given in §4.1, whenever $\alpha, \beta > 0$. We can write the forward exchange function for the bounded liquidity product function (4), using (12), as

$$f_1(\delta) = \min\left\{ R_2, \frac{\gamma\delta(R_2 + \beta)}{R_1 + \gamma\delta + \alpha} \right\}$$

The 'min' here comes from the definition of a CFMM: it will not accept trades which pay out more than the available reserves. The maximum amount that a user can trade with this market, which we will write as δ_1^-, is when $f_1(\delta_1^-) = R_2$, i.e.,

$$\delta_1^- = \frac{1}{\gamma}\frac{R_2}{\beta}(R_1 + \alpha).$$

(Note that this can also be derived by taking $f_1(\delta_1) = R_2$ in (12) with the invariant (4).) This means that

$$f_1^-(\delta_1^-) = \gamma\frac{\beta^2}{(R_1 + \alpha)(R_2 + \beta)},$$

is the minimum supported price for asset 1. As before, a similar derivation yields the case for asset 2. Writing $k = (R_1 + \alpha)(R_2 + \beta)$, we see that we only need to solve (14) if the price ν_1/ν_2 is in the active interval (17),

$$\frac{\gamma\beta^2}{k} < \frac{\nu_1}{\nu_2} < \frac{k}{\gamma\alpha^2}. \tag{18}$$

Otherwise, we know one of the two 'boundary' solutions, δ_1^- or δ_2^-, suffices.

References

1. Adams, H., Zinsmeister, N., Salem, M., Keefer, R., Robinson, D.: Uniswap V3 Core (2021). https://uniswap.org/whitepaper-v3.pdf
2. Angeris, G., Agrawal, A., Evans, A., Chitra, T., Boyd, S.: Constant Function market makers: multi-asset trades via convex optimization. In: Tran, D.A., Thai, M.T., Krishnamachari, B. (eds.) Handbook on Blockchain. Springer Optimization and Its Applications, vol. 194, pp. 415–444. Springer, Cham (2022). https://doi.org/10.1007/978-3-031-07535-3_13
3. Angeris, G., Chitra, T.: Improved price Oracles: constant function market makers. In: Proceedings of the 2nd ACM Conference on Advances in Financial Technologies, pp. 80–91. ACM (2020). https://doi.org/10.1145/3419614.3423251
4. Angeris, G., Chitra, T., Evans, A.: When does the tail wag the dog? Curvature and market making. Cryptoecon. Syst. **2**(1) (2022)
5. Angeris, G., Evans, A., Chitra, T., Boyd, S.: Optimal routing for constant function market makers. In: Proceedings of the 23rd ACM Conference on Economics and Computation, pp. 115–128 (2022)
6. Angeris, G., Kao, H.T., Chiang, R., Noyes, C., Chitra, T.: An analysis of uniswap markets. Cryptoecon. Syst. (2020). https://doi.org/10.21428/58320208.c9738e64. https://cryptoeconomicsystems.pubpub.org/pub/angeris-uniswap-analysis
7. ApS, M.: MOSEK Optimizer API for Python 9.1.5. https://docs.mosek.com/9.1/pythonapi/index.html
8. Bertsekas, D.: Nonlinear Programming, 3rd edn. Athena Scientific (2016)
9. Bezanson, J., Edelman, A., Karpinski, S., Shah, V.: Julia: A fresh approach to numerical computing. SIAM Rev. **59**(1), 65–98 (2017). https://doi.org/10.1137/141000671
10. Boyd, S., Vandenberghe, L.: Convex Optimization, 1st edn. Cambridge University Press (2004)
11. Byrd, R.H., Lu, P., Nocedal, J., Zhu, C.: A limited memory algorithm for bound constrained optimization. SIAM J. Sci. Comput. **16**(5), 1190–1208 (1995)
12. Coey, C., Kapelevich, L., Vielma, J.P.: Solving natural conic formulations with Hypatia.jl (2021)
13. Danos, V., Khalloufi, H.E., Prat, J.: Global order routing on exchange networks. In: Bernhard, M., et al. (eds.) FC 2021. LNCS, vol. 12676, pp. 207–226. Springer, Heidelberg (2021). https://doi.org/10.1007/978-3-662-63958-0_19
14. Dantzig, G.B., Wolfe, P.: Decomposition principle for linear programs. Oper. Res. **8**(1), 101–111 (1960)
15. Dunning, I., Huchette, J., Lubin, M.: JuMP: a modeling language for mathematical optimization. SIAM Rev. **59**(2), 295–320 (2017). https://doi.org/10.1137/15M1020575. https://epubs.siam.org/doi/10.1137/15M1020575

16. Egorov, M.: StableSwap - efficient mechanism for Stablecoin liquidity, p. 6. https://www.curve.fi/stableswap-paper.pdf
17. Legat, B., Dowson, O., Garcia, J., Lubin, M.: MathOptInterface: a data structure for mathematical optimization problems (2021). https://doi.org/10.1287/ijoc.2021.1067. http://pubsonline.informs.org/doi/10.1287/ijoc.2021.1067
18. Martinelli, F., Mushegian, N.: Balancer: a non-custodial portfolio manager, liquidity provider, and price sensor (2019)
19. Morales, J.L., Nocedal, J.: Remark on "algorithm 778: L-BFGS-B: Fortran subroutines for large-scale bound constrained optimization". ACM Trans. Math. Softw. (TOMS) **38**(1), 1–4 (2011)
20. O'Donoghue, B., Chu, E., Parikh, N., Boyd, S.: Conic optimization via operator splitting and homogeneous self-dual embedding. J. Optim. Theor. Appl. **169**(3), 1042–1068 (2016). https://doi.org/10.1007/s10957-016-0892-3
21. Revels, J., Lubin, M., Papamarkou, T.: Forward-mode automatic differentiation in Julia. arXiv arXiv:1607.07892 [cs.MS] (2016)
22. Wang, Y., Chen, Y., Wu, H., Zhou, L., Deng, S., Wattenhofer, R.: Cyclic arbitrage in decentralized exchanges. In: Companion Proceedings of the Web Conference 2022, Virtual Event, Lyon France, April 2022, pp. 12–19. ACM (2022). https://doi.org/10.1145/3487553.3524201
23. Zhang, Y., Chen, X., Park, D.: Formal specification of constant product ($xy = k$) market maker model and implementation (2018)
24. Zhu, C., Byrd, R.H., Lu, P., Nocedal, J.: Algorithm 778: L-BFGS-B: Fortran subroutines for large-scale bound-constrained optimization. ACM Trans. Math. Softw. (TOMS) **23**(4), 550–560 (1997)

Attack Techniques, Defenses, and Attack Case Studies

Leveraging the Verifier's Dilemma
to Double Spend in Bitcoin

Tong Cao[1]$^{(\boxtimes)}$, Jérémie Decouchant[2], and Jiangshan Yu[3]

[1] Kunyao Academy, Shanghai, China
tongcaodaniel@gmail.com
[2] Delft University of Technology, Delft, The Netherlands
[3] Monash University, Melbourne, Australia

Abstract. We describe and analyze *perishing mining*, a novel block-withholding mining strategy that lures profit-driven miners away from doing useful work on the public chain by releasing block headers from a privately maintained chain. We then introduce the *dual private chain (DPC) attack*, where an adversary that aims at double spending increases its success rate by intermittently dedicating part of its hash power to *perishing mining*. We detail the DPC attack's Markov decision process, evaluate its double spending success rate using Monte Carlo simulations. We show that the DPC attack lowers Bitcoin's security bound in the presence of profit-driven miners that do not wait to validate the transactions of a block before mining on it.

Keywords: Bitcoin · Double spending · Block withholding attack

1 Introduction

Bitcoin's security level is traditionally measured as the proportion of the mining power that an adversary must control to successfully attack it. Nakamoto assumed that an adversary would not control the majority of the mining power [28]. If this assumption does not hold, an attacker is able to spend a coin twice and affect the system consistency in what is known as a double spending attack or 51% attack. The soundness of the honest majority assumption has been discussed in the literature and mechanisms have been proposed to harden the mining process against the 51% attack without completely eliminating it [8,10,23,37].

Despite rewarding miners with newly minted coins and transaction fees, the Bitcoin mining process has also been shown to be vulnerable to selfish behaviors. Using selfish mining, a miner withholds mined blocks and releases them only after

---

This work was partly performed while Tong Cao was with the University of Luxembourg.

J. Decouchant and J. Yu—These authors are listed in alphabetical order and contributed equally.

F. Baldimtsi and C. Cachin (Eds.): FC 2023, LNCS 13951, pp. 149–165, 2024.
https://doi.org/10.1007/978-3-031-47751-5_9

the honest miners have wasted computing resources mining alternative blocks. Selfish mining increases a miner's revenue beyond the fair share it would obtain by following the default Bitcoin mining protocol [19]. Using simulations, selfish mining has been shown to be profitable only after a difficulty adjustment period in Bitcoin for any miner with more than 33% of the global hash power [21,30]. Variants of selfish mining further optimize a miner's expected revenue [34].

Additionally, miners face the verifier's dilemma [7,26,36], where upon receiving a block header they have to decide whether they should wait to have received and verified the corresponding transactions, or whether they should start mining right away based on the block header. Different miners might react differently to this dilemma.

Following previous works, we say that a chain of blocks is public if the honest miners are able to receive all its content, while we say that a chain is private if some contents of the chain are kept hidden by the adversary. In this paper, we show that an adversary can leverage a novel block withholding strategy, which we call perishing mining, to slow down the public chain in an unprecedented manner. More precisely, perishing mining leads miners that react differently to the verifier's dilemma to mine on different forks. We then present the Dual Private Chain (DPC) attack, which further leverages the verifier's dilemma to double spend on Bitcoin. This attack is, to the best of our knowledge, the first attack where an adversary temporarily sacrifices part of its hash power to later favor its double spending attack, and the first attack where an adversary simultaneously manages two private chains. Intuitively, the first adversarial chain inhibits the public chain's growth, so that the second one benefits from more favorable conditions for a double spending attack.

To evaluate the impact of the distraction chain on the public chain we first establish the Markov decision process (MDP) of perishing mining. From this MDP, we obtain the probability for the system to be in each state, and quantify the impact of perishing mining on the public chain, i.e., its growth rate decrease. We further describe the DPC attack and its associated MDP. We then evaluate its expected success rate based on Monte Carlo simulations. Counterintuitively, our results show that the adversary increases its double spending success rate by dedicating a fraction of its hash power to slow the public chain down, instead of attacking it frontally with all its hash power.

Overall, this work makes the following contributions.

• We present perishing mining, a mining strategy that is tailored to slow down the progress of the public chain by leveraging the verifier's dilemma. Using perishing mining an adversary releases the headers of blocks that extend the public chain so that some honest miners mine on them while some honest miners keep mining on the public chain, which effectively divides the honest miners hash power. We present the pseudocode of the perishing mining strategy, establish its Markov chain model and quantify its impact on the public chain growth.

• Building on perishing mining, we describe the DPC attack that an adversary can employ to double spend by maintaining up to two private chains. The first chain leverages the perishing mining strategy to slow down the public chain's growth and ease the task of the second chain, which aims at double spending. We provide the pseudocode of the attack, and characterize the states and transitions of its Markov chain model.

- We evaluate the perishing mining strategy and the DPC attack based on extensive Monte Carlo simulations. Our results indicate that perishing mining reduces the public chain progress by 69% when the adversary owns 20% of the global power and 50% of the hash power belongs to miners that mine on block headers without verifying their transactions. In comparison, selfish mining, which aims at optimizing a miner's revenue share, would only decrease it down by 15%. Our evaluation also shows that an adversary that owns 30% of the global hash power can double spend with 100% success rate when 50% of the hash power belongs to optimistic miners who do not verify transactions (i.e., type 2 miners in Sect. 3.2). While we focus on the double spending threat, we also show that the DPC attack allows an adversary to obtain a higher revenue than the one it would obtain by mining honestly or following previously known strategies (Appx. ??).

This paper is organized as follows. Section 2 discusses the related work and provides some necessary background. Section 3 defines our system model. Section 4 provides an overview of the DPC attack. Section 5 details the perishing mining strategy and the DPC attack that builds on it. Section 6 presents our evaluation results. Section 7 provides a discussion on other aspects of the attack. Finally, Sect. 8 concludes this paper.

2   Related Work

Double Spending Attack. The double spending attack on Bitcoin was described in Nakamoto's whitepaper [28], and has been further analyzed since [25,33]. Nowadays, $z = 6$ blocks need to be appended after a block for its transactions to be considered permanent. An adversary with more than 50% of the global mining power is able to use a coin in a first validated transaction and, later on, in a second conflicting transaction. Nakamoto characterized the race between the attacker and the honest miners as a random walk, and calculated the probability for an attacker to catch up with the public chain after z blocks have been appended after its initial transaction. Our DPC attack aims at double spending, and improves upon the classical double spending's success rate.

Block-Withholding Attacks. Selfish mining was the first mining strategy that allows a rational miner to increase its revenue share [19], and was later shown to harm the mining fairness [9,15]. Selfish mining is not more profitable than honest mining when the mining difficulty remains constant despite the fact that the adversary is able to increase its revenue share [21,22]. Nayak et al. proposed plausible values for the selfish miner's propagation factor by utilizing the public overlay network data [29]. They pointed out that the attacker could optimize its revenue and win more blocks by eclipsing [24] honest miners when the propagation factor increases. Gervais et al. analyzed the impact of stale rate on selfish mining attack [21]. Negy et al. pointed out that applying selfish mining in Bitcoin is profitable after at least one difficulty adjustment period (i.e., after approximately two weeks at least) [30]. The DPC attack differs from these works in the sense that its main goal is not to increase the adversary's mining share but to double spend with higher probability than previous attacks.

Table 1. Notations.

Symbol	Interpretation
$\alpha \in [0, 0.5]$	Mining power of the adversary
$\beta \in [0, 1]$	Fraction of its mining power that the adversary dedicates to its first private chain
$\mu \in [0, 0.5]$	Mining power of type 2 miners
v_t	Value of the transaction the adversary inserts in a block when starting the DPC attack and attempts to double spend
v_b	Mining reward per block

Combining Selfish Mining and Double Spending. Previous works have shown that an adversary can combine the double spending attack with selfish mining [21,35]. In this attack, the attacker maintains a single chain, which lowers the double spending success rate compared to the initial double spending attack. Our DPC attack shows that an adversary can simultaneously manage two private chains to launch a more powerful double spending attack.

Blockchain Denial of Service Attacks. The BDOS attack proposed strategies to partially or completely shut down the mining network [27]. To do so, the adversary only sends the block header to the network whenever she discovers a block that is ahead of the public chain and there is no fork, and publishes the block body if the next block is generated by the honest miners. By doing so, the profitability and utility of the rational miners and Simplified Payment Verification (SPV) miners is decreased, so that they eventually leave the mining network. The objective of BDOS attacks is to halt the system. An adversary would need to spend approximately 1 million USD per day to shut down the system. Our DPC attack frequently separates other miners' hash power, which has some similarities with the BDOS attack's partial shut down case. However, the DPC attack allows the adversary to double spend.

3   System Model

This section introduces the categories of miners we consider, and the adversary that launches a DPC attack. Table 1 summarizes our notations.

3.1   Bitcoin Mining and the Verifier's Dilemma

Bitcoin mining is a trial-and-error process[1]. The public blockchain (or chain) is visible to all participants, and is maintained by honest miners. To achieve

---

[1] https://en.bitcoin.it/wiki/Block_hashing_algorithm.

consistency, honest miners accept the longest chain in case of visible forks [17,20, 31]. However, temporary block withholding attacks have been shown to threaten Bitcoin's security [19,25,33,34]. Honest miners monitor the network to verify block headers and verify transactions.

In the Bitcoin's network, block headers are often propagated faster than transactions. Bitcoin's incentive mechanism does not directly reward the verification of transactions, and BIP-152[2] introduced the compact block propagation optimization where each node can relay a block in a compact format before verifying its transactions. In this case, a miner that immediately mines on the block header of a correct block gets a time advantage to find the next block. If the miners instead wait and verify the included transactions before the next mining round, then they might sacrifice some non-negligible time in the mining race [7,12,26,36].

We assume that miners follow the traditional block exchange pattern [16,27] using the overlay network. Block dissemination over the overlay network takes seconds, whereas the average mining interval is 10 min. While accidental forks (which may occur every 60 blocks [16] on average) reduce the effective honest mining power on the public chain and makes our attack easier, we do not consider accidental forks created by honest miners in order for simplicity. We evaluate mining and double spending strategies using event-based simulations where an event is the discovery of a block by a category of miner. We note v_b the mining reward that miners obtain whenever a block they have discovered is permanently included in the blockchain.

3.2   Miner Categories

We consider two types of honest Bitcoin miners that react differently to the verifier's dilemma: *type 1 honest miners* and *type 2 honest miners*.

Type 1 honest miners always follow the default mining protocol and mine on the longest chain of fully verified blocks. In particular, these miners do not mine on a block header that extends a longer non-fully verified concurrent chain.

Type 2 honest miners are profit-driven. As Bitcoin allows miners to accept and generate new blocks without verifying their transactions, type 2 miners start mining on a new block or its header if it extends the longest chain without verifying the transactions it contains. Note that type 2 miners can verify transactions whenever they are received and stop mining on a block header when associated transactions are faulty, or if they successfully mine the next block without having received the previous transactions. In our experiments, we consider two opposite categories of type 2 miners that behave differently upon reception of successive block headers to evaluate the best and worst possible attack results.

– *Optimistic type 2 miners* miners always mine on the longest chain of blocks, which is possibly made of several block whose transactions have not yet been received. In particular, Simplified Payment Verification (SPV) miners [3–6] can

---

[2] https://github.com/bitcoin/bips/blob/master/bip-0152.mediawiki.

be categorized as optimistic type 2 miners. Upon finding a block, optimistic type 2 miners can create an empty block or include transactions that they know cannot create conflicts (e.g., internal transactions for mining pools).

- *Pessimistic type 2 miners* only accept to mine on a block header if it extends a chain of full blocks. In particular, a pessimistic type 2 miner that extends a block header would then mine on the last block with transactions not to waste time. If the missing transactions eventually arrive, they then release the next full block. While if they extend over the last full block, they then create a fork.

In practice, it would be difficult for the adversary to identify the exact proportion of the global mining power that each type 2 miner subcategory represents. However, the adversary can be conservative and assume that all type 2 miners are pessimistic, since our attack still improves over the state-of-the-art in that case. We also discuss evidence for SPV mining in Sect. 7, which is arguably the simplest type 2 mining strategy.

The adversary owns a fraction $\alpha \in [0, 0.5]$ of the global hash power and its aim is to double spend with higher probability than using previous attacks. When launching its attack the adversary introduces a transaction of value v_t in a block that is included in the public chain and that it attempts to double spend. We also assume that the adversary cannot break cryptographic primitives. Contrary to the selfish mining's adversary model [19,21], our model does not assume that the adversary has a privileged network access, which is required in selfish mining when the adversary releases a conflicting block it had pre-mined in reaction to the extension of the public chain by an honest miner. For simplicity, we consider that every newly discovered and propagated block is almost instantaneously received by all miners. Several works evaluated and modeled network propagation delays in various cryptocurrencies [12,13,16].

4   Attack Overview

This section provides a high-level description of the Dual Private Chain (DPC) attack, where an adversary maintains two private chains. It then summarizes the respective roles of adversary's two private chains and their interactions.

4.1   Intuition

In a DPC attack, the adversary maintains two private chains from which it might release block headers or full blocks with the ultimate goal of double spending. During the attack, both of the adversary's private chains compete with the public chain and may diverge from it starting from different blocks. At a given point in time, the adversary might dedicate its full hash power to one of its private chains, or divide its hash power to simultaneously extend both private chains.

The DPC attack starts when the adversary creates a transaction of value v_t that is the basis for its double spending attempt. Once the adversary generates the block that contains this transaction, she initializes both its private chains with it and starts mining on it. Initially, the two chains are therefore equal, but they might diverge or converge again later on depending on the created blocks. The double spending attack succeeds if the double spending chain becomes longer than the public chain and if the public chain contains $z = 6$ blocks that have been included after the block that contains the initial transaction of the adversary.

Role of the Distraction Chain. The first private chain that the adversary maintains is called the *distraction chain*. We present perishing mining, a strategy that the adversary employs to maintain its first private chain to waste the hash power of type 2 honest miners and slow down the public chain. Whenever the adversary divides its hash power to simultaneously mine on its two private chains, it dedicates β of its hash power to mine on its first private chain. This chain is private in the sense that the adversary never releases the full blocks, but only the corresponding block headers. The strategy that the adversary applies on its distraction chain divides the honest miners so that they mine on different blocks, and wastes the hash power of type 2 honest miners, which collectively account for hash power μ. The adversary leverages a BDOS-like attack to only share the header of blocks it discovers on the distraction chain (see Sect. 5). As the body of those blocks contain adversary-created transactions that are never publicly released, only type 2 honest miners mine on them. In this way, the adversary can distract type 2 honest miners from mining on the public chain.

Role of the Double Spending Chain. The adversary maintains a second private chain to attempt to double spend, and we therefore call this chain the *double spending chain*. Whenever the adversary is simultaneously mining on its two private chains it dedicates $\alpha(1-\beta)$ of the global hash power to its second private chain. This chain is private in the sense that, even though block headers might be released, the actual blocks it contains are only published if the double spending attack is successful. Following previous analyses [28,33], we consider that a double spending attempt is successful when: (i) the double spending chain's length is larger than or equal to the public chain's length; and (ii) $z-1$ blocks have been appended after the block that contains the adversary's initial transaction ($z = 6$ in Bitcoin).

4.2 Interplay Between the Two Private Chains

Whenever type 1 and type 2 miners are mining on the same block, the adversary divides its hash power to concurrently mine with hash power $\alpha\beta$ on the last block of its distraction chain, which is then equal to the public chain, and mine with mining power $\alpha(1 - \beta)$ on its double spending chain. The adversary's goal is then to create a fork and release a block header so that type 1 and type 2 honest miners mine on different blocks. Note that the adversary will use all its hash power on the second private chain as long as the first private chain is longer than the public chain. This hash power shifting between two private chains is at the core of the DPC attack, which is detailed in Sect. 5.2.

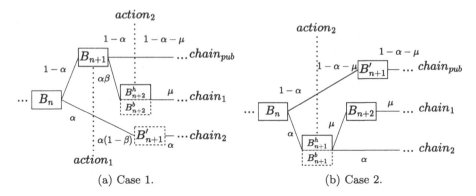

(a) Case 1.   (b) Case 2.

Fig. 1. Illustration of two possible cases that would lead type 2 miners to waste their hash power during a DPC attack. $B_n, B_{n+1}, B'_{n+1}, B_{n+2}$ are full blocks, B^h_{n+1}, B^h_{n+2} are block headers, and B^b_{n+1}, B^b_{n+2} are block bodies. We use solid rectangles when the content of a block is visible to honest miners, and a dotted rectangle when it is hidden by the adversary. We note interesting adversary's actions with $action_1$ and $action_2$ (see text for explanations).

In the DPC attack, the adversary executes different actions to lead the honest miners to mine on different blocks. Figure 1 shows two possible scenarios where the attack is initialized based on block B_n. The adversary generates a pair of conflicting transactions for its double spending attack. The first transaction is released to the public network and collected by the honest miners. The second transaction is kept private by the adversary. In both examples, after $action_1$, the adversary separates her hash power into two parts: she uses $\alpha\beta$ to work on public block lead B_{n+1}, and $\alpha(1 - \beta)$ to work on extending $chain_2$ to double spend. After $action_2$ the adversary releases the block header and uses all of her hash power to extend $chain_2$ for double spending. In both cases, type 2 honest miners (with μ of global hash power) are led to generate some blocks that will never be included in the public chain due to the adversary's block body withholding strategy. Consequently, the adversary's second private chain $chain_2$, which is used to attempt to double spend, benefits from the distraction of $chain_1$. We detail the DPC attack in Sect. 5.

5   The Dual Private Chains Attack

This section presents the details of the DPC attack, which attempts to lure type 2 honest miners away from extending the public chain, thus, facilitates a double spending attack. We first describe perishing mining, a strategy that a miner can use to slow down the progress of the public chain by making honest miners mine on different blocks. We then describe the full DPC attack that builds on perishing mining to maintain the adversary's first private chain. We provide an additional discussion on the DPC attack in Sect. 7.

5.1   Perishing Mining

We call *perishing mining* the strategy that the adversary uses on the distraction chain (whenever she is mining on it). After the initialization of the perishing mining strategy, the distraction chain and the public chain mine on the same block. The adversary's action then depends on whether the next block is discovered by the public miners or by itself (Please see our original analysis for details [11]). First, when the adversary discovers a block B_{n+1} that makes its distraction chain longer than the public chain, it releases the corresponding block header to the network. Upon receiving this header, type 2 miners start mining based on it, while type 1 miners continue working on block B_n. Second, when type 1 miners discover a block, the public chain is extended. Third, when type 2 miners find a block, the public chain is extended when the public chain is equal to the private chain. Otherwise, the block is abandoned due to the incomplete block verification, which wastes the hash power of type 2 miners. Note that when type 2 miners are optimistic the private chain is extended when it is not equal to the public chain.

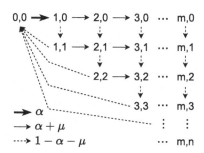

(a) With optimistic type 2 miners.

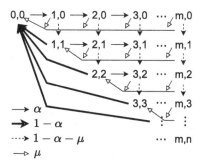

(b) With pessimistic type 2 miners.

Fig. 2. Perishing mining's Markov chain models with optimistic and pessimistic type 2 miners. Arrows that do not lead to a state (on the right subfigure) represent the wasted mining effort of pessimistic type 2 miners. Only the top-left transition on the left figure has probability α.

Figure 2 illustrates the MDP models of the perishing mining strategy assuming that type 2 miners are either optimistic or pessimistic. In this Markov chains, α, μ and $1-\alpha-\mu$, are respectively the probabilities for the adversary, type 2 and type 1 miners to discover a block. We use a tuple (i, j) to denote the state in perishing mining's MDP, where i and j are respectively the lengths of the private chain and the public chain. The fact that the adversary adopts the public chain whenever it is longer than the private chain implies that $i \leq j$. The adversary releases the header of the leading block to lure type 2 miners. When type 2 miners are optimistic (Fig. 2a), the adversary relies on type 2 miners that also attempt to extend the private chain. When type 2 miners are pessimistic

(Fig. 2b), the adversary is not able to use them to extend the private chain. We evaluate the negative impact of perishing mining on the public chain growth in Sect. 6.2.

5.2   Combining Perishing Mining and Double Spending

The DPC attack leverages the perishing mining strategy to distract type 2 miners and facilitate double spending.

We detail the attack's pseudocode in our original analysis [11], where l_1, l_2, and l_{pub} represent the length of the first private chain $chain_1$, the second private chain $chain_2$, and the public chain $chain_{pub}$ respectively.

During the DPC attack, the two invariants $l_2 \leq l_1$ and $l_{pub} \leq l_1$ are verified. The distraction chain is therefore always the longest chain among the three chains, and can adopt the public chain and the double spending chain when it is not the longest chain. For example, if it happens that the double spending becomes the longest chain then the distraction chain is set to be equal to the double spending chain. As a consequence, the type 2 miners would mine on the headers of the double spending chain, which would facilitate the double spending attack.

When the DPC attack starts, all three chains are equal and all miners mine on the same block. The adversary's actions are defined in reaction to block discoveries.

When the adversary finds a block on the distraction chain, it releases the corresponding block header so that type 2 miners mine on it, because the distraction chain is then the longest chain. If the two private chains are equal, the newly found block also extends the double spending chain. As a consequence, the adversary extends the distraction chain, and type 1 miners mine on the last full block of the public chain while type 2 miners mine on the last block header of the distraction chain. The adversary then allocates all its hash power (α) to mining on the double spending chain.

When the adversary finds a block on its double spending chain, it releases the block header if the second private chain becomes the longest chain. In this case, type 2 miners then mine on the double spending chain. The first private chain also adopts the second private chain so that the total hash power used to extend the double spending chain is $\alpha + \mu$. When the second private chain is shorter than the public chain, the adversary keeps mining on it with $1 - \beta$ of its hash power. As soon as the double spending chain becomes longer than the public chain and that at least 6 blocks have been appended to the public chain since the beginning of the attack, the adversary uses the double spending chain to override the public chain, and the DPC attack succeeds.

When type 1 miners find a block, they extend the public chain. If the public chain becomes the longest chain, then all honest miners will mine on the public chain and the adversary modifies its first private chain so that it adopts the public chain. The adversary then allocates $\alpha\beta$ of hash power to its distraction chain so that it tries to generate a block that will divide again the honest miners.

When type 2 miners find a block, three cases are possible. First, the double spending chain is extended if two private chains are equal and longer than the public chain. Second, the public chain and first private chain are extended if they are equal. Finally, in the other cases the newly discovered block is abandoned, which wastes the hash power of type 2 honest miners. The DPC attack can be tailored to optimistic or pessimistic type 2 miners.

5.3   Markov Decision Process of the DPC Attack

We establish the Markov decision process (MDP) of the DPC attack by simultaneously considering the two private chains and observing that each state is a 5-tuple $(l_{pub}, l_1, l_2, s_{(pub,1)}, s_{(1,2)})$. l_{pub}, l_1, and l_2 are respectively the lengths of the public chain $chain_{pub}$, the first private chain $chain_1$, and the second private chain $chain_2$. $s_{(pub,1)}, s_{(1,2)} \in \{\texttt{t(rue)}, \texttt{f(alse)}\}$ respectively indicate whether $chain_{pub}$ is equal to $chain_1$, and whether $chain_1$ is equal to $chain_2$.

Based on the relations between the three chains (synchronized or not), we identified 10 types of states in the presence of optimistic type 2 miners, and 9 types of states in presence of pessimistic type 2 miners. The corresponding transitions are presented in our original analysis [11]. Note that we were not able to obtain closed form formulas for the probabilities of each possible state due to the complexity of the DPC attack's MDP model. Nevertheless, we use Monte Carlo simulations to estimate the adversary's success rate and revenue, as in previous block withholding attacks [19,21,29].

Case 0 is the initial state of the attack. Case 4 captures the attack success, which happens if the public and the double spending chains contain more than 6 blocks, and if the double spending chain is longer than the public chain. Cases 1.x, 2.x, 3.x are all possible intermediary states and consider scenarios that differ based on the lengths of the chains, and whether or not they are equal, which happens when the adversary reinitializes one or both of its private chains.

We emphasize that an adversary that executes the DPC attack earns a mining reward only when the double spending chain succeeds. In this case, the adversary earns the block mining reward that corresponds to the private blocks it mined that end up in the public chain and the value of the transaction it managed to double spend. We use v_b for the value of blocks, and v_t for the value of the double spent transactions.

6   Analysis Using Monte Carlo Simulations

This section evaluates the perishing mining strategy and the DPC attack using Monte Carlo simulations that react based on the event of block discovery.

6.1   Methodology and Settings

We evaluate perishing mining and the DPC attack using random walks in their respective Markov decision processes. Our evaluations are based on Python

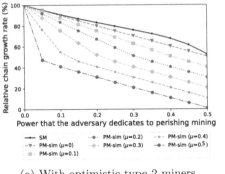

(a) With optimistic type 2 miners.

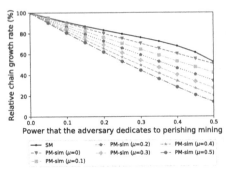

(b) With pessimistic type 2 miners.

Fig. 3. Relative growth rate of the public chain (compared to the attack-free case) when the adversary uses selfish mining (SM) or perishing mining (PM), where type 2 miners own a fraction μ of the global power.

scripts. In each scenario, we simulate the creation of 2,016 blocks, repeat each configuration 10,000 times, and report the average of the metrics of interest. Simulating the creation of 2,016 blocks maintains the mining difficulty constant during the experiment since Bitcoin's mining difficulty is adjusted every 2,016 blocks. We quantify the impact of perishing mining on the public chain's growth rate, and then evaluate the double spending success rate of the DPC attack. We compare the success rate of the DPC attack to the success rate of the classical double spending attack using the success rate formulas that were obtained by Nakamoto [28] and Rosenfeld [32]. We study the various strategies with $\alpha, \mu \in [0, 0.1, 0.2, 0.3, 0.4, 0.5]$ and $\beta \in [0, 1]$ (by 0.01 steps). Moreover, we analyze the adversary's expected revenue in our original analysis [11].

6.2   Impact of Perishing Mining on Chain Growth

In a DPC attack, the adversary leverages perishing mining strategy to inhibit public chain's growth. We now consider a scenario where the adversary constantly dedicates a fraction of its full hash power to perishing mining, so that we can quantify its effect on the growth rate of the public chain.

Figure 3 represents the relative public chain growth rate of a system under attack, which is expressed as a fraction (in %) of the public chain growth rate in the attack-free case. We compare perishing mining to selfish mining and vary the global hash power μ of type 2 miners 0 to 0.5 (i.e., ranging from 0% to 50% of the global hash power). The public chain is extended at a lower rate when the adversary's power increases and when the global power of type 2 miners increases. By comparing Fig. 3a and Fig. 3b, one can see that perishing mining has a stronger impact with optimistic type 2 miners than with pessimistic type 2 miners, as one could expect.

6.3 Double Spending Success Rate

Figure 4 illustrates the success rates of the DPC attack for different μ and with the best β value that we obtained experimentally. It is interesting to observe the differences between the partitions corresponding to a given μ with the best β value to see that maintaining distraction chain and double spending chain simultaneously makes a real difference. An adversary would be able to determine the best β after estimating μ, as we discuss in Sect. 7.

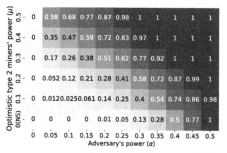
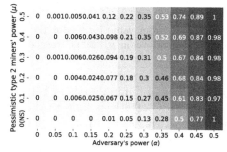

(a) With optimistic type 2 miners.   (b) With pessimistic type 2 miners.

Fig. 4. Success rate of the DPC attack depending on the hash power μ of the type 2 miners with the best value of parameter β within 2016 blocks. The "NS" line represents the success rate of the classical double spending attack (based on Nakamoto's evaluation). A darker color indicates a higher success probability.

In presence of type 2 miners (i.e., $\mu > 0$), the DPC attack's success rate is always higher than the one of the traditional double spending attack (i.e., 0(NS) in Fig. 4). The success rate of the double spending attack (with 6 confirmations) with $\alpha = 0.2$ (the power of the biggest mining pool) increases from 1% to 87% (or from 1% to 12%) via the DPC attack depending on μ as shown in Fig. 4a (or Fig. 4b). The impact of optimistic type 2 miners on DPC attack' success rate is more severe than pessimistic type 2 miners, for example, if $\mu = 0.2$ and $\alpha = 0.2$, the DPC attack's success rate is 28% in Fig. 4a while it is 7.7% in Fig. 4b.

Importantly, the DPC attack lowers Bitcoin's safety bound, i.e., the minimum hash power that the adversary needs to double spend or break the chain's consistency. For instance, when $\mu = 0.5, 0.4, 0.3, 0.2$ and type 2 miners are optimistic, a DPC adversary with 30%, 35%, 40%, 45% of the global hash power could completely manipulate the blockchain (i.e., 100% success rate in Fig. 4a), which is more threatening than the existing block withholding attacks [19,21,29].

Inspired by M. Rosenfeld [32], we further evaluate the safe transaction value (i.e., the suggested maximum value of transaction for clients) against double spending attack. Figure 5 plots the minimum value for $\frac{v_t}{v_b}$ that allows the DPC attacker to be more profitable than honest mining. When $\mu = 0.2$ and type 2 miners are optimistic, the adversary with $0.05, 0.1, 0.15, 0.2$ (the possible hash

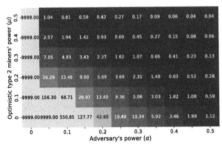
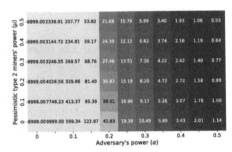

(a) With optimistic type 2 miners.   (b) With pessimistic type 2 miners.

Fig. 5. Minimum value for $\frac{v_L}{v_b}$ for the DPC attack to be more profitable than honest mining depending on μ. "9999" represents $\frac{v_L}{v_b} \geq 9999$.

power share of mining pools in Bitcoin) of global hash power is incentivized to perform DPC attack as long as the merchants are willing to accept the transaction with $26.29 * v_b, 13.49 * v_b, 9 * v_b, 5.69 * v_b$ BTC respectively (as shown in Fig. 5a). In the same case, when type 2 miners are pessimistic, the safe transaction value would increase and become $4026.56 * v_b, 329.86 * v_b, 81.4 * v_b, 30.97 * v_b$. Bitcoin's future block reward halving will decrease both the threshold to launch profitable DPC attacks and the safe transaction value, which confirms Carlsten et al.'s previous observation [14].

7   Attack Discussion

Attack Variants. We have presented the DPC attack we found to be the most effective when the adversary splits its hash power in two constant parts $\alpha\beta$ and $\alpha(1 - \beta)$. We foresee that one could devise variants of the DPC attack, e.g., using techniques that have been applied to selfish mining [19,25,33,34]. In these variants the adversary would mine on different blocks depending on the system's state, or dedicate a different fraction of its hash power to extend each of its two private chains. We leave the study of these variants to future work.

Estimating μ and Selecting β. It is sufficient for the adversary to approximate the value of μ, which is the proportion of the global hash power that belongs to type 2 miners, for a DPC attack to be successful, as our experimental results demonstrate. However, in practice, an adversary would be able to optimize its DPC attack by determining a precise value for μ. The adversary can estimate μ based on some public websites [3], or establish direct connections with the public mining pools to perform a statistical analysis. Moreover, the perishing mining strategy that we present in this paper can be used as a probing technique to measure μ. Indeed, the adversary can directly monitor the impact of perishing mining on the public chain and compute μ based on its growth rate. Once the exact value of μ is known, an adversary can find the best β for the DPC attack by replicating our experiments.

Attack Detection and Prevention. The DPC attack leverages the fact that type 2 miners, which include SPV miners, accept block headers without waiting for and verifying the corresponding transactions. One partial countermeasure against the DPC attack would consist in miners deliberately choosing to stop mining on block headers alone. However, it does not seem reasonable to assume that all miners would avoid this strategy because they can start working on the next block earlier than other miners and therefore increase their profit. Type 2 miners could also avoid mining on the adversary's blocks by accepting to mine only on blocks that were discovered from known mining pools. It is unclear whether this modification would have undesired security implications, e.g., regarding the decentralization of proof-of-work blockchains, or because pool sub-miners run a mining software that is developed internally and independently from the official protocol specification [18]. In addition, this modification would require type 2 miners to trust mining pools, and a malicious pool manager would still be able to execute the DPC attack.

Another idea would be for type 2 miners to stop mining on a block header if the associated transactions are not received before a maximum delay and then mine on the last full block. However, the adversary could also update its strategy to regularly send the unmatched block bodies so that type 2 miners keep mining on its blocks. It is unclear whether this countermeasure would be efficient, and in particular in practical settings. Moreover, the variation of message delays in Bitcoin's peer to peer network would sometimes lead type 2 miners to reject blocks that are generated by honest miners, and might imply possible DoS attacks.

Evidence of Type 2 Mining. In practice, it is difficult to know the exact strategy that miners follow. However, previous works have provided evidence of SPV mining [2–5,27]. Our assumptions in this work are not stronger since our pessimistic type 2 miners are more conservative than SPV miners. In 2020, 9+ mining pools representing 36% of the global power produced empty blocks, which one might consider evidence of SPV mining [1]. We analysed the Bitcoin blockchain and found that Antpool, Binance, F2pool, Huobi, Poolin, ViaBTC published empty blocks from 01/2021 to 02/2022 and collectively represent more than 60% of the global power.

8   Conclusion

In this paper, we proposed perishing mining, a novel adversarial mining strategy that slows down the public chain by leveraging the verifier's dilemma. We then described the dual private chain (DPC) attack where an adversary dedicates a part of its hash power to the perishing mining strategy and launches a parallel double spending attack. We established the Markov decision process of both the perishing mining and the DPC attack. We relied on Monte Carlo simulations to quantify the impact of perishing mining on the public chain growth, and evaluate the double spending success rate of the DPC attack. Our performance evaluation showed that the DPC attack is more powerful than the classical double spending attack as soon as a fraction of the miners mine on blocks without verifying their transactions. We also evaluated the revenue an adversary could expect from running the DPC attack, and showed that an adversary with sufficient funds or with sufficient hash power would maximize its revenue with the DPC attack.

References

1. Bitcoin miners are mining fewer empty blocks in 2020, and it may not all be due to chance. https://www.theblock.co/post/67928/bitcoin-miners-are-mining-fewer-empty-blocks-in-2020-and-it-may-not-all-because-of-chance. Accessed 2022
2. Empty Blocks. https://medium.com/@ASvanevik/why-all-these-empty-ethereum-blocks-666acbbf002. Accessed 2022
3. f2pool is doing SPV mining. https://bitcointalk.org/index.php?topic=700411.msg11790734#msg11790734. Accessed 2022
4. Half mining power were doing SPV mining. https://bitcoin.org/en/alert/2015-07-04-spv-mining#cause. Accessed 2022
5. SPV mining pools. https://en.bitcoin.it/wiki/Comparison_of_mining_pools. Accessed 2022
6. SPV mining. https://bitcoin.stackexchange.com/questions/38437. Accessed 2022
7. Alharby, M., Lunardi, R.C., Aldweesh, A., van Moorsel, A.: Data-driven model-based analysis of the ethereum verifier's dilemma. In: 2020 50th Annual IEEE/IFIP International Conference on Dependable Systems and Networks (DSN), pp. 209–220. IEEE (2020)
8. Badertscher, C., Lu, Y., Zikas, V.: A rational protocol treatment of 51% attacks. In: Malkin, T., Peikert, C. (eds.) CRYPTO 2021. LNCS, vol. 12827, pp. 3–32. Springer, Cham (2021). https://doi.org/10.1007/978-3-030-84252-9_1
9. Bonneau, J., Miller, A., Clark, J., Narayanan, A., Kroll, J.A., Felten, E.W.: SOK: research perspectives and challenges for bitcoin and cryptocurrencies. In: SP (2015)
10. Bonneau, J.: Why buy when you can rent? In: Clark, J., Meiklejohn, S., Ryan, P.Y.A., Wallach, D., Brenner, M., Rohloff, K. (eds.) FC 2016. LNCS, vol. 9604, pp. 19–26. Springer, Heidelberg (2016). https://doi.org/10.1007/978-3-662-53357-4_2
11. Cao, T., Decouchant, J., Yu, J.: Leveraging the verifier's dilemma to double spend in bitcoin. arXiv preprint arXiv:2210.14072 (2022)
12. Cao, T., Decouchant, J., Yu, J., Esteves-Verissimo, P.: Characterizing the impact of network delay on bitcoin mining. In: 2021 40th International Symposium on Reliable Distributed Systems (SRDS), pp. 109–119. IEEE (2021)
13. Cao, T., Yu, J., Decouchant, J., Luo, X., Verissimo, P.: Exploring the monero peer-to-peer network. In: Bonneau, J., Heninger, N. (eds.) FC 2020. LNCS, vol. 12059, pp. 578–594. Springer, Cham (2020). https://doi.org/10.1007/978-3-030-51280-4_31
14. Carlsten, M., Kalodner, H., Weinberg, S.M., Narayanan, A.: On the instability of bitcoin without the block reward. In: CCS (2016)
15. Croman, K., et al.: On scaling decentralized blockchains. In: Clark, J., Meiklejohn, S., Ryan, P.Y.A., Wallach, D., Brenner, M., Rohloff, K. (eds.) FC 2016. LNCS, vol. 9604, pp. 106–125. Springer, Heidelberg (2016). https://doi.org/10.1007/978-3-662-53357-4_8
16. Decker, C., Wattenhofer, R.: Information propagation in the bitcoin network. In: IEEE P2P (2013)
17. Dembo, A., et al.: Everything is a race and Nakamoto always wins. In: CCS (2020)

18. Eyal, I.: The miner's dilemma. In: IEEE Symposium on Security and Privacy (2015)
19. Eyal, I., Sirer, E.G.: Majority is not enough: bitcoin mining is vulnerable. In: Christin, N., Safavi-Naini, R. (eds.) FC 2014. LNCS, vol. 8437, pp. 436–454. Springer, Heidelberg (2014). https://doi.org/10.1007/978-3-662-45472-5_28
20. Gaži, P., Kiayias, A., Russell, A.: Tight consistency bounds for bitcoin. In: CCS (2020)
21. Gervais, A., Karame, G.O., Wüst, K., Glykantzis, V., Ritzdorf, H., Capkun, S.: On the security and performance of proof of work blockchains. In: CCS (2016)
22. Göbel, J., Keeler, H.P., Krzesinski, A.E., Taylor, P.G.: Bitcoin blockchain dynamics: the selfish-mine strategy in the presence of propagation delay. Perform. Eval. **104**, 23–41 (2016)
23. Han, R., Sui, Z., Yu, J., Liu, J.K., Chen, S.: Fact and fiction: challenging the honest majority assumption of permissionless blockchains. In: ASIA CCS (2021)
24. Heilman, E., Kendler, A., Zohar, A., Goldberg, S.: Eclipse attacks on bitcoin's peer-to-peer network. In: USENIX Security (2015)
25. Karame, G.O., Androulaki, E., Capkun, S.: Double-spending fast payments in bitcoin. In: CCS (2012)
26. Luu, L., Teutsch, J., Kulkarni, R., Saxena, P.: Demystifying incentives in the consensus computer. In: Proceedings of the 22nd ACM SIGSAC Conference on Computer and Communications Security, pp. 706–719 (2015)
27. Mirkin, M., Ji, Y., Pang, J., Klages-Mundt, A., Eyal, I., Juels, A.: BDoS: blockchain denial-of-service. In: CCS (2020)
28. Nakamoto, S.: Bitcoin: a peer-to-peer electronic cash system (2008)
29. Nayak, K., Kumar, S., Miller, A., Shi, E.: Stubborn mining: generalizing selfish mining and combining with an eclipse attack. In: Euro S&P (2016)
30. Negy, K.A., Rizun, P.R., Sirer, E.: Selfish mining re-examined. In: Bonneau, J., Heninger, N. (eds.) FC 2020. LNCS, vol. 12059, pp. 61–78. Springer, Cham (2020). https://doi.org/10.1007/978-3-030-51280-4_5
31. Pass, R., Seeman, L., Shelat, A.: Analysis of the blockchain protocol in asynchronous networks. In: Coron, J.-S., Nielsen, J.B. (eds.) EUROCRYPT 2017. LNCS, vol. 10211, pp. 643–673. Springer, Cham (2017). https://doi.org/10.1007/978-3-319-56614-6_22
32. Rosenfeld, M.: Analysis of bitcoin pooled mining reward systems. CoRR (2011)
33. Rosenfeld, M.: Analysis of hashrate-based double spending. arXiv preprint arXiv:1402.2009 (2014)
34. Sapirshtein, A., Sompolinsky, Y., Zohar, A.: Optimal selfish mining strategies in bitcoin. In: Grossklags, J., Preneel, B. (eds.) FC 2016. LNCS, vol. 9603, pp. 515–532. Springer, Heidelberg (2017). https://doi.org/10.1007/978-3-662-54970-4_30
35. Sompolinsky, Y., Zohar, A.: Bitcoin's security model revisited. arXiv preprint arXiv:1605.09193 (2016)
36. Teutsch, J., Reitwießner, C.: A scalable verification solution for blockchains. arXiv preprint arXiv:1908.04756 (2019)
37. Yu, J., Kozhaya, D., Decouchant, J., Verissimo, P.: Repucoin: your reputation is your power. IEEE Trans. Comput. (2019)

On the Sustainability of Bitcoin Partitioning Attacks

Jaehyun Ha[1] , Seungjin Baek[1] , Muoi Tran[2] , and Min Suk Kang[1(✉)]

[1] KAIST, Daejeon, South Korea
{jaehyunh1,seungjinb,minsukk}@kaist.ac.kr
[2] ETH Zürich, Zürich, Switzerland
dutran@ethz.ch

Abstract. A series of recent studies have shown that permissionless blockchain peer-to-peer networks can be partitioned at low cost (e.g., only a few thousand bots are needed), stealthily (e.g., no control plane detection is available), or at scale (e.g., the entire bitcoin network can be divided into two). In this paper, we focus on the *sustainability* of partitioning attacks in Bitcoin, which is barely discussed in the literature. Existing studies investigate new partitioning attack strategies extensively but not how long the partition they create lasts. Our findings show that, fortunately for Bitcoin, the permissionless peer-to-peer network can be partitioned but only for a short time. In particular, two recent partitioning attacks (i.e., Erebus [12], SyncAttack [10]) do not maintain partitions for more than 10 min in most cases. After analyzing Bitcoin's peer eviction mechanism (which makes the two original attacks difficult to sustain), we propose optimization strategies for the two attacks and calculate the total cost of the optimized attacks for a 1-hour attack duration. Our results complement the original attack studies: (i) the optimized Erebus attack shows that it requires at least one adversary-controlled Bitcoin node close to a target and a few additional expensive attack steps for sustainable attacks, and (ii) the optimized SyncAttack can create sustainable partitions only with excessive cost.

Keywords: Bitcoin · Partitioning Attacks

1 Introduction

Blockchain systems are desired to maintain highly reliable network connectivity across distributed nodes even in the face of severe network attacks or failures. However, Bitcoin and many permissionless blockchains are at risk of connection starvation attacks in which all available connections of public nodes are occupied by an adversary, leaving no resource for legitimate nodes. Connection starvation is first discussed as a part of the Eclipse attack in 2015 [5]. An adversary opens many connections to a target Bitcoin node and prevents other legitimate Bitcoin peers from establishing connections to it, effectively partitioning the target node from the rest of the peer-to-peer (P2P) network.

© International Financial Cryptography Association 2024
F. Baldimtsi and C. Cachin (Eds.): FC 2023, LNCS 13951, pp. 166–181, 2024.
https://doi.org/10.1007/978-3-031-47751-5_10

After the publication of the Eclipse attack, Bitcoin developers deployed several countermeasures, including a *peer eviction* mechanism in which a fully connected node terminates one of its existing connections to make room for a new incoming connection [2]. This peer eviction, along with several other measures, mitigates the Eclipse attacks by allowing legitimate nodes to connect to the partitioned target and thus deliver new blocks from the canonical chain; that is, the target node is no longer partitioned. In other words, the peer eviction mechanism makes the Eclipse attacks unsustainable.

Since then, there are two notable attacks showing partitioning the Bitcoin P2P network is still possible. In the Erebus attacks [12], a malicious autonomous system (AS) partitions a single target node by poisoning its internal peer database. SyncAttack [10] splits the entire Bitcoin P2P network into two partitions by monopolizing the incoming connection slots of all public Bitcoin nodes with a few tens of malicious peers. We observe, however, these studies have not properly evaluated the effect of the peer eviction mechanism against their attacks. Unfortunately, thus, sustainability of these attacks is left untested. Their original reports pay significant attention to the end-to-end attack evaluation, i.e., from the attack preparation phase to the attack completion phase with 100% connection occupation. Yet, the two studies do not show empirical evidence that their attacks are sustainable enough (e.g., partition continues while several blocks are generated), which is a critical condition for follow-up attacks, such as double-spending attacks or stubborn mining attacks [9]. The lack of rigorous evaluation on attack sustainability motivates us to test these partitioning attacks in our independent study.

To that end, we first test the *sustainability* of the original versions of the Erebus attack and SyncAttack. As we measure how long these attacks successfully partition a node (in the case of the Erebus attack) or two groups of nodes (in the case of the SyncAttack), we face a number of practical difficulties. For example, to accurately measure the moment when a partition ends, we should evaluate the Erebus attack in the Bitcoin mainnet, which has not been conducted in existing literature due to the challenging attack setup and ethical concerns. Evaluating SyncAttack accurately is even more challenging as it would create two partitions of thousands of nodes. We carefully apply several workarounds for these evaluations and estimate the attack sustainability effectively.

Our evaluation of the sustainability of these partitioning attacks, the first of its kind, shows that the two attacks would not maintain successful network partitioning to some meaningful extent, significantly limiting the effectiveness of these attacks in practice.

After learning that the two existing partitioning attacks in their original versions fail to last long enough (e.g., for 1 h) for follow-up exploits, we go one step further and optimize for their maximal sustainability. Our optimization requires thorough reviews of the original attack strategies and the current Bitcoin's peer connection mechanism. Our optimized attacks are designed against the up-to-date Bitcoin Core implementation v23.0 (as of October 2022).

We then measure the required cost of the optimized attacks when aiming to maintain partitions for a given duration (e.g., 1 h). For useful risk analysis of these attacks in practice, we define the attack cost as two-dimensional resources: (1) the number of unique, adversary-controlled network address groups, and (2) the distance (in network latency) from adversary-controlled nodes to the target client(s). Our analysis of the attack cost for these optimized attacks shows that the Erebus attack can be sustainable (e.g., maintain a partition for an hour) with moderately more attack resources (compared to what is described in its original version) and a few additional attack steps. In contrast, the SyncAttack shows its feasibility only with excessive cost.

The organization of the paper is as follows. We first provide a brief overview of recent partitioning attacks in Sect. 2. We then test the attack sustainability of two unmodified attacks in Sect. 3. In Sect. 4, we present our new optimized attack strategy based on Bitcoin's peer connection mechanism and calculate the cost of 1-hour sustainability with these optimized attacks.

2   Related Work

In this section, we review a few recent Bitcoin partitioning attacks [1,10–12]. We particularly focus on the Erebus attack and SyncAttack, and highlight their differences in Table 1. We also briefly review two partitioning attacks based on Internet routing manipulation (i.e., BGP hijacking), although evaluating their attack sustainability is beyond the scope of this paper.

Table 1. Comparison of two known Bitcoin partitioning attacks.

	Targets	Stealthiness	Attack resources	Preparation time	Peer table manipulation	Evaluation in the original paper	Deployed countermeasures
Erebus Attack	Single Bitcoin node	Yes	an AS	5–6 weeks	Required	No direct evaluation, only simulation with AS topology	Two deployed at Bitcoin Core
Sync Attack	Entire Bitcoin network	No	125 Bitcoin nodes	Not mentioned	Not required	No direct evaluation (measurement in mainnet, experiment in testnet)	None

2.1   Erebus: A Stealthy Single-Node Partitioning Attack

In the Erebus attack [12], a malicious AS, such as a tier-1 or tier-2 Internet Service Provider, fills a target node's peer tables (i.e., new and tried) with adversary-controlled IP addresses. Connections from the target to any of those IPs traverse through the adversary AS and therefore, are controlled by the adversary. The target is partitioned when all of its peer connections go through the adversary AS. As the sending rate of the attack payloads to the target is negligible and no routing manipulation is involved in both the data plane and control plane, it is difficult to detect the Erebus attacks. The original publication [12] shows that individual Bitcoin nodes can be partitioned, possibly in parallel, within 5–6 weeks of attack execution. Unfortunately, the attack sustainability is unknown since no experiments are given to show what happens after the Erebus attack successfully partitions a node.

2.2 SyncAttack: A P2P Network Splitting Attack

SyncAttack [10] aims to partition a group of Bitcoin nodes from the rest of the P2P network, i.e., splitting it into two. In the SyncAttack, the adversary occupies all inbound connection slots of all reachable nodes to prevent other nodes connect to them. The paper [10] argues that when all inbound slots of existing nodes are occupied, newly-joined nodes have no choice but to establish connections to the adversarial nodes. As a result, the P2P network would be split into two partitions: existing nodes versus new, arriving nodes. To make an existing node prioritizes the adversary-generated connections, the adversary sends fresh block and transaction data via 16 connections from the same IP and establishes other 99 connections from IPs with distinct network groups to it. Again, the attack sustainability is not properly evaluated in the original publication [10].

2.3 Bitcoin Partitioning Attacks Using Routing Manipulation

Apostolaki et al. [1] show that a malicious AS can perform BGP hijacking attacks against the IP prefixes hosting targeted Bitcoin nodes. Once the traffic to such prefixes is hijacked, the adversary AS drops Bitcoin traffic at the network layer, effectively cutting off the communication between targeted Bitcoin nodes and the rest of the P2P network. This is further extended in a multi-cryptocurrency attack by Saad et al. [11]. Since evaluating the sustainability of such attacks inherently requires measuring the sustainability of the routing manipulation, we leave it for future work.

3 Re-evaluating Existing Partitioning Attacks

We aim to evaluate the sustainability of the Erebus attack [12], and SyncAttack [10] — in the face of the peer eviction mechanism that has made the Eclipse attack unsustainable. In particular, we use *partitioning duration* as the metric to measure the sustainability of the two attacks. It indicates the time difference between the moment when the target node(s) is partitioned and the moment when it receives a new block from the canonical chain. To measure the partitioning duration, one needs to conduct the two attacks (i.e., partitioning a node or a group of nodes) successfully and waits for the partitions to cease. Thus, in this section, we test the sustainability of two existing partitioning attacks and provide empirical evidence that they do not create effective partitioning to any meaningful extent in practice. In the following Sects. 3.1 and 3.2, we describe how we re-evaluate the two attacks and measure their sustainability in practical test environments.

3.1 Re-evaluation of the Original Erebus Attack

Now, let us explain how we test the original Erebus attack with the sustainability metric.

Direct Implementation and Evaluation of the Original Attack. First, we explain how we are supposed to conduct the experiments of the original Erebus attack, according to its publication [12]. It follows five steps:

(i) Deploy a target Bitcoin node on the mainnet.
(ii) Send many adversary-chosen IPs (called shadow IPs) from a malicious ISP with various network groups to the target node.
(iii) Wait until the target node's peer table is filled with the shadow IPs and the target makes all its outgoing connections to the shadow IPs.
(iv) Monopolize the target node's inbound connections by making connections from the malicious ISP.
(v) Measure how long the target node is partitioned, checking the moment the target node receives new blocks.

Challenges. Measuring the sustainability of the Erebus attack, however, involves several challenges.

- *Mainnet experiment required.* For measuring the attack sustainability, we should identify the exact moment other benign Bitcoin nodes relay new blocks to the target node. Therefore, ideally, the experiment should be performed in the mainnet in order to reflect other real Bitcoin nodes' behavior.
- *Need huge network resources.* The original Erebus attack requires an adversary to be an autonomous system (AS), utilizing 500K shadow IPs for occupying the target node's peer table. To experiment it as is in the mainnet, we need to be an ISP or we need to own and control many Bitcoin nodes with many distributed IP addresses, both of which are extremely hard to achieve.
- *Long attack execution time.* The Erebus attack requires up to several weeks to be successfully mounted, which is too long for making practical evaluations in the mainnet.

Our Workarounds. Let us describe how we address the three challenges with our workarounds. To simplify the experiment, we only consider the target node's behavior *after* being partitioned. This is acceptable as we only measure the attack sustainability, not the end-to-end attack effectiveness. Instead of implementing the end-to-end Erebus attack, we make the target node behaves *as if* it is partitioned by the Erebus attack. For this attack emulation, we do the followings: (i) we set up a simple, temporary firewall to prevent the target node from making new outbound connections, and (ii) we occupy all inbound connections of the target by manually disconnecting its peers (via RPC calls). As a result, the target node cannot make outbound connections to other benign nodes, and all inbound connections are occupied by the attacker as if the Erebus attack is successfully

Table 2. Measured attack duration of the Erebus attack. The attack does not maintain partitions longer than 10 min in most cases.

Partitioning duration: average ± stdev	90% percentile	95% percentile
297 s ± 293 s	679 s	847 s

launched. This short-cut implementation of the Erebus attack for our sustainability evaluation can detour the challenges above: (a) we do not need to be an ISP or own/control large numbers of IP addresses, as we skip occupying the target node's peer table; (b) the attack does not require a long execution time because we manually disconnect all peers from the target node; (c) due to (a) and (b), our experiments now do not disturb other benign nodes in the mainnet.

Results. Table 2 shows the overall result of the original Erebus attack's partitioning duration from a mainnet experiment. The original Erebus attack maintains its partitioning to the target node for 297 s on average, where most of the experiments have ended within 900 s.

Why Does the Attack Not Last Long? The partition ends when a benign node delivers new blocks to the target; however, the original Erebus attack design does *not* have attack features that prevent such a partition-breaking event triggered by benign peers. The target node faces frequent inbound connections from other benign peers due to Bitcoin's peer eviction mechanism (see Sect. 4 for more details), and some of them would try relaying recent blocks right after establishing a connection. Even when only one benign node tries to relay blocks to the target node, as there is no barricade, the partition is broken by the delivered blocks.

The attack usually ends in less than 900 s, which is in sufficient for follow-up attacks. For example, double spending needs to make the target node confirm a fake transaction, which requires several blocks to be generated while the target is being partitioned.

3.2 Re-evaluation of the Original SyncAttack

Now, let us re-evaluate the original SyncAttack, by applying the same metric as we evaluated the original Erebus attack in the previous section. SyncAttck differs from the Erebus attack in a number of ways. The most notable difference is its scale; i.e., SyncAttack aims to split the *entire* Bitcoin network into two whereas the Erebus attack seeks to partition a *single* node. Therefore, we need to consider new challenges and strategies to make a reasonable SyncAttack evaluation.

Direct Implementation and Evaluation of the Original Attack. First, we explain how we conduct the sustainability experiments for the original SyncAttack. Experiments should follow these steps:

(i) Prepare a network with two benign partitions (i.e., existing nodes and arriving nodes) and a small group of adversary nodes.

(ii) Add a new node to the network and let this new node establishes new outbound connections referring to the DNS seeder.

(iii) Check whether the partition is maintained. We consider a partition ends when the new node establishes outgoing connections to both benign partitions.

(iv) Repeat (ii)-(iii), and end the experiment when the partition ends.

Challenges. Here, we list the challenges of the implementations above:

- *Implementation of a Large-Scale Network Split.* In contrast to the Erebus attack, evaluating the original SyncAttack requires a test network of thousands of Bitcoin clients to split into two. It is nearly impossible to conduct such an experiment in the mainnet. Simulating it would be challenging as well.
- *Implementation of Churn-Ins and Their Bootstrapping.* The Bitcoin network in practice experiences high churns, and new incoming nodes are important components for SyncAttack. When a new node enters the Bitcoin network, it requests reachable nodes' IP addresses to DNS seeds.

Our Workarounds. Let us explain how we realize the re-evaluation of SyncAttack with the following workarounds.

- *Evaluation with Over-Estimations.* Evaluating SyncAttack is challenging mainly due to the size and complexity of the attack execution. To reduce the experiments to a manageable size and manage the complexity while offering meaningful experiment results, we simplify our sustainability experiments with over-estimation. That is, we take a number of reduction strategies for our experiments to obtain the attack sustainability results that are strictly longer than the actual attack sustainability. We ensure at every reduction step that the attacks in our simplified evaluations are strictly easier to sustain than the large-scale attacks in the mainnet. We argue that this simplification makes an effective experiment for proving the *unsustainability* of SyncAttack. By showing that the strictly easier SyncAttack cannot achieve sustainability, we can show that the original SyncAttack must also be unsustainable.

  First, we reduce the size of the experiment by scaling down the original SyncAttack's strategy in the regtest network. Our regtest network consists of three types of nodes: 10 adversary nodes, and existing/arriving nodes with the same number. To use the terminologies in the original publications of SyncAttack [10], the adversary nodes take the roles of A_u (occupy all available inbound slots of reachable nodes) and A_r (occupy all available outbound slots of reachable nodes). This is a strict advantage to the adversary since it is easier to maintain the partition in a small-scale test network rather than in mainnet.

  Second, we make an assumption that the adversary occupies almost all inbound connection slots of reachable nodes. Under this assumption, the adversary has a higher chance of maintaining the partition because new partition-breaking connections from existing nodes would not occur.
- *Implementing Churn-Ins with a Real DNS Seeder.* In our evaluation framework, we continuously add new Bitcoin nodes into the network and test whether SyncAttack successfully continues to partition the target network. For a realistic experiment of SyncAttack, we deploy a custom DNS seeder [3], and include all IP addresses of existing nodes, arriving nodes and adversary nodes in our experiment setup into the seeder. Each new Bitcoin node fetches IP addresses from the DNS seeder and establishes 10 outgoing connections among them.

Table 3. Probability of maintaining partitions with SyncAttack for (i) every single arriving node, and (ii) multiple arriving nodes within an hour. Partitions do not last at all after having multiple arriving nodes in an hour.

Proportion of adversary nodes in seeder	71.4%	50%	33.3%
Prob. of maintaining the partition after single node arrival	12.5%	3.7%	1.5%
Prob. of maintaining the partition for 1 h	0	0	0

Results. Table 3 shows the probability of maintaining the partitioning in SyncAttack by varying proportion of adversary nodes in the seeder. The experiment is conducted 1,000 times for each condition, checking if partitioning can be maintained after a new single node arrives in the network. The partitioning duration of SyncAttack turns out to be *extremely short*. Even in the case where the adversary occupies half of the IP lists in the DNS seeder, the probability of maintaining the partition after *single* node arrival is 3.7%.

If the attacker tries to maintain the partitioning for an hour (i.e. minimum partitioning duration for performing double-spending), it has to withstand all new arriving nodes during that time. According to Bitnodes [13], 851 nodes joined the Bitcoin network every hour on average; the probability of maintaining the partitioning for an hour converges to zero. By looking at the fact that SyncAttack would not sustain in such advantageous conditions (i.e., controlling over the network with only a few dozen of nodes, and adversary occupying almost all inbound connection slots of reachable nodes), we claim that SyncAttack execution in mainnet is not feasible after all.

4 Optimization and Cost Analysis

Knowing that the two original attacks [10,12] are unsustainable in practice, we aim to improve these attacks to see whether sustainable Bitcoin partitioning attacks are possible in practice. To make stronger final conclusions about their sustainability, we aim to optimize the attacks by maximizing the partitioning duration in consideration of Bitcoin's peer eviction mechanism in Sect. 4.1.

For accurate and realistic cost analysis, we measure the attack resources required for the optimized attacks in practice. We define and model the necessary resources for these optimized attacks as a two-dimensional attack resource vector: (1) the number of distinct network groups controlled by the adversary (i.e., netgroup cost), and (2) the physical distance to the target node(s) (i.e., latency cost). Upon this, we derive the required cost of the optimized attacks when attempting to maintain partitioning for a given time duration (e.g., 1 h). Our optimization often requires significantly more attack resources than the original attacks to attain certain sustainability. Our analysis of the attack cost in these optimized attacks concludes that a node partition made by the optimized Erebus attack can be sustained with reasonably high investment (e.g., 100 unique network groups along with adversary closer to the target than 95%

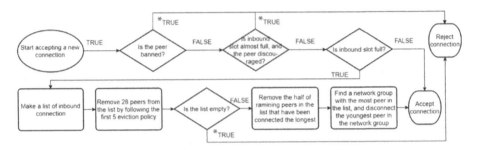

Fig. 1. Flow chart of Bitcoin's connection handling logic. An unmodified benign Bitcoin node always accepts new incoming connections, with the exception of three abnormal cases (marked with *) that occur by extremely unlikely chance.

of all inbound connections towards it) while the optimized SyncAttack becomes sustainable only with extremely high attack resources (e.g., 22K unique network groups along with adversary closer to each target in the reachable node than 95% of all inbound connections towards them).

4.1 Optimization of Two Original Attacks

We first look back at why the original partitioning attacks fail to sustain. A successful partitioning attack campaign begins to fail when a new benign connection is made to the target, and starts to deliver new blocks. This means that to maximize attack sustainability, we should prevent new benign connections from delivering new blocks to our target(s). To this end, we investigate Bitcoin's peer connection mechanism as it is where the decision to allow a new connection to the target node is made. Therefore, we investigate Bitcoin's peer connection management logic since now it is essential to know when and how a new connection is made to the target node. As we optimize the partitioning attacks, we optimize their attack strategies with respect to Bitcoin's peer connection management logic, particularly, the peer eviction mechanism.

Bitcoin's Peer Connection Management Logic. Figure 1 shows the overall flow diagram of Bitcoin's peer connection management logic. We analyze the CreateNodeFromAcceptedSocket() in net.cpp and extract this diagram without any omission. We summarize the two important design principles:

- *Admitting Inbound Connections (Almost) Unconditionally.* The Bitcoin client admits new inbound connections unconditionally in all practical scenarios except for the following three abnormal, unlikely cases:
  (i) the client has manually banned the new peer.
  (ii) the new peer has violated the Bitcoin protocol and is thus considered discouraged.
  (iii) the client has manually reduced the maximum number of inbound connections.

- *Evicting the Least Prioritized.* A new inbound connection may cause an eviction of an existing peer connection in order to free up one connection slot for this new inbound connection. Existing peer connections are ordered by their priority and only the least prioritized one is evicted.

Our conclusions drawn from these principles are two-fold. First, the remote attacker cannot prevent new benign connections from being made to the target node unless it can force the target and the benign nodes to turn into abnormal states, which is impossible. Second, therefore, partitioning adversaries have to evict any new benign connection before it delivers new blocks from the canonical blockchain.

Probability of Withstanding a *Single* Inbound Connection. Now, our goal is narrowed down to maintaining a partition by evicting new benign connections before they deliver new blocks to the target. As a target node may receive multiple new connections from other benign peers while being partitioned, we should evict multiple such benign connections. We can consider each new benign connection is made *independently* since benign peers are not coordinated in the permissionless Bitcoin network and also incoming connections do not change the target's internal state with respect to the peer eviction logic (unless the benign connection breaks the partition).

Let us define p_{pc} (partitioning continues), the probability the existing partitioning continues when a *single* new benign connection is made to the target. In other words, it is the probability that a new benign peer is evicted before delivering any new block. We want to ensure that we achieve p_{pc} very close to 1.0 since the target is partitioned until the first new inbound connection is made with the probability of $1 - p_{pc}$. Because all these events are independent, the expectation of the number of new inbound connections the adversary can withstand is $\frac{1}{(1-p_{pc})}$. For example, a five-nines probability for $p_{pc} = 0.99999$ ensures that partitioning can last after about $100,000$ new inbound connections on average.

Breaking Down p_{pc}. Given the current Bitcoin's peer connection management logic, we summarize and propose the two orthogonal optimization strategies for maximizing p_{pc}. These two optimizations must be conducted independently to maximize the overall partitioning duration.

The current Bitcoin's peer eviction policy has three rules[1] that prioritize 28 peer connections so that they are not evicted for a new (attacker's) connection:

- Rule ① *Netgroup-based prioritization.* Prioritize 4 peers with top-4 netgroup-key values.
- Rule ② *Ping-based prioritization.* Prioritize 8 peers with the lowest minimum ping times.
- Rule ③ *Message-history-based prioritization.* Prioritize 16 peers that have exchanged recent blocks and transactions.

The probability p_{pc} indeed is equivalent to the probability that the newly-made benign connection we want to evict is *not* prioritized by these rules. This is

---

[1] We exclude some rare-case rules found in the Bitcoin Core implementation, which are not useful for our current discussion.

because, after prioritizing 28 peer connections according to the rules above, the target Bitcoin node always selects a single, the least prioritized connection (i.e., the youngest peer in the network group with the most connections) to evict among the rest. Thus, now we analyze these three rules and the adversary's chance of having the benign connection not prioritized after all.

First, p_{nt4} (non-top-4), the probability that a new benign connection has non-top-4 netgroupkey value at the target. This can be increased by making many connections to the target with many unique netgroups.

Second, p_{ebp} (evicted-before-ping): the probability that a new benign connection is evicted before its ping time (with respect to the target) is calculated. This is related to how quickly an adversary can send new attack connection(s) to the target and evict the new benign connection before it finishes the ping calculation. This probability can be increased by locating the attacker's nodes very close to the target.

Third, p_{ebbt} (evicted-before-block/tx): the probability that a new benign connection is evicted before any blocks or transactions are sent to the target. This probability can also be increased by locating the adversary's nodes close to the target.

Designing Two Orthogonal Optimization Strategies. Finally, we design detailed attack strategies. We first separate out the optimization for p_{nt4} since an event of being prioritized by Rule ① is independent of the events of being prioritized by the latter two rules. This is because the network groups of inbound connections are irrelevant to how quickly the adversary's new connections can be made to the target. In other words, having many network groups as attack resources do not have a direct correlation with getting physically close to the target. Therefore, our first attack strategy deals with Rule ① should maximize p_{nt4} by raising the bar to be selected as the top-4 netgroupkey values.

Our second attack strategy aims to optimize p_{ebp} by minimizing the time to send attacker's new connections to the target so that the admitted benign connection is not prioritized either by Rule ② or Rule ③. In practice, ping time is always calculated before allowing a new peer to send any blocks or transactions. Thus, Rule ③ can be ignored since the second attack strategy, if successful, prevents any blocks or transaction messages from a benign connection after all.

Therefore, the probability p_{pc} is simply derived as the multiplication of the two independent probabilities p_{nt4} and p_{ebp}, which is given by

$$p_{pc} = p_{nt4} \cdot p_{ebp} \tag{1}$$

Let us provide some more details on these two orthogonal attack strategies.

Netgroup-Flooding. To maximize p_{nt4}, our attacker should flood connections to the target node with as many unique network groups as possible. To describe why such a simple (yet expensive) strategy ensures optimality, let us quickly sketch how the current Bitcoin implementation prioritizes nodes with certain netgroups. From Bitcoin 0.12.0, Bitcoin prioritizes four peer connections with the largest netgroupkeys among its inbound peers. The netgroupkey is calculated in a deterministic manner using a cryptographic hash function (i.e., SipHash) with a random seed that is known only to each node. The network group (i.e., the upper 16-bit of IPv4 addresses) is used as an input to the hash function and its digest becomes the netgroupkey of each peer. This way, the attacker cannot predict which network groups will be prioritized. As a result, the only way for the attacker to maximize p_{nt4} is to raise the bar for being selected as the top-4 netgroupkey value by flooding connections with many unique network groups.

Evict-Before-Ping. To maximize p_{ebp}, our attacker should make her new connections to the target node before it finishes the ping computation with the new benign connection. To achieve that, the attacker must first fill up all the available inbound connection slots of the target node in order to get notified whenever a new benign connection is made.

Next, to ensure that the target node receives and accepts the attacker's new connection request before finishing a ping computation of the new benign connection, the adversary should be located as close to the target as possible. We consider a number of practical scenarios to minimize the ping distance to the target node. First, if a target is in a public cloud (e.g., AWS, Google Cloud), an adversary can create instances at the same cloud data center and measure ping distance to the target until it obtains a small enough (e.g., a few milliseconds) ping value. Second, if a target is not in a public cloud but its approximate location is known by its IP address (e.g., [4,6,7]), an adversary may attempt to find bots or public clouds that are close enough to the target.

We accomplish the optimization strategies above by implementing the following steps with our simple attack script: (1) the adversary makes 114 connections (with nodes located close to the target node) to the target concurrently by establishing VERSION handshakes; (2) each connection performs a ping-pong exchange with the target every 2 min to stay alive; (3) each connection immediately reconnects to the target as soon as its TCP session with the target is terminated due to eviction. This way, we can ensure that the adversary is notified of the new benign connection, and evict it with minimum delays.

4.2   Cost Analysis of the Optimized Attacks

Finally, we evaluate the optimized attack strategies and estimate the required attack costs. Note again that we focus on the sustainability of these attacks and the cost incurred by maintaining an existing partition using the two attacks.

Cost Analysis with No Real-World Experiments. We estimate the required cost for the sustainability of the two attacks *without* real-world experiments because making several simplifying assumptions (as we did for the sustainability tests in Sects. 3.1 and 3.2) is not allowed here. Instead, we derive analytical frameworks that allow us to compute the attack duration of the two attacks for varying the two-dimensional attack costs.

As shown in Eq. (1), optimizing the sustainability of these partitioning attacks is composed of two orthogonal attack strategies. The two strategies require two different attack resources: maximizing p_{nt4} requires a large number of adversary-controlled IP addresses with unique netgroups (the more unique netgroups, the higher p_{nt4}) while maximizing p_{ebp} requires adversary-controlled nodes that are close to the target node (the closer to the target, the higher p_{ebp}). We describe how we derive two costs.

Table 4. Probability of maintaining partitions with the optimized Erebus attack for one hour. With significant attack resources (e.g., owning 100 unique network groups with $p_{ebp} = 0.95, 0.99$), partitions can be maintained with moderate probability.

Netgroup\ P_{ebp}	0.9	0.95	0.97	0.99
10	0.001	0.002	0.003	0.004
20	0.022	0.043	0.055	0.070
50	0.106	0.203	0.260	0.333
100	0.174	0.333	0.427	0.546
1,000	0.269	0.515	0.661	0.845
10,000	0.281	0.538	0.691	0.882
22,000	0.282	0.539	0.692	0.884

Netgroup Cost. As mentioned earlier, in each node, peers with top-4 netgroup-key values are prioritized. The adversary can raise the threshold for being chosen as the top-4 netgroupkey values by making connections from numerous distinct network groups. If the adversary can use G unique network groups to make connections to the target, p_{nt4} is simply derived as $\binom{G}{4}/\binom{G+1}{4} = \frac{G-3}{G+1}$ because its value should be smaller than top-4 values among $G + 1$ unique network groups (G from the adversary, 1 from the benign peer).

Latency Cost. For a successful evict-before-ping event, our adversary nodes should reconnect to the target earlier than a new benign connection. To be more specific, the adversary should reach the target *before* the target receives a *pong* message from the new benign connection. Analyzing the Bitcoin Core's network protocol, we learn that two round-trip times (RTTs) are required for a benign node to finish a ping-time calculation and the same two RTTs are needed for an adversary node to make another connection to the target after being notified of the new benign connection. Therefore, ignoring minor perturbations in end-to-end network latency between these nodes, an adversary can continue its partitioning (i.e., succeed evict-before-ping) if her node is *closer* to the target compared to the benign peer; otherwise, the partition may end because of this new benign connection. We empirically confirm this with five mainnet Bitcoin nodes in five different locations in Amazon EC2. From this, we state that the adversary can maximize p_{ebp} by getting closer than other benign nodes with respect to the target node.

Final Cost Estimation of the Two Optimized Attacks. We finally derive the estimated cost for the 1-hour sustainability of the two optimized attacks. Table 4 shows the probability of maintaining a partition with the optimized Erebus attack. Each value is derived by $p_{pc}^n = (p_{nt4} \cdot p_{ebp})^n$, where n is the

Table 5. Probability of maintaining partitions with the optimized SyncAttack for one hour, suggesting that SyncAttack is nearly impossible to sustain despite the optimization.

Netgroup\P_{ebp}	0.9	0.95	0.97	0.99
1,000	0.00	0.00	0.00	0.00
10,000	0.00	0.00	0.00	0.02
22,000	0.00	0.00	0.0013	0.44

number of benign peers that adversary has to withstand for one hour. In Sect. 3.1, we observe that about $n = 12$ ($\simeq 3,600/297$) new benign connections must be handled properly for the goal of 1-hour sustainability. As the Erebus attack partitions a single node, the adversary can locate her attack nodes close to the target and achieve a high p_{ebp} (e.g., 0.95, 0.97, 0.99). If the Erebus attacker owns 100 unique network groups (as it claims to be in the original paper), it can sustain the partitioning for an hour with a probability of 33% and 55% with p_{ebp}=0.95 and 0.99, respectively. With some more attack network resources, say 1,000 network groups, we can expect 52% and 85% of successful 1-hour attacks with p_{ebp}=0.95 and 0.99, respectively. Having unique network groups beyond 1,000, however, only marginally improves the attack duration. Note that the maximum unique netgroups we test is 22,000, which is the unique netgroups we find in a large Mirai botnet [8]

Table 5 shows the probability of maintaining a partition with the optimized SyncAttack. We assume benign reachable nodes are partitioned into two groups of size A and B, while the adversary owns G reachable nodes with unique network groups. Let us consider a single new arriving node to the network due to network churn. Each reachable node may end up establishing a new reliable connection from this new node with a probability $(1 - p_{pc})$ if the new node makes a connection request. Since the eviction process at each node is independent of each other, we can say that on average $A' = (1 - p_{pc})A$ nodes in one group and $B' = (1 - p_{pc})B$ nodes in the other group would be willing to establish reliable peer connections from the new benign node (again, if the benign node wishes to do so).

The new node can make a new connection to any of the three groups: A' nodes in one partition, B' nodes in the other partition, and X adversary nodes. The new node repeats reconnecting to other nodes when its connection is evicted quickly due to the optimal partitioning attack strategies until it finally makes a reliable peer connection to a reachable node. Thus, for the current partition to continue, a new connection from the new node should not be made to the first two groups at the same time (because that would bridge the two partitions). The probability for withstanding single arriving node P_{single} in SyncAttack would therefore be given by

$$P_{single} = \left(\frac{A' + G}{A' + B' + G} \right)^{10} + \left(\frac{B' + G}{A' + B' + G} \right)^{10} - \left(\frac{G}{A' + B' + G} \right)^{10}. \quad (2)$$

For Table 5, we consider two partitions of size 7,000 each (i.e., $A = B = 7,000$) [13]. For the number of new peer nodes per hour, we used the churn rate we measure earlier in Sect. 3.2; that is, we assume that 851 new peers appear on the mainnet for an hour on average. The overall probability for maintaining partition for an hour with the optimized SyncAttack is thus derived as P_{single}^{851}. SyncAttack turns out to be unsustainable in most cases even with optimization strategies. Even in the case where the adversary has attack resources with 22K network groups, it is hard to expect that SyncAttack would sustain for an hour (i.e., 0% with $p_{ebp} = 0.95$, 1% with $p_{ebp} = 0.97$). Our experiment shows that SyncAttack may maintain its partitioning with some reasonable probability of 44% *only* when it has a significant amount of attack resources. First, the adversary must control 22K or more nodes with unique network groups. This can be achieved only when the adversary has mega-size botnets (e.g., a Mirai botnet of 2.3M bots has 22K unique network groups). Second, the adversary should be close to all reachable nodes. That is, the adversary must be co-located with all the 14K reachable nodes in the Bitcoin network to achieve $p_{ebp} = 0.99$ (i.e., ensuring 99th percentile in terms of RTT distance for all the nodes). This appears to be challenging to achieve because reachable Bitcoin nodes are distributed in various networks.

5   Conclusion

That blockchain networks can be partitioned by unauthorized adversaries is still a serious threat to their security and safety. Our work helps us to further characterize existing partitioning attacks with the notion of attack sustainability, which is a critical yet less-emphasized metric for partitioning attacks. We hope this work guides the direction for developing additional countermeasures against partitioning attacks in Bitcoin and other blockchain networks.

Acknowledgment. This work was supported by Electronics and Telecommunications Research Institute (ETRI) grant funded by the Korean government [23ZR1300, Research on Intelligent Cyber Security and Trust Infra].

References

1. Apostolaki, M., Zohar, A., Vanbever, L.: Hijacking bitcoin: routing attacks on cryptocurrencies. In: Proceedings of the IEEE S&P (2017)
2. The peer eviction mechanism implementation of Bitcoin Core (Aug 2015). https://github.com/bitcoin/bitcoin/commit/2c701537c8fc7f4cfb0163ec1f49662120e61eb7
3. Custom DNS seeder. https://dnsseed.netsptest.com
4. db-ip IP Address Databases (2022). https://db-ip.com/db/
5. Heilman, E., Kendler, A., Zohar, A., Goldberg, S.: Eclipse attacks on Bitcoin's peer-to-peer network. In: Proceedings of the USENIX Security (2015)
6. IPinfo IP Address Databases (2022). https://ipinfo.io/products/ip-database-download

7. Maxmind GeoIP2 Databases. https://www.maxmind.com/en/geoip2-databases
8. Netlab360's Mirai Scanner. https://data.netlab.360.com/mirai-scanner/
9. Nayak, K., Kumar, S., Miller, A., Shi, E.: Stubborn mining: generalizing selfish mining and combining with an eclipse attack. In: 2016 IEEE European Symposium on Security and Privacy (Euro S&P), pp. 305–320. IEEE (2016)
10. Saad, M., Chen, S., Mohaisen, D.: SyncAttack: double-spending in bitcoin without mining power. In: ACM CCS (2021)
11. Saad, M., Mohaisen, D.: Three birds with one stone: efficient partitioning attacks on interdependent cryptocurrency networks. In: Proceedings of the IEEE S&P (2023)
12. Tran, M., Choi, I., Moon, G.J., Vu, A.V., Kang, M.S.: A sealthier partitioning attack against bitcoin peer-to-peer network. In: Proceedings of the IEEE S&P (2020)
13. Yeow, A.: Global bitcoin nodes distribution (2021). https://bitnodes.io/

Demystifying Web3 Centralization: The Case of Off-Chain NFT Hijacking

Felix Stöger[1]([envelope])[ORCID], Anxin Zhou[2][ORCID], Huayi Duan[1][ORCID], and Adrian Perrig[1][ORCID]

[1] ETH Zürich, Zürich, Switzerland
felix.stoeger@inf.ethz.ch, huayi.duan@inf.ethz.ch
[2] City University of Hong Kong, Kowloon, Hong Kong, SAR

Abstract. Despite the ambitious vision of re-decentralizing the Web as we know it, the Web3 movement is facing many hurdles of centralization which seem insurmountable in the near future, and the security implications of centralization remain largely unexplored. Using non-fungible tokens (NFTs) as a case study, we conduct a systematic analysis of the threats posed by centralized entities in the current Web3 ecosystem. Our findings are concerning: *almost every interaction between a user and a centralized entity can be exploited to hijack NFTs or cryptocurrencies from the user, through network attacks practical today.* We show that many big players in the ecosystem are vulnerable to such attacks, placing large financial investments at risk. Our study is a starting point to study the pervasive centralization issues in the shifting Web3 landscape.

1 Introduction

We are witnessing a trend of re-decentralizing web services provided by big corporations, which is portrayed as the transition from Web2 to Web3. In this envisioned Web3 paradigm, decentralized applications (DApps) are hosted on blockchains and other distributed infrastructures, without relying on any single entity for their governance and operation [23]. However, most DApps today deviate from this idealized model and, somewhat inevitably, employ centralized components for cost efficiency, performance, and usability. This creates profitable targets for attackers as observed in many real-world incidents [11,12,25]. Such architecture-level attack surface has not received equal attention from the research community compared with vulnerabilities in the underlying blockchain protocols [18,28], as we further discuss in Sect. 2. It is important and urgent to fill this gap, given the prevalence of centralized entities in the current Web3 ecosystem and their complex interactions with other parties.

We initiate a systematic study of the security issues *induced by centralization* in Web3, focusing on the sub-ecosystem around non-fungible tokens (NFTs). The reason for choosing NFTs as our subject of study is three-fold. First, they are among the most popular Web3 concepts with a multi-billion dollar market [31]. Second, NFTs establish the fundamental and ubiquitous notion of asset ownership, and therefore they will likely persist even if high market valuations decline.

F. Baldimtsi and C. Cachin (Eds.): FC 2023, LNCS 13951, pp. 182–199, 2024.
https://doi.org/10.1007/978-3-031-47751-5_11

After the initial standard [17], the Ethereum community has proposed a series of improvements to bring NFTs closer to a practical realm from usability [3] and legal perspectives [20]. Last but not the least, the NFT sub-ecosystem is sufficient to demonstrate common centralization issues, as it involves different centralized entities that interact with users and decentralized infrastructures in various ways. We are particularly interested in the security risks arising from such interactions, as they should not exist in a fully decentralized architecture.

Our work starts with the definition of a functional model that captures the essential entities in today's NFT ecosystem and their dynamics for the creation, tracking, and trading of NFTs. Instantiating this model with concrete architectures that employ different forms of centralization, we systematically examine vulnerable interactions that can be exploited through practical network attacks such as BGP or DNS hijacking. As a result, we find that *almost every interaction of a user with a centralized entity leads to an attack that can hijack NFTs or the associated cryptocurrencies.* Such hijacking is *off-chain* in that it involves no exploitation of the underlying blockchain or smart contracts. We also examine the detectability of these attacks. Some of them can be detected and prevented by prudent inspection of transaction parameters, whereas others require end-to-end data authentication in a decentralized architecture. We have validated most of our proposed attacks on OpenSea and a Ethereum testnet. Furthermore, our analysis of real-world service providers show that 6 out of 10 top NFT marketplaces and many other intermediary services are vulnerable.

Our study of NFTs is just a starting point to investigate the centralization risks in the broad and shifting Web3 ecosystem. The methodology we developed in this work is also applicable to analyzing DApps beyond NFTs.

2 Related Work

Research on NFT Security. Marlinspike [26] points out that DApps are not as decentralized as claimed because of their reliance on centralized servers. These servers can return arbitrary NFT-associated data to users, and marketplaces like OpenSea can unilaterally remove NFTs from their listings. This indicates a clear violation of DApps's fundamental principle that their operation should not be influenced by any centralized authority. Das et al. [15] examine today's NFT ecosystem and several security issues therein, including insufficient user authentication and unverified smart contracts, lack of persistent asset data storage, and trader malpractices. Wang et al. [33] measure the risks of disconnection between NFTs and their off-chain assets. Unlike these prior studies that discusses issues arising from (centralized) entities themselves, we inspect architecture-level vulnerabilities rooted in the *extra interactions* induced by centralized entities, and our attacks work *even if these entities themselves remain uncompromised.*

Attacks on DApps. Su et al. [30] analyze common transaction patterns of DApp attacks and develop a tool to automatically identify security incidents. Such attacks exploit design or implementation flaws in smart contracts and thus are orthogonal to the network-based attacks we consider.

As a major class of DApps, decentralized finance (DeFi) aims to remove traditional financial institutions like banks and exchanges. The transparency and high transaction latency of blockchains makes DeFi services subject to, e.g., front running [14] and sandwiching attacks [34]. Because of their reliance on centralized components like web servers and blockchain gateways, real-world DeFi platforms are also susceptible to the attacks presented in this paper.

Recently, Wang et al. [32] quantify the security risks of unlimited approval of ERC20 tokens that fuel many DApps. Some of our attacks also exploit the fact that trading NFTs requires their owners to delegate control to marketplaces.

Li et al. [24] find that centralized intermediary services used by DApps can be turned into attack vectors for denial of service (DoS). This demonstrates the risk of centralization from another interesting angle.

Blockchain Security. Many attacks on blockchains at the consensus [18,28] or network layer [4,21] have been discovered. In comparison, our work explores a new class of security threats arising from external entities which are not part of a blockchain but widely exist for practical reasons. Programming errors in smart contracts can often lead to vulnerabilities [5]. Different tools have been developed to find such security bugs [22,27]. These tools, however, cannot detect our attacks because we do not exploit flaws in smart contracts themselves.

Network Attacks. The Internet's core building blocks, including the Border Gateway Protocol (BGP) for inter-domain routing and the Domain Name System (DNS) for name resolution, are not secure by design. In a BGP hijacking attack, the attacker can maliciously announce the IP prefix of an autonomous system (AS) and thereby hijack its inbound network traffic; as for DNS, an off-path attacker can inject bogus data into a DNS server's cache and direct clients to malicious servers. These attacks in turn allow the subversion of a wide range of online systems [13], including public key infrastructures (PKIs) which underpin the widely deployed Transport Layer Security (TLS) protocol [29]. Unfortunately, security extensions to BGP and DNS, e.g., RPKI, BGPsec, and DNSSEC, have not received widespread deployment [10,19]. Therefore, network-based attacks are still practical and prevalent in today's Internet.

3   Modeling NFT Functionality

Despite the variety of entities in the current NFT ecosystem, they implement a common set of functions revolving around the creation, tracking, and trading of NFTs. We define a functional model to capture these essential functions and then instantiate it with concrete architectures for detailed security analyses. As depicted in Fig. 1, our model contains three types of users that interact with three services—ownership registry, asset storage, and NFT marketplace (NFTM)—via predefined interfaces. This model captures the typical life cycle of NFTs seen today, allowing us to systematically uncover vulnerable interactions involving different centralized entities.

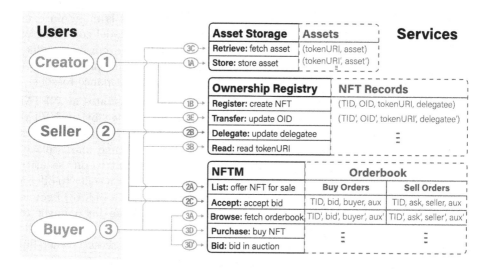

Fig. 1. Our model to capture the essential interactions (arrows) between different users (left) and services (right) commonly found in the current NFT ecosystem.

3.1   Data and Interfaces

Each service exposes a set of interfaces for users to access and modify its data (illustrated in the dashed boxes in Fig. 1).

Ownership Registry. In essence, NFTs are ownership records of digital or physical assets, and these records are stored in a (ideally) permanent ownership registry. Each record is defined by 4 fields. The first and foremost is TID, which uniquely identifies an NFT; in practice, this is implemented by pairing a globally unique smart contract address and a locally unique token index. The other three fields are: OID identifying the token's owner, tokenURI pointing to the underlying asset, and delegatee identifying an entity who can control the token on behalf of its owner. The registry exposes four interfaces: (1) Register to create a new record with all fields except delegatee properly initialized to non-empty values, (2) Transfer to change the owner of a token by updating its OID and clearing the delegatee field, (3) Delegate to set the delegatee for a token, and (4) Read to retrieve a record for a given TID. We explain several technicalities below.

The NFT standard EIP-721 [17] specifies only the Transfer and Delegate functions in our model. Our additional Register and Read explicitly describe the actions to (1) create NFTs and (2) read NFTs from the ownership registry. This allows us to identify subtle vulnerabilities that otherwise stay concealed. Another remark is that, in practice, tokenURI might not reference the asset directly, but instead a separately stored metadata object that contains a further pointer to the actual asset. This extra layer of indirection may increase the attack surface as well, but we refrain from overcomplicating our model with this subordinate interaction whose functions are already subsumed by the major interfaces. We further assume that once an NFT is created, its tokenURI cannot be updated. Finally, we do not consider the possible destruction of an NFT.

Asset Storage. The underlying data associated with NFTs is maintained in an asset storage. We consider a simple yet realistic storage model consisting of (`tokenURI`, `asset`) pairs and two interfaces to store and retrieve assets. Unlike the ownership registry that is hosted on a blockchain by default, practical asset storage systems are almost always off-chain for cost and performance reasons.

NFTM. NFTs must be tradable to create value. This necessitates an NFTM that connect buyers and sellers. The essential data maintained by an NFTM is an orderbook that keeps track of sell and buy orders. Each order contains a token identifier, a bid/ask price, the order's issuer, and some marketplace-specific auxiliary information (e.g., sale duration) not relevant to our security analyses. An NFTM provides 5 interfaces to users: (1) `List` for a seller to offer a token for sale, (2) `Accept` for a seller to accept a buy order or a bid, (3) `Browse` for users to read the catalog of tokens for sale, (4) `Purchase` for a buyer to buy a listed token, and (5) `Bid` for a buyer to bid on a token in auction. The NFTM updates its orderbook according to these actions and process a ownership transfer transaction whenever a buy order matches a sell order.

3.2 NFT Life Cycle

Users can take three roles: creator, seller, or buyer. We describe a typical NFT life cycle through users' interactions with the necessary services. We use the notation $\widehat{X}$ `action(in → out)` to represent the invocation of an interface `action`, which takes `in` as input from and returns `out` to the caller. The `in` or `out` parameters can be empty. We also omit non-critical data in some invocations.

Creation. The creator of an NFT can vary, for example an artist creating the digital asset, or a party entrusted by the asset creator with the task of tokenizing the asset. We do not distinguish these cases. To start with, the creator uploads an asset to the asset storage by calling $\widehat{1A}$ `Store(asset → tokenURI)`. With the returned `tokenURI`, it then creates a token by calling $\widehat{1B}$ `Register({OID, tokenURI} → TID)`, which stores a new record in the ownership registry.

Listing. The owner of a token offers it for sale through $\widehat{2A}$ `List({TID, OID, ask} →)`. The invoked marketplace needs permission to transfer the token without the seller's further involvement. This is done via $\widehat{2B}$ `Delegate({TID, Mkt} →)`, which sets the `delegatee` of token `TID` as the marketplace identified by `Mkt`.

Trading. A buyer interacts with all three service providers to buy an NFT. It starts by retrieving available sell orders from the marketplace via $\widehat{3A}$ `Browse(→ {TID, ask, seller})`. Here we assume only a single sell order is returned. To examine the associated asset, the buyer first gets the token's metadata by calling $\widehat{3B}$ `Read(TID→ tokenURI)` from the ownership registry and then fetches the asset by calling $\widehat{3C}$ `Retrieve(tokenURI→ asset)` from the storage provider. Marketplaces normally offer two buying options: direct purchase or auction. In the former case, the buyer directly offers the asked price and calls $\widehat{3D}$ `Purchase({TID, ask, buyer} →)`. In the latter case, the buyer places a bid via $\widehat{3D'}$ `Bid({TID, bid, buyer} →)`, which results in a buy order stored in the NFTM's orderbook. Upon a successful sale, the NFTM transfers the token to the new owner by calling ③E `Transfer({TID, buyer} →)` without the seller's involvement. This is legitimate because the NFTM has been approved by the seller in advance.

4   System Architecture and Attack Taxonomy

We consider four instantiations of our NFT model that exist (or could exist) in practice. The first one is a fully decentralized architecture where all services are hosted by decentralized infrastructures and all users access them through their own infrastructure nodes. Each subsequent architecture centralizes one service— that is, the service is either accessed by users through a centralized intermediary (CI), or otherwise hosted centrally and controlled by a single entity. Such centralization creates vulnerable links that can be intercepted to manipulate data communicated between users and services, enabling various attacks to hijack NFTs or cryptocurrencies from different users as summarized in Table 1.

Threat Model. We consider an off-path network adversary who is capable of intercepting communication between a user and a centralized entity through BGP or DNS hijacking. Even if the communication is secured by TLS, the adversary can still acquire a fraudulent certificate to impersonate the victim domain owned by a centralized entity [29]. We assume that decentralized infrastructures themselves, including blockchains and decentralized storage systems, are secure against the adversary, and that their data is always tamper-proof. For example, the adversary cannot attack their underlying consensus mechanisms [18,28] or prevent their users from retrieving data from honest nodes.

4.1   Architecture Type I: Fully Decentralized

In a fully decentralized architecture, the ownership registry and NFTM functions are implemented by smart contracts. Users access these services by sending blockchain transactions that encode function calls to these contracts. The asset storage can be on a blockchain or an off-chain storage system like IPFS or StorJ. We focus on IPFS as it is the de-facto standard decentralized storage system used by many DApps. In IPFS, a file is indexed by a content identifier (CID), a cryptographic token used to retrieve the file and verify its integrity.

Users in this architecture rely on their own blockchain and optionally IPFS nodes to access different services. We do not distinguish between a full blockchain node and a light client [8], because both of them allow a user to verify on-chain data. This idealized (yet still practical!) architecture requires users to use some specialized explorer software to retrieve, organize and render data (e.g., NFTM listings and orderbook) via their local nodes, without depending on any external web services that are prevalent today.

Security. In this architecture, users can locally validate all data they receive from the three services and all actions they perform. In interactions ③A and ③B, a user can read integrity-protected data from the blockchain through its local node. Interactions ①B, ③E, ②B, ②A, ②C, ③D, and ③D' are implemented by blockchain transactions cryptographically signed with the user's private key

Table 1. A summary of potential NFT hijacking attacks in different architectures. The third column indicates whether and how a user can detect attack attempts. Level 1: the user must carefully audit the transaction parameters to be signed to detect an attack attempt. Level 2: the user must obtain some authenticator (e.g., cryptographic digest or digital signature) for the relevant data (received from a centralized entity) in a secure way (e.g., through a decentralized infrastructure that the user is part of) and verify the data to detect an attack attempt. Level 3: the victim can detect the attacks only retrospectively after it notices the financial loss.

Attacks	Architecture	Detectability	Outcome
A1: ①Ⓐ	Type II	2/3*	NFT created with attacker-controlled asset
A2: ③Ⓒ	Type II	2/3*	Wrong NFT bought by buyer
A3: ①Ⓒ	Type III	3	Attacker siphons off royalty payments
A4: ②Ⓐ	Type III	1	NFT sold to attacker at a low price
A5: ②Ⓑ	Type III	1	NFT transferred to attacker
A6: ③Ⓐ	Type III	2/3**	Increased chance to buy attacker's NFT
A7: ③Ⓑ'	Type III	2	Wrong NFT bought by buyer
A8: ③Ⓒ'	Type III	2	Wrong NFT bought by buyer
A9: ③Ⓓ	Type III	1	Funds stolen from buyer Wrong NFT bought by buyer
A10: ③Ⓓ'	Type III	1	Buyer bids on wrong NFT Buyer's bid amount increased by attacker
A11: ②Ⓑ	Type III	1	Funds stolen from buyer
A12: ③Ⓑ:	Type IV	3	Wrong NFT bought by buyer

* 2 if IPFS or blockchain, 3 if centralized storage
** 2 if on-chain orderbook, 3 if centralized access or off-chain orderbook

and so they cannot be tampered with. If the asset storage is on-chain, users can verify the integrity of assets in interaction ①Ⓐ and ③Ⓒ; in the case of IPFS, users can also verify retrieved assets using their CIDs. To conclude, this architecture exposes no extra user interaction that can be exploited by our network attacker. Even if an attacker can intercept the communication between a user and other nodes in a decentralized infrastructure, it cannot alter the data undetected thanks to the infrastructure's built-in end-to-end data authentication.

4.2   Architecture Type II: Centralized Asset Storage

To lower the barriers to entry and reduce operational costs (e.g., the high gas fee in Ethereum), NFT participants in practice offer and use the services defined by our model in various centralized forms. We start by analyzing the asset storage.

Centralized Access. Even if many NFT assets nowadays are stored on a decentralized infrastructure by default, most users access them through Blockchain as a Service (BaaS) providers (e.g., Infura) or IPFS gateways [1]. These CIs provide convenient APIs as a service for users to access a decentralized infrastructure without running their own nodes. As the price of such convenience, however, users must trust these CIs for the authenticity of any received asset data.

For the case of IPFS, it may appear that end-to-end data authentication is still possible with assets' CIDs. However, data integrity verification is rarely implemented outside IPFS nodes. Moreover, IPFS gateways normally do not provide all the parameters[1] needed for data verification to users.

---

[1] For example, the file chunk size that influences the calculation of CID.

Centralized Hosting. Despite the pursuit of decentralization by NFT particpants, it is not uncommon that NFT assets are hosted directly on centralized systems [26]. For example, the Otherside project (otherside.xyz), whose NFTs have a sale volume of over 600K ETH, stores asset files on traditional web servers. Unlike decentralized storage, these centralized systems (including cloud storage) provide only simple checksum mechanisms for the detection of data corruption at best. An attacker capable of manipulating a file in transit can also forge its checksum[2]. Hereafter, we assume that end users cannot verify the authenticity of data received from a centralized storage system.

Attacks. We present attacks against interactions (1A) and (3C) (see Fig. 1). Both attacks arise from the loss of data verifiability due to centralized access or hosting of asset storage. We highlight the data modified by each attack in red.

$\mathcal{A}1$: `Store(asset →tokenURI)`. This attack aims to trick a creator into associating a new NFT with an unexpected asset. Specifically, the attacker can intercept the creator's communication with a CI for decentralized asset storage or directly with a centrally hosted asset storage, and then surreptitiously modify the returned `tokenURI`. As a result, the `tokenURI` included by the creator in a subsequent call to `Register` will reference an attacker-chosen asset.

A creator should normally delete its local copy of the asset file only after the file is uploaded successfully via `Store()`. This gives the creator chances to validate a received `tokenURI`, but such validation is indeed futile. For two of the three architecture variants, centralized access to on-chain assets and centrally hosted asset storage, the attacker can again intercept the creator's validation attempt to retrieve the asset file indicated by the fake `tokenURI`, misleading the creator with a false sense of security. For the case of centralized access to decentralized storage, the aforementioned limitations of IPFS mean that data verification (using CID) by end users is still not practical.

$\mathcal{A}2$: `Retrieve(tokenURI→asset)`. This attack deceives a buyer into purchasing a low-value NFT sold by the attacker, mistakenly believing it to be a high-value one. NFTs by the same creator are generally organized into a collection (e.g., Bored Ape Yacht Club) and have varying values. When a target buyer retrieves an attacker's "bait" asset from a CI or centrally hosted asset storage in interaction (3C), the attacker can intercept the communication and substitute the original dull asset with a more appealing one from the same collection. The buyer may end up investing the dull asset at a much higher price than necessary. The lack of end-user data verification in the architecture under discussion means that such an attack is hard to detect from a victim user's point of view.

Note that this attack is different from a simple counterfeit NFT where the attacker registers its own NFT with the same `tokenURI` as an expensive, legitimate NFT. Counterfeit NFTs are easily detected because they are not part of the same collection as the genuine NFTs.

---

[2] Note that a user in our model can retrieve an asset file's identifier and authenticator (e.g., a CID or digital signature) from a secure decentralized infrastructure.

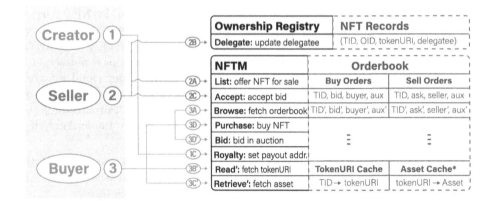

Fig. 2. Centrally hosted NFTM Architecture. The Asset Cache* is optional.

4.3 Architecture Type III: Centralized NFTM

At the hub of any NFT ecosystem are versatile marketplaces that bridge all other players. Because of its complex interactions with other entities, this service's centralization can pose most security risks, as explained in this section. Similarly to our previous analysis, we consider two variants of centralized NFTM (Fig. 2).

Centralized Access. Developing a full-fledged on-chain NFTM is challenging and inefficient, but it is possible to implement the core functions, including the maintenance of an orderbook and the matching and execution of orders, solely with smart contracts. Few NFMTs are of this type. One example is CryptoPunk, which is dedicated to one single collection of NFTs. Even with such a minimal on-chain NFTM, a non-expert user still needs BaaS CIs to access the underlying blockchain and must trust them for any received trading data.

Centralized Hosting. Most NFTMs today adopt this architecture (e.g., all of the top 10 listed on DappRadar.com). They implement the marketplace service as traditional web applications, allowing average users to manage and trade NFTs with ease. To facilitate our analysis, we assume that such an application, which typically consists of a web server and a database among many other components, is hosted entirely by a single *marketplace server* (MS).

The MS implements a user-facing storefront to simplify user interactions, stores the orderbook, provides users with buy- and sell order parameters to be signed, caches the `tokenURI` (replacing interaction ③B with ③B'), and optionally also caches the asset itself (replacing interaction ③C with ③C'). Nevertheless, the core functionality of buy- and sell order matching is still implemented in an NFTM smart contract. NFTMs can optionally also replicate the orderbook on-chain for improved auditability by the user.

Our classification of centrally hosted NFTMs is complementary to prior research [15], which classifies them according to which operations are implemented off-chain. We however do not consider fully centralized NFTMs which implement order matching off-chain.

NFTMs also allow NFT creators to earn upon secondary sales of their tokens by deducting a fraction of the sale price as royalties paid to the creator. EIP-2981 [7] describes an on-chain royalty mechanism, though it is not universally supported by NFTs and NFTMs. In its absence, NFTMs rely on proprietary mechanisms. We consider a common approach where the NFTM stores the creator's royalty payout address on the MS [15].

Attacks. The above architectures create the largest attack surface among all forms of centralization. We identify attacks exploiting 9 different interactions. All of them apply to centrally hosted marketplaces and the attack $\mathcal{A}6$ also applies to centrally accessed marketplaces.

$\mathcal{A}3$: SetRoyalties({addr, amount} →). This attack targets royalty mechanisms implemented by NFTMs where the payout address is stored exclusively on the MS. These NFTMs allow logged-in[3] NFT creators to change their payout address without additional authentication. By intercepting and replacing the addr parameter sent by the creator to the MS as part of SetRoyalties with its own address, an attacker will receive royalty payments from future sales of the NFT. The attack will likely remain unnoticed until a sufficient amount of royalties are siphoned off.

$\mathcal{A}4$: List({TID, OID, ask} →). This attack tricks the seller into selling an NFT to the attacker at an attacker-chosen price. To list an NFT for sale, the seller should cryptographically sign a sell order with its blockchain private key. The order's parameters {TID, OID, ask} are provided by the MS as part of ②A List. Intercepting the interaction and reducing the ask parameter results in the NFT being listed at a lower price than expected by the seller. This attack can be detected and prevented if the seller carefully audits the sell order's parameters before signing it. However, most crypto wallets fail to display transaction data in a structured and comprehensible way (beyond raw hex data), making transaction auditing difficult for unsophisticated users.

$\mathcal{A}5$: Delegate({TID, Mkt} →). This attack allows an attacker to directly steal a seller's NFTs. Recall that a seller should authorize an NFTM the right to transfer a listed NFT after a successful sale, by making the latter the NFT's delegatee. The Delegate call occurs right after the call to List, and similarly to the listing operation, the MS provides the corresponding parameters {TID, Mkt} to the seller. An intercepting attacker can change Mkt to make itself the delegatee and transfer the NFT to an account under its control. The detection of this attack is also similar to $\mathcal{A}4$:, but Mkt being a pseudorandom value further complicates manual transaction auditing.

$\mathcal{A}6$: Browse(→{TID, ask, seller}). This attack tricks the buyer into perceiving the attacker's NFT offerings as better value than they actually are. It applies to both centrally hosted and CI-accessed decentralized NFTMs. The buyer retrieves

---

[3] In the case of OpenSea, a user maintains a logged-in status if it cryptographically signed a "login-in" challenge in the last 24h.

a {TID,ask,seller} triplet for every NFT it browses from the NFTM's order-book stored on the MS. An attacker can increase the ask value of competing offerings, which makes the buyer perceive the attacker's offerings as better value. This attack can only be detected if a copy of the orderbook is stored on-chain, to which the buyer has untampered access. Centrally accessed NFTMs are also susceptible to this attack because the attacker can intercept and modify the triplet provided by the BaaS CI.

$\mathcal{A}7$: Read'(TID→tokenURI). Similarly to $\mathcal{A}2$, this attack misleads buyers into purchasing low-value fraudulent NFTs. A buyer retrieves a tokenURI through Read' for every TID retrieved previously through Browse. Intercepting and mod-ifying the tokenURI can cause the buyer to fetch unexpected assets in the subse-quent calls to Retrieve or Retrieve'. The buyer is thus tricked into associating a low-value, attacker-owned NFT with the asset of a more valuable NFT. If the buyer has untampered access to the ownership registry, it can detected the attack by comparing the retrieved tokenURI against that stored in the registry.

$\mathcal{A}8$: Retrieve'(tokenURI→asset). This attack also tricks the buyer into asso-ciating an attacker-owned NFT with another asset. It is functionally equivalent to $\mathcal{A}2$ and $\mathcal{A}7$, except that it targets NFTMs that cache assets on the MS instead of centralized asset storage.

$\mathcal{A}9$: Purchase({TID, ask, buyer} →). We describe two attacks against the Purchase interaction. The first deceives the buyer into purchasing an attacker-chosen NFT instead of the intended one. The second redirects the funds intended for purchasing an NFT to the attacker.

To purchase an NFT, the buyer signs a buy order blockchain transaction whose parameters {TID, ask, buyer} are provided by the MS, similarly to the sell order in $\mathcal{A}4$. By changing the TID parameter to that of an NFT sold by the attacker, signing the buy order causes the buyer to purchase the attacker's NFT.

Each blockchain transaction has a destination address as an additional parameter, which in our scenario is provided by the MS as the NFTM smart contract address. In the second attack, the attacker intercepts and replaces this address with that of its own smart contract. This causes the buyer to uninten-tionally send the buy transaction with the included funds to the attacker.

A buyer can detect both attacks by careful audit the transactions.

$\mathcal{A}10$: Bid({TID, bid, buyer} →). We describe four attacks against NFT auc-tions. The first attack tricks the buyer into bidding on an attacker-offered NFT, the second into placing unnecessarily high bids, the third into redirecting funds intended for purchasing an NFT to the attacker, and the fourth into bidding an attacker-chosen amount.

The first attack is functionally identical to the first attack of $\mathcal{A}9$, except that the attacker exploits the Bid function instead of Purchase.

The second attack increases the current highest bid amount retrieved by the buyer from the MS. This coerces the buyer into bidding more than necessary to win the auction. Detection is only possible if a copy of the current bids is stored on-chain, against which the buyer can compare the amount provided by the MS.

The third and fourth attack are complementary, and they target NFTMs implementing `Bid` as blockchain transactions or as interactions with the MS respectively. In both cases, `Bid` parameters {`TID`, `bid`, `buyer`} are provided by the MS. If `Bid` is a blockchain transaction, the funds are transferred to the NFTM as part of the transaction and held there for the duration of the auction. Wallets prominently display the amount of cryptocurrency attached to the transaction, making modifications easy to detect. The attacker can, however, stealthily modify the blockchain destination address as outlined in second attack of $\mathcal{A}9$ and thus extract the funds. If `Bid` is not a blockchain transaction, it is merely a signed commitment by the buyer to purchase the token upon winning the auction. As no cryptocurrency is transferred, the amount is not prominently displayed by wallets. Intercepting and increasing the `bid` tricks the buyer into bidding more than intended. Careful manual auditing can detect the attack.

$\mathcal{A}11$: `Delegate`({`TID`, `Mkt`} →). In bidding protocols where the funds are only transferred upon winning the auction, the NFTM must have access to the bidder's account to execute the winning bid. This is achieved by the buyer delegating tokens equal in value to the bid amount to the NFTM. On Ethereum, wrapped Ether (wETH), a fungible ERC-20 token, is commonly used. Intercepting and replacing `Mkt` provided by the MS with the attacker's address tricks the buyer into delegating the tokens to the attacker. Detection requires manual auditing and knowledge of the expected `Mkt` value.

4.4 Architecture Type IV: Centralized Ownership Registry

For this architecture, we only consider an on-chain ownership registry accessed through a BaaS CI, as by design NFT records should be stored on a blockchain.

$\mathcal{A}12$: `Read`(`TID`→`tokenURI`). This attack is functionally equivalent to $\mathcal{A}7$, except that it targets a centrally accessed ownership registry instead of an NFTM.

5   Attack Validation

We have validated our attacks on real systems used in today's NFT ecosystem. We focus on the case of centralized NFTMs, because (1) they are common in the real world, (2) they normally subsume the functions of other CIs like BaaS and IPFS as discussed earlier, and (3) they allow us to simulate complete attack procedures from the preparation (deploying fraudulent contracts, creating and listing bait NFTs, etc.) to the production of final outcomes (see Table 1).

```
1    class ChangeHTTPCode:
2        def request(self, flow: http.HTTPFlow) -> None:
3            graphql_id = "useCollectionFormEditMutation"
4            request_url = flow.request.pretty_url
5            raw_payload = flow.request.get_text(strict = False)
6            if not ("graphql" in request_url and graphql_id in raw_payload):
7                return
8            new_creator_fees = [{"address": attacker_account, "basisPoints":500}]
9            payload = json.loads(raw_payload)
10           payload['variables']['input']['collectionInput']['creatorFees'] = new_creator_fees
11           new_payload = json.dumps(payload)
12           flow.request.set_text(new_payload)
13   addons = [ChangeHTTPCode()]
```

Fig. 3. Python code for changing royalty payout address with `mitmproxy`.

Setup. We simulate the attacks using OpenSea—the largest NFTM today—on the Ethereum Rinkeby testnet. For user-side software, we use the Firefox browser with the MetaMask crypto wallet. To simulate a man-in-the-middle attacker, we use the `mitmproxy` tool and install a self-signed CA certificate into Firefox's trust store. This setup allows us to route all Firefox traffic to `mitmproxy`, where we can intercept and decrypt the HTTPS requests or responses and modify different data fields according to the simulated attacks.

Validation Details. Our attacks can be conducted in two ways: (1) directly modify data exchanged between the victim and the MS, or (2) exploit third-party JavaScript (JS) loaded in the NFTM storefront. While the first approach targets the victim's connection to the MS, the second approach targets the victim's connection to third-party JS providers. By intercepting and maliciously modifying JS loaded from these providers, the attacker can execute arbitrary JS in the victim's browser. The attacks against centralized NFTMs are further categorized based on their methodologies.

- **Royalty payout address change:** $\mathcal{A}3$
- **Change order or transaction parameters:** $\mathcal{A}4$, $\mathcal{A}5$, $\mathcal{A}9$, $\mathcal{A}10$, $\mathcal{A}11$
- **Wrong data fetched from NFTM:** $\mathcal{A}6$, $\mathcal{A}7$, $\mathcal{A}8$

We briefly explain the validation of attacks $\mathcal{A}3$ and $\mathcal{A}9$, which are representative for their respective attack category. We have also successfully validated the third attack category via straightforward modifications to data fetched from the MS.

Royalty payout address change. ($\mathcal{A}3$) In attack $\mathcal{A}3$, the attacker targets NFTMs that store the royalty payout address on their MS and replaces the creator's address with its own. In our validation, the creator submits a new payout address through OpenSea's user portal, and this is encoded as a GraphQL HTTPS request. We can intercept the request using `mitmproxy` and modify the address. Figure 3) shows the python code to implement the interception, including finding the request for changing the royalty payout address (lines 3–7) and replacing the address with an attacker's controlled account (lines 8–12).

Change Order or Transaction Parameters (.$\mathcal{A}9$) We have validated both versions of $\mathcal{A}9$. The first version causes the buyer to purchase an attacker-chosen

(a) Untampered transaction   (b) Tampered transaction

Fig. 4. Screenshots of MetaMask showing a genuine and a fradulent transaction. The latter claims to be from the NFTM and has the correct function name. Signing this transaction causes 1 ETH sent to the attacker.

NFT, and the second directs the buyer's buy-transaction to a malicious smart contract that extracts the attached cryptocurrency.

For the first attack, we simulate a buyer's request for an NFT through the OpenSea website, which generates an HTTPS request containing the sell-order ID `orderId` to the GraphQL endpoint on the MS. We can intercept this request using `mitmproxy` and change `orderId` to another attacker-controlled order. The MS will respond with the unsigned buy transaction corresponding to the malicious `orderId` and thus cause the buyer to inadvertently buy the attacker's NFT. The modification of `orderId` is minor and hard to notice, unless the victim carefully compares the NFT information displayed on the OpeaSea website and the parameters contained in the transaction to sign, which requires manual decoding of the raw, hex-encoded transaction data in MetaMask.

For the second attack, the attacker first deploys a malicious smart contract which extracts cryptocurrency from received transactions. When the buyer requests to buy an NFT, the attacker intercepts and replaces the `destination` field in the transaction data provided by the MS with that of its malicious smart contract. As seen in Fig. 4, the attack only causes visible changes to the destination address field and the icon associated with the address (both are pseudorandom values). MetaMask still displays the genuine OpenSea URL and the prominently displayed cryptocurrency amount is unchanged.

Ethical Consideration. Our experiments create test smart contracts and NFTs on a public blockchain intended for testing, including security research. They incur no real costs, even if tokens are accidentally purchased by other users. The test assets uploaded to IPFS disappear after some time if they are not cached by any node. Note that our attacks do not exploit the service providers'

Table 2. The susceptibility of the top 10 NFTMs (according to DappRadar.com) to prefix hijack attack. "Decentralized" allows trading without MS. We mark MSes loading JavaScript from JavaScript providers vulnerable to subprefix hijacking as "JS." An aggregator NFTM collects sell orders from other NFTMs. Its security thus depends on the security of the queried NFTMs.

NFTM	User Interaction	Interception Possible	Vulnerable JS Provider	Vulnerability
OpenSea	MS	No	-	-
CryptoPunks	Decentralized MS	No	-	-
LooksRare	MS	JS	cdn.jsdelivr.net	Max-Len
X2Y2	-	No		
Rarible	MS	JS	static.klaviyo.com	No ROA
SuperRare	Decentralized MS	JS	cdn.heapanalytics.com	Max-Len
Foundation	Decentralized MS	JS	cdn.segment.com	Max-Len
Decentraland	-	JS	cdn.segment.com	Max-Len
Element	Aggregator	No		
Golom	-	Yes/JS		Max-Len

systems but generic network vulnerabilities in centralized architectures. Service providers often consider man-in-the-middle attacks beyond their responsibility. We reported our findings through OpenSea's bug bounty program [2] and received the confirmation that our attacks are not within its scope.

6   Vulnerabilities of Real-World Entities

We analyze the susceptibility of popular real-world NFTMs and CIs to our attacks, by examining the BGP security of their networks. Specifically, we inspect whether they are vulnerable to subprefix hijacking, a practical and highly effective form of BGP hijacking attack that happens frequently in today's Internet. Using an open Internet data platform RIPEstat, we collected relevant information such as publicly announced IP prefix, source AS, and route origin attestation (ROA). The IP prefix of an entity is deemed vulnerable to subprefix hijacking if: (1) no valid ROA exists and the prefix length is less than 24, or (2) a valid ROA exists but the max-length field in the ROA is strictly greater than the prefix length and the prefix length is less than 24.

Our investigation results for NFTMs are shown in Table 2. One popular marketplace (Golom) has its MS directly originating from an IP prefix susceptible to subprefix hijacking. Six NFTMs rely on JavaScript code originating from risky IP prefixes; once these external JavaScript providers are hijacked by our network

Table 3. Popular CIs' susceptibility to prefix hijack attack

Centralized service	Vulnerable AS	Reason
IPFS Gateways		
4everland.io	AS16509	Max-Len
hardbin.com	AS14061	Max-Len
ipfs.eth.aragon.network	AS24940	Max-Len
jorropo.net	AS14061	No ROA
ipfs.runfission.com	AS14618	Max-Len
BaaS Gateways		
mainnet.infura.io	AS14618	Max-Len

attacker, so could be the NFTMs. This suggests that NFTMs should carefully audit their external dependencies to minimize their attack surface. We also identified 5 IPFS gateways and one major BaaS provider (Infura) that are subject to subprefix hijacking, as shown in Table 3. There are likely more in the wild.

Note that even if NFT service providers reside in secure networks that are resistant to BGP hijacking, our attacks can still be launched if users or their DNS servers locate in vulnerable ASes, or these servers are subject to DNS cache poisoning attacks [13]. A comprehensive demographic study of victim users is an interesting avenue for future research.

Most NFT service providers deploy TLS to secure their communication with users. A successful attack thus requires the attacker to obtain a fraudulent TLS certificate to impersonate a service provider's domain. This has been demonstrated to be practical in many ways, especially by attacking the domain validation process during certificate issuance [6, 29].

7 Conclusion

This paper makes a step in uncovering the security risks of centralization in the booming Web3 ecosystem. We focus on the case of NFT, a central application of Web3, and perform a systematic study of architecture-level vulnerabilities regarding the interactions between users and centralized entities. Our results confirm that centralization increases the overall attack surface by a wide margin. This is worrisome given the variety and practicality of such attacks, and the large financial investments in NFTs. Some of these attacks are relatively easy to detect if users take caution to audit blockchain transactions before signing them; the others are less so, requiring the shift to a truly decentralized architecture or extensive end-to-end data authentication.

Our findings also underscore the importance of secure Internet infrastructures for inter-domain routing and name resolution, which would prevent our attacks in the first place. A promising research direction is to evaluate how existing security extensions to the Internet as well as emerging clean-slate solutions [9, 16] can improve the Web3 ecosystem's resilience to attacks.

References

1. Official IPFS gateway. https://ipfs.io
2. OpenSea Bug Bounty Program. https://hackerone.com/opensea
3. Anders, L., Shrug: EIP-4907: Rental NFT, an Extension of EIP-721, March 2022. https://eips.ethereum.org/EIPS/eip-4907
4. Apostolaki, M., Zohar, A., Vanbever, L.: Hijacking Bitcoin: routing attacks on cryptocurrencies. In: Proceedings of the IEEE Symposium on Security and Privacy (S&P) (2017)
5. Atzei, N., Bartoletti, M., Cimoli, T.: A survey of attacks on ethereum smart contracts SoK. In: Proceedings of the International Conference on Principles of Security and Trust (POST) (2017)
6. Birge-Lee, H., Sun, Y., Edmundson, A., Rexford, J., Mittal, P.: Bamboozling certificate authorities with BGP. In: Proceedings of the USENIX Security Symposium (2018)
7. Burks, Z., Morgan, J., Malone, B., Seibel, J.: EIP-2981: NFT Royalty Standard. https://eips.ethereum.org/EIPS/eip-2981, September 2020
8. Chatzigiannis, P., Baldimtsi, F., Chalkias, K.: SoK: blockchain light clients. In: Proceedings of the International Conference on Financial Cryptography and Data Security (FC) (2022)
9. Chuat, L., et al.: The Complete Guide to SCION. From Design Principles to Formal Verification, 1st edn. Springer, Cham (2022). https://doi.org/10.1007/978-3-031-05288-0
10. Chung, T., et al.: A longitudinal, end-to-end view of the DNSSEC ecosystem. In: Proceedings of the USENIX Security Symposium (2017)
11. Cimpanu, C.: DNS hijacks at two cryptocurrency sites point the finger at GoDaddy, again. https://therecord.media/two-cryptocurrency-portals-are-experiencing-a-dns-hijack-at-the-same-time/. Accessed 01 Oct 2022
12. Cimpanu, C.: KlaySwap crypto users lose funds after BGP hijack. https://therecord.media/klayswap-crypto-users-lose-funds-after-bgp-hijack/. Accessed 01 Oct 2022
13. Dai, T., Jeitner, P., Shulman, H., Waidner, M.: From IP to transport and beyond: cross-layer attacks against applications. In: Proceedings of the ACM SIGCOMM Conference (2021)
14. Daian, P., et al.: Flash boys 2.0: frontrunning in decentralized exchanges, miner extractable value, and consensus instability. In: Proceedings of the IEEE Symposium on Security and Privacy (S&P) (2020)
15. Das, D., Bose, P., Ruaro, N., Kruegel, C., Vigna, G.: Understanding security issues in the NFT ecosystem. In: Proceedings of the ACM Conference on Computer and Communications Security (CCS) (2022)
16. Duan, H., Fischer, R., Lou, J., Liu, S., Basin, D., Perrig, A.: Rhine: robust and high-performance internet naming with e2e authenticity. In: Proceedings of USENIX Symposium on Networked Systems Design and Implementation (NSDI) (2023)
17. Entriken, W., Shirley, D., Evans, J., Sachs, N.: EIP-721: Non-Fungible Token Standard
18. Eyal, I., Sirer, E.G.: Majority is not enough: bitcoin mining is vulnerable. Commun. ACM **61**(7), 95–102 (2018)
19. Gilad, Y., Cohen, A., Herzberg, A., Schapira, M., Shulman, H.: Are we there yet? On RPKI's deployment and security. Cryptology ePrint Archive, Paper 2016/1010 (2016). https://eprint.iacr.org/2016/1010

20. Grimmelmann, J., Ji, Y., Kell, T.: EIP-5218: NFT rights management, July 2022. https://eips.ethereum.org/EIPS/eip-5218
21. Heilman, E., Kendler, A., Zohar, A., Goldberg, S.: Eclipse attacks on bitcoin's peer-to-peer network. In: Proceedings of USENIX Security (2015)
22. Jiang, B., Liu, Y., Chan, W.K.: Contractfuzzer: fuzzing smart contracts for vulnerability detection. In: Proceedings of the IEEE/ACM International Conference on Automated Software Engineering (ASE) (2018)
23. Johnston, D., et al.: The general theory of decentralized applications, DApps. Technical report (2014)
24. Li, K., Chen, J., Liu, X., Tang, Y.R., Wang, X.F., Luo, X.: As strong as its weakest link: how to break blockchain DApps at RPC Service. In: Proceedings of the Symposium on Network and Distributed Systems Security (NDSS) (2021)
25. Malwa, S.: Two Polygon, Fantom Front Ends Hit by DNS Attack. https://www.coindesk.com/tech/2022/07/01/two-polygon-fantom-front-ends-hit-by-dns-attack/. Accessed 01 Oct 2022
26. Marlinspike, M.: My first impressions of web3, January 2022. https://moxie.org/2022/01/07/web3-first-impressions.html. Accessed 01 Oct 2022
27. Permenev, A., Dimitrov, D., Tsankov, P., Drachsler-Cohen, D., Vechev, M.: VerX: safety verification of smart contracts. In: Proceedings of the IEEE Symposium on Security and Privacy (S&P) (2020)
28. Schwarz-Schilling, C., Neu, J., Monnot, B., Asgaonkar, A., Tas, E.N., Tse, D.: Three attacks on proof-of-stake ethereum. In: Proceedings of the International Conference on Financial Cryptography and Data Security (FC) (2022)
29. Schwittmann, L., Wander, M., Weis, T.: Domain impersonation is feasible: a study of CA domain validation vulnerabilities. In: Proceedings of the IEEE European Symposium on Security and Privacy (EuroS&P) (2019)
30. Su, L., et al.: Evil under the sun: understanding and discovering attacks on ethereum decentralized applications. In: Proceedings of USENIX Security (2021)
31. Verified Market Research (VMR). Non-Fungible Tokens Market Size And Forecast. Technical report (2022)
32. Wang, D., Feng, H., Siwei, W., Zhou, Y., Lei, W., Yuan, X.: Penny wise and pound foolish: quantifying the risk of unlimited approval of ERC20 tokens on ethereum. In: Proceedings of the International Symposium on Research in Attacks, Intrusions and Defenses (RAID) (2022)
33. Wang, Z., Gao, J., Wei, X.: Do NFTs' owners really possess their assets? A first look at the NFT-to-asset connection fragility. In: Proceedings of the ACM Web Conference (WWW) (2023)
34. Zhou, L., Qin, K., Torres, C.F., Le, D.V., Gervais, A.: High-frequency trading on decentralized on-chain exchanges. In: Proceedings of the IEEE Symposium on Security and Privacy (S&P) (2021)

Defending Against Free-Riders Attacks in Distributed Generative Adversarial Networks

Zilong Zhao$^{(\boxtimes)}$ ⓘ, Jiyue Huang ⓘ, Lydia Y. Chen ⓘ, and Stefanie Roos

TU Delft, Delft, The Netherlands
{z.zhao-8,j.huang-4,y.chen-10,s.roos}@tudelft.nl

Abstract. Generative Adversarial Networks (GANs) are increasingly adopted by the industry to synthesize realistic images using competing generator and discriminator neural networks. Due to data not being centrally available, Multi-Discriminator (MD)-GANs training frameworks employ multiple discriminators that have direct access to the real data. Distributedly training a joint GAN model entails the risk of free-riders, i.e., participants that aim to benefit from the common model while only pretending to participate in the training process. In this paper, we first define a free-rider as a participant without training data and then identify three possible actions: not training, training on synthetic data, or using pre-trained models for similar but not identical tasks that are publicly available. We conduct experiments to explore the impact of these three types of free-riders on the ability of MD-GANs to produce images that are indistinguishable from real data. We consequently design a defense against free-riders, termed DFG, which compares the performance of client discriminators to reference discriminators at the server. The defense allows the server to evict clients whose behavior does not match that of a benign client. The result shows that even when 67% of the clients are free-riders, the proposed DFG can improve synthetic image quality by up to 70.96%, compared to the case of no defense.

Keywords: Multi-Discriminator GANs · Free-rider attack · Anomaly detection · Defense

1 Introduction

Generative Adversarial Networks (GANs) are an emerging methodology to generate synthetic data [3,30,31], especially for visual data. GANs are capable of generating real-world-like images and are increasingly adopted by industry for data augmentation and refinement [21]. Their success is attributed to their unique architecture of training two competing neural networks, called discriminator and generator. The well-trained generator can then be used to generate synthetic data. If GANs are trained centrally, a single generator and discriminator are trained iteratively, where the former generates realistic images to fool

---

Z. Zhao and J. Huang—Equal contribution.

© International Financial Cryptography Association 2024
F. Baldimtsi and C. Cachin (Eds.): FC 2023, LNCS 13951, pp. 200–217, 2024.
https://doi.org/10.1007/978-3-031-47751-5_12

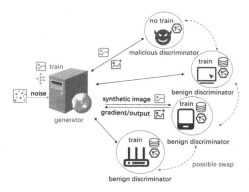

Fig. 1. Architecture of Multi-Discriminator GAN: one generator, and four discriminators, one of which being free-rider.

latter, and the latter then gives feedback to the former by comparing the generated and real images. As a consequence of privacy regulations imposed on data sources, e.g., GDPR [26], GANs often have to employ distributed architectures such that they can learn from multiple sources without illegally sharing the raw data.

Multi-Discriminator GAN (MD-GAN), Distributed GAN architectures have been adopted in medical (e.g., medical images) and financial (e.g., financial tabular data) domains [4,23,29], two areas that have stringent privacy constraints. Typically, as shown in Fig. 1, there are one generator and multiple discriminators, one discriminator for each data source. To learn such an MD-GAN, an iterative training procedure between generator and discriminators takes place. The generator synthesizes images that imitate the real data, whereas the discriminators provide feedback to the generator based on their local image set. A variant of MD-GAN further allows discriminators to exchange their local networks with peers to avoid overfitting [11]. Though such a distributed architecture guarantees that raw data is not shared, it comes with the risk of misbehaving discriminators and the need to defend against them.

Free-riders are a common threat to distributed systems in which the same task is executed by multiple parties, meaning that individuals can hide that they did not execute their task properly as the task is still completed by the other parties in the system. Examples are peer-to-peer file sharing [6] or Federated Learning systems [20,28]. Free-riders in Federated Learning systems [7,17] try to gain access to the so-called global model from the server, which is aggregated from local models of all contributors without sharing local data. Here, free-riders can simply return the previous global model (possibly with perturbation added) as their contribution. In the context of MD-GAN systems, free-riders aim to gain access to the valuable well-trained generator model without using any real data to train a discriminator. In contrast to Federated Learning systems, where the server model has the same structure as the client model, free-riders and benign discriminators in MD-GAN do not have any information about the concrete generator network. Moreover, it is no mean feat to detect free-riders in MD-GAN as the generator only receives the distributed feedback on how well the synthetic images compared to the real ones, i.e., gradients back-propagated from the discriminator.

In this paper, we aim to answer two research questions: what is the impact of free-riders on MD-GAN frameworks and how can benign participants defend against such free-riders? We conduct the first empirical characterization study on how different numbers and types of free-riders affect the quality of synthetic images of MD-GAN when training image benchmarks. We introduce three attack strategies for free-riders: They obtain a discriminator by i) using a randomly initialized discriminator model without training, ii) training a discriminator model on synthetic data, and iii) using a publicly available pre-trained discriminator model without any additional training. Note that the pre-trained discriminator is not for exactly the same task but for a related task with similar data. Our results show that having 30% or more free-riders considerably degrades MD-GAN's performance, as measured by the Fréchet Inception Distance (FID) score [13]. Free-riders who take advantage of the pre-trained model are less harmful than others but still, free-riders are shown to be a serious issue.

Consequently, we propose a novel **D**efense strategy against **F**ree-riders in MD-**G**AN, termed DFG, where the generator can filter out the contributions of free-riders. The two key steps of DFG are (i) the generator periodically sends out a probing dataset to all discriminators, and (ii) clusters their responses in combination with the reference responses of the "detector", a free-rider and a benign client trained on the generator side. If MD-GAN allows the discriminators to periodically swap models, DFG optionally contains a third defense step at the discriminators, enabling peers to reject swapping with potential free-riders. We evaluate DFG for different attacks, numbers of free-riders, and variants of MD-GAN on CIFAR10 and CIFAR100. Our results indicate that DFG can improve synthetic data quality for all considered scenarios. If the free-riders do not train its discriminator, which is the simplest scenario, DFG reduces FID by 45.05% (CIFAR10) and 33.64% (CIFAR100) with 1 free-rider and 5 benign clients in the system. When varying number of free-riders from 2 to 5, DFG averagely reduces FID by 73.71% (CIFAR10) and 68.39% (CIFAR100). If the free-riders use a pre-trained discriminator, which is the most stealthy type, DFG reduces FID by 60.86% on CIFAR100 dataset when half of the clients are free-riders, and by 70.96% on CIFAR10 dataset even when 67% of the clients are free-riders.

In summary, we make two novel main contributions: (1) A first characterization of three types of free-riders of MD-GAN. (2) Proposing a novel and effective defense strategy DFG and evaluating it on two image benchmarks (i.e., CIFAR10 and CIFAR100).

2   Background on MD-GAN and Free-Riders

In this section, we introduce the concept of MD-GANs and our adversarial model.

2.1   Preliminaries on MD-GAN

Key components of MD-GAN are one server and N clients maintaining one generator and N discriminators, respectively. In general, generator and discriminators are all deep neural networks[1] characterized by their model weights. The generator network, $\mathcal{G}$, aims to synthesize images that are indistinguishable from real ones. Each of the N discriminator networks, $\mathcal{D}_i, i \in \{1, 2, ..., N\}$, has direct access to its own set of real images, X_i. They aim to correctly differentiate fake images generated by the generator from real images. Figure 1 illustrates an example of one generator and four discriminators. For the MD-GAN setting in this paper, all of the clients must join for the full duration of the training process. After training, they obtain the model of the generator to synthesize data.

To train an MD-GAN, the generator and discriminators take turns to train and update their network weights over multiple rounds until reaching convergence. One training round consists of multiple mini batches of data. For batch j, discriminator i, and round t, $\mathcal{G}$ produces a synthetic dataset $S_{t,i}^j$ from a vector of Gaussian noise $z_{t,i}^j$. The discriminator trains on $S_{t,i}^j$ together with its real data.

Discriminator Training: The discriminator uses its local real images X_i^j (i.e., real image mini batch j at i^{th} discriminator) and the synthetic images $S_{t,i}^j$ from the generator to train itself. Specifically, the generator remains fixed during the discriminator training, we only optimize the discriminator loss and update the weights of discriminator networks through stochastic gradient descent algorithms [25].

Generator Training: When calculating generator loss, one can imagine that generator and discriminator are connected as one neural network. The ith discriminator calculates the loss for synthetic images $S_{t,i}^j$ from the generator and back-propagates gradients. After $\mathcal{G}$ receives all of the back-propagated gradients of synthetic images $S_{t,i}^j$ from every i^{th} discriminator, the generator accumulates all the gradients and updates its network weights. During generator training, the weights of the discriminators remain fixed.

2.2   Free-Rider Adversarial Model

We consider free-riders on the discriminator side, i.e., clients want to obtain the final generator model without contributing to the training of MD-GAN. Their goal is not to degrade the image quality of the generator. In this sense, they are rational parties rather than malicious. They deviate from the expected learning procedure to gain utility, namely access to the generator model, without having the necessary data. Free-riders aim to be *stealthy* to overcome any defenses employed by the generator. Such free-riders are local, internal, and active adversaries. In other words, they can only observe and participate in the communication and computation of their own training process. Moreover, free-riders **do not own any data** for training MD-GAN, nor do they have access to the data of others and they cannot observe the communication of others. They do

---

[1] We interchangeably use terms of networks and models.

(a) Real MNIST im-
ages

(b) Synthetic images
without free-riders

(c) Synthetic images
with 5 free-riders

Fig. 2. Real v.s. synthetic MNIST images from generators of MD-GAN encountering 0 and 5 free-riders with 5 benign discriminators.

not collude. The assumption of non-collusion is sensible as additional free-riders might decrease the quality of the final model they obtain, so parties are unlikely to reveal their free-riding to others.

3   Free-Rider Attacks in MD-GAN

This section explores different strategies for free riding discriminators. We describe the attack strategy and then evaluate their effectiveness.

3.1   Attacks

Free-riders aim to obtain the generator in the end of the training, such that they can synthesis data of high quality without contributing real data to the training process. To do so, they might need to bypass defenses aimed at detecting free-riding and hence want to be stealthy. A first method to achieve a certain degree of stealthiness is not to follow the random initialization method expected by the generator. The generator can easily compare the gradients provided by a discriminator to those produced by a random model with the same initialization method. If the provided gradients resemble those from a random model, the generator can identify the discriminator as a free-rider, a defense we explore more closely in the next section. To overcome such an straight-forward defense, free-riders can use a different initialization method. In our evaluation, we consider four initialization methods: (i) Kaiming initialization [12], (2) Xavier initialization [8], (3) uniform and (4) normal. Note that all benign clients follow Kaiming initialization (default method by Pytorch).

In order to consider more stealthy free-riders, we note that they have two potential sources of information that they can use to obtain a better model despite not having data to train: i) the synthetic data provided by the generator to generate the gradient feedback and ii) any publicly available pre-trained discriminator models for similar tasks, i.e., GANs for synthesizing images. In summary, we have the following adversarial behaviors for discriminators:

FR−L: Also termed lazy free-riders, they choose a random initialization method to initialize the model. Afterwards, they compute the gradients expected by the generator based on the random initial model without any training.

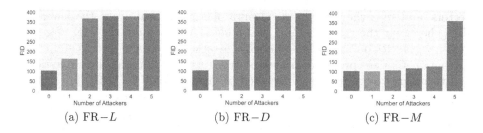

Fig. 3. Final FID of Multi-Discriminator GAN for different types of free-rider. Number of free-riders varies from 0 to 5, number of benign clients is fixed to 5.

FR$-D$: As detailed in Sect. 2.1, the generator provides mini batches of synthetic images to the discriminators. So, while a free-rider does not have real data to train on, they can still utilize the synthetic data, which is what FR$-D$ leverages. Concretely, the free-rider uses generated images provided by the generator as "real" data and randomly generates an equal number of images deemed as fake data by sampling every pixel from a uniform distribution. It then trains its discriminator using these two datasets in the same way as a benign client. In the later phase of the training, i.e., when the synthetic images from generator are very close to real images, FR$-D$'s model is likely relatively good, making it hard to detect them as a free-rider.

FR$-M$: A discriminator outputs whether the data is real and synthetic. Since the output is not class-related, a pre-trained discriminator, which has been used in another GAN framework, can potentially be re-purposed. Note that the generator and benign discriminators do not start training from a pre-trained model themselves because it can affect convergence negatively [1]. But for a free-rider, a well-trained discriminator could be less harmful than a random initial model. Therefore, we assume FR$-M$ is a free-rider that uses a pre-trained discriminator, e.g., one downloaded from the internet. We typically assume that datasets used to train the pre-trained discriminator are different from the ones used to train the current ones. However, to assess the impact of this assumption, we also consider a pre-trained discriminator for the same data in our evaluation.

3.2   Empirical Analysis on CIFAR-100

Here, we evaluate the effectiveness of our attacks on MD-GAN. We vary the number of attackers between 0 and 5 and always have 5 benign discriminators. CIFAR-100 [14] and MNIST [15] are used as the dataset. We evaluate the quality of generated images by measuring the Fréchet inception distance (FID) [13], which calculates the difference between real and generated images. It is defined as follows:

$$\mathrm{FID} = ||\mu_1 - \mu_2||^2 + \mathrm{tr}(\Sigma_1 + \Sigma_2 - 2(\Sigma_1 \Sigma_2)^{1/2})$$

where μ_1 and μ_2 denote the feature-wise mean of the real and generated images; Σ_1 and Σ_2 refer to the covariance matrix for the real and generated feature vectors; $||\mu_1 - \mu_2||^2$ refers to the sum-squared difference between the two mean vectors; and tr is the trace linear algebra operation. Intuitively, the lower the FID, the closer the generated and real images. We measure the FID of generated images with an increasing number of attackers. Neural networks and training parameters are provided in Sect. 5. We start by evaluating lazy free-riders and then turn to the more sophisticated behaviors. For $FR-M$ the pre-trained discriminator is trained on CIFAR100. In general, as stated above, we assume that the pre-trained model is trained on a dataset different from that used by benign clients. For simplicity, we use the same dataset here but provide more experiments on the role of the dataset in Sect. 5.

Baseline of -L We first visually motivate why free-riders are important to consider. Figure 2c shows that MD-GANs can create synthetic images that are very close to the original real MNIST images. Yet, if half the discriminators are free-riders, the images are barely readable and exhibit little similarity with the original images. We now quantify these difference using the FID for CIFAR-100. In Fig. 3a, we can observe that without free-riders, the FID is barely above 100 at the end of the training. With one free-rider, the FID only slightly increases. If two or more free-riders are present, the FID is close to 400, which is the FID without training. Thus, the random initialized discriminator cannot distinguish real and synthetic images and the gradients obtained from the lazy free-riders corrupt the utility of the final generator.

Free Data v.s. Free Model. We expect the more sophisticated free-riders to have less negative impact on the quality of the generated images. In Fig. 3, our three types of free-riders are compared. For all types, the impact increases with the number of free-riders, as a large amount of discriminators without useful data is bound to increase the impact. $FR-D$ (Fig. 3b) is only slightly better than $FR-L$ for one or two free-riders. For a higher number of attackers, the model is again almost of the same quality as a random initial model. We conclude that training on synthetic data without any real-world examples is not promising, at least not in the sense that it can result in a useful generator in MD-GAN, which is the goal of both the benign participants and the free-riders.

In contrast, pre-trained discriminators (Fig. 3c) are very effective. For one or two free-riders, the FID is largely unaffected by the free-riders. Even for 3 or 4 free-riders, the increase in FID is small, as it remains below 130, up from 104. If half of the discriminators are free-riders, only having a pre-trained model is insufficient for maintaining high quality, as indicated by Fig. 3c.

4   Defending MD-GAN Against Free-Riders

Reacting to the severe impact free-riders can have, in this section, we propose DFG, a defense strategy against free-riders in MD-GAN. The **objectives of DFG** are three-fold: **(1)** accurately detecting free-riders in each round and excluding their gradients from accumulation, **(2)** improving the FID for the case when free-riders are present but not considerably decreasing the FID in the absence of free-riders, and **(3)** entailing low additional overhead. Note that the first goal also implies that benign clients should not be classified as free-riders. Indeed, as a low number of free-riders can be tolerated, we consider accidentally

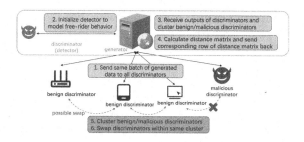

Fig. 4. Key steps of DFG.

classifying free-riders as benign less severe than vice versa. Classifying benign users as free-riders means that they cannot receive earned benefits in the form of the final model. Having a high risk of accidentally being declared a free-rider hence may disincentivize participation. The second part of the second goal is important as a defense that decreases the performance, e.g., by excluding benign clients, in the absence of an attack is unlikely to be adopted, especially if the impact of a low number of free-riders is less than the decrease in image quality caused by the defense. The last goal is necessary because the generator and discriminators might be unwilling to deploy a defense that considerably increases delays, computation, or communication overhead.

4.1 Protocol of DFG for MD-GAN

The core idea of DFG is to leverage a probing set and detect free-riders based on their responses to the probing set, using either clustering or outlier detection to distinguish responses of free-riders from benign ones. In the following, we detail the 6 steps of DFG, defending free-riders in MD-GAN. All steps are also summarized in Fig. 4.

Step 1: In our defense, $\mathcal{G}$ periodically, i.e., every L rounds, generates a probing set $\hat{S}$ to the clients. The set can act as a replacement for $S_{t,i}^j$ (i.e., synthetic images at round t and batch j of the ith discriminator). In contrast to the standard algorithm, DFG sends the same set $\hat{S}$ to all clients. The clients evaluate their discriminators on the set $\hat{S}$ and return the results in the form of a vector. Concretely, for each image s_k, with $1 \leq k \leq |\hat{S}|$, discriminator $\mathcal{D}_i$ computes $\mathcal{D}_i(s_k)$ and the returned vector is:

$$Pr_i(\hat{S}) = \left(\mathcal{D}_i(s_1), \mathcal{D}_i(s_2), \ldots, \mathcal{D}_i(s_{|\hat{S}|}) \right).$$

Step 2: Additionally, to detect free-riders, $\mathcal{G}$ makes use of two detectors. Concretely, the generator $\mathcal{G}$ randomly initializes two discriminators $\mathcal{D}_{N+1}$ and $\mathcal{D}_{N+2}$. $\mathcal{D}_{N+1}$ is used as a reference model of a free-rider and $\mathcal{D}_{N+2}$ is used as a reference model of a benign client. To train $\mathcal{D}_{N+2}$ in a same way as other benign clients, we assume that there is real data on the server side. $\mathcal{D}_{N+1}$ does not train during the whole training process. Every time when $\mathcal{D}_{N+1}$ and $\mathcal{D}_{N+2}$ receive $\hat{S}$, they compute $Pr_{N+1}(\hat{S})$ and $Pr_{N+2}(\hat{S})$ based on their local discriminators.

Step 3: After the generator collects all the vectors $Pr_i(\hat{S})$, $1 \leq i \leq N+2$, it applies binary clustering, e.g., k-means with k equal to 2., or anomaly detection (e.g. isolation forest) on all vectors $Pr_i(\hat{S})$. Clustering is a promising solution because it divides clients into two groups, which should be benign clients and free-riders. However, this might not work if two free-riders behave differently from each other. Then outlier detection, which identifies unusual behavior such as free-riding when training on local data is considered normal, can be more promising. We only apply clustering or outlier detection and not both. A combined defense, e.g., one that classifies a client as a free-rider if they are classified by any of the two, is bound to have a higher false positive rate, i.e., it accidentally classifies benign clients as free-riders, which we want to avoid. Intuitively, the $Pr_i(\hat{S})$ of a benign client is expected to have a low distance to the $Pr_i(\hat{S})$ of other benign clients, whereas they have a high distance to the $Pr_i(\hat{S})$ of the free-riders, including $\mathcal{D}_{N+1}$. Consequently, when a clustering algorithm is used, we classify all clients in the cluster that contains the $\mathcal{D}_{N+2}$ as benign clients, and the rest are free-riders. When an anomaly detection algorithm is used, all the clients are clustered into two groups: normal and abnormal. The clients in the normal group are considered benign. One exception is that when $\mathcal{D}_{N+2}$ is in the abnormal group, then we treat all the clients in abnormal group as benign clients and normal group members as free-riders. Note that there is a unique scenario where one group of the cluster or the abnormal group contains only $\mathcal{D}_{N+1}$ and another group contains the remaining clients. Accordingly, we believe this case to be no free-rider in the system.

Until now, step 1, 2 and 3 are all defense procedures for standard MD-GAN. But an advanced setting of MD-GAN allows all discriminators to periodically swap their weights between them, we denote this variant as MD-GAN^w. While helping to prevent the over-fitting of discriminator to local data, it also creates challenges for defenses. For this variant, a discriminator is not trained by one single client and hence it is hard to determine whether one party has (not) trained properly. Free-riders can obtain a properly trained discriminator by swapping. This exacerbate the difficulty of differentiating the gradients obtained from free-riders and benign discriminators. To introduce a discriminator-side defense, we take advantage of one information: the benign discriminators know that they are not free-riders. So once a benign client is asked to swap with another that is suspected to be a free-rider, it can refuse. The following steps are added:

Step 4: After the generator has all the vectors $Pr_i(\hat{S})$, $1 \leq i \leq N+1$, they compute a $(N+1) \times (N+1)$ matrix V of pair-wise L2 distances between the Pr vectors of the discriminators, including the detector, i.e., the element V_{ij} is $||Pr_i(\hat{S}) - Pr_j(\hat{S})||_2$. The generator shares the computed distances $V_{i1}, \ldots V_{i(N+1)}$ with the ith client.

Step 5: A benign client i then performs binary clustering or anomaly detection on these distances, excluding V_{ii}. The cluster with lower mean distances or the normal group judged by anomaly detection algorithm is taken to be the group of benign clients. The underlying assumption here is that the distance between two properly trained discriminators is less than the distance between benign discriminator and free-rider.

Step 6: A benign client only swaps with parties that are in the same cluster or group as it according to its local clustering or outlier detection, respectively.

5   Experimental Evaluation

In this section, we first introduce the experimental setups including datasets, baselines and the testbed. Then we clarify the evaluation metrics to demonstrate the effectiveness of DFG. Last, we summarize and analyze our experimental results for the different free-rider attack strategies with and without defense.

5.1   Experimental Setup

Testbed. Experiments are mainly run on two machines, both running Ubuntu 20.04. One machine hosts the generator, the other hosts all the discriminators. A third machine with same hardware is used to host 5 discriminators for the experiment with 10 free-riders. The machines are interconnected via 1G Ethernet links. The MD-GAN system is implemented using the Pytorch RPC framework. Our code is publicly hosted on github[2].

Datasets. We test our algorithms on two commonly used image datasets: CIFAR10 [14] and CIFAR100 [14]. CIFAR10 and CIFAR100 have 50 000 (10/100 classes) training images in color. Each benign client and the server individually possess 5 000 images, which are evenly distributed over all of the classes.

Baselines. To show the effectiveness of DFG, we simulate MD-GAN and MD-GAN^w with different types of free-riders (i.e., FR$-L$, FR$-D$ and FR$-M$) compared with scenarios without any defense. The pre-trained discriminator for FR$-M$ is trained in the traditional centralized setting with one generator and one discriminator. The pre-trained discriminator is trained on CIFAR100 with the whole dataset for 200 epochs. For both experiments on CIFAR10 and CIFAR100, we use the same pre-trained discriminator to determine the impact of using a similar dataset in contrast to the same dataset. Therefore, we can observe the transfer learning effect on the CIFAR10 experiment with the CIFAR100 pre-trained discriminator.

Notation. We use No_Def_Simple and No_Def_Swap to refer to MD-GAN and MD-GAN^w, respectively, for the scenario without defense. For the scenario with DFG, Def_Simple and Def_Swap are used. In step 3 and 5 of DFG, there are two choices to identify free-riders: (1) binary clustering and (2) anomaly detection. We refer to these two options as Def_X_C and Def_X_{AD} (X is either *Simple* or *Swap*).

---

[2] https://github.com/zhao-zilong/DFG.

Networks. For all experiments, we use the widely adopted and effective Wasserstein GAN with Gradient Penalty (WGAN-GP) [10] structure to train generator and discriminator models. The network of each discriminator consists of three repeated blocks. Each block concatenates 2D Convolution, Instance Normalization, and Leaky Relu layers. $\mathcal{G}$ is also composed of three concatenating blocks. Each block contains 2D Transposed Convolution, Batch Normalization, and Relu layers. The batch size B is set to 500. Since each client owns 5 000 images, there are 10 mini batches per training round. Due to the characteristics of WGAN-GP, the generator is trained once per 5 times the discriminators are trained. Therefore, for each round, the discriminator is trained by all 10 mini batches, but the generator is only trained twice. For DFG, when it evaluates the quality of the discriminators every 10 rounds, it only does that during the first training batch out of two within the round. We repeat each experiment 3 times and report the average.

We fix the number of **benign clients** to 5 for all experiments and vary the number of free-riders from 0 to 5, similar to [4,11] with the typical setting of 10 clients (in our paper, 5 free-riders + 5 benign clients) in the system. In order to show if and how the system deals with an extreme number of free-riders, we furthermore extend the number of free-riders to 10 for CIFAR10. For CIFAR100, we exclude this experiment due to the high computational overhead. The server broadcasts the initialization method (i.e., Kaiming initialization, default setting by Pytorch) for all discriminators and all benign clients apply this initialization. In contrast, free-riders randomly choose one of the four initialization methods introduced in Sect. 3.1. The "detector" on the server made up of $\mathcal{D}_{N+1}$ and $\mathcal{D}_{N+2}$ uses the same initialization method as benign clients. The total number of training rounds is 100. $\mathcal{G}$ generates 10 000 images every 5 rounds, which are used to evaluate $\mathcal{G}$'s performance in terms of FID. Every 10 rounds, we execute DFG: the generator sends the same probing set $\hat{S}$ of 500 images to all clients and the detectors, and $\hat{S}$ varies over rounds.

5.2 Evaluation Metrics

We compute the final performance of the generated data from $\mathcal{G}$ using the Fréchet inception distance (FID) [13], as introduced in Sect. 3. To further show the effectiveness of DFG, we use two different metrics. For MD-GAN without swapping, the **precision** and **recall** of the identified "free-riders" are reported. The precision quantifies the fraction of actual free-riders in the group of clients that are detected to be free-riders by our algorithm. The recall is to measure the fraction of free-riders identified by our defense. Here, a free-rider is labelled as Positive and a benign client as Negative for the calculation [22]. Note that recall is not defined in the absence of free-riders. For MD-GAN^w, our focus lies in preventing discriminator swapping between benign and malicious clients. If the DFG prevents a swapping request between two benign clients, we define this as a **wrong prevention**. And if DFG does not stop a swapping between a benign and a malicious client, we call this a **wrong permission**. Intuitively, for the client-side defense, misclassifying a free-rider as a benign client does not increase wrong prevention but increases wrong permission. And misclassifying a benign client

Table 1. Final FID for MD-GAN and MD-GAN^w on FR$-L$ (**A.** is short for the number of free-riders). Best result in **bold**.

Setup	CIFAR100						CIFAR10						
	0 A.	1 A.	2 A.	3 A.	4 A.	5 A.	0 A.	1 A.	2 A.	3 A.	4 A.	5 A.	10 A.
No_Def_Simple	104.6	165.6	369.3	381.4	381.7	396.5	79.5	146.5	390.9	439.0	443.8	454.1	470.8
Def_Simple$_C$	102.8	117.6	120.6	124.7	150.4	163.4	78.6	85.4	97.6	121.3	124.3	137.9	152.9
Def_Simple$_{AD}$	102.5	**109.9**	**115.4**	**119.9**	**120.3**	**128.8**	80.1	**80.5**	**92.6**	**116.0**	**118.5**	**128.7**	**140.2**
No_Def_Swap	110.7	193.4	397.9	418.8	418.9	420.8	80.1	193.7	420.8	465.9	470.3	472.1	477.5
Def_Swap$_C$	108.3	120.9	132.5	156.9	177.2	198.1	80.0	110.8	132.8	136.6	155.2	172.3	436.5
Def_Swap$_{AD}$	109.2	**119.8**	**120.1**	**123.0**	**124.2**	**124.6**	80.0	**89.8**	**100.0**	**118.6**	**120.5**	**128.9**	**427.7**

Table 2. Precision(%)/Recall(%) for MD-GAN and MD-GAN^w on FR$-L$.

Setup	CIFAR100						CIFAR10						
	0 A.	1 A.	2 A.	3 A.	4 A.	5 A.	0 A.	1 A.	2 A.	3 A.	4 A.	5 A.	10 A.
Def_Simple$_C$	100/-	100/97	100/92	96/83	95/79	95/65	100/-	100/100	100/100	100/89	95/79	95/53	98/37
Def_Simple$_{AD}$	100/-	100/100	100/100	100/100	95/83	98/73	100/-	100/100	100/100	100/100	90/83	85/62	86/45
Def_Swap$_C$	100/-	100/94	100/87	96/80	95/77	95/60	100/-	100/99	100/97	96/84	95/77	94/63	84/10
Def_Swap$_{AD}$	100/-	100/100	100/100	100/100	98/83	98/76	100/-	100/100	100/100	100/100	100/83	100/73	70/15

as a free-rider increases both wrong prevention and wrong permission. We count the numbers of the prevention and permission and report the percentages of **wrong prevention** and **wrong permission**.

5.3   Evaluation Results

Defense against FR$-L$ Table 1 shows the final FID of MD-GAN and MD-GAN^w with and without DFG. As the number of free-riders increases, so does the severity of the attack and the final FID. The random initialization used by the free-riders lead to wrong predictions and hence useless feedback for the generated data. Note that MD-GAN^w has a higher FID for all datasets and scenarios, including the one without free-riders. So swapping does not necessarily help convergence, e.g., when the data among discriminators has low heterogeneity.

DFG greatly improves the performance for both MD-GAN and MD-GAN^w. Even with 50% of the clients being free-riders, the achieved FID remains below 130 while it is around or even above 400 without a defense. In comparison, without an attack, the final FID is 104.6 and 79.5 for CIFAR100 and CIFAR10, respectively. Hence, the defense almost nullifies the attack in that it results in a FID only slightly higher than the FID in the absence of attacks. Even if there are 10 free-riders, i.e., the free-riders outnumber the benign clients 2:1, DFG still provides protection for MD-GAN. However, in line with our expectation that swapping hinders detection of free-riders, DFG provides little protection for MD-GAN^w if there are 10 free-riders.

Using isolation forest for anomaly detection always makes for a stronger defense than using clustering with 2-means. Clustering tends to fail as two free-riders that use different initialization methods end up with very different models

Table 3. Wrong Prevention(%)/Wrong Permission(%) for MD-GAN^w on FR$-L$.

Setup	CIFAR100						CIFAR10						
	0 A.	1 A.	2 A.	3 A.	4 A.	5 A.	0 A.	1 A.	2 A.	3 A.	4 A.	5 A.	10 A.
Def_Swap$_C$	0/-	0/8	10/12	31/35	37/42	37/45	0/-	0/8	5/12	30/33	35/35	39/40	55/68
Def_Swap$_{AD}$	0/-	0/0	0/0	10/0	20/10	33/14	0/-	0/0	0/0	15/0	18/10	24/20	52/50

Table 4. Final FID with FR$-D$ on CIFAR100

Setup	CIFAR100						CIFAR10						
	0 A.	1 A.	2 A.	3 A.	4 A.	5 A.	0 A.	1 A.	2 A.	3 A.	4 A.	5 A.	10 A.
No_Def_Simple	104.6	158.5	351.7	378.5	381.1	396.1	78.0	144.1	299.8	391.92	434.1	449.8	470.1
Def_Simple$_C$	102.8	106.9	127.9	128.4	156.4	163.6	77.8	102.7	110.6	122.3	125.3	131.7	180.8
Def_Simple$_{AD}$	103.5	**105.5**	**110.4**	**116.5**	**125.0**	**132.1**	77.1	**98.2**	**106.8**	**117.2**	**120.2**	**129.2**	**135.6**

and hence are not clustered together. In contrary, they are both seen as outliers in comparison to benign clients under isolation forest, so anomaly detection is more effective.

Let us zoom in to consider the precision and recall of DFG, shown in Table 2 for both CIFAR10 and CIFAR100. Almost all clients identified as free-riders by our defense are indeed free-riders, so the precision is close to 100 for nearly all settings. Indeed, if the number of free-riders is less than 3, the precision is 100. Recall is lower than precision. As we argue in Sect. 4, precision is more important than recall as a low number of free-riders can be tolerated and we do not want to disincentivize participation from benign clients. As long as less than 50% of the clients are free-riders, the recall is still above 75%. Once the number of free-riders is at least equal to the number of benign clients, it becomes hard to identify them, especially if swapping and 10 free-riders are present.

For MD-GAN^w, we evaluate the impact of step 4–6 of our defense. Table 3 shows the percentage of wrong prevention and wrong permission. In line with the results on FID, precision, and recall, Def_Swap$_{AD}$ performs better than Def_Swap$_C$ in all the experiments. Concretely, there are no wrong permission for Def_Swap$_{AD}$ for up to three free-riders whereas Def_Swap$_C$ can have up to 35% of wrong permission. The fraction of wrong prevention is slightly higher for Def_Swap$_{AD}$ than the fraction of wrong permission. Note that for Def_Swap$_C$, the fraction of wrong prevention is lower than the fraction of wrong permission. For 10 free-riders, more than 50% of prevention and permission are incorrect. The result is in line with what we observe for the final FID in Table 1: DFG fails when there are a lot of free-riders and swapping is applied. With the free-riders making up the majority of the clients, it becomes almost impossible to distinguish them initially and once discriminators have been swapped, free-riders can utilize the already-trained discriminators to appear like they participate in the training.

Defense against FR$-D$ FR$-D$ utilizes its synthetic data and data from the generator to train the generator. Thus, for FR$-D$, the expectation is that it can leverage the knowledge obtained from generator to train a better discriminator than FR$-L$. The results are displayed in Table 4. Comparing to Table 1, we find that without a defense, FR$-D$ exhibits a slightly lower FID for a low number of attackers than FR$-L$. So the negative impact of the attack is slightly less since FR$-D$ performs actual training. Given that randomly generated data instead of real data is used, the positive impact is minimal in terms of improved data quality. Yet, free-riders applying FR$-D$ are still quite different from benign clients and can hence be detected. In the presence of DFG, FR$-D$ leads to a similar performance as FR$-L$. Hence, DFG works for multiple attack strategies.

Defense against FR$-M$ In FR$-M$, free-riders use a pre-trained discriminator model. Recall that for both datasets, the pre-trained discriminator is based on CIFAR100. Based on [1], training a GAN from a pre-trained discriminator means that the loss function of the GAN is saturated and the learning process is slow or unstable. Overall, using a pre-trained discriminator results in the least negative impact of all considered attack strategies. The result is expected as these free-riders provide discriminators of actual relevance rather than ones that are random or trained on random data (Table 5).

Table 5. Final FID with FR$-M$.

Setup	CIFAR100						CIFAR10						
	0 A.	1 A.	2 A.	3 A.	4 A.	5 A.	0 A.	1 A.	2 A.	3 A.	4 A.	5 A.	10 A.
No_Def_Simple	104.6	**101.4**	**108.7**	**118.9**	**128.9**	362.8	77.6	87.6	107.1	120.1	125.4	174.3	475.9
Def_Simple$_C$	102.4	110.4	118.9	131.0	136.3	**142.0**	77.5	**82.0**	**94.2**	**106.9**	**110.6**	**116.5**	**138.2**
Def_Simple$_{AD}$	104.2	104.3	110.1	125.3	134.4	172.3	77.9	85.9	98.3	108.7	116.1	139.6	143.8

The exact results differ slightly depending on the combination of training dataset and choice of pre-trained discriminator. If CIFAR100 is used both for the pre-trained discriminator and the training dataset for MD-GAN, using DFG actually decreases the performance slightly if the number of attackers is less than 50%. DFG struggles to distinguish benign clients and free-riders. Indeed, the free-riders appear very similar to each other as they all start from the same pre-trained generator. In contrast, the benign clients are initially more diverse, which can make them accidentally be considered as outliers. Thus, DFG removing clients just degrades the performance and does not remove any negative influence from the training. If 5 clients are free-riders, FID does not converge without a defense. DFG here improves the situation, though the results are worse than for FR$-L$ and FR$-D$ as detection is harder. For CIFAR10, the pre-trained discriminator is for a different dataset than the training dataset. Thus, the discriminator is less suitable and degrades the FID more than for CIFAR100 if no defense is applied. However, the FID is still better than for other types of free-riders. DFG again largely nullifies the impact of the attack. A key difference when defending against FR$-M$ in comparison to previous attacks lies in the choice of defense. For FR$-M$, clustering is more effective than anomaly detection while the opposite is observed for $FR-L$ and $FR-D$. While the pre-trained discriminators may be different from the actual discriminators trained by benign clients, they are not different enough to be considered an anomaly .

All results indicate that DFG is an effective defense that only fails if the number of free-rider considerably exceeds the number of benign clients. It hardly ever excludes benign clients and only has minimal impact in the absence of attacks. Notably, DFG is effective against different types of free-riders.

6   Related Work

In this section, we summarize the related studies on multi-discriminator GAN frameworks and free-rider attacks in distributed learning systems.

MD-GAN: Overcoming the data privacy issues of centralized GANs [16,18], distributed GANs [4,9,11,23,24,32] enable multiple data owners to collaboratively train GAN systems. Existing distributed GAN frameworks can be summarized as Federated Learning GANs (FLGANs) [9,24,32] and MD-GANs [4, 11,23]. In FLGANs, a client trains both a generator and a discriminator network and a server aggregates both networks from all clients. Consequently, FLGANs require all participants to have high computational capacity. In contrast, MD-GAN architectures offload the intensive training of the generator to the server and keep the lighter training of the discriminator on the client side. In this manner, MD-GANs are also able to involve a massive number of edge nodes [5,27]. The various architectures of MD-GAN differ with regard to model exchange between discriminators. AsynDGAN [4] elementary MD-GAN architecture where discriminators only directly communicate with the generator. In order to improve the drawbacks of MD-GAN when discriminators only own small datasets, Hardy et al. [11] propose that discriminators are swapped between clients, opening an opportunity for free-riders to act stealthily.

Free-Riders: The concept of free-riders first emerged in economics [2] but has been essential in various distributed systems. In peer-to-peer file-sharing systems, free-riders join to download files without uploading any files [19]. In Federated Learning systems [20,28], Lin et. al. [17] first propose stealthy free-rider attacks for image classification: instead of sending a random model, free-riders send the global model of the previous round back with small perturbation noises added or provide a fake gradient using the previous difference of weights. Defenses are designed accordingly based on the DAGMM [33] network, which is a recent anomaly detection method so as to catch the differences on deep feature by gradients for free-riders. Fraboni et. al. [7] further explore the attack of adding perturbation noises [17] and provide a convergence guarantee of the global model in the presence of a single free-rider. However, as both studies are concerned with Federated Learning systems, where the clients and the server are curating models of the same structure, they are not directly applicable to MD-GAN systems where the server and client train different types of models.

Additionally, none of them has provided a systematic study on the influence of (multiple) free-riders. To the best of our knowledge, this paper is the first to study free-riders in MD-GANs.

7 Conclusion

In this first study of free-riders on MD-GAN, we explore multiple types of free-rider attacks. They all can severely degrade the quality of the trained generator, emphasizing the need for a defense. Our defense, DFG, distinguishes free-riders from benign clients through clustering or anomaly detection. It is highly effective and efficient. With the FID being about 100 without attacks and 400 with attacks and no defense, DFG enables the system to maintain an FID of less than 130 in the presence of attacks, even if the attackers make up 50% of the clients. Future work should target more malicious adversaries that actively aim to degrade performance.

References

1. Arjovsky, M., Bottou, L.: Towards principled methods for training generative adversarial networks. In: 5th International Conference on Learning Representations, ICLR 2017, Toulon, France, April 24–26, 2017, Conference Track Proceedings (2017)
2. Baumol, W.J.: Welfare economics and the theory of the state. In: The encyclopedia of public choice, pp. 937–940. Springer, Boston (2004). https://doi.org/10.1007/978-0-306-47828-4_214
3. Brock, A., Donahue, J., Simonyan, K.: Large scale GAN training for high fidelity natural image synthesis. In: 7th International Conference on Learning Representations, ICLR 2019, New Orleans, LA, USA, May 6–9, 2019 (2019)
4. Chang, Q., et al.: Synthetic learning: learn from distributed asynchronized discriminator GAN without sharing medical image data. In: 2020 IEEE/CVF Conference on Computer Vision and Pattern Recognition, CVPR 2020, Seattle, WA, USA, June 13–19, 2020, pp. 13853–13863. Computer Vision Foundation/IEEE (2020)
5. Correia, C., Correia, M., Rodrigues, L.: Omega: a secure event ordering service for the edge. In: 50th Annual IEEE/IFIP International Conference on Dependable Systems and Networks, DSN 2020, Valencia, Spain, June 29–July 2, 2020, pp. 489–501. IEEE (2020)
6. Feldman, M., Papadimitriou, C.H., Chuang, J., Stoica, I.: Free-riding and white-washing in peer-to-peer systems. IEEE J. Sel. Areas Commun. 24(5), 1010–1019 (2006)
7. Fraboni, Y., Vidal, R., Lorenzi, M.: Free-rider attacks on model aggregation in federated learning. In: Banerjee, A., Fukumizu, K. (eds.) The 24th International Conference on Artificial Intelligence and Statistics, AISTATS 2021, April 13–15, 2021, Virtual Event. Proceedings of Machine Learning Research, vol. 130, pp. 1846–1854. PMLR (2021)
8. Glorot, X., Bengio, Y.: Understanding the difficulty of training deep feedforward neural networks. In: Teh, Y.W., Titterington, D.M. (eds.) Proceedings of the Thirteenth International Conference on Artificial Intelligence and Statistics, AISTATS 2010, Chia Laguna Resort, Sardinia, Italy, May 13–15, 2010. JMLR Proceedings, vol. 9, pp. 249–256. JMLR.org (2010)

9. Guerraoui, R., Guirguis, A., Kermarrec, A., Merrer, E.L.: FeGAN: scaling distributed GANs. In: Silva, D.D., Kapitza, R. (eds.) Middleware '20: 21st International Middleware Conference, Delft, The Netherlands, December 7–11, 2020, pp. 193–206. ACM (2020)
10. Gulrajani, I., Ahmed, F., Arjovsky, M., Dumoulin, V., Courville, A.: Improved training of wasserstein GANs. arXiv preprint arXiv:1704.00028 (2017)
11. Hardy, C., Merrer, E.L., Sericola, B.: MD-GAN: multi-discriminator generative adversarial networks for distributed datasets. In: 2019 IEEE International Parallel and Distributed Processing Symposium, IPDPS 2019, Rio de Janeiro, Brazil, May 20–24, 2019, pp. 866–877. IEEE (2019)
12. He, K., Zhang, X., Ren, S., Sun, J.: Delving deep into rectifiers: surpassing human-level performance on imagenet classification. In: Proceedings of the IEEE International Conference on Computer Vision, pp. 1026–1034 (2015)
13. Heusel, M., Ramsauer, H., Unterthiner, T., Nessler, B., Hochreiter, S.: GANs trained by a two time-scale update rule converge to a local nash equilibrium. In: Guyon, I., et al. (eds.) Advances in Neural Information Processing Systems, vol. 30. Curran Associates, Inc. (2017)
14. Krizhevsky, A., Hinton, G., et al.: Learning multiple layers of features from tiny images (2009)
15. LeCun, Y., Bottou, L., Bengio, Y., Haffner, P.: Gradient-based learning applied to document recognition. Proc. IEEE 86(11), 2278–2324 (1998)
16. Li, C., Alvarez-Melis, D., Xu, K., Jegelka, S., Sra, S.: Distributional adversarial networks. In: 6th International Conference on Learning Representations, ICLR 2018, Vancouver, BC, Canada, April 30–May 3, 2018, Workshop Track Proceedings (2018)
17. Lin, J., Du, M., Liu, J.: Free-riders in federated learning: attacks and defenses. CoRR abs/1911.12560 (2019)
18. Liu, G., Khalil, I., Khreishah, A.: ZK-GanDef: a GAN based zero knowledge adversarial training defense for neural networks. In: 49th Annual IEEE/IFIP International Conference on Dependable Systems and Networks, DSN 2019, Portland, OR, USA, June 24–27, 2019, pp. 64–75. IEEE (2019)
19. Locher, T., Moor, P., Schmid, S., Wattenhofer, R.: Free riding in bittorrent is cheap. In: Kohler, E., Minshall, G. (eds.) 5th ACM Workshop on Hot Topics in Networks - HotNets-V, Irvine, California, USA, November 29–30, 2006. ACM SIGCOMM (2006)
20. McMahan, B., Moore, E., Ramage, D., Hampson, S., y Arcas, B.A.: Communication-efficient learning of deep networks from decentralized data. In: Singh, A., Zhu, X.J. (eds.) Proceedings of the 20th International Conference on Artificial Intelligence and Statistics, AISTATS 2017, 20–22 April 2017, Fort Lauderdale, FL, USA. Proceedings of Machine Learning Research, vol. 54, pp. 1273–1282. PMLR (2017)
21. Peres, R.S., Azevedo, M., Araújo, S.O., Guedes, M., Miranda, F., Barata, J.: Generative adversarial networks for data augmentation in structural adhesive inspection. Appl. Sci. 11(7), 3086 (2021)
22. Powers, D.M.W.: Evaluation: from precision, recall and f-measure to roc, informedness, markedness and correlation. CoRR abs/2010.16061 (2020)
23. Qu, H., Zhang, Y., Chang, Q., Yan, Z., Chen, C., Metaxas, D.: Learn distributed GAN with temporary discriminators. In: Vedaldi, A., Bischof, H., Brox, T., Frahm, J.-M. (eds.) ECCV 2020. LNCS, vol. 12372, pp. 175–192. Springer, Cham (2020). https://doi.org/10.1007/978-3-030-58583-9_11

24. Rasouli, M., Sun, T., Rajagopal, R.: FedGAN: federated generative adversarial networks for distributed data. CoRR abs/2006.07228 (2020)
25. Robbins, H., Monro, S.: A stochastic approximation method. Ann. Math. Stat. **22**(3), 400–407 (1951)
26. Union, E.: Regulation (eu) 2016/679 of the European parliament and of the council of 27 April 2016 on the protection of natural persons with regard to the processing of personal data and on the free movement of such data, and repealing directive 95/46/ec (general data protection regulation). Official Journal L110 59, 1–88 (2016)
27. Wang, Z., Xu, H., Liu, J., Huang, H., Qiao, C., Zhao, Y.: Resource-efficient federated learning with hierarchical aggregation in edge computing. In: 40th IEEE Conference on Computer Communications, INFOCOM 2021, Vancouver, BC, Canada, May 10–13, 2021, pp. 1–10. IEEE (2021)
28. Yang, Q., Liu, Y., Chen, T., Tong, Y.: Federated machine learning: concept and applications. ACM Trans. Intell. Syst. Technol. **10**(2), 12:1–12:19 (2019)
29. Zhao, Z., Birke, R., Kunar, A., Chen, L.Y.: Fed-TGAN: federated learning framework for synthesizing tabular data. arXiv preprint arXiv:2108.07927 (2021)
30. Zhao, Z., Kunar, A., Birke, R., Chen, L.Y.: CTAB-GAN: effective table data synthesizing. In: Balasubramanian, V.N., Tsang, I. (eds.) Proceedings of The 13th Asian Conference on Machine Learning. Proceedings of Machine Learning Research, vol. 157, pp. 97–112. PMLR (2021)
31. Zhao, Z., Kunar, A., Birke, R., Chen, L.Y.: CTAB-GAN+: enhancing tabular data synthesis. arXiv preprint arXiv:2204.00401 (2022)
32. Zhao, Z., Wu, H., van Moorsel, A., Chen, L.Y.: GTV: generating tabular data via vertical federated learning. arXiv preprint arXiv:2302.01706 (2023)
33. Zong, B., et al.: Deep autoencoding gaussian mixture model for unsupervised anomaly detection. In: 6th International Conference on Learning Representations, ICLR 2018, Vancouver, BC, Canada, April 30–May 3, 2018, Conference Track Proceedings (2018)

Empirical Studies and more
Decentralized Finance

Dissecting Bitcoin and Ethereum Transactions: On the Lack of Transaction Contention and Prioritization Transparency in Blockchains

Johnnatan Messias[1]([⊠])(iD), Vabuk Pahari[1], Balakrishnan Chandrasekaran[2], Krishna P. Gummadi[1], and Patrick Loiseau[3]

[1] MPI-SWS, Saarbrücken, Germany
{johnme, vpahari, gummadi}@mpi-sws.org
[2] Vrije Universiteit Amsterdam, Amsterdam, The Netherlands
b.chandrasekaran@vu.nl
[3] Inria, FairPlay Team, Paris, France
patrick.loiseau@inria.fr

Abstract. In permissionless blockchains, transaction issuers include a fee to incentivize miners to include their transactions. To accurately estimate this prioritization fee for a transaction, transaction issuers (or blockchain participants, mjohnme@mpi-sws.orgore generally) rely on two fundamental notions of transparency, namely contention and prioritization transparency. Contention transparency implies that participants are aware of every pending transaction that will contend with a given transaction for inclusion. Prioritization transparency states that the participants are aware of the transaction or prioritization fees paid by every such contending transaction. Neither of these notions of transparency holds well today. Private relay networks, for instance, allow users to send transactions privately to miners. Besides, users can offer fees to miners via either direct transfers to miners' wallets or off-chain payments—neither of which are public. In this work, we characterize the lack of contention and prioritization transparency in Bitcoin and Ethereum resulting from such practices. We show that private relay networks are widely used and private transactions are quite prevalent. We show that the lack of transparency facilitates miners to collude and overcharge users who may use these private relay networks despite them offering little to no guarantees on transaction prioritization. The lack of these transparencies in blockchains has crucial implications for transaction issuers as well as the stability of blockchains. Finally, we make our data sets and scripts publicly available.

Keywords: Contention transparency · Prioritization transparency · Private transactions · Bitcoin · Ethereum · MEV

1 Introduction

The rate at which users issue transactions in permissionless blockchains, e.g., Bitcoin [31] and Ethereum [47], is often much higher than the rate at which

© The Author(s) 2024
F. Baldimtsi and C. Cachin (Eds.): FC 2023, LNCS 13951, pp. 221–240, 2024.
https://doi.org/10.1007/978-3-031-47751-5_13

miners can include them in a block [10,21,25,28,29]. Users typically issue transactions using a wallet software, whose primary functionality is determining an "appropriate" fee for a given transaction. We use the term "fee" to refer generally to the incentive offered by a user to miners for prioritizing the inclusion of their transaction in a block, albeit its exact form may vary, e.g., *fee rate* in Bitcoin and *gas price* in Ethereum. This (prioritization) fee varies, unsurprisingly, as a function of the level of congestion in the blockchain [29] as well as the distribution of fees across available transactions. Inferring either of these is, however, deceptively complicated.

At first glance, these tasks appear straightforward, since every transaction is broadcast to all miners in the blockchain. A user could simply gather all transactions broadcast over time and reconstruct the set of uncommitted transactions available to a miner (i.e., contents of the miner's Mempool) at any point of time [28]. We refer to this assumption of a public and uniform view (across miners) of all available transactions as *contention transparency*. If contention transparency exists, a user could rank order available transactions by their fee (based on which miners should select transactions for inclusion) and estimate the commit delay of any transaction [29]. Consequently, they could determine the fee that they must pay to guarantee inclusion of their transaction in a given block. We label this assumption that the (prioritization) fee offered by a transaction is only that publicly declared by that transaction as *prioritization transparency*. Neither the contention transparency nor the prioritization transparency, however, holds today in permissionless blockchains.

Lack of Contention Transparency.   Not all transactions are publicly broadcast. Users can submit transactions to a subset of miners or mining pools via *private channels* or *relays* that are opaque to the public (i.e., transactions remain private to the relay, until they are committed). Users may also submit their transaction to a specific mining pool that assures them a fast commit time. This paper reveals that such private mining practices (i.e., where transactions are submitted to only a subset of the miners) are becoming commonplace and analyzes the characteristics of these private transactions.

Lack of Prioritization Transparency.   The fees offered by a transaction could be substantially more than that publicly declared by it. A transaction could, for instance, privately offer additional fees to a miner to "accelerate" its inclusion in a block. Many such transaction-accelerator (or *front-running as a service (FRaaS)*) platforms exist for Bitcoin [4,45] and Ethereum [12,18,40,41]. Furthermore, the same transaction could offer different fees to different mining pools (via their relays). The presence of such hidden or dark-fees could fundamentally erode the reliability of any fee prediction: Transaction issuers may end up paying substantially large fees without receiving proportional or any reduction in commit delays. This paper characterizes the prevalence of such dark-fee transactions and analyzes the most popular private relay network available in Ethereum, Flashbots [18]. Furthermore, we conduct active experiments in both Bitcoin and Ethereum to validate our assumptions regarding the prioritization transparency. In addition to showing that transaction fees may not be uniform across miners, we claim that, given the lack of contention transparency, the lack of prioritization transparency may become more widespread than it is now.

The lack of contention and prioritization transparencies stem from real, nontrivial concerns of transaction issuers. The risk of transactions being front-run by bots [9,12,42,46], for instance, creates the need for transaction privacy. Mining pools that address this need also facilitate, unsurprisingly, off-chain payments via which transaction issuers can (privately) incentivize the miners [4,29,45]. We view these developments as natural and logical steps in the evolution of blockchains and back our assertions with empirical observations. We claim, therefore, in contrast to prior work [9,41], that it is only the opacity of the overall fees issued by a transaction issuer that poses a fundamental threat to the stability of blockchains: Transaction issuers cannot, for instance, precisely infer the fee required to commit their transactions into the next block, and miners can, consequently, overcharge them as the "real" fees are opaque to the rest of the network [46].

We summarize our contributions as follows. We characterize the lack of contention transparency in both Bitcoin and Ethereum: We show that the use of private channels or relay networks to submit transactions directly to a subset of miners is becoming widespread. This practice will likely erode prioritization transparency, as transaction issuers may not be able to estimate the appropriate fees, none of which are publicly visible. We characterize the prevalence of such private transactions fees. We found that Flashbots bundles represent 52.11% of all Ethereum blocks. With the lack of prioritization transparency, miners might overcharge users when they send their transactions privately. We also show that Bitcoin miners collude (with an aggregate hashing power of more than 50% of the network's total hashing power) when including dark-fees transactions. Finally, we release our data sets and the scripts used in our analysis to enable the scientific community to reproduce our results [30].

2   Related Work

There is a rich literature on block rewards as incentives for mining [7,16,17, 19,23,32,33,36,39,48]. Recent work also analyzed the implications of relying on transaction fees separately [6] and in conjunction with block rewards [43], as well as the relationship between such incentives and transaction waiting times [10]. These prior work assume that transactions are broadcast to all miners and the fees offered is uniform across miners. None of them acknowledge the issue of transparency.

Basu *et al.* [3] and Lavi *et al.* [25] addressed the inefficiencies in transaction-fee setting mechanisms (i.e., first-price auctions) by proposing alternative mechanisms. They claim that miners might be dishonest, albeit they present no empirical evidence. Siddiqui *et al.* [38] used simulations to show that, if transaction fees are the only incentives, miners will select transactions greedily, thereby increasing the commit times of many transactions. Prior work also analyzed the Ethereum fee (i.e., gas price) mechanism to determine the gas price for a given transaction [1,26,27,44]. The fee estimation and fee-based prioritization schemes in these studies do not take into account dark-fees or private mining.

Many transaction-accelerator, or FRaaS, platforms exist for both Bitcoin [4,45] and Ethereum [12,18,40]. Transaction issuers might resort to such acceleration or off-chain payment channels to hide their true fee from competitors and avoid being front-run [9,41]. Tim Roughgarden [37] discussed the incentives for off-chain agreements (such as dark-fees) between miners and users for first-price auctions and different deviations of the new Ethereum fee mechanism *EIP-1559 protocol* [5].[1] Roughgarden showed that miners and users cannot strictly increase their joint utility through off-chain payments under EIP-1559 because on-chain bids can be easily replaced by the off-chain bids. However, utility here is only based on the revenue of bidding for block space. The author did not take into account that utility might depend on other factors, such as transaction issuers wanting to keep their actual bids for block space hidden through off-chain payments, which strictly increases their chances of prioritization, as other bidders cannot counter bid, as they are unaware of the bid itself.

Closest to our work are two that analyze private mining. Strehe and Ante [41] investigated *exclusive mining* (or private mining), where transactions issuers and miners collude to include transactions that have been sent through a private network. In this case, the transactions are not publicly disclosed until they have been included in a block; besides, the fees can remain opaque to everyone forever, as such off-chain agreements may use fiat currencies. Weintraub *et al.* [46] measured the popularity of *Flashbots*, the most used private relay network for Ethereum. Our work, in contrast, extensively investigates private transactions in both Bitcoin and Ethereum blockchains. Through active measurements, we empirically show that Bitcoin miners collude and highlight the colluding mining pools. We show that Flashbots bundles are quite prevalent in Ethereum and are mainly used for calling Decentralized Exchanges (DEX) contracts to take advantage of *Maximal Extractable Value (MEV)* opportunities. Finally, we discuss why our findings are still valid after "The Merge"—an Ethereum hard fork deployed on September 15th, 2022 [13,14].

3   On Contention Transparency

3.1   The Rise of Private Relay Networks

With the lucrative market of Decentralized Finance (DeFi) in Ethereum, today, bots engage in predatory front-running behaviors such as sandwich attacks and transaction-replay attacks [9,24,34,35,42,46,49]. Relay networks help users to counter such attacks: They provide users with a private channel for communicating with miners, who have to prove their identity to participate in the relay. Relay networks help users completely bypass the P2P network: Users send their transactions to the relay network, which in turn relays them to its participant miners. The relay network and its participants claim (a) not to front-run these transactions and (b) to keep them private until they are included in a block [18].

---

[1] The EIP-1559 went live in the Ethereum's London hard fork upgrade on August 5th, 2021, at block number 12,965,000.

These transactions, hence, by construction, experience no front-running issues. Relay networks are centralized; if miners misbehave, they may lose their network membership and forfeit their future profits. Multiple relay networks (e.g., bloXroute, Taichi Network [40], and others [8,15]) exist today, but we focus on Flashbots [18], the largest relay network for Ethereum.

Flashbots.   Flashbots's users *bundle* one or more transactions in some specific order [18]. Miners are expected to mine the entire bundle (retaining the ordering of transactions within the bundle) and place it at the top of their blocks. The miners receive a fee (paid via a direct transfer to their wallets) for including the bundle in addition to the (traditional) fees associated with the transactions in that bundle. If there are two competing bundles—capturing the same financial opportunity, e.g., liquidations—miners will choose the one with the highest reward (i.e., maximizing financial incentives). The other bundle is *discarded* (since the financial opportunity no longer exists after having been captured by the included bundle), albeit its transactions do *not* expend *any* gas. Therefore, except for a network base fee introduced in EIP-1559, arbitrageurs and liquidators can participate without having any balance in their wallet: If they successfully capture a financial opportunity, they pay the miner from the profit secured and pocket the rest [18]. Flashbots is a *free* to use relay network, and they allow anyone to query whether a transaction used their relay network and the private fees paid to the miner (after it has been committed in a block). We use this publicly available data for analyzing the transactions issued (privately) on Flashbots. Flashbots, however, does not list the discarded bundles (or its transactions): we have access, hence, only to committed transactions.

3.2   Characterizing Private Relay Networks

We gathered all Ethereum blocks mined over a 9-month time period—from September 8th, 2021 to June 30th, 2022—to investigate the behavior of Ethereum mining pools. This data set contains 347,629,393 issued transactions and 1,867,000 blocks (from block number 13,183,000 to 15,049,999). We used miners' wallet addresses to infer the block owners, but we failed to identify the owners of 46,895 blocks (or 2.51% of the total); we grouped the latter into one category, "Unknown." Figure 1a shows the distribution of blocks and transactions mined in Ethereum by the top-20 mining pools. We also retrieved 6,937,292 transactions (2% of all issued transactions) contained in 3,284,886 bundles from Flashbots; these are transactions sent privately to miners. 972,911 (52.11%) of blocks in the data set have at least one such Flashbots transaction: *Private transactions are becoming quite common across most of the powerful mining pools in Ethereum.*

Flashbots labels its bundles (and constituent transactions) into one of three categories: (i) *flashbots*, which represent those sent through their private relay; (ii) *rogue*, referring to those delivered to a (Flashbots) miner, but via a different relay network; and (iii) *miner payout*, indicating a bundle containing payouts to users of a mining pool [46]. We find 58.82%, 27.93%, and 13.25% of transactions belonging to the flashbots, miner payout, and rogue categories, respectively. We

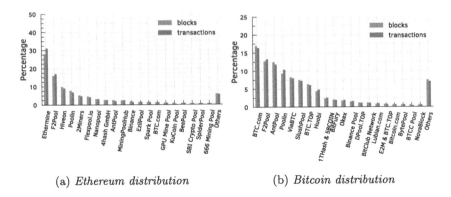

(a) *Ethereum distribution*   (b) *Bitcoin distribution*

Fig. 1. Blocks mined and transactions confirmed in (a) Ethereum and (b) Bitcoin by the top-20 mining pools; "Others" consolidates the remaining mining pools.

also noticed that 70,260 (1.01%) of all Flashbots transactions failed to execute after inclusion in a block. A small fraction of transactions is, hence, not successfully executed despite using private relays.

Flashbots claims to have $\approx 85\%$ of the total Ethereum hash rate [18]. Per our analyses, however, the majority of the mining pools (47 out of 48—barring EthPool) use Flashbots, accounting for 99.99% of the total Ethereum hash rate, A recent work also corroborates our findings [46].

Some of the most powerful mining pools like Spark Pool[2] (which cooperates with Taichi Network [40]), Ethermine [15], and F2Pool (part of Eden Network [8]) offer their own relay networks. As these networks allow transaction issuers to send transactions exclusively to a specific miner, we hypothesize that miners would prefer (or prioritize) these transactions to those sent via the public P2P network. Crucially, payments from these private transactions are guaranteed, while those from publicly issued transactions are not—they are available to any miner willing to commit them. *Miners, hence, would likely offer preferential treatment for private transactions.*

3.3   On Preferential Treatment of Private Transactions

We substantiate our hypothesis of preferential treatment for private transactions via an active experiment conducted on September 8th, 2021. We issued 8 transactions, where 4 were sent privately via the Taichi Network, powered by Spark Pool, and 4 through the public Ethereum network (refer Table 4 in Appendix 1).

While running the experiment, we checked if the popular Ethereum blockchain explorers (i.e., Etherscan, Blockchain.com, and Blockchair) observed any of our private transactions; if they did, it would imply that the Taichi Network leaked the transactions to the public. While the public transactions

---

[2] Spark Pool suspended their mining services on Sept. 30th, 2021, due to regulatory requirements introduced by Chinese authorities [20].

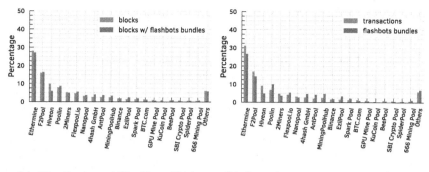

(a) *Distribution of Flashbots blocks*   (b) *Distribution of Flashbots bundles*

Fig. 2. Distribution of (a) blocks with at least one Flashbots bundle and (b) bundle of transactions per block, per mining pool. Ethermine included 27.05% of all blocks with a Flashbot bundle and 26.63% of all Flashbots bundles, while mining around 28.05% and 31.11% of all blocks and transactions, respectively.

appeared in these blockchain explorers, right after we sent them through the public P2P network, the private transactions were not observed by any of them until the transactions were included in a block. More importantly, our private transactions were *not* flagged by Etherscan (which relies on Flashbots API and more recently on EigenPhi [11]) as private, *even after inclusion in a block*. Measuring the prevalence of private transactions is, hence, challenging; it is likely that our estimates of the volume of private transactions based on such tools represent, hence, a lower bound.

Babel Pool included 2 out of our 4 private transactions. Spark Pool technically supports this mining pool, implying that they "collaborate" in committing private transactions sent over the Taichi network [2]. Our transactions were included, however, in the appropriate position in the block based on their fees. We delve into the prioritization of transactions in the next section.

We also characterize the prevalence of private transactions in Ethereum and indicate that mining pools can each have a distinct set of private transactions in their Mempool. Users, as a result, can no longer rely on the public Mempool alone to estimate their transaction fee. Given the absence of other data, they are highly likely to end up with a false estimate of the "appropriate" transaction fees for their transactions.

4   On Prioritization Transparency

4.1   Prevalence of Transaction Bundling

Flashbots bundles are prevalent in Ethereum (refer Sect. 3.2). Each Flashbots bundle contains at least 1 transaction and at most 631 transactions; on average they contain 2.11 transactions, with a median of 1 and a standard deviation of 6.47. We noticed that Ethermine alone included more than a quarter (26.63%)

of all 3,284,886 bundles (Fig. 2). Also, blocks contain at most 40 bundles, with an average of 3.38, a median of 3, and a standard deviation of 2.64.

Maximal Extractable Value (MEV).   Flashbots allows users to bundle together a set of transactions, thereby specifying the order in which they are executed. The bundles can also include public transactions, propagated over the public P2P network. A public transaction that buys a coin on a DEX can, for example, lead to an arbitrage opportunity [35]. A user can include this transaction in a bundle along with one of their own to capture this arbitrage opportunity. The last transaction in the bundle usually pays the miner (based on the profit made) in ether via a direct transfer (i.e., *coinbase transfer*) to their wallet addresses. This essentially means that miners are being offered different prices for mining the same transaction. In other words, miners have a financial incentive for including transactions that are in a bundle at the top of a block, even though the public fee offered through gas price in the transaction data is very low. Hence, each transaction in the bundle has a normal gas price and a *bundle gas price*, which is calculated using the total gas used by all transactions in the bundle and the total miner reward for mining the bundle.

Bundling Public Transactions.   To identify bundles with transactions that were probably sent through the public P2P network, we rely on a simple heuristic. Specifically, we focus on transaction bundles of size 2 and 3, and search for transactions that have likely resulted in a publicly sent transaction being bundled. Then, we find bundles issued from different issuers that include a zero and non-zero *max-priority fee*[3] transactions. The intuition is that miners have no incentive to include transactions that offer a zero max-priority fee, as they receive no rewards for mining these transactions. Unless they receive extra payment (through Flashbots coinbase transfer). Hence, transactions that have a non-zero max-priority fee were likely sent publicly.

For transaction bundles of size 2, we look for transactions whose issuers are not the same. Furthermore, we look for cases where the first transaction offers a non-zero max-priority fee, with no coinbase transfer to the miner, and the second transaction offers a 0 max-priority fee and a non-zero coinbase transfer.

For transaction bundles of size 3, we look for signs of sandwich attacks [34]. We look for bundles where the first and last transactions have the same issuer, but the second transaction has a different issuer. Additionally, we check that the first and third transactions offer a 0 max-priority fee, meaning that the miner receives no reward from the gas price for mining these transactions. Then, we ensure that the second transaction offers miners a non-zero max-priority fee, while the third offers miners a fee through direct coinbase transfer. This scenario might be a classic sandwich attack, where public transactions are bundled between two private transactions, sent by the same issuer, and the miner gets paid via a coinbase transfer from the third transaction [34].

---

[3] The *max-priority fee* was introduced in EIP-1559 as the unique financial incentive miners get for including publicly announced transactions. The other fees are burned.

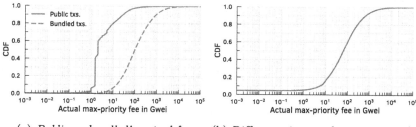

(a) *Public vs bundled's actual fee*   (b) *Difference in actual max-priority fee*

Fig. 3. Diff. between the actual max-priority fee of public transactions and Flashbots bundles; bundles typically offer a larger *effective* fee to the miners.

We found 853,394 transactions in 426,697 bundles of length 2, and 1,231,695 transactions in 410,565 bundles of length 3. From those, we found that 110,401 (25.87%) and 37,447 (9.12%) bundles, of lengths 2 and 3, respectively, fit our heuristic. We then calculate the *actual max-priority fee* for these bundles, as the total gas used by all transactions in the bundle divided by the total miner reward (from gas usage and coinbase transfer). Figure 3 shows the price difference miners get for including publicly and bundled transactions. Note that around 40% of transactions differ in the actual max-priority fee by 100 gwei-per-units-of-gas. Flashbots bundles offers much higher gas prices in comparison to the public announced max-priority fee alone.

Towards Liquidations Through Bundling. Lending protocols rely on *over-collateralization* of assets: In order to borrow assets from these protocols, a user has to deposit a collateral of at least 150% of the borrowed amount. To borrow 1 USDC on AAVE, for example, a user would have to collateralize at least 1.5 USDC worth of another asset (e.g., in ETH or BTC). If the ratio of the collateral asset versus the borrowed asset falls below 1.5, the user's position can be liquidated by any other participant until the ratio stabilizes to 1.5 again. The liquidator then pays back a portion of the user's debt to receive the collateral asset at a discount. In order to assess an asset's on-chain value, lending protocols rely on oracle services, e.g., Chainlink Data Feeds. In the case of the two largest lending platforms, AAVE V2 and Compound, for instance, Chainlink provides the price of each asset in ETH and USD, respectively.

We found 16,418 liquidations in AAVE and 6387 liquidations in Compound. Out of these, there were 4863 AAVE liquidations and 2036 Compound liquidations that were sent privately through Flashbots. In AAVE, the three largest collateral assets that were liquidated were WETH (57.58%), LINK (11.84%), and WBTC (8.99%). The debt assets paid for, i.e., the assets borrowed by the users, were USDC (33.77%), USDT (22.27%), DAI (19.39%), and GUSD (5.12%), all of which are stablecoins and account for over 80% of the assets repaid by liquidators. In Compound, the three largest collateral assets that were liquidated were WETH (69.7%), WBTC (10.31%), and UNI (5.5%). The debt assets were

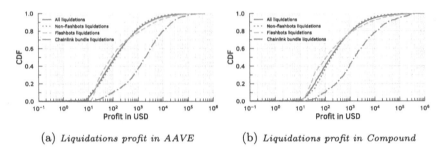

(a) *Liquidations profit in AAVE*   (b) *Liquidations profit in Compound*

Fig. 4. Profits of liquidators in (a) AAVE and in (b) Compound. Liquidations bundled with Chainlink updates generally provide higher profits.

USDC (38.9%), DAI (30.45%), USDT (23.38%), and TUSD (2.7%), all of which are stablecoins and account for over 90% of the assets repaid by liquidators.

Liquidation with Bundled Oracle Updates.   To check the adverse effect of bundling oracle updates, we looked at bundles with Chainlink oracle updates as they are a key part of liquidations. We identified 1165 AAVE liquidations distributed within 1154 bundles (2662 transactions including 1301 oracle updates) that contained at least one oracle update. In Compound, we found 648 liquidations distributed within 641 bundles (1457 transactions including 751 oracle updates) that contained oracle updates. In AAVE, out of 1154 bundles, there were 994 (86.14%) bundles that contained an oracle update followed by a liquidation, and 52 (4.51%) with two oracle updates followed by liquidations. In Compound, out of 641 bundles, there were 548 (85.49%) bundles that contained an oracle update followed by a liquidation, and 39 (6.08%) with two oracle updates followed by liquidations. Out of the total 1813 liquidations in AAVE and Compound we found that only 24 were possible in the previous block. Almost 98.68% of such liquidations were, hence, only possible because of the Chainlink updates in that block.

In order to calculate the profit made by the liquidators, we get the amount of debt that was repaid and the amount of the underlying collateral that was received by the liquidator. We calculate the price of each token at the time of liquidation by looking at the on-chain oracle price from Chainlink at the same block number, where the liquidation took place. For AAVE and Compound, we specifically use the Chainlink on-chain price used by AAVE and Compound in their respective protocols. AAVE uses the price in ETH as a reference for its tokens, whereas Compound's price oracles are denominated in USD. For AAVE, in order to calculate the profit made by each liquidation, we calculate the profit in ETH, and then multiply the profit by the current Chainlink on-chain price of ETH in USD. Per Fig. 4, liquidations that are bundled with a Chainlink update also have larger profits for liquidators, which implies that the lucrative liquidations are more likely to be bundled together with a Chainlink update.

Characterizing Transaction Bundling.   To investigate which DEXes protocols are called within Flashbots bundles, we focus on the following contract calls: 0x Protocol, Balancer, Bancor, Curve, SushiSwap, and Uniswap V1 and V3. In our set of 3,284,886 Flashbots bundles, we find that 2,231,051 (67.92%) unique Flashbots bundles (and 3,076,760 transactions) called at least one of these contracts. Table 1 shows the distribution of the number of transactions and the number of bundles for each of these contracts. We see that Uniswap and SushiSwap are the most bundled DEXes protocols in Flashbots.

4.2   Side Channel (dark-Fee) Payments and Transaction Acceleration

We now focus on the Bitcoin blockchain to study dark-fees transactions.

Prevalence of Transaction Acceleration.   Dark-fee transactions (or accelerated transactions) are transactions that offer additional fees to specific mining pools via an opaque and non-public side-channel payment [29]. Messias *et al.* show that in Bitcoin the top 5 mining pools, BTC.com [4], AntPool, ViaBTC [45], F2Pool, and Poolin, deploy transaction acceleration services, which enables users to "accelerate" the confirmation of their transactions by offering mining pools dark-fees [29]. These (dark-)fees are paid in fiat currency through a direct bank transfer or via other crypto coins to the mining pool. They are, therefore, opaque or dark to other participants. Strangely enough, these fees are also non-refundable as the miner receives them regardless of whether they include the transaction in a block or not—a guaranteed payment. The fees paid by the transaction issuer are, furthermore, not made public: only the user and the miner knows the actual fee paid by the transaction inclusion. Since transaction issuers pay the fees off-chain, miners have an incentive for prioritizing these transactions despite the low fee rate offered on-chain. It also implies that the transaction issuer offers a miner a different fee compared to that offered to other miners for including their transaction in a block. Miners do not disclose such private fees paid by issuers. This behavior is different from that of Flashbots in Ethereum: The latter discloses the final dark-fee after the transaction is committed (see Sect. 4.1).

Characterizing Transaction Acceleration.   In order to detect accelerated transactions, Messias *et al.* [29] proposed a metric called *signed position prediction error (SPPE)* and *position prediction error (PPE)*. The idea behind these measures is that transactions that have been accelerated through off-chain fees are likely to have been "misplaced" in a block based on the on-chain fee they

Table 1. There are 2,231,051 (67.92%) unique Flashbots bundles, and 3,076,760 (44.35%) transactions, that called the following decentralized exchange contracts in Ethereum: 0x Protocol, Balancer, Bancor, Curve, SushiSwap, Uniswap V1, or V3. Note that a single transaction or bundle might call one or more contracts.

	Balancer	Bancor	Curve v1 & v2	Uniswap v2 & Sushiswap	Uniswap v3	0x Protocolv1, v2 & v3	Total
# of bundles	85,422 3.83%	96,122 4.31%	53,296 2.39%	1,710,985 76.69%	1,337,715 59.96%	28,753 1.29%	2,231,051 67.92%
# of transactions	87,865 2.86%	99,040 3.22%	58,188 1.89%	2,533,084 82.33%	1,692,485 55.01%	29,100 0.95%	3,076,760 44.35%

offer. Figure 5 shows that the top-6 mining pools in our Bitcoin data set engage in transaction acceleration. Large SPPE values imply that a transaction that should have been included at the bottom is included at the top of the block, confirming acceleration. We rely on this methodology to infer transaction acceleration in Bitcoin and present our data set and findings below.

To identify accelerated transactions, we gathered all Bitcoin blocks mined from Jan. 1st 2018 to Dec. 31st 2020. In total, there are 161,954 blocks from block height 501,951 to 663,904, and 313,575,387 transactions. In Bitcoin, mining pools may indicate their ownership of the block by including a *signature* or *marker* in the *Coinbase* transaction (i.e., the first transaction of every block). We used such markers for identifying the mining pool (owner) of each block following techniques from prior work [22,29,36]. We failed to identify, however, the owners of 4911 blocks (approximately 3% of the blocks) and grouped these blocks under the label "Unknown." Figure 1b shows the distribution of the count of blocks mined and transactions confirmed by the top-20 mining pools. We further removed 65,902,514 (21.02%) *child-pays-for-parent (CPFP)* transactions from our acceleration analyses.

To estimate the prevalence of accelerated transactions in blocks mined by different mining pools, we compute the fraction of blocks mined by the top-15 mining pools, based on their hash rates in our data set (refer to Fig. 1b), that contained transactions with SPPE ≥ 99%. Per Fig. 6, we find that many large mining pools such as BTC.com, F2Pool, and ViaBTC are likely including accelerated transactions in a sizeable fraction of their mined blocks, with ViaBTC including it in over 40% of their blocks.

If we consider all mining pools' transactions with an SPPE ≥ 50% (1,869,043 transactions, in total), from 2018 to 2020, users transferred in total 11,631,217 BTC (or ≈ 223.55 billion USD[4]). The accelerated transactions accounted for 240,226 BTC (or ≈ 4.62 billion USD), corresponding to approximately 2.07%.

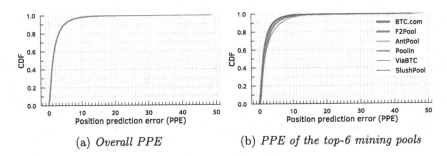

(a) *Overall PPE* (b) *PPE of the top-6 mining pools*

Fig. 5. Bitcoin position prediction error (PPE). (a) There are 160,962 blocks with non-CPFP txs; 80% of all blocks has PPE less than 3.06% (mean is 2.09% and std. deviation is 2.75.). (b) PPEs of top-6 mining pools per their normalized hash rate, showing that all large mining pools engage in transaction acceleration.

---

[4] Based on the Bitcoin exchange rate on October 19th 2022, 1 BTC = 19,219.90 USD.

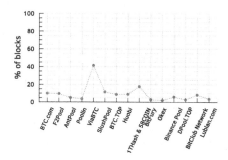

Fig. 6. Blocks with accelerated transactions (with SPPE ≥ 99%) are quite common among the top 15 mining pools. In Bitcoin, the mining pools with a high percentage of such blocks are ViaBTC (41.36%), 1THash & 58COIN (17.58%), SlushPool (11.58%), BTC.com (10.03%), and F2Pool (9.63%).

Aggregated Power of Colluding Miners.   In order to check the impact of transactions acceleration services on commit time of transaction, we ran active real-world experiments. Specifically, we paid ViaBTC [45] to accelerate selected transactions (see Table 5 in Appendix 2) during periods of high congestion between November 26th and December 1st, 2020. From 10 Mempool snapshots during this period, we selected transactions that offered a very low fee-rate (i.e., 1–2 sat-per-byte) for acceleration. To keep our acceleration costs low, we selected transactions with the smallest size (which was 110 bytes) within this set. For each of the 10 snapshots, we had multiple transactions with such low fee-rates and small size, for a total of 212 transactions across all the snapshots. We randomly selected one transaction from each snapshot (i.e., 10 transactions) and paid ViaBTC 205 EUR to accelerate them.

Table 2. Accelerated transactions have fewer delays and are included at the top of the block, i.e., at higher positions compared to non-accelerated transactions.

metrics	delay in # of blocks		perc. position in a block	
	acc.	non-acc.	acc.	non-acc.
minimum	1	9	0.07	17.47
25-perc	1	148	0.08	75.88
median	2	191	0.09	87.92
75-perc	2	247	0.20	95.00
maximum	3	326	4.39	99.95
average	1.8	198.5	0.79	84.46

We then compare the priority with which the accelerated transactions and the 202 (= 212 − 10) non-accelerated transactions with similar fee rates and sizes were included in the Bitcoin blockchain. The impact of acceleration was strikingly apparent as shown in Table 2. All 10 accelerated transactions were included within 1–3 blocks after their acceleration, with an average delay of 1.8 blocks. In contrast, the minimum delay for the 202 non-accelerated transactions of comparable fee-rates and sizes was 9 blocks, with an average delay of 198.5 blocks. Interestingly, 38 of the non-accelerated transactions were yet to be included in the blockchain by December 4th, 2020. Similarly, the accelerated transactions were included in top 0.07–4.39 percentile positions, with an average 0.79 percentile position, while the non-accelerated transactions were included in the beyond top 17.47–99.95 percentile positions, with an average 84.46 percentile position. From the above observations, it is clear that the transactions we accelerated were included with high priority, meaning Bitcoin mining pools take off-chain fees into account when prioritizing transactions.

Although, we accelerated our transactions using ViaBTC mining pool, our 10 transactions were included by 5 different mining pools, namely F2Pool, AntPool, Binance, Huobi, and ViaBTC. As we accelerated transaction during time of high congestion in Bitcoin, no mining pool would have included a transaction offering 1–2 sat-per-byte, unless they were accelerated. Since we only paid the ViaBTC mining pool, this implies that ViaBTC is colluding with other mining pools to accelerate transactions that offer off-chain fees. Except for Binance, all these colluding pools rank amongst the top-8 mining pools in terms of their hash rates at the time of our experiments. Table 3 shows the individual as well as the combined hash rates of these 5 colluding mining pools over the last day, last week, and last month before the conclusion of our experiment on December 1st, 2020. The most striking and the most worrisome fact is that the combined hash rates of these colluding mining pools exceeds 55% of the total Bitcoin hash rate. Additionally, if mining pools are colluding to include accelerated transactions, then they might also potentially collude in malicious ways.

Table 3. If we rank the miners who confirmed the accelerated transactions based on their daily, weekly, and monthly hash rate power, at the time these experiments were conducted, the combined hash power of these mining pools exceeds 55% of the Bitcoin's total hashing power.

Mining Pool	Hash-rate		
	last 24h	last week	last month
F2Pool	19.9%	18.7%	19.9%
AntPool	12.5%	10.6%	10.2%
Binance	9.6%	10.3%	10.0%
Huobi	8.1%	9.3%	9.8%
ViaBTC	5.1%	7.1%	7.7%
Total	55.2%	56%	57.6%

Furthermore, due to the lack of transparency into their queue, miners can charge higher prices for their acceleration services when colluding. It means that they can overcharge the transaction issuers for including their transactions.

5   Concluding Discussion

In this section, we discuss the implications of our findings regarding the lack of transparency in transaction contention and prioritization. We also argue why our findings and implications would be relevant even in the face of recent changes to blockchain protocols, e.g., Ethereum Improvement Protocol (EIP) 1559 and the Ethereum Paris Network Upgrade (a.k.a. the Merge).

Implications for Publicly Mined Transactions.   Most wallet software and crypto-exchanges today rely on reconstructing the current public Mempool state in order to suggest a suitable fee to transaction issuers. With the lack of contention and prioritization transparency, transaction issuers can no longer accurately recreate the current Mempool state for different miners. Consequently, they cannot reliably estimate the fees transactions need to pay for their desired prioritization. Worse, as the fraction of privately mined and accelerated transactions keeps rising, the transaction fees will become less (reliably) predictable in the future.

Implications for Privately Mined Transactions.   The problem of reliable fee estimation for a desired level of prioritization is even worse for privately mined transactions that are announced on private relay networks. When transaction issuers announce on a private relay network today, they are often unsure what fraction of total hash rate is controlled by the miners listening to the private relay network. It is important to estimate the hash rate controlled by private mining pools to estimate the commit (waiting) times for transactions. Furthermore, transaction issuers on private relay networks are completely blind to other competing transactions. This opacity allows miners offering private mining and transaction acceleration services to overcharge and demand exorbitant fees to commit transactions. For example, in the Ethereum blockchain, users are observed to be overcharged by miners for having their transactions confirmed with high priority through Flashbots bundles [46].

Relevance of Findings in Light of EIP-1559 and the Ethereum Merge.   Our observations about the lack of transparency and their implications are fundamental to the current blockchain architectures and hold both before and after the recent major improvements to blockchains, e.g., EIP-1559 and the Ethereum Merge. While EIP-1559 attempts to improve the estimation of transaction fees that need to be offered, it does not address the problems associated with the lack of transaction contention and prioritization transparency. Similarly, after the Ethereum Merge, *validators* that stake a certain amount of ETH rather than *miners* would be responsible for selecting and validating transactions to include in the next block [13]. Our observations about private mining would still hold for private validation and the implications would still be valid after the Merge.

In conclusion, our work shows that with private mining and accelerated transactions, the promise of the public decentralized blockchain does not hold. Firstly, mining pools with combined hash rates of over 50% are colluding with each other, showing a centralization in the system. Then, they can also censor certain transactions, breaking the ethos of decentralized public blockchains with no central authorities. Second, it breaks the assumption that all activities in the blockchain are transparent. Although this is true for transactions included in the blockchain, prioritization of transactions is becoming more opaque with the rise of private mining and off-chain fees. Hence, we make the case that to fulfill the transparency promise of public blockchains, prioritization of transactions should be transparent as well. Third, with private mining in Ethereum, Flashbots is increasingly being used for malicious and predatory activities such as sandwich attacks, which essentially levies a tax on users interacting with financial institutions on the blockchain (e.g., in DEX). These concerns need to be addressed if public blockchains are going to live up to their promises.

Acknowledgments. This research was supported in part by a European Research Council (ERC) Advanced Grant "Foundations for Fair Social Computing", funded under the European Union's Horizon 2020 Framework Programme (grant agreement no. 789373). It was also supported by MIAI @ Grenoble Alpes (ANR-19-P3IA-0003) and by the French National Research Agency under grant ANR-20-CE23-0007.

Appendix 1   Ethereum Private Transaction Experiment

We conducted 4 active experiments where we issued 8 Ethereum transactions; half issued publicly and the other half privately through a private-channel network known as Taichi Network [40]. Table 4 summarizes the transactions in our experiment. Spark Pool and Babel Pool included all private transactions (2 transactions each) sent directly to these miners through Taichi Network.

Table 4. We conducted 4 active experiments in Ethereum by simultaneously accelerating transactions privately and publicly via Taichi Network. Private transactions were included only by Spark Pool and Babel Pool. If we rank these mining pools according to their hash-rate, they account for 27.72% of the total Ethereum hash-rate.

#	type	tx hash	block number	miner	tx. position per # of txs.	block delay (in blocks)	fee paid (in Ether)	base fee (Gwei)	max fee (Gwei)	max priority fee (Gwei)	gas price (Gwei)	block timestamp in UTC
1	public	bbe88e···a4f000	13,183,516	Nanopool	305/336	1	0.00190489	88.98082939	116.52835749	1.72836605	90.70919543	2021-09-08 06:39:18
	private	c46b75···ead538	13,183,520	Babel Pool	29/39	5	0.00225209	105.51391459	120.56586232	1.72836605	107.24228063	2021-09-08 06:40:29
2	public	6d994f···c1aadd	13,183,561	Binance	209/213	2	0.00244137	114.95482846	137.64014705	1.30100683	116.25583529	2021-09-08 06:49:26
	private	a4d4ae···42ebf5	13,183,565	Spark Pool	294/296	6	0.00240978	113.45059961	137.64014705	1.30100683	114.75160643	2021-09-08 06:50:12
3	public	725743···0a6c45	13,183,634	Unknown	124/126	2	0.00263298	123.27216185	135.21393222	2.10805685	125.38021870	2021-09-08 07:06:31
	private	f2beec···15cdf1	13,183,635	Spark Pool	321/340	3	0.00257468	120.49562077	135.21393222	2.10805685	122.60367762	2021-09-08 07:06:44
4	public	e21695···2c1574	13,183,679	Ethermine	280/302	13	0.00223433	104.69510748	108.95262574	1.70164453	106.39675202	2021-09-08 07:18:37
	private	4c482b···87c76f	13,183,690	Babel Pool	150 / 212	24	0.00179917	83.97323655	108.95262574	1.70164453	85.67488108	2021-09-08 07:20:12

Appendix 2   Bitcoin Transaction Acceleration Experiment

Table 5. We conduct 10 transaction acceleration experiments in Bitcoin. If we rank the miners whose included these transactions based on their daily hash-rate power as (D) and weekly hash-rate power as (W), together these mining pools corresponds to a hash-rate power of (D: 55.2%; W: 56%).

txid	block height	miner	tx. position	delay (in blocks)	acc. cost (BTC)	vsize (byte)	fee rate sat-per-vsize	Mempool # of txs.	vsize (MB)	timestamp in UTC
35b18e···52dbc1	658,805	Huobi	2nd	2	0.001254	110	2	36,644	44.63	2020-11-26 19:10
65765c···baede2	658,898	F2Pool	73rd	1	0.001254	110	2	20,998	32.55	2020-11-27 11:06
0c2098···29fbf0	658,912	AntPool	2nd	2	0.001254	110	1	30,126	38.01	2020-11-27 13:38
1515a7···179af3	658,971	Binance	2nd	3	0.001254	110	1	25,922	37.89	2020-11-27 21:55
48a0a5···0ddaec	659,335	ViaBTC	3rd	1	0.001045	110	1	15,605	9.82	2020-11-30 10:09
9a17cf···f3734c	659,341	Huobi	2nd	2	0.001045	110	1	14,945	9.41	2020-11-30 10:28
831b24···95d421	659,351	AntPool	2nd	1	0.001045	110	1	10,990	8.66	2020-11-30 12:22
1f59bf···47096c	659,355	F2Pool	111th	3	0.001045	110	1	17,093	11.40	2020-11-30 12:58
6942e0···8c06c3	659,362	Huobi	2nd	2	0.001045	110	1	30,836	19.06	2020-11-30 14:49
8e49e2···ae825f	659,481	ViaBTC	6th	1	0.001254	110	2	30,935	22.59	2020-12-01 10:40

We ran an active Bitcoin transaction acceleration experiment where we paid 205 EUR to ViaBTC [45] to accelerated 10 transactions from 10 different snapshots of our Mempool. To select these transactions, we checked whether the Mempool was congested (i.e., having more transactions waiting for inclusion than the next block would be able to include), with its size being at least 8 MB. Then, we considered only transactions with low fee rates—less than or equal to 2 sat-per-byte—to ensure that these transactions would be highly unlikely to be included soon in a subsequent block. Next, we sorted the remaining transactions by size to limit the experiment cost as the acceleration-service costs grow proportional to the transaction size. Finally, we select the transaction with the smallest size in bytes for our active experiment.

Table 5 summarizes the transactions used in our experiment. Most of these 10 accelerated transactions were included nearly in the next block, demonstrating the acceleration efficiency. Also, these transactions were wrongly positioned in the block: They appeared, for instance, at the top of the block, i.e., higher than the non-accelerated transactions, showing that miners indeed prioritized them (see Table 2). Further, we observed that although we had only accelerated transactions via ViaBTC, other top mining pools were also involved in confirming the accelerated transactions.

References

1. Antonio Pierro, G., Rocha, H., Tonelli, R., Ducasse, S.: Are the gas prices oracle reliable? a case study using the ethgasstation. In: 2020 IEEE International Workshop on Blockchain Oriented Software Engineering (IWBOSE) (2020)
2. Babel Finance: Economic Daily: Babel Finance Launches Ethereum Mining Pool (2021)

3. Basu, S., Easley, D., O'Hara, M., Sirer, E.G.: Towards a Functional Fee Market for Cryptocurrencies. CoRR abs/1901.06830 (2019)
4. BTC.com: BTC.com Transaction Accelerator (2022). https://pushtx.btc.com
5. Buterin, V., Conner, E., Dudley, R., Slipper, M., Norden, I., Bakhta, A.: "EIP-1559: Fee market change for ETH 1.0 chain. Ethereum Improvement Proposals (2019)
6. Carlsten, M., Kalodner, H., Weinberg, S.M., Narayanan, A.: On the instability of bitcoin without the block reward. In: Proceedings of the 2016 ACM SIGSAC Conference on Computer and Communications Security. CCS 2016 (2016)
7. Chen, X., Papadimitriou, C., Roughgarden, T.: An axiomatic approach to block rewards. In: Proceedings of the 1st ACM Conference on Advances in Financial Technologies. AFT 2019 (2019)
8. Piatt, C., Quesnelle, J., Sheridan, C.: Eden Network (2021)
9. Daian, P., et al.: Flash boys 2.0: frontrunning in decentralized exchanges, miner extractable value, and consensus instability. In: 2020 IEEE Symposium on Security and Privacy (SP) (2020)
10. Easley, D., O'Hara, M., Basu, S.: From mining to markets: the evolution of bitcoin transaction fees. J. Financ. Econ. (2019)
11. EigenPhi: EigenPhi Crypto & DeFi Analytics (2022). https://eigenphi.io
12. Eskandari, S., Moosavi, S., Clark, J.: SOK: transparent dishonesty: front-running attacks on blockchain. In: Bracciali, A., Clark, J., Pintore, F., Rønne, P.B., Sala, M. (eds.) Financial Cryptography and Data Security (2020)
13. Ethereum Foundation: Proof-of-Stake (PoS) (2022). https://ethereum.org/en/developers/docs/consensus-mechanisms/pos/
14. Ethereum Foundation: The Merge (2022). https://ethereum.org/en/upgrades/merge/
15. Ethermine: Ethermine MEV-Relay (2022). https://ethermine.org/mev-relay
16. Eyal, I., Sirer, E.G.: Majority is not enough: bitcoin mining is vulnerable. Commun. ACM (2018)
17. Fiat, A., Karlin, A., Koutsoupias, E., Papadimitriou, C.: Energy equilibria in proof-of-work mining. In: Proceedings of the 2019 ACM Conference on Economics and Computation (EC 2019) (2019)
18. Flashbots: Flashbots Docs (2022). https://docs.flashbots.net
19. Goren, G., Spiegelman, A.: Mind the mining. In: Proceedings of the 2019 ACM Conference on Economics and Computation. EC 2019 (2019)
20. Partz, H.: Second-largest Ethereum mining pool to suspend all operations. Cointelegraph (2021)
21. Huberman, G., Leshno, J.D., Moallemi, C.: Monopoly without a monopolist: an economic analysis of the bitcoin payment system. Rev. Econ. Stud. **88**, 3011–3040 (2021)
22. Judmayer, A., Zamyatin, A., Stifter, N., Voyiatzis, A.G., Weippl, E.: Merged mining: curse or cure? In: Data Privacy Management, Cryptocurrencies and Blockchain Technology (2017)
23. Kiayias, A., Koutsoupias, E., Kyropoulou, M., Tselekounis, Y.: Blockchain mining games. In: Proceedings of the 2016 ACM Conference on Economics and Computation (EC 2016) (2016)
24. Kiffer, L., Levin, D., Mislove, A.: Stick a fork in it: analyzing the Ethereum network partition. In: Proceedings of the 16th ACM Workshop on Hot Topics in Networks (2017)
25. Lavi, R., Sattath, O., Zohar, A.: Redesigning bitcoin's fee market. In: The World Wide Web Conference. WWW 2019 (2019)

26. Liu, F., Wang, X., Li, Z., Xu, J., Gao, Y.: Effective GasPrice prediction for carrying out economical Ethereum transaction. In: 2019 6th International Conference on Dependable Systems and Their Applications (DSA) (2020)
27. Mars, R., Abid, A., Cheikhrouhou, S., Kallel, S.: A machine learning approach for gas price prediction in Ethereum blockchain. In: 2021 IEEE 45th Annual Computers, Software, and Applications Conference (COMPSAC) (2021)
28. Messias, J., Alzayat, M., Chandrasekaran, B., Gummadi, K.P.: On blockchain commit times: an analysis of how miners choose bitcoin transactions. In: KDD Workshop on Smart Data for Blockchain and Distributed Ledger. SDBD 2020 (2020)
29. Messias, J., Alzayat, M., Chandrasekaran, B., Gummadi, K.P., Loiseau, P., Mislove, A.: Selfish & opaque transaction ordering in the bitcoin blockchain: the case for chain neutrality. In: Proceedings of the ACM Internet Measurement Conference (IMC 2021) (2021)
30. Messias, J., Pahari, V., Chandrasekaran, B., Gummadi, K.P., Loiseau, P.: Data sets and scripts used to analyze the contention and prioritization transparency in both Bitcoin and Ethereum blockchains (2023). https://github.com/johnnatan-messias/blockchain-transaction-ordering
31. Nakamoto, S.: Bitcoin: A Peer-to-Peer Electronic Cash System (2008)
32. Noda, S., Okumura, K., Hashimoto, Y.: An economic analysis of difficulty adjustment algorithms in proof-of-work blockchain systems. In: Proceedings of the 21st ACM Conference on Economics and Computation (EC 2020) (2020)
33. Pass, R., Seeman, L., Shelat, A.: Analysis of the blockchain protocol in asynchronous networks. In: Coron, J.-S., Nielsen, J.B. (eds.) EUROCRYPT 2017. LNCS, vol. 10211, pp. 643–673. Springer, Cham (2017). https://doi.org/10.1007/978-3-319-56614-6_22
34. Qin, K., Zhou, L., Gervais, A.: Quantifying blockchain extractable value: how dark is the forest? In: 2022 IEEE Symposium on Security and Privacy (SP) (2022)
35. Qin, K., Zhou, L., Livshits, B., Gervais, A.: Attacking the DeFi ecosystem with flash loans for fun and profit. In: Financial Cryptography and Data Security. FC 2021 (2021)
36. Romiti, M., Judmayer, A., Zamyatin, A., Haslhofer, B.: A deep dive into bitcoin mining pools: An empirical analysis of mining shares. In: Workshop on the Economics of Information Security. WEIS 2019 (2019)
37. Roughgarden, T.: Transaction fee mechanism design for the Ethereum blockchain: an economic analysis of EIP-1559. In: Proceedings of the 2021 ACM Conference on Economics and Computation. EC '21 (2021)
38. Siddiqui, S., Vanahalli, G., Gujar, S.: Bitcoinf: achieving fairness for bitcoin in transaction fee only model. In: Proceedings of the 19th International Conference on Autonomous Agents and MultiAgent Systems. AAMAS 2020 (2020)
39. Sompolinsky, Y., Zohar, A.: Secure high-rate transaction processing in bitcoin. In: Böhme, R., Okamoto, T. (eds.) Financial Cryptography and Data Security. FC 2015 (2015)
40. SparkPool: Taichi Network (2021). https://taichi.network
41. Strehle, E., Ante, L.: Exclusive mining of blockchain transactions. In: Scientific Reports 2020-Conference Proceedings of the Scientific Track of the Blockchain Autumn School 2020 (2020)
42. Torres, C.F., Camino, R., State, R.: Frontrunner jones and the raiders of the dark forest: an empirical study of frontrunning on the Ethereum blockchain. In: 30th USENIX Security Symposium (2021)
43. Tsabary, I., Eyal, I.: The gap game. In: Proceedings of the 2018 ACM SIGSAC Conference on Computer and Communications Security. CCS 2018 (2018)

44. Turksonmez, K., Furtak, M., Wittie, M.P., Millman, D.L.: Two ways gas price oracles miss the mark. In: 2021 IEEE International Conference on Omni-Layer Intelligent Systems (COINS) (2021)
45. ViaBTC: Transaction Accelerator (2022). https://www.viabtc.com/tools/txaccelerator/
46. Weintraub, B., Torres, C.F., Nita-Rotaru, C., State, R.: A flash(bot) in the pan: measuring maximal extractable value in private pools. In: Proceedings of the ACM Internet Measurement Conference (IMC 2022) (2022)
47. Wood, G., et al.: Ethereum: a secure decentralised generalised transaction ledger. Ethereum project yellow paper (2014)
48. Zhang, R., Preneel, B.: Lay down the common metrics: evaluating proof-of-work consensus protocols' security. In: Proceedings - IEEE Symposium on Security and Privacy (2019)
49. Zhou, L., Qin, K., Torres, C.F., Le, D.V., Gervais, A.: High-frequency trading on decentralized on-chain exchanges. In: 2021 IEEE Symposium on Security and Privacy (SP) (2021)

Forsage: Anatomy of a Smart-Contract Pyramid Scheme

Tyler Kell[1,3], Haaroon Yousaf[2,3]([✉]), Sarah Allen[1,3], Sarah Meiklejohn[2,3], and Ari Juels[1,3]

[1] Cornell Tech, New York, USA
[2] University College London, London, England
haaroon.yousaf@gmail.com
[3] IC3, Wahsington D.C., USA

Abstract. Pyramid schemes are investment scams in which top-level participants in a hierarchical network recruit and profit from an expanding base of defrauded newer participants. They have existed for over a century, but their historical opacity has prevented in-depth studies.

This paper presents an empirical study of Forsage, a smart-contract-based pyramid scheme with unprecedented transparency. Our study focuses on the period around 2020, when Forsage was one of the largest contracts (by gas usage) in Ethereum. In 2022, some months after initial release of this work, the U.S. SEC dubbed Forsage a "fraudulent crypto pyramid and Ponzi scheme" and filed charges against its creators and promoters.

We quantify the (multi-million-dollar) gains of top-level participants as well as the losses of the vast majority (around 88%) of users. We analyze Forsage code both manually and using a purpose-built transaction simulator that we release as open source software to uncover the complex mechanics of the scheme. Through complementary study of promotional videos and social media, we show how Forsage promoters leveraged the unique features of smart contracts to lure users with false claims of trustworthiness and profitability, and how Forsage activity is concentrated within a small number of national communities.

Our analysis is the most complete study of a pyramid scheme to date.

1 Introduction

Cryptocurrencies and smart contracts are new and powerful technologies that promise a range of benefits, including faster monetary transactions, innovative financial instruments, and global financial inclusion for the world's unbanked. Conversely, though, these same technologies have fueled new forms of fraud and theft [29,38] and new ways of perpetrating existing types of crime [20,27].

Pyramid schemes are a prevalent type of scam in which top-tier participants in a hierarchical network recruit and profit at the expense of an expanding base of new participants. They have existed for more than a century, but have recently emerged in a new form: as smart contracts on blockchains such as Ethereum.

© International Financial Cryptography Association 2024
F. Baldimtsi and C. Cachin (Eds.): FC 2023, LNCS 13951, pp. 241–258, 2024.
https://doi.org/10.1007/978-3-031-47751-5_14

Smart contracts are in some ways an ideal medium for pyramid schemes and other scams. Because they run in decentralized systems, they cannot easily be dismantled by law enforcement agencies. They can instantaneously ingest payments from victims across the globe. They provide privacy protection for their creators in the form of pseudonymous addresses. Finally, as so-called "trustless" applications—with world-readable (byte)code—they present a veneer of trustworthiness to unsuspecting users.

The flip side of such transparency is that smart contracts offer researchers a degree of visibility into the mechanics of online (and offline) scams that is without historical precedent. Not only is the (byte)code specifying the scam's mechanics visible on chain, but so is every transaction performed by every participant.

In this paper, we take advantage of this newfound visibility to conduct an indepth measurement study of the largest smart contract-based pyramid scheme to date, called *Forsage Smartway* or *Forsage* for short.

Forsage came into existence in late January 2020. It was at one point the second most active contract in Ethereum by daily transaction count and spent almost 1/3 of the year—100 d—as one of the top five contracts by number of transactions per day. As we show throughout this paper, it is a classic pyramid scheme, defined by the SEC as "a type of fraud in which participants profit almost exclusively through recruiting other people to participate in the program" [3]. Indeed, in 2022, the SEC declared Forsage a "fraudulent crypto pyramid and Ponzi scheme" and filed charges against eleven individuals involved in the creation and promotion of the scheme [30].

The Forsage contract requires players to send currency (Ether) in order to participate. Funds sent by newly recruited users immediately pass through the contract to existing players, with those at the top of the (smart contract-defined) pyramid obtaining the largest returns.

Understanding the success of Forsage requires study of not just the contract itself, but also its community of hundreds of thousands of users, many of whom have actively discussed and marketed the scam. Consequently, to paint a detailed picture of how Forsage lures and defrauds users, our study combines measurement and analysis of a range of complementary forms of data, including source code, on-chain transaction data, and social media interactions.

Forsage was not just a blip: it was a major consumer of resources on Ethereum at its height, producing more transaction fees than even the most popular smart-contract-based cryptocurrency exchanges for 67 d. While the largest smart contract pyramid scheme identified to date, Forsage was not the only active pyramid scheme we identified on Ethereum and will not be the last. As a focused measurement study (see, e.g., [5, 26] for important examples of such work), our work can act as a template for further, in-depth understanding of blockchain pyramid schemes more generally. New such schemes, as we explain, often closely resemble Forsage.

1.1 Main Study Results

We believe that our study's findings are not just relevant to Forsage, but provide durable insights into the conception, mechanics, and evolution of smart-contract scams and financial scams more generally. They also point to effective strategies that government authorities and the cryptocurrency community can use to combat pyramid schemes and other scams, as we discuss in the full version of our paper [1].

Our focus is on the peak period of activity for the contract in the year 2020. (After that time, the contract saw little use, giving way to later, similar schemes.)

1.2 Summary of Contributions

In summary, the main contributions of our study of Forsage in this paper are:

- *Contract measurement study:* In a measurement study of Forsage contract activity on Ethereum, we document the flow of 721k ETH (226M USD) and show monetary losses by the vast majority of users. One of our most striking findings is characteristic of pyramid schemes: The vast majority of Forsage players have lost money, with net losses for over 88% of players. A small few at the top of the pyramid have profited handsomely, e.g., the contract owner, who has received over 5000 ETH (1.2M USD). To the best of our knowledge, our study offers the first precise quantification of payouts and losses in any large pyramid scheme, internet-based or historical. We also quantify the cost of Forsage's complexity in terms of on-chain transaction fees, showing that Forsage transactions are more expensive for its users than normal transactions.
- *Community-dynamics study:* By tagging claims in promotional videos and studying social media interactions, we shed light on the evolution of the community, documenting tactics used to attract users and combine location data from various social networks to identify the user geographical distribution. We show that Forsage activity is internationally broad, but highly concentrated within a few geographies (e.g., western Africa).
- *Contract deconstruction:* Using a tool for transaction simulation that is of possible independent interest, we detail the operating rules of Forsage and show the concentration of power and wealth at the top of its defined pyramid(s).

We emphasize that our results, which reveal a combination of classic and smart contract-specific scam characteristics, offer insights not just into Forsage, but into both blockchain and non-blockchain scams more generally.

Section 3 provides an overview of the inner workings of Forsage. Section 4 analyzes measurement data and provides statistics of the usage and profitability of the Forsage smart contract. Section 5 uses social media analysis to find out the geographical distribution of Forsage victims. Further information can be found in the full version of the paper [1], including a detailed evaluation of the Forsage smart contract and an analysis of Forsage promotional and social media content.

2   Background

Smart Contracts: The most popular public (permissionless) blockchain for smart contracts today is *Ethereum* [10]. Ethereum smart contracts are launched in the form of bytecode that runs in a Turing-complete environment known as the Ethereum Virtual Machine (EVM). *Transactions* sent to smart contracts by users are processed by contract code and are publicly visible on chain.

Transactions may send money to a contract from user accounts or other contracts and must specify payment of execution fees to block creators in the form of *gas*, a parallel currency converted into ETH upon transaction execution. This conversion is calculated by multiplying the amount of work performed by a transaction (its "gas consumed") by the price of gas in ETH set by user when submitting the transaction [32].

Correctness of contract execution is enforced by the consensus mechanism underlying the Ethereum blockchain, so a miner's execution of contract code in the EVM must be agreed upon by all network participants to be included in a confirmed block.

Other permissionless blockchains with similarly constructed smart contract functionality are growing in popularity, e.g., Tron [12], to which Forsage has also been ported. Ethereum, however, remains the dominant smart contract platform.

Scams: Scams, i.e., fraudulent schemes involving financial deception, have been documented for centuries. Many scams involving large populations of victims assume the form of *pyramid schemes*. The U.S. Securities and Exchange Commission (SEC) defines a pyramid scheme as "a type of fraud in which participants profit almost exclusively through recruiting other people to participate in the program" [3]. Pyramid schemes, which are illegal in most jurisdictions, have many variants. One variant is a *Ponzi scheme*, which specifically involves investment in financial instruments. *Multi-level marketing* (MLM) schemes, which involve the sale of a product or service, are related to pyramid schemes. They are legal in the U.S., but outlawed in some jurisdictions (e.g., China) [2].

Blockchain Scams: A multitude of scams have arisen within the blockchain ecosystem. Some scams have solicited investments from victims in new blockchain technologies. Examples include Onecoin, a Ponzi scheme that involved a fake (centralized) blockchain in which victims invested $19+ billion [18], Bitconnect, a token that promised returns of 1% per day and saw investment of $3.5 billion from victims, as well as other, related $1+ billion schemes such as Plustoken and WoToken.pro [8,24].

Other scams instead use blockchain technology to realize variants of scams, such as pyramid schemes, that were seen well before the advent of blockchains. Prominent examples are Million.Money[1] and Doubleway.io[2], which are both currently active, and the defunct Bullrun.live.[3] All three have similarities with For-

---

[1] https://million.money.

[2] https://doubleway.io/.

[3] http://bullrun.live.

sage: they use similar promotional materials, have a similar structure for the user dashboard, and use similar language and terminology (e.g., a referrer to the program is called an "upline"). We explore Forsage user interactions with multiple scam contracts in Sect. 4.2.

3 Forsage Overview

The creators and promoters of Forsage advertise it as a *matrix* MLM scheme, despite the lack of a service or product. It operates primarily on Ethereum, where its initial Matrix contract has been active since January 31st, 2020. Since then, Forsage creators have also launched a Forsage contract on Tron (TRX), an additional, followup smart contracts called Forsage xGold on both Tron and Ethereum, and a Forsage Binance Smart Chain (BSC) contract.

The Forsage Website: Users interact with Forsage using the forsage.io website, which shows how much they have paid into and earned from the contract. The website encourages the use of user-friendly cryptocurrency tools. It shows users how to purchase cryptocurrency using Trust Wallet, a user-friendly tool to exchange fiat for cryptocurrency, and how to use MetaMask, a browser extension that allows users to easily transact with cryptocurrency. The combination of these tools makes Forsage accessible to novice users who may not previously have used cryptocurrencies or smart contracts. Screenshots of the Forsage website prior to SEC takedown show the different matrices and their structure, can be found in the full version of the paper [1].

Forsage Use and Structure: A new Forsage user must pay a minimum of 0.05 ETH, which opens up the *slot* at the first *level* in the two matrix systems, called X3 and X4. Each matrix consists of 12 slots. To unlock the ability to use the next slot (at level $i + 1$), a user must pay twice as much ETH as for their currently highest slot (at level i). In both X3 and X4, the first slot costs 0.025 ETH, while the twelfth and final slot costs 51.2 ETH. This means that the total cost to open all slots in either matrix is 102.375 ETH. Figure 1 shows the correlation between profitability of participants and how many slots they unlocked.

Each Forsage user has a *referral code*, created at the time they register. The referral code links a recruited user's account to the account that recruited them, called their *upline*. These referral codes thus organize Forsage users into pyramids, with the oldest accounts at the top. Payments flow upwards within a pyramid as additional users join it. The pyramids of users linked by chains of referral code are referred to as Forsage *teams*. It is possible to join Forsage without entering a referral code; users who do so are assigned the referral code of the creator of Forsage.

The full version of the paper [1] contains detailed description and simulation of the logic for payment flow of user funds sent through the Forsage contract. Briefly, users earn money in the X3 and X4 matrices as follows:

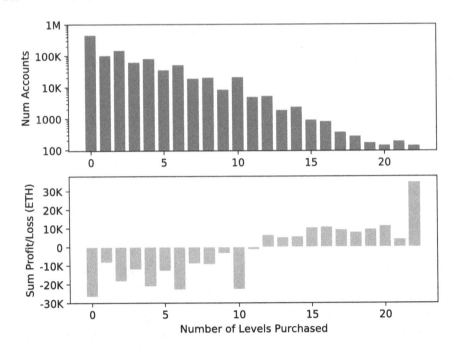

Fig. 1. The distribution of how many users had unlocked a given number of levels in the contract (on top, and at log scale), and the collective amount of money gained or lost by the users who had unlocked this number of levels (on bottom, and at linear scale). Users that bought the most levels were on average the most profitable.

X3: In X3, users earn income by recruiting others into the system. A user must recruit three additional users to recoup their initial investment within each slot. Any recruits beyond the first three per slot will generate income for the recruiting user and those further up in their pyramid. Each subsequent slot costs more to open, but its resulting payout if filled with recruits will be higher because the expected payout for each three recruits is equal to the initial cost to open the slot for the recruiter. After a user fills a slot (i.e. recruits 3 users into that slot), Forsage *blocks* the filled slot, causing the user to forfeit future earnings from it until it is unblocked. Unblocking means paying to open the slot at the next level up in the system, at which point this lower-level slot cannot become blocked again.

X4: In X4, users can earn both by recruiting other users and by being on an active team. When a user recruits the six additional users necessary to recoup their initial investment in an X4 slot (twice as many as are required in X3), that slot becomes blocked and the user will have received the same amount of money paid to open the slot, with others in their team getting paid as well. X4 also has an element of competition: If a newer user on a team is more active than the user whose referral code they used to join Forsage, that user

Table 1. Summary statistics of the four official Forsage smart contracts and one clone. The USD value was calculated by taking a sum of the payments per day and multiplying it by the average of the 24-hour high and low on the respective day.

Contract	Total TXs	Unique sending addresses	Total coins	Total USD	Launch date	Address
ETH Matrix	3M	1M	721k	225M	Jan 31, 2020	0x5a...
TRX Clone	217k	78k	537M	14M	July 25, 2020	TJRv...
TRX Matrix	1M	342k	1B	31M	Sept 6, 2020	TREb...
TRX xGold	307k	105k	90M	2M	Nov 7, 2020	TA6p...
ETH xGold	37k	17k	8k	9M	Jan 4, 2021	0x48...

can switch spots on the team, giving the more active, newer user the profits that would otherwise flow to the older, referring account [23].

4   Measurement Study

In this section, we present the results of our measurement study of Forsage contract transactions, which encompasses all monetary transactions in the scheme. A description of our data collection process is in the full version of the paper [1]. We first present statistics capturing the degree of user interaction with the various Forsage contracts on Ethereum and Tron (Sect. 4.1). We then present an analysis of the account behaviour and profits over the Forsage user population (Sect. 4.2), in particular analyzing where funds are obtained and how funds flow through the five most profitable accounts.

4.1   Scheme Statistics

Table 1 shows summary statistics for the four official Forsage contracts and an additional contract, TRX Clone, a clone of the Ethereum Matrix contract operating on Tron. This clone launched before the official TRX Matrix contract, and has a different domain[4] but with graphics and style akin to the official website. The official Forsage website added a warning after the clone's appearance, asking users to "beware of fake resources" and stating that the "forsage.io" website is the only official domain.

In total, the table shows that the official Forsage contracts amassed over 267M USD within the first year of operation. Among all of these contracts, the ETH Matrix contract brought in the most money and raised the highest amount on a single day: 3.7 million USD on August 1, 2020. The more recent xGold contracts (deployed on both Ethereum and Tron) were sent a combined 11.53 million USD in ETH and TRX in less than two months.

Figure 2 shows the number of transactions received by each contract over time. For each contract introduced after the original ETH Matrix one, we observe a large number of initial transactions followed by a substantial drop. We also

---

[4] forsagetron.io.

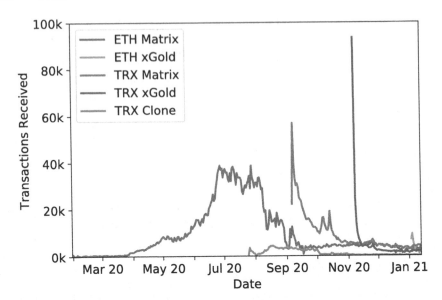

Fig. 2. Number of transactions sent from users to the four Forsage contracts across Ethereum and Tron and to an unofficial Tron-based clone.

see a decline in the number of transactions sent to the original ETH Matrix contract after other contracts become available. Given the particular longevity and popularity of the ETH Matrix contract, it is our main focus in the rest of this section.

To illustrate the popularity of Forsage, Fig. 3 shows the number of daily transactions associated with the six most popular contracts across a six-month period in 2020. Of these contracts, Tether and USDC are stablecoins; Uniswap is a decentralized exchange; and Easy Club, MMBSC Global, and Forsage are believed to be scams/pyramid schemes. We can see that Tether is consistently the most popular contract and that for most of its peak from June to August, Forsage (as represented by ETH Matrix) had the second highest transaction rate among Ethereum smart contracts. This data is supported by Google Trends results for 2020: From April to August of 2020, Forsage had the highest search traffic globally of any of the smart contracts we studied, including both Tether and Uniswap, the two most heavily used smart contracts on the network as of the time of writing.

4.2 Account Behavior and Profitability

To understand how Forsage users obtained the funds needed to interact with the contract, we looked at the transactions that sent ETH to their accounts, and at when their accounts first became active. Figure 4 shows the ETH received by Forsage users over time and the cumulative count of active Forsage-related accounts (i.e., the first time an account was used that later interacted with the

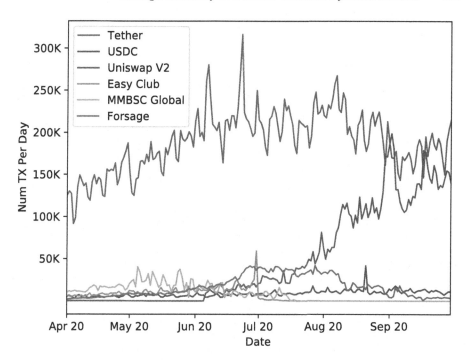

Fig. 3. The daily transaction count associated with the six most transacted contracts between April 1 and September 30, 2020. Here Forsage refers to the ETH Matrix contract.

Forsage contract), with a vertical line indicating when Forsage was deployed. It is clear that these accounts became active and began to receive substantially more ether after the deployment of Forsage; in fact, 98.89% of Forsage users had accounts that did not exist (or at least did not transact) before Forsage. We found a similar increase when looking at the number of transactions conducted by these users as well: prior to the deployment of Forsage, 11k accounts were involved in 278k transactions, but after Forsage's release this increased to 1.04M users engaging in 16M transactions. While the curve in Fig. 4 looks steep given the timescale, it in fact reflects a steady growth in the first appearance of accounts between April and August 2020, which aligns with the peak of Forsage we saw in Fig. 3. Each of these months saw thousands of new accounts appearing per day, on average: 1659 in April, 3653 in May, 8272 in June, 10,798 in July, and 4987 in August. In contrast there were at most 20 new accounts appearing per day for each month in 2019 (except December, when there were 68).

To identify which types of services were the source of this money, we used tags from Etherscan. Of the ETH sent to Forsage users, over 56% (1.5M) came from untagged sources, and only 15% came from known exchanges, with 5% of this coming from the decentralized exchange Uniswap. As mentioned in Sect. 3, Forsage promotional material recommends that users obtain ETH from

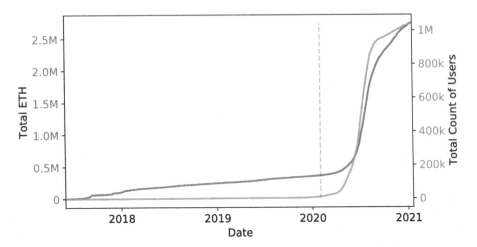

Fig. 4. Total ether received by Forsage users over time and total number of Forsage users according to when their accounts were first used, with a dashed line indicating the Forsage creation date.

Table 2. Top five profitable accounts interacting with Forsage.

Address	Profit (in ETH)	Notes/First Seen
0x81...	5409.6	Owner of the contract
0x44...	3445.0	March 22, 2020
0xde...	1954.9	March 22, 2020
0x4a...	1943.2	January 31, 2020
0x59...	1573.0	June 4, 2020

TrustWallet. This is a non-custodial service, which means accounts are associated with individual users rather than with the exchange. Thus, if most users followed this advice, we would expect to see that most of the ETH came from untagged sources.

Figures 6 and 7 show a histogram of all of the accounts that interacted with the ETH Matrix contract organized by the amount of money either gained or lost by each account (including the amount spent on transaction fees) as of January 14, 2021. In total, of the 1.04 million Ethereum addresses that took part in the ETH Matrix scheme, only 11.8% (123,979) earned a profit. These profitable accounts made 265,618.52 ETH collectively, and the loss-making accounts (919,194 in total) lost 305,785.44 ETH collectively (0.33 ETH on average). We revisit these profit-making accounts below. Users incur additional losses from the high transaction fees paid for transacting with the contract. This is demonstrated by the right-shifted peak in the Forsage curve relative to that of all ETH transactions in Fig. 5. The reasons for this are further explained in the full version of the paper.

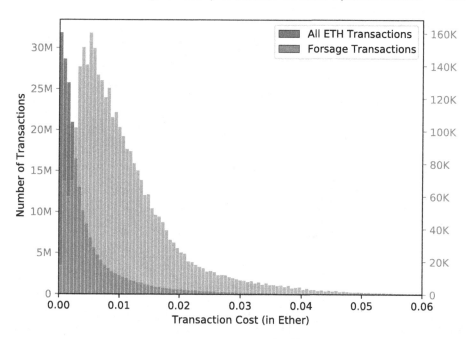

Fig. 5. Histogram of transaction costs on the Ethereum blockchain—from January 31, 2020 to January 14, 2021—that involve successful smart contract function calls. Blue bars indicate the number of all transactions that paid fees within the given bucket. Orange bars indicate the same data, but only for transactions sent to the Forsage smart contract. The data excludes outlier transactions with fees above 0.06 ETH, which is above the 99th percentile of all transactions from this time period. (Color figure online)

Profit-Making Accounts: The five addresses with the highest profits in Forsage can be found in Table 2. Perhaps unsurprisingly, the most profitable Forsage user is the owner of the contract, who earned 5409.6 ETH, or 2.04% of the total profits. Collectively, the five most profitable users made 14,325.7 ETH, or 5.4% of profits, despite representing only 0.0004% of users. The top 1000 users made 50% of the total profits.

Examination of the five most profitable addresses shows that the most profitable address is another Ethereum contract created by the owner of the ETH Matrix contract. Of the money received by this contract, 99% came from ETH Matrix. The fourth highest earner sent 9% of received ETH directly back to Forsage. In fact, if we follow all the addresses to which this user sent money, we see over 1321 ETH sent back to Forsage eventually. Similarly, the fifth highest earner sent 204 ETH directly back to Forsage.

Some of the top addresses interact directly with other known scams, such as Beurax.com and TorqueBot.net, meaning they sent or received coins directly from addresses associated with these scams. The top five profit-making accounts received 6.987 ETH from these scams.

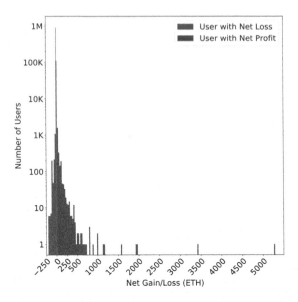

Fig. 6. Profit/loss histogram of Ethereum accounts that interacted with the Forsage smart contract, on a log scale. This graph shows the number of accounts that made a profit or loss for each range of ETH. The majority of accounts incurred a small net loss, less than 1 ETH.

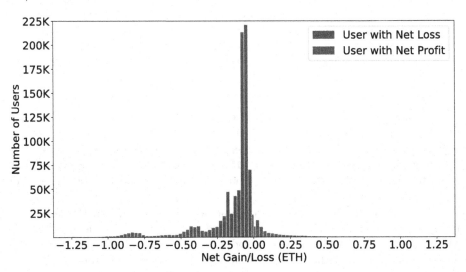

Fig. 7. Profit/loss histogram of Ethereum accounts that interacted with the Forsage smart contract, centered around 0 and on a linear scale. The vast majority of user accounts that interacted with Forsage lost between 0 and 0.25 ETH, with the peak occurring between 0.038 and 0.063 ETH.

Interestingly, the first transaction sent to the address that deployed Forsage was from 0xb1..., which is the Ethereum address that deployed Million.money. This suggests interaction between smart contract-based scam operators.

Finally, we consider the extent to which users who profited by interacting with the Forsage ETH Matrix contract also interacted with other Forsage contracts. The ETH xGold contract has 17,560 users, of which 17,129 (97.5%) also interacted with ETH Matrix. Furthermore, the highest earner in xGold was the third highest earner in Matrix, the fourth highest xGold earner was the seventh highest earner in Matrix, and the eighth highest earner in xGold was the second highest earner in Matrix. These three earners (all of which are within the ten wealthiest Matrix users) hold 21.85% of net profits in xGold. This suggests that at least some prominent users of Matrix did indeed migrate over to xGold.

5   Study of Forsage Community

Methodology: We studied the Forsage community by examining the presence of Forsage on social media. The Forsage website promotes official social media presences on Facebook, Instagram, Telegram, Twitter, and YouTube. All of these services have official APIs to collect data, but some of the research we conducted required manual interaction with the various social websites via a web browser, or more sophisticated data collection techniques like web scraping. In summary we identified over 403,029 distinct Facebook members in various Forsage Facebook groups, 285,788 people signed across 49 telegram channels and over 57,551 Youtube promotional videos. This is explained in more detail in the full version of the paper [1].

5.1   Forsage User Geography

Since transactions on the Ethereum network do not carry any inherent geographic metadata, we turned to social media analysis in order to gain a sense of the geographic placement of people interested in Forsage. In the data we collected on members of Forsage-related Facebook groups, we found 771 users that publicly listed a country location on their Facebook profile. We also found 10,200 unique Twitter accounts that publicly posted their geographic location. YouTube does not expose information about geographic location of the consumers of YouTube videos, but YouTube channels that produce videos can choose to include country location in their channel profile. Despite having a substantial population and being the nationality of the founders of Forsage, Russia was not a large source of Twitter or Facebook content, although the country did produce a large number of YouTube videos and content about Forsage.

The high number of Forsage users in the Philippines may explain why the Philippines SEC was first to take action to raise awareness about the malicious intent behind Forsage [21,22]. Likewise, Nigeria has high penetration rates for both cryptocurrency and Forsage, and has recently banned cryptocurrency payments from its banking sector [4]. While each of these five countries had high

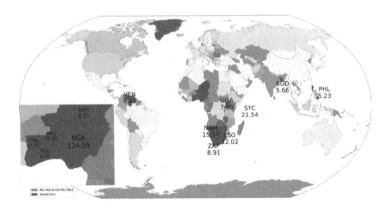

Fig. 8. Forsage social media interaction heat map by country. Country labels indicate the ISO-alpha-3 name of the country and the number of Forsage users per 100k people in that country. The data reflects the public location of members in a popular Forsage Facebook group and Twitter users that tweeted about Forsage. Countries depicted in gray had no Forsage interaction. The intensity of color from white to red is scaled linearly from the 0th percentile of data to the 90th percentile, and everything above 90% of the data is colored the same shade of dark red. This slightly understates the relative depth of penetration in outlier countries like Nigeria. (Color figure online)

Forsage activity in absolute terms, they also have large populations. We thus normalized our Facebook and Twitter data relative to the specific populations on each service for each country (i.e., the number of people per country divided by a public estimate of the number of Facebook and Twitter users in that country) to get a sense of the number of Facebook and Twitter users, per 100,000 users, that interacted on each platform with the Forsage topic. Statistics for the number of Facebook and Twitter users per country came from Miniwatts Marketing Group, WeAreSocial, and Hootsuite [13,15]. We did not include the YouTube data because the sample size was too small. We gave equal weight to the numbers for Facebook and Twitter to produce the heat map in Fig. 8.

Our normalized data showed that Forsage is most popular in Nigeria and the African continent, the Philippines, and Venezuela. Greenland, the Seychelles, and some Caribbean islands may be outliers due to small population sizes. Google Trends traffic and geographic data agree with our conclusions: Google Trends shows the greatest amount of population-adjusted search traffic in Nigeria and surrounding West African countries, and shows a peak in user search interest in July 2020, which is when we observed a similar peak in transactions involved Forsage in Fig. 2.

Familiarity with cryptocurrency does not appear to have any correlation with interest in Forsage: The 2021 Statista Global Consumer Survey [9] lists the top countries globally with the reported highest number of cryptocurrency users. Vietnam (#2) and China (#3) both had relatively high levels of cryptocurrency use, but low levels of interest in Forsage. Similarly, familiarity with cryptocurrency does not appear to prevent people from falling for the Forsage scam, as in the case of Nigeria and the Philippines (#1 and #3 globally for cryptocurrency usage). Nigeria may be a special case, as Statista found that almost a third of Nigerians said they used cryptocurrency, far beyond most countries. It is also an outlier in the data for interest in Forsage.

6 Related Work

Previous measurement studies of particular attack instances have been critical to the community's understanding of adversarial behaviour. Examples include Antonakakis et al.'s analysis of the Mirai botnet [5] and Pearce et al.'s characterisation of the ZeroAccess click-fraud botnet [26]. Case studies of other topics, including [17, 19, 37], have also been impactful to the security community.

Past research has examined scams running on Ethereum and Bitcoin. For Ethereum-based scams, Chen et al. [11] used data mining and machine learning to detect Ponzi schemes while Yu et al. [36] modeled Ponzi scheme identification and detection as a node classification task. Bartoletti et al. [7] compared the code and promotion of Ethereum Ponzi schemes, finding that scammers use the public nature of Ethereum to inspire confidence in their victims. Vasek et al. [31] and Bartoletti et al. [6] both worked to detect and model Bitcoin-based scams. These included Ponzi schemes that collect Bitcoin from victims, the former finding that most scams last less than one week. Paquet-Clouston et al. [25] and Xia et al. [33] studied specialized scams that leverage Bitcoin payments, namely threats of revealing intimate data and fake fundraising for COVID-19 research and relief.

Apart from our work, studies of existing scams' migration onto blockchains include [14, 16, 34], which examine chat-service based pump-and-dump schemes on cryptocurrencies. Some scams are new to blockchains, such as honeypot smart contracts, which include financial traps within the contract itself [29].

In past work characterizing the victims of blockchain-enabled scams, Phillips et al. [27] showed that victims tend to send funds from fiat-accepting cryptocurrency exchanges, making the scams accessible to novice cryptocurrency users. They also found that scammers often create multiple similar scams running in parallel. Yousaf et al. showed that scammers use shifting services to convert Ether into other coins to thwart tracking by law enforcement [35].

7 Conclusion

We presented an in-depth measurement study of Forsage, at one time the second most actively used contract in Ethereum. Our study required multiple data-gathering approaches and the creation of new open source tools to analyze the Forsage contract. These tools enabled us to provide detailed insights into the mechanism design, transaction costs, and other features of Forsage.

A key finding is that the vast majority of Forsage accounts—over 88%—incurred losses, for a combined total loss of 305,785 ETH. The contract owner and a few other accounts at the top of the pyramid earned over 5000 ETH (well over 1M USD). Social media analysis led us to discover the existence of geographically distinct communities, with scammers based mainly in Russia and victims mainly in Nigeria, the Philippines, Venezuela, Indonesia, and India.

Public warnings about Forsage by entities such as the Philippines SEC appeared to have little effect, as the creators continued to launch new lucrative variants, some on blockchains other than Ethereum. On August 1, 2022, some months after the initial release of our work, the SEC charged eleven members of Forsage including the founder [28] for operating a pyramid scheme. Since then, the website has been partially blocked. At present, it is inaccessible in some countries, such as the United States and United Kingdom, but still accessible in others, such as Switzerland.

Acknowledgements. This work was funded by NSF grants CNS-1704615, CNS-1933655, CNS-2112751 and generous support from IC3 industry partners.

References

1. https://arxiv.org/abs/2105.04380
2. MLM law of China: 'Prohibition of Chuanxiao'. http://www.gov.cn/zwgk/2005-09/03/content_28808.htm (2005)
3. Investor alerts and bulletins:beware of pyramid schemes posing as multi-level marketing programs. https://www.sec.gov/oiea/investor-alerts-bulletins/investor-alerts-ia_pyramidhtm.html, Oct 2013
4. Hannah, A.: Nigeria's crypto ban fuels mistrust in government. Coindesk
5. Antonakakis, M., et al.: Understanding the mirai botnet. In: 26th {USENIX} security symposium ({USENIX} Security 17), pp. 1093–1110 (2017)
6. Bartoletti, M., Pes, B., Serusi, S.: Data mining for detecting bitcoin ponzi schemes. In: 2018 Crypto Valley Conference on Blockchain Technology (CVCBT), pp. 75–84 (2018)
7. Bartoletti, M., Carta, S., Cimoli, T., Saia, R.: Dissecting ponzi schemes on ethereum: identification, analysis, and impact. Futur. Gener. Comput. Syst. **102**, 259–277 (2020)
8. Nick, B.: The most famous financial pyramids in the crypto world. https://cointelegraph.com/news/the-most-famous-financial-pyramids-in-the-crypto-world (2020)
9. Katharina, B.: How common is crypto?. https://www.statista.com/chart/18345/crypto-currency-adoption/ Accessed 21 March 2021
10. Vitalik, B., Vitalik, B.: A next-generation smart contract and decentralized application platform. ethereum white paper (2014)
11. Weili, C., Zibin, Z., Jiahui, C., Edith, N., Peilin, Z. Yuren, Z.: Detecting ponzi schemes on ethereum. In: Proceedings of the 2018 World Wide Web Conference on World Wide Web - WWW 18 (2018)
12. Tron Foundation. Tron: advanced decentralized blockchain platform. whitepaper version: 2.0. 2018
13. Miniwatts Marketing Group. Internet world stats: Usage and population statistics. https://www.internetworldstats.com/ (2021)
14. Hamrick, J.T., et al.: The economics of cryptocurrency pump and dump schemes. SSRN Electronic Journal, 01 (2018)
15. Hootsuite and WeAreSocial. Digital in 2021: National reports. https://datareportal.com/library (2021)

16. Kamps, J., Kleinberg, B.: To the moon: defining and detecting cryptocurrency pump-and-dumps. Crime Sci. **7**, 11 (2018)
17. Koscher, K., et al.: Experimental security analysis of a modern automobile. In: 2010 IEEE Symposium on Security and Privacy, pp. 447–462 (2010)
18. Madeira, A.: Onecoin: a deep dive into crypto's most notorious ponzi scheme. https://cointelegraph.com/news/onecoin-a-deep-dive-into-crypto-s-most-notorious-ponzi-scheme (2020)
19. Mowery, K.:. Security analysis of a full-body scanner. In: 23rd USENIX Security Symposium (USENIX Security 14), pp. 369–384, San Diego, CA, August 2014. USENIX Association
20. US Department of Justice Office of Public Affairs. Three north korean military hackers indicted in wide-ranging scheme to commit cyberattacks and financial crimes across the globe. https://www.justice.gov/opa/pr/three-north-korean-military-hackers-indicted-wide-ranging-scheme-commit-cyberattacks-and (2021)
21. Republic of the Philippines Securities and Exchange Commission. Forsage. https://www.sec.gov.ph/advisories-2020/forsage/ (2020)
22. Republic of the Philippines Securities and Exchange Commission. Sec warns against forsage, other schemes. https://www.sec.gov.ph/pr-2020/sec-warns-against-forsage-other-schemes/ (2020)
23. FORSAGE Official. Forsage overview: Earn ethereum daily! https://www.youtube.com/watch?v=m0NzYwFfGH4 (2020)
24. Palmer, D. https://www.coindesk.com/chinese-authorities-have-seized-a-massive-4-billion-in-crypto-from-plustoken-scam (2020)
25. Paquet-Clouston, M., Romiti, M., Haslhofer, B., Charvat, T.: Spams meet cryptocurrencies: Sextortion in the bitcoin ecosystem. In: Proceedings of the 1st ACM Conference on Advances in Financial Technologies, AFT '19, pp. 76–88, New York, NY, USA (2019). Association for Computing Machinery
26. Pearce, P., et al.: Characterizing large-scale click fraud in zeroaccess. In: Proceedings of the 2014 ACM SIGSAC Conference on Computer and Communications Security, pp. 141–152 (2014)
27. Phillips, R., Wilder, H.: Tracing cryptocurrency scams: clustering replicated advance-fee and phishing websites (2020)
28. United States Securities and Exchanges Commission. Sec charges eleven individuals in $300 million crypto pyramid scheme
29. Torres, C.F., Steichen, M.: Radu state. the art of the scam: demystifying honeypots in ethereum smart contracts. In: 28th USENIX Security Symposium (USENIX Security 19), pp. 1591–1607, Santa Clara, CA (2019). USENIX Association
30. U.S. Securities and Exchange Commission (SEC). SEC charges eleven individuals in $300 million crypto pyramid scheme. SEC Press Release. https://www.sec.gov/news/press-release/2022-134 (2022)
31. Vasek, M., Moore, T.: There's no free lunch, even using bitcoin: tracking the popularity and profits of virtual currency scams. In: Financial Cryptography (2015)
32. Wood, G.: Ethereum: a secure decentralized generalized transaction ledger (2020)
33. Xia, P., et al.: Don't fish in troubled waters! characterizing coronavirus-themed cryptocurrency scams (2020)
34. Xu, J., Livshits, B.: The anatomy of a cryptocurrency pump-and-dump scheme. In: 28th USENIX Security Symposium (USENIX Security 19), pp. 1609–1625, Santa Clara, CA, August 2019. USENIX Association (2019)
35. Yousaf, H., Kappos, G., Meiklejohn, S.: Tracing transactions across cryptocurrency ledgers. In: 28th USENIX Security Symposium (USENIX Security 19), pp. 837–850, Santa Clara, CA, August 2019. USENIX Association (2019)

36. Yu, S., Jin, J., Xie, Y., Shen, J., Xuan, Q.: Ponzi scheme detection in ethereum-transaction network (2021)
37. Zhang-Kennedy, L., Assal, H., Rocheleau, J., Mohamed, R., Baig, K., Chiasson, S.: The aftermath of a crypto-ransomware attack at a large academic institution. In: 27th USENIX Security Symposium (USENIX Security 18), pp. 1061–1078, Baltimore, MD, August 2018. USENIX Association (2018)
38. Zhao, X., Chen, Z., Chen, X., Wang, Y., Tang, C.: The dao attack paradoxes in propositional logic, pp. 1743–1746 (2017)

Understanding Polkadot Through Graph Analysis: Transaction Model, Network Properties, and Insights

Hanaa Abbas[1]([✉]) [iD], Maurantonio Caprolu[1] [iD], and Roberto Di Pietro[2] [iD]

[1] Hamad Bin Khalifa University (HBKU) - College of Science and Engineering (CSE), Division of Information and Computing Technology (ICT), Doha, Qatar
{haab09879,macaprolu}@hbku.edu.qa
[2] RC3 Center, CEMSE Division, King Abdullah University of Science and Technology (KAUST), Thuwal, Saudi Arabia
roberto.dipietro@kaust.edu.sa

Abstract. In recent years, considerable efforts have been directed toward investigating the large amount of public transaction data in prominent cryptocurrencies. Nevertheless, aside from Bitcoin and Ethereum, little efforts have been made to investigate other cryptocurrencies, even though the market now comprises thousands, with more than 50 exceeding one billion dollars of capitalization, and some of them sporting innovative technical solutions and governance. This is the case for Polkadot, a relatively new blockchain that promises to solve the shortcomings in scalability and interoperability that encumber many existing blockchain-based systems. In particular, Polkadot relies on a novel multi-chain construction that promises to enable interoperability among heterogeneous blockchains.

This paper presents the first study to formally model and investigate user transactions in the Polkadot network. Our contributions are multifolds: After defining proper and pseudo-spam transactions, we built the transaction graph based on data collected from the launch of the network, in May 2020, until July 2022. The dataset consists of roughly 11 million blocks, including 2 million user accounts and 7.6 million transactions. We applied a selected set of graph metrics, such as degree distribution, strongly/weakly connected components, density, and several centrality measures, to the collected data. In addition, we also investigated a few interesting idiosyncratic indicators, such as the accounts' balance over time and improper transactions. Our results shed light on the topology of the network, which resembles a heavy-tailed power-law distribution, demonstrate that Polkadot is affected by the rich get richer conundrum, and provide other insights into the financial ecosystem of the network. The approach, methodology, and metrics proposed in this work, while being applied to Polkadot, can also be applied to other cryptocurrencies, hence having a high potential impact and the possibility to further research in the cryptocurrency field.

Keywords: Polkadot · Cryptocurrency · Multi-chain Blockchain · Decentralization · DeFi · Graph Analysis · Network Science

© International Financial Cryptography Association 2024
F. Baldimtsi and C. Cachin (Eds.): FC 2023, LNCS 13951, pp. 259–275, 2024.
https://doi.org/10.1007/978-3-031-47751-5_15

1   Introduction

Over the years, blockchain-based cryptocurrencies have witnessed rapid acceleration in terms of protocols evolution, market capitalization growth, and widespread public and business acceptance. Consequently, considerable efforts have been directed toward investigating the large amount of transactions data in cryptocurrency blockchains. Many complex systems are modeled using network science (or complex network theory) in various applications, such as computer networks, social networks, linguistics and even biology. By applying graph analysis to cryptocurrency networks, researchers were able to discover groundbreaking insights, uncover interesting properties, and characterize major activities on these systems. When these techniques have been applied to cryptocurrencies, some works revealed security concerns manifested in the form of unusual economical patterns. For instance, in Bitcoin, Ron and Shamir (2013) [20] discovered abnormally long and "fork-merge" chains in the transaction graph, which led to the identification of some malicious entities possibly abusing Bitcoin for money laundering, fraud, or other illegal activities. Graph analysis also allows identifying the topological properties of the network; where most cryptocurrency networks are usually found to exhibit small-world structures and power-law distributions [7]. Other studies used clustering algorithms to find hidden relations between different accounts to deanonymize users [14] and investigate unknown transaction patterns [4]. So far, all these techniques have been applied only to the two most diffused cryptocurrencies, Bitcoin and Ethereum. However, the current cryptocurrency landscape includes several other projects that, for capitalization and architectural advantages, certainly deserve the same level of attention. Moreover, these recent proposals also introduce elements of novelties, since they try to address the technical limitations the first proponents have discovered with time, as well as novel governance mechanisms. These latter features, in particular, require to be investigated with scientific method.

In this study, we investigate Polkadot, a recent cryptocurrency launched in May 2020. Despite its recent mint, it has successfully secured a spot amongst the top 10 cryptocurrencies by market capitalization[1]. Polkadot is known for being a fully *"sharded"* blockchain, whose design principles are based on sharding [18,23]—a database splitting technique—that enables multiple chains to process their transactions in parallel. Each blockchain shard is called a *"parachain"* which is connected to the *Relay Chain*. Parachains are heterogeneous blockchains that can be customized per project needs; for example, to host smart contracts or bridges [24]. The Relay Chain acts as the main hub of the system, orchestrating the network's Nominated Proof-of-Stake (NPoS) consensus [2] which requires the cooperation of DOT holders, validators (block authors), and nominators. Furthermore, Polkadot serves as an interoperability platform; i.e., it allows cross-communication between heterogeneous blockchains including external ones, such as Bitcoin and Ethereum.

---

[1] Data sourced from https://coinmarketcap.com/.

Due to the novelty of multi-chains, there is a definite need to investigate their network operations, especially within an active ecosystem such as Polkadot. Despite achieving a good standing in the market, Polkadot has not yet received the same level of attention from academia commanded by other proposals, such as Bitcoin and Ethereum. In fact, to the best of our knowledge, this paper presents the first study on Polkadot that leverages graph analysis to characterize its transactions network. In detail, we investigate the Polkadot network using graph analysis to identify major network characteristics, including, but not limited to, statistical and topological properties. We examine how DOT, Polkadot's native currency, are transferred between user accounts. We collect all transactions that were committed on Polkadot's Relay Chain from Genesis to #11,320,000. Although it is to be noted that the transfer function was enabled on Polkadot on August 18, 2020 (block height #1,205,128). From the data, we construct the transactions graph and measure common graph metrics, such as: degree distribution, strongly/weakly connected components (SCC/WCC), and degree centrality. We believe that our analysis, enriched with data driven considerations, can help forecast the prospect growth and uses of both Polkadot and similar multi-chain blockchains, as well as opening up a few novel investigation avenues.

Contributions. Our main contributions are as follows:

1. We model the transactions among regular users in the Polkadot network. To this end, we first provide a formal definition of a Polkadot transaction, further divided into proper and improper transactions. Then, we model the transactions corresponding to money flow as a weighted directed multigraph.
2. We parse the Polkadot ledger, from the genesis block (May 2020) to block 11,320,000 (July 2022), to build the transaction graph representing the money flow among users.
3. We analyze the transaction graph by measuring global and local metrics. We obtain many new observations and insights on the structure of the network, useful to better understand the Polkadot ecosystem.
4. We identify and quantitatively analyze two different types of abnormal transactions, that we call self-loop and zero-transfer transactions, highlighting their patterns in terms of daily frequency and transaction values.
5. We empirically verify that Polkadot is affected by the *rich get richer* problem by studying user balances over time.
6. To the best of our knowledge, this is the first study that, leveraging graph theory and network science, analyzes transaction data and measures statistical properties of the Polkadot network.
7. The code used to collect the data and build the graph analyzed in this study is released as open source[2].

---

[2] https://github.com/m-caprolu/Polkadot-graph-analysis.

Paper Organization. The remainder of the paper is organized as follows. Section 2 explores related work in the literature. We model the transactions among Polkadot users in Sect. 3, then we describe the process of building the transaction graph in Sect. 4. In Sects. 5, 6, 7, and 8, we present and discuss the results of our analysis. Lastly, we report some concluding remarks in Sect. 9.

2   Related Work

Several works utilized graph-based analysis to investigate prominent blockchain-based networks, mainly Bitcoin and Ethereum [15,21]. Graph-based modeling allows to reveal insights into cryptocurrency transactions and user interactions, including other important tasks such as: cryptocurrency price prediction [13], address clustering [9,16,22], user deanonymization [10], attack forensics, detection of malicious activities such as phishing scams, counterfeit tokens, or money laundering [6], and detection of anomalies (e.g., in smart contracts execution) [5,11]. The graphs are built from the blockchains' publicly available transactions data. However, the architectural differences existing between transaction-based blockchains (e.g., Bitcoin) and account-based blockchains (e.g., Ethereum and Polkadot) require different graph analysis approaches. In this paper, we focus on account-based methods.

In account-based networks, native currency or tokens are represented as a balance that can be deposited to or withdrawn from the user's account. Each transaction can have only one input and one output. A node in the transaction graph represents a unique address and an edge represents a transaction. Since there are no works thus far pertaining to Polkadot, we summarize works from the literature about Ethereum. [8] found that Ethereum transactions volume, components size, incoming or outgoing transaction relations can be approximated by a power-law distribution, which exhibits a heavy-tailed structure. Additionally, [15] found that the growth rate (size of nodes and edges) and graph density are correlated with the price of ETH. Also, the degree distribution of the network follows a power law, and the transaction network is non-assortative. Non-assortativity means that nodes do not tend to communicate with only low-degree or only high-degree nodes [17].

There are a few works in the scientific literature that investigate Polkadot. The work in [1] presented a data-driven study that details the architecture of Polkadot and identifies several of its limitations and design contradictions. Their investigation shows that due to the restriction on the number of allowed validators in the network, a high minimum stake requirement was enforced which varied with the size of the validators set. In addition, a majority of the validators were found to charge 100% commission, thus excluding nominators from monetary incentivization and violating the basic principles of the NPoS economic security. Our work investigates Polkadot from a different perspective through graph-based modeling. Graph analysis allows us to extract refined insights into not only the structure of the network but also the transaction patterns, allowing us to highlight a few abnormal features in the transactions graph.

3   Modeling the Polkadot Transaction Graph

In this section, we model the economic interactions among users in the Polkadot environment. To this end, we first formally define a transaction, either in its proper or abnormal form. This distinction allows us to formally separate transactions that have effectively moved money between two accounts from those that, even if successful, have not had any real effect on the involved balances.

3.1   Polkadot Transactions

Polkadot uses the term "extrinsics" to refer to state changes emerging from the outside world, which include balance transfers. However, for the sake of simplicity, we refer to `balances.transfer` extrinsics as "transactions" in the rest of the paper. We define a transaction in Polkadot as follows:

Definition 1 (Transaction). *A transaction is a signed extrinsic submitted to the blockchain by a user account via a* `balances.transfer` *call or part of a* `utility.batch` *call, where its general attributes are:*

- *signed $= True$;*
- *$module_i d = $ "Balances";*
- *and, $call_i d$ in("transfer", "$transfer_k eep_a live$", "$transfer_a ll$");*

Furthermore, transactions can be formally divided as proper and improper, according the the definitions provided in the following. Let A be the set of all addresses present in the Polkadot ledger, and *ExtrinsicSuccess* is the system event triggered if the transaction is successful. We model a transaction t as a tuple $(In, Out, \lambda, \tau, \phi)$, where $In, Out \in A$ and $\lambda, \phi \in \mathbb{R}^+$, meaning that the account In is paying, at the time τ, λ DOTs to the account Out. In addition, ϕ represents the fee payed for issuing the transaction.

Definition 2 (Proper Transaction). *We say that t is a proper transaction if it satisfies the following properties:*

- *$ExtrinsicSuccess = 1$;*
- *$Value > 0$; and,*
- *$In \neq Out$.*

Definition 3 (Pseudospam Transaction). *We say that t is a pseudo-spam, also called improper, transaction if it satisfies the following properties:*

- *$ExtrinsicSuccess = 1$; and,*
- *$Value = 0$ or $In = Out$.*

In other words, a transaction is considered proper when the given transaction amount, greater than zero, is withdrawn from the sender's account and deposited to the receiver's account successfully. Conversely, an improper transaction is a successful transaction with no impact on the account's balance other than the deduction of the transaction fee, because the sender and receiver addresses are the same and/or the value of the transaction is 0.

Following our analysis of the entire Polkadot ledger, we have identified two forms of pseudospam transactions: (1) *zero transfers* where the transaction value is zero DOT; and, (2) *self-loops* where the destination address is the same as the sender's address. It is important to emphasize that an improper transaction is not a failed transaction; in fact, in the Polkadot network, all transactions are stored on the blockchain, even if they have failed. However, only a successful transaction returns an *ExtrinsicSuccess*. Consequently, we do not consider failed transactions as abnormal. Examples of failed transactions include: transactions whose destination address was not found, or those attempting a balance transfer while having insufficient funds to cover the transaction fee or the transfer value. In addition, we disregard Balances extrinsics that called methods intended for use by Root origin only (Note: Sudo user was removed only after the NPoS scheme was enabled in June 2021). Even though the use of sudo-level functions might have had a malicious intent, such transactions were scarcely found in the dataset, and more importantly, they have failed.

3.2   Polkadot Transaction Graph

Since Polkadot is an account-based blockchain, similar to Ethereum, the money flow among users can be formally modeled as a weighted directed multigraph $M := (A, T)$, where A is the set of all addresses, i.e., user accounts, and T is the set of successful transactions, as defined in definitions 2 and 3.

Figure 1 shows an example of the Polkadot transaction graph. A multi-graph allows an arbitrary number of edges to exist between a pair of nodes in any direction (e.g., Nodes A-B) and also supports self-loops (e.g., Node D). In this example, Node C is the most central node—all other nodes are connected through it. The graph is weighted, where weights are attributes that describe the graph's edges. The attributes include the transaction value in DOT and transaction timestamp. Incorporating timestamps in the graph analysis is essential for investigating temporal properties and evolution of the network, e.g., monthly progress.

4   Building the Transaction Graph

To build the transaction graph, we followed a methodology that includes multiple steps. First, we parsed the Polkadot ledger and we imported the transaction data into a relational database. Then, we queried from the database all the transactions that met the conditions listed above in Definition 1. Finally, using the NetworkX[3] python library, we built a *MultiDiGraph* and we analyzed it under different perspectives.

For the experimental part of this work, we set up a development environment on a DELL workstation, running a Windows 10 PRO OS, that includes a python

---

[3] https://networkx.org/.

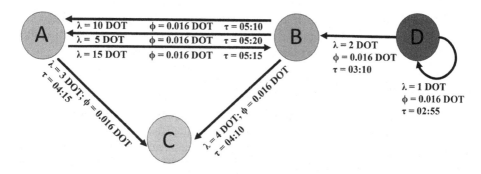

Fig. 1. Graph Representation of a Weighted MultiDiGraph in Polkadot.

(v3.10.2) IDE, a MySQL database (v8.0.28), and a Polkadot full node. The hardware specifications are as follows: Intel(R) Core(TM) i9-9900KS CPU@4 GHz, 64 GB RAM, and 2 TB SSD. We configured the full Polkadot node on an Ubuntu 20.04 LTS running on the Windows Subsystem for Linux (WSL), since Substrate—the framework on which Polkadot is built—is not natively compatible with Windows. We run the node in archive mode to access past states of the chain at any point in time. After fully syncing the blockchain storage on the node, we query and parse the blocks data into the MySQL database, starting from genesis and ending with block #11,320,000. Nonetheless, the actual analysis of transactions data starts at block #1,205,128, because Polkadot balance transfers were enabled only after the specified block height. Even though an archive node takes up large disk space (the collected data corresponding to 11.32 million blocks occupies up to 457 GB on disk), we opted for running our own node instead of querying the data from publicly available RPCs to guarantee data integrity and validity.

We implemented a software that comprises two main components: (1) a blockchain data parser; and (2) a graph analyzer. Our code base in Python follows a modular approach: The data parser queries blocks stored on Polkadot's Relay Chain, along with their extrinsics and events data, and stores the collected data on a MySQL database, whereas the graph analyzer generates a directed multi-graph abstraction of the transactions network. From the generated graph, the analyzer computes relevant metrics that define the network structure and characteristics. We also perform statistical analysis of the transactions data through direct SQL queries. To interface with the Polkadot node, we use two open-source Python libraries implemented by Parity: `substrate-interface` (API for Substrate nodes, which provides different methods for querying data storage and interacting with the chain) and `scalecodec`—needed for decoding/encoding SCALE Codec format that is used by the Substrate runtime. Moreover, we choose NetworkX library to perform the network analysis in Python, since it offers a vast choice of algorithms and tools to produce various metrics, including but not limited to: clustering, connectivity, assortativity, connected components and graph flows. It also supports graph visualization and serialization into different formats such as GraphML, JSON, GIS Shapefile, or a Python Pickle object. Our graph builder module relies on graph pickling functionality to store the graph object and deserialize it for faster processing.

5 Transaction Graph Analysis

In this section, we perform an in-depth study of the transaction network based on various graph properties which can be classified as global properties, i.e., related to the whole graph, and local properties, i.e., related to single nodes. In the following section, we elaborate on what the metrics suggest in terms of the network's structure.

Global Properties. The graph has a total of 2,149,679 nodes (corresponding to unique addresses) and 7,613,325 edges (corresponding to transactions), which include pseudospam transactions to be explored in more detail in the next section (Sect. 6). In the following analysis, we omitted pseudospam transactions then computed the graph metrics accordingly. Excluding pseudospam transactions reduced the count of edges and nodes by 53,121 (transactions) and 1,722 (accounts), respectively. This is an interesting finding as it suggests that 1,722 accounts have been involved with only pseudospam transactions throughout the history of the network. Among the global properties, we studied the graph's connected components, in addition to assortativity, reciprocity, density, clustering, and transitivity, displayed in Table 2.

Connected Components. Graph connectivity is an important measure of the network's resilience. A graph is said to be connected if there exists a path between every pair of nodes. A connected component is a subgraph in which every node is reachable from every other node. For Strongly Connected Components (SCCs), edge direction is taken into account, whereas for Weakly Connected Components (WCCs), direction is ignored. In Fig. 2, we plot the distributions of SCCs in blue and WCCs in green. For both, the result demonstrates that the network is composed of a single giant component—the largest connected subgraph—and many, much smaller components. The components size distribution resembles power-law distribution and is heavy tailed as shown in Fig. 2. This indicates that the network has a few central nodes (hubs) involved in a very large number of transactions with other nodes, forming a giant connected subgraph; while, the majority of the other nodes transact with just a small number of nodes. The hubs in this network carry out a significant role; that is, connecting a significant number of users together. Table 1 lists the node composition of the giant SCC and WCC components, each consisting of 62% and 99.97% of the nodes, respectively. Almost all nodes in the network can be reached from another node by some path, ignoring edge direction.

Degree Assortativity Coefficient. Assortativity measures the correlation between nodes in the graph with respect to their degree. For Polkadot's transactions network, the assortativity coefficient is reported as -0.255, indicating weak disassortativity. A negative assortativity value indicates that the graph's degrees are

Table 1. Summary of Graph Connected Components: SCC and WCC

#SCC	Giant SCC		#WCC	Giant WCC	
	#Nodes (% of nodes)	#Edges (% of edges)		#Nodes (% of nodes)	#Edges (% of edges)
806747	1,332,655 (62%)	5,870,608 (77.7%)	257	2,147,265 (99.97%)	7,559,472 (99.99%)

Table 2. Polkadot Transactions Graph's Global Properties

#Nodes	#Edges	Assortativity	Reciprocity	Density	Clustering	Transitivity
2,147,957	7,560,204	−0.255	0.017	1.64e-6	0.256	9.07e-6

negatively correlated. Notably, it indicates that high-degree nodes (aka 'hubs', such as crypto market exchanges) tend to form connections with nodes of lower degrees and that the network's topology does not behave like the so-called "rich club" phenomenon [25]. High degree nodes connect with smaller ones rather than with similarly high degree nodes.

Reciprocity. Reciprocity measures the likelihood of nodes in a directed network to be mutually linked (i.e., having bidirectional edges) [12]. Reciprocity is computed as 0.017, which is a value approaching 0. This indicates that just a small number of nodes transact in both directions. Even though the majority of the nodes are somehow connected in Polkadot, they tend to transact mostly in a uni-directional manner.

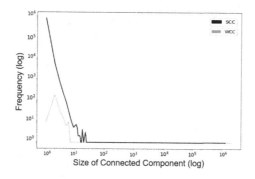

Fig. 2. Connected Components Size Distribution

Density, Clustering, and Transitivity. These three metrics are computed over the undirected graph. *Density* is the ratio of existing edges divided by the maximum possible edges in a graph [12]. The small density value (1.64e-6) indicates a less-dense graph that has more nodes than edges. Meaning, it is likely that users tend to create new accounts while executing new transactions to increase their anonymity [15]. *Global clustering coefficient* evaluates the extent to which nodes in a graph tend to cluster together [5]. The coefficient approximates to

0.256 ($\approx \frac{1}{4}$), indicating that user accounts are likely to form clusters; i.e., if two accounts transact with a third account, it is likely that the former will also transact with the other two. *Transitivity* can be used to find the community structure in blockchain graphs [12]. The transitivity of the graph, a small value in the order of 10^{-6}, suggests the lack of community structure possibly due to the presence of high-degree nodes that are "loner-stars" connected mainly to low-degree nodes.

Local Properties. Next, we investigate common local properties which are node degree distribution (including in- and out- degree) and degree centrality.

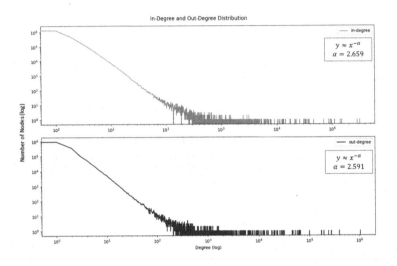

Fig. 3. Transactions Graph In-Degree and Out-Degree Distribution

Degree Distribution. For cryptocurrency networks, the degree distribution provides a high-level outlook about the transaction relations and how nodes are connected in the network. The in-degree and out-degree values of a node correspond to incoming and outgoing transactions, respectively. Figure 3 shows the in- and out- degree distributions, in log-log scale, of the transaction network. For both distributions, the power-law model ($y \sim x^{-\alpha}$) provides a reasonable fit. The tail/end segment is heavier than pure power law distributions, indicating that the number of high-degree nodes (influential nodes, e.g., market exchanges) is relatively much smaller than low-degree nodes (e.g., regular users). The larger the value of α, shown in Fig. 3, the less variable the node degrees are.

Degree Centrality. Centrality measures help to identify the most important nodes in a network. Table 3 lists the top 10 accounts based on normalized degree centrality, which is the fraction of addresses each node is connected to. We also list the in-degree and out-degree coefficients whose sum adds up to the degree value. The max degree centrality belongs to address $1exaAg...T6EGdE$. Upon further search, we found that the address has been identified by the online community as belonging to Binance [19], a prominent cryptocurrency exchange marketplace. This Binance node has been inactive since January 2022; however, before it went inactive, it transferred large sums of DOT to a new address $1qnJN7FViy3H...8GT7$ (listed in row 3), which we believe is the new Binance node—it has achieved high degree centrality in a relatively short time span.

Table 3. Top-10 Most Important Nodes Evaluated By Degree Centrality

#	Account	Known Identity/Role	Degree	In-degree	Out-degree
1	1exaAg2VJRQ...EGdE	Binance	0.614	0.133	0.481
2	12xtAYsRUrm...XkLW	Nominator	0.275	0.149	0.126
3	1qnJN7FViy3H...8GT7	Binance	0.227	0.045	0.182
4	15kUt2i86LH...XAkX	N/A	0.163	0.052	0.111
5	15SbxvcrYSQz...jy82	N/A	0.150	0.069	0.081
6	16hp43 × 8DUZt...4oEd	N/A	0.090	0.044	0.046
7	14Kazg6SFiUC...dQhv	N/A	0.090	≈ 0	0.090
8	12wVuvpApgp...Lchb	N/A	0.065	0.065	≈ 0
9	16HNPJqej7E...L8cj	N/A	0.049	0.018	0.031
10	157PD8GV7pJ...B2KR	N/A	0.049	0.019	0.030

6   Statistical Analysis of Self-loop Transactions

The collected data contains 31,961 (0.41%) self-loop and 4,677 (0.06%) zero-transfer transactions out of 7,613,325 transactions. Both of these transaction types account for much less than 1% of all transactions; however, it is important to investigate them since they do not comply with typical economical interactions. In this paper, we focus mostly on self-transfers since they occur more often.

First, we investigated self-loop transactions in the literature. We found one mention in [12], where the authors interpreted the presence of self-loops in Ethereum according to two trivial scenarios: users verifying if it is possible to send Ether to themselves, or due to a mistake while specifying the receiver address. However, in the case of Polkadot, further investigation is needed to understand the cause of this trend, as the frequency of those transactions suggests different scenarios.

Figure 4 shows the value and volume of self-loop transactions over time. Self-loop transactions were found to exist on a daily basis with arbitrary values (sometimes constant and sometimes following a pattern) and occur throughout the day. Figure 4a reveals interesting patterns in self-loop values and peculiar user behaviors. For example, 1 is the most frequent transaction value, constantly used over time, together with other multiples and sub-multiples of 10. In addition, the figure also highlights the values adopted by the two accounts with the highest number of self-loops. The first one, represented with red asterisks, issued 635 transactions over three months, with different values, sometimes decreasing according to a specific pattern. The second one, represented with blue circles, issued 145 transactions over a year, almost all with the same value of 0.0001.

From Fig. 4b, instead, it can be observed that self-loop transactions appear on a daily basis in the Polkadot ledger. In particular, every day we can observe around 50 self-loops, with a few huge spikes, and almost the double during the last observed months.

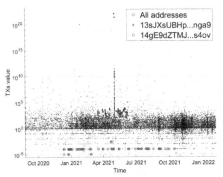 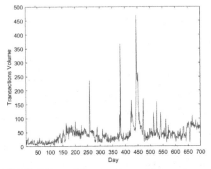

(a) Self-loop Transaction: Values over Time

(b) Self-loop Transactions: Volume over Time

Fig. 4. Polkadot Self-loop Transactions: (a) Values over Time — all users (black circles) and the two most active accounts (red asterisks and blue circles); (b) Volume over Time (Color figure online)

7   Analysis of Polkadot Accounts' Balance

We investigated the distribution of the total balance in DOT for all Polkadot accounts. Overall, there is a total of 1,042,149 active accounts in the network as of July 25, 2022. As shown in Fig. 5a, the distribution of DOTs over all accounts in Polkadot indeed resembles power-law distribution with a heavy-tailed structure. The majority of the accounts (over 1 million accounts) hold small balances, in the range 0-499K DOTs, and only a few own balances float in the range from 500K to over 50 million DOTs—50M DOTs have a market value of 300+ millions USD as of the 19th of October 2022.

We also examined the percentage of DOT held per account type (See Table 4): nominators, validators, council members, and others which may include regular users and proxy accounts. Proxy accounts are addresses created to perform a limited number of actions on behalf of the main account. Nominators own the largest fraction of DOT ($\approx 57\%$), whereas validators on the other hand hold only $\approx 0.1\%$ of all available DOTs.

Table 4. Balance Share per Account Type (in July 2022)

Type	Count	Share
Nominators	21,404	57.275%
Validators	297	0.152%
Council	13	0.006%
Others	1,020,435	42,567%

The previous observation is interesting given that, as shown in [1], over 60% of the validators in April 2022 charged 100% commission and retained block/era rewards to themselves. Hence, it was expected that validators should comparatively have higher balances, but in reality validators contribute little (around 0.2%) to total staking. We find that the typical interaction of nominators and validators in Polkadot is as depicted in Fig. 6. Nominators declare their intent to vote for their validator(s) by staking their DOTs. The validators collect a large-enough stake from nominators that allows them to join the active set. After every era (24 h), the era rewards are relatively equally distributed to all validators. 100%-commissioned validators retain rewards to themselves, whereas other validators can trigger a payout action to nominators according to their share in the total stake. In the case of Binance—the world's largest crypto exchange [3], the rewards amassed by its validators are forwarded to an intermediary address (called rewards address) which then forwards all its balance to the exchange address (top central node as listed in Table 3). We would like to point out that this behavior does not violate the protocols set out by Polkadot, nor does it pose major security risks because block production is not affected by validator stake [24]. These observations only identify limitations towards a 'true' decentralization of the network, due to the presence of highly capitalized, centralized, crypto exchanges [1].

To investigate the "rich get richer" phenomenon in Polkadot, we measured the users' balance evolution over time. A user is considered rich if his/her balance is higher than the average user balance. Formally, the hypothesis is that *the k richest users at time t are richer that the k richest users at time $t' < t$* [7]. To verify this hypothesis, we first define the Wealth Ratio (wr) as the average balance of the k richest users over the average balance of all the other ($|A| - k$) active users in the Polkadot network. Then, we check if the k richest accounts in M_t are richer than the k richest accounts in $M_{t'}$ by computing wr over time, as follows:

$$wr_t = \frac{\sum_{a \in K_t} \frac{b_t(a)}{|K_t|}}{\sum_{a \in \{A_t \setminus K_t\}} \frac{b_t(a)}{|A_t \setminus K_t|}} \qquad (1)$$

where $b_t(a)$ is the balance of account a at time t, and A_t and K_t are the set of all active accounts and the set of the k richest accounts, respectively, at time t. With M_t we refer to the graph induced by transactions having timestamp less than t. For our investigation, we set $k = 100$, while t varies appropriately to consider

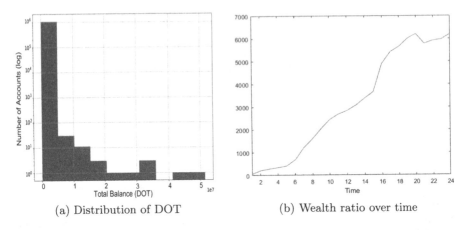

(a) Distribution of DOT   (b) Wealth ratio over time

Fig. 5. Analysis of Polkadot Accounts' Balance. (a) Account balance distribution; (b) Ratio between the Top-100 richest accounts average balance with respect to all (Active) accounts' average balances.

monthly snapshots of the Polkadot ledger over the observation period. Figure 5b shows that wr clearly increases over time. This means that the disparity between richest nodes and all the other accounts grows over time, empirically confirming the *rich get richer* hypothesis.

8 Discussion

It is a common phenomenon for real-world networks to contain hubs that are highly connected to many nodes. The presence of hubs gives the degree and component size distribution a long (heavy) tail, indicating that: there are a few nodes, with a much higher degree than most other nodes, also at the center of the network's giant components. These characteristics, specifically the power law approximation, are associated with what is known as a scale-free network [8].

Based on what discussed in Sect. 5, we can conclude that Polkadot's topology resembles a scale-free network, where at its center is Binance, a crypto market exchange, that dominates the network in terms of centrality and influence. As well-known in the literature, networks with power law degree distributions may introduce potential vulnerabilities. Indeed, if the central hubs, or the nodes with high degrees, are controlled or compromised, the entire network's functionality will get affected [8]. Having exchange centers and mining/staking pools with stronger connectivity than other nodes eventually leads to concentration/centralization of power, which is a phenomenon that is not desirable in decentralized blockchains. In the specific case of Polkadot, the most central entity in the network, Binance, also actively participates in the consensus protocol with nominator/validators accounts, potentially exacerbating the vulnerabilities above mentioned.

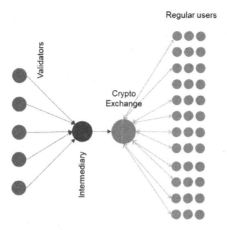

Fig. 6. Typical Interaction among Binance-supported validators, Binance-owned accounts, and regular users.

Other interesting insights on the Polkadot environment come from Sect. 7, where we showed that about 57% of DOT's total supply is owned by nominators, which accounts for only 2% of active users. In addition, we found that the disparity between rich accounts and regular users is increasing over time, demonstrating that Polkadot suffers from the *rich get richer* phenomenon.

9   Conclusion and Future Work

To the best of our knowledge, this study is the first one to formally model Polkadot's transactions data, probing statistical and structural properties of the network, and investigating its properties. By means of graph analysis, we have identified that Polkadot resembles a scale-free network and discovered the presence of a hub, attributable to Binance, dominating the network in terms of centrality and influence. We have also identified abnormal transaction patterns, which we term "pseudo-spam", that include two categories: self-loops (sender address is the same as the receiver address) and zero-transfers (transfer value equals to zero DOT). Both categories effectively have no economic value or impact on the owner's account balance. However, they still frequently appear in the ledger and, sometimes, exhibit fuzzy patterns that deserve further investigation in future work. In addition, we investigated the users' balance over time, finding that the distribution of DOT over all accounts resembles a heavy-tailed power-law distribution, and that the Polkadot network, as many other cryptocurrencies, is affected by the *rich get richer* problem.

The contributions provided in this paper, other than shedding light on a novel proposal in the cryptocurrency ecosystem (multichains), also highlight a few existing critical structural issues and point out transactions' suspicious patterns, possibly stimulating further research in the field.

Acknowledgments. This publication was partially supported by the Qatar National Research Fund (QNRF), a member of The Qatar Foundation, through the awards [NPRP-S-11-0109-180242] and [NPRP11C-1229-170007]. The information and views set out in this publication are those of the authors and do not necessarily reflect the official opinion of the QNRF.* Dr. Roberto Di Pietro produced part of his contributions while he was at HBKU-CSE.

References

1. Abbas, H., Caprolu, M., Di Pietro, R.: Analysis of polkadot: architecture, internals, and contradictions. In: 2022 IEEE International Conference on Blockchain (Blockchain), pp. 61–70 (2022). https://doi.org/10.1109/Blockchain55522.2022.00042

2. Ali, I.M., Caprolu, M., Di Pietro, R.: Foundations, properties, and security applications of puzzles: a survey. ACM Comput. Surv. **53**(4), 1–38 (2020). https://doi.org/10.1145/3396374

3. Aysan, A.F., Khan, A.U.I., Topuz, H., Tunali, A.S.: Survival of the fittest: a natural experiment from crypto exchanges. Singapore Econ. Rev. 1–20 (2021)

4. Caprolu, M., Pontecorvi, M., Signorini, M., Segarra, C., Di Pietro, R.: Analysis and patterns of unknown transactions in bitcoin. In: 2021 IEEE International Conference on Blockchain (Blockchain), pp. 170–179 (2021). https://doi.org/10.1109/Blockchain53845.2021.00031

5. Chen, T., et al.: Understanding Ethereum via graph analysis. ACM Trans. Internet Technol. (TOIT) **20**(2), 1–32 (2020)

6. Di Battista, G., Di Donato, V., Patrignani, M., Pizzonia, M., Roselli, V., Tamassia, R.: Bitconeview: visualization of flows in the bitcoin transaction graph. In: 2015 IEEE Symposium on Visualization for Cyber Security (VizSec), pp. 1–8. IEEE (2015)

7. Di Francesco Maesa, D., Marino, A., Ricci, L.: Data-driven analysis of bitcoin properties: exploiting the users graph. Int. J. Data Sci. Analytics **6**(1), 63–80 (2018)

8. Guo, D., Dong, J., Wang, K.: Graph structure and statistical properties of Ethereum transaction relationships. Inf. Sci. **492**, 58–71 (2019)

9. Harrigan, M., Fretter, C.: The unreasonable effectiveness of address clustering. In: 2016 Intl IEEE Conferences on Ubiquitous Intelligence Computing. Advanced and Trusted Computing, Scalable Computing and Communications, Cloud and Big Data Computing, Internet of People, and Smart World Congress (UIC/ATC/ScalCom/CBDCom/IoP/SmartWorld), pp. 368–373. IEEE, Toulouse, France (July (2016)

10. Jawaheri, H.A., Sabah, M.A., Boshmaf, Y., Erbad, A.: Deanonymizing tor hidden service users through bitcoin transactions analysis. Comput. Secur. **89**, 101684 (2020) https://doi.org/10.1016/j.cose.2019.101684, https://www.sciencedirect.com/science/article/pii/S0167404818309908

11. Khan, A.: Graph analysis of the Ethereum blockchain data: a survey of datasets, methods, and future work. In: 2022 IEEE International Conference on Blockchain (Blockchain), pp. 250–257 (2022). https://doi.org/10.1109/Blockchain55522.2022.00019

12. Lee, X.T., Khan, A., Sen Gupta, S., Ong, Y.H., Liu, X.: Measurements, analyses, and insights on the entire Ethereum blockchain network. In: Proceedings of The Web Conference 2020, pp. 155–166 (2020)

13. Lin, D., Wu, J., Yuan, Q., Zheng, Z.: Modeling and understanding Ethereum transaction records via a complex network approach. IEEE Trans. Circ. Syst. II Express Briefs **67**(11), 2737–2741 (2020). https://doi.org/10.1109/TCSII.2020.2968376
14. Di Francesco Maesa, D., Marino, A., Ricci, L.: An analysis of the Bitcoin users graph: inferring unusual behaviours. In: COMPLEX NETWORKS 2016 2016. SCI, vol. 693, pp. 749–760. Springer, Cham (2017). https://doi.org/10.1007/978-3-319-50901-3_59
15. Motamed, A.P., Bahrak, B.: Quantitative analysis of cryptocurrencies transaction graph. Appl. Netw. Sci. **4**(1), 1–21 (2019)
16. Neudecker, T., Hartenstein, H.: Could network information facilitate address clustering in bitcoin? In: Brenner, M., et al. (eds.) Financial Cryptography and Data Security, pp. 155–169. Springer International Publishing, Cham (2017)
17. Piraveenan, M.R.: Topological Analysis of Complex Networks Using Assortativity. University of Sydney (2010)
18. Polkadot: Polkadot v1.0: Sharding and economic security. https://polkadot.network/blog/polkadot-v1-0-sharding-and-economic-security/. Accessed 10 Oct 2022
19. Polkadot.js: Polkadot.js phishing known addresses. https://github.com/polkadot-js/phishing/blob/master/known.json. Accessed 10 Oct 2022
20. Ron, D., Shamir, A.: Quantitative analysis of the full bitcoin transaction graph. In: Sadeghi, A.-R. (ed.) FC 2013. LNCS, vol. 7859, pp. 6–24. Springer, Heidelberg (2013). https://doi.org/10.1007/978-3-642-39884-1_2
21. Serena, L., Ferretti, S., D'Angelo, G.: Cryptocurrencies activity as a complex network: analysis of transactions graphs. Peer-to-Peer Netw. Appl. **15**(6), 1–15 (2021)
22. Victor, F.: Address clustering heuristics for Ethereum. In: Bonneau, J., Heninger, N. (eds.) FC 2020. LNCS, vol. 12059, pp. 617–633. Springer, Cham (2020). https://doi.org/10.1007/978-3-030-51280-4_33
23. Wang, G., Shi, Z.J., Nixon, M., Han, S.: SoK: sharding on blockchain. In: Proceedings of the 1st ACM Conference on Advances in Financial Technologies, pp. 41–61 (2019)
24. Wood, G.: Polkadot: vision for a heterogeneous multi-chain framework. White Pap. **21**, 2327–4662 (2016)
25. Zhou, S., Mondragón, R.J.: The rich-club phenomenon in the internet topology. IEEE Commun. Lett. **8**(3), 180–182 (2004)

Short Paper: Estimating Patch Propagation Times Across Blockchain Forks

Sébastien Andreina[1]([⊠])(iD), Lorenzo Alluminio[2], Giorgia Azzurra Marson[1](iD),
and Ghassan Karame[3](iD)

[1] NEC Labs Europe, Heidelberg, Germany
{sebastien.andreina,giorgia.marson}@neclab.eu
[2] Clearmatics, London, UK
lorenzo.alluminio@clearmatics.com
[3] Ruhr-Universität Bochum, Bochum, Germany
ghassan@karame.org

Abstract. The wide success of Bitcoin has led to a huge surge of alternative cryptocurrencies (altcoins). Most altcoins essentially fork Bitcoin's code with minor modifications, such as the number of coins to be minted, the block size, and the block generation time. In this paper, we take a closer look at Bitcoin forks from the perspective of vulnerability patching. By mining data retrieved from the GitHub repositories of various altcoin projects, we estimate the time it took to propagate relevant patches from Bitcoin to the altcoins. We find that, while the Bitcoin development community is quite active in fixing security flaws of Bitcoin's code base, forked cryptocurrencies are not as rigorous in patching the same vulnerabilities (inherited from Bitcoin). In some cases, we observe that even critical vulnerabilities, discovered and fixed within the Bitcoin community, have been addressed by the altcoins tens of months after disclosure.

Keywords: Bitcoin forks · Vulnerabilities · Patch propagation

1 Introduction

The wide success of Bitcoin has led to an explosion in the number of so-called "altcoins", i.e., cryptocurrencies designed as a fork of the Bitcoin-core code base. Altcoins exhibit minor differences to Bitcoin, e.g., some feature a different block-generation time (e.g., Dogecoin and Litecoin), use a different hash function (e.g., Litecoin and Namecoin), or impose a different limit on the supply amount (e.g., Dogecoin, Litecoin). Despite these subtle differences, most altcoins share—to a large extent—the same technical foundations of Bitcoin. In the past decade, research has shown that Bitcoin (and many of its descendants) are vulnerable to a wide variety of attacks [4]. However, owing to strong development support, the Bitcoin-core software is routinely monitored and promptly patched (even including research results). Early studies about the security of proof-of-work

© International Financial Cryptography Association 2024
F. Baldimtsi and C. Cachin (Eds.): FC 2023, LNCS 13951, pp. 276–287, 2024.
https://doi.org/10.1007/978-3-031-47751-5_16

blockchains [10] already hinted that some altcoins might offer weaker security compared to Bitcoin, owing to the ad-hoc parameters they adopt.

In this paper, we investigate the security of altcoins from the perspective of vulnerability patching. To this end, we select prominent vulnerabilities reported in Bitcoin, and study how their patches were propagated through (Bitcoin-based) altcoins. Our approach relies on the inspection of GitHub repositories of popular cryptocurrencies, to identify relevant bugs and corresponding patches in the commit history of GitHub-hosted altcoin projects. Concretely, we study whether and how quickly various altcoin projects have addressed disclosed security issues. Unfortunately, retrieving detailed timing information associated to code changes in GitHub emerges as a challenging task. The reason is that most patches are taken directly from the main project repository and applied to the fork via a `rebase` operation which only exposes a reliable timestamp for the original patch (applied to the main project), and not the actual time when the patch was ported (to the fork) [5]. Moreover, the original commits are no longer referenced after `rebase` occurs. As Git prunes unreferenced commits periodically, the timestamps associated to a given patch are lost with every subsequent `rebase` invocation. While prior studies on Bitcoin forks rely on code similarities to compare altcoins' software with Bitcoin Core [14,15], they cannot infer patches that were ported via `rebase`.

To overcome this problem, we devised an automated tool to measure patch propagation times in Git-hosted forked projects even in the case of patches ported via `rebase`. Our tool leverages GitHub's event API and GH archive to estimate the time when a given patch is applied to a forked project. Namely, while GitHub follows the same practices as Git with pruning unreferenced commits, it keeps a log for all commits that ever existed. This information can be retrieved through GitHub's API, as long as one can reference the relevant commits. By traversing the graph of commits from the GH archive, we locate the (original) commit associated to the target patch and estimates the propagation time using three methods (cf. Sect. 2.2). Leveraging our tool, we analyze the patch-propagation time of various open-source altcoin projects (Dash [7], Digibyte [8], Monacoin [19], Litecoin [17], and Dogecoin [9]) which we selected among GitHub-based Bitcoin forks to ensure diversity in terms of market cap, popularity, and vision. For each of the aforementioned altcoin projects, we estimate the time it took to apply relevant patches ported from Bitcoin. Specifically, we consider 47 patches comprising 11 vulnerabilities disclosed in academic papers, 23 Bitcoin's Common Vulnerabilities and Exposures (CVEs), 3 major CVEs in libraries used by Bitcoin, 3 Bitcoin improvement proposals, and 7 major bugs found on the GitHub repository with tags related to the peer-to-peer network, covering crucial vulnerabilities reported in the last decade (see Table 1).

Our results (cf. Sect. 3) indicate that Bitcoin patched 55.3% of the vulnerabilities before their disclosure, while this number drops to 28.5%, 21.4%, 25%, 10.7% and 10.7%, for Litecoin, Dash, Dogecoin, Digibyte and Monacoin, respectively. For all selected altcoins, most patches have been applied with considerable delay compared to the disclosure time, thereby leaving many users vulnerable for several months or even years. We plan to release our tool as open-source to better aid the community in extracting timing information from re-based alt-coins and other GitHub contributions[1]. Our results motivate the need to build automated analysis tools for forked Bitcoin projects in order to precisely explore whether a given vulnerability applies to any of those projects. This would indeed facilitate responsible disclosure of vulnerabilities to all affected forks prior to any publication of the vulnerability.

2   Measuring Patch Propagation Times in Git

Most altcoins port software patches (that have been applied to Bitcoin Core) via `rebase` operations. Unfortunately, every `rebase` invocation modifies the history of the fork's repository—effectively altering the timestamps of all commits re-applied to the fork. In what follows, we study the problem of analyzing the propagation times of patches in Git across forked projects (i.e., the time to port a patch from the main project to the forked project), and introduce our tool, `GitWatch`, as an effective solution to this problem.

2.1   Git Operations

Commit We define a commit as a pair $C = (M, D)$ of *metadata* and *data*—the latter indicates the applied changes. Metadata information is essential for examining the *history* of a repository. It includes a commit hash h (a.k.a. commit ID) that uniquely identifies the commit, a parent p referencing the previous commit, an author a and a committer c, and corresponding author timestamp t_a and committer timestamp t_c recording the creation time of the commit, respectively, the time when the commit was last modified. The commit ID h is a cryptographic hash over the changes D along with the remaining metadata: $h = H(p, a, c, t_a, t_c, D)$. Git allows associating *tags* to commit operations, e.g., to mark released versions of software. A tag τ contains a reference h to the target commit, a timestamp t, and a human-readable label.

Push. A "batch" of commits authored by a user u forms a sequence $(C_1, \ldots, C_m)$ defined implicitly by the references to parent commits. Author and committer initially coincide with the user pushing the commits, and similarly author and committer timestamps coincide.

Fork. A *fork* of an existing repository R is a repository R^χ that shares a common history with R—the latter is called the *main branch*. The latest commit that R and R^χ have in common is called *base commit*. Let $\mathcal{CH}$ and $\mathcal{CH}^\chi$ denote the commit histories of R and R^χ respectively. Then $\mathcal{CH} = (C_0, \ldots, C_m, \ldots, C_{m+s})$ and $\mathcal{CH}^\chi = (C_0, \ldots, C_m, C_1^\chi, \ldots, C_r^\chi)$, for $r > 0$, where C_m denotes the base commit and all commits C_i^χ diverge from the main branch.

Rebase. This operation allows integrating changes from the main branch R (e.g., Bitcoin) to a fork R^χ (e.g., an altcoin) by re-applying all commits pushed

---

[1] https://github.com/nec-research/GitWatch.

to R^χ starting from a new base commit in R—hence the term *rebase*. This operation is usually adopted to fetch the latest version of the original repository. Invoking `rebase` effectively "re-builds" the changes made in the fork on top of the new base commit, thereby modifying the commit history of the fork. Formally, let $\mathcal{CH} = (C_0, \ldots, C_m, \ldots, C_{m+s})$ and $\mathcal{CH}^\chi = (C_0, \ldots, C_m, C_1^\chi, \ldots, C_r^\chi)$ be the commit histories of the two repositories. Invoking `rebase` on R^χ with new base commit C_{m+k}, with $k > 0$, replaces $\mathcal{CH}^\chi$ with $(C_0, \ldots, C_{m+k}, C_1'^\chi \ldots, C_r'^\chi)$, where each commit $C_i'^\chi$ updates the original commit C_i^χ adapting the metadata to the new base commit C_{m+k}—the committed changes D remain the same. This update modifies the first parent commit which, in turn, triggers a chain reaction and modifies all subsequent parent commits. Formally:

$$C_1'^\chi.p \leftarrow C_{m+k}.h \quad \wedge \quad C_i'^\chi.p \leftarrow C_{i-1}'^\chi.h \quad \forall i = 2, \ldots, r. \tag{1}$$

Rebasing has the crucial effect of updating the committer timestamp with the current time (while author timestamps remain unchanged):

$$C_i'^\chi.t_c \leftarrow \text{current time} \quad \wedge \quad C_i'^\chi.t_a = C_i^\chi.t_a. \tag{2}$$

Rebasing Makes Timestamps Unreliable. Rebasing can cause the loss of relevant timing information in the case of multiple `rebase` operations being performed on the same repository. Every `rebase` invocation preserves the author timestamp t_a of the original commits, however, it resets all committer timestamps t_c in the commit history to the current time—thereby overwriting all timestamps of previous `rebase` operations. This behavior is illustrated in Fig. 1. After a rebase, the old commits $C_1^\chi, \ldots, C_r^\chi$ become unreferenced and are "dangling". For saving up space, dangling commits are automatically pruned by Git. However, when a rebase replaces C_i with C_i', the two commits are factually different (due to differing metadata) and are initially both accessible in GitHub via their respective commit IDs. Assuming no pruning, this observation provides us with a strategy to retrieve the timestamp of rebases: by listing all the different versions of a commit C_i and their respective committer timestamp. Our methodology (c.f. Sect. 3) is based on this intuition to estimate the timing of rebases, yet it is compatible with the pruning of dangling commits.

2.2 Extracting Rebase Timing

GitHub generates events for all operations on subscribable public repositories. To extract meaningful information about patch propagation time—even when the patch is applied via rebasing—we rely on two main resources: GitHub's event API and GH archive. GH archive [12] is an open service providing the history of all GitHub

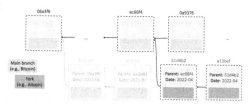

Fig. 1. Effect of `rebase` on commit metadata: commit ID, parent commit, and committer date are modified. Dotted boxes represent commits, arrows point to parent commits.

events since 2011. We notice that while rebases create dangling commits that are not retrieved when cloning, these commits can still be queried through GitHub's API by requesting the corresponding hash. Our tool, GitWatch, relies on this to retrieve the timestamps of dangling commits.

To measure the patch propagation times for a GitHub project χ, GitWatch first reconstructs the tree of commits that ever existed in χ, building a graph $\mathcal{G}_\chi = (V, E)$ containing all commits C in χ (including dangling commits) as vertices, and with edges representing the parent to child relationship, i.e., $C \in V$ and $(C.p, C) \in E$. To do so, it crawls GH archive for all events pertaining to χ in order to retrieve all commits from GitHub's API. Using $\mathcal{G}_\chi$, GitWatch locates the commit (if any) applying a target patch to χ and estimates the corresponding timestamp using three different heuristics: patch-commit finder (PCF), patch-event finder (PEF), and patch-tag finder (PTF). The patch propagation time Δ, from Bitcoin to the altcoin, is then derived by comparing these estimates with the original timestamp of the Bitcoin patch. The reliance on all three heuristics helps in eliminating possible false positives that may arise due to missing events in the GH archive. Whenever we obtain different results from the heuristics, GitWatch returns the smallest timeframe by default.

Patch-Commit Finder (PCF). Here, given a patch commit $C_i \in \mathcal{CH}^{BC}$, we traverse $\mathcal{G}_\chi$ to collect all non-Bitcoin commits C_j containing C_i in their history. Concretely, we construct a list $\mathrm{nbcc}_\chi(C_i)$ of "non-Bitcoin child commits" defined as follows:

$$C_j \in \mathrm{nbcc}_\chi(C_i) \iff C_j \notin \mathcal{CH}^{BC} \wedge C_j \in \mathcal{CH}^\chi \wedge \exists (E_1, .., E_n) \in \mathcal{G}_\chi :$$
$$E_1.\texttt{from} = C_i \wedge E_n.\texttt{to} = C_j \wedge \forall i \in [1, n-1], E_i.\texttt{to} = E_{i+1}.\texttt{from}. \tag{3}$$

PCF then locates in $\mathrm{nbcc}(C_i)$ the earliest commit C^* such that:[2]

$$C^* \in \mathrm{nbcc}_\chi(C_i) \wedge C^*.t_c \leq C_j.t_c \; \forall C_j \in \mathrm{nbcc}_\chi(C_i). \tag{4}$$

The estimated patch-propagation time is $\Delta^{\mathrm{PCF}} \leftarrow C^*.t_c - C_i.t_a$.

Patch-Event Finder (PEF). In addition to $\mathcal{G}_\chi$, our second heuristic relies on inspecting GitHub events. Events are associated to one or more commits: a push event e contains the list of commits $(C_1, \ldots, C_m)$ pushed by the author, i.e., $e = (\boldsymbol{C}_e, t_e)$ with $\boldsymbol{C}_e = (C_1, \ldots, C_m)$ and t_e is the event timestamp. We denote by ϕ the mapping from commits to events, i.e., $\phi(C_i) := e$ for all $i = 1, \ldots, m$. Slightly abusing notation, we write $C_i \in e \Leftrightarrow \phi(C_i) = e$. Similarly to PCF, we look for the earliest non-Bitcoin commit C^* that contains patch C_i in its history, however, we measure elapsed time with respect to event timestamps rather than commit timestamps. We estimate the patch propagation time as the time span between the creation of the patch commit C_i and the oldest event that references a commit C_j that has C_i in its history. Let $\mathcal{E}_\chi := \{e \mid \exists C \in \mathcal{CH}^\chi : \phi(C) = e\}$

---

[2] C^* following this property may not be unique, as multiple commits can have the same timestamp.

denote the set of events pertaining to the altcoin χ and recorded in the GH archive. PEF characterizes a relevant commit C^* as follows:

$$C^* \in \mathrm{nbcc}_\chi(C_i) \ \wedge \ \phi(C^*) \in \mathcal{E}_\chi \ \wedge \phi(C^*).t \leq \phi(C_j).t \ \forall C_j \in \mathrm{nbcc}_\chi(C_i) \cap \mathcal{E}_\chi. \quad (5)$$

The estimated patch propagation time is $\Delta^{\mathrm{PEF}} \leftarrow \phi(C^*).t - C_i.t_a$.

Patch-Tag Finder (PTF). Our third heuristic relies on timestamps recorded for relevant tags. Intuitively, we estimate the patch propagation time as the interval between the creation of the Bitcoin patch C_i and the creation of the first non-Bitcoin tag associated to a commit in χ that has C_i in its history. We define "non-Bitcoin child tag" analogously to that of non-Bitcoin child commit:

$$\tau \in \mathrm{nbct}_\chi(C_i) \iff \tau.h \in \mathrm{nbcc}_\chi(C_i) \ \wedge \tau \in Tags_\chi \wedge \tau \notin Tags_{BC}. \quad (6)$$

PTF identifies a relevant tag $\tau^* \in \mathrm{nbct}_\chi(C_i) \ \wedge \ \tau^*.t \leq \tau.t \ \forall \tau \in \mathrm{nbct}_\chi(C_i)$, and estimates the patch propagation delay as $\Delta^{\mathrm{PTF}} \leftarrow \tau^*.t - C_i.t_a$.

Comparison. Assuming successful retrieval of all dangling commits, our methodology lists all different versions of the relevant commit C^* (one per rebase), allowing us to select the most accurate commit timestamp. Our three heuristics therefore overcome the problem of retrieving reliable timestamps in the presence of rebasing (c.f. Sect. 2.1). The major limitation of PCF and PEF is that they may under-approximate the patching time in case a developer creates the patch locally (or on a dev branch) and pushes the patch to the main branch at a later time (e.g., for testing the patched code locally). PCF further relies on the developer's local clock, which could be skewed. PTF is not affected by these limitations, as it outputs the most conservative timestamp. We therefore expect PTF to output the most accurate estimate in typical scenarios, in particular because most users do not compile the latest modifications based on the current version of the main branch (which may be unstable); they are more likely to use released versions of the code, which are marked with tags. Notice that PCF, PEF, and PTF exclusively inspect commits that are either rebased or merged with the same code base: patches introduced with a different code base may therefore not be identified.

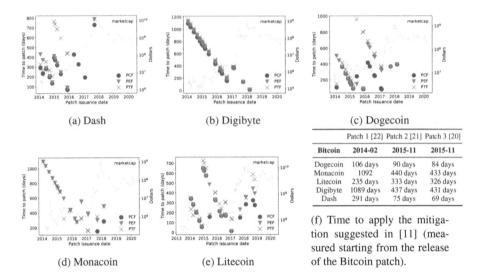

(a) Dash   (b) Digibyte   (c) Dogecoin

	Patch 1 [22]	Patch 2 [21]	Patch 3 [20]
Bitcoin	2014-02	2015-11	2015-11
Dogecoin	106 days	90 days	84 days
Monacoin	1092	440 days	433 days
Litecoin	235 days	333 days	326 days
Digibyte	1089 days	437 days	431 days
Dash	291 days	75 days	69 days

(f) Time to apply the mitigation suggested in [11] (measured starting from the release of the Bitcoin patch).

(d) Monacoin   (e) Litecoin

Fig. 2. Time for a patch issued by Bitcoin-core to be included to the different altcoins. Blue circle, orange triangle, and green cross represent respectively the output values given by the PCF, PEF, and PTF approaches; the market capitalization over time of each coin is plotted as a black dotted line against the values on the right y-axis. (Color figure online),

3   Methodology and Evaluation

3.1   Dataset

In our evaluation, we restrict our analysis to bugs and patches related to Bitcoin, in particular, how they are propagated through altcoins that are based on the same code base. Since we are interested in patches that are not specific to Bitcoin but relevant to most altcoins, we mainly focus on reported bugs on the peer-to-peer layer as this layer is generally inherited by altcoins (including those that introduce non-negligible modifications to the code base).

We analyze five altcoins, which we selected among existing open-source forks of Bitcoin: Dash [7], initially known for its early adoption in darknet markets, currently worth 2.65 Billion USD; Digibyte [8], a cryptocurrency advertised for its improved functionality and security, currently worth 1.12 Billion USD; Monacoin [19], aimed to become a national payment system in Japan, currently worth 0.11 Billion USD; Litecoin [17] and Dogecoin [9], which emerges among the most popular first-generation derivatives of Bitcoin with a market capitalization of 14.82 Billion USD and 40.07 Billion USD respectively. We then selected a list of 47 Bitcoin commits, 11 representing patches suggested by top-tier publications [11,13,16], 23 representing patches of CVEs, 3 representing Bitcoin improvement proposals (BIP), 3 representing CVEs in libraries used by Bitcoin and the remaining 7 representing bugs found on the GitHub repository with tags related to the peer-to-peer network. These patches include the majority of network and peer-to-peer vulnerabilities that were reported in the last decade.

3.2 Validation of `GitWatch`

To validate the effectiveness of `GitWatch`, we manually identified publication dates of relevant patches (by investigating release notes), and we compared these dates with the output of `GitWatch` for the same vulnerability. Our results, shown in Fig. 2f, confirm that for all the ground-truth data points we found, the actual patching time falls within the interval reported by the three heuristic used by `GitWatch` (i.e., between the minimum and maximum estimated propagation time). As expected, PTF provides the most accurate results, especially since release notes are usually part of a new release to which a tag is assigned.

Table 1. Estimated patching time (in days) based on our dataset. A dash (-) indicates that `GitWatch` could not find the patch in the altcoin.

Name	Pub Date	Description	Bitcoin	Litecoin	Dash	Dogecoin	Digibyte	Monacoin
		Total Number of fixes	47/47	41/42	21/28	23/28	25/28	26/28
Paper [13]	2015-08-14	deterministic random eviction	-143	19	15	92	681	684
Paper [13]	2015-08-14	random selection sha1	-143	19	15	92	681	684
Paper [13]	2015-08-14	random selection sha2	-143	19	15	92	681	684
Paper [13]	2015-08-14	test before evict	935	285	-	392	13	285
Paper [13]	2015-08-14	feeler connections	375	58	327	256	162	165
Paper [13]	2015-08-14	more buckets	-143	19	15	92	681	684
Paper [13]	2015-08-14	more outgoing connections	1482	-	-	-	-	-
Paper [11]	2015-10-16	no inv messages	44	326	69	84	430	433
Paper [11]	2015-10-16	filtering inv by ip address	38	333	75	90	437	440
Paper [11]	2015-10-16	penalizing non-responding nodes	-615	235	291	106	1089	1092
Paper [16]	2012-10-18	forward double spending attempts	617	202	281	362	950	953
Vulnerability	-	limit the number of IP learned from each DNS	0	103	-	392	13	103
Vulnerability	-	ensure tried table collisions eventually get resolved	0	281	-	-	-	-
GitHub bug	-	fixes fee estimate and peers files only when initialized	0	119	198	279	867	870
GitHub bug	-	check block header when accepting headers	0	56	135	216	804	808
GitHub bug	-	introduce block download timeout	0	8	87	168	756	759
GitHub bug	-	de-serialization bug where AddrMan is corrupted	0	169	426	367	273	276
GitHub bug	-	don't deserialize nVersion into CNode	0	15	194	94	376	167
CVE-2014-0160	2014-04-07	Remote memory leak via payment protocol	1	176	233	0	1030	1034
BIP 66	2015-02-13	FakeConf: Strict DER signatures	-12	4	61	142	731	734
BIP 65	2015-11-12	FakeConf: OP_CHECKLOCKTIMEVERIFY	-143	159	229	147	591	322
CVE-2016-10724	2018-07-02	DoS: Alert memory exhaustion	-836	216	-	414	320	323
CVE-2018-17144	2018-09-20	Inflation: Missing check for duplicate inputs	-3	1	1	-	155	1
CVE-2017-18350	2019-06-22	Buffer overflow from SOCKS proxy	-632	151	727	91	140	1
CVE-2018-20586	2019-06-22	Deception: Debug log injection	-229	41	380	-	106	244
CVE-2014-0224	2014-06-05	OpenSSL CVE	0	118	174	0	972	975
CVE-2018-12356	2018-06-14	Regex bug	1	184	-	291	50	184
CVE-2019-6250	2019-01-13	Vulnerability in the ZeroMQ libzmq library	5	31	-	-	-	31
		Average	7.53	114.85	188.0	185.17	519.55	503.3

3.3   Evaluation Results

As shown in Fig. 2, `GitWatch` provides consistent timing estimates, which converge in most cases. Dash (Fig. 2a) appears to port patches more quickly, compared to the other blockchains, most of the times with a delay between 200 and 400 d. Dogecoin and Litecoin instead (Figs. 2c

Table 2. Ground-truth data to validate `GitWatch`.

Vulnerability	Altcoin	Time	PCF	PEF	PTF
BIP 65	Litecoin	179 d [2]	159	160	181
BIP 65	Dogecoin	958 d [1]	244	147	958
BIP 66	Dogecoin	194 d [3]	142	142	194
CVE-2013-4627	Litecoin	33 d [18]	17	45	18
CVE-2013-4165	Litecoin	28 day [18]	10	529	13

and 2e) show more variable patching delays, ranging between 50–600 days, respectively, and 100–500 days on average. Digibyte and Monacoin (Figs. 2b and 2d) exhibit an apparent linearly decreasing delay. This peculiar behavior suggests that `rebase` operations to import the Bitcoin's patches are executed on a regular pace, in a manner that appears to be decoupled from the actual patch release. This would explain the downward trend in the plots, indicating that groups of patches are actually ported on the corresponding fork at the same time. To summarize, all five analyzed altcoins apply patches with a delay between several months to a few years. We include the detailed results of our study in Table 1. Out of the 47 selected commits, we omitted 5 CVEs that were patched before any of the altcoins were created, and 13 CVEs and 1 BIP where only Litecoin was released. Those 14 patches were ported by Litecoin with an average delay of 97 d. Our results show that Bitcoin issues patches to most critical vulnerabilities and CVEs in a prompt manner, often before the publication of vulnerability (i.e., in compliance with the responsible disclosure process).

4   Case Studies

We now look more closely at two specific vulnerabilities found in Bitcoin, which we selected because they are prominent and recent (disclosure in 2015 and 2017 resp.).

Case Study 1: Tampering with the Delivery of Information in Bitcoin [11] In order to sustain higher throughput and scalability, Bitcoin implemented a number of optimizations and scalability measures. In [11], it was shown that some of those measures come at odds with the security of the system. As a direct outcome of this vulnerability, a resource-constrained adversary could mount a large-scale Denial-of-Service attack on Bitcoin—effectively halting the delivery of all blocks and transactions in the system. The authors suggested various improvements that resulted in multiple patches:

- Patch 1 - f59d... [22], penalizing nodes that do not respond to block requests.
- Patch 2 - 5029... [21], preventing adversaries from filling up the advertisement table.
- Patch 3 - 5026... [20], replacing the advertisement message with the full block header.

As shown in Fig. 2f, Dash and Dogecoin took almost 3 months to port these patches from Bitcoin; Monacoin, Litecoin and Digibyte required between 7 months and 3 years.

Case Study 2: CVE-2017-18350. [6] This buffer-overflow vulnerability of the Bitcoin-core software was located in the proxy support, and would enable a malicious proxy server to overwrite the program stack, allowing it to perform remote code execution. However, to be vulnerable, the wallet needs to be configured to use a malicious proxy, therefore reducing the general risk on the users. Since remote code execution could allow any third party full access to the machine running the node, we deemed that this CVE to be of particular interest due to its potential drastic impact. This vulnerability was discovered on September 21st 2017, was patched two days later, on September 23rd and the patch was merged with the main branch of the Bitcoin-core repository four days later on September 27th, 2017. To give enough time to the users for applying the patch, the CVE itself was published only on the June 22nd, 2019. While this patch was applied directly to most of the different altcoins based on the Bitcoin-core software, Dash [7] only patched it several months after it was published, on November 19th, 2019. Dash users were seemingly using a vulnerable software with no available update for several months after the disclosure of the vulnerability. Dogecoin, Digibyte, Monacoin and Litecoin took respectively 91 d, 140 d, 151 d and 151 d to patch this vulnerability after it was discovered. While they all patched it before the vulnerability was disclosed, the software still remained unpatched for several months.

5 Conclusion

In this paper, we showed that various altcoins exhibit weaker stability compared to Bitcoin Core. Beyond confirming the folklore result that patch propagation is slow for some altcoins, we introduced a new technique to estimate the time for altcoins to propagate security patches, and determine which altcoins are faster in adopting a patch. For instance, Dash patched CVE-2017-18350 5 months after the public release of the CVE. Moreover, among the five altcoins we analyzed (some of which are worth several billions), Litecoin is the only project to have consistently ported patches within 1 year of their release. We hope that our work further motivates the need for a proper responsible disclosure of vulnerabilities to all forked chains prior to any publication of the vulnerability.

Acknowledgements. This work was partially funded by the Deutsche Forschungs-gemeinschaft (DFG, German Research Foundation) under Germany's Excellence Strategy - EXC 2092 CASA - 390781972 and the European Union (INCODE, Grant Agreement No 101093069). Views and opinions expressed are however those of the author(s) only and do not necessarily reflect those of the European Union. Neither the European Union nor the granting authority can be held responsible for them.

References

1. Dogecoin v1.14 alpha release note (2018). https://github.com/dogecoin/dogecoin/releases/tag/v1.14-alpha-1
2. Litecoin v0.10.4 release note (2015). https://github.com/litecoin-project/litecoin/blob/v0.10.4.0/doc/release-notes-litecoin.md
3. Dogecoin v1.10 release note (2015). https://github.com/dogecoin/dogecoin/releases?q=BIP66&expanded=true
4. Böhme, R., Eckey, L., Moore, T., Narula, N., Ruffing, T., Zohar, A.: Responsible vulnerability disclosure in cryptocurrencies. Commun. ACM **63**(10), 62–71 (2020). https://doi.org/10.1145/3372115
5. Businge, J., Moses, O., Nadi, S., Berger, T.: Reuse and maintenance practices among divergent forks in three software ecosystems. In: Empirical Software Engineering (2021)
6. Cve-2017-18350 (2019). https://medium.com/@lukedashjr/CVE-2017-18350-disclosure-fe6d695f45d5
7. Dash (2022). https://www.dash.org/
8. Digibyte (2022). https://digibyte.org/en-us/
9. Dogecoin (2021). https://dogecoin.com/
10. Gervais, A., Karame, G.O., Wüst, K., Glykantzis, V., Ritzdorf, H., Capkun, S.: On the security and performance of proof of work blockchains. In: Weippl, E.R., Katzenbeisser, S., Kruegel, C., Myers, A.C., Halevi, S. (eds.) Proceedings of the 2016 ACM SIGSAC Conference on Computer and Communications Security, Vienna, Austria, 24–28 October 2016. pp. 3–16. ACM (2016). https://doi.org/10.1145/2976749.2978341
11. Gervais, A., Ritzdorf, H., Karame, G.O., Capkun, S.: Tampering with the delivery of blocks and transactions in bitcoin. In: Ray, I., Li, N., Kruegel, C. (eds.) Proceedings of the 22nd ACM SIGSAC Conference on Computer and Communications Security, Denver, CO, USA, 12–16 October 2015. pp. 692–705. ACM (2015). https://doi.org/10.1145/2810103.2813655
12. Gh archive (2022). https://www.gharchive.org/
13. Heilman, E., Kendler, A., Zohar, A., Goldberg, S.: Eclipse attacks on bitcoin's peer-to-peer network. In: Jung, J., Holz, T. (eds.) 24th USENIX Security Symposium, USENIX Security 2015, Washington, D.C., USA, 12–14 August 2015, pp. 129–144. USENIX Association (2015), https://www.usenix.org/conference/usenixsecurity15/technical-sessions/presentation/heilman
14. Hum, Q., Tan, W.J., Tey, S.Y., Lenus, L., Homoliak, I., Lin, Y., Sun, J.: Coinwatch: A clone-based approach for detecting vulnerabilities in cryptocurrencies. In: IEEE International Conference on Blockchain, Blockchain 2020, Rhodes, Greece, 2–6 November 2020, pp. 17–25. IEEE (2020). https://doi.org/10.1109/Blockchain50366.2020.00011
15. Jia, A., et al.: From innovations to prospects: what is hidden behind cryptocurrencies? In: MSR, pp. 288–299. ACM (2020)
16. Karame, G., Androulaki, E., Capkun, S.: Double-spending fast payments in bitcoin. In: Yu, T., Danezis, G., Gligor, V.D. (eds.) the ACM Conference on Computer and Communications Security, CCS 2012, Raleigh, NC, USA, 16–18 October 2012, pp. 906–917. ACM (2012). https://doi.org/10.1145/2382196.2382292
17. Litecoin (2020). https://litecoin.com/en/
18. Litecoin v0.8.4.1 release note (2013). https://litecoinmirror.wordpress.com/2013/09/04/litecoin-0-8-4-1-release-notes/amp/

19. Monacoin (2018). https://monacoin.org/
20. Bitcoin patch propagation 3 (2015). https://github.com/bitcoin/bitcoin/commit/50262d89531692473ff557c1061aee22aa4cca1c
21. Bitcoin patch propagation 2 (2015). https://github.com/bitcoin/bitcoin/commit/5029698186445bf3cd69d0e720f019c472661bff
22. Bitcoin patch propagation 1 (2014). https://github.com/bitcoin/bitcoin/commit/f59d8f0b644d49324cabd19c58cf2262d49e1392

Game Theory and Protocols

DeFi and NFTs Hinder Blockchain Scalability

Lioba Heimbach(✉)⑩, Quentin Kniep⑩, Yann Vonlanthen⑩,
and Roger Wattenhofer⑩

ETH Zurich, Zurich, Switzerland
{hlioba,qkniep,yvonlanthen,wattenhofer}@ethz.ch

Abstract. Many classical blockchains are known to have an embarrassingly low transaction throughput, down to Bitcoin's notorious seven transactions per second limit. Various proposals and implementations for increasing throughput emerged in the first decade of blockchain research. But how much concurrency is possible? In their early days, blockchains were mostly used for simple transfers from user to user. More recently, however, *decentralized finance (DeFi)* and *NFT marketplaces* have completely changed what is happening on blockchains. Both are built using *smart contracts* and have gained significant popularity. Transactions on DeFi and NFT marketplaces often interact with the same smart contracts. We believe this development has transformed blockchain usage. In our work, we perform a historical analysis of Ethereum's transaction graph. We study how much interaction between transactions there was historically and how much there is now. We find that the rise of DeFi and NFT marketplaces has led to an increase in "centralization" in the transaction graph. More transactions are now interconnected: currently, there are around 200 transactions per block with 4000 interdependencies between them. We further find that the parallelizability of Ethereum's current interconnected transaction workload is limited. A speedup exceeding a factor of five is currently unrealistic.

Keywords: Blockchain · Ethereum · smart contract · decentralized finance · scalability · parallelization · workload characterization · transaction graph

1 Introduction

When the first blockchain, Bitcoin [31], was launched in 2008, it allowed the execution of financial transactions without relying on a central authority. With its promise, Bitcoin sparked the creation of many more cryptocurrencies, most notably Ethereum [41], which introduced smart contracts in 2015. However, even though cryptocurrencies are continuously reaching new levels of popularity, the transaction throughput of the most popular[1] ones remains incredibly low.

---

[1] Measured by total fees users are willing to pay to use the blockchain (see https://cryptofees.info) Ethereum is orders of magnitude more popular than other smart contract-enabled blockchains, such as Avalanche and Cardano.

© International Financial Cryptography Association 2024
F. Baldimtsi and C. Cachin (Eds.): FC 2023, LNCS 13951, pp. 291–309, 2024.
https://doi.org/10.1007/978-3-031-47751-5_17

Given the low throughput of blockchains, especially in comparison to established payment systems such as Visa or PayPal, many suggestions to tackle low blockchain throughput levels have been introduced as well as implemented. Layer 2 protocols [11,23,32,34], handling transactions off-chain, sharding protocols [3,10,17,21,28,40,44], and moving from *Proof-of-Work (PoW)* to *Proof-of-Stake (PoS)* [16] are amongst the most adopted scaling solutions. In addition to the development of the aforementioned solutions, the potential of concurrency control for multithreaded execution has been explored thoroughly.

However, these solutions do not focus on the implications of the changing nature of blockchain transactions. Before the rapid rise of *decentralized finance (DeFi)* and NFT marketplaces, transactions were largely simple transactions between two parties. Consequently, dependencies between a large set of transactions in a block were rare. In the face of few dependencies, transaction throughput can be increased with the proposed solutions – as they rely on the parallel execution of transactions to increase throughput. However, DeFi and NFT marketplaces have brought new challenges when scaling throughput.

While DeFi employs smart contracts hosted on the blockchain to offer many of the services provided by traditional finance, NFT marketplaces utilize smart contracts to facilitate NFT purchases. Core smart contracts building DeFi and NFT marketplaces are involved in many of a block's transactions and create dependencies between a significant proportion of transactions. This new reality on Ethereum greatly challenges the parallelization of transaction execution.

In this work, we explore the limits of transaction parallelization on Ethereum. We analyze these limits by investigating the connectedness of the Ethereum mainnet transaction graph over time. The identification of the largest connected component and clique in terms of the required execution workload in a block's transaction graph allows us to explore the potential of concurrent execution over time. In particular, we point out that DeFi's most important smart contracts are central in the transaction graph and responsible for the vast majority of transaction dependencies. Thus, a handful of smart contracts present a significant parallelization bottleneck, especially given the widespread adoption of DeFi and NFT marketplaces starting in 2020.

This development presents a tremendous challenge in the quest to reach throughput levels of established payment systems. We, therefore, conclude by outlining three areas to tackle in order to increase the parallelizability of Ethereum's workload and allow concurrency mechanisms to reach their full potential. These areas should not only be targeted by Ethereum, the focus of our analysis, but also by blockchains with comparable smart contract designs and usage patterns, as we expect them to have similar bottlenecks.

2 Related Work

Blockchain throughput has been one of the first topics of Bitcoin research, and many solutions have emerged to tackle the issue, e.g., layer 2, sharding. Here, we concentrate on those solutions that aim to parallelize the workload through concurrent execution. These works directly study the parallelization of the workload, whose bounds we quantify.

Sergey and Hobor [37] are among the first to explore smart contract concurrency for the parallel execution of blockchain transactions. They provide an analogy between smart contracts and concurrent programming. In the scheme introduced by Zhang and Zhang [46], miners use concurrency control techniques to pre-compute a serializable schedule that can be utilized by validators replaying the block. By employing a dependency graph based concurrency control technique, Amiri et al. [1] find a valid schedule execution that allows for non-conflicting transactions to execute in parallel. Our work, on the other hand, explores the blockchain transaction dependency graph to quantify the existing real-world potential of parallelization.

Additionally, a recent line of work surrounding smart contracts' concurrency leverages speculative execution. Dickerson et al. [13], and Anjana et al. [2] pre-compute a serializable concurrent schedule for a block's transactions through speculative execution, while Gelashvili et al. [19] propose Block-STM, a parallel execution engine that avoids pre-computation. An estimation of the potential concurrency of speculative execution by miners is offered by Saraph and Herlihy [36]. Chen et al. [9] take speculative execution to a new level by speculatively executing transactions that are waiting to be included in a block. In contrast, we explore the limits of concurrency given the nature of blockchain transactions in light of the recent rise of DeFi and NFT marketplaces.

Pîrlea et al. [33] and Murgia et al. [30] utilize static analysis to parallelize execution. They statically determine which transactions can safely be executed in parallel and which contracts can be placed on different shards. While static analysis is valuable for identifying dependencies ahead of time, the existing approaches do not remove inherent dependencies from the workload, which are at the center of our findings.

A parallel line of work studies the transaction graphs of popular cryptocurrencies. Ron and Shamir [35] first analyzed the Bitcoin transaction graph. While their work studies the full transaction graph statically, Kondor et al. [24] also examine changes in the Bitcoin transaction network over time. Several studies also explore the Ethereum transaction network [4, 8, 18, 20, 22, 26, 27, 29, 42, 43, 47, 47] through temporal graph analysis. Instead of solely studying the evolution of Ethereum's full transaction network, we focus on the impacts of the increased smart contract usage on the connectedness of Ethereum's block-wise transaction graphs and quantify the implications for parallelizability of the current and historical transaction workload.

In their study of Ethereum's transaction network, Zanelatto et al. [45] focus on understanding the evolution of connected components in the network. Their work precedes the rise of DeFi and NFT marketplaces on Ethereum and therefore does not capture the increased trend of more and more interplay between transactions and different smart contracts. Our work focuses on this increased connectivity and discusses its implications on the blockchain.

3   Background

In the following, we introduce the essential preliminaries concerning transaction execution on the Ethereum blockchain and DeFi smart contracts.

3.1   Ethereum Transaction Execution

Ethereum is a smart contract platform, i.e., it does not only support Ether transfers. Instead, it runs a general-purpose virtual machine, the *Ethereum virtual machine (EVM)*, that executes a specific byte code instruction set. Thus, Ethereum allows functions defined in smart contracts to be called in transactions. Smart contract functions can call functions of other smart contracts, generating *internal calls*. The EVM distinguishes between the following different types of function calls: (1) *call* performs operations scoped to the *called* contract's storage, (2) *delegate call* performs operations scoped to the *calling* contract's storage, (3) *static call* is like a regular call but with read-only access to the storage, and (4) *call code* is a deprecated version of delegate call. Thus, all calls are scoped to a specific contract and have either read/write or read-only access to its storage.

We call two transactions *conflicting* or *dependent* if they have calls with the same scope and one of them has write access on that scope. Note that two transactions that interact with the same smart contract might not necessarily touch the same storage cell. However, taking this coarser view on conflicts simplifies large scale analysis and is easier to reason about for smart contract developers.

There are also EVM instructions (BALANCE, EXTCODESIZE, EXTCODEHASH, EXTCODECOPY), which allow a contract to read global state (including the current Ether balance and smart contract code) of any address, regardless of the current scope. In practice, out of these mostly EXTCODESIZE is used to detect whether an address is a smart contract. In our analysis we disregard potential conflicts, which could be caused by these instructions.

Ethereum introduced the *access list* [5,6], which specifies a list of addresses and storage keys that the transaction wants to access, giving a gas discount on these accesses. However, it is optional and not yet widely adopted. We found that out of more than 600 million transactions, only 2 million included an access list and their accuracy and completeness is unclear. Building complete and accurate access lists of just addresses would also be easier for smart contract developers and end users. Further, previous work could not gain a significant advantage by parallelizing at the storage key level [36] as opposed to the address level.

Code execution on the EVM is paid for in *gas*, which is automatically converted from the sender's Ether balance. Gas is a measure of how expensive code execution is for validators on Ethereum [15]. Thus, we use gas as a proxy measure for real execution time (including computation and storage accesses). This way assumptions about the underlying implementation, runtime environment, and hardware are kept to a minimum. Further, we define *sequential gas* as the highest cumulative gas cost of any sequential execution in a parallel schedule.

3.2   Decentralized Finance Smart Contracts

DeFi offers many financial services from traditional finance. Instead of relying on intermediaries, DeFi utilizes smart contracts. We elaborate on the functionality of some of DeFi's most important smart contracts in the following.

ERC-20 Tokens are smart contracts that implement fungible tokens, i.e., they can represent anything that can be owned and exchanged in integer quantities, and adhere to a specific interface standard, the ERC-20 (Ethereum Request for Comments 20) [14]. These implement at least a given set of nine functions, including `transfer` (transferring an amount of tokens from the callers address to a given address) and `balanceOf` (getting token balance of a given address).

Routers are implemented by DEXs as a central frontend to their trading interfaces. These routers are stateless, they simply specify via which *liquidity pools*, trading venues for ERC-20 tokens, trades are routed. The router makes the calls to the liquidity pools according to a pre-defined route.

4   Data Collection

We run an Erigon client [25] to collect Ethereum blockchain data. In particular, we query trace data for the whole blockchain history to better understand the parallelizability of the Ethereum mainnet workload, as well as trends over time. Trace data provides us with the internal calls executed by each transaction. In the following evaluation, we look at historical data by sampling 65 blocks per day at random over the whole history of Ethereum's mainnet blockchain. With the historical analysis, we can observe long-term trends in Ethereum's workload and parallelizability thereof. Additionally, we also look at recent data in more detail by considering every single block over the three-month period from 1 June 2022 through 31 August 2022. Through the recent data, we hope to get an accurate view of the current state of parallelizability on the Ethereum blockchain.

5   Ethereum Mainnet Workload

In the following, we consider changes in the Ethereum mainnet workload over time. In Fig. 1a, we compute and plot the average number of transactions of the blocks in our data set each month along with the 95% confidence interval. Alongside this, we also show the Ether price.

While the number of transactions per block is initially only small, i.e., less than ten transactions, we notice a first significant rise in the number of transactions per block starting in early 2017 and peaking in late 2017 at around 200 transactions per block. During this time, there were unprecedented levels of speculation surrounding cryptocurrencies; this hype likely drove the rapid increase in the Ether price and the number of transactions on the Ethereum mainnet. The market's subsequent cool-down is reflected in a transaction number decrease to around 100 per block and a sharp Ether price decrease. In fact, until the end of

2019, the number of transactions per block and the Ether price are highly correlated, i.e., the Pearson correlation coefficient is 0.77. Later, another increase in the average transaction number occurred in 2020 during the DeFi and the subsequent NFT boom. Since then, the average number of transactions per block was stable at around 200, and the average number of transactions did not significantly surpass the previous peak. With the rise of DeFi and NFTs, the correlation between the number of transactions and the Ether price also decreased, i.e., the Pearson correlation coefficient drops to 0.60 from 2020 onward.

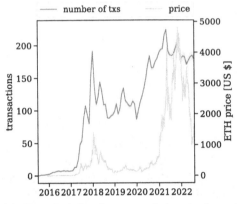
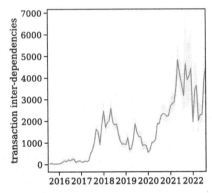

(a) Historical development of the number of transactions per block on Ethereum mainnet and the Ether price.

(b) Historical development of the number of transaction interdependencies per block.

Fig. 1. Visualization of the average number of transactions per block (cf. Fig. 1a) and the average number of transaction interdependencies per block (cf. Fig. 1b). We randomly sample 65 blocks per day and plot the daily average along with the 95% confidence interval.

We further plot the number of transaction interdependencies in Fig. 1b, i.e., the number of transaction pairs that access the same smart contract. While the impact of DeFi and NFT marketplaces on the number of transactions does not significantly surpass previous levels, this does not hold for the number of transaction interdependencies. Notice that there were, on average, around 2000 transaction interdependencies per block during the initial peak. However, the increased usage of smart contracts starting from 2020 also increased the average number of transaction interdependencies per block to 5000 at its peak and never significantly dropped afterward. Note that these interdependencies are largely created by a few core DeFi smart contracts, i.e., popular ERC-20 tokens, DEX routers, and NFT marketplaces. Thus, the widespread adoption of these smart contracts presents a significant challenge to the parallelization of Ethereum transactions.

6   Transaction Graph Representation

To explore trends in parallelization potential we consider a graph representation of the transaction data. There are two graph representations commonly utilized for Ethereum transaction data: *address-based* and *transaction-based*. We provide a definition for the address-based graph in Definition 1 and visualize an example in Fig. 2a. Observe that transaction tx_3 involves four addresses, $D \to C \to A \to B$, while tx_2 only involves two addresses, $B \to C$.

Definition 1 [Address-based Graph ($AG_{n,m}$)]. *The address-based graph for blocks $n, \ldots, m$, $n \leq m$, is represented as $AG_{n,m}(V, E, \{\omega_e\}_{e \in E})$. Here, V is the graph's set of vertices, each $v \in V$ is an address and V is the set of all addresses that appeared in blocks $n, \ldots, m$, i.e., were the sender or receiver of one of the (internal) calls of one of the block's transactions. E is the graph's set of edges, each edge $e = (v, u)$ shows a call of contract u by contract v in blocks $n, \ldots, m$. The weight of edge e, ω_e, is given by the amount of gas utilized by the corresponding internal call.*

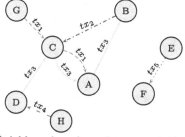
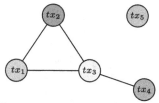

(a) Address-based graph representation of a sample set of Ethereum transactions, where vertices are addresses (contracts or wallets) and edges are calls. The color and style of an edge indicates which transaction the call belongs to.

(b) Transaction-based graph representation of a sample set of Ethereum transactions, where vertices are transactions and the edges indicate dependency between two transactions. Transactions that interact with the same address are dependent.

Fig. 2. Two types of graph representations of the same sample set of five Ethereum transactions. The edge colors indicate belonging to a transaction in the address-based graph representation (cf. Fig. 2a), the transaction-based graph representation has the same transaction set as vertices.

In Definition 2, we define the transaction-based graph and draw the corresponding example in Fig. 2b. Note that the address-based representation induces the transaction-based representation. In the transaction-based graph, neighboring transactions cannot safely be executed in parallel. Therefore, in the example shown in Fig. 2b, transaction tx_4 cannot be executed while tx_3 executes as they both interact with address D (cf. Fig. 2a). Cliques in the transaction-based representation indicate that all transactions in the clique have to be executed sequentially. Thus, the execution of transactions tx_1, tx_2 and tx_3 cannot be parallelized. In the following, we will largely consider the address-based representation, but will also draw unique insights from the transaction-based representation, i.e., calculate the graph's biggest clique to explore the limits of parallelization.

Definition 2 [Transaction-based Graph ($\mathbf{TG}_{n,m}$)]. *The transaction-based graph for blocks $n, \ldots, m$, $n \leq m$, is represented as $TG_{n,m}(V, E, \{\omega_v\}_{v \in V})$. Here, V is the graph's set of vertices, each $v \in V$ is a transaction and V is the set of all transactions that appeared in blocks $n, \ldots, m$. The weight of a vertex v, ω_v, is the amount of gas utilized by transaction v. E is the graph's set of edges, each edge $e = \{v, u\}$ shows a dependency between transaction v and u in blocks $n, \ldots, m$. A dependency is induced when the two transactions interact with the same address, i.e., the address appears as sender or receiver of an (internal) call for each of the two transactions.*

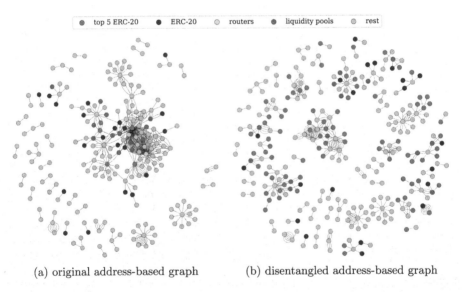

(a) original address-based graph   (b) disentangled address-based graph

Fig. 3. Address-based visualisation of block 15,348,042 (mined 15 August 2022). Figure 3a shows the original graph, while Fig. 3b visualizes a disentangled version of the graph (cf. Section 6.1). In both graphs, we highlight some core DeFi smart contracts, namely, ERC-20 tokens, DEX routers, and DEX liquidity pools. Note that the biggest connected component of the disentangled graph is significantly smaller than that of the original graph.

In Fig. 3a we visualize the address interactions of block 15,348,042 (mined 15 August 2022) and highlight some core DeFi smart contracts. The pink vertices are the top five ERC-20 tokens (WETH, USDC, USDT, DAI, and LINK)

in terms of the number of transfers, while the purple vertices are the remaining ERC-20 token addresses that appeared in block 15,348,042. We highlight the following DEX routers in yellow: Uniswap V2, Uniswap V3, SushiSwap, and 1inch, and utilize blue to flag the Uniswap V2, Uniswap V3, SushiSwap, and Curve liquidity pools. Notice that the majority of the block builds a single connected component and that the vast majority of the labeled DeFi contracts are part of this connected component. With some, mainly the top 5 ERC-20 and the DEX routers, being central in this connected component and thereby contributing greatly to the dependencies between the different transactions in a block.

6.1 Disentangled Transaction Graph Representation

Observing the persistently high degree (in the address-based transaction graph) of these DeFi contracts across the majority of the blocks since the rise of DeFi, we noticed that many of the dependencies introduced by these smart contracts, which are a central part of the DeFi ecosystem, are by no means essential. Especially the apparent dependencies introduced by ERC-20 token contracts and DEX routers in the smart contract level, would not manifest in the storage key level. These two examples of non-essential dependencies are relatively easy to spot by validators as we outline in the following.

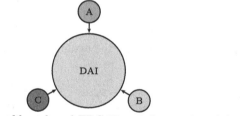 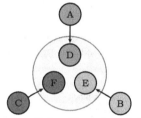

(a) address-based ERC-20 transfer graph   (b) disentangled address-based ERC-20 transfer graph

Fig. 4. Address-based graph representation of three transfers of DAI, an ERC-20 token, between the following wallets: address A to address D, address B to address E, and address C to address F. In Fig. 4a we show the actual address-based representation. Observe that the three transfers appear dependent on each other. In Fig. 4b we show how we disentangle the graph to avoid this dependency.

For example, consider three transfers of DAI, an ERC-20 token, between the following addresses: address A to address D, address B to address E, and address C to address F. As DAI is not the Ethereum blockchain's native currency, we only observe calls from the DAI senders to the DAI smart contract, which keeps track of fungible DAI tokens (cf. Fig. 4a). Thus, the three transfers appear dependent, which would not be the case for three equivalent ETH transfers. Therefore, we disentangled the transaction graph representation in Fig. 4b.

Instead of having the transaction's sender call the token contract, we pretend that they call the memory location of the receiver in the DAI smart contract. In addition to making these adjustments for the ERC-20 `transfer` function, we also make respective adjustments for the following ERC-20 contract functions: `balanceOf`, `transferFrom`, `approve`, and `allowance`. Note that we only perform this disentanglement for the top five ERC-20 tokens: WETH, USDC, USDT, DAI, and LINK. These five ERC-20 tokens are the five largest in terms of the number of transfers and together account for 34% of all ERC-20 transfers. Further, we choose to restrict ourselves to this small number of ERC-20 tokens to show: (1) their impact on the connectedness of a block's transactions and (2) ensure that the tokens do not have any unexpected behavior, e.g., transferring a proportion to a third party [12].

DEX routers are also involved in many transactions and, thereby, lead to increased connectedness in the transaction graph. As the DEX routers themselves are stateless and only perform calls to the indicated liquidity pools on the user's behalf, the dependencies in the smart contract level are therefore not necessary. Thus, we remove routers from the transaction graph. In particular, we re-route all the router edges to the sender of the respective transaction. In the later analysis, we perform this disentanglement for the routers of the following DEXs: Uniswap V2, Uniswap V3, SushiSwap, and 1inch.

7   Parallelizability

In the following exploration of Ethereum's transaction graphs, we quantify the limited parallelization potential. In Sect. 7.1, we discuss the evolution over time

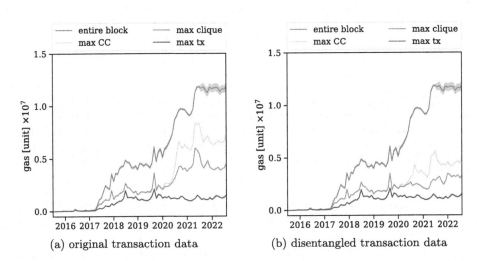

(a) original transaction data   (b) disentangled transaction data

Fig. 5. We plot the gas used by: (1) the entire block, (2) the block's heaviest connected component (CC), (3) the block's heaviest clique, and (4) the block's heaviest transaction. Fig. 5a analyzes the original transaction data and Fig. 5b the disentangled transaction data. Note that we plot the monthly average along with the 95% confidence interval from randomly sampling 65 blocks per day.

– cementing the impact of DeFi and NFTs – and, in Sect. 7.2, the current state of parallelization potential on the Ethereum mainnet. We define *parallelizability* of a block as the highest speedup factor (total gas used by the block divided by sequential gas of a schedule) that can be achieved. For our analysis, we look at specific schedules as well as graph metrics, which serve as upper and lower bounds on the parallelizability under our definition of conflicts.

7.1 Parallelizability over Time

In the following, we analyze the parallelization potential on Ethereum's mainnet by considering the connectedness of the transaction graphs. We randomly sample 65 blocks per day over the entire blockchain history up until the last block on 31 August 2022 – allowing us to observe the trends over time.

The adoption of DeFi and NFT marketplaces is clearly visible when looking at trends over time in gas usage, a proxy for the execution time. In Fig. 5a, we plot the amount of gas per block in blue. Notice the sharp increase starting in 2020 with the rise of DeFi. Whereas these new applications did not increase the number of transactions to unprecedented levels, they caused the amount of gas per block to skyrocket due to the increasing complexity of transactions.

To provide an enhanced understanding of the parallelizability of these increasingly heavy blocks, we also plot the size of the heaviest connected component, drawn in yellow, and the size of the heaviest clique, shown in pink, in Fig. 5a. Note that we measure the weight of a connected component or clique by the total amount of gas used by its transactions. Thereby, these weights indicate the time required to execute the contained transactions.

Connected components are equivalent in the address-based and transaction-based graph representations. Across both views, the weight of the heaviest connected component offers a lower bound for the parallelization potential of a block's execution. Any schedule that runs as many transactions as possible in parallel, i.e., in each time step executes a maximal independent set of transactions, will not exceed the time required to execute the heaviest connected component sequentially. We want to note that to obtain the dependencies between transactions, one has to have access to a statically provided access list or first execute all transactions. However, this is done only once by the validator. Once the block was executed, a parallel schedule could be made available to everyone else for validation. Further, we utilize the transaction-based graph representation to find the heaviest clique. For this, there is no direct analogue in the address-based graph. The heaviest clique specifies an upper bound for the parallelization potential of a block's execution. Any schedule must handle all transactions in a clique sequentially – assuming atomic transaction execution. We, in fact, ran a simple list scheduling algorithm to find a schedule. It generates a partial ordering and always allows execution of a maximal independent set in parallel. We find that, while the schedule occasionally requires longer to execute than the heaviest clique would, the relative error is negligible (cf. Appendix A). Thus, the upper bound of the parallelization potential is almost achievable with a simple schedule. Note that our transaction graph might overestimate dependencies as we are coming from the smart contract level and not the storage key level.

Looking at our data, we observe that the heaviest connected component currently makes up more than half of the block (cf. Fig. 5a). Further, the difference between the average heaviest connected component and the average heaviest clique has grown since the popularization of DeFi in 2020. This could be explained by interactions between the different protocols and smart contracts of the DeFi ecosystems. Since the rise of DeFi, the transactions in the heaviest connected component tend to interact with popular ERC-20 tokens, DEX liquidity pools, and lending protocols. However, mostly those that interact with the same smart contract are in a clique. We note that the largest clique typically consists of those transactions that interact with WETH, i.e., the most popular ERC-20 token (in terms of the number of transfers).

As previously stated, transactions interacting with WETH generally form the heaviest clique in the original transaction data. However, as we show in Sect. 6.1, the apparent dependencies in the smart contract level view are simply a consequence of implementing ERC-20 tokens as smart contracts as opposed to native tokens. To obtain a more accurate picture, we perform the previously outlined disentanglement, we observe a significant reduction in both the size of the heaviest connected component and clique (cf. Fig. 5b) since the adoption of DeFi. In fact, from 1 July 2020 to 31 August 2022, the disentanglement decreased the size of the heaviest connected component by a factor of 1.78 on average. Further, the size of the heaviest clique decreased by a factor of 1.88 on average.

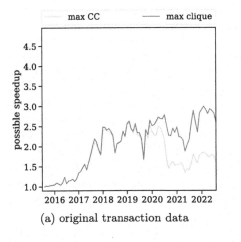
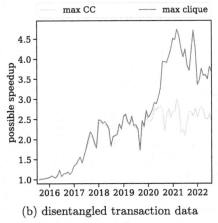

(a) original transaction data   (b) disentangled transaction data

Fig. 6. We visualize the achievable execution speedup (aggregated monthly) through parallelization for the original transaction data (cf. Fig. 6a) and the disentangled transaction data (cf. Fig. 6b). We obtain the lower bound for the parallelization potential through the identification of the heaviest connected component and the upper bound from the heaviest clique. Note both the heaviest connected component and clique are weighted by gas.

We also plot the size, in terms of gas used, of the heaviest transaction per block in both Fig. 5a and Fig. 5b.[2] The size of the heaviest transaction in a block indicates a further, looser upper bound for the parallelization potential that disregards any dependencies between transactions. By neglecting all dependencies, we automatically omit any nonessential dependencies. This looser upper bound thus only assumes that transactions must execute atomically. However, we find that, on average, the heaviest transactions are a significant proportion of the entire block – a ninth on average over the entire history. Thus, parallelization is not only limited by the ever-increasing size of the heaviest clique but is similarly bounded by individual large transactions.

We plot the lower and (realistic) upper bound for the achievable speedup in Fig. 6. In Fig. 6a, we show these bounds for the original transaction data, and in Fig. 6b, we show the same bounds for the disentangled transaction data. Similar to our previous observations, the lower (given by the size of the heaviest connected component) and the upper bound (given by the size of the heaviest clique) of the realistically achievable speedup are close to each other up until the rise of DeFi in 2020. Further, we observe the performed disentanglement also only shows its effects from 2020 onward, as it targets DeFi smart contracts. From 2020, we notice an increase in the difference between the lower and upper bound of the achievable speedup. Further, in the original transaction data, we

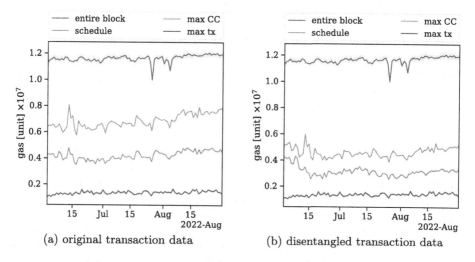

(a) original transaction data   (b) disentangled transaction data

Fig. 7. We plot the gas used by: (1) the entire block, (2) the block's heaviest connected component (CC), (3) our naive schedule (sequentially), and (4) the block's heaviest transaction. Fig. 7a analyzes the original transaction data and Fig. 7b the disentangled transaction data. Note that we plot the daily average along with the 95% confidence interval. Further, we use the sequential gas of our schedule as a proxy for the size of the heaviest clique.

---

[2] Note that the disentanglement does not impact the size of the heaviest transaction, and neither the total gas of a block.

observe that both the lower and the upper bound for the realistically achievable speedup decrease once DeFi becomes adopted (cf. Fig. 6a). In the disentangled transaction data, on the other hand, we notice that the lower bound for the possible speedup does not decrease after the introduction of DeFi, but instead remains more or less constant (cf. Fig. 6b). It is even more remarkable that the upper bound for the realistically achievable speedup even increases after the introduction of DeFi for the disentangled transaction data. We presume this stems from the increasing number of transactions in the same period (cf. Fig. 1a). Further, it is likely impacted by most DeFi transactions being dependent on each other over a given number of hops in the graph representation but not necessarily being all in one clique.

7.2   Current Limits of Parallelizability

To better gauge the current limits of parallelizability, we expand on the previous analysis by analyzing all blocks from 1 June 2022 to 31 August 2022 – allowing us to obtain a complete picture of the current state of the Ethereum mainnet. In Fig. 7, we plot the amount of gas used by: (1) the entire block, (2) the block's heaviest connected component, (3) our schedule (sequentially), and (4) the block's heaviest transactions. Note that we only plot the sequential gas used by our schedule and not the heaviest clique, as finding the heaviest clique is time intensive. Our analysis in Appendix A shows that our schedule almost reaches the same parallelization potential.

When examining Fig. 7, we notice that there are few fluctuations in both the daily mean size of the blocks and the daily mean size of the heaviest transactions. We only observe two collapses, of around 10%, in the mean size of the entire block at the end of July and the beginning of August. When looking at the daily average size of the heaviest connected component and the daily average amount of sequential gas used by our schedule in the original transaction data (cf Fig. 7a), a similar picture paints itself. In general, both averages make up approximately one-half (connected component) and one-third (schedule) of the block size on average. There is one peak in the average gas used by the heaviest connected component and the schedule around 15 June 2022 that we do not observe in the block size. The daily price movements of Ether were very high during this time (cf. Appendix C, Fig. 12b) due to the anticipation of and the release of the CPI data [39]. As a consequence, the Ether trading volume on DEXs like Uniswap V3 experienced a rapid increase [38], which we presume lead to an increased size of both the heaviest connected component and clique in relation to the block size. We want to point out that, while the 95% confidence interval is tight around the daily mean for all four graphs, the fluctuations of values for all four graph measures are substantial as shown in Appendix B (cf. Fig. 11). For instance, shortly around the time at which we observe the peak in gas usage, the 99th percentile of the heaviest transaction reaches almost the 99th percentile of the block size. Thus, there are some blocks in which a single transaction makes up almost the entire block – allowing for little to no parallelization in those blocks. Still, we observe that the daily average of gas usage by the heaviest connected component and by the heaviest clique, for which we use our schedule as a proxy, make up a relatively stable proportion of the block in the recent (original) transaction data.

Turning to the disentangled transaction data (cf. Fig. 7b), we notice a stable reduction in the daily average of the gas used by the heaviest connected components (by a factor of 1.6) and the sequential gas used by the schedule (by a factor of 1.5). It is most remarkable that the reduction is less significant in early June than in the remaining data set. We presume that this is a consequence of the significant price drop of Ether in the same period (cf. Fig. 12a), which likely led to exceptional DeFi usage patterns that further interconnected the workload. In the remaining data set, the reduction achieved by the disentanglement is very stable, but the achievable speedup still only reaches around a factor four (cf. Appendix B, Fig. 10).

Finally, in order to simulate higher transaction throughput, we consider batches of ten consecutive blocks and explore the connectedness of the corresponding transaction graphs (cf. Fig. 8). Even with this (rather exaggerated) simulated increase in block size, the sequential gas of our schedule increases proportionally, thus not changing this upper bound for the realistically achievable speedup. On the other hand, the lower bound (indicated by the heaviest connected component) even becomes much looser. This suggests that, when merging blocks, the largest cliques of all blocks merge into one, whereas connected components are even merged from within the same block. This is in line with our analysis that the heaviest cliques are always induced by the same few contracts – indicating that increasing block size does not improve concurrency potential.

8   Discussion and Conclusion

Our work quantifies the parallelizability of the Ethereum mainnet workload. We find that currently, the level of concurrency is very limited. Thus, it does not suffice to only devote efforts to finding ways to best exploit the existing potential for concurrency. Instead, we believe that part of the focus must be shifted towards ensuring that the workload is parallelizable in the first place. Concretely, we believe that the following three areas must be targeted to enable the existing concurrency mechanisms to achieve much higher speedups.

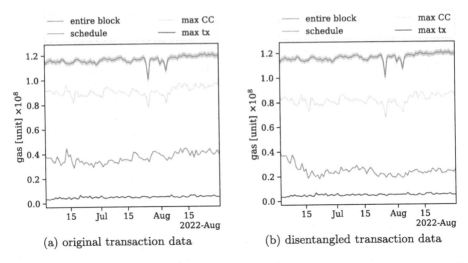

(a) original transaction data   (b) disentangled transaction data

Fig. 8. We plot the gas used by: (1) 10 consecutive blocks, (2) their heaviest connected component (CC), (3) our naive schedule (sequentially), and (4) their heaviest transaction. Figure 8a analyzes the original transaction data and Fig. 8b the disentangled transaction data. Note that we plot the daily average along with the 95% confidence interval.

Investigate dependencies. As we outline, some of DeFi's core smart contracts appear in many transactions. Thus, we believe that transaction dependencies must be investigated on a more fine-grained basis, for example at the storage key level. Furthermore, smart contracts could be redesigned to avoid unnecessary dependencies in the transaction graph.

Incentivize "simple" transactions. The heaviest transaction in a block currently makes up around one-tenth of the average block size. Thus, these individual transactions present a limit on the parallelization potential. We therefore believe that the blockchain should discourage such frequent heavy transactions and instead encourage simple transactions. One possible approach would be charging for computation superlinearly.

Increase predictability of dependencies. The incredibly low usage of the access list, indicates that it is currently not viable for transaction senders to provide the addresses and storage keys their transaction will touch. Predictability of dependencies would take care of this situation and would allow for increased parallelization during execution.

Only once the workload on the Ethereum mainnet is truly parallelizable will the speedup suffice to make the 100,000 transactions per second [7] stated by the Ethereum Foundation achievable.

Appendix

See the full version of the paper at https://fc23.ifca.ai/preproceedings/136.pdf.

References

1. Amiri, M.J., Agrawal, D., El Abbadi, A.: Parblockchain: leveraging transaction parallelism in permissioned blockchain systems. In: 2019 IEEE 39th International Conference on Distributed Computing Systems (ICDCS), pp. 1337–1347. IEEE (2019)
2. Anjana, P.S., Kumari, S., Peri, S., Rathor, S., Somani, A.: Optsmart: a space efficient optimistic concurrent execution of smart contracts. Distributed and Parallel Databases, pp. 1–53 (2022)
3. Avarikioti, G., Kokoris-Kogias, E., Wattenhofer, R.: Divide and scale: formalization of distributed ledger sharding protocols. arXiv preprint arXiv:1910.10434 (2019)
4. Bai, Q., Zhang, C., Xu, Y., Chen, X., Wang, X.: Evolution of ethereum: a temporal graph perspective. arXiv preprint arXiv:2001.05251 (2020)
5. Buterin, V., Swende, M.: Eip-2929: gas cost increases for state access opcodes (2022). http://eips.ethereum.org/EIPS/eip-2929
6. Buterin, V., Swende, M.: Eip-2930: Optional access lists (2022). http://eips.ethereum.org/EIPS/eip-2930
7. Cavicchioli, M.: Ethereum will reach 100,000 transactions per second (2022). http://en.cryptonomist.ch/2022/07/22/ethereum-reach-100000-transactions-second/
8. Chen, T., et al.: Dataether: data exploration framework for ethereum. In: 2019 IEEE 39th International Conference on Distributed Computing Systems (ICDCS), pp. 1369–1380. IEEE (2019)
9. Chen, Y., Guo, Z., Li, R., Chen, S., Zhou, L., Zhou, Y., Zhang, X.: Forerunner: constraint-based speculative transaction execution for ethereum. In: Proceedings of the ACM SIGOPS 28th Symposium on Operating Systems Principles, pp. 570–587 (2021)
10. Dang, H., Dinh, T.T.A., Loghin, D., Chang, E.C., Lin, Q., Ooi, B.C.: Towards scaling blockchain systems via sharding. In: Proceedings of the 2019 International Conference on Management of Data, pp. 123–140 (2019)
11. Decker, C., Wattenhofer, R.: A fast and scalable payment network with bitcoin duplex micropayment channels. In: 17th International Symposium on Stabilization, Safety, and Security of Distributed Systems (SSS), Edmonton, Canada (August 2015)
12. DeFi Cartel: Salmonella (2022). http://github.com/Defi-Cartel/salmonella
13. Dickerson, T., Gazzillo, P., Herlihy, M., Koskinen, E.: Adding concurrency to smart contracts. In: Proceedings of the ACM Symposium on Principles of Distributed Computing, pp. 303–312 (2017)
14. Ethereum Foundation: ERC-20 token standard (2022). http://ethereum.org/en/developers/docs/standards/tokens/erc-20/
15. Ethereum Foundation: Gas and fees (2022). http://ethereum.org/en/developers/docs/gas
16. Ethereum Foundation: The merge (2022). http://ethereum.org/en/upgrades/merge/

17. Ethereum Foundation: Sharding (2022). http://ethereum.org/en/upgrades/sharding/
18. Ferretti, S., D'Angelo, G.: On the ethereum blockchain structure: a complex networks theory perspective. Conc. Comput. Practice Exper. **32**(12), e5493 (2020)
19. Gelashvili, R., et al.: Block-stm: scaling blockchain execution by turning ordering curse to a performance blessing. arXiv preprint arXiv:2203.06871 (2022)
20. Guo, D., Dong, J., Wang, K.: Graph structure and statistical properties of ethereum transaction relationships. Inf. Sci. **492**, 58–71 (2019)
21. Han, R., Yu, J., Zhang, R.: Analysing and improving shard allocation protocols for sharded blockchains. Cryptology ePrint Archive (2020)
22. He, N., et al.: Understanding the evolution of blockchain ecosystems: a longitudinal measurement study of bitcoin, ethereum, and eosio. arXiv preprint arXiv:2110.07534 (2021)
23. Kalodner, H., Goldfeder, S., Chen, X., Weinberg, S.M., Felten, E.W.: Arbitrum: scalable, private smart contracts. In: 27th USENIX Security Symposium (USENIX Security 2018), pp. 1353–1370 (2018)
24. Kondor, D., Pósfai, M., Csabai, I., Vattay, G.: Do the rich get richer? an empirical analysis of the bitcoin transaction network. PLoS ONE **9**(2), e86197 (2014)
25. ledgerwatch: Erigon (2022). http://github.com/ledgerwatch/erigon
26. Lin, D., Chen, J., Wu, J., Zheng, Z.: Evolution of ethereum transaction relationships: toward understanding global driving factors from microscopic patterns. IEEE Trans. Comput. Social Syst. **9**(2), 559–570 (2021)
27. Lin, D., Wu, J., Yuan, Q., Zheng, Z.: Modeling and understanding ethereum transaction records via a complex network approach. IEEE Trans. Circuits Syst. II Express Briefs **67**(11), 2737–2741 (2020)
28. Luu, L., Narayanan, V., Zheng, C., Baweja, K., Gilbert, S., Saxena, P.: A secure sharding protocol for open blockchains. In: Proceedings of the 2016 ACM SIGSAC Conference on Computer and Communications Security, pp. 17–30 (2016)
29. Motamed, A.P., Bahrak, B.: Quantitative analysis of cryptocurrencies transaction graph. Appli. Netw. Sci. **4**(1), 1–21 (2019)
30. Murgia, M., Galletta, L., Bartoletti, M.: A theory of transaction parallelism in blockchains. Logical Methods Comput. Sci. **17** (2021)
31. Nakamoto, S.: Bitcoin: a peer-to-peer electronic cash system. Decentralized Bus. Rev., 21260 (2008)
32. Optimism Foundation: Optimism (2022). http://www.optimism.io
33. Pîrlea, G., Kumar, A., Sergey, I.: Practical smart contract sharding with ownership and commutativity analysis. In: Proceedings of the 42nd ACM SIGPLAN International Conference on Programming Language Design and Implementation, pp. 1327–1341 (2021)
34. Poon, J., Dryja, T.: The bitcoin lightning network: scalable off-chain instant payments (2016)
35. Ron, D., Shamir, A.: Quantitative analysis of the full bitcoin transaction graph. In: Sadeghi, A.-R. (ed.) FC 2013. LNCS, vol. 7859, pp. 6–24. Springer, Heidelberg (2013). https://doi.org/10.1007/978-3-642-39884-1_2
36. Saraph, V., Herlihy, M.: An empirical study of speculative concurrency in ethereum smart contracts. arXiv preprint arXiv:1901.01376 (2019)
37. Sergey, I., Hobor, A.: A concurrent perspective on smart contracts. In: Brenner, M., et al. (eds.) FC 2017. LNCS, vol. 10323, pp. 478–493. Springer, Cham (2017). https://doi.org/10.1007/978-3-319-70278-0_30
38. Uniswap Labs: Ether (2022). http://info.uniswap.org/#/tokens/0xc02aaa39b223fe8d0a0e5c4f27ead9083c756cc2

39. U.S. Bureau of Labor Statistics: Schedule of releases for the consumer price index (2022). http://www.bls.gov/schedule/news_release/cpi.htm
40. Wang, G., Shi, Z.J., Nixon, M., Han, S.: SoK: sharding on blockchain. In: Proceedings of the 1st ACM Conference on Advances in Financial Technologies, pp. 41–61 (2019)
41. Wood, G., et al.: Ethereum: A secure decentralised generalised transaction ledger. Ethereum Project Yellow Paper **151**(2014), 1–32 (2014)
42. Xie, Y., Jin, J., Zhang, J., Yu, S., Xuan, Q.: Temporal-amount snapshot multigraph for ethereum transaction tracking. In: Dai, H.-N., Liu, X., Luo, D.X., Xiao, J., Chen, X. (eds.) BlockSys 2021. CCIS, vol. 1490, pp. 133–146. Springer, Singapore (2021). https://doi.org/10.1007/978-981-16-7993-3_10
43. Xie, Y., et al.: Understanding ethereum transactions via network approach. In: Xuan, Q., Ruan, Z., Min, Y. (eds.) Graph Data Mining. BDM, pp. 155–176. Springer, Singapore (2021). https://doi.org/10.1007/978-981-16-2609-8_7
44. Zamani, M., Movahedi, M., Raykova, M.: Rapidchain: scaling blockchain via full sharding. In: Proceedings of the 2018 ACM SIGSAC Conference on Computer and Communications Security, pp. 931–948 (2018)
45. Zanelatto Gavião Mascarenhas, J., Ziviani, A., Wehmuth, K., Vieira, A.B.: On the transaction dynamics of the ethereum-based cryptocurrency. J. Complex Netw. **8**(4), cnaa042 (2020)
46. Zhang, A., Zhang, K.: Enabling concurrency on smart contracts using multiversion ordering. In: Cai, Y., Ishikawa, Y., Xu, J. (eds.) APWeb-WAIM 2018. LNCS, vol. 10988, pp. 425–439. Springer, Cham (2018). https://doi.org/10.1007/978-3-319-96893-3_32
47. Zhao, L., Sen Gupta, S., Khan, A., Luo, R.: Temporal analysis of the entire ethereum blockchain network. In: Proceedings of the Web Conference 2021, pp. 2258–2269 (2021)

Cryptoeconomic Security for Data Availability Committees

Ertem Nusret Tas[ID] and Dan Boneh[✉][ID]

Stanford University, Stanford, USA
{nusret,dabo}@stanford.edu

Abstract. Layer 2 systems have received increasing attention due to their potential to scale the throughput of L1 blockchains. To avoid the cost of putting data on chain, these systems increasingly turn to off-chain data availability solutions such as data availability committees (DACs). However, placing trust on DACs conflicts with the goal of obtaining an L2 architecture whose security relies solely on the L1 chain. To eliminate such trust assumptions, we propose a DAC protocol that provides financial incentives to deter the DAC nodes from adversarial behavior such as withholding data upon request. We then analyze the interaction of rational DAC nodes and clients as a dynamic game, with a Byzantine adversary that can corrupt and bribe the participants. We also define a notion of optimality for the DAC protocols, inspired by fairness and economic feasibility. Our main result shows that our protocol is optimal and guarantees security with the highest possible probability under reasonable assumptions on the adversary.

1 Introduction

Layer 2 systems [19,21,30] are an important approach to scaling the throughput of Layer 1 blockchains such as Ethereum. One of the key challenges in securing an L2 system is *data availability*: how to ensure that the state of the L2 system is always available and can be reconstructed when needed? This data is needed to safely restart the L2 system after a failure, and for basic operations such as deposits and withdrawals. The data availability problem comes up in other contexts as well, such as in decentralized storage systems [22,25,29].

There are three general approaches to data availability in L2 systems:

- *On-chain data:* Rollup systems [21] store all transaction data on a Layer 1 *parent* chain, such as Ethereum. These systems rely on the security of the L1 nodes to ensure that the data is always available.
- *Off-chain data stored by a Data Availability Committee (DAC):* Other systems such as StarkEx [4], zkPorter [5] and EigenLayr [1] use a DAC to store data off-chain across a number of trusted nodes [26]. While the DAC provides a gas-efficient alternative to on-chain data, these systems rely on the correct operation of the DAC nodes to ensure that the data remains available.

© International Financial Cryptography Association 2024
F. Baldimtsi and C. Cachin (Eds.): FC 2023, LNCS 13951, pp. 310–326, 2024.
https://doi.org/10.1007/978-3-031-47751-5_18

– *Off-chain data with (repeated) Data Availability Sampling (Celestium* [27]*):*
An enhancement to DACs employs data availability sampling [7,11,17,31] so
that light clients, such as rollup users, can identify unavailable blocks created by the DAC without attempting to download the full block. This approach is being used by modular blockchains such as Celestia [6] and Polygon
Avail [24] that specialize in preserving other chains' data. However, DAS does
not remove the trust assumption placed on the DAC nodes for data availability, since it requires DAC members to reply to DAS queries for data recovery.
DAS also cannot ensure that data remains permanently available [12].

Providing a standalone data availability service, such as Celestia and others,
reflects a general trend towards modularity in the design of blockchains.

In this paper, we focus on the security of Data Availability Committees
(DAC), namely the last two bullets on the previous page. A DAC consists of
multiple DAC members, which we call *nodes*, that store copies of the data that
should be made available (*e.g.*, data sent by the rollup sequencer). These nodes
are expected to provide the data to querying clients in a timely manner. Since
malicious DAC members can withhold the data, DACs typically replicate the
data on each DAC node for fault tolerance. Thus, as long as one member is
honest, rollup clients would receive the data upon request. Although the storage
requirement of the DAC scales linearly in the number of nodes due to replication, this redundancy can be reduced through the use of erasure codes and
polynomial commitments. For instance, the semi-AVID-PR scheme [23] uses linear erasure-correcting codes and homomorphic vector commitments to guarantee
data availability as long as over $2/3$ of the nodes faithfully follow the protocol.

A major drawback of DACs is the need to trust the DAC members. Consider
a compromised DAC, where the adversary can prevent the reconstruction of the
data, for example, by controlling more than $1/3$ of the DAC members. Such a
DAC can evolve the rollup state using unavailable transaction data, and withhold
this data from the rollup clients. This prevents clients from issuing transactions,
and enables the adversary to steal client funds through ransom attacks [14].
Thus, using a DAC hinders the goal of realizing a trust-minimized scaling architecture that relies solely on the security of the L1 chain for the safety and liveness
of the rollup[1]. Liveness signifies that the clients can submit new transactions to
the rollup system, and the system processes these transactions.

Data availability sampling (DAS) does not improve the liveness guarantees
over the basic DAC architecture. If the DAC is not compromised, then DAS
helps rollup clients verify that the rollup data is available without downloading
all the data from the DAC. However, if the DAC is compromised, DAS provides
no guarantees for data availability. The compromised DAC can update the rollup
state with unavailable transactions, and ignore all DAS queries from the clients.
Hence, DAS needs the trust assumption placed on the DAC members for liveness.

---

[1] Although current rollup systems typically rely on a single honest sequencer to evolve
the rollup state, as long as the rollup data is available (*e.g.*, on the L1 chain), any
rollup full node can step up to fulfill the sequencer's role if it fails.

Incentive-Based Data Availability. One way to strengthen the security of a DAC is to rely on financial incentives to deter the DAC members from adversarial behavior such as withholding data and lazy validation, where the DAC members *pretend* as if the data was stored. There are solutions such as Proofs of Custody [16] using financial disincentives (*e.g.*, slashing) to encourage the lazy DAC members to store the entrusted data. However, as withholding data is not a provable offense, it not clear how to enforce the slashing of the adversarial members' stake when they do indeed store the data, yet refuse to reveal it upon request (even if DAS is being used). Moreover, any incentive-based data availability proposal must be analyzed in the face of rational DAC members who may respond to bribes, and Byzantine adversaries who may offer bribes.

Our main contribution is a DAC protocol that introduces a *slashing* mechanism for malicious DAC nodes that withhold data. The bulk of the paper is a technical analysis of the protocol, and proves its security under certain assumptions on the adversary's power. Moreover, we show that our protocol is optimal in a rigorous sense. We define the security model and the optimality notions in Sects. 2 and 4.

We model the interactions of the DAC as a dynamic game involving multiple parties:

- DAC members, *i.e.*, **nodes**, are denoted by $\mathcal{P}_1, \ldots, \mathcal{P}_N$, where N is the number of nodes. These nodes store the data provided by an external entity.
- A **client** $\mathcal{V}$ sends a sequence of data queries to the N nodes. Every node can either respond to $\mathcal{V}$ with the requested data, or not respond. We assume the data held by the nodes is signed by the data provider, so that integrity of the response is easily verified. If a response contains incorrect data, it is treated as a non-response.
- A **contract** running on the L1 chain is used to resolve disputes and punish misbehaving DAC nodes. In particular, all N nodes are staked, and the stake is held in the contract. If the nodes do not respond to $\mathcal{V}$ with the requested data, $\mathcal{V}$ can send its query to the contract. In this case, the nodes are obliged to post their responses to the contract. If a node provably fails to do so, the contract can slash that node by confiscating part of its stake. Part of the slashed stake is given to the client as compensation and the rest is burned. The size of the per-node stake and the behavior of the contract are the key design decisions for a DAC protocol.

Nodes and clients are rational agents that seek to maximize their utilities. An adversary $\mathcal{A}$ who fully controls f corrupt nodes may try to bribe the remaining $N - f$ nodes to cause a client query to fail. This will make the requested data unrecoverable. Our goal is to design a DAC, so that under reasonable assumptions on the size of f and on the adversary's budget, every query from the client will succeed with probability at least $1 - \epsilon$, for some small ϵ.

Queries from the client model data requests needed for normal operations such as withdrawals. For instance, in a rollup system, clients might have to prove their account balances with respect to the latest state root, and they do so by presenting a Merkle proof for their account. A non-responsive DAC storing the latest state can delay withdrawals by refusing to provide these Merkle proofs. In this case, each client can post a query to the contract, and force the nodes to place the requested proof on the L1 chain. Our model for the DAC system and the incentivize mechanism enforced by the contract has applications beyond data availability, and can be used to incentivize the honest participation of nodes in any committee outside the L1 chain that provides a service (*e.g.*Decentralized Oracle Networks [9,15]). We discuss use cases for our DAC system in Sect. 2.

The DAC Protocol. Suppose every query requires at least k nodes out of N to respond either directly to the client, or to the contract, for the client to obtain an answer to its query. If no erasure coding is used and the data is replicated across all nodes, then $k = 1$, otherwise k could be bigger than 1.

The protocol proceeds in four steps:

- *step 1:* the client $\mathcal{V}$ sends its query to all DAC nodes over the network.
- *step 2:* if k or more nodes respond, then the client obtains the requested data and the protocol terminates.
- *step 3:* if by a certain timeout the client does not receive k responses, it posts its query to the contract on chain. For this purpose, the client has to send a base payment to the contract, which is needed to deter spamming clients. We discuss the choice of client payment amount in Sect. 6.
- *step 4:* all N nodes are then asked to post their responses to the query on chain. The protocol terminates once a certain timeout is reached.

It remains to describe what the contract does once the timeout is reached in step 4. Every node that does not post its response to the contract by the timeout loses part or all of its stake. The precise *slashing function* is explained in Sect. 3. Moreover, if by the timeout in step 4 the client does not obtain an answer to its query through the responses, the client is compensated by the contract using the funds obtained from the slashed nodes.

The question is how to analyze the security and performance of a contract in comparison to other contracts. In Sect. 4 we present four desirable properties that a slashing function should satisfy. Informally, these properties are:

- *Symmetry.* Motivated by fairness, the slashing function does not depend on the identities of the nodes, only on their actions.
- *No Reward.* The slashing function does not pay out any rewards to the responsive nodes. This is motivated by economic feasibility as the contract should maintain a non-negative balance, and discourage the nodes from forcing an on-chain interaction for extra payoff rather than answering over the network. (No rewards rule does not rule out flat rewards by other means.)

- *Security Under No Attack.* The slashing function ensures that the client promptly learns the correct response to its query, if the adversary does not offer any bribes. This captures a minimal notion of security.
- *Minimal Punishment.* The slashing function keeps the slashed amounts of non-responsive nodes at a minimum when the client obtains an answer to its query. Thus, when most nodes are responsive, those that fail to respond due to benign failures, *e.g.*, crash faults, are not heavily penalized.

We then define a notion of optimality for these functions:

Definition 1 (Informal). A slashing function is **optimal** with respect to a set of slashing functions $\mathcal{F}$, if the function satisfies the following two conditions: (i) upon sending its query to the contract, the client obtains an answer with the maximum probability from among all the functions in $\mathcal{F}$ given the worst adversary, and (ii) when the client obtains an answer, the function imposes the minimal punishment on non-responsive nodes from among the functions in $\mathcal{F}$.

In Sect. 4, we show that our slashing function is optimal for both *risk-neutral* and *risk-averse* nodes among the set of all functions that satisfy the four desirable properties described above. We also analyze the security of a dynamic game among a rational client and the DAC nodes. We identify the conditions under which the client obtains an answer to its query without calling the contract. The analysis of Sect. 4 is the most technical part of the paper, and is our core contribution.

Evaluation. In Sect. 5, we evaluate the real-world performance of our optimal contract. To match the number of Ethereum validators and the minimum value that can be staked as an independent validator on Ethereum, we set the total number of DAC nodes to $N = 300,000$ and the amount staked per node to 32 ETH. Then, given risk-neutral nodes, the adversary has to offer a total bribe of $\approx 3.2 \cdot 10^3$ ETH (≈ 3.9 million USD[2]) to the nodes, to reduce the security probability per query by a tiny amount, namely to reduce the probability that a client learns the answer to its query from 100% to 99.9%. To prevent clients from learning the answers over repeated queries, the adversary has to spend at least 3.9 million USD *for each query*. As our contract is optimal, no other contract can force the adversary to pay a higher bribe for the same security probability. The minimum bribe needed by the adversary to reduce the security probability increases as N or the collateral grows, or as the nodes become more risk-averse.

2 Model

Notation. We denote the security parameter by λ. We say that an event happens with negligible probability, if its probability, as a function of λ, is $o(1/\lambda^d)$

---

[2] Ethereum to USD conversion rate, 1 ETH ≈ 1231.0 USD, is the average Ethereum price on July 15, 2022 [3].

for all $d > 0$. We say that an event happens with overwhelming probability if it happens except with probability negligible in λ. If an event happens with probability $q + \text{negl}(\lambda)$ or $q - \text{negl}(\lambda)$, where q is a non-negligible constant, for simplicity, we say that the event happens with probability q. We assume that except with probability negligible in λ, the contract implements the specified slashing function correctly, the underlying cryptographic primitives are secure, and messages can be posted to the contract within bounded time. We use the shorthand $[N]$ to denote the set $\{1, 2, \ldots, N\}$.

Environment and the Adversary. Time is slotted, and the clocks of the client and nodes are synchronized[3]. Messages, *e.g.*, queries and replies, can only be sent at the beginning of a slot, and are delivered to the recipient by the end of the same slot by the environment $\mathcal{Z}$.

Adversary $\mathcal{A}$ is a probabilistic polynomial time algorithm. Before the execution starts, $\mathcal{A}$ corrupts f nodes, which are subsequently called adversarial. These nodes can deviate from the protocol arbitrarily (Byzantine faults) under $\mathcal{A}$'s control, which has access to their internal states. The remaining $N - f$ nodes and the client are utility maximizing agents and can choose any action that gives them a higher utility. In the subsequent analysis, we will assume that $\mathcal{P}_i$, $i = N - f + 1, \ldots, N$ represent the adversarial nodes, and $f \leq N - k$. Otherwise, it is impossible to guarantee the recovery of the answer to a query as the adversarial nodes can withhold their responses from the client and the contract.

Before the protocol execution starts, the adversary can also offer *bribes* to the *remaining* nodes and the client subject to constraints. It has a supply of p_0 coins, which can be distribute to any subset of the nodes as additional payoff if the nodes adopt an adversarial action during the game. Similarly, the adversary can give up to p_1 coins to the client if it adopts an adversarial action. Such an adversary is called a (p_0, p_1)-adversary. When the bribe offered to the client is irrelevant, we use the notation p_0-adversary. (p_0 and p_1 are adversary's resources that are *beyond* the f nodes corrupted by the adversary.) Upon hearing an offer, each participant can independently choose to accept or reject the bribe depending on the expected utility. Once a participant accepts the bribe, the adversary can monitor through the environment and contract if the specified action was taken. Although the action and exchange of the bribe might not happen atomically, the adversary and the nodes can ensure that no party deviates from its promise via a trusted third party, or repeated games ([28, Section 4.4]).

Actions, Payoffs, and the Game. We next describe the dynamic game played by the client and the DAC nodes. Before the game starts, the client $\mathcal{V}$ and the nodes are input a single query by the environment $\mathcal{Z}$. Given a query, each node $\mathcal{P}_i$ can instantaneously generate a response c_i, called the *clue*. We assume that the correctness of these clues can be verified by the clients and the contract[4].

---

[3] Bounded clock offsets can be captured by the network delay.

[4] For instance, correctness of the data shards in PoS Ethereum can be verified with respect to a KZG commitment on the blockchain [12, 17, 20].

The contract accepts a clue by a node if and only if it is the first correct response by the node to a query posted to the contract. It records the time slots when each query or clue was received, in a contract state. At the beginning of each slot, the participants learn about the state recorded at the end of the previous slot.

Let p_s be the amount staked by a node to function as a DAC member. It costs p_c coins for the client to send a query to the contract, and p_w coins for each node to prepare and post the corresponding clue to the contract. It is free to send a clue to the client over the network. These parameters are summarized in Table 1. We assume that each node starts the game with a baseline payoff of $C = p_s + p_w$, as it has p_s coins staked in the contract, and is assumed to have enough funds to post clues to the contract during the game[5]. The client starts the game with an initial payoff of 0.

The actions available to the client $\mathcal{V}$ and nodes $\mathcal{P}$ at any slot t are as follows:

$\mathcal{S}_r$: $\mathcal{P}$ sends a correct clue to $\mathcal{V}$ over the network at slot t.

$\mathcal{S}_q$: $\mathcal{V}$ sends a query to the contract for the first time at slot t.

$\mathcal{S}_p$: For a query, $\mathcal{P}$ sends a correct clue to the contract for the first time at t.

The notation $\neg(.)$ is used to denote the opposite of the specified action. At any time slot, a node can take an action (a, b), where $a \in \{\mathcal{S}_r, \neg\mathcal{S}_r\}$ and $b \in \{\mathcal{S}_p, \neg\mathcal{S}_p\}$. Similarly, the client can take an action from $\{\mathcal{S}_q, \neg\mathcal{S}_q\}$. Although the clients and nodes can exchange messages other than queries and clues, only the queries, clues or their absence can lead to a change in their payoffs. Since the participants play a dynamic game, the actions chosen at later slots can depend on the actions observed at the earlier ones.

The game ends, and the payoffs are realized at the beginning of slot T_{answer}. If $\mathcal{V}$ finds out the correct answer to its query through the clues, either posted to the contract or sent over the network, by slot T_{answer}, it receives a payoff of p_f coins. We set $T_{\text{answer}} = 4$ though it can be any sufficiently large constant. In our model, T_{answer} should be at least 4 to guarantee any meaningful security. The payoffs of the participants depend on the bribes p_0 and p_1, the collateral p_s, the variables p_f, p_c, p_w selected by $\mathcal{Z}$, and the contract's *slashing function*.

Utility of a participant is given as a function $U(.)$ of the payoff obtained at the end of the game. In the subsequent sections, we will first consider risk-neutral nodes with a linear utility function $U(x) = x$, where x is the net payoff at the end. We will then analyze risk-averse nodes with a strictly concave utility function of the form $U(x) = (x)^\nu$, where $\nu \in (0, 1)$. We do not consider risk-seeking nodes with strictly convex utility functions, *e.g.*, $U(x) = (x)^\nu$, $\nu > 1$, as such a function violates the law of diminishing marginal utility for the payoffs.

We will later also consider a sub-game that focuses exclusively on the interaction between the nodes and the contract. In the game, a query appears in the contract at some slot t, and the nodes choose to post clues or not at slot $t + 1$, after which the payoffs are realized. These payoffs depend on the bribe p_0, the collateral p_s, the cost p_w, and the slashing function.

---

[5] For risk-neutral nodes, the baseline is normalized to be 0.

Security. We say $T_{\mathtt{answer}}$-security is satisfied if the client receives k or more correct clues from the nodes either over the network or through the contract by the *beginning* of slot $T_{\mathtt{answer}}$ with overwhelming probability.

Application. The game above models the withdrawal of client funds from a blockchain or rollup. Each client has an account, represented as a key-value pair, and the balances of these accounts constitute the blockchain state. The hashes of the key-value pairs are organized in a vector commitment, *e.g.*, a sparse Merkle tree, with a constant size commitment, called the state root. The state data is preserved by the DAC nodes and state commitments are posted to the chain.

To prove its account balance, a client requests a witness from the nodes for the inclusion of its account within the latest state. If it does not receive a witness over the network, the client can complain on a *smart contract* by sending a query that contains the hash of the account's key-value pair. If the hash is a hiding commitment, the client can also ensure that no observer learns its balance. It can always prove its balance to a select third party by revealing the key-value pair at the pre-image of the hash, the latest state root on chain, and the witness.

Upon receiving a query, the contract expects a witness to be provided by the DAC nodes within a bounded time, *e.g.*, the chain's confirmation latency. Correctness of this witness can be verified by the contract and the client with respect to the state commitment on the chain. If the query is for an account not included in the latest state, the nodes can convince the contract of this fact via a proof of non-inclusion. If there are multiple queries, instead of sending the witness for each query, the nodes can compute a SNARK proof that verifies the inclusion of all the queried accounts within the state. Clients can then verify the inclusion of the queried accounts by checking the proof with respect to the latest state root, and the hashes of the queried accounts. Succinctness of the SNARK proof enables achieving bounded delay on the response time.

3   The Optimal Contract

A contract can reward or punish the nodes depending on whether it received clues from the nodes for a query within a timeout period. We normalize this

Table 1. Parameters in our model

Parameter	Explanation
N	Number of nodes
p_0	Total payoff the adversary can offer to the nodes
p_1	Total payoff the adversary can offer to the client
$p_{\mathtt{comp}}$	Compensation for the client if reconstruction fails
p_f	Client's payoff from a valid reply within 4 slots
p_c	Cost of sending a query to the contract
p_w	Cost of constructing and sending a clue to the contract
p_s	Collateral per node

timeout to be a single slot for all contracts[6]. Let $x_i = 1$ if the node $\mathcal{P}_i$ sends a valid clue at slot $t + 1$ in response to a query posted at some slot t, and $x_i = 0$ otherwise. We characterize a contract by a slashing function f that maps actions $\mathbf{x} = (x_1, \ldots, x_N) \in \{0, 1\}^N$ to payoffs $(f_1(\mathbf{x}), \ldots, f_N(\mathbf{x})) \in \mathbb{R}^N$ for the nodes, and the payoff $f_{\mathcal{V}}(\mathbf{x}) \in \mathbb{R}$ for the client. Since the contract cannot punish the nodes more than the staked collateral, $f_i(\mathbf{x}) \geq -p_s$ for every action $\mathbf{x} \in \{0, 1\}^N$. We will hereafter use slashing function and the contract interchangeably.

The proposed optimal contract and the associated slashing function is parameterized by a small number $\epsilon > 0$:

$$f_i(\mathbf{x}) = \begin{cases} 0 & \text{if } x_i = 1 \\ -p_s & \text{if } x_i = 0, \; \sum_{j=1}^{N} x_j < k \\ -p_w - \epsilon & \text{if } x_i = 0, \; \sum_{j=1}^{N} x_j \geq k \end{cases}$$

$$f_{\mathcal{V}}(\mathbf{x}) = \begin{cases} 0 & \text{if } \sum_{j=1}^{N} x_j \geq k \\ p_{\text{comp}} & \text{if } \sum_{j=1}^{N} x_j < k \end{cases}$$

Here, $p_{\text{comp}} < p_s, p_f$, and $p_{\text{comp}} > p_c$ to ensure that the client's net payoff stays above zero if it does not receive sufficiently many clues through the contract.

The contract burns, *i.e.*, slashes the collateral p_s put up by each node that has not sent a valid clue by the end of slot $t + 1$, if there are less than k clues. In this case, the contract also awards p_{comp} of the slashed coins to $\mathcal{V}$. Otherwise, if there are k or more clues in the contract by slot $t + 1$, it punishes the non-responsive nodes by a modest amount, namely $p_w + \epsilon$.

4 Analysis

In Sect. 4.1, we formalize the desirable properties and notions of optimality for slashing functions. In Sect. 4.2, we show that the slashing function of Sect. 3 is optimal for risk-neutral and risk-averse nodes. In Sect. 4.3, we generalize the analysis to a dynamic game with a rational client.

4.1 Contract Properties

The desirable properties for slashing functions f (Sect. 1) are formalized below:

- *A1: Symmetry.* A slashing function f is symmetric if $f(\pi(\mathbf{x})) = \pi(f(\mathbf{x}))$ for every action $\mathbf{x} \in \{0, 1\}^N$ and permutation π.
- *A2: No Reward.* A slashing function f offers no rewards if for every action $\mathbf{x} \in \{0, 1\}^N$, $f_i(\mathbf{x}) \leq 0$, $\forall i \in [N]$, and $f_{\mathcal{V}}(\mathbf{x}) + \sum_{i \in [N]} f_i(\mathbf{x}) \leq 0$.

---

[6] In a network with temporary partitions, the timeout can be increased to guarantee the timely inclusion of the messages sent to the contract.

– *A3: Security Under No Attack.* A slashing function f guarantees security under no attack if for all $(0,0)$-adversaries, it achieves T_{answer}-security with overwhelming probability in all Nash equilibria of the game.

– *A4: B-Minimal punishment.* A slashing function f offers B minimal punishment if for every action $\mathbf{x} \in \{0,1\}^N$ such that $\sum_{i=1}^{N} x_i \geq k$, we have that $f_i(\mathbf{x}) \geq -B$ for all $i \in [N]$.

Definition 2. A slashing function f is said to be **compliant** if it satisfies the axioms A1–A3, and the axiom A4 for some constant $B \in \mathbb{R}^+$.

Definition 3. A compliant slashing function f is said to be (p_0, q)-**tolerant** if for all p_0-adversaries, when a query is received by the contract at some slot t, there are k or more correct clues in the contract at slot $t + 1$, with probability at least q, in all Nash equilibria.

The value q of a (p_0, q)-tolerant contract can be interpreted as the minimum probability for security given that the client received no responses over the network and sent its query to the contract.

We next introduce two notions of optimality for the contract. A security-optimal function ensures that for any p_0, security is violated with the minimum possible probability in the equilibrium with the largest failure probability.

Definition 4. A compliant slashing function f is said to be **security-optimal** if for all $p_0 \geq 0$, there exists a $q_0 \in [0,1]$ such that f is (p_0, q_0)-tolerant, and there does not exist any compliant, (p_0, q)-tolerant function f', where $q > q_0$.

A punishment-optimal contract imposes the minimum punishment on the unresponsive nodes (*e.g.*, due to benign errors) if security was not compromised.

Definition 5. A compliant slashing function f is said to be ϵ-**punishment-optimal** if it satisfies B-minimal punishment, and no compliant slashing function f' can satisfy B'-minimal punishment for some $B' < B - \epsilon$.

Finally, we combine the two notions of optimality in a single definition:

Definition 6. A family of slashing functions f_ϵ, parameterized by ϵ, is said to be **optimal** if each member f_ϵ of the family is compliant, security-optimal and ϵ-*punishment-optimal*.

4.2   Analysis of the Optimal Contract

We prove the following theorem for risk-neutral and risk-averse nodes.

Theorem 1. *The family of slashing functions described in Sect. 3 is optimal.*

Theorem 1 follows from Theorems 2, 3, and 4. Their proofs for risk-neutral and risk-averse nodes are given in [28, Appendices A and B] respectively.

We first showing that the slashing function is compliant:

Theorem 2. *Each slashing function from Sect. 3, parameterized by $\epsilon > 0$, satisfies symmetry (A1), no reward (A2), security under no attack (A3), and $(p_w + \epsilon)$-minimal punishment (A4).*

The axioms A1, A2 and A4 follow by inspection, whereas A3 is shown by Lemma 1. Proof of Lemma 1 is given in [28, Appendices A and B] for risk-neutral and risk-averse nodes respectively.

Lemma 1. *Given the slashing function of Sect. 3, for any $(0,0)$-adversary $\mathcal{A}$, 4-security is satisfied with overwhelming probability in all Nash equilibria.*

When $p_{\text{comp}} > p_c$, the client is incentivized to send its query to the contract if it receives less than k clues over the network. Then, the nodes post their clues to the contract to avoid slashing of their stakes, and the contract ensures security with overwhelming probability.

Remark 1. If $p_{\text{comp}} \leq p_c$, for any contract that offers no rewards to the nodes, and for any $(\epsilon, 0)$-adversary where $\epsilon \geq 0$, there exists a Nash equilibrium such that 4-security is violated with overwhelming probability. Consider the action profile, where the nodes do not send their clues to the client $\mathcal{V}$ over the network, and do not post their clues to the contract. Given these actions, if $p_{\text{comp}} \leq p_c$, $\mathcal{V}$'s payoff can at most be 0, and the maximum payoff is achieved if $\mathcal{V}$ does not send a query to the contract, even when it does not receive clues over the network. In this case, the normalized payoff of each node becomes 0 as well, which is the maximum payoff attainable by any node. Hence, the nodes do not have any incentive to deviate from the action profile above, which constitutes a Nash equilibrium.

We next show that the slashing function is ϵ-punishment optimal.

Theorem 3. *Consider a slashing function that is symmetric (A1), offers no rewards (A2), and satisfies B-minimal punishment for some $B < p_w$ (A4). Then, for $k > 1$, there exists a $(0,0)$-adversary $\mathcal{A}$ and a Nash equilibrium, where 4-security is violated with non-negligible probability. Thus, no compliant slashing function can satisfy B-minimal punishment for some $B < p_w$.*

When $B < p_w$, punishment for a node that does not post its clue to the contract while the other nodes send their clues is smaller than the cost of posting the clue. This leads to a free-rider problem, and results in an equilibrium with a non-negligible failure probability for security, where each non-adversarial node trusts the others to send clues to the contract.

Finally, we prove security-optimality:

Theorem 4. *The slashing function of Sect. 3 is security optimal.*

Consider the sub-game, where the contract receives a query at some slot t. For a given contract and utility function $U(x) = x^\nu$, let $q_\nu^{\mathcal{A}}$ denote the probability that given a p_0-adversary $\mathcal{A}$, there are less than k valid clues in the contract at slot $t + 1$ in the Nash equilibrium with the largest probability of failure. Then, the proof of Theorem 4 for risk-neutral nodes follow from Theorem 5:

Theorem 5. *Suppose $p_0 < (N - f - k + 1)(p_s - p_w)$ and the nodes are risk-neutral with the utility function $U(x) = x$. Then, for any p_0-adversary $\mathcal{A}$, the slashing function of Sect. 3 satisfies*

$$q_v^{\mathcal{A}} \leq q^* = \frac{p_0}{(N - f - k + 1)(p_s - p_w)}$$

Moreover, there exists a p_0-adversary $\mathcal{A}$ such that for any compliant slashing function, $q_v^{\mathcal{A}} \geq q^*$.

The p_0-adversary $\mathcal{A}$ of Theorem 5 offers a bribe of $\frac{p_0}{N-f-k+1}$ to $N - f - k + 1$ non-adversarial nodes, e.g., $\mathcal{P}_i$, $i \in [N - f - k + 1]$. In return, it requests these nodes to collectively withhold their clues from the contract with probability q^*.

Remark 2. If $p_0 \geq (N - f - k + 1)(p_s - p_w)$, there exists a Nash equilibrium, where 4-security is violated with overwhelming probability. Adversary offers a payoff of $p_s - p_w$ to each of the $N - f - k + 1$ nodes, and requests them to withhold their clues from the contract. In the equilibrium, the offer is accepted and the nodes do not post their clues to the contract.

Remark 3. Sending repeated queries to the contract does not reduce the failure probability by more than a linear factor in latency. Suppose the client $\mathcal{V}$ is allowed to send the same query to the contract up to ℓ times. Then, if there are less than k valid clues in the contract at slot $t + 1$, $\mathcal{V}$ might want to repeat the sub-game up to ℓ times with the hope of eventually learning the answer to its query. In this case, the adversary $\mathcal{A}$ can offer a payoff of $\frac{p_0}{N-f-k+1}$ to the nodes $\mathcal{P}_i$, $i \in [N - f - k + 1]$, and in return, ask them to collectively withhold their clues in *all* of the games with probability q^*/ℓ. As in the proof of Theorem 5, this adversary ensures $q_v^{\mathcal{A}} \geq q^*/\ell$ for any compliant slashing function.

Finally, we characterize the failure probability for the optimal contract. Suppose the contract of Sect. 3 is $(p_0, 1 - q^*_{p_0,\nu})$-tolerant per Definition 3, where the failure probability $q^*_{p_0,\nu}$ is depends on the total bribe p_0 and the nodes' utility function $U(x) = x^\nu$, e.g., $q^*_{p_0,1} = q^*$ by Theorem 5. Although Theorem 4 proves that the contract of Sect. 3 is security optimal, unlike Theorem 5, its proof does not provide an explicit expression for $q^*_{p_0,\nu}$ when $\nu < 1$, i.e., for risk-averse nodes. Instead, we identify an optimization problem whose solution gives $q^*_{p_0,\nu}$ [28, Appendix C]. As the optimization problem is not convex for $\nu < 1$, in lieu of solving the problem, we provide bounds on $q^*_{p_0,\nu}$ that characterize its asymptotic behavior in terms of ν, p_0 and N.

4.3   Analysis of the Dynamic Game

In this section, we analyze the interaction among a rational client and the nodes during the dynamic game. For a specified slashing function, let $q(p_0, \nu)$ denote the maximum probability that 4-security is violated in the Nash equilibrium with the largest probability of failure, across all p_0-adversaries.

Theorem 6 shows that when $k > 1$, the slashing function of Sect. 3 achieves the minimum $q(p_0, \nu)$ among all compliant slashing functions, and this probability equals $q^*_{p_0,\nu}$. Proofs of the subsequent theorems are in [28, Appendix D].

Theorem 6. *Consider* (p_0, p_1)*-adversaries such that* $p_1 < p_{\mathrm{comp}} - p_c$ *and* $p_0 < (N - f - k + 1)(p_s - p_w)$*. Then, for the slashing function of Sect. 3, it holds that* $q(p_0, \nu) \leq q^*_{p_0,\nu}$.

Moreover, given any compliant slashing function, if $k > 1$*, then, there exists a* $(p_0, 0)$*-adversary and a subgame perfect equilibrium such that 4-security is violated in the equilibrium with probability* $q^*_{p_0,\nu}$.

Theorem 6 proves that even if the adversary does not offer any bribe to the client, *i.e.*, $p_1 = 0$, if $k > 1$, there exists a subgame perfect equilibrium where security is violated with the maximum probability $q^*_{p_0,\nu}$.

Remark 4. If $p_1 > p_{\mathrm{comp}} - p_c$, there exists a Nash equilibrium, where 4-security is violated with overwhelming probability. Suppose the adversary $\mathcal{A}$ asks the nodes to *not* send their clues to $\mathcal{V}$ or to the contract, and requests $\mathcal{V}$ to *not* post its query to the contract. If $\mathcal{V}$ never sends its query to the contract, nodes achieve a strictly better utility by accepting the adversary's offer. Similarly, $\mathcal{V}$ cannot increase its utility by deviating from the adversarial action. This is because, if $\mathcal{V}$ rejects its bribe and sends a query to the contract, given the nodes' actions, its payoff becomes $p_{\mathrm{comp}} - p_c$, less than the bribe p_1. Hence, given $\mathcal{A}$, the specified actions indeed constitute a Nash equilibrium.

Theorem 7 analyzes the game when $k = 1$.

Theorem 7. *Consider any compliant slashing function and* (p_0, p_1)*-adversaries such that* $p_1 < p_{\mathrm{comp}} - p_c$ *and* $p_0 < (N - f - k + 1)(p_s - p_w)$*. Suppose there are* N *nodes, and* $k = 1 \leq N - f$*. Then, if* p_1 *satisfies*

$$(1 - q^*_{p_0,\nu})(p_f - p_c + p_1)^\nu + q^*_{p_0,\nu}(p_f - p_c + p_1 + p_{\mathrm{comp}})^\nu \geq (p_f)^\nu,$$

there exists a (p_0, p_1)*-adversary and a subgame perfect equilibrium such that 4-security is violated with probability at least* $q^*_{p_0,\nu}$*, i.e.,* $q(p_0, \nu) \geq q^*_{p_0,\nu}$.

Via Theorems 6 and 7, for all values of k and all (p_0, p_1)-adversaries with a sufficiently large p_1, the slashing function of Sect. 3 achieves the minimum possible failure probability for 4-security among all compliant slashing functions. If p_1 satisfies formula (7), then the adversary can incentivize $\mathcal{V}$ to send a query to the contract regardless of whether $\mathcal{V}$ received clues over the network. This in turn discourages the nodes from sending clues over the network, and helps sustain an equilibrium where security rests solely on the clues sent to the contract. In this context, slashing function of Sect. 3 minimizes the failure probability for security, which becomes $q^*_{p_0,\nu}$.

On the other hand, if p_1 is too small to satisfy formula (7), p_0 is sufficiently small (but non-zero) and $k = 1$, given the optimal slashing function of Sect. 3, 4-security can be satisfied, without any query sent to the contract, with probability exceeding $q^*_{p_0,\nu}$. This prevents the adversary from making the contract the default method for retrieving the data and bloating the blockchain.

Theorem 8. *Consider the slashing function of Sect. 3 and (p_0, p_1)-adversaries such that $p_1 < p_{\text{comp}} - p_c$, $p_0 < (N - f)p_w$, and p_1 satisfies*

$$(1 - q^*_{p_0, \nu})(p_f - p_c + p_1)^\nu + q^*_{p_0, \nu}(p_f - p_c + p_1 + p_{\text{comp}})^\nu < (p_f)^\nu.$$

Suppose there are N nodes, and $k = 1 \leq N - f$. Then, 4-security is satisfied with overwhelming probability in all Nash equilibria, without the client sending its query to the contract.

When $\nu = 1$, *i.e.*, for risk-neutral nodes, formula (7) implies $p_1 \geq p_c$. As p_c can be as small as the gas cost of sending a query, for most (p_0, p_1)-adversaries, we expect p_1 to exceed p_c, *i.e.* to satisfy formula (7).

5   Evaluation

We next calculate the bribe p_0 needed to violate security in the equilibrium with the largest failure probability, when a query is sent to the optimal contract of Sect. 3 on Ethereum. When the clues are SNARK proofs as argued in Sect. 2, assuming that sending and verifying a SNARK proof on Ethereum requires 650000 gas [10], and the gas cost is 34.77 Gwei[7], we estimate the cost of posting a clue to the contract as $p_w \approx 0.0226$ ETH. We set the collateral p_s to be 32 ETH to match the minimum amount that can be staked in Ethereum by an independent node. Assuming that the adversary can control up to 1/3 of the N DAC nodes, and clues from 1/3 of the nodes are sufficient to recover the answer to the client queries, we set $N - f - k + 1$ to be $N/3$. The 1/3 bound for the adversarial DAC nodes matches the maximum tolerable adversary fraction shown for the security of Casper FFG [13], the finality gadget of PoS Ethereum. We consider $N < 300,000$, which has the same magnitude as the number of validators on PoS Ethereum [8].

Let ϵ denote the maximum failure probability for DAC security that the clients are willing to tolerate. Suppose $\epsilon = 0.1\%$. For risk-neutral nodes, Theorem 5 implies that $\epsilon = \min(1, \frac{1}{N - f - k + 1} \frac{p_0}{p_s - p_w})$. For risk-averse nodes with the utility function $U(x) = x^\nu$, upper and lower bounds on ϵ is calculated in [28, Appendix C]. Using the above parameters, the formula for ϵ for risk-neutral nodes and the bounds for risk-averse nodes, we calculate the following bounds[8] for the minimum bribe p_0 needed to violate security with probability $\epsilon = 10^{-3}$ (0.1%), as a function of the utility parameter ν (details in [28, Appendix C]).

The exact value of p_0 increases as ν decays, *i.e.*, as the nodes become more risk averse. This increase becomes more stark at small values of the maximum failure probability ϵ. A plot of the lower bound on p_0 as a function of $N \in [1, 300000]$, for $\nu = 0.1, 0.5, 0.8, 1.0$ and $\epsilon = 10^{-6}$ (as opposed to $\epsilon = 0.1\%$) is presented in [28, Appendix C] to illustrate this point. The lower bound curve increases as ν decreases. Since Table 2 considers $\epsilon = 10^{-3}$, unlike the case with $\epsilon = 10^{-6}$, the lower bound expression for p_0 does not grow as ν gets smaller.

---

[7] The gas cost is the average gas price for July 15, 2022 [2].

[8] 1 ETH ≈ 1231.0 USD, is the average Ethereum price on July 15, 2022 [3].

Table 2. Lower and upper bounds on p_0 in ETH and USD as a function of the utility parameter ν, where 1 ETH ≈ 1231.0 USD, the number of DAC nodes N is $300,000$, and the failure probability is $\epsilon = 0.1\%$.

ν	Lower bound on p_0	Upper bound on p_0
0.1	3197.9 ETH (3.9 Million USD)	13257.7 ETH (16.3 Million USD)
0.5	3197.9 ETH (3.9 Million USD)	6082.5 ETH (7.5 Million USD)
0.8	3197.9 ETH (3.9 Million USD)	3977.5 ETH (4.9 Million USD)
1.0	3197.9 ETH (3.9 Million USD)	3197.9 ETH (3.9 Million USD)

6 Discussion and Future Work

Preventing Centralization of Storage. DAC members have an into pool their resources and pay for a central data repository, *e.g.*, a cloud provider. They then answer the client queries by querying the central repository, and split the cost of the repository among themselves. However, if this single repository loses the data, then all is lost. Thus, a DAC protocol should discourage data centralization, and this can be done using a cryptographic Proofs of Replication (POR) [18] that forces every node to store a different incompressible version of the data. However, POR introduces a significant computation overhead. Interestingly, the data centralization problem is not addressed by data availability or storage systems such as Celestia [6] and Arweave [29].

While our protocol does not solve the problem, arguably, it discourages data centralization. A node that participates in a centralization scheme is putting its trust in the repository to preserve the data. However, the repository has little to lose if the data is lost, while the node will lose its entire stake. Hence, the node is incentivized to store the data locally rather than to trust a third party.

Preventing Client DoS Attack. Clients can send queries to the contract frequently, at the cost of p_c coins per query. Although p_c can be as low as the gas cost of posting an account information on chain (*cf.*Application in Sect. 2), which implies a potential DoS vector, the contract can increase this cost to disincentivize DoS attacks. The value of p_c can even be adaptively chosen as a function of the number of queries to reduce congestion. Then, as long as p_c is not subsidized by the bribe p_1, no rational client would send a query unless the nodes withhold their clues. However, p_c should not be too high as that would hurt the contract balance by requiring a high p_{comp} (*cf.*Remark 4), and discourage rational clients from sending queries for accounts with smaller balances (*i.e.*, p_f). An interesting future work is to determine the optimal p_c that would not impose a high burden on most accounts while making spamming attacks costly.

Utility Functions. The analysis in Sect. 5 demonstrates how risk-aversion implies a higher bribe for the adversary to violate security. However, the exact shape of the utility function depends on the marginal utility for the coin in which the payoffs are provided. Quantifying this marginal utility and identifying the correct function is important future work to accurately assess the affect of bribery on security. Further discussion on bribery and collusions among nodes is presented in [28, Section 6].

Acknowledgments. This work was supported by NSF, ONR, the Simons Foundation, NTT Research, and a grant from Ripple. Additional support was provided by the Stanford Center for Blockchain Research.

References

1. Eigenlaye. https://www.layrlabs.com/ Accessed 1 Aug 2022
2. Ethereum average gas price. https://ycharts.com/indicators/ethereum_average_gas_price Accessed 15 Jul 2022
3. Ethereum historical data. https://www.investing.com/crypto/ethereum/historical-data Accessed 15 Jul 2022
4. StarkEx v4. https://docs.starkware.co/starkex-v4/ Accessed 1 Mar 2022
5. zkPorter: a breakthrough in L2 scaling (2021). https://blog.matter-labs.io/zkporter-a-breakthrough-in-l2-scaling-ed5e48842fbf
6. Al-Bassam, M.: Lazyledger: a distributed data availability ledger with client-side smart contracts. arXiv:1905.09274 (2019)
7. Al-Bassam, M., Sonnino, A., Buterin, V., Khoffi, I.: Fraud and data availability proofs: detecting invalid blocks in light clients. In: Borisov, N., Diaz, C. (eds.) FC 2021. LNCS, vol. 12675, pp. 279–298. Springer, Heidelberg (2021). https://doi.org/10.1007/978-3-662-64331-0_15
8. Anderrson, S.: ETH 2.0 crosses 300,000 validators, Ether deposits worth 28.9B already locked (2022). https://www.thecoinrepublic.com/2022/03/05/eth-2-0-crosses-300000-validators-ether-deposits-worth-28-9b-already-locked/
9. Breidenbach, L., et al.: Chainlink 2.0: Next steps in the evolution of decentralized oracle networks. Whitepaper (2021). https://research.chain.link/whitepaper-v2.pdf
10. Buterin, V.: On-chain scaling to potentially ~500 tx/sec through mass tx validation (2018). https://ethresear.ch/t/on-chain-scaling-to-potentially-500-tx-sec-through-mass-tx-validation/3477
11. Buterin, V.: 2D data availability with kate commitments (2020). https://ethresear.ch/t/2d-data-availability-with-kate-commitments/8081
12. Buterin, V.: Proto-danksharding faq (2022)
13. Buterin, V., Griffith, V.: Casper the friendly finality gadget. arXiv:1710.09437 (2019). https://arxiv.org/abs/1710.09437
14. Drake, J.: Starkex validium ransom attack (2020). https://notes.ethereum.org/DD7GyItYQ02d0ax_X-UbWg?view
15. Ellis, S., Juels, A., Nazarov, S.: Chainlink a decentralized oracle network. Whitepaper (2017). https://research.chain.link/whitepaper-v1.pdf
16. Feist, D.: Proofs of custody (2021). https://dankradfeist.de/ethereum/2021/09/30/proofs-of-custody.html
17. Feist, D.: New sharding design with tight beacon and shard block integration (2022). https://notes.ethereum.org/@dankrad/new_sharding

18. Fisch, B.: Poreps: Proofs of space on useful data. Cryptology ePrint Archive:2018/678 (2018). https://eprint.iacr.org/2018/678
19. Gudgeon, L., Moreno-Sanchez, P., Roos, S., McCorry, P., Gervais, A.: SoK: layer-two blockchain protocols. In: Bonneau, J., Heninger, N. (eds.) FC 2020. LNCS, vol. 12059, pp. 201–226. Springer, Cham (2020). https://doi.org/10.1007/978-3-030-51280-4_12
20. Kate, A., Zaverucha, G.M., Goldberg, I.: Constant-size commitments to polynomials and their applications. In: Abe, M. (ed.) ASIACRYPT 2010. LNCS, vol. 6477, pp. 177–194. Springer, Heidelberg (2010). https://doi.org/10.1007/978-3-642-17373-8_11
21. McCorry, P., Buckland, C., Yee, B., Song, D.: Sok: validating bridges as a scaling solution for blockchains. Cryptology ePrint Archive:2021/1589 (2021). https://eprint.iacr.org/2021/1589
22. Miller, A., Juels, A., Shi, E., Parno, B., Katz, J.: Permacoin: Repurposing bitcoin work for data preservation. In: IEEE Symposium on Security and Privacy, pp. 475–490. IEEE Computer Society (2014)
23. Nazirkhanova, K., Neu, J., Tse, D.: Information dispersal with provable retrievability for rollups. arXiv:2111.12323 (2021). in ACM Advances in Financial Technologies - AFT 2022
24. Polygon: Avail - the data availability blockchain (2021). https://github.com/maticnetwork/data-availability
25. Psaras, Y., Dias, D.: The interplanetary file system and the filecoin network. In: DSN (Supplements), p. 80. IEEE (2020)
26. Sriram, A., Adler, J.: The Ethereum Off-Chain Data Availability Landscape (2022). https://blog.celestia.org/ethereum-off-chain-data-availability-landscape/
27. Sriram, A., Adler, J., Al-Bassam, M.: Quantum gravity bridge: Secure off-chain data availability for ethereum l2s with celestia (2022). https://blog.celestia.org/celestiums/
28. Tas, E.N., Boneh, D.: Cryptoeconomic security for data availability committees. arXiv:2208.02999 (2022)
29. Williams, S., Diordiiev, V., Berman, L., Raybould, I., Uemlianin, I.: Arweave: A protocol for economically sustainable information permanence. Yellow paper (2019). https://www.arweave.org/yellow-paper.pdf
30. Yee, B., Song, D., McCorry, P., Buckland, C.: Shades of finality and layer 2 scaling. arXiv:2201.07920 (2022)
31. Yu, M., Sahraei, S., Li, S., Avestimehr, S., Kannan, S., Viswanath, P.: Coded merkle tree: solving data availability attacks in blockchains. In: Financial Cryptography. Lecture Notes in Computer Science, vol. 12059, pp. 114–134. Springer (2020)

Kadabra: Adapting Kademlia
for the Decentralized Web

Yunqi Zhang🆔 and Shaileshh Bojja Venkatakrishnan$^{(\boxtimes)}$🆔

The Ohio State University, Columbus, USA
{zhang.8678,bojjavenkatakrishnan.2}@osu.edu

Abstract. Blockchains have become the catalyst for a growing movement to create a more decentralized Internet. A fundamental operation of applications in a decentralized Internet is data storage and retrieval. As today's blockchains are limited in their storage functionalities, in recent years a number of peer-to-peer data storage networks have emerged based on the Kademlia distributed hash table protocol. However, existing Kademlia implementations are not efficient enough to support fast data storage and retrieval operations necessary for (decentralized) Web applications. In this paper, we present Kadabra, a decentralized protocol for computing the routing table entries in Kademlia to accelerate lookups. Kadabra is motivated by the multi-armed bandit problem, and can automatically adapt to heterogeneity and dynamism in the network. Experimental results show Kadabra achieving between 15–50% lower lookup latencies compared to state-of-the-art baselines.

Keywords: Multi-armed bandit · Decentralized protocol · Kademlia p2p routing

1 Introduction

Decentralized peer-to-peer applications (dapps) fueled by successes in blockchain technology are rapidly emerging as secure, transparent and open alternatives to conventional centralized applications. Today dapps have been developed for a wide gamut of application areas spanning payments, decentralized finance, social networking, healthcare, gaming etc., and have millions of users and generate billions on dollars in trade [11]. These developments are part of a growing movement to create a more "decentralized Web", in which no single administrative entity (e.g., a corporation or government) has complete control over important web functionalities (e.g., name resolution, content hosting, etc.) thereby providing greater power to application end users [1,44].

A fundamental operation in dapps is secure, reliable data storage and retrieval. Over the past two decades, the cloud (e.g., Google, Facebook, Amazon) together with content delivery networks (CDNs; e.g., Akamai, CloudFlare) have been largely responsible for storing and serving data for Internet applications. Infrastructure in the cloud or a CDN is typically owned by a single

© International Financial Cryptography Association 2024
F. Baldimtsi and C. Cachin (Eds.): FC 2023, LNCS 13951, pp. 327–345, 2024.
https://doi.org/10.1007/978-3-031-47751-5_19

provider, making these storage methods unsuitable for dapps. Instead dapps—especially those built over a blockchain (e.g., ERC 721 tokens in Ethereum)—directly resort to using the blockchain for storing application data. However, mainstream blockchains are notorious for their poor scalability which limits the range of applications that can be deployed on them. In particular, realizing a decentralized Web that supports sub-second HTTP lookups at scale is infeasible with today's blockchain technology.

To fill this void, a number of recent efforts have designed decentralized peer-to-peer (p2p) data storage networks—such as IPFS [5], Swarm [42,43,45], Hypercore protocol [20], Safe network [36] and Storj [40]—which are seeing rapid mainstream adoption. E.g., the IPFS network has more than 3 million client requests per week with hundreds of thousands of storage nodes worldwide as part of the network [44]. In these networks, each unique piece of data is stored over a vast network of servers (nodes) with each server responsible for storing only a small portion of the overall stored data unlike blockchains. The networks are also characterized by their permissionless and open nature, wherein any individual server may join and participate in the network freely. By providing appropriate monetary incentives (e.g., persistent storage in IPFS can be incentivized using Filecoin [14,21]) for storing and serving data, the networks encourage new servers to join which in turn increases the net storage capacities of these systems.

A key challenge in the p2p storage networks outlined above is how to efficiently locate where a desired piece of data is stored in the network. Unlike cloud storage, there is no central database that maintains information on the set of files hosted by each server at any moment. Instead, p2p storage networks rely on a distributed hash table (DHT) protocol for storage and retrieval by content addressing data. While tens of DHT constructions have been proposed in the past, in recent years the Kademlia DHT [29] has emerged as the de facto protocol and has been widely adopted by practitioners. For instance, IPFS, Swarm, Hypercore protocol, Safe network and Storj are all based on Kademlia. To push or pull a data block from the network, the hash of the data block (i.e., its content address) is used to either recursively or iteratively route a query through the DHT nodes until a node responsible for storing the data block is found.

For latency-sensitive content lookup applications, such as the Web where a delay of even a few milliseconds in downloading webpage objects can lead to users abandoning the website [46], it is imperative that the latency of routing a query through Kademlia is as low as possible. Each Kademlia node maintains a routing table, which contains IP address references to other Kademlia nodes in the network. The sequence of nodes queried while performing a lookup is dictated by the choice of routing tables at the nodes. Today's Kademlia implementations choose the routing tables completely agnostic of where the nodes are located in the network. As a result, a query in Kademlia may take a route that criss-crosses continents before arriving at a target node costing significant delay. Moreover, the open and permissionless aspects makes the network inherently heterogeneous: nodes can differ considerably in their compute, memory and network capabilities which creates differences in how fast nodes respond to queries;

data blocks published over the network vary in their popularity, with demand for some data far exceeding others; the network is also highly dynamic due to peer churn and potentially evolving user demand for data (e.g., a news webpage that is popular today may not be popular tomorrow). Designing routing tables in Kademlia that are tuned to the various heterogeneities and dynamism in the network to minimize content lookup delays is therefore a highly nontrivial task.

Prior works have extensively investigated how to design location-aware routing tables in Kademlia. For example, the proximity neighbor selection (PNS) [7] advocates choosing routing table peers that are geographically close to a node (more precisely, peers having a low round-trip-time (RTT) ping delay to the node), and proximity routing (PR) [7] favors relaying a query to a matching peer with the lowest RTT in the routing table. While these location-aware variants have been shown to exhibit latency performance strictly superior to the original Kademlia protocol [29], they are not adaptive to the heterogeneities in the network. PNS is also prone to Sybil attacks which diminishes its practical utility [32]—an adversary controlling a large number of fake Kademlia nodes at a location can cause a nearby node's routing table to be completely filled with adversarial IP addresses. Real world Kademlia implementations in libp2p [28], IPFS and other file sharing networks therefore have resorted to maintaining the peer routing tables largely per the original Kademlia protocol. S/Kademlia [4] is a particularly popular implementation which uses public-key cryptography for authentication and proof-of-work puzzles to avoid Sybil attacks.

We propose Kadabra, a decentralized, adaptive algorithm for selecting routing table entries in Kademlia to minimize object lookup times (to push or get content) while being robust against Sybil attacks. Kadabra is motivated by the (combinatorial) multi-armed bandit (MAB) problem [6,37], with each Kademlia node acting as an independent MAB player and the node's routing table configurations being the arms of the bandit problem. By balancing exploring new routing table configurations with exploiting known configurations that have resulted in fast lookup speeds in the past, a node is able to adaptively discover an efficient routing table that provides fast lookups. Importantly, the discovered routing table configuration at a node is optimized precisely to the pattern of lookups specific to the node. Our proposed algorithm is fully decentralized, relying only on local timestamp measurements for feedback at each node (time between when a query was sent and its corresponding response received) and does not require any cooperation between nodes. To protect against Sybil attacks, Kadabra relies on a novel exploration strategy that explicitly avoids including nodes that have a low RTT to a node within the node's routing table with the RTT threshold specified as a security parameter. At the same time, Kadabra's exploration strategy also avoids selecting nodes very far from a node. To accelerate discovery of an efficient routing table configuration, Kadabra decomposes the problem into parallel independent MAB instances at each node, with each instance responsible for optimizing peer entries of a single k-bucket. In summary, the contributions of this paper are:

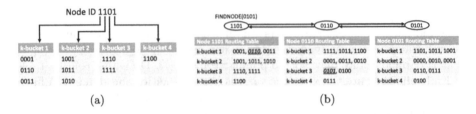

Fig. 1. (a) Example of k-buckets at a node in a network with 4-bit node IDs. (b) Example of a recursive routing path taken to lookup key 0101. A yellow-highlighted node ID is a peer to which the query is forwarded for the next hop. (Color figure online)

1. We consider the problem of efficient routing table design in Kademlia and formulate it as an instance of the multi-armed bandit problem. Using data-driven techniques for optimizing lookup speeds in structured p2p networks has not been proposed before, to our best knowledge.
2. We propose Kadabra, a fully decentralized and non-cooperative algorithm for learning the routing table entries to accelerate lookups. Kadabra is adaptive to both the traffic demand patterns of the users and the heterogeneities in the network.
3. We validate Kadabra through simulations under various network and traffic settings. In each case, we observe Kadabra to consistently outperform baselines by between 15–50% in latency.

2   Background

2.1   Kademlia

Overview. Kademlia is arguably the most popular protocol for realizing a structured p2p system on the Internet today. In a Kademlia network, each node is assigned a unique binary node ID from a high-dimensional space (e.g., 20 byte node IDs are common). When the network size is large, it is difficult for a node to know the node ID of every single node in the network. A node may have knowledge of node IDs of only a small number (such as logarithmic in network size) of other nodes. The most basic operation supported by Kademlia is *key-based routing* (KBR) wherein given a key from the node ID space as input to a node, the protocol determines a routing path from the node to a target node whose ID is the 'closest' to the input key. Closeness between a key and a node ID in Kademlia is measured by taking the bitwise-XOR between the two binary strings, and converting the resultant string as a base-10 integer. The basic KBR primitive can be used to realize higher-order functions such as a distributed hash table (DHT). In a DHT, a (key, value) store is distributed across nodes in the network. A (key, value) pair is stored at a node whose node ID is the closest to the key according to the XOR distance metric. To protect against node failures, in practice a copy of the (key, value) is also stored at a small number (e.g., 20) of sibling nodes that are nodes whose IDs are closest to the initial storing node. To store a (key, value) in the network a node invokes a STORE(key, value) remote procedure call (RPC), and to fetch a value corresponding to a key the node calls a FINDVALUE(key) RPC [4,29]. KBR is implemented as a FINDNODE(key) RPC, which returns the Kademlia node having the closest ID to key.

Routing. Each Kademlia node maintains a routing table containing node ID, IP address and port information of other peers using which STORE, FINDVALUE or FINDNODE queries are routed to their appropriate target nodes. For node IDs that are n bits long, the routing table at each node comprises of n k-buckets, where each k-bucket contains information about k peers. The IDs of peers in the i-th k-bucket of a node's routing table share the first $i - 1$ bits with the node's ID, while differing in the i-th bit (Fig. 1a). For a network with m nodes, it can be shown that on average only the first $\log(m)$ k-buckets can be filled with peer entries while the remaining k-buckets are empty due to lack of peers satisfying the prefix constraints.

Queries in Kademlia are routed either recursively or iteratively across nodes. In a recursive lookup, a query is relayed sequentially from one node to the next until a target node is found. The response from the target node is then relayed back on the reverse path to the query initiator. In an iterative lookup, a query initiating node itself sequentially contacts nodes until a target node is found, and receives a response directly from the target node. We focus primarily on recursive routing in this work (Fig. 1b).

When a query for key x is received at a node v, the node searches for a peer v' within its routing table with an ID that is closest to x. If the distance between the IDs x and v' is less than the distance between x and v, then v forwards the query to node v'. Later when v receives a response to the query from v', v relays the response back to the node from whom it received the query. If the distance between x and v is less than than distance between x and v', the node v issues an appropriate response for the query to the node from whom v received the query. To avoid lookup failures, a query initiator issues its query along α (e.g., $\alpha = 3$) independent paths. This basic lookup process described above is fundamental to implementing the STORE, FINDVALUE and FINDNODE functions. We point the reader to prior papers [4,29] for more details on the lookup process.

2.2 Lookup Latency and Node Geography

A Kademlia node may include any peer it has knowledge of within its k-buckets, provided the peer satisfies the required ID prefix conditions for the k-bucket. Nodes get to know of new peers over the course of receiving queries and responses from other nodes in the network. As node IDs are assigned to nodes typically in a way that is completely independent of where the nodes are located in the world, in today's Kademlia it is likely that the peers within a k-bucket belong to diverse geographical regions around the world without any useful structure. E.g., a recent study [44] measuring performance on the IPFS network reports a 90-th percentile content storing latency of 112 s with 88% of it attributed to

DHT routing latency. For retrieving content, the reported 90-th percentile delay is 4.3 s which is more than 4× the latency of an equivalent HTTPS lookup. Similar observations have been made on other Kademlia systems in the past as well [10].

There has been an extensive amount of work on reducing lookup latencies in DHTs by taking the physical location of nodes on the underlay [19,22,25, 33,35,49]. For instance, Kaune et al. [26] propose an algorithm that takes the ISPs of nodes into consideration, and also uses network coordinates for reducing latencies. Jimenez et al. [23] tune the number of parallel lookup queries sent or bucket size to achieve speedup. Chen et al. [9] minimize the mismatch between Kademlia's logical network and the underlying physical topology through a landmark binning algorithm and RTT detection. Gummadi et al. [16] do a systematic comparison of proximity routing and proximity neighbor selection on different DHT protocols. The algorithms proposed in these and other prior works are hand-crafted designs, which are not tuned to the various heterogeneities in the network. Moreover, security in these proposed methods has not been discussed as a first-order concern. Indeed, today's DHT implementations have not adopted these proposals into their systems.

2.3 Security in Kademlia

A Kademlia node is susceptible to various attacks, especially in permissionless settings. We consider the following attacks in this work.

Eclipse and Sybil attacks. In an Eclipse attack, an attacker blocks one or more victim nodes from connecting to other nodes in the network by filling the victim nodes' routing table with malicious nodes. In a Sybil attack, the attacker creates many fake nodes with false identities to spam the network, which may eventually undermine the reputation of the network. Today's Kademlia implementations circumvent these attacks using ideas largely inspired from S/Kademlia [4]. In S/Kademlia, the network uses a supervised signature issued by a trustworthy certificate authority or a proof-of-work puzzle signature to restrict users' ability to freely generate new nodes.

Adversarial routing. In Kademlia, a malicious node within an honest node's routing table may route messages from the honest node to a group of malicious nodes. This attack is called adversarial routing, and it may cause delays and/or make the queries unable to find their target keys. To alleviate adversarial routing, S/Kademlia makes nodes use multiple disjoint paths to lookup contents at a cost of increased network overhead.

Churn attack. Attackers can also enter and exit the network constantly to induce churns to destabilize the network. Kademlia networks handle these kind of attacks by favoring long-lived nodes [27,29].

3 System Model

We consider a Kademlia network over a set of nodes V with each node $v \in V$ having a unique IP address and a node ID from ID space $\{0,1\}^n$. Each node maintains n k-buckets in its routing table, with each k-bucket containing the IP address and node ID of up to k other peers satisfying the ID prefix condition. We consider a set S of (key, value) pairs that have been stored in the network; each (key, value) pair $(x, y) \in S$ is stored in k peers whose IDs are closest to x in XOR distance. We let S_x denote the set of keys in S. Time is slotted into rounds, where in each round a randomly chosen node performs a lookup for a certain key. If a node $v \in V$ is chosen during a round, it issues a lookup query for key $x \in S_x$ where x is chosen according to a demand distribution p_v, i.e., $p_v(x)$ is the probability key x is queried. We focus primarily on recursive routing in this paper. When a node v initiates a query for key x, it sends out the query to α closest (to x, in XOR distance) peers in its routing table. For any two nodes u, w, $l(u, w) \geq 0$ is the latency of sending or forwarding a query from u to w. When a node w receives a query for key x and it has stored the value for x, the node returns the value back to the node u from whom it received the query. Otherwise, the query is immediately forwarded to another node that is closest to x in w's routing table. When a node w sends or forwards a value y to a node u, it first takes time $\delta_w \geq 0$ to upload the value over the Internet followed by time $l(w, u)$ for the packets to propagate to u. We do not model the time take to download the value, as download bandwidth is typically higher than upload bandwidth. Thus, for a routing path v, u, w with v being the query initiator and w storing the desired value, the overall time taken for v to receive the value is $l(v, u) + l(u, w) + \delta_w + l(w, u) + \delta_u + l(u, v)$. The above outlines our lookup model for the DHT application. For KBR, we follow the same model except only a single query (i.e., $\alpha = 1$) is sent by the initiating node. We assume each node has an access to the IP addresses and node IDs of a small number of random nodes in the network.

Problem statement. For each of the KBR and DHT applications, our objective is to design a decentralized algorithm for computing each node's routing table such that the average time (averaged over the distribution of queries sent from the node) taken to perform a lookup is minimized at the node. We consider non-cooperative algorithms where a node computes its routing table without relying on help from other nodes.

4   Kadabra

4.1   Overview

Kadabra is a fully decentralized and adaptive algorithm that learns a node's routing table to minimize lookup times, purely based on the node's past inter-actions with the network. Kadabra is inspired by ideas from non-stationary and streaming multi-armed bandit problems applied to a combinatorial bandit setting [2,8,31]. A Kadabra node balances efficient routing table configurations it has seen in the past (exploitation) against new, unseen configurations (exploration) with potentially even better latency efficiency. For each query that is initiated or routed through a Kadabra node, the node stores data pertaining to which peer(s) the query is routed to and how long it takes for a response to arrive. This data is used to periodically make a decision on whether to retain peers currently in the routing table, or switch to a potentially better set of peers. Treating the routing table as the decision variable of a combinatorial MAB problem leads to a large space and consequently inefficient learning. We therefore decompose the problem into n independent subproblems, where the i-th subproblem learns only the entries of the i-th k-bucket. This decomposition is without loss of generality as each query is routed through peers in at most one k-bucket. In the following we therefore explain how a Kadabra node can learn the entries of its i-th k-bucket.

In Kadabra, a decision on a k-bucket (i.e., whether to change one or more entries of the bucket) is made each time after b queries are routed via peers in the bucket (e.g., $b = 100$ in our experiments). We call the time between successive decisions on a k-bucket as an epoch. Before each decision, a performance score is computed for each peer in the bucket based on the data collected over the epoch for the bucket. Intuitively, the performance score for a peer captures how frequently queries are routed through the peer *and* how fast responses are received for those queries. By comparing the performance scores of peers in the bucket during the current epoch against the scores of peers in the previous epoch, Kadabra discovers the more efficient bucket configuration which is then used as the k-bucket for the subsequent epoch.[1] To discover new (unseen) bucket configurations, Kadabra also explores random bucket configurations according to a user-defined schedule. In our implementation, one entry on the k-bucket is chosen randomly every other epoch. The overall template of Kadabra is presented in Algorithm 1.

4.2   Scoring Function

During an epoch with k-bucket Γ_{curr}, let $q_1, q_2, \ldots, q_r$ be the set of queries that have been sent or relayed through one or more peers in the k-bucket. For each query $q_i, 1 \leq i \leq r$, let $d_i(u) \geq 0$ be the time taken to receive a response upon sending or forwarding the query through peer u for $u \in \Gamma_{\text{curr}}$. If q_i is not sent or forwarded through a peer $u \in \Gamma_{\text{curr}}$ we let $d_i(u) = \Delta$ where $\Delta \geq 0$ is a user-defined penalty parameter.[2] A large value for Δ causes Kadabra to favor peers that are frequently used in the k-bucket, while a small value favors peers from which responses are received quickly. In our experiments, we choose Δ to be a value that is slightly larger than the moving average of latencies of lookups going through the bucket. The function SCORINGFUNCTION$(u, \mathcal{D})$ to compute the score for a peer u is then defined as score$(u) = $ SCORINGFUNCTION$(u, \mathcal{D}) = -\sum_{i=1}^{r} d_i(u)\ \forall u \in \Gamma_{\text{curr}}$. The overall score for the k-bucket is then given as SCOREBUCKET$(\Gamma_{\text{curr}}, \mathcal{D}) = -\sum_{u \in \Gamma_{\text{curr}}} \text{score}(u)/|\Gamma_{\text{curr}}|$. For a k-bucket that is empty, we define its score to be $-\Delta$.

---

[1] To increase stability under churn, we may choose to replace only unresponsive peers—as in the original Kademlia protocol—in each epoch.

[2] Notice that $d_i(u)$ is well-defined for both recursive and iterative routing.

Algorithm 1: Algorithm outline for updating entries of i-th k-bucket of node v in each epoch.

---

input : data $\mathcal{D}$ on queries sent during current epoch; peers Γ_{curr} and Γ_{prev} in k-bucket of current and previous epochs respectively; total score PrevScoreBucket of previous k-bucket; flag F indicating whether to explore in next epoch; list $\mathcal{L}$ of peers eligible to be included within k-bucket; security parameter ρ;

output: updated set of peers Γ_{next} for next epoch;

```
/* Score each peer in Γcurr using a scoring algorithm based on
   measurements collected during epoch                          */
```
$\mathrm{score}(u) \leftarrow \mathrm{SCOREPEER}(u, \mathcal{D})$, for each peer $u \in \Gamma_{\mathrm{curr}}$

if *flag F is true* **then**


```
/* Replace worst peer with a random peer during next epoch      */
```
    $u^* \leftarrow \mathrm{argmin}_{u \in \Gamma}\ \mathrm{score}(u)$

    $\Gamma_{\mathrm{next}} \leftarrow \Gamma_{\mathrm{curr}} \backslash \{u^*\} \cup \mathrm{SELECTRANDOMPEER}(\mathcal{L}, \rho)$

else


```
/* Choose best peer set between current and previous epoch as
   decision for next epoch                                      */
```
    if $\mathrm{SCOREBUCKET}(\Gamma_{curr}, \mathcal{D}) >$ PrevScoreBucket **then**

        $\Gamma_{\mathrm{next}} \leftarrow \Gamma_{\mathrm{curr}}$

    else

        $\Gamma_{\mathrm{next}} \leftarrow \Gamma_{\mathrm{prev}}$

    end

end

4.3   Random Exploration

To discover new k-bucket configurations with potentially better performance than past configurations, a Kadabra node includes randomly selected peers within its bucket through the SELECTRANDOMPEER() function as outlined in Algorithm 1. The Kadabra node maintains a list $\mathcal{L}$ of peers eligible to be included within its k-bucket, which satisfy the required node ID prefix conditions. In addition to the peer IP addresses, we assume the node also knows the RTT to each peer in the list. For a random exploratory epoch, the node replaces the peer having the worst score from the previous epoch with a randomly selected peer from the list. The number of peers in the bucket that are replaced with a random peers can be configured to be more than one more generally.

A key contribution in Kadabra is how peers are sampled from the list of known peers to be included in the k-bucket. Depending on the number of nodes in the network, and the index of the k-bucket, the number of eligible peers can vary with some peers close to the node while some farther away (in RTT sense). A naïve approach of sampling a node uniformly at random from the list, can eventually lead to a bucket configuration in which all peers are located close to the node. This is due to the algorithm 'discovering' the proximity neighbor selection (PNS) protocol which has been demonstrated to have efficient latency performance compared to other heuristics [4,16]. However, as with PNS, the routing table learned with a uniformly random sampling strategy is prone to a Sybil attack as it relatively inexpensive to launch a vast number of Sybil nodes concentrated at a single location close to a victim node(s) [34,39]. While the PNS peer selection strategy does not have an efficient performance in all scenarios (e.g., if the node upload latencies are large; see §5), in cases where it does, Kadabra would be susceptible to attack. What we desire, therefore, is to learn a routing table configuration in which not all peers are located close to the node. Such a routing table configuration may not be performance efficient (e.g., PNS may have a better latency performance in certain scenarios), but is more secure compared to PNS.

We capture this intuition by introducing a security parameter $\rho \geq 0$, that is user-defined, to restrict the choice of peers that are sampled during exploration. For a chosen ρ value, a Kadabra node computes a subset $\mathcal{L}_{>\rho} \subseteq \mathcal{L}$ of peers to whom the RTT is greater than ρ from the node. The SELECTRANDOMPEER($\mathcal{L}, \rho$) then samples a peer uniformly at random from $\mathcal{L}_{>\rho}$. A high value for ρ selects peers that are at a distance from the node, providing security against Sybil attacks at a cost of potentially reduced latency performance (and vice-versa).

5   Evaluation

5.1   Experiment Setup

We evaluate Kadabra using a custom discrete-event simulator built on Python following the model presented in §3.[3]

Baselines. Since the main focus of Kadabra is on how to configure the routing table, we compare our algorithm against the following baselines with differing (i) routing table (bucket) population mechanisms, and (ii) peer selection methods during query forwarding:

(1) Vanilla Kademlia [4,29]. The original Kademlia protocol in which a node populates its buckets by randomly adding peers from node ID ranges corresponding to the buckets. When forwarding a query, the node chooses the peer whose node ID is closest (in XOR distance) to the query's target node ID from the appropriate bucket.

(2) Proximity routing (PR) [4,16]. In PR buckets are populated exactly as in vanilla Kademlia. However, when routing a query the query is sent to the peer in the appropriate k-bucket that is closest to the node in RTT.

(3) Proximity neighbor selection (PNS) [4,16]. In PNS the node picks peers which are closest to itself (in terms of RTT) from among eligible peers to populate each k-bucket. When forwarding a query, the node chooses the peer whose node ID is closest to the target node ID from the appropriate bucket.

---

[3] We do not use the erstwhile popular OverSim [3] and PeerSim [30] simulators, as they are outdated and no longer maintained by their authors. Kadabra simulator is available at https://github.com/yunqizhang99/KadabraSim/..

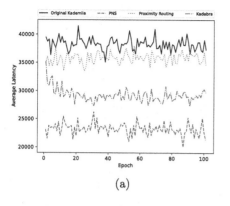
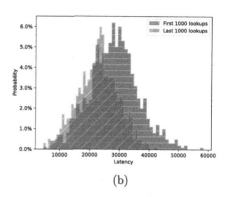

(a)   (b)

Fig. 2. Nodes in a square under uniform demand: (a) Average latency of queries in each epoch for queries routed through the 1st k-bucket of an arbitrary node. (b) Histogram of lookup latencies in Kadabra during the first and last 1000 rounds in a 10 million query run.

Network settings. We consider two network scenarios: nodes distributed over a two-dimensional Euclidean space, and nodes distributed over a real-world geography.

(1) Nodes in a square. In this setting, 2048 nodes are assigned random locations within a 10000 × 10000 square. The latency $l(u,v)$ between any two nodes u, v is given by $l(u,v) = ||u-v||_2 + w(u,v)$, where $||u-v||_2$ is the Euclidean distance between u and v on the square and $w(u,v)$ is random perturbation from an uniform distribution between 100 and 5000. Each node has a node latency (δ in §3) sampled uniformly between 100 and 2000.

(2) Nodes in the real world. We again consider 2048 nodes located in various cities around the world, as reported by Ethereum node tracker [13]. The latency between nodes in any pair of cities is obtained from a global ping latency measurement dataset [47].[4] Each node has a node latency sampled from an exponential distribution of mean 1000ms.

Application and traffic patterns. We first consider the KBR application under the following three traffic patterns:

(1) KBR under uniform demand. In this setting, a node during a round (see §3) issues a lookup to another node chosen uniformly at random from among the available nodes.

(2) KBR under demand hotspots. In this setting, there are 20% of keys (nodes) that form the target destination for 80% of lookups. The hotspot nodes are randomly chosen.

---

[4] For cities not included in the ping dataset, we measure the latency to the geographically closest city available in the dataset.

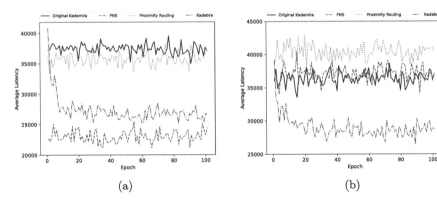

(a)   (b)

Fig. 3. Nodes in a square: (a) Average latency during each epoch for queries routed through the 1st k-bucket of an arbitrary node with demand hotspots. (b) Performance of a node within a region of high node latency nodes.

(3) KBR under skewed network bandwidth. To model regions around the world with poor Internet speeds, we consider a subset of geographically close nodes whose node upload latencies (see §3) are twice as large as the average node latency in the network.

In a full version of this paper [48], we have presented additional results for the settings mentioned above, and have also considered the DHT application, iterative routing, and network instability.

5.2   Results

Nodes in a square. Figure 2a plots the average latency between forwarding a query through the 1st k-bucket and receiving a response during each epoch for an arbitrarily chosen node within the square. We observe that starting with a randomly chosen routing table configuration (at epoch 0), Kadabra continuously improves its performance eventually achieving latencies that are 15% better. Compared to the latencies in the original Kademlia protocol, Kadabra's latencies are lesser by more than 20%. For this specific network setting, PNS shows the best performance (at the cost of poor security). We have used ρ values of [400, 350, 300, 250, 200, 150, 100, 50, 0] for the different k-buckets (1st to last) in Kadabra, which results in slightly higher latencies compared to PNS.

To show that all nodes in the network benefit from Kadabra, we conduct an experiment lasting for 10 million rounds (1 query per round from a random source to a random destination), with the sequence of first 1000 queries being identical to the sequence of the last 1000 queries. Figure 2b plots a histogram of the query latencies for the first and last 1000 queries in Kadabra. We observe the 90-th percentile latency of Kadabra during the last 1000 queries is lesser than that in the beginning by more than 24%.

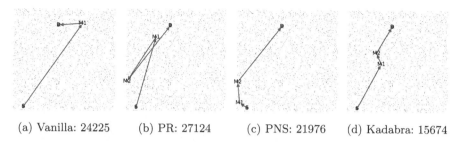

(a) Vanilla: 24225   (b) PR: 27124   (c) PNS: 21976   (d) Kadabra: 15674

Fig. 4. Nodes in a square: Paths and latencies (below the plots) of an example lookup. Kadabra is trained for 50 epoch under uniform demand. Mi refers to a node that is on the path but is not the source or destination node.

Figure 3a shows the average query latency over epochs for queries routed through the 1st k-bucket of an arbitrary node under hotspot demand. With certain keys being more popular than others, Kadabra adapts the node routing tables biasing them for fast lookups of the popular keys—a capability that is distinctly lacking in the baselines. As a result, we observe Kadabra outperforming the original Kademlia and PR by more than 25%.

To show that Kadabra adapts to variations in the Internet capacities of nodes, we consider an experiment where nodes within an area (2000 × 2000 region in the center of the square) alone have a higher node latency (5000 time units) than the default node latency values. This setting models, for instance, low-income countries with below-average Internet speeds. For a node within the high node latency region, PNS ends up favoring nearby peers also within that region which ultimately severely degrades the overall performance of PNS (Fig. 3b). Kadabra, on the other hand, is cognizant of the high node latencies in the region, and discovers k-bucket entries that provide more than 25% improvement in latency performance compared to PNS.

In Fig. 4, to better understand how Kadabra achieves better performance than the baseline heuristics, we present an example of the paths taken for a lookup from the same source to the same destination using different heuristics. We observe that, after a 50-epoch training, Kadabra is able to achieve significantly lower path latency by choosing a relatively straight path with low node latencies. In the figure, node D's node latency is 1000. For vanilla Kademlia, node M1's node latency is 1400. For PR, node M1's node latency is 800 and M2's node latency is 1400. For PNS, node M1's node latency is 2000 and M2's node latency is 1400. For Kadabra, node M1's node latency is 100 and M2's node latency is 100.

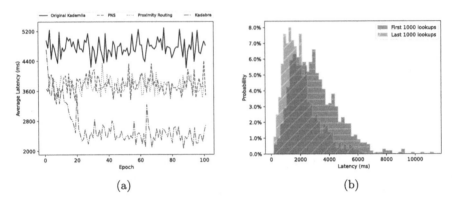

(a)   (b)

Fig. 5. Nodes in the real world: (a) Performance of queries routed through the 1st k-bucket of a node in Frankfurt. (b) Histograms of query latencies before and after learning in Kadabra with 10 million lookups.

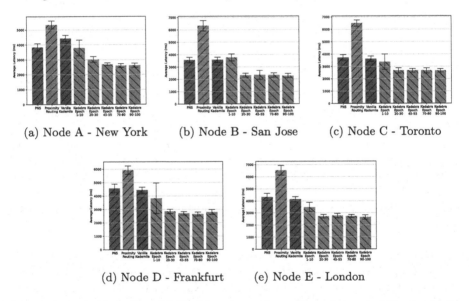

(a) Node A - New York   (b) Node B - San Jose   (c) Node C - Toronto

(d) Node D - Frankfurt   (e) Node E - London

Fig. 6. Nodes in the real world: Performance under uniform demand at five randomly sampled nodes around the world.

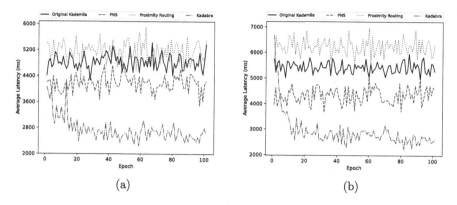

Fig. 7. Nodes in the real world: (a) Performance when there are demand hotspots. (b) Performance when 4% of nodes near New York City have above average node latencies.

Nodes in the real world. Unlike the square setting where nodes are uniformly spread out, in the real world setting nodes are concentrated around certain regions in the world (e.g., Europe or North America). Moreover the node latencies are also chosen to reflect retrieval of large files [44,51]. Figure 5a shows the latencies for queries routed through the 1st k-bucket of an arbitrary node (in this case, the node is located in Frankfurt). Kadabra has 50% lower latencies compared to the original Kademlia protocol and 35% lower latencies compared to PNS and PR. This is because the baseline algorithms are not aware of the different node latencies of the peers, whereas Kadabra is able to focus its search on peers having low node latencies. As in the square case, Fig. 5b shows the benefit of Kadabra extends to the entire network. To show that the presented behavior is general, and not occurring only at a few nodes, in Fig. 6 we show performance of Kadabra and baselines at five randomly chosen nodes in major cities across the world. In all cases, we observe a similar qualitative behavior.

Figure 7a shows performance when there are demand hotspots. Compared to uniform demand, both PNS and PR worsen in performance increasing the gap to Kadabra. A similar trend is observed in Fig. 7b when we consider a region of nodes (near New York City in our experiments) and set their node latency to double the default average value. While even Kadabra shows a slight degradation, it is still more than 40% more efficient compared to PNS.

In addition, we evaluate the security of Kadabra by setting 20% of the nodes as adversarial, which deliberately delay queries passing through them by 3× their default node latencies. While all algorithms degrade in this scenario, Fig. 8a shows that when the adversarial nodes are located at random cities Kadabra discovers routes which avoid the adversarial nodes resulting in overall quicker lookups. Even when the adversarial nodes are concentrated in one region close to a victim node, Fig. 8b shows how a victim running Kadabra can effectively bypass the adversarial nodes while PNS takes a huge performance loss at more that 2× the latency of Kadabra.

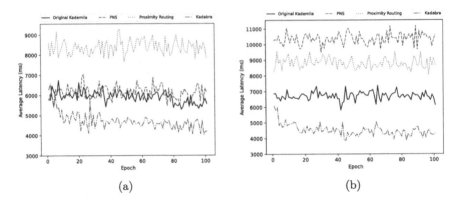

Fig. 8. Nodes in the real world: Kadabra outperforms baselines even when 20% of the nodes are adversarial in the network. (a) Adversarial nodes are randomly located. (b) Adversarial nodes are concentrated in one region close to the victim node. Performance is measured at the victim node.

6   Related Work

A great many number of prior works have studied how to speedup DHTs by being aware of the peer locations in the underlying physical Internet [23,26]. However, all of these works propose hand-crafted heuristics which do not adapt to network heterogeneity. Using parallel lookups and increasing the number of content replicas are some of the early methods. R/Kademlia enhances Kademlia routing with recursive overlay routing instead of iterative routing from vanilla Kademlia [18]. Some algorithms utilize caching to accelerate lookups by identifying hotspots [15] and lowering the load on congested nodes [12]. Heck et al. [17] evaluate the network resilience of Kademlia. Jain et al. [22] compare performance of various DHTs against measurement-based overlays. In Kanemitsu et al. [24], the authors propose KadRTT which uses RTT-based target selection and ID arrangement to accelerate lookups. Ratnasamy et al. [35] use landmark nodes and binning to optimize latencies in overlay networks. Steiner et al. [38] proposes an integrated content lookup protocol to reduce content retrieval times in Kad, a popular file-sharing application built using Kademlia. Stutzback et al. [41] advocate for parallel lookups and study optimal system parameters in Kad. Zhu et al. [50] presents a storage algorithm for Kademlia against load imbalance. To the best of our knowledge, Kadabra is the first effort to accelerate DHTs through a data-driven approach.

7   Conclusion

We have presented Kadabra, a decentralized data-driven approach to learning the routing tables in Kademlia for accelerated lookups. Unlike existing heuristics, Kadabra is cognizant to heterogeneity in network conditions resulting in routing tables that are tuned to the network and demand patterns. Our proposed protocol is also secure against Sybil, Eclipse and adversarial routing attacks. While these attacks are important, a thorough analysis of Kadabra's robustness against other known attacks [27] is a direction for future work. In our experiments, we observe Kadabra typically converges in a few epochs. Testing Kadabra's convergence and performance in a real world network (e.g., IPFS and Swarm) and obtaining a theoretical understanding on the convergence are also important directions for future work.

Acknowledgements. We gratefully thank Dr. Petar Maymounkov for providing valuable comments on our work.

References

1. Alabdulwahhab, F.A.: Web 3.0: the decentralized web blockchain networks and protocol innovation. In: 2018 1st International Conference on Computer Applications & Information Security (ICCAIS), pp. 1–4. IEEE (2018)
2. Assadi, S., Wang, C.: Exploration with limited memory: streaming algorithms for coin tossing, noisy comparisons, and multi-armed bandits. In: Proceedings of the 52nd Annual ACM SIGACT Symposium on Theory of Computing, pp. 1237–1250 (2020)
3. Baumgart, I., Heep, B., Krause, S.: OverSim: a flexible overlay network simulation framework. In: 2007 IEEE Global Internet Symposium, pp. 79–84. IEEE (2007)
4. Baumgart, I., Mies, S.: S/Kademlia: a practicable approach towards secure key-based routing. In: 2007 International Conference on Parallel and Distributed Systems, pp. 1–8. IEEE (2007)
5. Benet, J.: IPFS - Content Addressed, Versioned, P2P File System. arXiv preprint arXiv:1407.3561 (2014)
6. Bubeck, S., Cesa-Bianchi, N.: Regret analysis of stochastic and nonstochastic multi-armed bandit problems. Found. Trends® Mach. Learn. **5**(1), 1–122 (2012)
7. Castro, M., Druschel, P., Hu, Y.C., Rowstron, A.: Exploiting network proximity in distributed hash tables. In: International Workshop on Future Directions in Distributed Computing (FuDiCo), pp. 52–55. Citeseer (2002)
8. Cavenaghi, E., Sottocornola, G., Stella, F., Zanker, M.: Non stationary multi-armed bandit: empirical evaluation of a new concept drift-aware algorithm. Entropy **23**(3), 380 (2021)
9. Chen, Z., Huang, M., Tan, Q.: The design of Kademlia system base on network topology matching. In: 2010 Second International Workshop on Education Technology and Computer Science, vol. 2, pp. 146–149. IEEE (2010)
10. Crosby, S.A., Wallach, D.S.: An analysis of BitTorrent's Two Kademlia-Based DHTs. Technical Report (2007)
11. Cointelegraph Report: DApp daily users surge to 2.4 M in Q1 2022 despite headwinds. https://cointelegraph.com/news/report-dapp-daily-users-surge-to-2-4m-in-q1-2022-despite-headwinds
12. Einziger, G., Friedman, R., Kantor, Y.: Shades: expediting Kademlia's lookup process. Comput. Netw. **99**, 37–50 (2016)
13. Ethereum Node Tracker. https://etherscan.io/nodetracker
14. Filecoin. https://filecoin.io/

15. Guangmin, L.: An improved Kademlia routing algorithm for P2P network. In: 2009 International Conference on New Trends in Information and Service Science, pp. 63–66. IEEE (2009)
16. Gummadi, K., Gummadi, R., Gribble, S., Ratnasamy, S., Shenker, S., Stoica, I.: The impact of DHT routing geometry on resilience and proximity. In: Proceedings of the 2003 Conference on Applications, Technologies, Architectures, and Protocols for Computer Communications, pp. 381–394 (2003)
17. Heck, H., Kieselmann, O., Wacker, A.: Evaluating connection resilience for the overlay network Kademlia. In: 2017 IEEE 37th International Conference on Distributed Computing Systems (ICDCS), pp. 2581–2584. IEEE (2017)
18. Heep, B.: R/Kademlia: recursive and topology-aware overlay routing. In: 2010 Australasian Telecommunication Networks and Applications Conference, pp. 102–107. IEEE (2010)
19. Hildrum, K., Kubiatowicz, J.D., Rao, S., Zhao, B.Y.: Distributed object location in a dynamic network. In: Proceedings of the Fourteenth Annual ACM Symposium on Parallel Algorithms and Architectures, pp. 41–52 (2002)
20. Hypercore Protocol. https://hypercore-protocol.org/
21. The IPFS-Filecoin Interface. https://github.com/filecoin-project/specs/issues/143
22. Jain, S., Mahajan, R., Wetherall, D.: A study of the performance potential of DHT-based overlays. In: 4th USENIX Symposium on Internet Technologies and Systems (USITS 03) (2003)
23. Jimenez, R., Osmani, F., Knutsson, B.: Sub-Second Lookups on a Large-Scale Kademlia-Based Overlay. In: 2011 IEEE International Conference on Peer-to-Peer Computing, pp. 82–91. IEEE (2011)
24. Kanemitsu, H., Nakazato, H.: KadRTT: routing with network proximity and uniform ID arrangement in Kademlia. In: 2021 IFIP Networking Conference (IFIP Networking), pp. 1–6. IEEE (2021)
25. Karger, D.R., Ruhl, M.: Finding nearest neighbors in growth-restricted metrics. In: Proceedings of the Thirty-Fourth Annual ACM Symposium on Theory of Computing, pp. 741–750 (2002)
26. Kaune, S., Lauinger, T., Kovacevic, A., Pussep, K.: Embracing the peer next door: proximity in Kademlia. In: 2008 Eighth International Conference on Peer-to-Peer Computing, pp. 343–350. IEEE (2008)
27. Koutrouli, E., Tsalgatidou, A.: Taxonomy of attacks and defense mechanisms in P2P reputation systems-Lessons for reputation system designers. Comput. Sci. Rev. 6(2–3), 47–70 (2012)
28. Libp2p Kademlia. https://github.com/libp2p/go-libp2p-kad-dht
29. Maymounkov, P., Mazières, D.: Kademlia: a peer-to-peer information system based on the XOR metric. In: Druschel, P., Kaashoek, F., Rowstron, A. (eds.) IPTPS 2002. LNCS, vol. 2429, pp. 53–65. Springer, Heidelberg (2002). https://doi.org/10.1007/3-540-45748-8_5
30. Montresor, A., Jelasity, M.: PeerSim: a scalable P2P simulator. In: 2009 IEEE Ninth International Conference on Peer-to-Peer Computing, pp. 99–100. IEEE (2009)
31. Nobari, S.: DBA: dynamic multi-armed bandit algorithm. In: Proceedings of the AAAI Conference on Artificial Intelligence, vol. 33(01), pp. 9869–9870 (2019)
32. Pecori, R.: S-Kademlia: a trust and reputation method to mitigate a Sybil attack in Kademlia. Comput. Netw. 94, 205–218 (2016)
33. Plaxton, C.G., Rajaraman, R., Richa, A.W.: Accessing nearby copies of replicated objects in a distributed environment. In: Proceedings of the Ninth Annual ACM Symposium on Parallel Algorithms and Architectures, pp. 311–320 (1997)

34. Putman, C., Nieuwenhuis, L.J., et al.: Business model of a botnet. In: 2018 26th Euromicro International Conference on Parallel, Distributed and Network-based Processing (PDP), pp. 441–445. IEEE (2018)
35. Ratnasamy, S., Handley, M., Karp, R., Shenker, S.: Topologically-aware overlay construction and server selection. In: Proceedings. Twenty-First Annual Joint Conference of the IEEE Computer and Communications Societies, vol. 3, pp. 1190–1199. IEEE (2002)
36. Safe Network. https://safenetwork.tech/
37. Slivkins, A.: Introduction to multi-armed bandits. Found. Trends® Mach. Learn. **12**(1–2), 1–286 (2019)
38. Steiner, M., Carra, D., Biersack, E.W.: Faster content access in KAD. In: 2008 Eighth International Conference on Peer-to-Peer Computing, pp. 195–204. IEEE (2008)
39. Steiner, M., En-Najjary, T., Biersack, E.W.: Exploiting KAD: possible uses and misuses. ACM SIGCOMM Comput. Commun. Rev. **37**(5), 65–70 (2007)
40. Storj Labs Inc.: Storj: a decentralized cloud storage network framework. https://www.storj.io/storjv3.pdf
41. Stutzbach, D., Rejaie, R.: Improving Lookup Performance over a Widely-Deployed DHT. In: Proceedings IEEE INFOCOM 2006. 25TH IEEE International Conference on Computer Communications, pp. 1–12. IEEE (2006)
42. Swarm. https://www.ethswarm.org/
43. SWARM-storage and communication infrastructure for a self-sovereign digital society. https://www.ethswarm.org/swarm-whitepaper.pdf
44. Trautwein, D., et al.: Design and evaluation of IPFS: a storage layer for the decentralized web. In: Proceedings of the ACM SIGCOMM 2022 Conference, pp. 739–752 (2022)
45. Trón, V.: The Book of Swarm: storage and communication infrastructure for self-sovereign digital society back-end stack for the decentralised web, V1. 0 pre-Release 7 (2020)
46. Website Load Time Statistics: why speed matters in 2022 - load speed can make or break a website. https://www.websitebuilderexpert.com/building-websites/website-load-time-statistics/
47. WonderNetwork Pings. https://wondernetwork.com/
48. Zhang, Y., Bojja Venkatakrishnan, S.: Kadabra: adapting Kademlia for the decentralized web. arXiv preprint arXiv:2210.12858 (2022)
49. Zhao, B.Y., Joseph, A., Kubiatowicz, J.: Locality aware mechanisms for large-scale networks. In: Proceedings of the FuDiCo, vol. 2 (2002)
50. Zhu, L., Zheng, K.: An improved Kademlia algorithm based on Qos. In: Proceedings of 2014 International Conference on Cloud Computing and Internet of Things, pp. 128–130. IEEE (2014)
51. Zichichi, M., Ferretti, S., D'Angelo, G.: On the efficiency of decentralized file storage for personal information management systems. In: 2020 IEEE Symposium on Computers and Communications (ISCC), pp. 1–6. IEEE (2020)

Optimality Despite Chaos in Fee Markets

Stefanos Leonardos[1]([✉])[iD], Daniël Reijsbergen[2,4][iD], Barnabé Monnot[3][iD],
and Georgios Piliouras[4][iD]

[1] King's College, London, UK
stefanos.leonardos@kcl.ac.uk
[2] Nanyang Technological University, Singapore, Singapore
daniel.reijsbergen@ntu.edu.sg
[3] Ethereum Foundation, Berlin, Germany
barnabe.monnot@ethereum.org
[4] Singapore University of Technology and Design, Singapore, Singapore
georgios@sutd.edu.sg

Abstract. Transaction fee markets are essential components of block-chain economies, as they resolve the inherent scarcity in the number of transactions that can be added to each block. In early blockchain protocols, this scarcity was resolved through a first-price auction in which users were forced to guess appropriate bids from recent blockchain data. Ethereum's EIP-1559 fee market reform streamlines this process through the use of a base fee that is increased (or decreased) whenever a block exceeds (or fails to meet) a specified target block size. Previous work has found that the EIP-1559 mechanism may lead to a base fee process that is inherently chaotic, in which case the base fee does *not* converge to a fixed point even under ideal conditions. However, the impact of this chaotic behavior on the fee market's main design goal – blocks whose long-term average size equals the target – has not previously been explored. As our main contribution, we derive near-optimal upper and lower bounds for the time-average block size in the EIP-1559 mechanism despite its possibly chaotic evolution. Our lower bound is equal to the target utilization level whereas our upper bound is $\approx 6\%$ higher than optimal. Empirical evidence is shown in great agreement with these theoretical predictions. Specifically, the historical average was $\approx 2.9\%$ larger than the target rage under Proof-of-Work and decreased to $\approx 2.0\%$ after Ethereum's transition to Proof-of-Stake. We also find that an approximate version of EIP-1559 achieves optimality even in the absence of convergence.

1 Introduction

In the seminal Bitcoin whitepaper [19], the concept of a *blockchain* was introduced as a secure data structure maintained by *nodes* in a peer-to-peer network. A blockchain consists of elementary database operations called *transactions* that modify a global state – e.g., cryptocurrency ownership or the state of smart contracts. Nodes provide an essential service to the blockchain's users by broadcasting their transactions and responding to queries about the global state [11]. As

S. Leonardos and D. Reijsbergen—Contributed equally.

F. Baldimtsi and C. Cachin (Eds.): FC 2023, LNCS 13951, pp. 346–362, 2024.
https://doi.org/10.1007/978-3-031-47751-5_20

such, a large and diverse network of nodes enhances *decentralization* in the sense that the availability and integrity of blockchain-enabled services do not depend on a handful of entities. As nodes execute every new transaction to maintain their view of the latest global state, the *computational cost* of new transactions must be limited to avoid excluding all but the most powerful nodes. In Ethereum [3], this computational cost is measured through the notion of *gas*, and each block has a gas *limit* that is decided by the nodes. In Ethereum's original design, each transaction has a *gas price* that indicates how much its creator is willing to pay for its inclusion on the blockchain. This mechanism behaves like a *first-price auction*, and shares all of its drawbacks [20]: users tend to bid untruthfully relative to the true valuation of their transaction, which leads to guesswork and overbidding that is detrimental to the user experience.

Ethereum Improvement Proposal (EIP) 1559 [2] simplifies Ethereum's fee market through a protocol-set *base fee*. Instead of aiming to fill each block to the limit, it aims to achieve a long-term average *target*, which is half the maximum size of each block. The base fee is automatically updated to reflect market conditions: if a block is larger than the target, then demand for transaction inclusion is too high at the current price so the base fee is increased (and vice versa for smaller blocks). The base fee hence aims to reflect the constantly-changing *market-clearing price*, which is the theoretical price at which demand for transactions is precisely such that block sizes equal the target. To add a transaction to the blockchain, users pay the base fee per unit of spent gas – this payment is permanently destroyed or *burned* [12]. This mechanism is provably incentive-compatible in the sense that users bid close to their true valuation unless demand is extremely high [22,23]. However, whether the protocol is *optimal* in the sense that it achieves its main design goal – a long-term average block size that equals the target – has not previously been explored. Previous work has found that the base fee may *not* converge to the market-clearing price [15] even when market conditions remain unchanged, as the base fee process exhibits (Li-Yorke) *chaos* in a wide range of market conditions. As the base fees need not converge to the market-clearing price, it is natural to ask whether the long-term average block sizes in fact converge to the target.

In the current work, we investigate whether optimality is possible in fee markets that exhibit non-convergent behavior. Specifically, we show that the default EIP-1559 mechanism is *approximately optimal* even if the block sizes are chaotic. We find that, unless market conditions are such that the base fee converges to a fixed point, EIP-1559 1) overshoots the target but 2) by at most ≈6.27%. These results hold *regardless* of the specific market conditions beyond convergence, or the nature of the block creation protocol. This suggests that we can still analyze the system even if it does not reach an equilibrium, which is a very stringent condition to be met in practice. Furthermore, our results allow us to quantify the maximum degree to which excessively large blocks impact nodes with limited processing power. We have validated our theoretical results using historical data, as displayed in Fig. 1 (see full version): since its introduction, blocks in EIP-1559 were initially ≈2.9% larger than the target, and after a major change

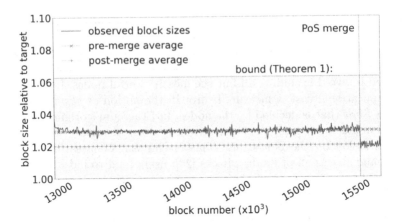

Fig. 1. Evolution of the relative block size since EIP-1559: the blue line without marks depicts the observed average block size over batches of 5000 consecutive blocks. The red and green lines with marks depict the averages over the periods before and after Ethereum's switch to proof-of-stake, respectively. The colored region indicates the range of potential long-run averages covered by the bound of Theorem 1 (Color figure online).

to Ethereum's block creation protocol, the PoS "Merge" [13], this overshoot dropped to ≈2.0%. In particular, Ethereum's consensus protocol switched form Proof-of-Work to Proof-of-Stake (PoS), which, as a by-effect, caused the time between the creation of new blocks to become constant. Both of our main theoretical findings – blocks overshoot the target, but to a limited degree – have therefore been borne out in practice. Moreover, the persistence of excessive block sizes throughout the observation period suggests that this is not merely a honeymoon effect [21]. We also observe the tightness of our bound in a wide range of simulation experiments (see full version).

In practice, the baseline variant of EIP-1559 is a linear approximation of an exponential update rule that is computationally inefficient to implement [8]. As a further contribution, we investigate the average-case performance of this ideal mechanism, deemed *exponential* EIP-1559. Our analysis suggests that exponential EIP-1559 *always* achieves the long-term average target, even if the base fee does not converge to the market-clearing price. We find that the manner in which EIP-1559 approximates an exponential function creates the observed overshoot – as such, this suggests an interesting direction for future protocol updates.[1]

Outline: The outline of our work is as follows. After a discussion of the context of our work (Sect. 2) and our model of a blockchain economy (Sect. 3), we present a unifying framework for the dynamics of different transaction fee market mech-

---

[1] In the full version of the paper, we further discuss such designs including a recent proposal that sets base fees using the principles behind Automated Market Makers (AMMs) [4] and general dynamic posted price mechanisms [9].

anisms, including the default EIP-1559 mechanism, its exponential variation, and alternative proposals (Sect. 4). In Sect. 5, we present our formal analysis. In Sect. 6, we discuss the generality of our results, and Sect. 7 concludes the paper.

2   Background and Related Work

In this section, we provide a high-level description of Ethereum's fee market and EIP-1559, and present some concepts that we have not discussed previously. We conclude the section with an overview of related work on fee markets.

Ethereum: Ethereum is a cryptocurrency platform that supports *smart contracts*, i.e., software programs that are executed in a decentralized network. Ethereum's global state consists of the state of all smart contracts and the amount of Ethereum's native cryptocurrency token – *Ether* or ETH – in each user account. The purpose of Ethereum transactions is to transfer ETH from one account to another, or to create or call a smart contract. A selection of nodes have the ability to periodically group transactions into a new *block* and broadcast it to the network. Although the exact nature of these nodes depends on the consensus mechanism, we will refer to such nodes as *"miners"* for brevity. Each block points to a previous block, forming a *blockchain*. Each operation in a transaction consumes gas, and the amount of ETH that a user is willing to pay for each unit of gas depends on the user's *valuation* of the transaction – i.e., how much utility she expects to derive from the transaction's inclusion on the blockchain. Before EIP-1559, users would specify a gas price for each transaction that determines the amount of ETH spent per unit of gas. Demand for gas fluctuates over time, e.g., due to temporal patterns and events such as NFT drops, so non-expert users were forced to guess appropriate gas prices from recent data.

EIP-1559: EIP-1559 simplifies Ethereum's original fee market design through the use of a dynamically adjusted base fee. The base fee at each time serves as a *posted price* that users need to pay to have their transaction processed at the next block. When users pay a transaction fee, an amount of ETH equal to the base fee is burned – however, a small amount of ETH can be awarded to the miner by the user in the form of a *miner's tip*. Without the miner's tip, miners would have no incentive to process transactions, which could cause them to create empty blocks instead. The base fee is continuously updated to reflect changing market conditions: if blocks are larger (smaller) than a fixed *target* size, then the base fee is increased (decreased) to reduce (increase) demand. The target has been set to roughly equal the maximum block size before EIP-1559 (i.e., 15M gas) – meanwhile, the maximum block size has been increased to 30M gas (i.e., twice the target). A higher maximum block size (relative to the target) increases the risk that nodes are overwhelmed during demand bursts.

Related Work: In [22,23], three desirable properties for transaction fee markets are investigated: whether (1) users are incentivized to bid their true valuation, (2) miners are incentivized to follow the protocol's inclusion rule, and (3) miners and users have no incentive to form cartels to subvert the protocol. It is shown that EIP-1559 always satisfies property (1) and (3), and (2) only when demand is "stable" [23]. Ethereum's original fee market (being a first-price auction) does not satisfy property (1), whereas property (3) would not hold if the base fee were awarded to miners instead of burned. The compatibility of these properties under general conditions is further explored by [6,10,24] in the context of transaction fee markets and by [17] in the context of NFT auctions.

In [15,18], the behavior of the base fee under stable market conditions is investigated – it is found that the base fee exhibits Li-Yorke chaos [15], which in practice results in the prevalence of sequences of alternating full and empty blocks. This behavior was later confirmed to occur in practice [21]. In [9], the *social welfare* of fee market mechanism is investigated, and two alternative mechanisms to EIP-1559 are proposed that perform better on this metric. In [16], the impact of EIP-1559 on various user-centric measures such as average transaction fees, waiting times, and consensus security is investigated. In [7], an extension of EIP-1559 is considered in a setting in which the base fee depends on the availability of multiple fungible resources (i.e., beyond gas use). Finally, fee market design has been studied for other cryptocurrency platforms, e.g., Bitcoin [1,14].

The question of whether the fee market ensures that the long-term average block size indeed equals the target size has not been considered in these works, although [16] finds that the average size of blocks as measured in terms of the network load (which does not capture the gas use of, e.g., smart contract function calls) has increased from 64.05 to 78.01 kB.

3   Model and Notation

In this section, we introduce our notation to describe transaction fee markets mathematically. We have EIP-1559 in mind (cf. Sect. 2), but the description applies to variations of EIP-1559 and other related mechanisms as well.

Base Fee and Target Block Size: The main element of EIP-1559 like transaction fee markets is a dynamically adjusted *base fee*, b_n, that is updated after every block, $B_n, n \geq 0$. The goal of the mechanism is to update the base fee in such a way that blocks achieve a pre-defined target block size. Let T denote the target block size and let kT denote the maximum block size, for some integer $k \geq 1$. Currently, in the Ethereum blockchain, k is set at $k = 2$, i.e., the target is equal to half the maximum block size.

Users (Transactions) and Valuations: Users (transactions) arrive to the pool according to a stochastic process. Without any loss of generality, we assume that each transaction uses 1 unit of gas, and use the random variable N_n to describe the number of transactions that arrive between two consecutive blocks B_n, B_{n+1} for $n \geq 0$. Let $\lambda_n = \mathbb{E}(N_n)/T$ be the ratio of the expected value of N_n to the target T. We make no assumptions about the distribution of N_n beyond it having a finite mean, i.e., $\lambda_n < \infty$. To avoid trivial cases, we will assume that $\lambda_n > 1$, i.e., that the arrival rate is larger than the target block size. For the theoretical analysis, we will assume that users leave the pool if their transaction is not included in the next block and return according to the specified arrival process.[2] Whenever necessary, we will index users (transactions) with $i, j \in \mathbb{N}$.

Users' Valuations: Each transaction, indexed by $i \in \mathbb{N}$, has a valuation, v_i. Valuations at time t are drawn from a distribution function F_n with support included in $\mathbb{R}^+$. Typically, the support of F_n is bounded, i.e., there exists a maximum possible valuation $M \gg 0$.[3] We will write $\overline{F}_n(x) := 1 - F_n(x)$ to denote the so-called *survival function* of the distribution F_n. For simplicity, we will assume that $\lambda_n \equiv \lambda$ and $F_n \equiv F$ for all $n \geq 0$, i.e., that λ and F are independent of the block height. We discuss how our results are straightforwardly generalized to a setting with time-dependent distributions in Sect. 6.

Bids and Tips: User bids in EIP-1559 consist of two elements: (1) the *max fee*, f, which is the maximum amount per gas unit that the user is willing to pay for their transaction to be included and (2) the *max priority fee*, p, which is the maximum tip per gas unit that the user is willing to pay to the miner who includes their transaction. We assume that users bid truthfully and rationally, i.e., a user with valuation v_i will bid $(f, p) = (v_i, \epsilon)$ where $\epsilon > 0$ is the minimum amount that covers the miners' cost to process the transaction. Combining with the above, this generates the inclusion requirement: miner's tip $= \min\{f - b_n, p\} \geq \epsilon$.

Block Sizes: Let $g_n := g(b_n)$ denote the number of transactions that get included in block B_n when the base fee is equal to $b_n, n \geq 0$. Given a number of transactions $N_n = n$ and valuations $v_1, \ldots, v_n$, we have that $g(b_n) = \min\{kT, \sum_{i=1}^{n} \mathbf{1}(v_i \geq b_n)\}$, i.e., the size of the block is equal to minimum between the block limit, kT, and the number of transactions whose max fee exceeds the base fee.[4] We note that $\mathbf{1}(v_i \geq b_n)$ has a Bernoulli distribution with probability $\mathbb{P}(v_i \geq b_n) = \overline{F}(b_n)$ of observing 1. For our analysis, we will consider the mean-field approximation of the stationary demand, which results in

$$g(b_n) = \min\left\{kT, \sum_{i=1}^{N_n} \mathbf{1}(v_i \geq b_n)\right\} = \min\{kT, \lambda T \overline{F}(b_n)\} \tag{1}$$

---

[2] This assumption only reduces unnecessary complexities in the analysis and is relaxed in the simulations without significant effect in the results.

[3] While unbounded valuations are unrealistic for practical purposes, we note that our results hold even for such cases.

[4] To simplify notation, we henceforth assume that each user's priority fee, p, is equal to the miners' breaken even cost ϵ. Equivalently, we only consider transactions that miners are willing to include and hence, we apply the indicator to b_n instead of $b_n + \epsilon$.

We denote the market-clearing price, i.e., the base fee for which $g(b^*) = T$, by b^*. From (1), we observe that $b^* = \bar{F}^{-1}(1/\lambda)$. Equation (1) also implies that $\lim_{b_n \downarrow 0} g(b_n) = kT$ since $\lambda > k$ by assumption, and $\lim_{b_n \to \infty} g(b_n) = 0$. To reflect practical settings, we will assume that b_n cannot become negative.

4   Fee Market Mechanisms: Base Fee Update Rules

Base fee update rules (BFURs), are functions $h : (0, \infty) \to (0, \infty)$. Their goal is to efficiently regulate block sizes via updates in the base fee, $b_{n+1} := h(b_n)$ with $b_0 > 0$. Intuitively, the base fee increases (decreases) whenever blocks are more (less) than the target and remains constant otherwise.

Design Goal: Achieving the target block size in *each* block, however, turns out to be a very difficult [16, 21] or even theoretically impossible goal [15]. To obtain a more tractable objective, it is still reasonable to ask whether the target block size is achieved *on average*. In symbols, let $G_N := \frac{1}{N} \sum_{n=1}^{N} g_n$ denote the average block size until block $N > 0$. Then, this requirement suggests that

$$\lim_{N \to \infty} G_N = T.$$

4.1   Proper Base Fee Update Rules

To avoid pathological cases, a base fee update rules h needs to satisfy some minimal regularity conditions. These our outlined in Definition 1.[5]

Definition 1. (Proper Base Fee Update Rules (PBFURs)) Let T be the target block-size. An update rule $h : (0, \infty) \to (0, \infty)$ is called *proper* if it satisfies the following

(A.1) non-divergence: $h(b_n) \geq b_n$ *if* $g(b_n) \geq T$ and $h(b_n) \leq b_n$ *if* $g(b_n) \leq T$.
(A.2) bounded relative differences: *there exists an* $\alpha \geq 1$ *such that* $\alpha^{-1} b_n \leq h(b_n) \leq \alpha b_n$.

Assumption (A.1) ensures that base fee updates are in the right direction, i.e., that the base fee does not decrease (increase) whenever the current block size is more (less) than the target. Assumption (A.2) excludes update rules with potentially unbounded updates. To include more general update rules, (A.2) can be relaxed to (the equivalent in flavor):

(A.2') *there exists* $\alpha > 1$ *and* $\beta > 0$ *such that* $\alpha^{-1} b_n - \beta \leq h(b_n) \leq \alpha b_n + \beta$.

---

[5] Apart from the current base fee, b_n, a base fee update rule may also depend on other parameters, θ_n, such as the target block size (time-independent) or the block size and efficient gas prices at time n (time-dependent). Whenever irrelevant, we will omit such parameters from the description of h. In the full version, we provide the generalized counterpart of Definition 1 that accounts for such dependencies.

PBFURs have the desirable property that they generate a bounded sequence of base fees. This is established in Lemma 1 which can be proved by induction (cf. full version).

Lemma 1. *If h is a PBFUR, and $0 < b_0 < \infty$, then*

$$\min\{b_0, \alpha^{-1}b^*\} \le b_n \le \max\{b_0, \alpha b^*\} \quad \text{for all} \quad n \ge 0.$$

4.2 Examples of PBFURs

EIP-1559: In the EIP-1559 transaction fee market [15,18,21], the base fee, b_n, is updated after every block (where blocks are indexed by their block height, $t > 0$) according to the following equation

$$b_{n+1} = b_n \left(1 + d \cdot \frac{g_n - T}{T}\right), \qquad \text{for any } n \in \mathbb{N}, \tag{EIP-1559}$$

where d denotes the *adjustment quotient* (or step-size or learning rate), currently set by default at $d = 0.125$. It will be convenient to use the notation $y_n := \frac{g_n - T}{T} \in [-1, 1]$, for the *normalized deviation at block t*, and

$$G_N := \frac{1}{N} \sum_{n=1}^{N} g_n \tag{2}$$

for the *average block size up to block N*. It is immediate to check that (EIP-1559) satisfies both A.1 and A.2 and is, thus, a PBFUR.

Exponential EIP-1559: Instead of the (EIP-1559) updates, we may consider the exponentially weighted updates

$$b_{n+1} = b_n \left(1 + d\right)^{\left(\frac{g_n - T}{T}\right)}, \qquad \text{for any } n \in \mathbb{N}. \tag{EXP-1559}$$

The standard (EIP-1559) update rule is the linear approximation (in the Taylor expansion of the function $d \mapsto (1+d)^{y_n}$) of the update rule in Eq. (EXP-1559). Again, it is immediate to check that (EXP-1559) satisfies non-divergence (A.1) and bounded relative differences (A.2) and is, thus, a PBFUR. Using the generalized Bernoulli inequality, it is also straightforward to show that the updates of Eq. (EXP-1559) are always less aggressive than (but in the same direction as) the updates of Eq. (EIP-1559). In other words, if a block is congested ($y_n > 0$), then the next base fee will increase with both methods, but it will be higher with (EIP-1559). Similarly, if a block is not congested ($y_n < 0$), then the next base fee will decrease with both methods, and it will be lower with (EXP-1559).[6]

---

[6] Ethereum researchers [8], also study an alternative exponential EIP-1559 form which relies on the exponential approximation $1 + dy_n \approx e^{dy_n}$ for dy_n small enough. Again, it is immediate to see that this rule satisfies (A.1) and (A.2) and is, thus, a PBFUR.

5   Analysis: Bounds on Average Block Sizes

5.1   EIP-1559

In this section, we are interested to obtain lower and upper bounds on the long-term average block sizes, $G_N, N \geq 0$, generated by the EIP-1559 update rule, cf. Eq. (EIP-1559). Our main result is summarized in Theorem 1.

Theorem 1. *Let $(g_n)_{t>0}$ denote the sequence of block sizes generated by the base fee $(b_n)_{t>0}$ of the EIP-1559 update rule (EIP-1559) with learning rate $d \in (0,1)$ for an arbitrary valuation distribution on $\mathbb{R}_+$. Then, the long-term average block size $\lim_{N \to +\infty} G_N$ satisfies*

$$T \leq \lim_{N \to +\infty} G_N \leq \left[1 - \frac{\ln(1+d)}{\ln(1-d)}\right]^{-1} 2T. \qquad (3)$$

In words, Theorem 1 implies that the EIP-1559 update rule either meets or *slightly* overshoots the target of T. The extent of possible overshooting (see upper bound in (3) of Theorem 1) depends on the choice of the learning rate d. For instance, at the current default level of $d = 0.125$, this yields a bound of approximately 1.0627 or 106% of the block size T. The upper bound for values of $d \in (0, 0.5]$ (which are of practical interest) is visualized in Fig. 2. As we see, this bound grows approximately linearly in d. This pattern continues for larger values of d till eventually growing exponentially fast and approaching 2 (or 200% of T) in the limit $d \uparrow 1$ (but such values are, at least currently, only of theoretical interest). The proof of Theorem 1 utilizes the following upper and lower linear bounds on the natural logarithm.

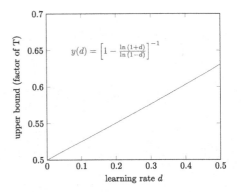

Fig. 2. Upper bound (scaling factor of maximum block size if $k = 2$) in Eq. (3) of Theorem 1. The upper bound grows almost linearly for the relevant values of d.

Lemma 2. *(i) Let $x > -1$. Then it holds that*

$$\ln(1+x) \leq x,$$

with equality if and only if $x = 0$. (ii) Let $d \in (0,1)$ and let $|x| \leq d$. Then, it holds that

$$\ln(1+x) \geq \alpha x + \beta,$$

with $\alpha = \frac{1}{2d} \cdot [\ln(1+d) - \ln(1-d)]$ and $\beta = \frac{1}{2} \cdot [\ln(1+d) + \ln(1-d)]$.

Using Lemma 2, we can now prove Theorem 1.

Proof. *(Proof of Theorem 1)* Let $d \in (0, 1)$. By taking the natural logarithm on both sides of Eq. (EIP-1559), we obtain that

$$\ln(b_{n+1}/b_n) = \ln\left(1 + d\frac{g_n - T}{T}\right)$$

Recall that $\frac{g_n - T}{T} \in [-1, 1]$ by definition. Thus, by applying Lemma 2 on the term $\ln\left(1 + d\frac{g_n - T}{T}\right)$ with $d\frac{g_n - T}{T} \in [-d, d]$, we obtain that

$$\alpha d \cdot \frac{g_n - T}{T} + \beta \leq \ln(b_{n+1}/b_n) \leq d \cdot \frac{g_n - T}{T},$$

with α, β as above. Combining the above and solving for g_n, we obtain that

$$\frac{T \cdot \ln(b_{n+1}/b_n)}{d} + T \leq g_n \leq \frac{T \cdot \ln(b_{n+1}/b_n)}{\alpha d} + \left(1 - \frac{\beta}{\alpha d}\right) T.$$

Observe that if we sum up all terms from 1 to N, then the term involving $\ln(b_{n+1}/b_n)$ on both sides telescopes to

$$\sum_{n=1}^{N} \ln(b_{n+1}/b_n) = \sum_{n=1}^{N} (\ln b_{n+1} - \ln b_n) = \ln b_N - \ln b_1.$$

Thus, summing up all terms from 1 to N in the previous inequality, and using the notation $G_N = \frac{1}{N}\sum_{n=1}^{N} g_n$, we obtain that

$$G_N \leq \frac{T(\ln b_N - \ln b_1)}{N\alpha d} + \left(1 - \frac{\beta}{\alpha d}\right) T, \tag{4}$$

and

$$\frac{T(\ln b_N - \ln b_1)}{Nd} + T \leq G_N, \tag{5}$$

for the upper and lower bounds respectively. Concerning the term on the right hand side of the upper bound, observe that after some standard algebraic manipulation, we can write $\left(1 - \frac{\beta}{\alpha d}\right) \cdot T = \left[1 - \frac{\ln(1+d)}{\ln(1-d)}\right]^{-1} \cdot 2T$. To conclude observe that $\lim_{N \to +\infty} b_N < M$ for some $M > 0$, since $(b_n)_{n \geq 0}$ is bounded by Lemma 1.[7] This implies that

$$\lim_{N \to +\infty} \frac{T \ln b_N - \ln b_1}{N} = 0.$$

Thus, taking the limit $N \to +\infty$ on both sides of the inequalities in (4), (5), we obtain that

$$T \leq \lim_{N \to +\infty} G_N \leq \left[1 - \frac{\ln(1+d)}{\ln(1-d)}\right]^{-1} \cdot 2T,$$

as claimed.   □

----

[7] The limit is also bounded from above if transactions are no longer included by miners when the base fee becomes so high that the computational cost of processing transactions outweighs any potential miner's tip.

5.2   Visualizations: Bifurcation Diagrams and Long-Term Averages

To gain more intuition, we proceed to visualize the individual trajectories of the base fee dynamics and the resulting block sizes for a simulated demand realization. This is done in the *bifurcation diagrams* of Fig. 3.

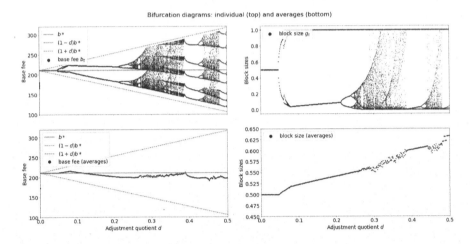

Fig. 3. EIP-1559: Individual trajectories of the base fee dynamics (top left) and block sizes (top right) for various values of the adjustment quotient, d, in $(0, 0.5]$ (horizontal axis). For every d, we plot 100 iterations after skipping 200 iterations. The bottom panels show averages of the trajectories in the top panels. Demand has been simulated from an exponential distribution on $[205, +\infty)$ with mean $\mu = 210$ and variance $\sigma^2 = 25$. The results are robust to different distributions and initializations (currently $b_0 = 100$), cf. full version. Despite the chaotic behavior of the individual trajectories (top), the long-term averages (bottom) exhibit mathematically tractable patterns. Note: Unlike Fig. 1, the scale of the $y-$axis in the block-size panels (right column) is between 0 (empty) and 1 (full) and the target is equal to 0.5. (The jupyter notebooks to generate these plots (and the similar ones in the Appendix) are available in this github repository.)

Individual Trajectories (Top Panels): The bifurcation diagram in the top left panel shows the individual trajectories of the base fee dynamics (blue dots) for different value of the adjustment quotient, d, (horizontal axis). Recall that the default value of d is 0.125. To generate the plots, we have drawn the user-valuations from a gamma distribution with mean $\mu = 220$ and standard deviation $\sigma = 10$. The depicted blue dots show the attractors (stable also for more iterations) after 100 iterations and a burn-in of 200 iterations. For low values of d (below 0.08), we see that the base fee dynamics converge to a single value, close to or exactly at the theoretical optimum, b^*. For larger values of d (approximately between 0.1 and 0.3), the dynamics oscillate between two values and

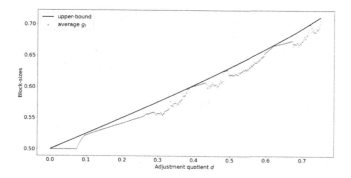

Fig. 4. Estimated upper bound (red line) of the average block-sizes as given by Theorem 1. The blue dots represent the average block-sizes for normally distributed simulated demand (user-valuations) with mean $\mu = 210$ and standard deviation $\sigma = 2.5$ at different values of the adjustment quotient, d, (horizontal axis). The long-term average block sizes grow linearly with d consistent with the estimated upper bound. Moreover, the upper bound is *tight*. We obtain qualitatively equivalent results for many demand distributions, e.g., uniform and gamma with arbitrary parameters (not presented here). (Color figure online)

for most remaining values of d (larger than 0.3 and for a small regime roughly between 0.08 and 0.1), the dynamics exhibit chaotic behavior (multiple dots dispersed over the whole interval between the two diagonal red lines). In all cases, the dynamics remain within the bounded region $[(1 - d)b^*, (1 + d)b^*]$.

The bifurcation diagram in the top right panel shows the resulting block sizes. Similar to the base fee dynamics, block sizes converge to the target value (0.5 or half-full) for low values of d, oscillate between full and (almost) empty for intermediate values of d and become chaotic for larger values of d.

In summary, the bifurcation plots in the two top panels show the effect of the adjustment parameter, d, on the individual trajectories of the base fees and the block sizes. These plots illustrate how small changes in the adjustment quotient, i.e., in the studied *bifurcation parameter*, can cause dramatic changes in the observable trajectories of both base fees and block sizes.

Averages (Bottom Panels): The bottom panels show the averages of the trajectories that are depicted in the top panels; base fees (bottom left) and block sizes (bottom right). We can see that the base fee slightly undershoots the ideal value of b^* and that the block sizes (slightly) overshoot the target of 0.5. Moreover, the deviation from this target grows linearly in the adjustment quotient d. At the current level, i.e., $d = 0.125$, the averages are approximately at 0.53.

Tight Upper-Bound on Block Sizes: The figures in the averages in Fig. 3 are not specific to the simulated demand and generalize to arbitrary demand distributions. Figure 4 shows the estimated upper-bound (red line) of Eq. 3 and the realized average block-sizes for user-valuations drawn from a normal distribution with mean $\mu = 210$ and standard deviation $\sigma = 10$. The upper-bound is tight and approximates very well the actual evolution of the block-size averages for various values of the adjustment quotient d. Qualitatively equivalent results obtain for arbitrarily parameterized uniform, normal and gamma user-valuation distributions (not presented here).

5.3   Exponential EIP-1559

As we show in Theorem 2, (EXP-1559) achieves time average convergence exactly to the target block sizes of T. However, (EIP-1559) is more relevant from practical purposes since it requires integer rather than floating point calculations.

Theorem 2. *For the dynamical system in Eq. (EXP-1559), it holds that*

$$\lim_{N \to +\infty} G_N = T,$$

i.e., the time average of the block sizes (or block occupancies), $(G_N)_{N \geq 1}$, converges to the target value T as the number, N, of updates grows to infinity.

The proof of Theorem 2 mirrors the steps in the proof of Theorem 1 and is therefore deferred to the full version. However, it is worth noting that there is nothing special about T; the time-average of the dynamic in Eq. (EXP-1559) would converge to any given target block-size (as it appears in the numerator of the exponent) within, of course, the admissible limits.

Convergence Rates. From the proof of Theorem 2, we can also reason about the convergence rate. After N time-steps, we have that the distance $d(G_N, T)$ between $G_N := \frac{1}{N} \sum_{t=0}^{N} g_n$ and the target T is equal to

$$d(G_N, T) = \frac{T(\ln b_N - \ln b_1)}{2 \ln(1 + d)} \cdot \frac{1}{N}$$

which drops linearly in N, i.e., $\mathcal{O}(1/N)$. The constant factor depends on T, $\ln 1 + d$, and the error due to initialization, $\ln b_N - \ln b_1$. Since b_N is bounded (cf. Lemma 1, we also know that $\ln b_N$ cannot grow (in absolute value) beyond certain bounds. Thus, all these terms vanish at a rate of $1/N$. Note, that in a similar fashion, we can get similar rates for the linear-EIP1559 update, cf. Theorem 1. In this case, we have that

$$\frac{T(\ln b_N - \ln b_1)}{2d} \cdot \frac{1}{N} \leq d(G_N, T) \leq \frac{T(\ln b_N - \ln b_1)}{2\alpha d} \cdot \frac{1}{N} - \frac{\beta}{\alpha d} \frac{T}{2}.$$

Again, the convergence rate is linear (by the same reasoning as above for $\ln b_N$ and the only thing that changes is the constant error term in the upper bound.

Visualizations for Exponential EIP-1559. Figure 5 shows the same data as Fig. 3 but for the exponential EIP-1559 update rule (cf. (EXP-1559)). The updates of both base fees (top left panel) and block sizes (top right panel) are more smooth (albeit not entirely non-chaotic). However, as can be seen from the left panels, the base fee dynamics tend to overshoot the actual ideal value. This behavior is slightly dependent on the initialization of the dynamics and is not consistent among all possible simulations in many of which the base fee dynamics meet b^* (not presented here). However, in all cases, the important observation concerns the block sizes and the fact that the target is met exactly (horizontal line at exactly 0.5 in the bottom right panel) regardless of the initialization and the value of the adjustment quotient d. This outcome is consistent with the theoretical prediction of Theorem 2.

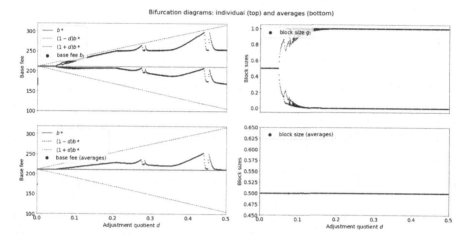

Fig. 5. Exponential EIP-1559: Individual trajectories of the base fee dynamics (top left) and block sizes (top right) for various values of the adjustment quotient, d (horizontal axis). The panels are the same as in Fig. 3. Exponential updates result in more regular (individual) trajectories and exactly achieve the block-size target on average. While the exact base fee trajectory is sensitive to b_0, it is not clear why the average base fee does not approach the market-clearing price, b^* (horizontal red line). (Color figure online)

6   Discussion

Overshoot. The inequality $\ln\left(1 + d \cdot \frac{g_n - T}{T}\right) \leq d \cdot \frac{g_n - T}{T}$ that is used to derive the lower bound of T in Theorem 1 (cf. inequality (i) in Lemma 2) holds with equality *if and only if* $d \cdot \frac{g_n - T}{T} = 0$, i.e., if and only if $g_n = T$. This implies that the long-term average block sizes will be equal to the target, T, if and only if the system equilibrates at a fixed point. However, the base fee dynamics are provably chaotic for almost all market conditions (demand and user valuations) that can be met in practice [15], and, thus, individual blocks will generally deviate from the target. Consequently, the lower bound will hold with *strict* inequality, implying a positive overshoot in EIP-1559 (almost) regardless of market conditions.

Generality and Robustness. We note that the proof of Theorem 1 does not in any way rely on F_n or the distribution of N_n, but only on the learning rate d. As such, our results hold regardless of the exact distribution of valuations or the block creation protocol. In fact, the only technical requirement is that for Lemma 1, we need the existence of a market-clearing price b^* to express our bounds. However, if we make the market-clearing price b^* time-dependent i.e., b_n^* instead of b^*, we only need to require that there exist $b_{\min}^* > 0$ and $b_{\max}^* < \infty$ such that $b_{\min}^* \leq b_n^* \leq b_{\max}^*$ for all $n \geq 0$ to obtain similar bounds. These are loose restrictions in practice. Our results also do not rely on k, e.g., if the maximum block size were set to 4 the target, then this would have no impact on the theoretical bounds. Interestingly, the upper bound in (3) is less than twice the target *regardless* of how small the target is relative to the maximum.

Although our theoretical results establish general bounds on the long-term average block size, the precise average values may depend on many factors, including the distribution of user valuations and the block creation protocol. We do observe from Fig. 1 that the observed block size averages over 5000-block batches exhibit remarkably consistent behavior both before and after the PoS merge. Since EIP-1559, market conditions have changed considerably: the base fee itself has changed from around 100 GWei (1 GWei = 10^{-9} ETH) in Jan. 2022 to around 10 Gwei in Aug. 2022. However, the average block size per batch has remained around 102.9% of the target throughout this period. Interestingly, the average block size dropped to around 102.0% immediately after the switch to PoS. The reason behind this drop is a stimulating direction for future research. One hypothesis is that before PoS, the inter-block times had an (approximately) exponential distribution, whereas they are constant in Ethereum's PoS protocol [5]. As such, the variance of N_n is smaller and block sizes are more regular. Another hypothesis is that blocks are less congested after the switch due to a decrease in inter-block times from roughly 13 s on average[8] to 12 s.

7   Conclusions

In this paper, we have formally analyzed the long-term performance of the standard EIP-1559 transaction fee market mechanism and its closely related variants; exponential EIP-1559 among others. Our findings provide a theoretical justification for the anecdotal evidence that blocks are slightly more full than normal. As our main contribution, we have found that both designs, the baseline EIP-1559 and its exponential variant, are approximately and exactly optimal, respectively, even under the prevailing chaotic conditions in inter-block sizes. Importantly, this implies that these mechanisms can still achieve their goals even if the underlying system does not equilibrate, a condition that is rarely met in practice. The

---

[8] https://ycharts.com/indicators/ethereum_average_block_time.

empirical data since the launch of EIP-1559 suggest that our results accurately capture reality: observable average block sizes are within the sharp approximation bounds predicted here and this is, in fact, robust to the underlying protocol functionality including both pre- and post-PoS merge periods.

Concerning future work, the current paper provides a framework to evaluate the performance and analyze the stability of transaction fee or other related cryptoeconomic mechanisms. Practical use cases suggest that blockchain economies are systems with complex dynamics: when these economies are close to their equilibrium state, they can re-adjust their parameters and self-stabilize. However, once they are pushed further away and/or lose their peg to their fundamentals, they start to spiral away and eventually collapse (e.g., the Terra/Luna crypto network). Determining the limits in which these instabilities emerge already before such mechanisms are launched in practice, is critical to improve their efficiency and avoid future financial catastrophes.

Contents of the Appendix

The Appendix, which can be found in the full version of the paper, includes (A) the omitted proofs of Lemma 1, 2 and Theorem 2, (B) the definition of *Generalized Proper Based Fee Update Rules* (GBFURs) and the analysis of some rules that fall in this category, including AMM-based mechanisms [4], Dynamic Posted-Price mechanisms [9] and our proposed *Effective Gas Price Correction Update Rule*, (C) the details of the empirical evaluation, and, in particular, the data that we used to construct Fig. 1, and, finally, (D) systematic simulations of the (EIP-1559) and (EXP-1559) BFURs.

Acknowledgements. This research is supported in part by the National Research Foundation, Singapore and DSO National Laboratories under its AI Singapore Program (AISG Award No: AISG2-RP-2020-016), NRF 2018 Fellowship NRF-NRFF2018-07, NRF2019-NRF-ANR095 ALIAS grant, grant PIESGP-AI-2020-01, AME Programmatic Fund (Grant No. A20H6b0151) from the Agency for Science, Technology and Research (A*STAR) and Provost's Chair Professorship grant with number RGEPPV2101. It is also supported by the National Research Foundation (NRF), Prime Minister's Office, Singapore, under its National Cybersecurity R&D Programme and administered by the National Satellite of Excellence in Design Science and Technology for Secure Critical Infrastructure, Award No. NSoE DeST-SCI2019-0009.

References

1. Basu, S., Easley, D., O'Hara, M., Sirer, E.G.: StableFees: a predictable fee market for cryptocurrencies. SSRN (2019). https://ssrn.com/abstract=3318327 or https://dx.doi.org/10.2139/ssrn.3318327
2. Buterin, V., Conner, E., Dudley, R., Slipper, M., Norden, I., Bakhta, A.: EIP1559: fee market change for ETH 1.0 chain (2019)
3. Buterin, V.: Ethereum: a next-generation smart contract and decentralized application platform (2014)

4. Buterin, V.: Make EIP 1559 more like an AMM curve. Ethereum Research (2021)
5. Buterin, V., et al.: Combining GHOST and Casper. arXiv preprint arXiv:2003.03052 (2020)
6. Chung, H., Shi, E.: Foundations of transaction fee mechanism design. arXiv preprint arXiv:2111.03151 (2021)
7. Diamandis, T., Evans, A., Chitra, T., Angeris, G.: Dynamic pricing for non-fungible resources. arXiv preprint arXiv:2208.07919 (2022)
8. Feist, D.: Exponential EIP-1559 (2022)
9. Ferreira, M.V., Moroz, D.J., Parkes, D.C., Stern, M.: Dynamic posted-price mechanisms for the blockchain transaction-fee market. In: Proceedings of the 3rd ACM conference on Advances in Financial Technologies, pp. 86–99 (2021)
10. Gafni, Y., Yaish, A.: Greedy Transaction Fee Mechanisms for (Non-)myopic Miners (2022). https://doi.org/10.48550/ARXIV.2210.07793
11. Gencer, A.E., Basu, S., Eyal, I., van Renesse, R., Sirer, E.: Decentralization in Bitcoin and Ethereum Networks. In: Meiklejohn, S., Sako, K. (eds.) FC 2018. LNCS, vol. 10957, pp. 439–457. Springer, Heidelberg (2018). https://doi.org/10.1007/978-3-662-58387-6_24
12. Karantias, K., Kiayias, A., Zindros, D.: Proof-of-burn. In: Bonneau, J., Heninger, N. (eds.) FC 2020. LNCS, vol. 12059, pp. 523–540. Springer, Cham (2020). https://doi.org/10.1007/978-3-030-51280-4_28
13. Kessler, S.: The Ethereum Merge is done, opening a new era for the second-biggest blockchain (2022)
14. Lavi, R., Sattath, O., Zohar, A.: Redesigning Bitcoin's fee market. ACM Trans. Econ. Comput. 10(1), 1–31 (2022)
15. Leonardos, S., Monnot, B., Reijsbergen, D., Skoulakis, E., Piliouras, G.: Dynamical analysis of the EIP-1559 ethereum fee market. In: Proceedings of the 3rd ACM Conference on Advances in Financial Technologies (AFT 2021), pp. 114–126. Association for Computing Machinery, New York (2021). https://doi.org/10.1145/3479722.3480993
16. Liu, Y., Lu, Y., Nayak, K., Zhang, F., Zhang, L., Zhao, Y.: Empirical analysis of EIP-1559: transaction fees, waiting time, and consensus security. arXiv preprint arXiv:2201.05574 (2022)
17. Milionis, J., Hirsch, D., Arditi, A., Garimidi, P.: A framework for single-item NFT auction mechanism design. arXiv e-prints arXiv:2209.11293 (2022)
18. Monnot, B., Hum, Q., Koh, C.S.M., Leonardos, S., Piliouras, G.: Ethereum's transaction fee market reform of EIP 1559. In: Proceedings of the WINE 2020 Workshop on Blockchain (2020)
19. Nakamoto, S.: Bitcoin: a peer-to-peer electronic cash system (2008)
20. Nisan, N., Roughgarden, T., Tardos, E., Vazirani, V.V.: Algorithmic Game Theory. Cambridge University Press (2007)
21. Reijsbergen, D., Sridhar, S., Monnot, B., Leonardos, S., Skoulakis, S., Piliouras, G.: Transaction fees on a honeymoon: ethereum's EIP-1559 one month later. In: 2021 IEEE International Conference on Blockchain (Blockchain), pp. 196–204 (2021). https://doi.org/10.1109/Blockchain53845.2021.00034
22. Roughgarden, T.: Transaction fee mechanism design for the ethereum blockchain: an economic analysis of EIP-1559 (2020). https://doi.org/10.48550/ARXIV.2012.00854
23. Roughgarden, T.: Transaction fee mechanism design. ACM SIGecom Exchanges 19(1), 52–55 (2021)
24. Shi, E., Chung, H., Wu, K.: What can cryptography do for decentralized mechanism design? arXiv preprint arXiv:2209.14462 (2022)

Author Index

Printed in the United States
by Baker & Taylor Publisher Services